THE TRUTH ABOUT THE TERRITORY:

CONTEMPORARY NONFICTION FROM THE NORTHWEST

edited by Rich Ives

Owl Creek Press
1620 N. 45th St.
Seattle WA 98103

CONTENTS

Editor's Note   4
Acknowledgements   6

William Kittredge, *Redneck Secrets*   10
         Drinking and Driving   19
         Silver Bullets   32
Joan Swift, *Recovery*   39
John Hildebrand, *Kaltag*   60
Raymond Carver, *My Father's Life*   70
David Quammen, *The Troubled Gaze of the Octopus*   79
         Rumors of a Snake   84
         Has Success Spoiled the Crow?   89
H. L. Davis, *A Walk in the Woods*   94
         The Brook   104
Rich Ives, *A Place Near Home*   115
Barry Lopez, *Arctic Dreams*   123
Thomas McGuane, *Me and My Bike and Why*   136
         Molly   142
Clyde Rice, *A Heaven in the Eye*   149
Richard Hugo, *The St. James Lutheran 5*   159
         James Wright   170
Jack Olsen, *Give a Boy a Gun*   186
Will Baker, *The Winged Worm*   196
         Father White Mouse   201
Richard Ford, *The Three Kings*   217
John Haines, *Lost*   236
         Wolves   239
         The Art of Pulling Hearts   242
Rich Baker, *The "Hero" of the Eagle's Nest*   252
Marilyn Stablein, *After the Hurricane*   256
         Intrusions in Ice   261
Kim Stafford, *The Barn and the Bees*   268
         A Few Miles Short of Wisdom   279
Gretel Ehrlich, *Looking for a Lost Dog*   291
         To Live in Two Worlds   294

Annie Dillard, *Lenses*   312
                Teaching a Stone to Talk   316
                Total Eclipse   323
Richard K. Nelson, *The Gifts*   337
William Stafford, *Down in My Heart*   353
Brenda Peterson, *Growing Up Game*   360
Monica Sone, *We Are Outcasts*   364
John McPhee, *Coming into the Country*   376
Madeline De Frees, *Requiem for the Outfitter*   391
Tess Gallagher, *To Work and Keep Kind*   403
                My Father's Love Letters   408
Ralph Beer, *Holding to the Land*   429
Jack Cady, *Transcendentalism and the American Road*   441
Ivan Doig, *Flip*   456
Geoffrey Wolff, *The Duke of Deception*   486
Ken Kesey, *Tranny Man Over the Border*   510

Notes on the Authors   530

EDITOR'S NOTE

With this volume Owl Creek Press completes its coverage of contemporary Northwest writing. The first anthology in the series, *Rain in the Forest, Light in the Trees: Contemporary Poetry from the Northwest* is under revision and will be released soon in a second, updated edition. The press will also attempt to keep both *From Timberline to Tidepool: Contemporary Fiction from the Northwest* and *The Truth About the Territory: Contemporary Nonfiction from the Northwest* in print and up to date. A growing, enthusiastic readership for Northwest writing, the support of the National Endowment for the Arts, the support of teachers using the anthologies in the classroom and the encouragement and support of the writers themselves have all been important to the success of the project. My gratitude and thanks to all of you.

Since it is the nature of much of the best nonfiction writing to defy boundaries, perhaps even genres, I have, for this anthology, extended the borders of the Northwest to welcome nonfiction writers to this anthology from nearby geographical areas with similar concerns as well as writers whose nonfiction subjects and/or settings, if not their geographical home bases, are distinctly Northwestern. In a genre where "subject" is of such obviously central concern, this seemed only natural and could, perhaps, be constructively revealing as well.

These anthologies are intended to be self-contained introductions to a wide variety of writers but, even so, the selections can represent only a sampling of the work of each included author. I have attempted to open doors to these worlds, but the lives inside them continue elsewhere. Don't stop here.

No editorial perusal of a region as rich in literary talent as the Northwest can hope to be totally comprehensive, and I wish to extend my apologies to any writers I may have overlooked. If these anthologies continue to receive the support they have enjoyed since 1983 when *Rain in the Forest, Light in the Trees* was first released, I may have the opportunity to correct any such oversights in future editions. And I am very certain there will continue to be rewarding new works arising frequently from the fertile literary landscapes currently being explored by Northwest writers. I hope I can help bring these works the attention they deserve.

Rich Ives

ACKNOWLEDGEMENTS

In all cases permissions were first granted by the authors and followed, as requested, with permissions from the publishers.

"Redneck Secrets," "Drinking and Driving" and "Silver Bullets" reprinted from *Owning It All* by William Kittredge, Graywolf Press, copyright (c) 1987. "Recovery" by Joan Swift reprinted from *The Iowa Review*, Spring, 1978, (c) 1978. "Kaltag" by John Hildebrand is printed here for the first time, excerpted from an as yet untitled nonfiction work forthcoming from Houghton Mifflin, (c) 1987. "My Father's Life" by Raymond Carver reprinted from *Esquire*, Sept. 1984, (c) 1984. "The Troubled Gaze of the Octopus," "Rumors of a Snake" and "Has Success Spoiled the Crow?" reprinted from *Natural Acts* by David Quammen, published in hardback by Nick Lyons Books and in paperback by Dell, (c) 1985. "A Walk in the Woods" and "The Brook" reprinted from *Kettle of Fire* by H. L. Davis, William Morrow and Company, (c) 1959. "A Place Near Home" by Rich Ives appears here for the first time (c) 1987. "Arctic Dreams" reprinted from *Arctic Dreams* by Barry Lopez, Charles Scribner's Sons, (c) 1986. "Me and My Bike and Why" and "Molly" reprinted from *An Outside Chance* by Thomas McGuane, Farrar, Straus and Giroux, (c) 1980. "A Heaven in the Eye" reprinted from *A Heaven in the Eye* by Clyde Rice, Breitenbush, (c) 1984. "The St. James Lutheran 5" and "James Wright" reprinted from *The Real West Marginal Way* by Richard Hugo, W. W. Norton and Company, (c) 1986 by Ripley S. Hugo. "Give a Boy a Gun" reprinted from *Give a Boy a Gun* by Jack Olsen, (c) 1986. "The Winged Worm" and "Father White Mouse" reprinted from *Mountain Blood* by Will Baker, U. of Georgia Press, (c) 1986. "The Three Kings" by Richard Ford reprinted from *Esquire*, (c) 1985. "Lost" and "Wolves" reprinted from *Other Lives* by John Haines, Graywolf Press, (c) 1982. "The Art of Pulling Hearts" by John Haines from *The Montana Review 2* (c) 1980. "The 'Hero' of the Eagle's Nest" by Rich Baker reprinted with revisions from the Tacoma *News Tribune*, Sept. 23, 1984, (c) 1984. "After the Hurricane" and "Intrusions in Ice" by Marilyn Stablein appear here for the

This project is supported by a grant from the National Endowment for the Arts.

THE TRUTH ABOUT THE TERRITORY:

CONTEMPORARY NONFICTION FROM THE NORTHWEST

REDNECK SECRETS

Back in my more scattered days there was a time when I decided the solution to all life's miseries would begin with marrying a nurse.   Cool hands and commiseration.   She would be a second-generation Swedish girl who left the family farm in North Dakota to live a new life in Denver, her hair would be long and silvery blonde, and she would smile every time she saw me and always be after me to get out of the house and go have a glass of beer with my buckaroo cronies.

Our faithfulness to one another would be legendary. We would live near Lolo, Montana, on the banks of the Bitterroot River where Lewis and Clark camped to rest on their way West, "Traveler's Rest," land which floods a little in the spring of the year, a small price to pay for such connection with mythology. Our garden would be intricately perfect on the sunny uphill side of our 16 acres, with little wooden flume boxes to turn the irrigation water down one ditch or another.

We would own three horses, one a blue roan Appaloosa, and haul them around in our trailer to jackpot roping events on summer weekends. I wouldn't be much good on horseback, never was, but nobody would care. The saddle shed would be tacked to the side of our doublewide expando New Moon mobile home, and there would be a neat little lawn with a white picket fence about as high as your knee, and a boxer dog called Aces and Eights, with a great studded collar.   There would be a .357 magnum pistol in the drawer of the bedside table, and on Friday night we would dance to the music of old-time fiddlers at some country tavern and in the fall we would go into the mountains for firewood and kill two or three elk for the freezer. There would be wild asparagus along the irrigation ditches and morels down under the cottonwoods by the river, and we would always be good.

And I would keep a journal, like Lewis and Clark, and spell bad, because in my heart I would want to be a mountain man — "We luved aft the movee in the bak seet agin tonite."

We must not gainsay such Western dreams. They are not automatically idiot. There are, after all, good Rednecks and bad Rednecks. Those are categories.

So many people in the American West are hurt, and hurting. Bad Rednecks originate out of hurt and a sense of having been discarded and ignored by the Great World, which these days exists mostly on television, distant and most times dizzily out of focus out here in Redneck country.

Bad Rednecks lose faith and ride away into foolishness, striking back. The spastic utility of violence. The other night in a barroom, I saw one man turn to another, who had been pestering him with drunken nonsense. "Son," he said, "you better calm yourself, because if you don't, things are going to get real Western here for a minute."

Real Western. Back in the late '40's when I was getting close to graduating from high school, they used to stage Saturday night prizefights down in the Veteran's Auditorium. Not boxing matches but prizefights, a name which rings in the ear something like *cockfight*. One night the two main-event fighters, always heavyweights, were some hulking Indian and a white farmer from a little dairy-farm community.

The Indian, I recall, had the word "Mother" carved on his hairless chest. Not tattooed, but carved in the flesh with a blade, so the scar tissue spelled out the word in livid welts. The white farmer looked soft and his body was alabaster, pure white, except for his wrists and neck, which were dark, burned-in-the-fields red, burnished red. While they hammered at each other we hooted from the stands like gibbons, rooting for our favorites on strictly territorial and racial grounds, and in the end were all disappointed. The white farmer went down like thunder about three times, blood snorting from his nose in a delicate spray and decorating his whiteness like in, say, the movies. The Indian simply retreated to his corner and refused to go on. It didn't make any sense.

We screeched and stomped, but the Indian just stood there looking at the bleeding white man, and the white man cleared his head and looked at the Indian, and then they both shook their heads at one another, as if acknowledging some private news they had just then learned to share. They both climbed out of the ring and together made their way up the aisle. Walked away.

11

Real Western. Of course, in that short-lived partnership of the downtrodden, the Indian was probably doomed to a lifetime on the lower end of the seesaw. No dairy farms in a pastoral valley, nor morning milking and school boards for him. But that is not the essential point in this equation. There is a real spiritual equivalency between Redmen and Rednecks. How sad and ironic that they tend to hit at each other for lack of a real target, acting out some tired old scenario. Both, with some justice, feel used and cheated and disenfranchised. Both want to strike back, which may be just walking away, or the bad answer, bloody noses.

Nobody is claiming certain Rednecks are gorgeous about their ways of resolving the pain of their frustrations. Some of them will indeed get drunk in honkytonks and raise hell and harass young men with long hair and golden earrings. These are the bad Rednecks.

Why bad? Because they are betraying themselves. Out-of-power groups keep fighting each other instead of what they really resent: power itself. A Redneck pounding a hippie in a dark barroom is embarrassing because we see the cowardice. What he wants to hit is a banker in broad daylight.

But things are looking up. Rednecks take drugs; hippies take jobs. And the hippie carpenters and the 250-pound, pig-tailed lumberjacks preserve their essence. They are still isolated, outrageous, lonely, proud and mean. Any one of them might yearn for a nurse, a doublewide, a blue roan Appaloosa, and a sense of place in a country that left him behind.

Like the Indian and the buffalo on the old nickel, there are two sides to American faith. But in terms of Redneck currency, they conflict. On the one side there is individualism which in its most radical mountain-man form becomes isolation and loneliness: the standard country-and-western lament. It will lead to dying alone in your motel room: whether gored, boozed or smacked makes little difference. On the other side there are family and community, that pastoral society of good people inhabiting the good place on earth that William Bradford and Thomas Jefferson so loved to think about.

Last winter after the snowmobile races in Seeley Lake, I had come home to stand alongside my favorite bar rail and listen to my favorite skinny Redneck barmaid turn down propositions. Did I say *home?* Anyway, standing there and feeling at home, I realized that good Redneck bars are like good hippie bars: they are community centers, like churches and pubs in the old days, and drastically unlike our singles bars where every person is so radically on his or her own.

My skinny barmaid friend looked up at one lumberjack fellow, who was clomping around in White logger boots and smiling his most winsome. She said, "You're just one of those boys with a sink full of dishes. You ain't looking for nothing but someone dumb enough to come and wash your dishes. You go home and play your radio."

A sink full of dirty dishes. And laundry. There are aspects of living alone that can be defined as going out to the J.C. Penney store and buying $33 worth of new shorts and socks and t-shirts because everything you own is stacked up raunchy and stinking on the far side of the bed. And going out and buying paper plates at K-mart because you're tired of eating your meals crouched over the kitchen sink. You finally learn about dirty dishes. They stay dirty. And those girls, like my skinny friend, have learned a thing or two. There are genuine offers of solace and companionship, and there are dirty dishes and nursing. And then a trailer house, and three babies in three years, diapers, and he's gone to Alaska for the big money. So back to barmaiding, this time with kids to support, babysitters.

There is, of course, another Montana. Consider these remarks from the journals of James and Granville Stewart, 1862:

JANUARY 1, 1862. Snowed in the forenoon. Very cold in the afternoon. Raw east wind. Everybody went to grand ball given by John Grant at Grantsville and a severe blizzard blew up and raged all night. We danced all night, no outside storm could dampen the festivities.
JANUARY 2. Still blowing a gale this morning. Forty below zero and the air is filled with driving, drifting snow. After breakfast we laid down on the floor of the several rooms, on buffalo robes that Johnny furnished, all dressed as we were and slept until about

two-o'clock in the afternoon, when we arose, at a fine dinner, then resumed dancing which we kept up with unabated pleasure . . . danced until sunrise.

JANUARY 3. The blizzard ceased about daylight, but it was very cold without, about fourteen inches of snow badly drifted in places and the ground bare in spots. We estimated the cold at about thirty-five below, but fortunately there was but little wind. After breakfast all the visitors left for home, men, women, and children, all on horseback. Everyone got home without frost bites.

Sounds pretty good. But Granville Stewart got his. In the great and deadly winter of 1886-1887, before they learned the need of stacking hay for winter, when more than one million head of cattle ran the Montana ranges, he lost two-thirds of his cow herd. Carcasses piled in the coulees and fence corners come springtime, flowers growing up between the ribs of dead longhorn cattle, and the mild breezes reeking with decay. A one-time partner of Stewart's, Conrad Kohrs, salvaged 3,000 head out of 35,000. Reports vary, but you get the sense of it.

Over across the Continental Divide to where the plains begin on the east side of the Crazy Mountains, in the Two Dot country, on bright mornings you can gaze across the enormous swale of the Musselshell, north and east to the Snowy Mountains, 50 miles distant and distinct and clear in the air as the one mountain bluebell you picked when you came out from breakfast.

But we are not talking spring, we are talking winter and haystacks. A man we know, let's call him Davis Patten, is feeding cattle. It's February, and the snow is drifting three feet deep along the fence lines, and the wind is carying the chill factor down to about 30 below. Davis Patten is pulling his feed sled with a team of yellow Belgian geldings. For this job, it's either horses or a track-layer, like a Caterpillar D-6. The Belgians are cheaper and easier to start.

Davis kicks the lat remnant of meadow hay, still greenish and smelling of dry summer, off the sled to the trailing cattle. It's three o'clock in the afternoon and already the day is settling toward dark. Sled runners creak on the frozen snow. The gray light is murky in the wind, as though inhabited, but no birds are flying anywhere. Davis Patten is sweating under his insulated coveralls, but his beard is frozen around his mouth. He heads the team toward the barns, over under the cottonwood by the creek. Light from the kitchen windows shows through the bare limbs. After he has fed the team a bait of oats, then Davis and his wife Loretta will drink coffee laced with bourbon.

Later they watch television, people laughing and joking in bright Sony color. In his bones Davis recognizes, as most of us do, that the principal supporting business of television is lies, truths that are twisted about a quarter turn. Truths that were never truths. Davis drifts off to sleep in his Barca-Lounger. He will wake to the white noise from a gray screen.

It is important to have a sense of all this. There are many other lives, this is just one, but none are the lives we imagine when we think of running away to Territory.

Tomorrow Davis Patten will begin his day chopping ice along the creek with a splitting maul. Stock water, a daily chore. Another day with ice in his beard, sustained by memories of making slow love to Loretta under down comforters in their cold bedroom. Love, and then quickfooting it to the bathroom on the cold floors, a steaming shower. Memories of a bed that reeks a little of child making.

The rewards of the life, it is said, are spiritual, and often they are. Just standing on land you own, where you can dig any sort of hole you like, can be considered a spiritual reward, a reason for not selling out and hitting the Bahamas. But on his winter afternoons Davis Patten remembers another life. For ten years, after he broke away from Montana to the Marines, Davis hung out at the dragster tracks in the San Joaquin Valley, rebuilding engines for great, roaring, ass-busting machines. These days he sees their stripped red-and-white dragchutes flowering only on Sunday afternoons. The "Wide World of Sports." Lost horizons. The intricate precision of cam shaft adjustments.

In the meantime, another load of hay.

Up in towns along the highline, Browning and Harlem and Malta, people are continually dying from another kind of possibility. Another shot of Beam on the rocks and Annie Greensprings out back after the bars are closed. In Montana they used to erect little crosses along the highways wherever a fatality occurred. A while back, outside Browning, they got a dandy. Eleven deaths in a single car accident. *Guinness Book of World Records.* Verities. The highway department has given up the practice of erecting crosses: too many of them are dedicated to the disenfranchised.

Out south of Billings the great coal fields are being strip-mined. Possibilities. The history of Montana and the West, from the fur trade to tomorrow, is a history of colonialism, both material and cultural. Is it any wonder we are so deeply xenophobic, and regard anything east of us as suspect? The money and the power always came from the East, took what it wanted, and left us, white or Indian, with our traditions dismantled and our territory filled with holes in the ground. Ever been to Butte? About half the old town was sucked into a vast open-pit mine.

Verities. The lasting thing we have learned here, if we ever learn, is to resist the beguilements of power and money. Hang on to your land. There won't be any more. Be superstitious as a Borneo tribesman. Do not let them photograph our shy, bare-breasted beauties as they wash clothes along the stream bank. Do not let them steal your soul away in pictures, because they will if they get a chance, just as Beadle's Nickle-Dime Library westerns and Gene Autry B-movies gnawed at the soul of this country where we live. Verities have to be earned, and they take time in the earning — time spent gazing out over your personal wind-glazed fields of snow. Once earned, they inhabit you in complex ways you cannot name, and they cannot be given away. They can only be transmogrified — transformed into something surreal or fantastic, unreal. And ours have been, and always for the same reason: primarily the titillation of those who used to be Easterners, who are everywhere now.

These are common sentiments here in the mountain West. In 1923 Charlie Russell agreed to speak before the Great Falls Booster Club. After listening to six or seven booster speeches, he tore up his own talk and spoke. This is what he said:

In my book a pioneer is a man who turned all the grass upside down, strung bob-wire over the dust that was left, poisoned the water and cut down the trees, killed the Indian who owned the land, and called it progress. If I had my way, the land here would

16

be like God made it, and none of you sons of bitches would be here at all.

So what are we left with? There was a great dream about a just and stable society, which was to be America. And there was another great dream about wilderness individuals, mountain men we have called them, who would be the natural defenders of that society. But our society is hugely corrupt, rich and impossibly complex, and our great simple individuals can define nothing to defend, nothing to reap but the isolation implicit in their stance, nothing to gain for their strength but loneliness. The vast, sad, recurrent story which is so centrally American. Western Rednecks cherish secret remnants of those dreams, and still try to live within them. No doubt a foolish enterprise.

But that's why, full of anger and a kind of releasing joy, they plunge their Snowcats around frozen lakes at 90 miles an hour, coming in for a whiskey stop with eyes glittering and icicles bright in their whiskers, and why on any summer day you can look into the sky over Missoula and see the hang-gliding daredevils circling higher than the mountains. That's why you see grown men climbing frozen waterfalls with pretty colored ropes.

And then there seems to be a shooting a week in the doublewide village. Spastic violence. You know, the husband wakes up from his drunk, lying on the kitchen floor with the light still burning, gets himself an Alka-Seltzer, stumbles into the living room, and there is Mother on the couch with half her side blown away. The 12-gauge is carefully placed back where it belonged on the rack over the breakfront. Can't tell what happened. Must have been an intruder.

Yeah, the crazy man inside us. Our friends wear Caterpillar D-9 caps when they've never pulled a friction in their lives, and Buck knives in little leather holsters on their belts, as if they might be called upon to pelt out a beaver at any moment. Or maybe just stab an empty beer can. Ah, wilderness, and suicidal nostalgia.

Which gets us to another kind of pioneer we see these days, people who come to the country with what seems to be an idea that connection with simplicities will save their lives. Which simplicities are those? The condescension implicit in the program is staggering. If you want to feel you are being taken lightly, try

17

sitting around while someone tells you how he envies the simplicity of your life. What about Davis Patten? He says he is staying in Montana, and calling it home. So am I.

Despite the old Huckleberry Finn-mountain man notion of striking out for the territory, I am going to hang on here, best I can, and nourish my own self. I know a lovely woman who lives up the road in a log house, on what is left of a hard-earned farmstead. I'm going to call and see if she's home. Maybe she'll smile and come have a glass of beer with me and my cronies.

William Kittredge

DRINKING AND DRIVING

Deep in the far heart of my upbringing, a crew of us sixteen-year-old lads were driven crazy with ill-defined midsummer sadness by the damp, sour-smelling sweetness of night-time alfalfa fields, an infinity of stars and moonglow, and no girlfriends whatsoever. Frogs croaked in the lonesome swamp.

Some miles away over the Warner Range was the little ranch and lumbermill town of Lakeview, with its shorehouse district. And I had use of my father's 1949 Buick. So, another summer drive. The cathouses, out beyond the rodeo grounds, were clustered in an area called Hollywood, which seemed right. Singing cowboys were part of everything gone wrong.

We would sink our lives in cheap whiskey and the ardor of sad, expensive women. In town, we circled past the picture show and out past Hollywood, watching the town boys and their town-boy business, and we chickened out on the whores and drank more beer, then drove on through the moonlight.

Toward morning we found ourselves looping higher and higher on a two-truck gravel road toward the summit of Mount Bidwell, right near the place where California and Nevada come together at the Oregon border. We topped out over a break called Fandango Pass.

The pass was named by Wagon-train parties on the old Applegate cutoff to the gold country around Jacksonville. From that height they got their first glimpse of Oregon, and they camped on the summit and danced themselves some fandangos, whatever the step might be.

And we, in our ranch-boy style, did some dancing of our own. Who knows how it started, but with linked arms and hands we stumbled and skipped through the last shards of night and into the sunrise. Still drunk, I fell and bloodied my hands and stood breathing deep of the morning air and sucking at my own salty blood, shivering and pissing and watching the stunted fir and meadow aspen around me come luminous with light, and I knew our night of traveling had brought me to this happiness that would never bear talking about. No more nameless sorrow, not with these comrades, and we all knew it and remained silent.

Seventeen. I was safe forever, and I could see 70 miles out

across the beauty of country where I would always live with these friends, all of it glowing with morning.

We learn it early in the West, drinking and driving, chasing away from the ticking stillness of home toward some dim aura glowing over the horizon, call it possibility or excitement. Henry James once said there are two mental states, excitement and lack of excitement, and that unfortunately excitement was more interesting than lack of excitement. Travel the highways in Montana, and you will see little white crosses along the dangerous curves, marking places where travelers have died, many of them drunk, and most of them searching and unable to name what it was they were missing at home. It's like a sport: you learn techniques. For instance, there are three ways to go: alone, with cronies of either sex, or with someone you cherish beyond all others at that particular moment. We'll call that one love and save it for last.

Although each of these modes can get tricky, alone is the most delicate to manage. Alone can lead to loneliness, and self-pity, and paranoia, and things like that — the trip can break down into dark questing after dubious companionship.

The advantage of going it alone lies, of course, in spontaneity and freedom. You don't have to consult anybody but your inclinations. You touch that warm car, and you climb in for a moment and roll down the window, just to see what it would be like.

And then, it's magic — you're rolling, you're gone and you're riding. Shit fire, you think, they don't need me, not today. I'm sick. This is sick leave. You know it's true. You've been sick, and this day of freedom will cure your great illness. Adios.

Say it is spring, as in *to rise or leap suddenly and swiftly,* the most dangerous and frothy season, sap rising and the wild geese honking as they fly off toward the north. "Ensnared with flowers I fall on grass." Andrew Marvell.

It might be the first day of everything, in which we rediscover a foreverland of freedom and beauty before the invention of guilt. A day when the beasts will all lie down with one another. Hummingbirds in the purple lilac.

What we are talking about is the first day of high and classical spring here in the temperate zones, one of those pure and artless mornings somewhere toward the latter part of May or early June in the countries where I have lived, when the cottonwood leaves have sprung from the bud and stand young and pale green against the faint, elegant cleanliness of the sky. We are talking about walking outside into such a morning and breathing deeply.

Where I like to head out of Missoula is upstream along the Blackfoot River, the asphalt weaving and dipping and the morning light lime-colored through the new leaves on the aspen, with some fine, thin, fragile music cutting out from the tape deck, perhaps Vivaldi concerti played on the cello. Such music is important in the early day. It leaves a taste as clean as the air across the mountain pastures, and it doesn't encourage you to think. Later, there will be plenty of thinking.

But early on all I need is the music, and the motion of going, and some restraint. It always seems like a good idea, those mornings up along the Blackfoot, to stop at Trixie's Antler Inn just as the doors are being unlocked. One drink for the road and some banter with the hippie girl tending bar.

But wrong.

After the first hesitation, more stopping at other such establishments is inevitable. And quite enjoyable, one after another. The Wheel Inn on the near outskirts of Lincoln, Bowmans Corner over south of Augusta, with the front of the Rockies rearing on the western skyline like purity personified.

Soon that fine blue bowl of heaven and your exquisite freedom are forgotten, and you are talking to strangers and to yourself. No more Vivaldi. It's only noon, and you are playing Hank Williams tapes and singing along, wondering if you could have made it in the country music business. By now you are a long and dangerous way from home and somewhat disoriented. The bartenders are studying you like a serious problem.

You have drifted into another mythology, called lonesome traveling and lost highways, a place where you really don't want to be on such a fine spring day. Once, it seemed like pure release to learn that you could vote with your feet, that you could just walk away like a movie star. Or, better yet, load your gear in some old beater pickup truck and drive. Half an hour, the vain-glorious saying went, and I can have everything on rubber. Half an hour, and I'll be rolling. You just watch, little darling.

For some of us, the consequences of such escape tended to involve sitting alone with a pint bottle of whiskey in some ancient motel room where the television doesn't work. The concept was grand and theatrical, but doing it, getting away, was oftentimes an emotional rat's nest of rootlessness. Country music, all that worn-out drifter syncopation, turned out to be another lie, a terrific sport but a real thin way of life.

So, some rules for going alone: Forget destinations; go where you will, always planning to stay overnight. Stop at historical markers, and mull over the ironies of destiny as you drive on. By now you're listening to bluegrass, maybe a tape from a Seldom Seen concert. And you are experiencing no despair.

Think of elk in the draws, buffalo on the plains, and the complex precision of predator-prey relationships. Be interesting, and love your own company. There is no need to get drunk and kill somebody on the road. Quite soon enough it will be twilight, and you can stop in some little town, check in at one of the two motels along the river, amble down to the tavern, and make some new friends. Such a pretty life.

Traveling with cronies is another matter. Some obvious organizational efforts are implicit. There stands your beloved car, warm in the sun. You touch a fender and turn away and backtrack toward your telephone, which magically starts ringing. Others have the same idea. My rig, your ice chest, bring money we're traveling.

But the real logistical niceties lie in the chemistry of compatibility. Not just every good friend is a fit companion for the heedless expeditions of a summer drive. Each stop and turnoff must seem the result of consultation with mutual inclination. Nothing spoils traveling more quickly than endless debate, or any debate at all. Trust the driver. Everybody knows what we're looking for. Take us there.

Which is where? Looking for what? Call it ineffable — that which cannot be expressed or described and is not to be spoken of. Traveling with cronies can't be heedless without unspoken agreement.

Back when we were young and idiot, we would head up to The Stockman's in Arlee, hit the Buffalo Park in Ravali, move on to the 44 Bar north of St. Ignatius, and then make the Charlo turn to Tiny's. From there whim led the way until we ended up in the Eastgate Lounge in Missoula around midnight. The circuit was called The Inner Circle.

Say the afternoon sky is streaked white, and spring winds drive storm clouds over the peaks of Montana's Mission Mountains. This is the Flathead Valley, and the town is Charlo, and though it may seem impersonal now, it need not be. If you are in any way sensible, your next move should be simple and clear and rewarding. You and your companions will clump down the stairs and into Tiny's Tavern. The place used to be called Tiny's Blind Pig, *blind pig* being prohibition code for tavern. The old name, for those of us who stopped by when we were passing through, implied a connection with the romance we were seeking — an outlaw dream of prohibition, dusty black automobiles just in from a rum-run to Canada, blonde gum-snapping molls. As newcomers we ached to be a part of Montana — and here it was, the real goddamned item.

One night my brother was shooting pool at Tiny's with a wiry old man, an electrician by trade as I recall. During a lull in the bar talk I heard something that stood the hair on the back of my neck. "Son of a bitch," my brother said, "I wouldn't have to cheat to beat you."

Oh, pray for us, Lord. Outlanders in a bar filled with local ranchers and their brawny sons celebrating another victory for the best eight-man football team in the history of Montana. Do not let them beat on us — at least, not on me. Take my brother.

The rancher next to me, about a foot taller than I will ever be, looked sideways and grinned. "Don't know about you," he said, "but I ain't going over there. Them old black eyes take about three weeks to heal." By the time I had bought him and me a drink, my brother and the electrician were finishing their game without any further hint of warfare.

Well, I thought, got myself home again. Home is a notion such backcountry taverns seem to radiate — at least if they're places that long-time patrons and their barkeep hosts have imprinted with the wear and damage of their personalities. Tiny's was shaped as much as anything by the old man who owned it when I first went there — ancient and hurting, hobbling around on crutches, a former police chief from Miami, Florida, with a huge collection of memorabilia in glass cases around the bar — over 5000 different kinds of beer bottle, intimate snapshots of Hitler taken in the 1930's, fine obsidian arrowheads, gem-quality Kennedy half-dollars. Tiny is dead now, and they've changed the sign over the doorway. But his collections are still in place.

Homes and love, if they are to exist as more than fond children of the imagination, most often take us by surprise on back roads. On my way to Missoula almost every day I pass the old Milltown Union Bar, where Dick Hugo used to do his main drinking in the days when he was serious about it. Above the doorway white heads of mountain goat and bighorn sheep, sealed in plexiglass bubbles, contemplate those who enter. As Hugo said in a poem about the Milltown, "You were nothing going in, and now you kiss your hand." In another poem, about another barroom, Hugo named the sense of recognition and homecoming I expect upon going into one of the taverns I love. His poem begins, "Home. Home. I knew it entering."

Indeed, what are we looking for? In July of 1969 I came to Montana to stay, bearing a new Master of Fine Arts degree from the flooding heartland of Iowa. I had just finished up as a thirty-five-year-old, in-off-the-ranch graduate student in the Iowa Writer's Workshop, and I had lucked into a teaching job at the University of Montana. I was running to native cover in the west; I was a certified writer, and this was the beginning of my real life at last.

During that summer in Iowa City — drinking too much, in love with theories about heedlessness and possibility — I was trying to figure out how to inhabit my daydream. We lived in an old stone-walled house with a flooded basement out by the Carolville reservoir, listening to cockroaches run on the nighttime linoleum and imagining Montana, where we would find a home.

Every morning the corn in the fields across the road looked to have grown six inches, every afternoon the skies turned green with tornado-warning storms, and every night lightning ran magnificent and terrible from the horizons. My wife said they ought to build a dike around the whole damned state of Iowa and turn it into a catfish preserve. The U-Haul trailer was loaded. After a last party we were history in the Midwest, gone to Montana, where we were going to glow in the dark.

The real West started at the long symbolic interstate bridge over that mainline to so many ultimately heart-breaking American versions of heaven, the Missouri River. Out in the middle of South Dakota I felt myself released into significance. It was clear I was aiming my life in the correct direction. We were headed for a town studded with abandoned tipi burners.

But more so — as we drove I imagined Lewis and Clark and Catlin and Bodmer and even Audubon up to Fort Union on the last voyage of his life in 1843, along with every wagon train, ox-cart, cattle drive, and trainload of honyockers, all in pursuit of that absolute good luck which is some breathing time in a commodious place where the best that can be is right now. In the picture book of my imagination I was seeing a Montana composed of major post cards. The great river sliding by under the bridge was rich with water from the Sun River drainage, where elk and grizzly were rumored to be on the increase.

Engrossed in fantasies of traveling upriver into untouched territory, I was trying to see the world fresh, as others had seen it. On April 22, 1805, near what is now the little city of Williston in North Dakota, Meriwether Lewis wrote:

. . . immense herds of buffalo, elk, deer, and antelopes feeding in one common and boundless pasture. We saw a large number of beaver feeding on the bark of trees along the verge of the river, several of which we shot. Found them large and fat.

By 1832, at the confluence of the Missouri and the Yellowstone, the painter George Catlin was already tasting ashes while trying to envision a future — just as I was trying to imagine what had been seen. Catlin wrote:

. . . the native Indian in his classic attire, galloping his wild horse, with sinewy bow, and shield and lance, amid the fleeting herds of

elks and buffaloes. What a beautiful and thrilling specimen for America to preserve and hold up to the view of her refined citizens and the world, in future ages! A nation's park, *containing man and beast, in all the wild and freshness of their nature's beauty!*

Think of Audubon responding eleven years later, on May 17, 1843, in that same upriver country around Fort Union:

Ah! Mr. Catlin, I am now sorry to see and to read your accounts of the Indians you saw — how very different they must have been from any that I have seen!

On July 21, Audubon writes:

What a terrible destruction of life, as it were for nothing, or next to it, as the tongues only were brought in, and the flesh of these fine animals was left to beasts and birds of prey, or to rot on the spots where they fell. The prairies were literally covered with the skulls of victims.

On August 5 Audubon finishes the thought:

But this cannot last; even now there is a perceptible difference in the size of the herds, and before many years the Buffalo, like the Great Auk, will have disappeared; surely this should not be permitted.

In our summer of 1969 we poked along the edge where the Badlands break so suddenly from the sunbaked prairies, imagining the faraway drumming of hooves, Catlin's warriors on their decorated horses coming after us from somewhere out of dream. Not so far south lay Wounded Knee.

We studied the stone faces of our forefathers at Mount Rushmore and didn't see a damned thing because by that time in the afternoon we were blinded by so much irony on a single day. We retired for the night to a motel somewhere south of the Devil's Postpile in Wyoming. I was seeing freshly, but not always what I hoped to see. The distances were terrifying.

By the time we reached Missoula, I had disassociated my

sensibilities with whiskey, which gave me the courage to march up the concrete steps to Richard Hugo's house, only a block from the Clark Fork River, where the Village Inn Motel sits these days. I rapped on his door. He studied me a moment after I introduced myself. "You're very drunk," he said.

Well hell, I thought, now you've done it.

"Wait a minute," Hugo said. "I'll join you."

Home, I thought, childlike with relief. This was the new country I had been yearning for, inhabited by this man who smiled and seemed to think I should be whatever I could manage.

I was lucky to know Dick Hugo, and his collected poems, *Making Certain It Goes On*, heads my list of good books written about the part of the world where I live. Dick loved to drive Montana, his trips imaginative explorations into other lives as a way toward focusing on his own complexities. He made the game of seeing into art, and his poetry and life form a story that lies rock bottom in my understanding of what art is for.

Once we drove over to fish the Jefferson River on a summer day when we were both hung-over to the point of insipid visionary craziness. We didn't catch any fish, and I came home numb, simply spooked, but Dick saw some things, and wrote a poem:

SILVERSTAR

This is the final resting place of engines,
farm equipment and that rare, never more
than occasional man. Population:
17. Altitude unknown. For no
good reason you can guess, the woman
in the local store is kind. Old steam trains
have been rusting here so long, you feel
the urge to oil them, to lay new track, to start
the west again. The Jefferson
drifts by in no great hurry on its way
to wed the Madison, to be a tributary,
to the ultimately dirty brown Missouri.
This town supports your need to run alone.

What if you'd lived here young, gone full of fear
to that stark brick school, the cruel teacher
supported by your guardian? Think well
of the day you ran away to Whitehall.
Think evil of the cop who found you starving
and returned you, siren open, to the house
you cannot find today. The answer comes back wrong.
There was no house. They never heard your name.

When you leave, leave in a flashy car
and wave goodbye. You are a stranger
every day. Let the engines and the farm
equipment die, and know that rivers
end and never end, lose and never lose
their famous names. What if your first girl
ended certain she was animal, barking
at the aides and licking floors? You know
you have no answers. The empty school
burns red in heavy snow.

Each time I read "Silverstar" I rediscover a story about homes, and the courage to acknowledge such a need, a story about Dick and his continual refinding of his own life, and an instruction about storytelling as the art of constructing road maps, ways home to that ultimate shelter which is the coherent self. Montana is a landscape reeking with such conjunctions and resonances. They fill the silence.

Not long ago, on a bright spring morning, I stood on the cliffs of the Ulm Pishkun where the Blackfeet drove dusty hundreds of bison to fall and die. Gazing east I could dimly see the great Anaconda Company smokestack there on the banks of the Missouri like a finger pointing to heaven above the old saloon-town city of Great Falls where Charlie Russell painted and traded his pictures for whiskey — only a little upstream from the place where Meriwether Lewis wrote, having just finished an attempt at describing his first sight of the falls:

After writing this imperfect description, I again viewed the falls,
and was so much disgusted with the imperfect idea it conveyed of

28

*the scene, that I determined to draw my pen across it and begin
again; but then reflected that I could not perhaps succeed better* . .

After so many months of precise notation, all in the service of
Thomas Jefferson's notion of the West as useful, in one of the
most revealing passages written about the American West, Lewis
seems to be saying:

*But this, this otherness is beyond the capture of my words, this
cannot be useful, this is dream.*

The dam-builders, of course, did not see it his way.

Behind me loomed the fortress of the rock-sided butte Charlie
Russell painted as backdrop to so much history, with the Rockies
off beyond on the western horizon, snowy and gleaming in the
morning sun. This listing could go on, but I was alone and almost
frightened by so many conjunctions visible at once, and so many
others right down the road: Boone Caudill and Teal Eye and Dick
Summers over west on the banks of the Teton River, where it cuts
through the landscapes of *The Big Sky* — history evident all
around and the imaginings of artists and storytellers intertwined.
Charlie Russell and Bud Guthrie and Dick Hugo and Meriwether
Lewis created metaphoric territory as real as any other Montana in
the eye of my imagination.

We all play at transporting ourselves new into new country,
seeing freshly, reorienting ourselves and our schemes within the
complexities of the world. It is a powerful connection to history,
and the grand use we make of storytelling as we incessantly
attempt to recognize that which is sacred and the point of things.

Which brings us to our most complex option, traveling with
lovers. In Missoula, in the heart of winter, if you are me, you talk
in a placating way to the woman you love. It is about three days
after you forgot another country custom, *The Valentine Party*.
You suggest ways of redeeming yourself. You talk to friends. An
expedition forms.

This paragon of a woman owns an aging four-wheel-drive
Chevrolet pickup, three-quarter-ton, and she and I and her twin

boys set off in that vehicle. Only praying a little bit. Good rubber, but a clanking U-joint. The friends — a southern California surfer hooked on snow skiing of all varieties, and a lady of his acquaintance — set off in that lady's vintage Volvo. We also pray for them. The Volvo wanders in its steering, in a somewhat experimental way. But no need for real fear. These are Montana highways.

Out of Missoula we caravan south through the Bitterroot Valley, where — before the subdivisions — Tom Jefferson could have seen his vision of pastoral American happiness realized. The Volvo wanders, the U-joint clanks, and we are happy. We wind up over Lost Trail Pass, where Lewis and Clark experienced such desperate vertigo in the wilderness on their way west. At the summit we turn east, toward the Big Hole Basin and a town named Wisdom. At 6,000 feet, the altitude in the Big Hole is too much for deciduous trees. The only color is the willow along the creeks, the red of dried blood.

We pass along the Big Hole Battlefield, where Joseph and Looking Glass and the Nez Perces suffered ambush by Federal troops under General Oliver Otis Howard on the morning of August 11, 1877. Casualties: Army, 29 killed, 40 wounded; Nez Perce, by Army body count, 89 dead, most of them women and children. We are traveling through the rich history of America.

Winter has come down on this country like a hammer, but the defroster is working perfectly and there is a bar in Wisdom with dozens of stuffed birds and animals on display around the walls. The place is crowded with weekend snowmobile fans in their bright insulated nylon coveralls. There is a stuffed quail on a stand with its head torn off. All that's left is just a little wire sticking out of the neck. What fun that night must have been.

The bar is fine. No one cares when we bring in our own cheese and stoneground wheat crackers. We slice on the bar top, scatter crumbs. The bartender cleans up our mess. Smiles. The kids play the pinball machine all they want. We have hot drinks. So we are slightly tipsy, not to say on the verge of drunk, when we line out south toward Jackson. This is the deep countryside of Montana, and no one cares. The Volvo doesn't wander as erratically. The U-joint has made peace with itself. Which is something country people know about mechanical devices. They oftentimes heal. At least for a little while.

The Big Hole is called the "Land of 10,000 Haystacks." Nearby, a country man is feeding his cattle. Pitching hay with ice in his mustache. He has been doing it every day for two months. He has a month to go. Feeding cattle never was any fun. We do not think about such matters.

Beyond Polaris we head up a canyon between five-foot banks of snow, and we are arrived. Elkhorn Hot Springs. Right away, we like it. Snowshoeing and cross-country in all directions, and for our surfer friend, a dandy little downhill area only about three miles away. We have a cabin with a fireplace that works fine after the wood dries out. Up in the lodge they are serving family-style dinners. And cheap. You know — roast beef and meat loaf and real mashed potatoes and creamed corn and pickled beets. And on and on. Maybe this is the moment to break out the bottle of rum.

Eventually we wander down to the hot baths, the indoor sauna pools and the outdoor pool, and the snow falling into our mouths. Snowball fights in the water. Rowdiness. Young boys in swimming suits created from cut-off Levis. And the next day, sweet red wine in the snow and white chilled wine in the evening, and the ache from all the skiing melting out of our knees into the hot water.

But electricity is in fact the way nature behaves. Nothing lasts. That was winters ago. My surfer friend went off hunting the last good wave. He wrote from Australia, extolling the virtues of the unexamined life. The Volvo is dead; the U-joint is fixed. Desire and the pursuit of the whole is called love.

William Kittredge

SILVER BULLETS

There they are, hard-handed riders just topping the ridge beyond the arroyo. Squint and shade your eyes against the desert glare, watch them move with quiet assurance, and thrill to their presence. Imagine the harsh clacking mechanical sounds as they lever shells into the firing chamber. Pretty soon now, as we know, they will come riding in and kill to save us from strangers.

It's an old, smoked, and seasoned American scenario: rescue by heroes come from our wilderness, cowboys and mountain men, Shane and George S. Patton, Big John Wayne from the Monument Valley, Deerslayer after Deerslayer defending us from strangeness and dark tides, bad dreams, savages, and bankers. Our sweet farmstead family-centered life will last forever, so the implications go, if we simply trust in such horsemen to defend our property and virtue.

Heroes are an ancient problem. There is the cutting quickness of violence, the warfare so elementally ended, and then what? The good hero, Shane, rides away into the mystical Tetons and is never heard of again. Who was that masked man? Why did he leave this silver bullet?

Most of the species we are talking about live in a racist, sexist, imperialist idealogical framework of mythology as old as settlements and invading armies. It is important to understand that the mythology of the American West is also the primary mythology of our nation and part of a much older world mythology, that of lawbringing. Which means it is a mythology of conquest. In America, this secular vision went most public in a story called the Western.

The plot line was there in the early vernacular tales about the possibilities of freeholding and Daniel Boone leading yeoman farmers to conquer the Kentucky outback. It became self-conscious in the novels of James Fenimore Cooper, and was knocked indelibly into our national brains and souls by the oceanic thousands of popular pulp novels published in the last century by such outfits as Beadle's Dime Library. Think of it — 1,700 novels about Buffalo Bill and his buffalo killing. It's true.

Most rudimentarily, our story of law-bringing is a story of takeover and dominance, ruling and controlling, especially by strength. Our American version springs from a vision of the New World, the vast continent we found, natural and almost magically alive, capable of inspiring us to awe and reverence, and yet curled dangerously around a heart of darkness inhabited by savages.

A disenfranchised pastoral people came to this land from Europe, intent on establishing a civilization where all men were free and equal, and where any man could find and own property. The first problem was the damned Indians. They were already settled on the land, and they wanted to live as they always had, and they had laws of their own to respect. And our law did not always command much respect even from those who brought it: people seeking frontiers are often people seeking escape from law, bringing terrible demons with them — lust and greed, for property and power.

Historically, we know what happened. Our pastoral people killed and they kicked ass, they subjugated the Indians and they took the land, they plundered; and when the dust had settled they owned all things from sea to shining sea, forever. Gold. Water. Whatever.

But the Western, our enfranchising myth, tells a prettier story. In the classical version, a good magical warrior comes from outside society, the terrible land of freedom that exists beyond the law. He is an "outlaw," and because of his life in the wilderness he possesses two skills that have been given up by those who choose to live protected and constrained by law: magical speed of hand with guns, and the wilderness knowledge that it is sometimes necessary to kill in the name of goodness.

This hero saves our people from the savage forces of lust and greed. He alone has the magic, and the strength of character to do so. And he is sad because he has to go away after he is finished with the killing, back to the mythological wilderness. His willingness to embrace violence, even in the service of law, is a disruptive force in a society that cannot endorse his ways. He is a killer; he does our dirty work, then carries our social guilt away with him, leaving us to go about the empire-building work of our days with clean hands and souls.

This is our great paradoxical, problematic American teaching

33

story. It is also the plot of *Shane*. The holy and innocent hero comes from the wilderness and slays the dragon, then rides away like a movie star. It is the Western, a morality play that was never much acted out anywhere in the so-called Real West. Or anywhere else.

The actual West was bloody enough, but its inhabitants were never so obsessed with showdown gunfighting as our story would have us believe. Had they been, nobody would have been left alive. More people have been killed in Missoula in any recent year than in Dodge City in its heyday. Certainly the West was not much traveled by holy gunfighters engaged in the business of setting things right.

So the yeoman farmers are saved from the men of greed who covet their hard-earned agricultural land, and Shane, however wounded, must ride back to his mythological home in the Tetons, those most American, isolated and upreaching mountains. The holy outsider leaves his silver bullet behind in a morality play that excuses us our history of violence. No wonder we loved it — and yet Western movies, by all Hollywood evidence, are dead.

But are they, really?

Why would they be dead? Violence is everywhere, and guilt, and we all want excuses from school. Maybe it's just that our heroes got sick of horses and no sex, riding away gut-shot into the Tetons, and went to other movies.

The Western's so-called demise was already apparent in *High Noon*, which came out in 1952, the year before *Shane*. At the end of a long day, the town saved and the bad men dead in the streets, Gary Cooper looks with contempt on the weak mercantilist townspeople he has defended, who will not move to defend themselves, and he throws his badge down in the dust. Then he rides away in the buggy with Grace Kelly, the Quaker wife who has spent this day learning to respect his warrior skills. Sometimes it is necessary to kill.

A nice cold-war parable, in which the good society has lost its nerve. By *Bonnie and Clyde*, in the mid-sixties, the heroes had become true professional outlaws, and who could blame them? The good society had become a nasty Great Depression joke in which the rich get richer and the poor suck whatever tit they can find for thin watery sustenance indeed. Despite obscure sexual problems, Bonnie and Clyde fight the bad rich people, and like Robin Hood they return money and pride to the last remnants of the good society, the poor folks back on the farm.

From *Bonnie and Clyde* it was an easy step to the classical professional Western, with its outlaw heroes who live outside society. We were losing terrible face in Vietnam, Manifest Destiny gone loco with napalm, and our nation's children were ducking the draft, smoking dope, and dropping out. Anybody worth a damn was an outlaw, and they were everywhere, the last best hope of humankind gone renegade.

Our good society was deep into chicken-shit venality, and everything was upside down. All our ideological chickens were coming home to roost, and we were learning to despise ourselves. The TV news continually played on images designed to generate national self-loathing. Our heroes were left stranded, without a good society to defend. So they banded together, and went on alone. *The Wild Bunch* came out in 1969, the same year as *Butch Cassidy and the Sundance Kid*.

Aside from an oasis village of fiercely independent Indians living humanely with one another down in nontechnological Mexico, remnants of a lost life to be yearned for, the only good society was Peckinpah's Wild Bunch itself, a little band of heroic comrades living off the detritus of a culture in which notions of communal life were sunk far into a quicksand of commonplace money-grubbing treachery. Who could care if they killed a whole shitload of townspeople in a street war with the Pinkertons? The classical Western, with strong and independent men defending a good but passive society, had gone away and left nothing worth defending. Butch and Sundance confront an impervious bank safe, mechanically tuned and sophisticated beyond any threat from their six-gun magic, and leave for Bolivia. Freeze frame.

A few years later, John Wayne played a loving old man's eulogy for his life and genre in *The Shootist*, and that seemed the ultimate tip of the cowboy hat. *Adios,* Buckaroo. The hero was gone, and private citizens were left to their own devices, like Charles Bronson in that climax revenger's comedy, *Death Wish*.

We knew it couldn't be true.

And sure enough, there in the last good movie we could possibly identify as a Western, a movie about a war over California water, Jack Nicholson played our hero resurrected on the streets of Los Angeles, wisecracking as he leads us down through the circles of urban hell and irony, our own sweet Virgil, until the bottom falls out. It's *Chinatown*, Jake, where our man is left isolated without the solace of love or respect or even meaningful comrades, and it's hard to think where to turn from his defeat.

Adios, indeed, it seemed to say. Where's that opium? Our society had grown up believing in heroes who would come riding in to save us, and now we found ourself in a society that wasn't worth saving. Our mythological story was revealed as a horseshit excuse for bad conduct and the pursuit of greed, for ruling and controlling, especially by strength.

What we did was wait ruefully for some new mythic flowering from the fire of our troubles, uneasily hanging on to that remnant of the story that says it is at least okay to defend ourselves. Paranoia movies — *Taxi Driver, Death Wish* — had us rooting for random revenge. *Dirty Harry* nursed the same grudge.

But vigilantism is an uncivilized solution. There are other ways to go. In *48 Hrs*, a clean, well-lighted black man comes out of the penitentiary wielding the fastest mouth in America, and saves our thick-sliced white man's bacon. Our city-hero, the detective whose investigations lead us through to insights about our underworld thickets, has gone Third-World and criminal and hip. Wouldn't it be pretty to think of this film as the cutting edge of possibility — the justifiably embittered grandchildren of slaves and natives emerging from the disenfranchised masses to forgive and save us with hard wisdom learned in their downtown wilderness, the story carrying wonderful implications about common humanity in our fight against chaos? Tonto, now that the masked man is gone, did he leave you any of those silver bullets?

It looked like we might have stranded ourselves far enough out on the shores of killer nihilism to be finally driven toward accepting responsibility for our own troubles. Some such recognition as this, however dim, probably accounted for the surprising popularity of a film like *Gandhi*. Confronted with end-of-the-world dragons of our own making, we were finally willing to embrace a hero of decency, whose main weapons were strength of will, intelligence, and *refusal* of heroism as we have known the disease. His gun was his mind, and he used it to back down the whole imperialist British Empire.

But no. We went on to *Rambo*.

In the meantime, back at the ranch, most of our heroes had run away to deep space and comic books. *Star Wars* played out all the old Western movie stops, magical warriors battling the Empire of merciless technology over nothing specific, Luke Skywalker, armed only with the Force, shutting down his computer to go at the Death Star after Han Solo, the mercenary warrior, couldn't get the job done. Shane saves the Wild Bunch. But since nobody asked us to think the story had any validity beyond diversion we loved it again, and why not?

Didn't it seem right? Escape was what we were looking for, from our powerlessness in the paranoid land of Godfathers, and wasn't it bound to lie out there in the timeless, mythic lands of make-believe films like *Conan, Flash Gordon, Superman,* and that Punk-Mystic-Western series which started with *The Road Warrior?* In those other countries our heroes could still go about their violent work without anybody having to worry about identifying with the losers: those people our parents never warned us about, ourselves.

For weren't daily walking-the-streets moral decisions complex and ambiguous enough without our having to contend with films like *Breaker Morant*, where the warrior heroes were mercilessly executed by the state after their time of usefulness ran out? How much did we want to know about the sadness of our own yearning for such figures?

Around 1953, when I was an enlisted man in the Air Force stationed at Travis, just north of San Francisco, the little movie house next to the base ran for six months filled up with crowds for *Shane*. But a few years ago when I taught it in a University of Montana film course, my audience of undergrad sophisticates laughed. And I could see why. But underneath I was pissed. *The Wild Bunch* was coming soon, and I bet them they wouldn't laugh at Sam Peckinpah. Sure enough, not one snicker.

Obviously, things have changed since *Shane*, since 1953. Mostly it's the sight of ourselves we see reflected there. Alan Ladd comes riding toward us, clad in his mountain-man buckskins, wearing his gun, the Tetons at his back, and he speaks with quiet Southern courtliness, the individual who travels alone, the lonely man with rules. Even his shortness doesn't matter because he is just so damned competent and sure of himself. We know he yearns to be absolved of his loneliness, and don't blame him for falling in with the family unit of Van Heflin, Jean Arthur and Brandon De Wilde, and siding with them and their agricultural neighbors against the traditional forces of acquisitiveness, the brutal ruling-class ranchers and their hired gunfighter, Jack Palance.

Money is always the core of these troubles. Shane is victorious at the end, as we knew he would be. It's a story we responded to with love in 1953. It seems simple-minded and sentimental now.

What has changed? Just us, our sense of what is possible in our society. *The Wild Bunch* tells us no such fairy tales about the possible triumph of pastoral life. The Wild Bunch are criminals rather than mountain men, in search of a last good heist, pursued by one of their own kind, Robert Ryan, another outsider, the only man capable of corralling them. But among themselves they still have a code of conduct. At least they do not lie to one another, and we still respect that remnant of what was dreamed of as America.

In *The Wild Bunch* both Anglo and Mexican societies are irreversibly corrupt. An Anglo drunk gives temperance lectures, and a Mexican general is infatuated with his automobile. But the pastoral dream has not vanished. Hidden in villages there is another life which might survive, although we doubt it, and doubt that it could do so for long. As for the Wild Bunch themselves, they are doomed, and go to their doom with sad relish, recognizing that modern life is impossible for them.

And the final image is not the great ceremonial slaughter we all remember; as the credits come down, it is the Wild Bunch riding out from that pastoral village bathed in green light and song and deep in the heart of the last good time while we wait to be discovered by a new story with which to order our lives, in which the strong inherit the earth for better reasons than firepower.

William Kittredge

RECOVERY

Now the stage becomes dark, and Man challenges Nature — a stirring encounter during which Nature is bitten on the hip, with the result that for the next six months the temperature never rises above thirteen degrees . . .

Woody Allen

I first saw an artificial hip joint in the office of my San Francisco orthopedic surgeon. He was like a little boy with an erector set when he opened the drawer of his desk and pulled out what looked like a railroad spike with a knob on top. It was stainless steel and was used to replace the femur and ball part of the hip joint. His eyes gleamed. Pins, those metal sticks used to hold together the broken parts of a joint, would still be used in certain cases, but the astonishing material available now made it possible to replace entire joints. I remember a tiny old aunt who, one day while standing on the corner waiting for a bus, was swept up and away by a strong wind. Her hip was shattered when she landed on the pavement in front of a gas station and a pin was placed in it. Afterwards, she limped and had to swing her leg while holding onto the dining room table.

He didn't show me the plastic socket. In fact, I've seen one only as a shadowy outline on an x-ray of my own hip after surgery three or four years later in another city. It looked like the bell of a jellyfish or, greatly reduced in size, a hairdryer in a beauty parlor. The stainless steel spike with the knob and the plastic jellyfish together make a total hip joint. The procedure is called arthroplasty.

For years I was considered too young for arthroplasty. Surgeons disagreed among themselves on the longevity of the materials. Then, one morning last March, the sun traced another line across the sky and both my years and the metals were perfected. I saw them as two lines on a graph finally crossing.

Both the surgery and the recovery went well, except for a minor bladder infection. But then, infection anywhere in the body is dangerous when a prosthesis has been installed in human tissue. There is always the possibility it may attack the cells around the foreign material and render them incapable of accepting it. But the fevers were subdued and I left the hospital on schedule. It was a full year, though, before I was able to walk normally without pain.

Looking back across the months from the distance of my beachfront living room, I can still see the endless corridors as I saw them from the cart, converging like lines in stereopticon. And I can still see the wilderness of buildings, clouds, planes, rain, snow, and tossing branches I gazed at for thirteen days through the window of my hospital room. But I never hear the music anymore. I haven't heard it since the day I left. Once, playing the radio in the car, *Lara's Theme* enveloped me briefly like vapor from an aerosol can, but when I changed the station, it vanished. I can never hear that song without reliving the whole experience.

When I wake up I'm still in the operating room. My eyes are closed like a newborn kitten's, but I can hear the conversation of the nurses, the anesthesiologist who again is doing something to my arm. I'm vaguely aware the needle is gone. They're talking about karate. My doctor's voice, at first close, becomes more distant, then is gone. The others continue to talk. I can't feel my right leg at all, but something is pushing on my left one, something like a giant bellows squeezing and releasing. A minute or so passes before it squeezes, releases again. I don't like it. But even more uncomfortable is the pressure in my bladder. Besides my left leg, it's the only part of my body with any sensation. It occurs to me to ask for a bedpan, but I think better of the notion and wait. I can't even cross my legs. Although I was Hip Number Two and there is one more to follow me, no one seems to be in any hurry to get me out of there. I open my eyes and stare directly into the face of the anesthesiologist six inches away. He's removing a white cotton wrapping from my arm and seems startled by my gaze.

40

"Hi," I say, but he doesn't answer.

The position of my cart in the recovery room is opposite a wall with a clock. I see that it's shortly after noon and am relieved that everything has gone on schedule. I think about the x-ray of my right hip which loomed, brilliantly backlit, over the operating room and consider that it will never be part of my body again.

Two nurses walk back and forth between the carts, some of which bear bodies, others of which are empty. This is like a morgue, I think. On my right is a man who lies with his nose pointed solemnly at the ceiling. His eyes are closed and his head is swathed in yards of gauze and tape. There's nothing about him to suggest he's alive.

My bladder has swelled larger. One of the nurses swishes past and I ask her for a bedpan. She stops short, giving a little squeak.

"Did you say something?" she exclaims, leaning over and peering into my face as closely as I had peered into the face of the anesthesiologist.

"Bedpan." I realize now I'm slurring.

"You don't mean it!" she says, but turns and comes back shortly with a yellow plastic one which she has the skill to slide under my buttocks without disturbing my operated side.

I watch the clock proceed from twelve-thirty to one and then to one-thirty. I'm only vaguely aware of an I.V. bottle hanging over my left shoulder, the rubber tube descending from it, and the needle entering my arm. My bladder gets fuller and fuller, the membrane (I imagine it like the interior of a football) becoming more and more distended. The man beside me in the gauze and adhesive tape skull cap never moves. There are blue veins in his nose.

No use. At ten after two a decision is made to wheel me back to my room on Six Southwest. I'm not exactly sure just where that is in relation to the operating room in this part-new, part-old hospital, but I know Six Southwest is new. I don't notice much along the way, just that the bedpan has been removed and that something the size of a watermelon is occupying the space where my bladder should be.

In my room I meet for the first time the lovely nurse June.

Lovely because, besides being young and blonde, she understands.

"Your sphincter muscles," she announces, "are still under the
effects of the spinal anesthesia."

I beg her to catheterize me. I can't believe what I'm saying. No
one has ever asked to be catheterized.

She frowns.

"I'll have to consult your doctor. It could give you an infection
and that would be bad."

"Ask him, ask him," I prod.

"He doesn't make rounds until about seven."

"I can't wait." It occurs to me if I screamed it would help, but I
don't.

June is the RN on the floor. Rather, one of two RNs. She has
the private wing this week. She leaves for a moment, then returns,
having made a decision. She's carrying a tube and a large metal
pan. After a couple of minutes the large metal pan is full. She
calls for another receptacle. And then another. No one believes it.

My doctor is furious with her because, after that, I do get an
infection. Antibiotics are doubled.

I discover, soon enough, that I'm able to sleep only on my back.
Since infancy I've slept on my stomach, or at least fallen asleep in
that position. Now I can't fall asleep at all. For four days only
Demerol lets me drift away. One shot every four hours. First one
shoulder gets it, then the other. Finally they start making tracks
up and down my upper arms.

"What ever became of morphine?" I ask, longing for a deeper
submersion. Everyone gasps.

As the spinal anesthesia wears off, I become aware that
something is squeezing my right leg every couple of minutes, just
as I knew when I woke in the operating room that something was
squeezing my left. Both of my lower appendages are encased in
white plastic stockings to which are attached hoses leading to a
yellow compressed air tank. It sits at the foot of my bed, refugee
from some flight into space, and pumps into the stockings air
which massages like fingers the immobile muscles of my calves.

I'm told this prevents blood clots. I hated it earlier and I hate it now.

As well as the man who comes every day to make me inhale three-quarters of the earth's atmosphere which I must blow into his machine. I don't like him either. He wears a brown business suit, making me suspicious of his medical credibility. The huffing and puffing keeps my lungs clear and reduces the threat of pneumonia.

My right leg is suspended in a metal sling called a Zimmer. A length of lamb's wool reaching from my upper calf to my ankle supports it as it hangs in the air. Later, I'll exercise with it, they tell me.

My mind is alternately wild with energy, news, ideas, images, then set afloat on a blissful sea of unconsciousness after each Demerol injection. I'm on the phone with my daughter Emily, with friends Gen and Harriet. I call Lester at the office, my mother. I even phone City Hall about a neighbor's illegal fence. Everyone is amazed at my lucidity so soon after major surgery. My brain races, gets ahead of itself, maneuvers around corners and into tight crevices, emerges, and speeds on. But to erase the pain which becomes more and more evident as the spinal anesthesia wears off, I ring for the nurse who has the needle. Then it's as if a shade were pulled down, a blank shade without pictures. I doze off, not dreaming, not caring. The music hasn't started yet.

On the fourth day after surgery, I learn to live without Demerol. I don't know whose decision this is, perhaps my doctor's, but probably mine. Every square inch of both arms has been used and there's a large black-and-blue mark in the shape of a Rorschach ink blot on my right shoulder, where one of the nurses missed the muscle. Now the sleepless nights begin.

I'm lying in two a.m. darkness, my head aching and my stomach on fire, thinking about the pituitary gland. I read somewhere that it's shaped like a berry. Is it like a blueberry glistening with dew in the pre-dawn shadows deep inside the brain? With my eyes open I can make out the large rectangle of the window, the draperies' geometric squares in black, rust, and white. Light is sliding over the floor from some source I can't see like underwater lights in a swimming pool. With my eyes closed, I try to see the pituitary gland. Maybe it looks like a raspberry, the little round segments red and dusted with fuzz.

They've taken away the deep breathing machine. The yellow tank full of compressed air is gone too, along with the white plastic stocking which were fed by it every two minutes. I'm wearing white *elastic* stockings now and my legs expand and contract like the valves of a heart or the gills of a fish.

I feel like I'm lying on nails. I count the hours and for ninety-six of them I've been on my back, except for a half hour each night when three nurses push, lift, tug, and roll me over to my left side where I balance on my pelvic bone until they return and maneuver me onto my back again. Once the nurses worked me over to the edge of the bed and let my legs dangle over. They stood me up for fifteen seconds and I looked under my right arm to see the eleven-inch incision which begins part way down my thigh and disappears up and around the bend of my buttock. It was held together by a row of brown bristles like the whiskers of a walrus.

The pituitary gland must look, I think, a bit like a tiny clapper in a large bell. The slightest movement and there's ringing. The clapper is necessary for the merriest tinkle, the loudest gong. When the pituitary is still, the body is silent. But the body clangs and clangs when the pituitary swings unexpectedly. That's why my head pounds and my stomach aches, why my back contracts with pains. The spinal anesthesia ran south to the fork of my legs, then along the route of my nerves until my right side was paralyzed. But some part of it also ran north to my brain and the pituitary.

I'm lying in the valley of my eight good pillows. They surround me like snowy hills. They prop me, keep me in place, but they don't help me sleep. Nor does Seconal. I must complain about that in the morning.

It's not music at all when I first hear it. It's a sort of buzzing, a swarm of bees on the right side of the bed. Without thinking, I start to turn, then remember I can only twist. But there's nothing there.

44

)kay. I'll sleep. If I shift all my weight to my left side, maybe that will work. The nightstand beside the bed is a dark hulk, and the books, magazines, cards, purse, and Kleenex piled on top of it make a jagged outline against the window beyond. Another hospital is framed in the glass. Its windows look back at me.

Now I hear it for the first time: *Edelweiss, edelweiss, every morning you greet me, small and white, clean and bright . . .* where is it coming from? I push the button which raises the head of the bed until my body and my legs make an angle of about one hundred fifty degrees. Ninety degrees or less can dislocate the prosthesis. An all-male chorus is singing. I can't quite make out the words, but I know the tune. I lean closer to the nightstand containing the TV tuning apparatus and pull back the hair from around my left ear. The voices could be coming from the little round holes in the speaker. I turn the volume down as far as it will go. I push the on-off button to make sure it's really off. Nothing. I turn on the light and examine the printing above each knob. One says RADIO, and when I turn it, it stops in six places. Six stations. But there seems to be no way to turn it off. There's no way to turn it on either.

Is it the radio? The voices seem to be coming more from the direction of the window seat. I switch the light off and peer into the depths of the console. Maybe it's a faulty transistor.

The all-male chorus has finished its version of *Edelweiss* and now a string orchestra is playing the same melody. They get through it once and start over again. The second time, they stop halfway through and go back to the beginning. *Edelweiss, edelweiss* . . . the violins have deep smooth voices, but why do they keep repeating the same phrases over and over?

It's a rehearsal! That's it! But where? Zurich or Vienna or anywhere it's not three in the morning. Is my new hip joint picking up radio signals? I'm disregarding the fact that rehearsals aren't likely to be broadcast. I've heard of people whose silver inlays or fillings pick up radio stations. What if all my life now I'll have to listen to whatever the stainless steel head of my femur chooses to send pulsing to my inner ear. I move my leg to see if I can get it to play something else.

45

All at once the violins fade and the all-male chorus starts in again. Only briefly though. Suddenly birds are chirping the melody. *Edelweiss, edelweiss.* Robins and larks. They tweet right through to the end and go back to the beginning. Hundreds of birds have miraculously learned the tune. *Blossom of snow, may you bloom and grow, bloom and grow forever.* They haven't memorized the words, but I supply them.

For ten minutes the birds sing from some vague recess in the air. Then a man shouts, a piano plays lively dance music, and the number ends in a crash of keys.

I fall asleep.

I've never by habit arisen early. Those poets whose albas celebrate dawn have always puzzled me. Yet here in the hospital, I find myself looking forward to the sky's gradual graying, to the bustle in the hallway when nurses are changing shifts. It's seven a.m. I've had three hours sleep. Then I remember. It's Friday. I'm going to Physical Therapy today.

My impatience to be down there is related, I suppose, to the urge some women have to get out of bed mere hours after childbirth and scrub the floor. I imagine Physical Therapy as a kind of country, a land where beautiful mended bodies, shining and whole, some even healthily flushed with exertion, pedal or roll or pull under lights soft as the southern sun. It's a happy place and I'm anxious to go.

Everyone appears at once: a nurse's aide with a thermometer; a registered nurse with a little paper cup, the kind used for nuts at a children's party, full of pills; a practical nurse who takes from the bedstand a wash basin and soap; a girl in a green uniform bearing a tray with breakfast on it. I persuade her to open the draperies all the way so that I can see not only the hospital on the opposite hill but the powder-box roof of the new indoor stadium as well.

It's a typical March day: a huge black cloud in the upper right-hand corner of the window, baby blue on the left, and in between, tatters of sunshine on the roof of the building below. In a minute it's raining and the bare twigs of the birch trees whip around in the wind. I think of turning on the TV set.

46

Raising myself on my left elbow, I see it: the bedside console. It looks innocent enough. I put my ear to it as I did last night. Silence. But wait, far away, so far away . . . what is it? Yes. It's *Lara's Theme*. Somewhere, my love . . . da da dee da da da. The sound track from "The Sound of Music" and the one from "Dr. Zhivago" too!

I look at the console more closely: there's a metal label centered just below the controls:

Electronic Bedside Unit
120 VAC   60HZ   10AMP
Serial Number 17864
ES2 Not for Use In
Anesthetizing Location
HILL-ROM COMPANY, INC.
Division of Hillenbrand Industries
Batesville, Indiana

and

UL
Listed
Nurse Call Equipment
Electronic Bedside Unit
521 N

From now on I'll think of it as the Electronic Bedside Unit. It's more fitting. The sterility of its shelves for Kleenex and Swipes, its cupboard for the stainless steel bowl and yellow plastic bedpan, its brown plastic buttons and chrome knobs for summoning nurses or TV images, the wires and circuits inside: all beg for a more scientific designation than bedstand or console.

I remember the pinewash stand in my grandmother's rural Pennsylvania kitchen. Under its lid was a white washbasin ringed with green thistles. Next to it were a soap dish in the same pattern and a small rounded glass in the Wedgewood white for the family's seven toothbrushes. When the lid was closed, the grandest piece of the set stood on top, a big pitcher with a scalloped handle and pouring spout, thistles and white.

From the black speaker beside me *Lara's Theme* is illicitly seeping. I promise myself to get to the bottom of the affair.

"How do you turn the radio on?" I ask Madge Okada who comes in to wash my back.

"You can't," she says. "There's no radio in there."

She's referring to the Electronic Bedside Unit.

"It's wired for a radio, but not connected. Maybe when the building is finished they'll hook it up."

I remember then the man who sat in the admitting office with me Sunday afternoon. On top of his suitcase was a bright yellow table model radio, its brown cord wound around and around it, crisscrossing the dial and the speaker. He had come prepared.

It requires three people to hoist me from the bed to the cart. One of my eight pillows goes with me between my legs. I hook my right arm around the orderly's neck and with a heave I slide across the mattress. A nurse's aide lifts my legs. Another takes my robe from the closet and, laying it across my stomach, straps me firmly onto the cart. It's flatter than any medieval conception of the earth. It's as hard as quarry tile which I suspect is underneath the sheet covering it. All my bones poke into me.

It's pleasant though to take in new scenery. Chris, the orderly from Physical Therapy, wheels me deftly down the widely angled halls of Six Southwest and, although I walked them nervously the night before surgery, it's as if I've never seen them before. We pass a long row of windows lining a hall to another wing. Through them I see snow swirling against the panes. The sun is inexplicably shining.

Chris has a red beard and from my supine position I look straight up at its bushy bottom. Chris is a beard and two nostrils. He's an art student and has studied in New York. Now he pushes orthopedic patients to and from the Physical Therapy department of the hospital ten hours a day, seven days a week, followed by seven days off when he paints. I want to lie on my side, bend my knees, raise my head. But I can't.

The elevator takes us to the basement. Six Southwest opened

just three months ago. Some of the rest of the hospital is fairly new, remodelled four or five years ago. But Physical Therapy is located in the oldest part of the hospital still in use and the halls leading to it are already half torn away. Wires hang forlornly from exposed beams. The walls and ceilings are a patchwork of mortar, tile, and vizqueen. I see loudspeakers over doors opening on nothing.

It's like the line-up at the supermarket check-out stand. Only I'm in the basket. Chris jockeys my cart into a position against the wall, sixth from a yellow doorway, and goes away. I lie stiff as Nefertiti's mummy under my sheet. Pains shoot like arrows up and down my back and legs. There's no way I can keep the tears from running down my face. Like rain in gutters, they stream into my ears. Thunder crashes outside and from the room with the yellow doorway I hear a man's voice moaning no no no. Thunder rolls again, deep and close.

There's something brightly colored just over my head to the right. Twisting, I see it's a picture of two birds and I try to concentrate on their teal blue plumage. They perch on a vertical branch. The higher one holds a brown berry in its beak and leans to drop it in the open beak of the other. The lettering beneath is written in script and it takes me some minutes to make out what it says, reading it as I am from the bottom up. They're Passenger Pigeons, *Columbia Migratoria*, Male 1, Female 2. I notice as I'm finally wheeled through the yellow doorway that the entire hallway is lined with pictures of birds. I waited under an extinct breed.

His name is Bob. He has kind eyes but he tells me I must push my right leg out hard against the palm of his hand. There is a large rat in my thigh. Its teeth gleam in the desert moonlight. I feed it again and again with the only food I have until somewhere on the other side of the curtain, a telephone rings. I'm glad to be left alone while Bob takes the call although he instructs me to practice head lifts while he's gone.

All at once someone starts a machine in the next room. Water splashes, a motor whirrs. Probably the whirlpool bath in the room next to this one. I remember seeing it as I was wheeled past on the cart. How lovely it would be to lie with the warm water moving around my legs like soft, hungry house cats. Suddenly, quite distinctly out of the bubbling and churning, come the strains of a familiar song. I abandon the head lifts to listen more closely. It's *Auld Lang Syne*. It's Guy Lombardo and New Year's Eve in Times Square!

I'm told, although I've never seen it myself, of course, that propped in my hospital bed I'm like the star in a stage play. A row of lights flanks me on either side, ready to illuminate me. The Electronic Bedside Unit guards me on the left, on the right a table which slides up and over the bed or folds down. Above on a chain hangs the metal trapeze I grab for lifting myself. The Zimmer swings at the end of the bed. And the bed itself is electric, capable of folding me up in its middle if the wrong switch is activated.

I have the upper half raised so that I'm sitting up each morning when some representative of the medical profession arrives. Not my doctor, but one of his associates. There are five of them in all, I deduce. They usually appear while I'm eating breakfast.

"Hi," I say. Then, before he can dart behind the curtain and vanish for the day, "Please change me to another sleeping pill."

"Didn't the Seconal work?"

"I thought it was Nembutol."

"No, you were switched from Nembutol to Seconal."

"I thought I was switched from Seconal to Nembutol."

"It was the other way around."

"Can I try something else?"

"I'll leave an order for Dalmane," he said, and left, whoever he was.

I love being alone in my room, the door closed against hallway traffic, my ears alert for violins. Hearing Guy Lombardo in the whirlpool bath means the music can't be coming out of the Electronic Bedside Unit. Or does it?

Electronics. I confess to myself I don't know what it is. Those 747s flying low over the hospital on their approach to the airport: some of the passengers inside are wearing earphones, listening to taped music. Maybe the transistors in the Electronic Bedside Unit are picking up the waves even when the unit isn't turned on. No. It could be even more complicated than that. What about the dozens of electrical and electronic devices in the hospital: the x-ray machines, dialysis machines, equipment for electrocardiograms, ultrasound, microwave ovens, electric beds, even telephones and elevators? I'm surrounded by circuits and wires and transistors. Currents might easily cross, messages garble, the pulses of one machine vibrate through the veins of another.

But why am I the only one to hear the music?

I gaze at the collage I asked mother to scotch tape to the wall opposite my bed when she visited yesterday. It arrived in the morning mail, a large manila envelope with a rectangle of cardboard inside. On it Douglas had pasted clippings from magazines: a girl skiing, a Monterey cypress, a shell, seaweed, a seagull, blue sky, the bow of a boat, and, in the lower left-hand corner, a man and a woman walking along a beach, the sea and the rocky headland stretching clear to the upper left. Across the top in the cut-out letters of a ransom note: Get Well.

There are no mountains out there. No sand. No sea. There is no world beyond this hospital room. Apparently I'm the only one who knows this.

The man in the next room has a tape deck. One nurse mentioned it to another this afternoon, and since she'd forgotten to close my door when she left the room, I overheard her. I also overheard that his name is Mr. Morley.

He's another total hip. Seventy-three. He hasn't walked since he was eleven years old. He travelled from east of the mountains to this kingdom of insomniacs to lie, like the rest of us, in the changeless position of a fossil locked in its bed of stone. When the Seconal fails and the Nembutol, does he crave some lullaby to soothe him to sleep? He's taped *Edelweiss* and *Lara's Theme!* To the strains of *Somewhere, My Love* he's blissfully dreaming, the tape deck going around and around like a satellite in space, the music repeating.

I use nighttime now for plotting and experimenting. I try, for instance, to make the music stop by changing the position of my head. My metal bed would be a good conductor and so I push the button which raises the upper part of the mattress and when the angle is steep enough, I slide down until my feet are hanging over the end. There's no noticeable difference. I try clasping and unclasping the trapeze over my bed. I try swinging the Zimmer in all the directions it will go. I put my fingers in my ears to see if something's spinning in my head. So why not investigate the Sleep Tape Theory?

I push the nurse call button on the Electronic Bedside Unit. It, in turn, lights up a bulb above 602 at the nurses' station. In only a few seconds a dazzling brunette pokes her head around the white curtain I kept drawn in front of the closed door. She's a new one.

"You're going to think I'm mad," I began.

"Mad gr-r-r-r?"

I like her immediately. She tells me she's a "float," works this floor and this wing only every now and then, which is why I haven't seen her before. I explain about the music and my theory involving Mr. Morley's tape deck.

I've noticed among the night nurses a certain curiosity about the matter of the music. Except for Madge Okada, the nurses on day duty are preoccupied with baths and pills, with strapping you onto stretchers and carts in the most painful position possible. I asked Madge one day if she heard *Lara's Theme* coming from the speaker in the Electronic Bedside Unit when the radio that wasn't in it wasn't turned on. She put her ear to the speaker, shook her head, and announced, "Nope, she's gone back to Siberia."

The "float" is interested in my theory and scurries off to Mr. Morley's room.

"I'll pretend I'm checking his urinal," she says, her dark brown eyes gleaming.

In three minutes she's back.

"Nothing's moving," she says.

"You're sure the tape deck isn't going around?"

"I'm sure. Mr. Morley is asleep."

For a second my mind goes to the urinal. Was it full? Then I hear her suggest that maybe the woman in the room on the other side has brought her radio from home.

"I never hear her," I say in defense. "Only when one of her visitors pulls the folding chairs from the wall clamps. What's underneath?"

"Medical."

"What's that?"

"Heart patients. Cancer. Kidney disease. They sleep all night."

Do they dream too, I wonder?

"What's above us," I ask.

"The roof."

Ah, yes. The roof. I should have known that. On the cart, staring straight up from my lashed position, I've seen the brown stains around the accoustical tiles of the ceiling. Leaks. The new wing is imperfect.

The "float" leaves me to my ruminations. That's when I hear in quick succession, one scarcely letting the other sing itself out before the next begins, three new numbers. First, *Happy Birthday To You*, although I'm a Scorpio and this is March. Next, *Hi Lily Hi Lo*. And then, formidably, *The Battle Hymn of the Republic*. They come from behind the bed. I roll to my left side, grab the headboard with both hands and perilously hike myself up just far enough to peer over. Nothing. Nothing there but the eye of the nightlight spreading a faint fan of illumination over the floor.

My walker and I go walking every day now. Homo erectus. It's a strange kind of ambulation. I clutch the aluminum with both hands and shuffle forward, one foot at a time, heel, toe, heel, toe. My legs can't remember how to do it. Is it all right to bend my knee? Both knees? Not too much weight on the right one. Then the rat comes out of the crevice in the rocks and his eyes are gleaming ore.

Some adjustment in my inner ear must be responsible. Each time I return to my horizontal position and the room quiets and the clouds resume their usual cant in the sky, the entertainment begins. *Lara's Theme* floats from the TV speaker. *Edelweiss* drifts from the blower in the heating unit under the window seat. And now, another new tune! I lean closer to the speaker in the Electronic Bedside Unit. There's no doubt. *Five foot two, eyes of blue, oh what those five feet can do, has anybody seen my gal?* I can even make out the words!

I ring for the nurse.

"June, listen. This thing's playing and it's not even turned on!"

June dutifully leans over and puts her ear to the speaker in the Electronic Bedside Unit. She slowly shakes her head, then attempts to change the subject by mentioning cheerily that it's time for my pills. She whips into the hall and comes right back with a little paper cup full of green, red, yellow, orange, and brown capsules and tablets.

I stare at them.

Green is for iron. Brown for thyroid. Red for something I can't remember. The yellow one is a stool softener. Orange is the antibiotic I still take four times a day. Although my bladder infection has been cured, no chances are being taken.

"June," I say, "are you sure you don't hear *How Much Is That Doggy In The Window?*"

It occurs to me I'm hallucinating. Red, green, brown, yellow, orange. I'm drugged. Why didn't I think of it before? I'm having auditory hallucinations! In the eyes of the staff I'm a madwoman. I think of Moses and the voice of God booming from the one cloud over the Midian desert. I consider Joan of Arc, the whispers of saints in her ears.

On the wide windowsill blooms the Visiting Orchid. Brian said it should be placed there, to the far left where the sun as it traverses toward the west can endow it with its smile all afternoon. Gen thought it would do better on the shelf next to the TV set, where, should the sun come out, the light would be more diffuse. Three times the orchid went back and forth until finally it stayed on the windowsill, since it was a cloudy day.

I look at it now, the pale blossom which seems to be a lavender but up close is creamy with pale pink spots. It's perfect, for isn't that why people like orchids? Their perfection and their fragility. The calamities which can occur: bacteria, fungus, sunburn. And the perfection which is always possible in spite of it all. It leans out into the medicinal air, frail but sturdy on its twisting brown stalk. What did they say it's called? *Mixed Blessing.*

A change is occurring. *Lara's Theme* and *Edelweiss* are being replaced, perhaps for the sake of my questionable sanity. If I am indeed hallucinating, I'm doing it with the minds and ears of my mother and aunts. When they were young, my mother told me, they used to walk arm in arm every evening down the dirt street of their little country town. When they weren't looking for The Dipper or chattering, they sang. Songs like *In the Gloaming* and *Let The Rest Of The World Go By.* Idyllic, pastoral. Maybe they sang *Tramp, Tramp, Tramp, The Boys Are Marching.* And when my mother was old enough, she might have danced to *Put your little foot, put your little foot, put your little foot right there, put your little foot, put your little foot, put your little foot right there.*

Suddenly I realize that many of the lyrics concern *feet.* Or feet involved in some kind of activity. *Mine eyes have seen the glory of the coming of the Lord. They are TRAMPLING out the vintage where the grapes of wrath are stored. Five foot two, eyes of blue,* oh what those FIVE FEET CAN DO. TRAMP, TRAMP, TRAMP, *the boys are MARCHING.* Leslie Caron danced to *Hi Lily Hi Lo.*

I began pool therapy today. Wheeled down the long hall with the Audubon prints, I lay swathed in sheets. I wore a pink-and-white candy striped romper suit safety-pinned at the shoulders. Chris pushed me to the shallow end of the pool where I was unveiled. The sheets peeled off. I rolled to the edge of the water. How did my legs get in? I was clinging to the blue tile edge, walking sideways like a crab. Walking! At the deep end the water reached to my ribs. As I walked back and forth from one side to the other, I hung onto metal bars. It seems now I must have been wearing seven league boots. Or was I, for that short time, a butterfly emerged from a chrysalis of sheets? I moved in a biome of lightness.

Mr. Morely entered shortly after me in a canvas sling which lowered him gently into the pool. I'm ashamed now that I accused him of having a Sleep Tape. Although he appeared to be the kind who might like *Lara's Theme*. Tomorrow I'll go about things more scientifically.

The TV service man turns out to be a girl. I thought, before ruling out the possibility of some electronic malfunction in favor of auditory hallucinations, I should have the system checked.

The TV set, which sits on a high shelf opposite my bed, is connected to the Electronic Bedside Unit by some mysterious network of wires inside the walls. I can turn it off and on, raise and lower the volume, change channels, by twisting knobs. The sound flows out of the Bedside Unit's speaker.

The TV girl wants to know why I'd like the TV speaker's wires disconnected from the Electronic Bedside Unit's wires. I was certain she'd ask.

"Well," I start out. "Can you hear anything right now? Music, I mean. Can you hear someone singing *We'll build a sweet little nest somewhere in the west and let the rest of the world go by?*" I feel foolish.

She says no. But she doesn't laugh.

"I've got a radio at home that plays jazz when it's not plugged in," she says.

A wavelet of envy laps over me. She hears *South Rampart Street Parade* while I have to listen to *The Battle Hymn Of The Republic*.

But the experiment fails. She's pleased to play detective but when the two speakers are disconnected, some faint unrecognizable tune still floats around the room like a ghost whose soul is denied rest.

"It's funny," she says. "When I unplug my radio at home, I never hear anyone speaking. It's always just music and singing. And it always sounds like it's coming from so far away. Like it's coming from the moon."

I'm still considering that remark. It would explain why the numbers aren't contemporary, why they were popular years and years ago. The moon or some other distant body in space, maybe a *radio star*, received those signals decades ago and now is sending them back!

I'm rising in a bathysphere from some deep water place. The Mariana Trench had me chained in darkness. There were no dreams. Now I'm coming up. Up. Slowly. The water turns from black to deep luminous blue, then to a kind of feathery green. I'm nearing the surface. I'll drown if I can't breathe.

One of the night nurses stands beside the bed, in her hand the little paper cup.

"I'm sorry to wake you," she says. "You can have another sleeping pill if you want."

I swallow the antibiotic and then the Dalmane, which seems to work.

"This is the last time I'll have to get you up in the middle of the night. Doctor's taking you off antibiotics."

I try to remember what color it is. Red? Purple? Not green. That's iron.

I turn to get back into the bathysphere but both it and the water are gone.

There's something different about the room. Some motion, some force as subtle and pervasive as the change of seasons inhabits the air. Is it spring? I sense leaves pushing through membranes, bulging and flexing. Just outside the window, sap is driving upward in the trees. Nothing can stop it. It rises to the highest branches. Beyond the glass there is the fresh, heady roar of a city. The TV speaker is silent. The Electronic Bedside Unit is mute. The fan inside the window seat is blowing warm air into the room.

Suddenly I realize the violins are no longer playing. Not the smallest shred of a melody hangs in the air. The all-male chorus is gone and the lofty choir intoning *Mine eyes have seen the glory of the coming of the Lord.*

Which is the hallucination, I wonder. The silence? Or the day-and-nightlong pouring of song into my head? I feel for the first time since surgery that I might actually walk again someday without pain. Like Rogers and Astaire, the acetabulum and the ball head of the femur are partners in a dance. I see them gliding across the floor. Ginger is bending over Fred's outstretched arm until her hair brushes the hardwood. Nobody thinks about bone or plastic or stainless steel. Only the dance matters.

I never hear Guy Lombardo in the whirlpool bath anymore. Maybe my scraping and clumping along the Audubon hallway on my crutches drowns him out. Maybe he's gone back to Times Square. But through my room still waft the strains of twenty pieces. I escape only into the shower. There I soap what parts of me I can reach without narrowing too many angles and cling to the metal bars around the stall.

I'm not hallucinating. I haven't swallowed an antibiotic for seventy-two hours. Yet the music goes on. Now it's the holidays. *Jingle Bells* and *Silent Night*. What if the stainless steel in my hip joint is receiving signals, after all? When I'm finally home, will I pick up *Hark The Herald Angels Sing* clear from the moon?

This is my last day. An orderly from x-ray appears in the doorway shortly after ten in the morning. My hip is to be photographed one more time before I leave, the fifth picture-taking session in thirteen days. I think idly of radiation poisoning as I'm strapped to the cart and wheeled away.

X-ray hasn't improved during my stay. A series of right angle turns executed with military precision by the x-ray orderly takes us to the hospital's catacombs where the ubiquitous wires hang like stalactites from the ceiling. Carts are jammed in the hallway like logs. A young man with red hair and only one leg sits patiently in a wheelchair, his chin sunk on his chest. He doesn't look up. A white-haired old woman lies on a cart telling someone named Stella whom only she can see not to do it. Only two of the x-ray rooms are in use.

I'm finally wheeled into one of them. There a young technician arranges me on the wide table as if I were a bunch of flowers. The right leg must be turned just a little bit more this way, the left pelvic bone that way. When she gets me at last into a position not indigenous to the human species, she tells me to hold it and not breathe. I obey and am rewarded with a ten-by-twelve glossy of my new right hip joint.

My native ilium curves in shadows upward and disappears. The visible part of my pelvic cavity appears in the x-ray like one-half of a black valentine. The top of my thigh bone, the femur, has been neatly sawed off and a spike driven down into the marrow of its center, with flanges at the top to keep it from descending forever. I see the femur faint as a whisper. Above the flanges, the spike narrows and bends, then suddenly grows a large round top which fits into an equally round cup glued into the ilium. The cup is ghostly as my own bone because it's made of plastic, while the stainless steel spike is bold as a dagger. Between the cup and the pelvic cavity floats a bright little hat-shaped piece of metal. It looks like an Amish hat though when I ask my doctor about it, he says it's a sombrero. Its purpose is to prevent the glue from seeping into the vital organs.

Two dollars is added to my hospital bill and I take the x-ray home with me.

Patients are usually discharged between eleven a.m. and noon. Lester is tied up at a meeting until four, so I must wait. I have a plan. Between the time most patients are discharged and the time others are admitted, some of the rooms on Six Southwest may be empty.

I look in both directions up and down the hall. Even the nurses' station is momentarily deserted. I start off toward the long window at the end of the hall, inching my way along although I'm getting better with the crutches.

The first room I pass is Mr. Morley's. He's still in bed, his left leg hanging in the Zimmer. I see his tape deck is motionless. In the next room a nurse's aide is shaking linen about, changing the bed. The door to the third room is shut, a sign on it forbidding visitors. A fourth reveals through its open door a maid moving a mop around and around in circles on the tile floor.

At last I come to a room which is empty. The chair near the window has been placed at the angle it assumes when no one is about to sit in it. The bed is newly made and cranked high like a snow-white bier. I crutch around its foot and over to the Electronic Beside Unit. It's identical to the one in my room and probably to all those in the hospital. Leaning as far over as I can, I put my right ear close to the speaker. I don't breathe. Mine was in the middle of *Good King Wenceslaus* when I left. This one is silent. I don't know what it means.

Joan Swift

KALTAG

Sunday morning.

A cloud of seagulls rose up as I rounded the point of an island where I'd camped the night. The sun caught their white heads as the flock took shape in the wind. Wheeling and crying overhead, they overtook my canoe. Their rookery must have been close by because the gulls were in a bad temper, diving half-heartedly at my head and making a terrible screeching that sounded one minute like bicycle horns and the next like children crying. Splashing down ahead of the bow, they formed a cordon of stern gull faces. I bore down and would have gladly run them over but at last they flew off noisily, abandoning the river.

Coming upon Kaltag from the river you see the old Catholic church steeple and the village sprawled below, suspended between grey water and blue sky. The gravel beach below the village was lined with skiffs, their engines tilted against transoms. I parked my canoe among them and walked past racks of split salmon the color of tobacco leaves to the dirt road. A chained dog at the far end of the beach began to howl.

The village looked empty beneath the bright summer sky. The oldest buildings were crunched together beside the riverbank, squat cabins built in the Russian style with the weathered logs dovetailed at the ends and chinked with moss, while down the road was a new, pastel-colored high school. Kaltag appeared deserted except for three old men sitting on a bench. In every village along the Yukon there had been these old men, these sentinels, always looking upstream to see what the current would bring.

This morning the river had brought me, but the trio seemed disinterested. They were waiting for the priest to come down from Nulato to say mass. I had known a student from Kaltag at the university, but I had no idea whether she'd come back home.

"Does Violet Esmailka still live here?"

"Yes," said one of the men. "But her name is Burnham since she got married. They live in that house over there."

He pointed across the road to a red frame house with a hipped roof. It was the biggest house in the village. I walked across the road and knocked on the door. Nobody answered.

"It's Sunday morning," the old man said, turning the words

slowly in his mouth so I might comprehend the obvious. "They're sleeping."

So I asked about the portage trail to Unalakleet, the old trade route between the Interior Indian tribes and the Bering Sea Eskimos. It was a shortcut to the coast. By taking a ninety-mile dogleg inland and crossing the divide to the Unalakleet River, one could shave five hundred miles off the river route to the sea.

The old men just yawned and shook their heads in unison. The trail was very wet in summer, they said. A person would need hip boots to cross the swamps. When I explained that I only wanted to hike a little of the trail, this did little to shake the growing conviction that the Yukon delivered up only fools.

"That's brown bear country," one old man said smiling behind his sunglasses. "Lots of bears come down from the hills now that the fish are running."

His friend picked up the thread. "There was a fella that tried to walk over it last year. He came here in a canoe like you and asked a lot of fool questions about the portage and people told him not to go. He had canvas shoes and carried an axe. No rifle. He got lost in the swamp and a brown bear chased him. Someone from the village found him a few days later all ragged and cold on the riverbank."

"Maybe that fellow was afraid," the man with the sunglasses said. "You know a bear can smell if you're afraid."

The portage trail began as a wide lane cut into the birch and spruce at the end of the airfield. The morning had warmed up, and the good, astringent smell of labrador tea and sedge arose as I crushed them underfoot. After the first mile, the litter and empty plastic containers of snowmobile oil all but disappeared. The woods closed in, and I felt a long way from the village. From here the trail wound along the headwaters of the Kaltag River into the hills, crossed the divide near Old Woman Mountain and descended the Unalakleet River to the sea.

In the spring, when the snow crusted over, Koyukon Indians had crossed this route with dogsleds carrying fox and wolverine skins, beaver pelts, and carved wooden dishes; and when they returned from trading with the Eskimos, their sleds were loaded with seal oil, blubber from beluga whales, trade beads and domestic reindeer hides from Siberia. That trade relations had been cordial could be seen in the villagers' round, Eskimo features.

Over this same route came the first Russians to open the great interior to the fur trade. The Koyukons, who had set themselves up as middlemen between the Eskimos and other interior tribes, were reluctant to bring in competition. For four winters in a row, the Indians put the Russians off the trail by providing guides who led the foreigners over longer, more difficult routes. Finally Vasiliy Malakhov, a trader with the Russian American Company, found the trail out in 1838 and established a trading post the following year upriver at Nulato. A few winters later Lieutenant Lavrentiy Zagoskin of the Russian Imperial Navy set off on the portage trail from Unalakleet one December morning with five sleds and twenty-seven dogs. Halfway up the Unalakleet River, he came to an Indian village he called Ulak. In *Travels in Russian America,* Zagoskin wrote of the villagers: "It is rare to find an Ulukagmyut who is not a shaman — every single one of them is an excellent trader. As it is a matter of indifference to them by what means they get rich, they take by force or buy at their own price what they cannot acquire by trade or shamanistic manipulation."

These days, Indians drive snowmobiles over the trail to the coast only when they want a change of scenery. The Russians have long departed, leaving behind only their names among the villagers.

Heading downhill, the trail got wetter and spongier as it gave way to muskeg. I stopped to pick blueberries along the trail. Stooped over, I moved through the bushes, raking the branches like a bear until my fingers were stained a deep purple. I was in no hurry. A wind whipped through the birch trees, the trail moving in and out of shadow.

I wondered if fear, like sex, carries a perceptible cachet. I imagined it smells sour and overly ripe, like something dying. On the Yukon, I never thought to be frightened because there was only the river itself to fear, and that would be like fearing the ground or the sky. But sometimes, walking into a new village or alone in the woods, I caught a whiff of my own quaking timidity. Bears may not be the bloodhounds of fear, as the old men said, but if they were, then sooner or later they'd pick up my trail. This was only a premonition, like wind trembling leaves, but as another breeze moved the woods in shadow I started back for the village.

The man who answered the Burnham's door had a blond beard and carried a beer can in his hand. Behind him in the livingroom, two other men in their twenties crouched intently before a color television. One of them wore a baseball cap and motioned to us frantically.

"C'mon in for Christ's sake. Guy here's going to sink a big putt."

We rushed in to witness a golfer in a pink sports shirt choose a putter from his caddy. Hunched over the green, he tapped a white ball in a curving trajectory toward the hole. He missed.

"Tough break!" my companion hooted. "Poor jerk just kissed $50,000 goodbye."

The golf tournament was beamed live via satellite from Florida. To me, sitting in a log cabin village unconnected by road, the telecast could not have seemed more unreal had it been beamed from the dark side of the moon.

The man wearing a baseball cap shut off the set and got me a beer from the kitchen. He had a thin moustache with droopy ends that he continuously flicked with his tongue. The Burnhams, he explained, were away fishing and wouldn't be back until late afternoon. He and his friends were only boarding here. They worked for an outfit called Tel-Com, laying telephone cable to every house in every village from Kaltag up the Koyukuk River. They had just finished in Nulato where one potential customer threatened to shoot them if they persisted in digging a trench to his cabin. But for the most part, the villagers were pleased at the prospect of phone service. Then again, nobody had yet received a phone bill.

The Tel-Com men made the kind of fabled wages that lure young men north and can't help but arouse envy in the work-poor villages. In three months, they could earn enough money to take off the rest of the year. The man in the baseball cap had spent last winter traveling the South Pacific and showed me a handful of raw opals wrapped in velvet that he'd taken from an Australian mine. "And the real beauty of this job," he said, "is that when it's over I can go back to Oregon and collect unemployment all winter!"

This being their day off and the weather so lovely, the phone men suggested a fishing trip. Why not? Rolling a few joints to keep the morning's momentum, they rigged up fishing tackle, and we made a short parade down to the beach.

The clear Kaltag River enters the silty Yukon just above the village, and for a distance the two rivers flow side by side, unmixed, like vinegar and oil. Pellucid and lightly green in its depths, the tributary revealed a cutaway view of the riverbottom: a drowned tree with schools of whitefish shimmering in its branches.

One of our party had outfitted himself like a bankrobber with a pistol-grip shotgun that rocked in its sling across his back as we followed a slick, muddy trail up the alder bank. I watched the dappled leaf-light move across his shoulders until we stepped out onto a sunny gravel bar. Here the Kaltag River shrank to a good-sized creek, shallow and fast-running beside the tangled banks.

The fishermen began to flail at the river with their spinners, aiming at isolated Arctic char that hung in the smooth stretches of water between riffles. But mostly there were salmon. A river of salmon, each as long as my arm, their dorsal fins cutting the surface of the water. Nose upstream, they held steady in the current except for abrupt, lateral movements that carried them like cloud shadows over the pebbled streambed. These were chum or dog salmon, sea-green with a batik of gaudy red splotches along their sides. Among Yukon salmon, the summer-run chum were the most numerous but poorest eating; the Indians netted them only to feed their dogs. The chum salmon had begun to die as soon as they left salt water. Their rate of disintegration was faster than other species of salmon and by the time they reached the spawning streams they were rotting from the tail up. A few hook-jawed and battered males hung about, but most of the salmon in the river were females hovering dutifully over redds, depressions, scooped out in the gravel, where earlier, swimming flank to flank beside a male, they'd spewed their load of eggs into a pale mist of sperm.

The blond bearded fisherman snagged a salmon, and his buddies whooped and shouted as he horsed the fish to shore. The snagged salmon made one memorable run, the line slicing through the water as the fish shot upstream. But at last it came thrashing onto dry land, a treble hook in its tail. Pulling his lure loose, the fisherman pitched the salmon back into the river like a chunk of cordwood. He did not want the fish because its flesh would be soft and mealy.

I left the anglers and walked down the riverbank. It smelled like a fish market. Trampled in the soft mud were black bear tracks, the heel pad sunk deep like a man walking barefoot. In radiating lines from the woods were also the tracks of foxes, ravens, dogs — all brought down to the river by the stench to feast on spawned-out fish that had snagged on the shore. In some riffles, I came upon a salmon swimming close to shore to avoid the fast water. It was close enough to touch, and so, a little guiltily, I did. If a fish could sigh, it would have. My hand on its broad green back was just one more annoyance in a long series of trials unto death. As the salmon wriggled to deeper water, the current caught it sideways, sweeping it back over the ground it had gained, and I saw how battered the fish was. A milky fungus covered its fins and eyes, and I realized the salmon was swimming blind.

All down the Yukon, I had been half-conscious of this opposite traffic, the upriver migration of salmon a fathom or two below the surface. The salmon I'd seen had blundered into a net or fishwheel, ocean bright colors faded, their eyes holding the astonished look of drowned men. But here, having navigated by some mystery of scent or taste five hundred river miles to their homestream, they seemed elegant in their spawning and dying. There was no panic. Like true believers, they fought the inevitable, downward sweep of current.

The river slackened as I followed it downstream, until it formed a deep, glassy pool so transparent I could see clear down to the bouldery riverbed. Then I realized that what I had taken for rocks were, in fact, windrows of dead salmon that had drifted downstream to settle on the riverbottom. A fine grey layer of sediment covered the corpses so that the salmon looked fossilized, as if, having passed onto some further existence, they had turned to stones.

In the fading afternoon, the Burnhams returned, lugging camping gear and two small children up from their beach. I reintroduced myself to Violet. She has a pretty, roundish face, more Eskimo than Indian. I remembered her at college as bright and ambitious, illuminated by her own candlepower. After graduation, she'd worked a year as a bookkeeper, and now, with a husband and two children, seemed a little world-weary. She would like to get back to Fairbanks for a visit but won't because she hates riding in small planes.

The Burnhams kindly offered to put me up for the night in one of the upstairs dormers. My bunkmate was a quiet fellow who purchased salmon roe for the Japanese to turn into caviar. After supper, we all sat in the living room watching the evening news from Anchorage on the television. A tenement in an Eastern city had caught fire; there was a garbage strike somewhere — all of it seemed very distant and unrelated, yet we watched with great interest. Television had come to Kaltag three years before and, according to Violet, for the first year people scarcely ever left their homes. But the fascination with game shows and mini-series seemed to have worn off enough that everyone was visiting again. The Burnham's house, in fact, seemed a social hub with people dropping in all evening. One of them, a lean fellow from a village downstream, took a long, appraising look around the room. "Too many white people around here," he said and went out the door. For my part, I was glad to be caught up in a household again, even if only on the fringes.

While Violet put the kids in bed, her husband led us to a shed beside the house which held lumber, sleds, and a huge rack of antlers from a moose he had shot on the Innoko River. The spread between the tines was as broad as a sofa. A tall, big-shouldered man, Richard Burnham came to Alaska from Oregon for the big-game hunting, and now has to work it in when he's not working for the village government. He seems to have settled successfully into Kaltag, having married one of its daughters and started a family, and, like Joe Runyon, he's a dog musher.

On a hunting trip the previous fall, Richard and his brother-in-law chanced upon a black bear digging its den in the side of a cutbank ridge. The two men skulked away, but remembered the spot. In the winter they returned, and Richard's brother-in-law chopped through the frozen ridge-top until he penetrated the bear's den.

"He jabbed a stick a long way down the hole," Richard said, "and we watched until the stick began to move by itself. The bear's breathing made it move up and down. So we knew a bear was in there. Chopping the hole bigger, my brother-in-law lowered himself headfirst into the den and shot the bear in the head with a pistol.''

Then it was Richard's turn. He crawled through the entrance in the side of the cutbank, hoping the den held only a single resident. Inside, the air was warm and moist with the fetor of bear. Richard looped a rope around the bear's head, haloed in the shaft of light from above. Sliding out, he pulled on the rope with his brother-in-law until the bear, a glossy boar girdled with fat, emerged into the winter light.

Richard's story sparked a round of bear stories among the Tel-Com men, each more gruesome than the next. I didn't want to hear it. Saying goodnight, I drifted upstairs where the egg-buyer was already soundly snoring. I stretched out on the bunk and fell into a sleep heavy with the deaths of animals.

About three in the morning, I awoke. A window was open and the room had gotten very cold. Through the window, the noise of a domestic argument wafted up from the street below. I tried sleeping, but there was a painful familiarity to the recriminations and denials. For a moment, I thought I was home.

Looking out the window into the faint morning light, I saw a young woman walking down the road, followed at a short distance by a man. Her husband? Lover? Around the two of them a small crowd had assembled. The woman turned to face the man and screamed bitterly. "Liar! Bastard!" Stooping down, she picked up a stone and hurled it at the man who stood with his arms outstretched, a penitent. The stone struck his chest with an awful, hollow sound.

Weeping angrily, the woman turned her back and walked off, the ex-lover and crowd following silently. They stopped after a short distance and repeated the scene as if it were the next station in some private agony. I lay back and listened to her shouts fade as the procession moved down the street.

By morning the weather had turned — a leaden sky and wind-slanted drizzle. While the other men of the house went off to work, I dawdled behind, drinking coffee with Violet and her younger sister. I enjoyed being a guest and staying inside with the women. Violet was giving her son a haircut at the kitchen table while her sister and I watched the blank intrigues of a TV soap opera. Nobody mentioned the ruckus last night.

Late in the morning, the phone men returned. They looked sober and shaken. The one with the blond beard poured himself a cup of coffee and sat down at the table trembling. Violet asked him what was wrong.

"We found a dead man on the beach."

They'd been laying cable to one of the cabins along the riverbank, he said, when they looked down and saw a body stretched out on the gravel beach. It was a young man, seemingly asleep, but his face looked strangely pale. Then they saw the shotgun clutched to his chest.

Violet's sister must have known then who the phone man was describing because she clapped her hand over her mouth and ran out of the house.

Sad news travels fast, even without telephones, and soon everyone in the village knew about the suicide. According to Violet, the young man had been despondent for days and talked openly of taking his life. Last night he had not returned home but laid down on the gravel shore below the village, put a shotgun muzzle to his heart and blew his troubles into eternity.

The suicide was apparently unrelated to the scene I'd overheard from my bedroom window the night before. Two random tragedies. Still in my mind they were unalterably connected: the woman's scream, the muffled blast.

"Sometimes," Violet said, sweeping her son's hairclippings from the kitchen floor, "there's a wave of restlessness that goes through the village. You can almost feel it. There's no place to go, and people get restless." She shook her head. "It's so sad."

Already I felt restless." Dying men and dying fish. There were too many bad ions in the air or a bad moon rising. Whatever, I wanted to be back on the river again.

Saying goodbye to the Burnhams, I bought the gasoline I needed, and headed back in the rain to the beach. On the wet road, I passed a crowd bearing the body in an orange tarp to the village hall. For the next few days, villagers would bring food to the family of the deceased, and a potlatch would follow after the burial. The following spring, the young man's death would be remembered at the Stickdance, the traditional Feast of the Dead.

The men would sing the thirteen ancient songs and the women dance without moving their feet. Afterwards the ceremonial stick would be taken down, carried through the village, then broken and thrown over the riverbank. In this way, the souls of the departed would be remembered and hastened toward reincarnation.

As I filled my gas tank, a small throng of high school boys wandered up the beach, shouting and stopping to pick up stones to fling into the river. Maybe they were upset about the suicide or restless or just bored, but I could see what was coming. At that age they always flock together to give them the nerve they lack alone. As soon as one of them spotted me, the rest homed in because I was a stranger.

"What the fuck are you doing here, white guy?"

"Leaving," I said.

"Well, that's good because we were just about ready to wreck your boat!"

I gave them my best traveler's smile and shoved off. It was depressing to be razzed out of town by kids whose older brothers and sisters I might have taught in school. I wanted to knock their heads together and tell them that they had no reason to hate me. But there were too many of them, and this was their classroom, not mine.

August marks the beginning of the rainy season on the Lower Yukon, and overnight the river had turned into a cold, grey sea. Idling the engine, I drifted from Kaltag, the old church steeple passing overhead and then disappearing beyond the bank. I headed out into the middle of the river and opened the throttle. Out of nowhere, the seagulls rejoined me. Floating overhead on extended wings, they cried in harsh, urgent voices I could not comprehend.

John Hildebrand

My dad's name was Clevie Raymond Carver. His family called him Raymond and friends called him C.R. I was named Raymond Clevie Carver Jr. I hated the "Junior" part. When I was little my dad called me Frog, which was okay. But later, like everybody else in the family, he began calling me Junior. He went on calling me this until I was thirteen or fourteen and announced that I wouldn't answer to that name any longer. So he began calling me Doc. From then until his death, on June 17, 1967, he called me Doc, or else Son.

When he died, my mother telephoned my wife with the news. I was away from my family at the time, between lives, trying to enroll in the School of Library Science at the University of Iowa. When my wife answered the phone, my mother blurted out, "Raymond's dead!" For a moment, my wife thought my mother was telling her that I was dead. Then my mother made it clear *which* Raymond she was talking about and my wife said, "Thank God. I thought you meant *my* Raymond."

My dad walked, hitched rides, and rode in empty boxcars when he went from Arkansas to Washington State in 1934, looking for work. I don't know whether he was pursuing a dream when he went out to Washington. I doubt it. I don't think he dreamed much. I believe he was simply looking for steady work at decent pay. Steady work was meaningful work. He picked apples for a time and then landed a construction laborer's job on the Grand Coulee Dam. After he'd put aside a little money, he bought a car and drove back to Arkansas to help his folks, my grandparents, pack up for the move west. He said later that they were about to starve down there, and this wasn't meant as a figure of speech. It was during that short while in Arkansas, in a town called Leola, that my mother met my dad on the sidewalk as he came out of a tavern.

"He was drunk," she said. "I don't know why I let him talk to me. His eyes were glittery. I wish I'd had a crystal ball." They'd met once, a year or so before, at a dance. He'd had girlfriends before her, my mother told me. "Your dad always had a girlfriend, even after we married. He was my first and last. I never had another man. But I didn't miss anything."

70

They were married by a justice of the peace on the day they left for Washington, this big, tall country girl and a farmhand-turned-construction worker. My mother spent her wedding night with my dad and his folks, all of them camped beside the road in Arkansas.

In Omak, Washington, my dad and mother lived in a little place not much bigger than a cabin. My grandparents lived next door. My dad was still working on the dam, and later, with the huge turbines producing electricity and the water backed up for a hundred miles into Canada, he stood in the crowd and heard Franklin D. Roosevelt when he spoke at the construction site. "He never mentioned those guys who died building that dam," my dad said. Some of his friends had died there, men from Arkansas, Oklahoma, and Missouri.

He then took a job in a sawmill in Clatskanie, Oregon, a little town alongside the Columbia River. I was born there, and my mother has a picture of my dad standing in front of the gate to the mill, proudly holding me up to face the camera. My bonnet is on crooked and about to come untied. His hat is pushed back on his forehead, and he's wearing a big grin. Was he going in to work or just finishing his shift? It doesn't matter. In either case, he had a job and a family. These were his salad days.

In 1941 we moved to Yakima, Washington, wher my dad went to work as a saw filer, a skilled trade he'd learned in Clatskanie. When war broke out, he was given a deferment because his work was considered necessary to the war effort. Finished lumber was in demand by the armed services, and he kept his saws so sharp they could shave the hair off your arm.

After my dad had moved us to Yakima, he moved his folks into the same neighborhood. By the mid-1940s the rest of my dad's family — his brother, his sister, and her husband, as well as uncles, cousins, nephews, and most of their extended family and friends — had come out from Arkansas. All because my dad came out first. The men went to work at Boise Cascade, where my dad worked, and the women packed apples in the canneries. And in just a little while, it seemed — according to my mother — everybody was better off than my dad. "Your dad couldn't keep money," my mother said. "Money burned a hole in his pocket. He was always doing for others."

71

The first house I clearly remember living in, at 1515 South Fifteenth Street, in Yakima, had an outdoor toilet. On Halloween night, or just any night, for the hell of it, neighbor kids, kids in their early teens, would carry our toilet away and leave it next to the road. My dad would have to get somebody to help him bring it home. Or these kids would take the toilet and stand it in somebody else's backyard. Once they actually set it on fire. But ours wasn't the only house that had an outdoor toilet. When I was old enough to know what I was doing, I threw rocks at the other toilets when I'd see someone go inside. This was called bombing the toilets. After a while, though, everyone went to indoor plumbing until, suddenly, our toilet was the last outdoor one in the neighborhood. I remember the shame I felt when my third-grade teacher, Mr. Wise, drove me home from school one day. I asked him to stop at the house just before ours, claiming I lived there.

I can recall what happened one night when my dad came home late to find that my mother had locked all the doors on him from the inside. He was drunk, and we could feel the house shudder as he rattled the door. When he'd managed to force open a window, she hit him between the eyes with a colander and knocked him out. We could see him down there on the grass. For years afterward, I used to pick up this colander — it was as heavy as a rolling pin — and imagine what it would feel like to be hit in the head with something like that.

It was during this period that I remember my dad taking me into the bedroom, sitting me down on the bed, and telling me that I might have to go live with my Aunt LaVon for a while. I couldn't understand what I'd done that meant I'd have to go away from home to live. But this, too — whatever prompted it — must have blown over, more or less, anyway, because we stayed together, and I didn't have to go live with her or anyone else.

I remember my mother pouring his whiskey down the sink. Sometimes she'd pour it all out and sometimes, if she was afraid of getting caught, she'd only pour half of it out and then add water to the rest. I tasted some of his whiskey once myself. It was terrible stuff, and I don't see how anybody could drink it.

After a long time without one, we finally got a car, in 1949 or 1950, a 1938 Ford. But it threw a rod the first week we had it, and my dad had to have the motor rebuilt.

"We drove the oldest car in town," my mother said. "We could have had a Cadillac for all he spent on car repairs." One time she found someone else's tube of lipstick on the floorboard, along with a lacy handkerchief. "See this?" she said to me. "Some floozy left this in the car."

Once I saw her take a pan of warm water into the bedroom where my dad was sleeping. She took his hand from under the covers and held it in the water. I stood in the doorway and watched. I wanted to know what was going on. This would make him talk in his sleep, she told me. There were things she needed to know, things she was sure he was keeping from her.

Every year or so, when I was little, we would take the North Coast Limited across the Cascade Range from Yakima to Seattle and stay in the Vance Hotel and eat, I remember, at a place called the Dinner Bell Cafe. Once we went to Ivar's Acres of Clams and drank glasses of warm clam broth.

In 1956, the year I was to graduate from high school, my dad quit his job at the mill in Yakima and took a job in Chester, a little sawmill town in northern California. The reasons given at the time for his taking the job had to do with a higher hourly wage and the vague promise that he might, in a few years' time, succeed to the job of head filer in this new mill. But I think, in the main, that my dad had grown restless and simply wanted to try his luck elsewhere. Things had gotten a little too predictable for him in Yakima. Also, the year before, there had been the deaths, within six months of each other, of both his parents.

But just a few days after graduation, when my mother and I were packed to move to Chester, my dad penciled a letter to say he'd been sick for a while. He didn't want us to worry, he said, but he'd cut himself on a saw. Maybe he'd got a tiny sliver of steel in his blood. Anyway, something had happened and he'd had to miss work, he said. In the same mail was an unsigned postcard from somebody down there telling my mother that my dad was about to die and that he was drinking "raw whiskey."

When we arrived in Chester, my dad was living in a trailer that belonged to the company. I didn't recognize him immediately. I guess for a moment I didn't want to recognize him. He was skinny and pale and looked bewildered. His pants wouldn't stay up. He didn't look like my dad. My mother began to cry. My dad put his arm around her and patted her shoulder vaguely, like he didn't know what this was all about, either. The three of us took up life together in the trailer, and we looked after him as best we could. But my dad was sick, and he couldn't get any better. I worked with him in the mill that summer and part of the fall. We'd get up in the mornings and eat eggs and toast while we listened to the radio, and then go out the door with our lunch pails. We'd pass through the gate together at eight in the morning, and I wouldn't see him again until quitting time. In November I went back to Yakima to be closer to my girlfriend, the girl I'd made up my mind I was going to marry.

He worked at the mill in Chester until the following February, when he collapsed on the job and was taken to the hospital. My mother asked if I would come down there and help. I caught a bus from Yakima to Chester, intending to drive them back to Yakima. But now, in addition to being physically sick, my dad was in the midst of a nervous breakdown, though none of us knew to call it that at the time. During the entire trip back to Yakima, he didn't speak, not even when asked a direct question. ("How do you feel, Raymond?" "You okay, Dad?") He'd communicate, if he communicated at all, by moving his head or by turning his palms up as if to say he didn't know or care. The only time he said anything on the trip, and for nearly a month afterward, was when I was speeding down a gravel road in Oregon and the car muffler came loose. "You were going too fast," he said.

Back in Yakima a doctor saw to it that my dad went to a psychiatrist. My mother and dad had to go on relief, as it was called, and the county paid for the psychiatrist. The psychiatrist asked my dad, "Who is the President?" He'd had a question put to him that he could answer. "Ike," my dad said. Nevertheless, they put him on the fifth floor of Valley Memorial Hospital and began giving him electroshock treatments. I was married by then and about to start my own family. My dad was still locked up when my wife went into this same hospital, just one floor down, to have our first baby. After she had delivered, I went upstairs to give my dad the news. They let me in through a steel door and showed me where I could find him. He was sitting on a couch with a blanket over his lap. *Hey*, I thought. *What in hell is happening to my dad?* I sat down next to him and told him he was a grandfather. He waited a minute and then he said, "I feel like a grandfather." That's all he said. He didn't smile or move. He was in a big room with a lot of other people. Then I hugged him, and he began to cry.

Somehow he got out of there. But now came the years when he couldn't work and just sat around the house trying to figure what next and what he'd done wrong in his life that he'd wound up like this. My mother went from job to crummy job. Much later she referred to that time he was in the hospital, and those years just afterward, as "when Raymond was sick." The word *sick* was never the same for me again.

In 1964, through the help of a friend, he was lucky enough to be hired on at a mill in Klamath, California. He moved down there by himself to see if he could hack it. He lived not far from the mill, in a one-room cabin not much different from the place he and my mother had started out living in when they went west. He scrawled letters to my mother, and if I called she'd read them aloud to me over the phone. In the letters, he said it was touch and go. Every day that he went to work, he felt like it was the most important day of his life. But every day, he told her, made the next day that much easier. He said for her to tell me he said hello. If he couldn't sleep at night, he said, he thought about me and the good times we used to have. Finally, after a couple of months, he regained some of his confidence. He could do the work and didn't think he had to worry that he'd let anybody down ever again. When he was sure, he sent for my mother.

He'd been off from work for six years and had lost everything in that time — home, car, furniture, and appliances, including the big freezer that had been my mother's pride and joy. He'd lost his good name too — Raymond Carver was someone who couldn't pay his bills — and his self-respect was gone. He'd even lost his virility. My mother told my wife, "All during that time Raymond was sick we slept together in the same bed, but we didn't have relations. He wanted to a few times, but nothing happened. I didn't miss it, but I think he wanted to, you know."

During those years I was trying to raise my own family and earn a living. But, one thing and another, we found ourselves having to move a lot. I couldn't keep track of what was going down in my dad's life. But I did have a chance one Christmas to tell him I wanted to be a writer. I might as well have told him I wanted to become a plastic surgeon. "What are you going to write about?" he wanted to know. Then, as if to help me out, he said, "Write about stuff you know about. Write about some of those fishing trips we took." I said I would, but I knew I wouldn't. "Send me what you write," he said. I said I'd do that, but then I didn't. I wasn't writing anything about fishing, and I didn't think he'd particularly care about, or even necessarily understand, what I was writing in those days. Besides, he wasn't a reader. Not the sort, anyway, I imagined I was writing for.

Then he died. I was a long way off, in Iowa City, with things still to say to him. I didn't have the chance to tell him goodbye, or that I thought he was doing great at his new job. That I was proud of him for making a comeback.

My mother said he came in from work that night and ate a big supper. Then he sat at the table by himself and finished what was left of a bottle of whiskey, a bottle she found hidden in the bottom of the garbage under some coffee grounds a day or so later. Then he got up and went to bed, where my mother joined him a little later. But in the night she had to get up and make a bed for herself on the couch. "He was snoring so loud I couldn't sleep," she said. The next morning when she looked in on him, he was on his back with his mouth open, his cheeks caved in. *Gray-looking*, she said. She knew he was dead — she didn't need a doctor to tell her that. But she called one anyway, and then she called my wife.

Among the pictures my mother kept of my dad and herself during those early days in Washington was a photograph of him standing in front of a car, holding a beer and a stringer of fish. In the photograph he is wearing his hat back on his forehead and has this awkward grin on his face. I asked her for it and she gave it to me, along with some others. I put it up on my wall, and each time we moved, I took the picture along and put it up on another wall. I looked at it carefully from time to time, trying to figure out some things about my dad, and maybe myself in the process. But I couldn't. My dad just kept moving further and further away from me and back into time. Finally, in the course of another move, I lost the photograph. It was then that I tried to recall it, and at the same time make an attempt to say something about my dad, and how I thought that in some important ways we might be alike. I wrote he poem when I was living in an apartment house in an urban a rea south of San Francisco, at a time when I found myself, like my dad, having trouble with alcohol. The poem was a way of trying t connect up with him.

Photograph of My Father in His Twenty-Second Year

October. *Here in this dank, unfamiliar kitchen*
I study my father's embarrassed young man's face.
Sheepish grin, he holds in one hand a string
of spiny yellow perch, in the other
a bottle of Carlsberg beer.

In jeans and flannel shirt, he leans
against the front fender of a 1934 Ford.
He would like to pose brave and hearty for his posterity,
wear his old hat cocked over his ear.
All his life my father wanted to be bold.

But the eyes give him away, and the hands
that limply offer the string of dead perch
and the bottle of beer. Father, I love you,
yet how can I say thank you, I who can't hold my liquor either
and don't even know the places to fish.

The poem is true in its particulars, except that my dad died in June and not October, as the first word of the poem says. I wanted a word with more than one syllable to make it linger a little. But more than that, I wanted a month appropriate to what I felt at the time I wrote the poem — a month of short days and failing light, smoke in the air, things perishing. June was summer nights and days, graduations, my wedding anniversary, the birthday of one of my children. June wasn't a month your father died in.

After the service at the funeral home, after we had moved outside, a woman I didn't know came over to me and said, "He's happier where he is now." I stared at this woman until she moved away. I still remember the little knob of a hat she was wearing. Then one of my dad's cousins — I didn't know the man's name —

reached out and took my hand. "We all miss him," he said, and I knew he wasn't saying it just to be polite.

I began to weep for the first time since receiving the news. I hadn't been able to before. I hadn't had the time, for one thing. Now, suddenly, I couldn't stop. I held my wife and wept while she said and did what she could do to comfort me there in the middle of that summer afternoon.

I listened to people say consoling things to my mother, and I was glad that my dad's family had turned up, had come to where he was. I thought I'd remember everything that was said and done that day and maybe find a way to tell it sometime. But I didn't. I forgot it all, or nearly. What I do remember is that I heard our name used a lot that afternoon, my dad's name and mine. But I knew they were talking about my dad. *Raymond*, these people kept saying in their beautiful voices out of my childhood. *Raymond*.

Raymond Carver

THE TROUBLED GAZE OF THE OCTOPUS

In *Gravity's Rainbow,* Thomas Pynchon's great steaming slag-heap of a novel, there is a memorable scene in which an enormous octopus comes slouching out of the sea, grabs a young woman around the waist with one sucker-studded arm, and tries to drag her away back into the water. Echoes of King Kong and Fay Wray. The woman is rescued by Pynchon's hero, a certain Tyrone Slothrop who pummels the octopus over the head with a wine bottle (to no effect), and then distracts it by offering a tasty crab. "In their brief time together Slothrop forms the impression that this octopus is not in good mental health," Pynchon tells us. I have sometimes had the same feeling about Thomas Pynchon, but never mind. The point of recalling that octopus scene, in particular, is that I for one always took it to be luridly and outlandishly implausible, an excursion to the outback of the surreal, another hallucinatory cartoon caper like so much else that comes out of Mr. Pynchon's febrile imagination.

Turns out, though, that I was unduly skeptical. Turns out that this sequence might contain more truth than poetry. The details of anatomy and scale and behavior have a sound basis in science; only the matter of motivation remains unsettled. The species in question is *Octopus dofleini,* otherwise known as the giant Pacific octopus.

Does this creature really lay hold, in such peremptory manner, of unsuspecting human beach-goers? And if so, just what has it got in mind?

The concept of *mind* is not inappropriate as applied to the octopi, since these creatures have by far the most highly developed brain in their province of the animal kingdom. They belong to the phylum Mollusca, a large group of invertebrates mainly characterized by soft bodies, hard shells, and rather primitive patterns of anatomical organization, well suited to surviving inconspicuously on the sea bottom. Typical of the Mollusca are clams, oysters, snails; the octopi (and to a lesser extent their near relatives, the squids) are decidedly untypical. They are an evolutionary anomaly, a class of genius misfits who have advanced far beyond their origins.

The octopi have an elaborate fourteen-lobed brain, an organ so large that their brain-to-body-weight ratio exceeds that of most fish and reptiles. Mentally, they are more on a level with birds and mammals. They possess a capacity for learning, memory and considered behavior that makes them — with the exception of marine mammals — the most intelligent of all sea-dwelling animals. In a laboratory, they tend to be good at mazes, and perform well in tests of discrimination among visual symbols. This last talent depends partly upon their acute eyesight. Every octopus looks out at the world through a pair of extraordinary eyes — eyes about which, to a human, there is something unexpectedly and disquietingly familiar.

"The animal has eyes that stare back," according to Martin J. Wells, a British zoologist who is one of the world's experts in octopus physiology and behavior. "It responds to movement, cowering if anything large approaches it, or leaning forward in an alert and interested manner to examine small happenings in its visual field." Jacques Cousteau goes a bit farther: "When a diver sees a giant octopus in the dim water, its great eyes fixed on him, he feels a strange sensation of respect, as though he were in the presence of a very wise and very old animal, whose tranquility it would be best not to disturb." One of Cousteau's assistants adds: "I have often had the impression that they are 'reflecting.'" Other divers and lab researchers make the same sort of comment, describing the same eerie sense of encounter, recognition, even mutuality. Lately I've had occasion to experience it myself, during three evenings of octopus-watching in a small university room filled with quietly gurgling tanks: the potent, expressive gaze of the octopus. These animals don't just gape at you glassily, like a walleye. They make eye contact, as though they are someone you should know.

One of the reasons for the potency of that stare is simply a matter of proportion. Relative to the body size of a given octopus, the eyes are, like the brain, unusually large. (The ultimate record in this regard belongs to that octopus cousin, the giant squid — with an eyeball up to fifteen inches across, largest on Earth and twice the size of the eye of a blue whale.) Octopus eyes are also protrusive and mobile, bulging up periscopically when the creature's attention is caught, swiveling far enough fore and aft to cover all 360 degrees of horizon. But the real magic behind the octopod gaze is that those eyes bear a startling structural similarity to our own.

It's an exemplary instance of the phenomenon called *convergent evolution*. Two separate evolutionary paths are followed for millions of years by two disparate groups of creatures, arriving eventually at two separate but (coincidentally) very similar solutions to a common problem. In this case, the problem of translating incident light rays into coherent images conveyable to the brain. The vertebrate eye — the model we humans share with cougars and eagles and rattlesnakes, all having inherited the pattern commonly — is an ingenious contrivance combining a cornea, a crystalline lens, an adjustable iris, and a retina. That such an organ evolved even once, within the vertebrate line, represents a miraculous triumph of time and trial-and-error over improbability. The still larger miracle is that *two* very similar versions have appeared independently. The other belongs exclusively to the octopi and their close kin. Each of those squid and octopus eyes consists of a cornea, a crystalline lens, an adjustable iris, and a retina, functioning together in much the same way as ours.

And the octopi are also endowed with an eyelid, so that they can wink at us fraternally.

Among all the sea's vigilant octopod eyeballs, the most imposing belong to *Octopus dofleini*. This is the giant that has impressed Cousteau and others with its dignified presence, as though it were "a very wise and very old animal." The wisdom part is quite possible, but the great agedness is an illusion.

Octopi grow quickly to adulthood and die at an early age, in most cases right after their first breeding experience. Two or three years is a full lifespan, even for the larger Mediterranean octopi that might grow in that brief time from the size of a flea to the size of a collie. An octopus can achieve such speedy growth — almost doubling its weight each month throughout most of its life — because of its exceptional metabolic efficiency in converting food protein to octopus protein. And at this process, *O. dofleini* is probably unsurpassed. Surviving longer than other species, to the grand age of five or maybe a little beyond, some giant Pacific octopi attain awesome sizes.

They live mainly in sea-bottom caves along the coast of the northern Pacific, from California up through British Columbia and Alaska, and across to Japan. The caves give them security from predation and, during mating time, a good place to brood eggs. They seem to prefer that range of moderate depths from the intertidal zone down to 100 fathoms, and by most accounts they are exceedingly shy. Until three or four decades ago, *dofleini* were known almost solely from commercial fishermen, who occasionally, inadvertently, and probably to their own vast alarm, brought one up in a trawl net. After World War II, improved diving equipment (especially scuba) opened a new degree of human access to those deeper caves. Reports of larger and larger *dofleini* began to appear. Cousteau mentions one specimen, spotted off Seattle, with an arm-span of thirty feet and a weight of around 200 pounds. Another diver has told William High, of the National Marine Fisheries Service, about bringing up several 400-pound *dofleini* during his commercial octopus-fishing days, as well as a single huge individual that went 600 pounds.

Then the inevitable happened. Someone had a clever idea, and in 1956 hundreds of divers converged on Puget Sound, to compete in an event billed as the World Octopus-Wrestling Championship. It became an annual tradition.

The biggest specimens of *dofleini* were smoked out of their caves with solutions of noxious chemicals, and wrestled up onto land by divers working in teams, there to be weighed and measured and admired. Dealing underwater with an octopus that large requires — from a human in scuba gear — equal measures of skill, cool-headedness, and lunatic daring. *Doflieni* are naturally timid but also quite strong, and they do have four times as many arms. Panic-stricken *dofleini* have been known to pin a man's arms to his sides, pull off his face mask, yank out his mouthpiece. There have even been several instances when a big octopus pounced on the back of an unsuspecting diver, from a rock ledge overhead. If one diver becomes trapped, in a situation like that, the usual procedure seems to be for his buddy to commence slicing away octopod arms with a knife, or to go for the eye with a spear.

After those "wrestling" championships each year, the healthy octopi were carefully released back into the sea. No harm done. No permanent toll on the giant octopus population. Right? At least that was the assumption. But one woman diver who took part in the round-ups has told Cousteau: "It is hard to keep in mind that octopuses of the size and weight of these are really very fragile animals, highly developed and with a very sensitive nervous system. They seem to succumb easily to nervous disorders. If a diver is too rough with an octopus, even without actually hurting it physically, it happens that the animal goes into a state of emotional shock and sometimes dies."

*   *   *

Let me recapitulate. It seems that (1) octopi in the 200-pound range, or larger, cowering in sea caves off the coast near Seattle, and (2) known for their high-strung susceptibility to nervous disorders, have been (3) kidnapped and terrorized intermittently by strange visitors in black neoprene, these latter often armed with knives and spears. Consequently, it can be assumed that (4) eyeballs human-like but the size of grapefruit now gaze out from those caves, furtively, trepidatiously, some of them no doubt looking just a bit addled. Looking as though they might belong to animals that, like Pynchon's beast, are in not quite the best mental health.

My own view is this: Any giant octopus that grabs hold of a passing human probably has some pretty good reason. If not an unanswerable grievance, then at least a plausible insanity defense.

Or maybe the creature is just desperate to communicate. Snatching that lone human up by the rubber lapels. Exigent as the Ancient Mariner. Transfixing the man or the woman with a big glittering eye. *Listen. We know who you are. And we've seen what you do.* But unfortunately the octopi, for all their intelligence, for all their sensitivity, for all their remarkable evolutionary sophistication, are born mute.

David Quammen

RUMORS OF A SNAKE

What this world needs is a good vicious sixty-foot-long Amazon snake.

Don't look at me, it's not my private notion. There is a broader mandate of some murky sort, not biological but psychic, issuing from that delicately balanced ecosystem we call the human mind. *Give us a huge snake. A monster, a serpent out at the far fringe of imaginability. Let it inhabit the funkiest jungle. A horrific thing, slithering along in elegant menace, belly distended with pigs and missing children.* The evidence of this odd yearning is oblique but cogent: Lacking any such beast, we are eager to settle for rumors of one. Otherwise how to explain the breathless compoundment of hearsay, tall tale, and exaggeration that has always surrounded the anaconda?

A fair example appears in the memoirs of Major Percy Fawcett. In 1906 he was sent out from London by the Royal Geographical Society to make a survey along certain rivers in western Brazil. "The manager at Yorongas told me he killed an anaconda 58 feet long in the Lower Amazon. I was inclined to look on this as an exaggeration at the time, but later, as I shall tell, we shot one even larger than that." The disclaimer is a cagey stroke. Major Fawcett would have us take him for a hard-headed British skeptic.

Later he tells: "We were drifting easily along in the sluggish current not far below the confluence of the Rio Negro when almost under the bow of the *igarite* there appeared a triangular head and several feet of undulating body. It was a giant anaconda. I sprang for my rifle as the creature began to make its way up the bank, and hardly waiting to aim smashed a .44 soft-nosed bullet into its spine, ten feet below the wicked head . . . We stepped ashore and approached the reptile with caution. It was out of action, but shivers ran up and down the body like puffs of wind on a mountain tarn. As far as it was possible to measure, a length of forty-five feet lay out of the water, and seventeen feet in it, making a total length of sixty-two feet." The indisputable logic of good arithmetic. It might all be true but most likely it isn't.

An adventurer of the 1920s named F.W. Up de Graff offered a similar account, having observed his anaconda in shallow water. "It measured fifty feet for certainty, and probably nearer sixty.

84

This I know from the position in which it lay. Our canoe was a twenty-four footer; the snake's head was ten or twelve feet beyond the bow; its tail was a good four feet beyond the stern; the center of its body was looped up into a huge S, whose length was the length of our dugout and whose breadth was a good five feet." But size estimates made in a watery medium are notoriously unreliable — especially when that watery medium is the Amazon River.

Bernard Heuvelmans, in his feverish book about stalking mysterious animals, tells at third or fourth hand of another Brazilian specimen that was purportedly killed in 1948. "The snake, which was said to measure 115 feet in length, crawled ashore and hid in the old fortifications of Fort Tabatinga on the River Oiapoc in the Guapore territory. It needed 500 machine-gun bullets to put paid to it. The speed with which bodies decompose in the tropics and the fact that its skin was of no commercial value may explain why it was pushed back in the stream at once." Always for the gigantic individuals there is this absence of physical evidence, and always a waterproof reason for the absence: no camera on hand, rotting meat, even the skin was too heavy to carry out. One photograph did exist that, during the 1950s, was sold all over Brazil as a postcard, its caption claiming a length of 131 feet for the snake pictured. Unfortunately, no object of reference appeared in the photo with it. That snake might as easily have been a robust but miniscule twenty-footer.

My own modest sighting comes not from Brazil but from northeastern Ecuador, along the Rio Aguarico, in a remote zone of lowland jungle that may be as favorable to the production and growth of anacondas as almost anywhere in the Amazon drainage. Like those other wide-eyed witnesses Fawcett and Up de Graff, I was in a dugout canoe. Our guide was an intrepid and jungle-smart young man named Randy Borman, who spotted the big snake on a log tangle near the river bank while the rest of us were gawking elsewhere. He steered the boat in for a closer look.

Dark gunmetal gray with sides mottled in reddish brown, the anaconda was sunning itself placidly. Barely above the water on a low-riding log: protectively colored and patterned so that, even from ten yards away, it was virtually invisible. Randy edged the canoe closer. Do you see it now? Some of us did, several admitted they didn't. We moved closer. Here indeed was a formidable snake. Still motionless, still sunbathing dreamily. I was delighted with this glimpse of an anaconda in the wild but — amid the soft brushfire crackle of camera shutters — we had already ventured closer than I ever expected to get. Then closer still. A very tolerant and self-possessed snake. Beautiful big head. Thick graceful coils of body. Sizable brown eye. Hello, Randy? Just when I thought our guide would back the canoe off, instead he dove over the gunnel to grab this creature around the neck.

A deeply startling act. But Randy came up again, deftly, with a great armload of anaconda wrapping itself onto him in surprise and anger, squeezing with the authority of a species that does its killing by constriction. My face bore the contemplative expression of two eggs sunnyside in a white Teflon skillet.

Randy smiled calmly. "We'll take him back to camp for the others to see." An hour later, having been much fawned over and photographed, the animal was gently released back into its river. A few fast pulses of undulant swimming, then a dive beneath the brown water, and it was gone. There was a convenient absence of physical evidence.

So in recounting the story afterward (which I have not hesitated to do often, cornering people at parties and hoping the talk might turn to giant reptiles) I could make that poor snake any damn size I pleased. A piddling ten feet? Maybe eleven? Roughly the same girth as a man's biceps? In fact (so I would say, with engaging dismissiveness) it was rather dainty as this species goes. Still, an impressive beast.

Very little is known about the biology of *Eunectes murinus,* the anaconda; even less about its life history in the wild; and a sad fact is that no one seems much to care. Not a single field-research project (one expert has told me) is currently being done on it. The species has not yet found its George Schaller, its Diane Fossey, its Jane van Lawick-Goodall.

We know that it is a nonvenomous constrictor of the boa family. We know that it is aquatic, preferring slow rivers and swamps. That it bears live young (as opposed to laying eggs) in litters of up to eighty. That it is native to tropical South America east of the

Andes, and also to the island of Trinidad. That (unlike the other boas and pythons) it does poorly and dies soon in captivity. But as to the rest, its favored diet, its daily and seasonal rhythms, its mating and birthing behavior, physiology, growth rate, optimal longevity: almost a total blank. There is an absence of evidence.

Admittedly, the prospect of studying full-grown anacondas in their own habitat offers an array of uniquely forbidding logistical problems For that reason or whatever others, scientific consideration of *Eunectes murinus* has been limited almost entirely to the same simple question that so mesmerized those early explorers: *How big does it get?* Well, really quite big. Bigger than any other snake on earth. *But how big is that?*

A second sad fact about the anaconda: By scientific standards of verification, it just doesn't seem to be nearly so large as everyone seems to want to believe it is. Forget 131 feet. Forget 62 feet, even with faultless arithmetic. Discount the record-length skins, which generally have been stretched by a good 20 percent in the process of tanning. Scientists have their own unstretchable views on this matter.

One respected herpetologist, Afranio do Amaral, has posited a maximum length of the anaconda of about forty-two feet. But then Afranio do Amaral is a Brazilian, arguably with a vested patriotic interest. And after him the figures only get stingier. James A. Oliver of the American Museum of Natural History was willing to grant 37 1/2 feet, based on the measurement made by a petroleum geologist, with a surveyor's tape, of a snake shot along the Orinoco River. But again in this case there was the problem of physical evidence: "When they returned to skin it, the reptile was gone," we are told. "Evidently it had recovered enough to crawl away." Teddy Roosevelt is said to have offered $5,000 for a skin or skeleton thirty feet long, and the money was never claimed. Sherman and Madge Minton, authors of several reliable snake books, declare that "To the best of our knowledge, no anaconda over twenty-five feet long has ever reached a zoo or museum in the United States or Europe." And Raymond Ditmars, an eminent snake man at the Bronx Zoo early in this century, wouldn't believe anything over nineteen feet.

Can these people all be discussing the same animal? Can Ditmars's parsimonious nineteen feet be reconciled with the eyewitness account of Major Fawcett?   Does Roosevelt's unclaimed cash square with Heuvelmans's 115 feet of worthless rotting meat? It seems impossible.

But new evidence has lately reached me that suggests an explanation for everything.   The evidence is a small color photograph.   The explanation is relativity.

Not Einstein's variety, but a similar sort, which I shall call *Amazonian relativity*. It's very simple: The *true genuine size* of an anaconda (this theory applies equally well to piranha and bird-eating spiders) is relative to three other factors: (1) whether or not the snake is alive; (2) how close you yourself are to it; and (3) how close both of you are, at that particular moment to the Amazon heartland. A live snake is always bigger than a dead one, even allowing for posthumous stretch. And as the other two distances decrease — from you to the snake, from you to the Amazon — the snake varies inversely toward humongousness.

This small color photograph, of such crucial scientific significance, arrived in the mail from an affable Dutch-born engineer, a good fellow I met on that Rio Aguirico trip. Unlike me, he carried a camera; sending the print was meant as a favor. In its foreground can be seen the outline of my own dopey duck-billed hat. The background is a solid wall of green jungle. At the center of focus is Randy Borman, astride the stern of his dugout, holding an anaconda. Dark gunmetal gray with sides mottled in reddish brown.

The snake is almost as big around as his wrist. It might be five feet long. Possibly close to six. But photographs can be faked. I don't believe this one for a minute.

David Quammen

HAS SUCCESS SPOILED THE CROW?

Any person with no steady job and no children naturally finds time for a sizable amount of utterly idle speculation. For instance, me — I've developed a theory about crows. It goes like this:

Crows are bored. They suffer from being too intelligent for their station in life. Respectable evolutionary success is simply not, for these brainy and complex birds, enough. They are dissatisfied with the narrow goals and horizons of that tired old Darwinian struggle. On the lookout for a new challenge. See them there, lined up conspiratorially along a fence rail or a high wire, shoulder to shoulder, alert, self-contained, missing nothing. Feeling discreetly thwarted. Waiting, like an ambitious understudy, for their break. Dolphins and whales and chimpanzees get all the fawning publicity, great fuss made over their near-human intelligence. But don't be fooled. Crows are not stupid. Far from it. They are merely underachievers. They are bored.

Most likely it runs in their genes, along with the black plumage and the talent for vocal mimicry. Crows belong to a remarkable family of birds known as the Corvidae, also including ravens, magpies, jackdaws and jays, and the case file on this entire clan is so full of prodigious and quirky behavior that it cries out for interpretation not by an ornithologist but a psychiatrist. Or, failing that, some ignoramus with a supple theory. Computerized ecologists can give us those fancy equations depicting the whole course of a creature's life history in terms of energy allotment to every physical need, with variables for fertility and senility and hunger and motherly love; but they haven't yet programmed in a variable for boredom. No wonder the Corvidae dossier is still packed with unanswered questions.

At first glance, though, all is normal: Crows and their corvid relatives seem to lead an exemplary birdlike existence. The home life is stable and protective. Monogamy is the rule, and most mated pairs stay together until death. Courtship is elaborate, even rather tender, with the male doing a good bit of bowing and dancing and jiving, not to mention supplying his intended with food; eventually he offers the first scrap of nesting material as a sly hint that they get on with it. While she incubates a clutch of four to six eggs, he continues to furnish the groceries, and stands watch nearby at night. Then for a month after hatching, both parents dote on the young. Despite strenuous care, mortality among fledglings is routinely high, sometimes as high as 70 percent, but all this crib death is counterbalanced by the longevity of the adults. Twenty-year-old crows are not unusual, and one raven in captivity survived to age twenty-nine. Anyway, corvids show no inclination toward breeding themselves up to huge numbers, filling the countryside with their kind (like the late passenger pigeon, or an infesting variety of insect) until conditions shift for the worse, and a vast population collapses. Instead, crows and their relatives reproduce at roughly the same stringent rate through periods of bounty or austerity, maintaining levels of population that are modest but consistent, and which can be supported throughout any foreseeable hard times. In this sense they are astute pessimists. One consequence of such modesty of demographic ambition is to leave them with excess time, and energy, not desperately required for survival.

The other thing they possess in excess is brain-power. They have the largest cerebral hemispheres, relative to body size, of any avian family. On various intelligence tests — to measure learning facility, clock-reading skills, the ability to count — they have made other birds look doltish. One British authority, Sylvia Bruce Wilmore, pronounces them "quicker on the uptake" than certain well-thought-of mammals like the cat and the monkey, and admits that her own tamed crow so effectively dominated the other animals in her household that this bird "would even pick up the spaniel's leash and lead him around the garden!" Wilmore also adds cryptically: "Scientists at the University of Mississippi have been successful in getting the cooperation of Crows." But she fails to make clear whether that was as test subjects, or on a consultative basis.

From other crow experts come the same sort of anecdote. Crows hiding food in all manner of unlikely spots and relying on their uncanny memories, like adepts at the game of Concentration, to find the caches again later. Crows using twenty-three distinct forms of call to communicate various sorts of information to each other. Crows in flight dropping clams and walnuts on highway pavement, to break open the shells so the meats can be eaten. Then there's the one about the hooded crow, a species whose range includes Finland: "In this land Hoodies show great initiative during winter when men fish through holes in the ice. Fishermen leave baited lines in the water to catch fish and on their return they have found a Hoodie pulling in the line with its bill and walking away from the hole, then putting down the line and walking back on it to stop it sliding, and pulling it again until (the crow) catches the fish on the end of the line." These birds are bright.

And probably — according to my theory — they are too bright for their own good. You know the pattern. Time on their hands. Under-employed and over-qualified. Large amounts of potential just lying fallow. Peck up a little corn, knock back a few grasshoppers, carry a beak-full of dead rabbit home for the kids, then fly over to sit on a fence rail with eight or ten cronies and watch some poor farmer sweat like a sow at the wheel of his tractor. An easy enough life, but is this *it*? Is this *all*?

If you don't believe me just take my word for it: Crows are bored.

And so there arise, as recorded in the case file, these certain . . . no, *symptoms* is too strong. Call them, rather, *patterns of gratuitous behavior.*

For example, they play a lot.

Animal play is a reasonably common phenomenon, at least among certain mammals, especially in the young of those species. Play activities — by definition — are any that serve no immediate biological function, and which therefore do not directly improve the animal's prospects for survival and reproduction. The corvids, according to expert testimony, are irrepressibly playful. In fact, they show the most complex play known in birds. Ravens play toss with themselves in the air, dropping and catching again a small twig. They lie on their backs and juggle objects (in one recorded case, a rubber ball) between beak and feet. They jostle each other sociably in a version of "king of the mountain" with no real territorial stakes. Crows are equally frivolous. They play a brand of rugby, wherein one crow picks up a white pebble or a bit of shell and flies from tree to tree, taking a friendly bashing from its buddies until it drops the token. And they have a comedy-acrobatic routine: allowing themselves to tip backward dizzily from a wire perch, holding a loose grip so as to hang upside down, spreading out both wings, then daringly letting go with one foot; finally, switching feet to let go with the other. Such shameless hot-dogging is usually performed for a small audience of other crows.

There is also an element of the practical jokester. Of the Indian house crow, Wilmore says: ". . . this Crow has a sense of humor, and revels in the discomfort caused by its playful tweaking at the tails of other birds, and at the ears of sleeping cows and dogs; it also pecks the toes of flying foxes as they hang sleeping in their roosts." This crow is a laff riot. Another of Wilmore's favorite species amuses itself, she says, by "dropping down on sleeping rabbits and rapping them over the skull or settling on drowsy cattle and startling them." What we have here is actually a distinct subcategory of playfulness known, where I come from at least, as Cruisin' For A Bruisin'. It has been clinically linked to boredom.

Further evidence: Crows are known to indulge in sunbathing. "When sunning at fairly high intensity," says another British corvidist, "the bird usually positions itself sideways on to the sun and erects its feathers, especially those on head, belly, flanks and rump." So the truth is out: Under those sleek ebony feathers, they are tan. And of course sunbathing (like ice-fishing, come to think of it) constitutes prima facie proof of a state of paralytic ennui.

But the final and most conclusive bit of data comes from a monograph by K. E. L. Simmons published in the *Journal of Zoology*, out of London. (Perhaps it's for deep reasons of national character that the British lead the world in the study of crows; in England, boredom has great cachet.) Simmons's paper is curiously entitled "Anting and the Problem of Self-Stimulation." *Anting* as used here is simply the verb (or to be more precise, participial) form of the insect. In ornithological parlance, it means that a bird — for reasons that remain mysterious — has taken to rubbing itself with mouthfuls of squashed ants. Simmons writes: "True anting consists of highly stereotyped movements whereby the birds apply ants to their feathers or expose their plummage to the ants." Besides direct application, done with the beak, there is

92

also a variant called *passive anting:* The bird intentionally squats on a disturbed ant-hill, allowing (inviting) hundreds of ants to swarm over its body.

Altogether strange behavior, and especially notorious for it are the corvids. Crows avidly rub their bodies with squashed ants. They wallow amid busy ant colonies and let themselves become acrawl. They revel in formication.

Why? One theory is that the formic acid produced (as a defense chemical) by some ants is useful for conditioning feathers and ridding the birds of external parasites. But Simmons cites several other researchers who have independently reached a different conclusion. One of these scientists declared that the purpose of anting "is the stimulation and soothing of the body," and that the general effect "is similar to that gained by humanity from the use of external stimulants, soothing ointments, counter-irritants (including formic acid) and perhaps also smoking." Another compared anting to "the human habits of smoking and drug-taking," and maintained that "it has no biological purpose but is indulged in for its own sake, for the feeling of well-being and ecstasy it induces . . ."

You know the pattern. High intelligence, large promise. Early success without great effort. Then a certain loss of purposefulness. Manifestations of detachment and cruel humor. Boredom. Finally the dangerous spiral into drug abuse.

But maybe it's not too late for the corvids. Keep that in mind next time you run into a raven, or a magpie, or a crow. Look the bird in the eye. Consider its frustrations. Try to say something stimulating.

David Quammen

A WALK IN THE WOODS

Nothing leaves a man's thoughts so much room to circulate and develop free from distorting influences as walking through the woods, plodding aimlessly along some half-overgrown trail through the timber to see what is around the next turn, or maybe the next one after that. It shouldn't matter much whether anything is there or whether the trail goes anywhere. To a detached and contemplative mind, a trail that goes nowhere has as much food for reflection about it as one with practicality and usefulness. Sometimes it can have more.

Once I followed the weathered tracks of a farm wagon through some broken pine-timber country in Southeastern Oregon, mostly for the sake of following something, and finally came on a wagon standing rusty and weather-bleached in the middle of an abandoned camp. With it were a half-rotten old tent, a pile of tattered bedding, a few dishes, some rocks piled for a fireplace, some battered cooking utensils and pieces of harness scattered around with grass grown almost over them and a woman's ivory-backed hand mirror hanging from a tree limb by a piece of baling wire. There was nothing to show what kind of people the outfit had belonged to or why they had come there. The land was worthless, the grass sparse, the trees scrawny and twisted and there was no water. They may have taken to the woods to settle a quarrel, or to hide from the authorities, or to hunt for a lost gold mine, or maybe they were a young couple eloping. One explanation was as good as another. The less one knows about such things, the more room there is to guess at them.

To a person used to walking in the woods, an obvious purpose in anything can knock all the interest out of it. Small things like fir seeds drifting loose in the sunlight or grouse feathers scattered in a clearing where a hawk struck can turn out to be unforgettable, while incidents that a practical world might regard as triumphs seem mere passing distractions — the more dramatic, the more annoying.

When I was young a great-uncle of mine in Southwestern Oregon took to wandering around the open timber that lay along the creek bottom below his hay meadows in his old age, and spent almost all his time at it, always carrying a double-bitted ax to keep his neighbors from inventing fool theories about why he was doing it. He was interrupted in his excursion one morning by the hired man, who had snagged a large Chinook salmon in the creek while the horses were watering and was having trouble keeping his line from tangling with the horses' feet. My uncle got the horses out of the creek and helped bring the salmon to land as absorbedly as if he had hooked it himself. Then, after a moment's reflection, he picked it up and hove it back into the creek, threw the hired man in after it and went silently back to the house for the rest of the day.

It was a long time before I came to understand what he had been so resentful about. Salmon was a useful article of diet, and anybody already occupied with a couple of horses was likely to need help in landing one. His strenuousness began to seem rational one fall when I was out with a deer-hunting expedition in a logged-off area of the Coast Range Mountains in Western Oregon. I had injured my right hand in an automobile accident and couldn't handle a rifle, so I spent the time lazing around camp while the rest of the party tramped the hills looking for deer which, as usually happens, kept themselves painstakingly out of sight until the hunting season was over.

Lying around camp got monotonous after a few days, so I started out to explore the line of an old logging railroad that followed a little creek back into the mountains. It wasn't a hunting trip, there were no firearms left in camp to hunt with, and I couldn't have handled a gun anyway.

I did take a folded-up paper sack, on the chance there might be blackberries along the creek, but I didn't use it. There were too many things worth watching — coveys of mountain quail dodging through the salal brush, always with one quail perched on a low limb as a watchman; bumblebees in the patches of fireweed; places where the old logging train had derailed and scored the weather-cracked gray ties for fifty feet with its wheel flanges, and where a trestle across the creek had burned out, leaving the rusty rails hanging helpless in mid-air like half-melted sticks of candy; deer and rabbit trails leading down through the underbrush to the creek, and some bleached crawfish shells scattered along the wet sand where a marten had dined; a flock of band-tailed pigeons that settled on a big madrona tree to eat the scarlet berries, not perching on limbs as birds ordinarily do, but clinging to the outside foliage as if they had been pasted on it for ornament, and then flapping away in panic because one of them lost his hold and let out an alarmed squawk; a huddle of board shanties that had been a logging camp, with galvanized oil drums and some cast-off overalls peering shyly from among the wild blue asters and a greasy old donkey engine bolted to a stump with red-hipped wild roses growing over it, covering its dirt with cleanness.

Finally a wild blackberry patch did come into sight near the end of the logged-off area. It looked tempting, and there was no sign that even bears had molested it, but it was in a swale at the bottom of a long slope overgrown with mountain laurel. There was no sign of a trail through it, and it was so high that even the fallen trunks of a few huge firs uprooted in some windstorm were almost hidden by it. I sat down on a piece of crumbly rock in the middle of the right of way to decide whether the blackberries would be worth my climbing all that way down.

There were reasons for doing it and reasons against it. The blackberries would be something to show the deer hunters when they got back to camp; but it was past midafternoon, picking them would take time and there would be the job of climbing back through the underbrush after they were picked, which was tiresome; I wished the blackberry patch hadn't been there, or that I hadn't seen it.

The sky over the fir timber had a curious effect of depth and tenseness about it; the spaces behind the sun were as vast and lucid and quivering as the space in front of it. I got up, deciding that the blackberries were too much trouble, and the rock I had been sitting on crumbled into pieces. I picked up a piece and tossed it down the slope as a sort of parting flourish, and a three-point buck deer started up from his concealed bed in the underbrush, took a long jump to clear a fallen tree, landed in a deep hole that had been too overgrown for him to see and broke his neck. He was dead when I climbed down to him, his head wrenched so far back that one prong of his antlers was driven an inch into his shoulder.

He was too heavy to carry uphill through all that brush. It was all I could do even to move him, with only one hand usable, but it would have been sinful to leave a whole deer for the buzzards when the hunters in camp had been walking their legs off for a week trying to get sight of one. So I did a one-handed dressing job on him with a pocket knife and lugged the haggled sections back to the old logging-camp shanties to wait for a pack horse. It was backbreaking drudgery, lacking the slightest feeling of communication with wild nature, but even if it had been easy I would have resented it. To get a deer by tossing a rock into a brush pile was not a triumphant climax to the day's impressions. The only gain was that I knew for the first time how my great-uncle felt about having to help land the salmon when he had intended to go out walking. He was a little ahead of me in having a hired man handy on whom to take out his injured feelings. It must have helped.

Walking through a completely wild and untracked stretch of woods never has much in it that is worth remembering. A forest in a primitive state, especially in the West, is invariably cut up with gullies and choked and tangled with underbrush and dead branches and fallen trees. Getting through it on foot and keeping directions straight make such demands on the mind and muscles that there is no room left for any fleeting wayside impressions.

Following a trail is always better, any kind of trail is better than none. Even a deer trail or an overgrown trap line will lighten the strain of remembering landmarks and deciding which way to head next. Once, on a Government survey in the mountains of Central Washington, I spent most of a day plodding through a beautiful high-altitude stand of mixed white pine and cedar along a faintly marked old trail, and had a thorough good time. There were chipmunks and pine squirrels and ruffed grouse, and I got so absorbed watching an old she-bear with two half-grown cubs on a rock slide across a canyon that I strayed off the trail a couple of times and had to go back and hunt for it.

Toward midafternoon, the trail ended in a scattering of bleached bones between two fallen trees, a bent piece of rusty iron and some links of chain sticking up from among the deep pine needles. It was the skeleton of a big timber wolf, with a heavy steel trap locked around one of its forelegs. Following the trail had landed me in the middle of nowhere, and I had to backtrack till almost dark to find out where I had been. Still, it had been serene and leisurely and reflective, and I didn't regret it. Once, while the old she-bear was working her way up the rock slide, one of the cubs sat down and refused to keep up, and she came back and turned him across her knee and spanked the stuffing out of him. Setting a compass course would have been more efficient, but it wouldn't have led to anything like that, or I would have been too busy crawling through underbrush and climbing dead logs to notice it.

Nothing knocks the color out of walking in the woods like forcing some purpose into it. Carrying along a camera gives a man the sneaking feeling he ought to be taking pictures. It is even worse with a gun. Even the most unobtrusive shooting iron will stir in a man an involuntary alertness for some excuse to shoot something. He is not walking, he is hunting. If he doesn't see anything to shoot, the hunt is a failure; if he does, the walk is a failure.

The kind of walking that holds its color longest usually starts with something small and trivial — an odd noise in the blackberry thicket back of a roadside shanty, which turns out to be a loose board flapping or a broken-down windmill creaking. Or maybe it's something moving in the weeds at the turn of the old wood road beyond the shanty's back fence that might be a cock pheasant or sunlight reflecting from a blackberry leaf, or a haw bush with a handful of ripe haw berries on it in a patch of yellowing bracken a dozen yards on, or a trout jumping in a deep hole below a rickety pole bridge, or a stretch of corduroy road beyond it, with skunk cabbage and coarse yellow waterlilies and black-ringed snakeweed crowded where the water seeps out into the black leaf mold below it.

A parable of some kind could be worked up from looking into mountain water on a still day. At a distance, it reflects what is around it — grass, trees, sky; when you lean close, the reflection is of yourself. Lean close enough to drink from it, and you will see down past all the reflections to the reality of underwater life — bugs, worms, tadpoles, fingerling trout, drowned weeds, sprays of reddish lichens. But the water itself, through which both reflections and reality exist, is so still and colorless that it is never really visible at all.

Sometimes the clearings along the old wood roads turn out to be merely wild grass meadows reaching into the timber, or the remains of an old homestead hayfield, its old fence rails matted so deep under dead grass and wild blackberry vines that it is hard to tell what they were intended to enclose. But these clearings do sometimes come up with something unexpected.

It is hard to imagine human beings living in one of those back-country areas, reached only by old wood roads that look scarcely passable for a pack horse, but some people do. It was only a few years back, following a rocky old wagon track along a ridge through the oak timber in Northern California, that I ran into a regular assortment of them. First I found some woodcutters stripping tanbark from a patch of oaks, then I saw a young cowboy of not over eighteen, big and towheaded and bashful, living in a homemade camp wagon between two rows of half-dead olive trees and herding a couple of dozen scrub cows to pasture on some worn-out vineyards, filling in his spare time by laying a fieldstone terrace in front of his camp wagon after a pattern in a magazine. Then I met an alert-looking little man in a summer shirt who came down the wood road carrying a camp hatchet with a couple of dogs following him. He explained that he had a permit from the mortgage company to trap its lands down the ridge, and was out marking trees for one of his trap lines. He had a couple of lines already in among the abandoned farms down in the timber, and though he hadn't made much of a start at catching strictly fur-bearing animals, he had caught over ninety full-grown outlaw house cats, not counting undersized ones.

A mile or so farther on, where the gray-green oaks gave way to thickets of small Douglas fir, I saw what looked like an abandoned farm in the middle of some grassland halfway down the slope of the ridge. It was a huddle of gray board shanties with a faint trail of scrawny, climbing rosebush wandering through the tarweed. Four or five full-grown deer were eating green plums and wormy apples from the overgrown orchard while a half-dozen fawns pranced and circled and chased one another around what was left of a high picket fence that had been put up to keep them out. When the door of one of the shanties opened and an old man came out, they merely edged away from him and went on stripping the twisted old trees of their underripe fruit. The man went over to the well curb and hung a cloth on it to dry, picked up a dead limb, and went back indoors with it, taking no more notice of the deer than they did of him.

It seemed a comedown for the country, as I thought it over. Here was a man of supposedly mature judgment who insisted on living on a worn-out farm and lacked get-up enough to keep it from falling to pieces around him, who picked up dead tree limbs for fuel instead of cutting a few solid oak trees into cordwood, who couldn't even rustle up a firearm to keep the wild animals from overrunning him.

In the old days, homesteading in these remote areas was a sign of courage and independence and resourcefulness. A man did it because he felt capable of standing up to Nature at her meanest, and preferred that kind of tussle to being beholden to his fellow men. Now, seemingly, it was a sign of worthlessness; people clung to these run-down weed patches to shirk the responsibility of standing up to anything.

That was probably true as a general observation, but as it turned out the old man shuffling out among the deer was not a good illustration. A heavy-set younger man working another old orchard farther up the ridge explained that the old man's place was run down so badly because he was blind. The deer weren't afraid of him because they knew it. The old man had stayed with his homestead because he was used to it and knew where to find things without having to see them. People hauled in supplies for him when they thought of it, and he drew a small pension from somewhere.

The heavy-set man who explained all this was something of a specimen himself — big, red-complexioned and awkward-looking, with a week's beard caked whitish with orchard dust. He had only one eye, which shifted incessantly as he talked, like the antennae of an insect, and he seemed to be straining between agonizing self-consciousness and desperate wistfulness. His name was Hulse, or something that sounded like it, and his orchard had been in his family a long time. He was one of four brothers born and raised on it. The others had run into trouble, and he was the only one left.

"They was a little bit headstrong sometimes, and these newcomers around here always go out of their way to make trouble for people," he said. "So they had to leave the country for a while, so I've got the place on my hands till things blow over. One thing is, it makes it easy for people to find me. When they want to know which one of the Hulse boys I am, I can tell 'em I'm the one that's never shot anybody.''

Walking through these back-country areas you learn that letting a place run down can bring gain as easily as loss. In the high Cascade Mountains of Central Oregon there used to be a washed-out freight road that followed a creek past a flume. It was a good place to walk and reflect in, because the country changed color and character every mile or so and made a man feel that he was covering ground without having to exert himself. At first it was open and dusty, with grayish clumps of scrub oak, deer brush and dwarf pine drooping in the heat and quail whistling in the dead grass or yellowing the sunlight with dust from a wallow among the pine needles in the road. Then the road edged down close to the creek through a stretch of logged-off Douglas fir grown up in little thickets of willow and hazel and blue elderberry. The farms were small and close together and crowded against the old flume line as rigidly as beads on a string. The buildings were small and paintless — too small to be lived in, some of them looked — with the remains of a flower garden in front and few dozen scrubby and twisted fruit trees alongside where white-tailed deer came to feed on the rusty pears and little red-streaked apples.

Down the slope toward the creek where the ground had been fertilized by the ashes of a brush fire there were great swales of ripe, wild blackberries, torn into ragged lanes by the bears who had fed on them. New coveys of big blue grouse clucked and pecked at them like flocks of chickens. Nearer the creek where the shade was deeper, there were clumps of black raspberries and hazel bushes loaded with nuts as big as plums. Among the huckleberries under the deep fir and alder along the creek there were little sharptailed grouse known locally as native pheasants, and whole packs of ruffed grouse all clucking at once, and sounding like somebody picking a comb over an empty rain barrel.

The glare of light that struck through the deep timber came from the clearing around the remains of the old sawmill. All that was left were a few fire-blackened timbers and scraps of rusty iron scattered around a rectangle of naked ground, a weather-blackened sawdust pile cut with blots of dark yellow where the deer had made a trail across it and a half-wrecked log dam that had backed up the creek for a mill pond. There were broken boards and timbers scattered in the dead grass where the flume had been wrecked, and several neat green-lettered signs were tacked on stumps, marking the boundary of the national forest. The signs showed what the sawmill had been doing and why it was no longer in business. One of the standard lumberman's tricks in the uninhibited old days was to buy up a small patch of forest land adjoining some big tract of Government timber, and then to forget about property lines and log off everything in sight until somebody in authority showed up with a crew of surveyors and a court injunction. The lumberman would then pull out, expressing deep contrition for the error, and go do the same thing somewhere else.

Halting such operations protected public property against private pillage, but it usually bore hard on the back-country settlements, which had come to depend on the mill as a market for their produce. Closing this one mill had wiped out a community of from two or three hundred human beings. All the work they had done to bring the country from wilderness to the production of something useful had to be written off as wasted.

Not that it was all wasted, if one took a long view of it. Nature had come in again after they moved out, and was producing probably four or five times as much usable food from the abandoned clearings and stump lands as they had managed to wrest from the country with all the work they had put into it.

It would be impossible to place any concrete value on walking in the woods, but one can sometimes make a tentative estimate from what people have been willing to pay for it. Eight or ten years ago I was spending a winter on a hill ranch in Northern California. Walking out through the oak timber after a big three-day rainstorm, I ran into the elderly Italian vineyardist who owned the adjoining farm. He was strolling thoughtfully along an old horse trail through the wet leaves, his hands tucked under the bib of his overalls, a big man, heavy-set, red-faced, slow in his movements — a nice old fellow. He was somewhere around seventy, and his vineyard, on which he did most of the work himself, was accounted the best-kept in that part of the country. He explained that he was walking around to see if the rain had brought out any mushrooms.

We sat down on a dry boulder to visit a little, and he got to telling about himself, how he had worked on a farm in Northern Italy as a boy, had run away to Switzerland, gone to work in a machine shop in Zurich, married a Swiss girl and started saving so they could come to America. He worked in Zurich for eight years, at the end of which the Swiss girl eloped with a traveling salesman, taking his accumulated wages with her. He moved across into Germany, working in machine shops and iron foundries all the way down the Rhine as far as the Ruhr, and then across to England, where he worked for a few years in Sheffield and Birmingham.

He finally saved enough to come to the United States where he worked for awhile in New Jersey and Pennsylvania, and then came west to California. He worked for a San Francisco iron works for eight or ten years, and then in one of the big railroad shops, until he had enough money saved to buy his vineyard and the equipment to work it. It had taken time. He had started working toward it in his early youth, and he had got it only when he was on the verge of old age. That was too long, probably. Still, people always had to wait too long for what they wanted, and he had at least done better than some. He had finally got it and had been on it ten years, and here he was, out hunting mushrooms in the oak timber and having a good time at it.

"I don't think you'll find many mushrooms," I said. "It's too soon after the rain for them."

He sat on the rock and looked at the sweep of wet yellow grass down the hillside, the leafless gray-tan oaks and black oaks, the dark-green live oaks and holly oaks, the bright green of the pepperwoods and manzanita shrubs.

"I don't care much," he said. "I like to walk around and look. It don't matter much if there's any out or not. I worked forty-six years to get so I could walk through the trees like this and not care whether I got anything out of it or not. Now I'm seventy-two years old, and I've got to do as much of it as I can."

H. L. Davis

THE BROOK

One fall, a good many years ago, I was working on a General Land Office survey of some high-altitude timber in the Cascade Mountains of Central Washington. The timber was mixed white pine and cedar running along the flank of a high ridge, with an undergrowth of red fir so dense and closespread overhead that we had worked through it for two days without seeing any sunlight except, sometimes, as a faint and elusive path of ghostly radiance about as big as a man's hand, and with no water except where some accidental snow-seep had been dug underground for storage by one of the little mountain marmots. On the afternoon of the third day, the ridge tapered down and spread out into a clearing: a grassy tract of level ground where two little mountain streams came together, closing it in on two sides in the shape of a triangle. It was at the bottom of a small canyon, but it was the only part of the woods where the sun reached at all — the dark-gold autumn sunlight of the mountains that sometimes seems tangible enough to dip one's hand in — and somebody had built a log cabin on it, with the door and windows taking the afternoon sun exactly where it reflected back from the junction of the two streams.

There were many cabins in remote parts of the woods then, put up by wandering sharpshooters to pin down homestead rights on valuable timber. Most of them were merely the four walls, roof and two windows required by land-office regulations, with no great care shown in finishing even them. This one had real workmanship in it: the logs all of a size, with the corners squared and the tops and bottoms grooved and slotted to fit together without chinking, the hand-split planking of the floor and partition dressed smooth and joined tight, and the slab doors set in casings and fitted with iron latches and hinges instead of the cast-off harness straps commonly used in homestead shanties in that country. There was glass in the windows, and a fireplace. Everything about it showed that whoever had built it had intended to live in it. It never had been lived in, and, considering the location, never could have been, because of the communications. It was thirty-five miles from the nearest wagon-road, with twelve miles of the roughest and wildest kind of mountain country between it and even a practicable horse-trail. We had back-packed

104

in to finish with our survey, but we had to do it only once. For a man to settle himself in a place where everything had to be back-packed in over twelve miles of mountains would have made any ordinary brand of foolishness look spindling; and still, I couldn't help sympathizing with him. The sight of running water always gets hold of something inside me, and the little sunlit rise of ground between the two streams would have made me feel like doing exactly what he had done. I wouldn't have gone as far with it as he had, but I knew how he must have felt, squaring his logs and siting his windows to look out on the water sweeping past the russet alder and pink dogwood and yellow rockmaple, and I envied him the lonely exultation he must have felt in working it all out without anybody around to remind him how impractical it was.

It would have been different, probably, if he had figured out some way to live in the cabin after he got it finished. Admiration for a place by running water is something I can understand and share, but asserting possession over it always sets the wrong way with me, as I suppose it does with most country-raised people. There was an elderly retired wheat-farmer in one of the mountain valleys of Central Oregon once who took it into his head to build himself a house astraddle of one of the creeks that ran through it, with a trap-door in the kitchen floor through which he could haul up trout within only a couple of steps of the frying pan on the stove. None of the neighbors seemed exactly carried away by the idea, and none of them acted quite broken up when the spring floods knocked his house off its foundations and he had to be carried out to high ground by a party of rescuers swimming their horses in to reach him. He had no business trying to yard off the creek for himself to begin with; and catching trout within reach of the frying pan was impractical, because it left out of account that they had to be cleaned before being cooked.

A brook reached its highest importance when it ran through a town. Few in the Northwest do nowadays, having been tunneled under in the interests of street-lines and real-estate subdivisions, or else ditched off to make a log-pond for some sawmill, but the town I lived in had one in years past, and it helped immeasurably in keeping one's consciousness widened out beyond the limits of the town itself, which were narrow in more ways than one. Merely watching its changes from season to season was keeping track of what was happening in places upstream as remote from anything the town knew as if they had been in a different hemisphere: the water surging under the street-bridges clouded yellowish from an early rain in the high farmlands, or milky pink from some fall of wet snow carrying down red earth from the timber, or shrunk to a dark thread when some hard mountain frost had slowed down the springs that fed it. To know the brook was to live in a big section of country instead of a small one, and in a variety of different climates and types of scenery and economics and social values instead of merely one.

It was not much of a stream, even for a brook. There was no place in it deep enough to swim in — it was too cold for swimming anyway — and except in the spring freshets a man could jump across it in most places and wade it without getting in over hip-deep anywhere. But it did touch a big and varied assortment of country in its thirty-mile course from the town, ninety feet above sea level, to its source in some mountain snow-springs seven thousand feet up, and there was always something about it worth seeing at any time of the year. Even in the dead of winter, the clouds of pale-red willow and smoke-blue alder holding patches of old snow against the black water were beautiful, and looking at them could bring to mind what it must be like up at the headwaters — the green-white quaking aspens buried in snow halfway up into their branches, the little forest-ranger cabin with only the line of its gray roof sticking out above the snow from some yarded deer moving in it to keep warm, snow sliding down from a dead tree-snag in a cloud of gleaming diamond-dust, the shadow of a hawk across the snow, the shadow of a big white snowshoe rabbit squatted against a dead log — to know a brook is to know all of it at once, so that looking at one part of it will bring up what it is like at any given moment along its full length.

Some brooks have sections that, for one reason or another, are not worth turning out for at any season. Every part of this one was good during some part of the year. The salmon trout made their run around late March and early April, and they could be caught along the truck farms and small orchards at the very edge of town, and sometimes even in the town itself. Beyond the truck farms, the brook ran in a long shallow riffle over colored pebbles, closed on both sides by a grove of tall black oaks where the ruffed grouse came around the middle of April to carry on their courting ceremonies. The noise the water made rattling over its bed of pebbles was so loud in places that a man had to raise his voice to be heard over it, but the noise the cock-grouse made drumming among the oaks was so thunderous and startling that it would drown out any ordinary speaking-voice completely. I have read somewhere that the cock-grouse produces his drumming sound by beating his wing-tips on a hollow log or a stump, and I wouldn't argue the point against published authority, but there were mornings in the spring when I could hear at least two dozen grouse drumming in as many directions simultaneously, and the entire oak grove didn't have more than half a dozen stumps in it, and no hollow logs at all.

Their courting always seemed to get results, whether it was done according to the books or not. By early summer, the oak grove and the hills back of it and the patches of undergrowth along the brook would be alive with full-fledged families of them, the two old ones and anywhere from ten to a dozen three-quarter-grown young. They usually stayed clear of the orchards above the grove because the ground under the fruit trees was kept plowed so it had no cover, but there was one good-sized orchard belonging to two elderly unmarried brothers who had killed each other in some family argument, and since they had no heirs it had been left to grow up in a tangle of deer-brush and wild sweetbrier and wild hay that drew grouse coveys during the early summer by the dozen.

The grouse-hunting season didn't open until October, but the grouse in the old orchard were so plentiful and brazen that sometimes the temptation to take time by the forelock a little was more than flesh and blood could resist. Once, having let go and knocked down a couple of them that kept whirring up in my face and then settling twenty feet ahead to do it again, I had to spend the whole afternoon hiding in the tall grass from a neighboring orchardist who had been appointed deputy game warden for the district, and, panting for something to use his badge on, combed the orchard up, down and sideways until dark trying to find me. It was too big an area for him to cover thoroughly, and the grass where I was hiding was full of dead-ripe windfall apricots, so I didn't make out too badly, except that I had dropped my gun and the two grouse somewhere back in the deer-brush when I heard him coming, and I had to stay till daylight the next morning to find them. It was uncomfortable, especially in the cold hours before dawn, but the discomfort didn't outlast the night, and the first sun on the tall grass-heads, the sleek dark water of the brook lit with yellow flashes where the light caught it, and the flights of little white-and-gray birds almost striking their wings in it as the light changed it from dark to pale-green, have lasted unchanged and undimmed over all these years. It was a pity about the two grouse: they were bright harmless creatures, worth a lot more to look at than to eat, but it was the truth that four out of five of them always got hauled off by predatory animals before fall, so shooting them may merely have been getting in ahead of some coyote, bobcat, lynx-cat, weasel, hawk, eagle, or something else that might have made more ragged work of it. They were too speculative and incautious to have stayed alive long.

Beyond the abandoned orchard the brook ran in a series of deep pools and small waterfalls past a colony of Swiss-French who had settled there far back in the eighteen-seventies and had kept themselves steadfastly apart from the people around them ever since, still speaking only broken English, or, in a considerable number of cases, no English at all. They were vineyardists, and since neither the soil nor the climate around them was adapted to grape culture, some of their neighbors held the theory that they kept to themselves to avoid being twitted about their foolhardiness in staying with it, but there was something deeper than that back of it. Once, when I was working as a county sheriff's deputy, one of their men got killed from ambush under circumstances that could hardly have meant anything but a carefully prearranged murder. We hurried up to investigate, thinking that a little extra zeal and expeditiousness in the case might help to convince the people in the colony that they were members of society the same as everybody else, and that the State felt itself as responsible for protecting their lives as it did for collecting their taxes. We discovered, after questioning eight or ten of them, that they were not only not interested in having the case cleared up, but were doing their utmost to keep us from finding out anything about it. It was some issue among themselves, apparently, and whether they were pleased with the way it had been settled or not, they were determined to keep outsiders from mixing into it. They were successful, too. We were never able to get the slightest hint from any of them as to who had done it, or why, or anything about it. Living with a murderer in their midst should have made some of them nervous enough to drop a few chance remarks after the excitement had died down, but it didn't seem to. They weren't of a nervous temperament.

The string of deep pools that the brook made in passing their farms was the only part of it that abounded in crawfish, possibly because the table-scraps they habitually dumped into it were a diet that crawfish throve on. Elsewhere along the brook they were scarce, usually no bigger than a man's thumb, and almost black in color. In the pools fronting the vineyard colony they were big, dark red, and swarming into every pool that held forth the shadowiest promise of anything to eat. Once I left a string of half a dozen medium-sized trout in the shallow water at the edge of a pool to go talk to somebody up on the road, and, coming back after three-quarters of an hour, discovered that crawfish were piling four or five deep over the whole string and had eaten the trout almost up to the gills. One would have expected them to spread farther on upstream to widen their food supply instead of having to fight over it constantly, but they never got beyond the limits of the vineyard colony. Something about its atmosphere or temperament may have been congenial to them.

It was curious what changes of color the brook water went through in the short mile between the end of the colony vineyards and its entrance into the deep canyon leading up to the falls. Along the alder-shaded pools fronting the vineyards, it had a darkish cast, a little like the fluted edge of an obsidian arrowhead held up to the light. Farther up, in the open sunlight among the wild gooseberry thickets where a big flock of prairie chickens bedded during the afternoon, it was the dark steel-blue of a new gun except at the riffles which were greenish-white, and in the wild tumble of foam-streaks and rapids where it came out of the shaded canyon it was dark gray-green, as it sometimes was in its course through the town when winter was breaking up. Above the rapids it was blocked by an old beaver-dam that had backed it up and spread it out over the canyon floor in a sort of slough, with a foot or so of water covering a mixture of swamp-grass, dead weeds and bushes, and mud. There was no way to get through it except by wading, which involved some risk because of the deep under-water holes that the beavers had dug as rear entrances to their houses out in the main backwater. It was impossible to see where they were, and stepping into one of them meant dropping ten feet straight down a narrow shaft full of thin mud and ice-water, with no time to yell and no room to elbow out again. Beavers are useful and industrious animals, but it used to strike me sometimes that there was something a little self-centered in their habit of changing the course of a stream and the character of the land adjoining it, merely to work out a few private entrances to their houses.

The upper end of the canyon was deep and narrow, with the brooks sliding dark and unbroken down a channel worn out of black stone. There was one place in it so deep that one could look up from it at the sky and see the stars shining, even in the middle of the day. Beyond were the falls, which filled the canyon for nearly half a mile down with spray like a heavy rain. A trail up a steep rimrock-slide led around them to the upper country.

The upper country was the best part of the whole brook. It was a high-floored mountain valley with big yellow pine timber topping the hills on both sides. Down the slopes there were thickets of hazel and arrowwood and vine maple and mountain ash, separated by open stretches of grassland. On the flat bordering the brook there were fir and rock-maple, dogwood, alder, and wild raspberry bushes. The places where people lived were all half a mile or more up the hillside above it. The land along it had all been homesteaded for timber along in the eighteen-nineties, and had been abandoned after it was logged off. Most of the homestead buildings were still standing, with old half-wild overgrown orchards that still bore rusty pears and blue and yellow plums and little red-striped apples all through the late summer and fall. They were mostly merely deserted frame houses, a little spooky to stay in after dark, but there was a one-room log cabin a few miles farther up, so much older and simpler in design that there was something impersonal about it, where I spread down for the night sometimes when it was cold or threatening rain. Its door wouldn't go all the way shut and its window was nothing but a square hole cut in the logs, but it had a stone fireplace at one end and a fir-tip bed in one corner, and keeping a fire going made it seem warmer than outdoors, even if the difference in actual temperature was too small to argue about. A fir-tip bed was made by filling a rectangle of logs with the small end-tips of fir-boughs, stood upright and packed tight so they couldn't lean over or flatten down under one's weight. It took a fair-sized fir tree and a day's hard work to make one, but they were luxurious to sleep on, and since the twigs got springier and more resilient in drying out, they would last for years.

It was a pleasant place to stay in, in spite of porcupines that sometimes came poking in through the half-open door at night after the fire had burned low, on a little grass-flat grown up in clumps of vine maple, facing a half-wrecked pole bridge that led across the brook to a thicket of chinquapins — the only trees of that species I ever saw in the Northwest — and on past them to a little draw where there were masses of huckleberries, and usually, in the season when they were ripe, one or two black bears. It was at its best in the fall, when the vine maples had changed color and the air was tinged bluish from the fallen leaves drying and fruit ripening in the old orchards. Sometimes, being usually off work in late September and October, I used to take books up to read during the slack afternoons, and there are poems of Rossetti and Browning that I couldn't look at now without remembering the vine maple clumps flaming deep red like geraniums, the bluish air tinged with the fragrance of huckleberries, and the sound of the brook washing among the old bridge-timbers and underneath a fallen tree a little distance downstream, much more clearly than I remember anything in the poems. It was tempting to speculate sometimes on what the man had been like who had put up the cabin to begin with: some early-day pelt-hunter, possibly, since its workmanship was more that of a camp than a permanent residence, and there were racks built for drying meat in the fir grove above it, and no sign around it of the flubbed-up pretense at agriculture required by the General Land Office for issuing a homestead patent. He hadn't bothered about ownership, seemingly. The country was too overgrown to amount to much for hunting, but there was hunting country within reach of it, and he may have picked it as a site for his cabin because it was a place to be, which it was.

The settlers who had taken homesteads up the hillside away from the brook were mostly small cattle raisers, with a few seasonal sidelines like cutting wild hay for a big cattle company on the far side of the valley and hauling cordwood down to sell in the town when it was going through one of its regular winter fuel shortages. The land they had taken up was not particularly good, but it adjoined open country where they could run their cattle without having to involve themselves in leases or grazing permits, and it had the additional advantage that they could occasionally knock over one or two cattle company steers and lay the blame for it, if it was noticed, on mountain lions or wolves or half-breed Indians. The company cowboy assigned to patrol that section of its range worked hard at it, but it was a big area to keep tab on single-handed, and he had never been able to work up sociable relations with the settlers because, though he knew his work and looked like something out of Frederic Remington's paintings, he couldn't speak any language except Welsh.

They were a shy, loud-voiced, old-fashioned set of people — their school was probably the last place in the country where the youngsters still played such obsolete games as hatball and black-man and bull-pen — expert at out-of-date skills like axemanship and ten-horse-team skinning and diamond-hitch packing, and given to old-time forms of social diversion that sometimes tended to upset all the standard notions of what old-time social diversions were like. I went one winter to a neighborhood candy-pull at one of their houses, supposing, from various patronizing allusions in old books and magazines, that it would amount merely to boiling molasses down to a caramel, setting it out in buttered plates till it cooled, handing it out for the guests to pull till it got pale-yellow and brittle, and then sitting around licking it and playing something like forfeits, or clap-in-and-clap-out. It turned out to be not in the least like that. The only form of group diversion it could have been compared to was a knock-down-and-drag-out riot. The point of the entertainment was that after the molasses had cooled and been handed around to start pulling, the men started trying to steal gobs of it from everybody and getting into fights with the other men over it. The spectacle of two sedate-featured men of middle age locked in a clinch and wrestling their way down the front steps into a snowdrift with one hand apiece while clutching a mass of coagulated molasses in the other would have been funny if they hadn't been in such dead earnest about it. None of the candy ever got pulled, and the casualties for the evening included two broken ribs, a dislocated shoulder, some smashed knuckles, a set of lacerated fingers that got into somebody's mouth by mistake, and everybody's clothes completely wrecked. None of the guests seemed to think the tally of injuries was anything unusual; it was about average for a candy-pull, they agreed, especially one where the people were all in high spirits and not holding back from enjoying themselves.

They showed the same strenuousness in their notions about hunting. Once I ran into a half-dozen of them taking a wagon up to the end of the road to start a three-weeks' hunt in the mountains, and their entire equipment for it, besides guns and ammunition, consisted of flour, salt, coffee, two belt-axes, a frying pan, and a tin bucket. There were no blankets, no tent, no bed-canvas; their system for keeping warm at night was to put up a fir-bough lean-to with a fire in front of it, which worked as well or better. As for food to supplement the flour and coffee, that was what they were headed into the woods for. A hunting party that couldn't bring in enough game to feed itself had no business going out on a hunt at all. Their faith in the country's game supply was stronger than mine would have been, but they came back at the end of the three weeks looking sleek and hearty, so it must have been well-founded. An outsider might have suspected them of filling in a few empty corners with huckleberries and wild raspberries, which were ripe in the mountains at that season, but nobody who knew them would have given the idea house-room. They were not opposed to wild berries, but picking them was work for women and Indians, and a man who would do it to make up for his incapacity as a hunter was apt to find his standing in the community sunk too low to be recognizable for the next year or two.

Another of their prejudices had to do with fishing, which, without laying down any iron-clad doctrine on the subject, they were inclined to frown on as undignified for men and unladylike for women. The brook above the abandoned homesteads leveled off into a long reach of still water, so motionless and colorless that it looked shallow though in most places it was around four feet deep, full of big trout that refused to take the slightest interest in any fishing lure ever invented. I was at work trying everything on them one afternoon when a fifteen-year-old girl from one of the homesteads came past with an old .22 rifle, stalking a little native pheasant in the snow-brush up the hillside, and offered to show me how it was done. She rigged a horsehair noose on the end of a switch, and, by manipulating it carefully in the deep water close to the bank, yanked out six trout in less than twenty minutes. Then she got up, leaving them lying in the grass, and started on up the hill after her pheasant. A native pheasant, dressed, would weigh possibly a pound. The trout she had caught would have weighed easily five times that much. I tried to talk her into taking them, but she refused. Noosing trout was well enough for children to fool away their time at, but grown people didn't bother with such things. She was grown.

The place where the brook headed was only a few miles past the still place where the big trout were. It was on the slope of a high mountain, so near the top that it seemed almost like a break in the skyline, near the edge of a great lawnlike sweep of open grassland that people in the Northwest used to call a mountain meadow: a half-dozen clear springs, so cold it hurt to drink from them, that joined together and ran down past the white snags of dead trees and the dark fir-clumps swiftly, but without a ripple to break the silence. Standing beside the little forest-ranger shack where the highest spring came out was like standing with one's head and shoulders drawn into the sky, completely separated from the far-off sound of wind in the firs that went on constantly under it; but the silence reached all the way to the ground, too — down into the grass and the dead tree-snags and the water racing past them toward the quaking aspens and the gray alders of the canyon below. It was not so much looking at a landscape as living through something of which the landscape and the silence were both a part. All the brook's miles of clatter and usefulness could not touch the silence, but it touched and deepened them, all the way down to the town and through the big culvert under the railroad tracks where it spread out into the river and vanished.

H. L. Davis

A PLACE NEAR HOME

I have come here with a small trailer pulled behind a pickup. Both belong to my parents. I have been visiting. I sit in the trailer, refugee from more than a cold wind, and think, half of my reason for being here.

Kicking Horse Reservoir, between St. Ignatius and Ronan in northwestern Montana, sprawls, manmade, under the morning shadow of the Mission Mountains, never more than a few feet deep, explosive with life, an important link in the local agricultural chain of survival based on a water supply created for the ranches and farms in the valley.

The cold seeps in with help from the wind. I had planned to stay two or three days in this small trailer to fish and think. The fishing does not look promising. I am the only one on the lake or, more properly, reservoir. Wetting a line briefly in the cold wind, I quickly grew hungry. Darkness is coming on fast under thick clouds.

Along the bank of the reservoir, three Great Blue Herons are examining the shallows, several degrees of patience and skill beyond even my imagination of fishing determination. But my life depends on other things, for which I have only begun learning adequate patience. Here such patience is basic, essential to the physical requirements of thousands of dependent lives. I am surrounded by mortality.

In my memory a cricket calls from the tall grass by the cemetery fence next to a wheat field a half a mile north of Groton, South Dakota. Another answers. A chorus. Then silence. The sun has not yet disappeared beneath the horizon, but it will soon. A cock pheasant and three hens slip from the field through the shorter freshly-mowed grass to the gravel road in search of grit to help digest the grain they've been eating. They scratch at the gravel in peace. No one is here. Except Patricia, my sister.

The cloud cover has thickened. I pee out the door and a gusty sidewind spreads thin gold liquid across the damp earth, still wet from last night's rain. I drench a dry cow-pie left by one of the cattle grazing on the edge of the reservoir. Two canvasbacks fly over, wings whistling in the wind. I come, for a moment, dangerously close to praising this "natural" world full of such delightful surprises. Then another gust of wind cuts through my clothing and I remember again why I have come here. A stark beauty haunts this place, despite the cold. Other visits, other seasons, clouds of mosquitoes, the penetrating stale reek of stagnant water, an ominous lack of trees. It's the kind of place that won't let you escape realities. It's also the kind of place that encourages imagination. They are not opposites. I have come here on this journey within a journey because my father has cancer and I must make room for that fact in my life.

Patricia would be 37 now. In my imagination, she is a loving, conservative woman, a little bulky and tall, who married a farmer and remained in South Dakota when the rest of the family moved. In my imagination, she would have been 15 when she married. She has married young and has three children, all boys, who work on the farm. No matter how hard I try, I cannot separate her from that wheat field.

It has, perhaps, too much to do with loss, too much because there may be a danger of becoming so involved in capturing the past, sorting its importance, that the present will have become part of the past before it reaches us. And it has to do with love because that is where we feel our losses most deeply. And it has to do with sex because sex leads us so easily to loss, and sometimes to the children inside us. And, when we're lucky, to a better understanding of parents.

It happens in the imagination, and in the heart, but it happens in locations. By accident and by choice, it *takes place.* And place becomes a way of understanding it.

My father is in his fourth week of seven weeks of radiation treatment for lung and neck cancer. The neck cancer is less serious and the spot in his lung is responding to the treatments by shrinking. My mother, who recovered from cervical cancer resulting in a hysterectomy when I was eight years old, is ever the optimist, a positive supporting companion with a history of ulcers and the removal of part of her stomach to stop a bleeding ulcer behind her. I am 35 and have suffered nothing more severe than a broken heart and a few sleepless nights. I tend to be overly emotional, hiding it at times in over-intellectualization and, like my mother, I worry. I carry antacid tablets in my pocket with the parking meter change and at least two pens. Recently life has been kind and my confidence is high. That pleases but does not help my father.

A hawk flies up from a fencepost in the field near the trailer as I open the door again to check on the weather. He hangs in a small gust of wind I cannot feel. Briefly the world seems motionless and the grass smells like wheat. I think of Patricia, and I think of the small animals I cannot see whose lives hang on the whims of the wind that may carry the hawk near them at the wrong moment. I cannot see them, but I know they are there, just as they are in a cemetery carved out of a wheat field in an overlooked patch of trees near Groton, South Dakota.

Loss clings like a veil drawn over the senses to those who have feared it too much, until it becomes a part of them. It changes its color, its mood, even its meaning, a badge of sympathy worn on the tongue. We have all met the sad relatives whose lives stopped the day they lost a spouse or a child because they cannot imagine anything so important ever happening again. But that is not what I should mean when I speak of suffering because they have stopped traveling through life. They have not really *suffered* loss. They have come to a place with that name and now they exist there like a historical monument few tourists notice and all the townspeople have forgotten. No one even bothers to argue about how it happened or why or what it means now because it no longer means motion and motion is life. Someone has stared at the statue so long it's hard to tell which of them might move first. The statue, at least, seems to have been riding that muscular horse somewhere, wearing a uniform that stood for a struggle. But any creature who has given up is not suffering. He is waiting for the world to confirm his acceptance of death.

Still, we can all admire struggle and statues and sympathize with pain and loss. The father who turns from the river his child has drowned in without a sound and stands days later in a quiet public assembly and screams, the mother who nearly buries the remaining child in misplaced affection and finally turns back to the dead child's father, the child who quietly conducts a ritual burial for a dead pet in the backyard at midnight after parents and friends have forgotten and drifted off to dreamless sleep, these people are suffering loss. That figure before the statue, becoming a statue, he is not suffering loss. And his tragedy did not *take place*, it took everything. *Where* loss happens, *where* suffering is acknowledged is a place that matters, not because it serves as a constant reminder but because it changes.

The trailer is rocking. I throw on some clothes and step out the door, yelling. It doesn't occur to me till later that it might be vandals wanting exactly that reaction. Or thieves armed with frustration and anger, if not guns. But there's nothing there and the wind is silent. I walk around the trailer in the cold early morning on the soggy earth and a cow eyes me suspiciously and trots off. Later, I remember an incident at a gravel pit about twenty miles south. A man was killed there about four years ago when someone who didn't even know him shot into his tent. I don't worry about that. I worry about more immediate difficulties like getting stuck moving the trailer back to the road on the soft earth. The cows are bellowing. Killdeer cry and a hawk floats over the field. The alarm clock I didn't set ticks loudly.

I remember a snowstorm once in Montana, a white-out. I was trying to drive home. I lived on the edge of Missoula, only four or five miles from the University, where I worked as a librarian. I had driven within three blocks of home during a break in the blizzard. Suddenly I was blind. Then every minute or two a glimpse of some object and a tentative inching forward. I was unable to place the scene into any landscape leading home. Simply moving forward was all I could do, less than three blocks from home and unsure if I was even still headed there. Yet the radio and the familiar details of the car's interior were enough to tell me I was not lost. In Montana snowstorms people have been known to freeze to death less than a hundred yards from safety. That I might freeze to death was a possibility. But I was not lost. Lost is a place that has forgotten itself.

Loss is something else. Loss turns even the familiar strange. I would not have noticed how worn and dirty the car seat had become. I would have heard only personal meaning in every song on the radio.

There was a time once when I feared losing a lover returning to her estranged husband. I floundered, too young to understand how self-indulgent and unnecessary my suffering was when I relentlessly imagined how she might act with him every time *Behind Closed Doors* echoed through my "empty" apartment or surfaced with such seemingly deliberate hostility from the canned depths of my Volkswagen's AM radio. I would have imagined any human event in some way symbolic of my loss. Only the snow would seem inviting, a purer loss than my own. In it I might have become lost, with all my personal baggage blinding me and the snow an event to blame it on. But the wind spoke to me of the cold in gusty breaths and I learned then to appreciate the silence in what it said.

The sun is up now and it remains cold. A small flight of Canada Geese honks to a huddled quiet on the mudflats. The reservoir is low.

A killdeer calls from the meadow. A large hawk surveys the field from a leaning fencepost near the trailer. The wind continues to blow and the water churns on the reservoir. The wind sings. The wind howls. I listen and wait. Moments later it's gone. The wind dies and a new world replaces everything. A hawk floats over the shoreline, a piece of the sky until the sky falls and a careless creature rises to a world it had not imagined.

Dusk. A long day with little to show for it. I caught many perch, bass and trout, but none big enough to provide dinner for me, though perhaps, thrown back, they will for that large bass I hope to catch tomorrow. I tried to drive into the mountains to fish at the Jocko Lakes (strange name for a lake on the Flathead Indian Reservation), but signs warned of toxic algae. My sure thing (in more than two dozen trips while living in Montana only once did I go home empty-handed) fizzled out. The Jocko Lakes ride the ridge between Seeley Lake and Arlee, high on the southern slope of the Mission Mountains. Anything toxic here is a sobering thought. And so down the winding pothole-ridden road to Twin Lakes, where a family of four hauled in rainbow trout while I, using the same bait, couldn't even get a nibble. I tried the fly rod and a few small minnows pecked at the fly. Then back to Kicking Horse Reservoir where the perch and bass hit steadily till dark, all of them too small. I startled a family of muskrats along the shore and watched a skunk waddle down a dry irrigation channel toward a hawk who wisely retreated.

And so, fishless, tonight's fare is homemade chili, my father's speciality. He has been doing the cooking while my mother watches their store, a gift shop, too tired from his radiation treatments to work much. He has been a workaholic all his life and not working is hard on him. Now that I have found my own interest in work, though some would not call writing work, I can see more of him in me. Once, a few years ago, I remember a surprising touch of fear in the middle of a laugh when I realized how much I sounded like my father. Unlike my father, I will not smother the chili in pepper and eat it with peanut butter.

Imagine Patricia playing with the kids. The three boys roughhouse with her, a little big to be treating their mother this way. Patricia rolls on the freshly-mowed lawn (the oldest boy's first proud solo with the mower), alive with laughter, tumbling like an overweight rodeo clown. Her husband — let's call him Les — gets a kick out of watching them and wishes he could join in, but a long hard day in the fields has left him barely enough time to eat before dark. Another long day of harvesting awaits him, and he may have to work at night if the work goes too slow the next few days. A fresh breeze would be welcome after the hard day if it didn't carry a reminder of colder weather on its way.

Abandoned nesting boxes on the island like a cluster of Indian burial boxes. They seem to drift in the fog. I have felt it several times on this trip, that moment of deep and difficult emotional disorientation.

Patricia is, for me, a strange loss, one I see reflected in my parents only on rare occasions. She lived only a few hours, an enlarged and rebellious heart at birth. She is rarely mentioned, but I remember clearly the sense of awe and a surprising lack of fear when my parents took me as a young child to place flowers on her grave.

And I remember that graveyard, the stone, the wheatfield surrounding it, the exact swish and clatter of the caretaker mowing the lawn, the tilt of his head as he peered ahead of the blades to watch for stones thrown by cars from the shoulder of the county highway. Or by kids like me.

Patricia died before I was born, but she has her place in my life because, in part, she has her place in the literal world. And my imagination begins there.

My father is a stubborn man. I am a stubborn son. His chili was delicious. It gave me heartburn. I am eating the rest of it for dinner. Two bass and a half a dozen perch worth keeping out of several dozen caught. The weather was erratic — moments of cold intense wind, an hour or two of relative warmth and sunshine, occasional rain. Enough time inbetween showers to partially satisfy my current obsession with fishing. Why do men find fishing and hunting so satisfying? Some primal instinct for the role of provider? Is that why it seems comforting to me to be successful at it again during a difficult time? Or is it the need for a quiet place to conduct serious thinking alone that brings me here? I suspect it is all this and much more — a sorting of the meanings of place, male roles, the past, and with luck, the future.

A few miles south of here is the Four Winds Village, a tourist stop consisting of old Western buildings, a Western curio store and a train museum. A couple of years ago I photographed a model train in the museum that became a book cover, ironically, for a collection of poems by a German poet. I remember now my surprise at discovering that many of the best collections of Indian Art are in Germany. Imagination and art show little consideration for time, and place means only what we allow it to mean in imagination. I had hoped to shoot some more pictures, but the museum was closed. I shot a dozen photos of weathered buildings etched with the personality of long exposure to changing climate before rain ended the shooting. Weather is never really the cliche it seems. And it is often a bridge. My past is framed in such pieces. I read my father's face into the lines and color of these buildings. It is in them more, for me, than any picture I have ever seen of him. His character is in these buildings and in pieces of association certain places in the world contain because they hold my imagination. A parent is never easy to see clearly for a child grown. Time and distance are the tools. You can learn or you can build masks. Most of us do a little of both. This is a time to tear away the masks, even the ones with smiles on them. For my father, like many fathers, to directly voice anger, frustration, and especially fear would be to become another person, these men who do not share such feelings easily. This has always been the hardest mask for him to remove.

My own masks are still forming. They take on the darker tones of the earth. Several have been handed down through generations of fathers and sons. It's seldom clear when they're given, quiet notions of life, and sometimes death, spoken as if some other less important thing were the subject, but *where* they're received, sometimes months, years, a lifetime later, is always a solid and wondrous place, in the real world, on the map of the heart. It could have been another lake, a river, a mountain campsite, a rocky stretch of ocean beach. It could be a room in the house you have lived in most of your life, a place where so much you could have ignored matters. But you are there again, where you have been before, differently now, thinking and bringing together some pieces of a life. Only from such places can suffering lead home.

Rich Ives

Three of us were driving north on the trans-Alaska pipeline haul road, pulling a boat behind a pickup. For miles at a time we were the only vehicle, then a tractor-trailer truck — pugnacious and hell-bent — would shoulder past, flailing us with gravel. From Fairbanks to Prudhoe Bay the road parallels the elevated, gleaming pipeline. Both pathways in the corridor have a manicured, unnatural stillness about them, like white-board fences running over the hills of a summer pasture. One evening we passed a lone seed-and-fertilizing operation, spraying grass seed and nutrients on the slopes and berms of the road, to prevent erosion. There would be no unruly tundra here. These were the seeds of neat Kentucky grasses.

One day we had a flat tire. Two of us changed it while the third stood by with a loaded .308 and a close eye on a female grizzly and her yearling cub, rooting in a willow swale 30 yards away. We saw a single wolf — a few biologists in Fairbanks had asked us to watch for them. The truckers, they said, had shot most of the wolves along the road; perhaps a few were drifting back in, with the traffic so light now. Short-eared owls flew up as we drove along. Single caribou bulls trotted off in their light-footed way, like shy waterfowl. Moose standing along the Sagavanirktok River were nodding in the willow browse. And red foxes, with their long black legs, pranced down the road ahead of us, heads thrown back over their shoulders. That night I thought about the animals, and how the road had come up amidst them.

We arrived at the oil fields at Prudhoe Bay on an afternoon when light blazed on the tundra and swans were gliding serenely in rectangles of water between the road dikes. But this landscape was more austere than any I had ever seen in the Arctic. Small buildings, one or two together at a time, stood on the horizon. It reminded me of West Texas, land throttled for water and oil. Muscular equipment sitting idle like slouched fists in oil-stained yards. It was no business of mine. I was only here to stay overnight. In the morning we would put the boat in the water and head west to the Jones Islands.

The bungalow camp we stayed in was wretched with the hopes of cheap wealth, with the pallid, worn-out flesh and swollen bellies of supervisors in ball caps, and full of the desire of young men for women with impossible shapes; for a winning poker hand; a night with a bottle gone undetected. The older men, mumbling of their debts, picking through the sweepings of their despair alone in the cafeteria, might well not have lived through the misery, to hear the young men talk of wealth only a fool would miss out on.

We left in the morning, bound for another world entirely, the world of science, a gathering of data for calculations and consultations that would send these men to yet some other site, the deceit intact.

Months later, on a cold March morning, I came to Prudhoe Bay for an official visit. I was met at the airport by a young and courteous public relations officer, who shook hands earnestly and gave me the first of several badges to wear as we drove around the complex. The police at road checkpoints and at building entrances examined these credentials and then smiled without meaning to be cordial. Here was the familiar chill of one's dignity resting for a moment in the hand of an authority of artificial size, knowing it might be set aside like a small stone for further scrutiny if you revealed impatience or bemusement. Industrial spying, it was apologetically explained — disgruntled former employees; the possibility of drug traffic; or environmental saboteurs.

We drove out along the edge of the sea ice and examined a near-shore drill rig from a distance — too chilly to walk over, said my host, as though our distant view met the letter of his and my responsibilities.

We ate lunch in the cafeteria of the oil company's headquarters building, a sky-lit atrium of patrician silences, of slacks and perfume and well-mannered people, of plants in deferential attendance. The food was perfectly prepared. (I recalled the low-ceilinged cafeterias with their thread-bare, food-stained carpets, the cigarette-burned tables, the sluggish food and clatter of Melmac where the others ate.)

On the way to Gathering Station #1 we pull over, to be passed by the largest truckload of anything I have ever seen: a building on a trailer headed for the Kuparuk River. In the ditch by the road lies a freshly fallen crane, the wheels of the cab still turning in the sunshine. The man with me smiles. It is —28 degrees Fahrenheit.

124

At Gathering Station #1 the oil from four well areas is cooled. Water is removed. Gas is separated off. Above ground for the first time, the primal fluid moves quickly through pipes at military angles and sits under pressure in tanks with gleaming, spartan dials. The painted concrete floors are spotless. There is no stray tool or wipe rag. Anything that threatens harm or only to fray clothing is padded, covered. The brightly lit pastel rooms carry heat from deep in the earth and lead to each other like a series of airlocks, or boiler rooms in the bowels of an enormous ship. I see no one. The human presence is in the logic of the machinery, the control of the unrefined oil, the wild liquid in the grip of pipes. There is nothing here for the oil but to follow instructions.

Tempered, it flows to Pump Station #1.

The pavilion outside the fence at the pump station is drifted in with snow. No one comes here, not in this season. I climb over the drifts and wipe wind-crusted snow from Pexiglass-covered panels that enumerate the local plants and animals. The sentences are pleasant, meant to offend no one. Everything — animals, oil, destiny — is made to seem to fit somewhat naturally together. People are not mentioned. I look up at Pump Station #1, past the cyclone fencing and barbed wire. The slogging pumps sequestered within insulated buildings on the tundra, the fields of pipe, the roughshod trucks, all the muscular engineering, the Viking bellows that draws and gathers and directs — that it all runs to the head of this seemingly innocent pipe, lined out like a stainless-steel thread toward the indifferent Brooks Range, that it is all reduced to the southward journey of this 48-inch pipe, seems impossible.

No toil, no wildness shows. It could not seem to the chaperoned visitor more composed, inoffensive, or civilized.

None of the proportions are familiar. I stand in the wind-blown pavilion looking at the near and distant buildings. I remember a similar view of the launch complexes at Cape Canaveral. It is not just the outsize equipment lumbering down the roads here but the exaggerated presence of threat, hidden enemies. My face is beginning to freeze. The man in the blue Chevrolet van with the heaters blasting is smiling. No guide could be more pleasant. It is time to eat again — I think that is what he is saying. I look back at the pipeline, this final polished extrusion of all the engineering.

There are so few people here, I keep thinking. Deep in the holds of those impersonal buildings, the only biology is the dark Devonian fluid in the pipes.

On the way back to the cafeteria the man asks me what I think of the oil industry. He has tried not to seem prying, but this is the third time he has asked. I speak slowly. "I do not know anything about the oil industry. I am interested mostly in the landscape, why we come here and what we see. I am not a business analyst, an economist, a social planner. The engineering is astounding. The true cost, I think, must be unknown."

During dinner he tells me a story. A few years ago there were three birch trees in an atrium in the building's lobby. In September their leaves turned yellow and curled over. Then they just hung there, because the air in the enclosure was too still. No wind. Fall came when a man from building maintenance went in and shook the trees.

Before we drove the few miles over to Deadhorse, the Prudhoe Bay airport, my host said he wanted me to see the rest of the Base Operations Building. A movie theater with tiered rows of plush red velour seats. Electronic game rooms. Wide-screen television alcoves. Pool tables. Weight-lifting room. Swimming pool. Squash courts. Running track. More television alcoves. Whirlpool treatment and massage. The temperatures in the different rooms are different perfectly. Everything is cushioned, carpeted, padded. There are no unpleasant sounds. No blemishes. You do not have to pay for anything. He shows me his rooms.

Later we are standing at a railing, looking out through insulated glass at the blue evening on the tundra. I thank him for the tour. We have enjoyed each other. I marvel at the expense, at all the amenities that are offered. He is looking at the snow. "Golden handcuffs." That is all he says with his wry smile.

It is hard to travel in the Arctic and not encounter industrial development. Too many lines of logistic support, transportation, and communication pass through these sites. I passed through Prudhoe Bay four or five times in the course of several years, and visited both lead-zinc mines in the Canadian Archipelago, the Nanisivik Mine on Strathcona Sound on Baffin Island, and the

126

Polaris Mine on Little Cornwallis Island. And one winter I toured Panarctic's facilities at Rae Point on Melville Island, and their drill rigs on the sea ice off Mackenzie King and Lougheed islands.

I was drawn to all these places for reasons I cannot fully articulate. For the most part, my feelings were what they had been at Prudhoe Bay — a mixture of fascination at the sophistication of the technology; sadness born out of the dismalness of life for many of the men employed here, which no amount of red velour, free arcade games, and open snack bars can erase; and misgiving at the sullen, dismissive attitude taken toward the land, the violent way in which it is addressed. At pretensions to a knowledge of the Arctic, drawn from the perusal of a public relations pamphlet and from the pages of pulp novels. A supervisor at an isolated drill rig smiled sardonically when I asked him if men ever walked away from the buildings on their off-hours. "You can count the people who care about what's out there on the fingers of one hand." The remark represents fairly the situation at most military and industrial sites in the Arctic.

Away from the carefully tended environment of a corporate showcase base of operations, the industrial scene is much bleaker. In the most distant camps, to my sensibilities at least, were some of the saddest human lives I have ever known. The society is all male. The tedium of schedules is unrelieved. Drugs and alcohol are smuggled in. Pornographic magazines abound, which seems neither here nor there until one realizes that they are nearly inescapable, and that they are part of a resentful attitude toward the responsibilities of family life. There is a distrust, a cursing of women, that is unsettling. Women and machinery and the land are all spoken of in the same way — seduction, domestication, domination, control. This observation represents no new insight, of course, into the psychology of development in Western culture; but it is not academic. It is as real as the scars on the faces of flight attendants I interviewed in Alaska who were physically and sexually abused by frustrated workmen flying to and from Prudhoe Bay.

The atmosphere in some of the camps is little different from the environment of a small state prison, down to the existence of racial cliques. This is part of factory life in America, an ugly way the country has arranged itself, a predicament from which economic and political visionaries would extricate us. There is a lurking suspicion among the workers I spoke to that in spite of their good wages they were somehow being cheated, that any chance for advancement from their menial situation was, for most of them, an illusion. And they were convinced that someone, somewhere, was to blame. Their frustration was predictably directed at their employers, at overeduated engineers or petroleum geologists, and at vague political and ethnic groups whom they saw as confused and impractical critics of growth, of progress. Some of these men felt that the Arctic was really a great wasteland "with a few stupid birds," too vast to be hurt. Whatever strong men could accomplish against the elements in such a place, they insisted, was inherently right. The last words of many of these discussions, whether they were delivered quizzically or cynically or in disbelief, were summary — what else is it good for?

Many arctic oil and mine workers are hard-pressed to explain — and mostly not interested in — what it is good for, beyond what is in the ground; or in what its future will be; or in the fate of its people and animals. "Technology is inevitable," a drilling supervisor told me with finality one day. "People just got to get that through their heads." The sensibility of many of the foremen and crew chiefs, to characterize the extreme, is colonial. The tone of voice is impatient and the vocabulary is economic. The mentality is largely innocent of history and arctic ecology, cavalier about human psychological requirements, and manipulative. And the attitude of the extremist, at least in this regard, filters down. These thoughts are parroted by other workers who feel defensive, or embattled by critics. Men who make such extreme statements often give the impression of not having thought through what they are saying. They only mean to keep their jobs, or talk themselves out of doubt.

In the mines and oil fields, of course, were other, different men, who criticized in private conversation what was being done "for the money." As a group, they felt a responsibility for what they were doing. They did not see their jobs solely as a source of income. Many told me they wanted to return to the Arctic after making enough money to go back to school. They wanted to travel in the Arctic and read more about it. They meant no harm, and were uneasy themselves about the damage they were capable of doing. In Canada they feared the collusive force that government and industry were capable of bringing to bear — that the restraints against it were too weak. These were mostly younger men; and the sentiments were not rare among them.

More memorable somehow, and ultimately more gratifying, were the thoughts of several older men who spoke to me on different occasions about the conditions under which they worked. (It was one of them who had suggested the parallel with prison life.) These were seasoned men of dignified bearing in their forties and fifties, the sort of people you have regard for instantly, regardless of the circumstances. They were neither insistent nor opinionated in offering their observations, which made it easier to speculate in their presence; and they gave an impression of deliberation and self-knowledge.

They shook their heads over industrial mismanagement, that humorless, deskbound ignorance that brings people and land together in such a way that both the land and the people suffer. They said, without any condescension, that the companies that employed them sometimes clearly erred, and that they acted in high-handed and sometimes illegal ways. But these were more acknowledgments of a state of affairs than criticism. They spoke as much of their families, of their wives and children. They spoke of them with indulgence and unconscious admiration. You could build anything on the decency of such men.

In the wake of these latter conversations the world seemed on balance to me, or at least well intentioned. Part of what was attractive about these men was that their concern for the health of the land and their concern for the fate of people were not separate issues. They were not for me, either. And one evening, lying in my bunk, it became clear that the fate of each was hinged on the same thing, on the source of their dignity, on whether it was innate or not.

The source of their dignity — not among themselves, but in a larger social context — was the approval of their superiors, an assessment made by people who were not their peers. (Largely unfamiliar with modern Eskimo life, these men nevertheless had an intuitive and sympathetic response to the predicament of Eskimos constantly being scrutinized and judged by outsiders.) Their dignity as workmen, and therefore their self-respect, was not

129

whole. To an outside viewer they, like the land, were subject to manipulation. Their dignity was received. It grew out of how well they responded to directions.

In my experience, most people in the Arctic who direct activities of employees or who seek to streamline the process of resource extraction without regard to what harm might be done to the land, do so with the idea that their goals are desirable and admirable, and that they are shared by everyone. Their own source of dignity, in fact, derives from a belief that they are working in this way "for the common good." In their view the working man must provide cheerful labor, be punctual, and demonstrate allegiance to a concept of a greater good orchestrated from above. The Eskimo, for his part, must conduct himself either as a sober and aspiring middle-class wage earner or, alternately, as an "authentic, traditional Eskimo," that is, according to an idealized and unrealistic caricature created by the outsider. The land, the very ground itself, the plants and the animals, must also produce something — petroleum, medicines, food, the setting for a movie — if it is to achieve any measure of dignity. If it does not, it is waste. Tundra wasteland. A waste of time.

Without dignity, of course, people are powerless. Strip a person or the land of dignity and you can direct any scheme you wish against them or it, with impunity and with the best of motives. To some this kind of efficiency is a modern technique, lamentable but not evil. For others it is a debilitating degradation, a loss of integrity and spirit that no kind of economic well-being can ever justify.

The solution to this very old and disconcerting situation among the men I spoke to, when I asked, was utopian. They believed in the will of good people. They thought some way could be found to take life-affecting decisions away from ignorant, venal, and unimaginative persons. Yes, they said, an innate not a tendered dignity put individuals in the best position to act, to think through the difficult problems of what to do about technologies that mangled people and mangled the land. But they did not know where you started, where the first, hard changes had to be made.

I was traveling with a friend once, in northern Baffin Island. We were in a hunting camp at the edge of the sea ice with about thirty Eskimos. It was damp and windy — raw weather. Out of the sky one morning — we had been in this atmosphere long enough to make the event seem slightly confusing at first — came a helicopter, which landed at the camp. A man got out and walked over to the tent where we were staying. He was the president of a shipping company. He was concerned that an icebreaking ore ship that had recently been in Admiralty Inlet might have adversely affected hunting for the Eskimos or made travel over the sea ice more difficult for them. (The ship's track had relieved pressure in the ice, which would cause it to break up in an unusual pattern as spring progressed. The track might possibly lure narwhals into a fatal savssat. Or the noise of the ship's engines might frighten narwhals away from the floe edge, where the Eskimos were hunting.)

There were several unusual aspects to this man's visit. First, Eskimos virtually never get to talk directly with "the head man," the person whose decisions vitally affect the direction of their lives. They are usually held at bay by dozens of intermediaries. Second, important men more often have pressing schedules and retinues with them, which preclude protracted or serious conversation. Third, it is unusual for anyone at all to show a concern this pointed, this knowledgeable. The man offered to fly several hunters out along the 40 miles of ship track in the helicopter so they could inspect it. He would land wherever they wanted. The hunters went with him, and were glad for the opportunity to see the situation from the air.

That accomplished, the man could have left, feeling a wave of genuine gratitude from the Eskimos for his thoughtfulness. But he stayed. He sat in a tent in the hunting camp and ate the "country food" that was offered, along with bannock and tea. He did not try to summarize or explain anything. He did not ask a lot of questions to demonstrate his interest. He just sat quietly and ate. He handed a gawking child a piece of bannock and said a few things about the weather. By his simple appreciation of the company, by his acceptance of these unfamiliar circumstances, he made everyone in the tent feel comfortable. The dignity of the occasion arose from an atmosphere of courtesy that he alone could have established.

He sat for more than an hour. And then he said Good-bye and

left. One incident in the vastness. But it was a fine moment, a gesture you could carry away with you.

One brilliant July morning I flew out of Resolute on Cornwallis Island for the Canadian weather station at Eureka, on northern Ellesmere Island. I traveled with a flight map in my lap. From this height, and with the map, I found a corroboration of what I knew of the land — from history books, from walking around in it, from talking to people long resident here, from eating food the land produced, from traveling over it with people who felt defined by it. There were walrus in the upper part of Wellington channel. We passed over Grinnell Peninsula, long thought an island, named for the generous Henry Grinnell. Far to the west I could see the dark waters of a perennial polynya in the ice in Penny Strait, and to the east country I wanted one day, if ever there was a chance, to see from the ground, at the head of Jones Sound and the southern end of Simmons Peninsula. In winter.

We drew up on the southeast corner of Axel Heiberg Island, which Otto Sverdrup had explored. Good Friday Bay. Surprise Fiord. Wolf Fiord. At the head of these fiords were glaciers that did not reach tidewater — huge hesitations on the brown earth of the valleys. In the east light I was reminded of the mountain ranges of Arizona, of the colors of canyons on the Colorado Plateau — ocherous browns, washed tans, flat yellows. I was mesmerized by the view of Axel Heiberg: distant mountains in a sky of clear air; steep slopes of gray scree tumbled out onto the backs of white glaciers, the lime-green tongues of vegetation etched so sharply against the darker mountains it seemed in the morning light that the scene occurred behind polished glass. I realized this island was as remote as anything I could imagine, and for the first time in all the months I had spent North, I felt myself crossing a line into the Far North. It was as though I had passed through one of those walls of pressure one feels descending from mountains. I had a clarity of mind that made the map in my lap seem both wondrous and strange in its approximations. I looked west into Mokka Fiord, to a chain of lakes between two whitish gypsum domes. Beyond was the patterned ground of the mesic tundra. The browns and blacks and whites were so rich I could feel them. The beauty here is a beauty you feel in your flesh. You feel it physically, and that is why it is sometimes terrifying to approach. Other beauty takes only the heart, or the mind.

I lost for long moments my sense of time and purpose as a human being. In the walls of Axel Heiberg I found what I had known of mountains as a child; that from them came a knowledge that was received, for which there were no words, only, vaguely, prayers. What I loved as a man, the love for parents and wife and children and friends, I felt suffused with in that moment, flushed in the face. The fierce testament of life in abeyance on the winter tundra, the sharp taste of *irok* on evening walks on Baffin Island, the haunting sound of oldsquaw in the ice, *ahaalik, ahaalik*. At the sudden whiteness of a snowbank on the brown earth at Mokka Fiord, I remembered vividly arctic hares, three feet tall and running on their hind legs, hundreds of them, across Seward Peninsula. In the stillness of Axel Heiberg I felt for the first time the edges of an unentered landscape.

That intense reverie came because of the light, the clearness of the air, and certainly the desire to comprehend, which, however I might try to suspend it, was always there. I found in adumbrations of the land, in suggestions of the landscape and all that it contained, the ways human life sorts through itself and survives. To look at the land was never to forget the people it contained.

For a relationship with landscape to be lasting, it must be reciprocal. At the level at which the land supplies our food, this is not difficult to comprehend, and the mutuality is often recalled in a grace at meals. At the level at which landscape seems beautiful or frightening to us and leaves us affected, or at the level at which it furnishes us with the metaphors and symbols with which we pry into mystery, the nature of reciprocity is harder to define. In approaching the land with an attitude of obligation, willing to observe courtesies difficult to articulate — perhaps only a gesture of the hands — one establishes a regard from which dignity can emerge. From that dignified relationship with the land, it is possible to imagine an extension of dignified relationships throughout one's life. Each relationship is formed of the same integrity, which initially makes the mind say: the things in the land fit together perfectly, even though they are always changing. I wish the order of my life to be arranged in the same way I find the light, the slight movement of the wind, the voice of a bird, the heading of a seed pod I see before me. This impeccable and indisputable integrity I want in myself.

One of the oldest dreams of mankind is to find a dignity that might include all living things. And one of the greatest of human longings must be to bring such dignity to one's own dreams, for each to find his or her own life exemplary in some way. The struggle to do this is a struggle because an adult sensibility must find some way to include all the dark threads of life. A way to do this is to pay attention to what occurs in a land not touched by human schemes, where an original order prevails.

The dignity we seek is one beyond that articulated by Enlightenment philosophers. A more radical Enlightenment is necessary, in which dignity is understood as an innate quality, not as something tendered by someone outside. And that common dignity must include the land and its plants and creatures. Otherwise it is only an invention, and not, as it should be, a perception about the nature of living matter.

The plane, that so well designed, dependable, and ubiquitous workhorse of the Canadian Arctic, the Twin Otter, swung out over Fosheim Peninsula, a rolling upland, far northern oasis, on its approach to the Eureka airstrip. I could see muskoxen feeding to the north.

There is a peninsula at the southern end of Baffin Island called Meta Incognita, named by Queen Elizabeth. The words are often translated as the "Unknown Edge" or the "Mysterious Land." (Frobisher thought this the shore of North America.) It is possible, however, that Elizabeth had another meaning in mind. The word *meta*, strictly speaking, means "cone." In classical Rome the towers at either end of the race course in the Colosseum, around which the chariots turned, were called *metae*. It may have been that Elizabeth meant to suggest a similar course, with London the *meta cognita*, the known entity, and the land Frobisher found the unknown entity, the *meta incognita*. North America, then, was the turn at the far end of the course, something England felt herself reaching toward, and around which she would eventually make a turn of unknown meaning before coming home.

The European culture from which the ancestors of many of us came has yet to make this turn, I think. It has yet to understand the wisdom, preserved in North America, that lies in the richness

134

and sanctity of a wild landscape, what it can mean in the unfolding of human life, the staying of a troubled human spirit.

The other phrase that comes to mind is more obscure. It is the Latin motto from the title banner of *The North Georgia Gazette: per freta hactenus negata*, meaning to have negotiated a strait the very existence of which has been denied. But it also suggests a continuing movement through unknown waters. It is, simultaneously, an expression of fear and of accomplishment, the cusp on which human life finds its richest expression.

The plane landed. Light was lambent on the waters of Slidre Fiord. From the weather station six dogs came toward us, lumbering like wolves, a movement that suggested they could drop buffalo. I reached out and patted one of them tentatively on the head.

Barry Lopez

ME AND MY BIKE AND WHY

Like many who buy a motorcycle, there had been for me the problem of getting over the rather harrowing insurance statistics as to just what it is that is liable to happen to you. Two years in California — a familiar prelude to acts of excess — had made of me an active motorcycle spectator. I watched and identified, finally resorting to bikers' magazines; and evolved a series of foundationless prejudices.

Following the war, motorcycling left a peculiar image in the national consciousness: porcine individuals wearing a sort of yachting cap with a white vinyl bill, the decorative braid pulled up over the hat, their motorcycles plated monsters, white rubber mud flaps studded with ruby stars hung from both fenders. Where are those machines now? Surely Andy Warhol can't have bought them all. Not every one of them is a decorative planter in a Michigan truck garden. But wherever they are, it is certain that the ghosts of cretinism collect close around the strenuously baroque plumbing of those inefficient engines and speak to us of an America that has gone.

It was easy for me initially to deplore the big road bikes, the motorcycles of the police and Hell's Angels. But finally even these "hogs" and show bikes had their appeal, and sometimes I had dark fantasies of myself on El Camino Real, hands hung overhead from the big chopper bars, feet in front on weirdly automotive pedals, making all the decent people say: "There goes one."

I did it myself. Heading into San Francisco with my wife, our Land Rover blaring wide open at 52 miles per, holding up a quarter mile of good people behind us, people who didn't see why anybody needed four-wheel drive on the Bayshore Freeway, we ourselves would from time to time see a lonesome Angel or Coffin Cheater or Satan's Slave or Gypsy Joker on his big chopper and say (either my wife or myself, together sometimes): "There goes one."

Anyway, it was somewhere along in here that I saw I was not that type, and began to think of sporting machines, even racing machines, big ones, because I had no interest in starting small and working my way up as I had been urged to do. I remember that I told the writer Wallace Stegner what I intended, and he asked, "Why do you people do this when you come to California?"

"It's like skiing," I said, purely on speculation.

"Oh, yeah? What about the noise?"

But no one could stop me.

There was the dire question of money that ruled out many I saw. The English-built Triumph Metisse road racer was out of the question, for example. Some of the classics I found and admired — Ariel Square Fours, Vincent Black Shadows, BSA Gold Stars, Velocette Venoms or Phantom Clubmen, Norton Manxes — had to be eliminated on grounds of cost or outlandish maintenance problems.

Some of the stranger Japanese machinery, two-cycle, rotary-valved engines, I dismissed because they sounded funny. The Kawasaki Samurai actually seemed refined, but I refused to consider it. I had a corrupt Western ideal of a bike's exhaust rap, and the tuned megaphone exhausts of the Japanese motorcycles sounded like something out of the next century, weird loon cries of Oriental speed tuning.

There is a blurred moment in my head, a scenario of compulsion. I am in a motorcycle shop that is going out of business. I am writing a check that challenges the contents of my bank account. I am given ownership papers substantiated by the state of California, a crash helmet, and five gallons of fuel. Some minutes later I am standing beside my new motorcycle, sick all over. The man who sold it to me stares palely through the Thermopane window covered with the decals of the noble marques of "performance." He wonders why I have not moved.

I have not moved because I do not know what to do. I wish to advance upon the machine with authority but cannot. He would not believe I could have bought a motorcycle of this power without knowing so much as how to start its engine. Presently he loses interest and looks for another tormented creature in need of a motorcycle.

Unwatched, I can really examine the bike. Since I have no notion of how to operate it, it is purely an *objet*. I think of a friend with a road racer on a simple mahogany block in front of his fireplace, except that he rides his very well.

The bike was rather beautiful. I suppose it still is. The designation, which now seems too cryptic for my taste, was

"Matchless 500," and it was the motorcycle I believed I had thought up myself. It is a trifle hard to describe the thing to the uninitiated, but, briefly, it had a 500-cc., one-cylinder engine — a "big single" in the patois of bike freaks — and an eloquently simple maroon teardrop-shaped tank that is as much the identifying mark on a Matchless, often otherwise unrecognizable through modification, as the chevron of a redwing blackbird. The front wheel, delicate as a bicycle's, carried a Dunlop K70 tire (said to "cling") and had no fender; a single cable led to the pale machined brake drum. Over the knobby rear wheel curved an extremely brief magnesium fender with, instead of the lush buddy-seat of the fat motorcycles, a minute pillion of leather. The impression was of performance and of complete disregard for comfort. The equivalent in automobiles would be, perhaps, the Morgan, in sailboats the Finn.

I saw all these things at once (remember the magazines I had been reading, the Floyd Clymer books I had checked out of the library), and in that sense my apprehension of the motorcycle was perfectly literary. I still didn't know how to start it. Suddenly it looked big and mean and vicious and no fun at all.

I didn't want to experiment on El Camino Real, and moreover, it had begun to rain heavily. I had made up my mind to wheel it home, and there to peruse the operation manual, whose infuriating British locutions the Land Rover manual had prepared me for.

I was surprised at the sheer inertial weight of the thing; it leaned toward me and pressed against my hip insistently all the way to the house. I was disturbed that a machine whose place in history seemed so familiar should look utterly foreign at close range. The fact that the last number on the speedometer was 140 seemed irresponsible.

It was dark by the time I got home. I wheeled it through the back gate and down the sidewalk through a yard turned largely to mud. About halfway to the kitchen door, I somehow got the thing tilted away from myself, and it slowly but quite determinedly toppled over in the mud, with me, gnashing, on top of it.

My wife came to the door and peered into the darkness. "Tom?" I refused to vouchsafe an answer. I lay there in the mud, no longer struggling, as the spring rains of the San Francisco peninsula singled me out for special treatment. I was already composing the ad in the *Chronicle* that motorcycle people dream of finding: "Big savings on Matchless 500. Never started by present owner. A real cream puff." My wife threw on the porch light and perceived my discomfiture.

The contretemps had the effect of quickly getting us over the surprise that I had bought the motorcycle, questions of authorization, and so on. I headed for the showers. Scraped and muddy, I had excited a certain amount of pity. "I'll be all right."

No one told me to retard the spark. True enough, it was in the manual, but I had been unable to read that attentively. It had no plot, no characters. So my punishment was this: when I jumped on the kick starter, it backfired and more or less threw me off the bike. I was limping all through the first week from vicious blowbacks. I later learned it was a classic way to get a spinal fracture. I tried jumping lightly on the kick starter and, unfairly, it would blast back as viciously as with a sharp kick. Eventually it started, and sitting on it, I felt the torque tilt the bike under me. I was afraid to take my hands off the handlebars. My wife lowered the helmet onto my head; I compared it to the barber's basin Don Quixote had worn into battle, the Helmet of Mambrino.

I slipped my toe up under the gearshift lever, lifted it into first, released the clutch, and magically glided away and made all my shifts through fourth, at which time I was on Sand Hill Road and going 50, my shirt in a soft air bubble at my back, my Levi's wrapped tight to my shins, my knuckles whitening under the giddy surge of pure undetained motion as I climbed gently into the foothills toward Los Altos. The road got more and more winding as I ascended, briskly but conservatively. Nothing in the air was lost on me as I passed through zones of smell and temperature as palpable transitions, running through sudden warm spots on the road where a single redwood 100 feet away had fallen and let in a shaft of sunlight. The road seemed tremendously spacious. The sound was behind me, so that when I came spiraling down out of the mountains and saw some farm boy had walked out to the side of the road to watch me go by, I realized he had heard me coming for a long time. And I wondered a little about the racket.

These rides became habitual and presumably more competent. I often rode up past La Honda for a view of the sea at the far edge of a declining cascade of manzanita-covered hills, empty and foggy. The smell of ocean was so perfectly evocative in a landscape divided among ranches and truck gardens whose pumpkins in the foggy air seemed to have an uncanny brilliance. A Japanese nursery stood along the road in clouds of tended vines on silver redwood lattice. I went past it to the sea and before riding home took a long walk on the ribbed, immense beach.

A fascinating aspect of the pursuit, not in the least bucolic, was the bike shop where one went for mechanical service, and which was a meeting place for the bike people, whose machines were poised out front in carefully conceived rest positions. At first, of course, no one would talk to me, but my motorcycle ideas were theirs; I was not riding one of the silly mechanisms that purred down the highways in a parody of the equipment these people lived for.

One day an admired racing mechanic — "a good wrench" — came out front and gave my admittedly well-cared-for Matchless the once-over. He announced that it was "very sanitary." I was relieved. The fear, of course, is that he will tell you, "The bike is wrong."

"Thank you," I said modestly. He professed himself an admirer of the "Matchbox," saying it was "fairly rapid" and had enough torque to "pull stumps." Ultimately, I was taken in, treated kindly, and given the opportunity to ride some of the machinery that so excited me: the "truly potent" Triumph Metisse, an almost uncontrollable supercharged Norton Atlas from New Mexico, and a couple of road-racing machines with foot pegs way back by the rear sprocket and stubby six-inch handlebars — so that you lay out on the bike and divide a sea of wind with the point of your chin.

One day I "got off on the pavement," that is, crashed. It was not much of a crash. I went into a turn too fast and ran off the shoulder and got a little "road burn" requiring symbolic bandages at knees and elbows. I took the usual needling from the crew at the bike shop, and with secret pleasure accepted the temporary appelation, "Crash Cargo." I began taking dawn trips over the mountains to Santa Cruz, sometimes with others, sometimes

140

alone, wearing a wool hunting shirt against the chill and often carrying binoculars and an Audubon field guide.

Then one day I was riding in my own neighborhood when a man made a U-turn in front of me and stopped, blocking the road. It was too late to brake and I had to put the bike down, riding it like a sled as it screeched across the pavement. It ran into the side of the car and I slid halfway under, the seat and knees torn out of my pants, scraped and bruised but without serious injury. I had heard the sharp clicking of my helmet against the pavement and later saw the depressions that might have been in my skull.

The man got out, accusing me of going 100 miles an hour, accusing me of laying for a chance to create an accident, accusing me of being a Hell's Angel, and finally admitting he had been daydreaming and had not looked up the street before making his illegal maneuver. The motorcycle was a mess. He pleaded with me not to have physical injuries. He said he had very little insurance. And a family. "Have a heart."

"You ask this of a Hell's Angel?"

At the motorcycle shop I was urged to develop nonspecific spinal trouble. A special doctor was named. But I had the motorcycle minimally repaired and sent the man the bill. When the settlement came, his name was at the top of the stationery. He was the owner of the insurance agency.

Perhaps it was the point-blank view from below of rocker panels and shock absorbers and the specious concern of the insurance man for my health that gave my mortality its little twinge. I suddenly did not want to get off on the pavement anymore or bring my road burn to the shop under secret bandages. I no longer cared if my bike was rapid and sanitary. I wanted to sell it, and I wanted to get out of California.

I did both those things, and in that order. But sometimes, in the midst of more tasteful activities, I miss the mournful howl of that big single engine as it came up on the cam, dropped revs, and started over on a new ratio; the long banking turns with the foot pegs sparking against the pavement and the great crocodile's tears the wind caused to trickle out from under my flying glasses. I'm behind a sensible windshield now, and the soaring curve of acceleration does not come up through the seat of my pants. I have an FM radio, and the car doesn't get bad mileage.

Thomas McGuane

MOLLY

I have been bird hunting since I was ten years old. I was not much good at it when I was ten, and many years of experience have not made me any better. Sometimes, when asked about the results of my shooting, I am ashamed. Sometimes so ashamed that I lie about it vividly and recklessly.

I have a seven-year-old pointer. When she was a puppy she was wild, flushing birds far from the gun. She ran deer and often didn't come home at night at all. My dog has six hunting seasons under her belt now and, if anything, she is worse than ever. Her remote barking in the deep forest is the sound of bird hunting to me.

But this was to be the year when my dog Molly and I would get it all together. We were starting out clean. She doesn't blame me, knowing I have worries. And I, who despise negative reinforcement and the electrical collar, have come to see my dog as a person as rich in neurosis as Oblomov. Like me, though, she aims to please.

I always have a kind of private opening day, simply because my vague orientation as a hunter keeps me from getting the news. My opening day is liable to be weeks into the season. This year was no exception. The first hard frost wiped out what was left of our garden. Last year the horses beat the frost by three weeks, moving brutally among the tomato vines and oak-leaf lettuce plants with their pie-plate-size hoofs and yellow piano-key teeth. Anyway, the garden was shot. Jack Frost was in the air, and the departure of a long list of summer houseguests and a long line of sour-mash dead soldiers was enough to send this sojourner into the field.

There is an unsuccessful motif that has long threatened to eclipse my hunting life. I feel it began one late fall day long ago in a duck blind with my father at the mouth of a Michigan river. We'd had a good morning's pass shooting. (Those were the days when blacks, redheads, and canvasbacks were not the sort of thing one was inclined to send to the taxidermist.) It was very cold, and my father kindly offered to pick up the decoys, with their icy lines, if I would clean up the blind.

142

While he rowed around in the blowing sleet, I tidied up. We had a Zenith radio to listen to the Lions game and a chaste little briquette fire upon which to smokelessly prepare various snacks between flights. I put the empty tins and papers in a neat pile next to the radio to take home. I leaned my 20-gauge in the homeward corner of the blind next to our limit of ducks. And, just how I shall never know, I set my father's 12-gauge butt-first in the fire.

Then I went outside and dawdled. Our blind was on a long, old dike of dredging from the construction of the Livingstone Channel. It spanned the U.S.-Canadian border. The inner-sanctum duck gunners in my hometown took licenses in both countries, owned a hundred cedar decoys, a sneak boat, and usually a layout boat. The prestige gun was a Winchester Model 12 with a 30-inch full-choke barrel that was as close to riflery as shotgunners ever get. There was a mild kind of disparaging rivalry between Canadian and American hunters, and not much more fraternization between the lines than there was in the First World War between the Hun and the doughboy. We knew in our hearts that Canadians slaughtered ducks on the water, shot gulls, and guzzled weird diuretic ales in their Ontario public houses.

When my father brought the boat ashore and tilted the Evinrude down against the transom, I helped him pull the bow up against the granite dredging. He climbed out on the rocks and went into the blind. Then he came from the blind and asked me why I had done it. In his hands was his Winchester. Much smoke poured from the wrong end. The buttstock extended about 2 1/2 inches behind the trigger guard.

"I would have thought," said my father without rancor, "that you could have smelled the recoil pad burning. It's rubber."

I don't suppose either of us could have known on that day, there in the driving sleet on the American frontier, that in some way the most resonant chord of my life as a hunter had been struck.

But, frankly, the hell with that. Out here in the northern Rockies the sky is big. Cowboys still gaze coolly upon the dudes from inside their air-conditioned Wagoneers. Out behind the old prefab the sage still turns blue in the spring. Here and there tranquilizer-junkie grizzly bears slump in the junipers with hypodermic projectiles buried in their fundaments. And I felt it was not unreasonable to think of a fresh start in hunting.

As I say, I had the dog. Molly. Born in Michigan of an old line of Arkansas hunting machines, the kind that roar in your ears and run up and down that kennel wire like orangutans.

The breeder had brought out two armloads of seven-week-old pointers, wrinkling their eyes in the sunshine and groaning. He put them all in the grass, where they began to wander around and pounce on each other. I had done my homework in gundog books, and had any number of Nash Buckingham-level prejudices of classical fanaticism. My opinions were emphatically not based upon the actual slumberous yard dogs of my own life and experience.

I knew how to spot a bold, promising pup and how not to take guff from wily Snopesian dog handlers. But as I surveyed the tumbling fat puppies on the lawn, I began to notice an isolated nut case: a pup who didn't want to play, who was afraid, and who sat by herself blinking slowly — a dog with absolutely no future on the concrete runs of a serious dog kennel.

The wily Snopesian dog handler could not believe his luck when I forked over hard cash for that one. My brother was with me, and my action inspired him to cough up for a weirdo himself. We headed home with the speckled babies in the front of the car, crawling around the gearshift and crying for their mother. We were moved.

In no time flat I had my dog dancing to a bird's wing on a fishing rod. I also had a piece of clothesline, an Acme Thunderer dog whistle, and a blank pistol, props for an outlandish charade that was to last many many years.

In the meantime, another friend, Jim Harrison, had also acquired a pointer, a crazed muscle-bound hyena who once swam over the horizon in Lake Michigan while our wives wept on the beach. We would hunt our dogs in tandem that first fall on Mister Partridge, the Einstein of the Northern forest.

I drove up to Jim's and brought Molly into the house. Molly and Jim's dog Missy did their best to recapture the magic of the tiger scene in *Little Black Sambo* where everything turns to butter. They did leg springs off the backs of chairs so that the chairs would still be doing figure eights in midair long after the dogs had left the room. They would lie side by side on their backs under the sofa and pull out all the stuffing. They would try to shatter glass with their voices when a car pulled into the driveway, micturating all the while on a couch, a pillow, a doily, or anything precious that they could evaluate. Jim explained that this was how it was with hunting dogs. Jim's wife had a reply that I sincerely believe it will someday be possible to print.

Zero hour. We roll through the cedar gloom of the Northern fastness. The two dogs are looking out of the window. I have come to think of them as existentialists. Jim and I feel instinctively that the forest is stiff with birds of the grouse persuasion. We're bucking along in my Land Rover, whose odometer is giving 100,000 miles a long hard look.

We pull off the road into a grove of trees and get out of the Rover. Then we run all those numbers around the car that hunters like to get into: racking open the guns, donning ammo belts and canvas coats, last hits on the coffee thermos, and light war-zone chatter that is pointedly not about hunting.

The dogs are still inside the car, pouring around behind the glass, jumping from front to back, back to front, scrambling for traction on the upholstery. You know how it goes.

A moment of silence, and Jim says, "Uh, shall we let the dogs out?"

"Sure," I say, almost gaily. I open the front door a little and am rudely slammed back as the two evil hounds vault for the forest like voltage jumping a gap.

Of all instruments, the Acme Thunderer seems the least appropriate for playing dirges, but over and again Jim tried, I tried. A bluish pallor fell across our faces. From the distance the yapping of the fun couple rang in the swamps.

Later Jim and I decided to go hunting. We walked miles in a forest less than entirely stiff with game birds. Ultimately, a partridge sprang into the air. Jim and I fired simultaneously. The bird fell. We ran from converging courses to the bird and came darkly close to forming an encounter group over its expired person. An autopsy with an examination of shot was considered. We would carefully shred the corpse with a carrot grater, placing each bit of shot on a sheet of white paper to be measured in the micrometer. But this was ruled out because we were both shooting 7 1/2s.

The pitch of the dogs' barking suddenly changed. They apparently had treed a coon.

Later in the day our dogs came back to relax and warm up in the car. We sealed them inside the Land Rover, then wedged our way through the doors to be sure neither of them tried anything cheap like another 40-mile-per-hour swamp crossing. But the dogs were content to save themselves in the back, studying migrating songbirds high in the sky through the window and listening to the radio.

We crossed the county. A grouse had been seen in a cherry orchard that week, and we were headed for that cherry orchard. A short time later we were slithering up a wet clay road that ended in an open field. Jim instructed me to head across, toward the woods and orchard at the other side.

I shifted the Land Rover into low and started out onto the level field. A minute later this machine, which had proven itself all over the world — in desert and in swamp — lurched to a stop within whimpering distance of a thousand white cottages. We got out and rather formally looked under the car. The differential was resting neatly in the crotch of a cherry-tree stump. I got back in and put it in four-wheel drive, compound low, and goosed hell out of it. Nothing. This went on for about an hour. Finally I got out of the car and the dogs shot between my legs and went shrieking into the sunset. We saw a grouse depart the orchard as they barreled through.

Sometime later we called a wrecker. How strange it all seems now, the big white wrecker in a level open field, hauling that safari vehicle off a cherry stump while the dogs prospected for county lines at incalculable land speeds. And how strange, finally, to be standing out there in the absolute middle of nowhere, presenting one's AAA card to a service-station attendant.

But why go over that? It's morbid to think that the past lays its dead hand on all our days. It's been twenty years since I burned my father's shotgun and more than five since the wrecker came. I've been in Montana for some seasons now. It's a different time, a different place. I have a private opening day to look forward to.

Molly is ready, too. She comes into my room and stares at my hunting boots for long periods of time. She howls when my son mistakenly shuts her in the bathroom. But, except that it is bird

146

season, what was she doing in the bathroom anyway? And she does irresponsible things that indicate that her mind is not on the routine domesticities of out-of-season dog life. For example, yesterday she ate a two-volume edition of *Anna Karenina*.

This will be our day together.

My son's playmates are here, and as I have trained them, they are throwing things for the dog to make her run around so that on hunting days like this one she will be tired before we ever start and not so inclined to clear out on a strafing mission.

I put dog and gear into the same old Land Rover, now as thoroughly pocked as a Spalding Dot, and head north of our ranch to an area of fertile, dry-land farming I know to be full of fat grain-fed pheasants.

The drive takes nearly an hour, and from time to time I study my dog's eyes for indications of lunacy and the grossly unpredictable. She looks as sound as a silver dollar. Even *I* feel a trifle seasoned. I wonder if she has noticed that, or if, in fact, she's found any little reason for admiring me.

I leave the Rover by a grove of thornbushes. The open country lies in fast-intersecting declinations that fall from the foothills of the Crazy Mountains. I am on a plateau and can see the Absaroka Range to the south, already snowy. It's slightly stormy, and plumes of snow are whirling out of the higher passes. But down here the sun plays all around us.

As I get ready Molly stays close to me, prancing like a cheerleader. A small cloud of butterflies dances across the tractor ruts and Molly makes after them like a rocking horse but returns to my side when I whistle.

All right, ready to go. "Find some birds," I tell her. She gives me one last look, as though from the cockpit of a fighter plane, and pours it on. I don't believe this. My heart begins to sink as she ticks off the first 880 and I realize nothing has changed.

I walk gloomily along a shelterbelt of Lombardy poplars with only the vaguest reference to the shrinking liver-and-white form in the distance. At the far edge of the field I see her stop, lock up on point, then selfishly pounce into the middle of the birds. Gloom. Gloom. Pheasants scatter. But wait — *my God!* They're flying this way.

Like the lowest kind of dry-gulch artist, I crouch in the hedgerow. The pheasants keep coming, Molly yelping along behind. At 50 yards I rise to the balls of my feet. At 20 I stand up out of the brambles and . . . *shoot a double!* Two cock pheasants tumble. I scramble around to gather them up before my dog can rend and eat them.

I hang the handsome birds from my belt. Their rich, satisfying odor keeps man's best friend trotting along at my side. Now and again I hear her teeth click lightly. There is a spring I know near the thorn grove where I gather some wild, peppery watercress for our game dinner.

At last that perfect symbiosis between a man and his dog! I finally feel that Molly is as good a hunter as I am.

We approach the Land Rover. The cloud of butterflies blows across the tractor ruts again, and I check myself from pursuit.

Thomas McGuane

A HEAVEN IN THE EYE

Late in the afternoon we were passing through great redwood groves when we saw a place where we could get our truck off from the road to a level area where the trees towered all about and there was little undergrowth. We all left the truck to explore and were pleased with what we found. We trooped back to our ailing transportation to find a car stopped behind it. It was Lenore — Bessie's sister-in-law — the one who stayed in the Drake house when Annie Marge was with us. Laughing and hugging each of us in turn she said, "I knew it could only be you, Clyde. That spotted steer hide over the top of the chicken coop gave you away." She had her mother and father and her young son with her. They too were going to Oregon, so we camped together in a clear space in the grove. They set up a tent across from our truck and trailer with the campfire spot in between. We let our chickens and animals out as usual, but first we made a little cooking fire. We had a steel plate — a long narrow one — and we made a narrow fire under it, so we could have several pots and a frying pan cooking in a row. Nordi had greased her frying pan and left it heating at one end of the plate. Heidi, always curious about our ways, was making slow, dumb observations. A pet with no fear of humans, she wandered in between the truck and tent and, as we watched, stared at the frying pan and then leaning nearer stuck her big flat nose into the hot grease, and with her slow reactions, held it there a moment while it sizzled then leaped into delayed reaction and went charging away, tail high in the air and her udders swinging wildly about, till at some distance she turned and gave us a glance full of distrust and hurt. Nordi salved her nose and everybody patted her and made over her till it seemed to me that her expression was that of a spoiled child — bovine of course.

There were little harmless, pink centipedes about by the thousands and our chickens rushed about grabbing up the succulent morsels till dark. Zadee sneaked around camp hoping she could grab a loaf of bread and make a break for it. We were ten around the fire, counting our important-feeling animals. By now they seemed to enjoy the evening fire as much as we. After eating, Nordi cooked our next day's lunch and set it to cool — but high, where Zadee couldn't get it. We laid aside the cooking plate

149

and let the fire's light shimmer and flicker on our encampment — all our ten faces staring into the flames. Carl uttered sort of an inner snicker and told a story about his childhood and the story was just right for the moment. Though our animals probably didn't get the point of it, they liked the talking of people and moved a step closer. Nordi made some laughing remark about his tale and he told another about a strange mate he had had on shipboard. I found I was leaning my back against one of Heidi's forelegs and Nordi's hand was smoothing Zadee's long velvet ears, as Lenore told of a boyfriend — a Swede — who became enamored of a tribe of Indians in Round Valley and joined them and was locally famous for his loud tribal yells when drinking. Lenore's parents were rather silent people but good listeners — they didn't interrupt you with a tale of their own.

Encouraged, I began a funny story, one that Nordi and Carl had heard me tell again and again. Most off-color stories start out very pure and lose the pallor of innocence as they move toward the raffish end. This one ran the opposite way: it started out at an explicitly described orgy and ended up with the girl of the story being refused a berth in a convent as being too angelic and pure. "Cover that marvelous ass of yours," said the abbess, "and uncover the beauty of your saint-like face, and, walking among sinners, lead them to the light."

But trying to tell it differently — hoping to spare Nordi and Carl the oft-heard phrases — I got mixed up, forgot the punch line and, avoiding the word "shit," said "dung," which had the timbre of a very dull bell and certainly no shit-like meaning. I tried to liven up the story and to remember the punch line, but Nordi and Carl began talking loudly about Gortel Dwalmanson and his sister Dwalma Gortelson. This was an in joke, the aforesaid siblings being hypothetical friends I had invented to gossip about when I had been skipper of the *Sonoma*. They were over-large Norwegians, who seemed always to adapt to how we expected them to act. For Norwegians, they were extremely malleable.

Now Carl began talking of Gortel and of a big brick chimney he had laid in a day. Nordi said, "I bet Dwalma helped him."

"No," he replied, "she was back in Norway trying to win the Nobel Prize for physics. She took her track shoes with her, not being sure just how the event went."

"That's right," said Nordi. "Now I remember. And she also took a bale of chittum bark along — to show them how it's done in Oregon. Don't they make a physic out of chittum bark?"

"Of course," said Carl. "She thought maybe showing them she knew the source of physics might help her win the Prize."

By now Lenore's mother's smile no longer glimmered with the dew of anticipation — or even of comprehension. Abandoning my already scuttled story, I joined in.

"Well, Gortel's no slouch either," I said. "When I think of the wonderful feats of strength he's done — like leading choir at church. I tell you, the mellow golden tones in his voice had half the women there bawling."

"Good old Gortel," Carl broke in. "I tried wrestling with him once, but couldn't even budge him. Why the fellow's made of *iron.*"

"Yeah, Carl, I know," I said. "Knuckle? Not him. He'll brazen it out with that steely look of his."

"And the gals running after him the way they do," said Nordi. "He's got lead in his pencil all right."

"Oh, I don't know," said Carl. "He's not much to look at with that heavy acne on his face and neck."

"Not any more," I said. "After going to skin doctors for years, he finally went to an old sea captain who turned the trick. The old skipper took Gortel down to the drydock, where they chipped him and gave him a coat of redlead. That stopped it, and it's never come back."

Lenore's father got up suddenly and stepped into their tent, that awful corn getting to him at last. Then he reached out and grabbed his wife and pulled her in behind the flap too. Lenore's eyes danced in spite of the extreme silliness of it, for she was pleased to see her father show emotion. Her parents were very staid people and vivid Lenore was not.

Our two roosters kept fussing around outside the perimeter of firelight. I went out to them. At once they started to lead the way into the darkness. I went back and counted the hens roosting in the cage atop the trailer. There were only eight, two were missing. We lit our lanterns and Nordi and Carl and Lenore and Bunky and I all followed the roosters through the woods to where vine maples writhed out among the redwoods. There they stopped and looked up, so we did too. Vaguely in the lantern light we saw the two hens roosting high above us. Bunky shinnied up and threw them down and the roosters set after them and gave them an awful pecking and drove them to camp and into the cage, whose door we closed. Then we sought our beds in the top of the truck.

In the morning we fed our stock as our friends pulled down their tent. We were ready to go, but watched them leave in their new shiny car, watched them go down the long straightaway, dwindling and then gone. The joy and the release from tension went with them and our faces fell, as we turned to our shabby transportation. I removed the spotted steer hide and stowed it under the mattresses of our beds. That day we passed Crescent City and, several hours later, crossed the border into Oregon. On we went, always filling our milk cans with water for the leaky radiator. We found that the sharp curves were heavily banked and, coming into one, as the mechanic had said, our weight on the steering gear — not made for such forces — tried to drag us across the road and down into the ravine. It was a wonder I was able to bring it out of it — pure luck, really. It taught me to watch as I had never watched before, but they were very few here and we moved along until, on a long downgrade, I lost control. The brake band no longer gripped. There was no way to slow down or stop. All I could do was steer and hope. Nordi was crowded into the cab with us. We were fairly rocking along now, when we came around a turn almost on two wheels and saw a long, straight, level road before us. Far out on it we stopped and we all got out. I was frantic, angry at myself that I was endangering them so, but Carl was pleasant. They all said, "sink or swim." They were with me. We are trying to get to a new life, they said. Carl said, "Fine, forget it, let's go."

So I opened up the plate that covered the bands and fiddled around until I got the brake band tightened and the other two a bit better adjusted and on we went, crossing Rogue River on a long bridge, rolling slowly along until we passed Port Orford. Coming down a hill into town the brake band held this time. We ate cold food that evening and I sent them to bed and, lashing a coal oil lantern to the back of the trailer and another to the front fender, went on moving in the light of a full moon. Most of it was long straight runs. At fifteen miles an hour I could handle it. I made twenty-seven miles — not once did I see another car on the road. Finally I pulled over, fed and watered the stock that Nordi had tended earlier and, climbing up, slept with them on the top of the load.

We were now going to Toledo, a big lumber town a few miles back from the port of Newport, way up the coast ahead of us. Carl's parents lived there. Carl for some obscure reason hated his father as much as he loved his mother. Why, he never divulged. He snorted and sighed, as he thought of his meeting with them. He would not go on with us as we'd planned, for he was in as depressed a state of mind as when he came to us that winter's night. He had never driven an automobile, but now he pestered me to drive and continued pestering me. I finally showed him how to work the foot pedals and such, and eventually let him drive.

After he had driven for about an hour, he saw ahead of us a gas station perched on a bit of flat land on a cliff above the sea. He drove across the highway and into it to get gas. I saw what he was doing in time and as we came abreast of the pump I jerked the wheel from his hands and spun it. In a very tight turn we stayed within the cliff's boundaries as we made a complete circle and were once more heading north on the highway. I wish I could have seen that top-heavy load and the trailer with the cow and goat spinning around on the edge of the cliff.

Carl was furious, but I made him get out and change places with me. Finally I made him see that using the handbrake with the weight we had would not stop it, and at the speed he had entered the station, we would all be dead at the foot of the cliff if I had not acted. This incident made him more sullen than ever. He might brighten up a bit at times, but in a few hours self-hatred would take over and a cynical look would half hide his despair. Both Carl and Pushells were gifted in many ways, quick and clever. It was strange that they got involved in political movements that, in their own way, were as half-cocked as capitalism. Neither of them were much interested in women and each in time found his shield of irony good for the glancing blows of most adversaries, but useless in fending away the knives of introspection.

We came down an area of sharp turns and through a small city, crossed Coos Bay by ferry that same night, and headed on. We found a place to exercise our animals and chickens and Nordi cooked, then we went on. And later in moonlight while they slept, I proceeded as I had the night before. In the morning by ferry we crossed the Umpqua and, as we made a brief camp, I slept.

That day it seemed our truck was about to give up. We crawled along over hills. We were three hours getting up over Cape Perpetua. Night came but we stopped only to get water for our radiator. Clouds covered the moon. I cut small fir branches and, walking ahead with the lantern, I put a branch where I could see it at the beginning of a banked curve, and going on to where my wheels would leave the ditch at the end of the curve, I deposited another branch.

I did this for what I assumed was four miles, then came back and, putting a lantern on the inner fender also, drove slowly on, safe with boughs indicating my way around the curve — where to put the wheels in the ditch and where to bring them back on the road. I did this chore twice that night, going on eight miles while walking sixteen. The next night and day were the same. In early evening we boarded the ferry to cross Yaquina Bay to the town of Newport. The tide was low and we had a difficult time getting our rig aboard. Somehow we made it and I wondered how we should get ashore. I went to the deckhands and explained that I was an old ferryboat man myself, then I pointed out my predicament. I would need a shove to get off. They spoke to some other people aboard whom they knew and when we landed there were six men besides Carl pushing as we crept up the gangway. We could never have made it under our own power. Ahead of us was a very steep street. I told Carl to run alongside of us with a brakeblock and, if I didn't make it, to block her at once. Then I charged the hill. Oh, it was a weary charge. Near the top the engine balked and Carl blocked us from rolling back and Nordi was there blocking the other wheel. I got out and saw that our engine could never pull us up to the top of that grade. Then a big logger, smelling of the pitch of firs, was at my elbow.

"What's the trouble?" he said.

"We can't pull this hill."

He looked the situation over. "I could help you with my old Packard if you got a rope."

"I've got one," I said, and from our load I drew a big strong rope. Our savior told his four passengers to get in the back seat for weight over his back wheels. Then, at his signal, we tried once more and, burning rubber, he pulled us as we struggled up and over the hill. I hurried to thank him but he had untied the rope from his axle and was gone. I sat down at the top of the hill and wept, for I was pretty well worn out. Then we drove on to Toledo.

A neighbor instructed us, and we drove up to Carl's father's house. Carl looked at it as if in terror, but finally we went to the door and knocked and went in. Carl embraced his very surprised mother. They didn't have a great deal to say to each other. After a bit he asked for his father. She said, "He's probably in the coffee shop down the street."

Carl wanted me to come with him. He was obviously agitated. They hadn't seen one another or corresponded in ten years. We entered and saw him at the counter reading a newspaper as he sipped his coffee. Carl walked over and took a seat next to him. The old man sat reading for several minutes and then turned to see who sat beside him. He recognized his son. "Hello," he said, quietly. "How about a cup of coffee?"

And Carl, suddenly not our Carl, but the son of this man, said, "Yeah, I could use a cup."

After a bit he came back to me and said, "I suppose you're going to demand it, so here's a hundred and seventy-five dollars. It's all I have left. I'm going to stay here."

I took it. I had to. (It was our own money anyway.) I left, sick of him and wanting to get away.

We drove on and camped. I slept a long time and the next day Nordi was in the cab with me all the time, and there was room for Bunky. We sang a lot that day. We worked our way up the steep curvy road of Otter Crest, stopping every quarter of a mile or so, as the radiator boiled over and we had to let the engine cool a bit before we poured in more water, then on again. Now there were a great many more cars and log trucks all whizzing by us at a great rate. Nordi kept her hand on my arm as we drove, and then the road left the coast and headed inland toward Portland, eighty-five miles away. There we camped and in the morning started across the coast range. God, how that radiator leaked! Just before the first of the two crests we were to cross, we ran out of water. Bunky and I took one of the five-gallon milk cans and went down through the woods into what we assumed was a draw.

We must have gone two miles before we came to a stream. We filled the can and started back. The can was unwieldy and rather heavy and we were in an area of small trees and dense brush. Eventually we came out a mile down the road from where we came in, worn out from dragging the can over big logs and through thick hazel brush. When we got to the truck we just laid down for a while before filling the radiator. Again we chugged along, climbing the steep grades and suddenly we were on top, rolling along, and made the second pass without incident and eased down to a great plain that led east between rolling hills. That night, as we camped beside the road, a cop on a motorcycle stopped by and asked us if there was anything he could do. We thanked him and asked him if there were any more steep grades between us and Portland.

"One the other side of Newberg," he said. "But you'll make it if you've come this far."

At noon we were stalled past Newberg, on the steep hill. Three times we had to stop and cool and water our engine, but we carried plenty of water and finally topped it. From then on we rolled right along. Maybe it was as sluggish travel as were all the miles behind us, but it didn't seem so. A grand sense that we were passing from one life to another was in me. Even as we ascended the hills that backed the city their steepness caused us no concern. We had a glimpse of the city below us and then the road turned going down — a wide road. Cars surrounded us. We flowed with them toward the city.

Signs informed us. We made the right turns and, avoiding the city center, rolled with many others out on the Ross Island Bridge. Oh, such joy was welling up in me. We were home where we belonged. Home to make a new start. Our rig bore us and ours down the other side of the bridge. We had crossed the Willamette and were crossing Seventh Street where my mother and I were born. Oh, God, how good it was to be alive! I looked at Nordi. She gave me a cold glance.

"I can't forgive you for the embarrassment of this trip," she said. "You left the furniture — all the things that make home."

I'd earned all this a hundred times. Not that I was mean about things or weak or stupid; but in my search for simple living — in my avoidance of the encirclement of softness — I was out of step

156

with even those others who had the same goals as mine.

"Okay," I said, slowing the car, wondering what people would think if they knew we had no brake, that it had worn out just north of San Francisco, ten days before. I stepped on the gas, looking for a side street where I could turn off for Oregon City and Molalla and the land — the stump-littered land that seemed my only hope. "Okay," I said again, "but I needed the plow and tools, all that stuff back there, to make a go of it, Nordi."

"I know," she answered. "But I want things. Not the things in the back of the truck. I want things like other people have."

"Like polychrome floorlamps?" I asked. We had both laughed about these pretentious floorlamp monstrosities for years, but now she turned in her seat and stared at me without humor.

A feeling of brink came over me then, a feeling of great loss, not gain, as she said, "Yes, polychrome floorlamps. And all the rest of it."

And so I came home to Oregon. I cleared land and lost it. I painted again, I carved a woman in spruce, I made some miniatures and built a house of rammed earth on the Clackamas River, where I still live. Eventually, I built a sea-going boat, and then I built a small mill.

The boat was ecstasy from start to finish, for my son helped me build it. It was big, forty-six feet. I knew the pride of broadaxe work and I learned the delicate joy of adzing timbers with a superb adze. The adze is gone now, stolen long ago, and I still mourn it. It was light and lipped and its handle was curved and when you held it in your hands and bent your back as adzemen do and the thin crumbly chips spun from your hewing you were like a god and knew intimately the countless tiny planes that make an adzed surface luminous. The three-pound hammer seemed always in my hand and often the slick, that great god of chisels, was in the other. I grew to rely on the honesty of the barefoot auger and even my dreams were filled with the rough touch of oak and fir. I steamed them and bent them and wedged them in place and drove home the blunt-cut nails that still hold those planks against the pounding sea. I lost the boat in Pedro. She still fishes off Mexico.

As for the small mill, it was there that I learned the power and the priesthood of being a sawyer. It was sexual in a way, like unfolding a woman. You were dedicated to search and claim the best, and on the other side of the saw the offbearer observed your way with the log, as did the turn-down man behind you. These men loved logs — the grain and plumpness of timber — as you did, and there had to be a courtliness in your arrangement of each log's charms. You were also dedicated to the whining hunger of the saw and to the engine, and to the sweet sawdust and to the shift. Your shame was the logged-off area, the trash-ridden tear you made in the mountain's garment. About you the big logging horses, Frank and Jim, thundered their hooves in the straining, while old men who once had prowess in the woods came and watched with fierce gleams in the sadness of their eyes. While you ate your lunch they sat beside you and gave you pointers on the way it was done long ago.

Clyde Rice

THE ST. JAMES LUTHERAN 5

In the late 30s, the St. James Lutheran church of White Center, Washington, had a basketball team. Just barely. Just barely because we had only five players, and just barely because we had no coach, no plays, no organization. We didn't have uniforms either. We played in our trousers, stripped to the waist. The few times we won, we won by luck, a little defense and, for 13- and 14-year olds, some rough play under the boards. But mostly luck. Elmer Matson and I were the best shots and we were terrible. We just came closer than Benny Fiedler, Karl Schalka and Eddie Nelson.

We lacked experience of even the most basic kind. Highland Park grammar school, which we all attended, had no baskets. How impoverished St. James Lutheran came to have baskets, I don't know. They hung at either end of the small rec room that served as the church auditorium and social hall. For several years, the high point of a church social affair came when Mr. Clark, who was related to Benny Fiedler in some way, sang "We Just Couldn't Say Goodbye." We clapped and clapped when Mr. Clark had finished. I never remember Mr. Clark singing any other song. If we applauded long enough, Mr. Clark sang "We Just Couldn't Say Goodbye" again.

Our team was not in a league. The wind forbid. Once we were defeated 42 to 3 at the Seattle downtown YMCA by a bunch from West Seattle. They'd attended schools that had baskets and basketballs, and they'd picked up some fundamentals along the way. Little things we didn't know, like breaking for the basket, screening, passing and shooting.

I started Sunday School at St. James when I was three. Grandmother saw to it I did not miss. I hated it and went under the threat of a beating if I resisted, since Grandmother's beatings were no laughing matter. I never stopped hating it all ten years I had to attend. I detested every step through the woods on the trail that led from our backyard to 16th, though I loved that trail itself, then south a half block on 16th to Cambridge, and west on Cambridge to 18th where the old frame brown church sat on the crest of the small hill. I ran every loving step of freedom back the same route when we were finally released.

One day in Sunday school we were discussing right and wrong, good and evil, and I eagerly pointed out that Eddie Cantor was a good man because he gave newcomers a chance to sing on his radio show. Both Deanna Durbin and Bobby Breen got their start there. "But," Mrs. Brandt, our teacher, said, "Remember Eddie Cantor is a Jew, and a Jew's right hand always knows what his left hand is doing." I was hurt that my contribution had been rejected. Why wasn't Eddie Cantor good if he did good things? And what did hands have to do with it? What was a Jew, anyway?

As I got older I found some saving things about the church, namely the baskets, the basketball and a kitchen window I could jimmy. I would shoot baskets alone for hours inside the locked church. The thud of the ball on the floor echoed spookily in light that seemed gray once it entered the small windows. Once when I had stopped to rest, the church bells started to ring. I froze in fear as the room filled with clangs, and I imagined the bells ringing themselves. When the bells stopped I bolted home without locking the door or putting the ball away.

The degradation I associated with the church, with the pitifully small congregation of the early and mid 30s, the spiritless self-conscious singing of hymns, as if the singers were afraid they might be heard, the two posturing insecure sons of a woman who had a mustache and hairs growing from her chin, the torn yellow wallpaper (or was it flaking yellow plaster?), was never more felt than when I was thirteen and had to take confirmation. If I didn't take confirmation I was assured I'd be thrown out of the house to make my own way in the world. That was threat enough. I had little courage or character.

I was the only boy in the confirmation class. That reinforced my suspicion that religion was unmanly and only for girls. Grandmother was ultra-religious while Grandfather was indifferent. He went to church seldom, and when he did he looked uncomfortable and bored.

The five or six girls in the class and I sat in the church kitchen under the bare overhead lightbulb and took religious instruction. At least the girls took it. I didn't ready any of the assignments. During class I stared at the floor, embarrassed and depressed, and refused to speak. I didn't listen to the others, and if called on mumbled anything that would get them off my back so I could return to whatever fantasy I was playing before the interruption.

One day at grammar school, some of my colleagues on the softball team told me they had spied on the class through the kitchen window. Shame flooded my stomach and my face burned. I wanted to lash out at them, their grinning faces. I wanted to run away forever. God damnit, other boys didn't have to take confirmation. In the confirmation class picture I looked as uncomfortable as I felt.

If the church and religion were feminine, basketball was not. The high points of the season were when we beat Fauntleroy twice, both times by one or two points. I'm not sure how we did that. They were boys from affluent homes two miles west of White Center, and they were disciplined players, well coached and drilled in fundamentals. Were they psyched out playing boys from the legendary tough White Center district? I doubt that. We weren't tough, except for Eddie Nelson, and he was not a hostile boy.

We played both times at Fauntleroy. We never played anyone at St. James, since the gym there was not really a gym. There were no seats, or even room for seats, and no showers. Fauntleroy's well groomed mothers and staid looking fathers in suits and ties (really, or am I making that up?) came to cheer their sons on.

What a good team Fauntleroy was. Their passing dazzled and befuddled us as they broke plays that to our untutored reflexes seemed performed in dream. Eddie and I picked up the boy streaking to the basket with the ball just in time, when we did. I suppose we beat them both times because their shooting was off and Eddie and I, the two biggest boys, grabbed our share of rebounds. Our offense consisted of standing around with the ball looking for someone to pass to, hoping Elmer Matson could find room and time for a shot. Yet both times we left the Fauntleroy parents disappointed when we headed back home happy with our narrow victory.

It was around the time of the short lived St. James Lutheran basketball team that Frank Capra's *Lost Horizon* came to George Shrigley's White Center Theatre. How I admired Ronald Coleman. What class. And how I wanted to be like him, calm and detached while being kidnapped, the plane headed who knows where deeper and deeper into the mountain ranges of west China. But I was like the others, concerned, nervous, frightened, unable to summon any dignity in the face of the uncertain and unknown.

And think of Shangri La, where people are always nice to each other, where you have a right to be simply because you are alive, where people live to be hundreds of years old protected from this mean world by gorgeous mountain ranges. It was almost too much for this 13-year-old. Don't leave, Mr. Coleman. Don't ever leave. But he did, and suddenly a lovely young woman was an old hag dead in the snow, and he was wandering aimlessly through the bitter weather alone. And then, just when all hope seemed gone, he found it again, that secure valley of paradise, and the bells rang, and Mr. Coleman's eyes glowed with the hope of all people, and blubberer that I was I've never blubbered harder in a movie. I was shattered. It took the whole newsreel and the cartoon which I'd already seen, before I was composed enough to go out into the streets of White Center.

Karl Schalka lived closest to us. He was an even-tempered boy who seemed to get along with everyone. He lived in a big house on the crest of First Hill, two blocks east of us, on what, for us, was the eastern horizon. His house might have dominated the landscape but it was obscured by the thick near tropical growth of the Pacific Northwest. Karl looked a little bit like the actor Jimmy Lydon, who played Henry Aldrich in the movies.

I knew Benny Fiedler best. We were in the same class in grammar school. Benny was a talented child and his mother saw to it he took music and dancing lessons. By the time he was seven or eight he had tapdanced on the stage of the Orpheum Theatre in downtown Seattle. Benny was a bit sissified in grade school, and since dancing itself was not considered masculine, some of the boys in our class disdained him. He seemed to have few friends when he was little and he wasn't good at sports though he could run fast. He may have been on the track team at Highland Park, I'm not sure.

Elmer Matson was small, graceful, quick. He had delicate features as a boy and suffered much of the time from colds. He overdressed, sweaters, jackets, overcoats, and he often wore rubbers at his mother's insistence. He was the only boy I knew who wore rubbers. The one time I remember being in his house it was suffocatingly hot, and I suspected Elmer wouldn't have so many colds if he weren't overheated most of the time. He looked like he might be temperamental but he wasn't. I remember him as unusually civilized for a boy in his beginning teens.

Eddie Nelson lived alone with his father. I think his mother was dead. Eddie's father was a house painter, I believe. Eddie was blond, near albino and husky. He had little personality and few complicated emotions. You'd expect him not to be temperamental and you'd be right. I can't imagine Eddie being psyched out in a game, his play affected by moods or the reputation of the opposition. He was rugged and simple.

When I thought about White Center, I often thought of the Tonkins and Wilbur Fordyce and Mr. and Mrs. Baker. I think Wilbur was Mrs. Tonkin's son by another marriage, and the Bakers were related also but I don't know how. The Tonkins and Wilbur lived across the street from us in the house long occupied by the Brockermans before they finally moved away to Bremerton. They were coarse people. That's a funny adjective for me to use but I can't think of another one that is so fitting. I seldom think of people that way and I imagine anyone who knows me would be surprised to hear me use the word 'coarse' when speaking of people. Yet, as a young boy, that's how I saw them. Jack Smith, who lived in the other house across the street, broke me up one day after the war when he remarked that he had been so hard up at times during the war that he could have given Wilhelmina Tonkin a bad time. She was a huge unattractive woman with a loud voice. Mr. Tonkin limped badly.

The Tonkins, the Bakers and Wilbur seemed such low class people that living in the same neighborhood with them was a source of degradation. Junk littered their yard. An old car partly torn down. Cooking pans. Mr. Baker beat Louise and Buddy, his children, frequently, harshly and often for less than cause. Once after Buddy had done something quite minor, Mr. Baker yelled, "bend your ass over that car," and when Buddy complied across the fender, beat him with a thick rope knotted at the end. The rope looked like something from a Russian prison.

Mrs. Baker was a young woman who looked old. Her hair was gray and stringy, and her clothes were faded and limp from too many washings. She was a sad looking, silent woman, someone who had been defeated always, and she aged daily it seemed, almost as you looked at her, as if she were in another cycle of time.

Wilbur was around my age but I had little to do with him. He was gone much of the time, maybe back to some other place he'd lived where old friends remained. Wilbur seemed crude and ill mannered, tough too, and a trifle bitter. I found myself as intolerant of him as I was of the others.

One night in the White Center Theatre, I saw Mrs. Tonkin grinning inanely at a terribly produced, unfunny Marie Wilson comedy. I saw that as typical of White Center and my own heritage. No Taste. No Class. The evening Louise came out onto the gravel road that was our street, weeping violently, I mocked her and yelled "Louise got a spanking." For years I was haunted by my sudden cruelty. And when I remembered that, I realized I was from White Center too, as vile, as crude as I considered the others, and I made private vows to better myself. For many years whenever I did something I was ashamed of, I felt, in addition to the shame itself, a sense of failure. Would I ever be any better?

When I started high school in West Seattle, I found a place that seemed in more ways than just miles far from Wilbur Fordyce, the Tonkins, the Bakers. The streets, unlike ours, were all paved, and the homes were middle class, freshly painted and well kept, with trimmed lawns, some with clipped hedges. Both Elmer Matson and Karl Schalka were from middle class homes but that didn't impress itself on me. I wanted to pull away from all things White Center which I lumped into one undesirable past. I tried to cultivate new friends among the boys from West Seattle, and so in the next few years I lost contact with the members of the St. James Lutheran basketball team. It was a big high school, around 2000 students, and so it was possible to look for other circles in which to move. If I was to find any dignity, any confidence, any self-improvement, it would be with people from West Seattle. It didn't occur to me that the gang I found myself a part of in my senior year had no one as genteel as Matson, Schalka or Fiedler. I was so prejudiced toward places, I generalized beautiful girls in White Center into homely ones, plain girls in West Seattle into glamorous sirens.

For me, Betty Bolin epitomized the social superiority of West Seattle. Petite, pretty, well groomed, poised, she lived in a large home on top of the Admiral Way hill. Below her home, Elliott Bay, and across the bay all Seattle opening like a gift against the far backdrop of the Cascade mountains. I would never have had the nerve to ask her for a date but over a long period I developed an obsessive urge to speak to her. The day I finally found the courage to try I was so frightened words began to gush out faster than I could think. Her stare was as level as her posture, and I couldn't meet it for even a second it seemed. I stammered out of control until I was so embarrassed it was impossible to go on. I walked off fast, sweating and blushing, not realizing then that my fears were not just juvenile but signs of a sexual timidity that would cripple me for many years to come, and I found some remote spot where I could regain some composure. I hated Betty Bolin, not being sophisticated enough to know that it was really me I hated for having humiliated myself.

Benny Fiedler had gotten interested in tumbling early and by the time he was a junior in high school he was a muscular young man. His shoulders were wide and his chest and arms were huge. But as his body developed his eyesight, never very good, got worse. He made the football squad and sat on the bench until late in the season when the coach sent him in at defensive guard. I felt warm when Benny ran onto the field. The sissy boy from Highland Park in a high school football game. When the ball was centered, Benny knocked the opposing lineman down and raced into the backfield so fast it seemed impossible that he hadn't been offside. There he was, a lone West Seattle player in the middle of a play that was just forming, with a chance to throw the play for a big loss. But he didn't. His eyesight was so bad he couldn't find the ball carrier.

Eddie Nelson filled out and became a very fine first string player for West Seattle, a defensive bear who either made all city or came close to it. He was savage on the field, quiet off of it. Given the accidental development of social affairs at that age, I found myself one night at a party with Eddie in West Seattle. Eddie's well-built date teased him into dominating her and he easily wrestled her to the couch as she giggled and protested inconvincingly. I was impressed with Eddie's masculinity, ashamed of my lack of it.

All five of us from the now defunct basketball team graduated from high school in the early 40s, and we all went into the service in Word War II. Eddie and Karl joined the marines. Elmer Matson joined the navy. Benny Fiedler was drafted into the Army, and I joined the Army Air Corps. Three of us came back.

Benny Fiedler was killed in Belgium. The citation said that with the rank shot out from the front of the company, Benny led a charge of 1000 yards across Belgium soil under heavy German tank fire before he was cut down. I got that from Benny's father who took some pride in it. Since I came back with a DFC for a mission where the bombs fell in some remote Alpine region that might have been Switzerland, I was cynical about citations, but I didn't let Mr. Fiedler know it. In Benny's case, I hoped the citation was true, that those sneering bullies from Highland Park Grammar School would be wrong forever. But I was young then and at times righteousness was vital.

Benny had no business in the Army at all. The Army drafted him despite his bad eyesight and assured him he would see only limited service. Mr. Fiedler told me this with bitterness. Those were the days when a clerk inadvertently using the wrong rubber stamp on your records might seal your destiny.

Eddie Nelson bought it at Tarawa in the invasion assault. One day I ran into Ed Jersey, a White Center boy, in an old tavern down by the Duwamish slough. He suffered from malaria and the depression some men experience after being frightened too many times in combat. He said he thought he had seen Eddie Nelson's body at Tarawa but he couldn't be sure. The body he'd seen had been in two pieces and he hadn't stopped to study it.

I saw Eddie's father after the war, in the streets of White Center. He was shuffling aimlessly along as if he had no destination. I didn't speak to him. He seemed so forlorn I imagined the immediate air about him looked gray.

A year or so after the war, I saw Elmer Matson. He had recently married and was living in an apartment only a couple of blocks from our place in White Center. He seemed happy and on his way to a full life, and I envied him. I thought he couldn't miss, a well-mannered, good-looking young man like that.

And it was in the first year after the war that I was drinking beer with a couple of old friends from White Center in the Swallow Tavern when Mr. Baker was suddenly at our table, the way people are suddenly at your table in taverns. Mrs. Baker had just died and he wanted to talk about it with someone. He hated himself for the hard life he'd given his wife, and he blamed himself for her death. Now and then his eyes misted up. We sat and drank beer late into the night and talked intimately like old friends.

I was no longer interested in the church but I heard about it now and then from Grandmother. It rode the post-war religious revival to modernization. Now it was a large brick building, not the old frame one, and the congregation had multiplied. The old timers still came, many nearing death, those strange sad people who had kept the church going during the Depression years. But now successful business people from White Center attended. Some assumed positions of power in the church. At one point the Fiedlers thought of finding another church. Some of the new, "highly respectable" members ridiculed Mr. Fiedler for the way his face looked when he passed the collection plate. He had passed the collection plate for years but now his expression wasn't dignified enough. Too matter of fact.

Betty Bolin looked no different when I saw her in 1960 at a University of Washington football game. She introduced me to her husband. Both looked like well-heeled alumni. They were living in one of the fashionable suburbs that had developed east of Lake Washington after the war. We fell into a brief conversation. When she told me how hard it was becoming to cross over the lake to Seattle, I said, "Don't worry, you'll have a second bridge in a matter of forty years." She laughed brightly. It was a local joke. Authorities had been discussing and seemingly doing little else about a second bridge for years.

How easy it was to talk with her. Maybe it always had been. She was just a nice woman, down to earth and unaffected. As she disappeared into the crowd making its way back for the second half, I wondered if she had remembered that day, at least twenty years before when I'd humiliated myself in front of her. If she did, she had the graciousness not to show it.

In those years I was living a sort of dual life. I dressed up and went to work in the office at the Boeing Company, the middle class man hoping for anonymity, hoping my surface was conventional enough to pass myself off as one of the rest. But we lived, my wife and I, in run down, old out-of-the-way houses we found to rent, where we could let things go, the yard outside, the rooms within.

We made plenty of money and we lived as if we were poor. Both of us were irresponsible with money and we managed to spend all we got. So, in a way, we kept ourselves poor enough to belong where we lived. When we decided to go to Europe it took but a little over a year to save 8000 dollars so we could make the trip.

I saw Karl Schalka in 1963. Someone organized a neighborhood reunion party at a downtown hotel. Men only but not a "stag party." No girls or dirty movies. We drank in a banquet room into the night and talked about our lives. My wife and I were planning to leave for Italy soon and I was glad we hadn't gone before this affair. It was good, though in some cases sad, to see what had become of some of the White Center-Highland Park bunch. Karl and I happened to sit next to each other.

Deep into the evening Karl said to the group. "I'm not surprised Dick became a poet. Dick always had things to say and we always used to listen to Dick. He seemed to understand things." I was drunk enough to show that I was pleased but not so drunk that I wasn't surprised and a little embarrassed. When you hear something that contradictory to what you remember, you know everything you write is a damned lie. I looked back on my life and could remember few moments when I found any wisdom to call on. More than anything, I remembered a series of phony roles, an attempt to imitate men I admired who seemed to be making it through life with confidence and dignity, silly posturings calculated to make me look masculine and courageous, posturings calculated to change me into someone other than my inadequate self, a life based often on fantasy because reality was elusive and would not do.

New businesses and many new people have moved into White Center, the neighborhood streets were paved long ago, and one White Center restaurant is reputed to be pretty good. Modest, nice homes sit close to each other where I remember woods, ponds and swamps. West Seattle, mostly built up by the 40s, has seen fewer changes. The widened thoroughfares, the continuum of pavement and housing seem to have shortened the distance between White Center and West Seattle. Fauntleroy seems only a stone's throw now. If they are not one district, at least the borders, once vividly defined by my insecurities, are impossible to locate.

I'm just finishing a White Center poem. For years I was never poet enough to do much with White Center. My attempts at poems about my home town seemed blocked by allegiances to memory. That was the trouble: they were *about* White Center. The imagination had no chance in the face of facts.

A long time back, maybe twenty-five years ago, a reviewer in the *Hudson Review* ridiculed William Carlos Williams for saying that one reason a poet wrote was to become a better person. I was fresh out of graduate school, or maybe still there, filled with the New Criticism, and I sided with the reviewer. But Williams was right and I know now what he was talking about. It wasn't some theory of writing as therapy, nor the naive notion that after writing a poem one is any less depraved. It was the certainty that writing is a slow, cumulative way of accepting your life as valid, of accepting yourself over a lifetime, of realizing that your life is important. And it is. It's all you've got. All you ever had for sure.

It may have been time and the attendant losses — Benny, Eddie, Mrs. Baker, a lot of others — and the slow discovery that many of us meet eventually, in our joy as well as our despair, no matter who we are or where we come from, that finally made me realize the relative social values of places are a silly concern. But I like to think writing was a necessary part of that process. I often found the sources of poems in the lonely reaches of the world, the ignored, forlorn, and, to me, beautiful districts of cities, like the West Marginal Way area in Seattle, the sad small towns of Washington and Montana, the villages and countryside of Southern Italy, wherever I imagined life being lived as amateurishly as we had once played basketball.

With its cynical disregard of relative values, the imagination is one hell of a durable democracy. The Bakers, Wilbur, the Tonkins, Betty Bolin, the St. James Lutheran Five, Hermann Goering, Groucho Marx and the London Philharmonic might sit comfortably together in the same poem. Arrogant as it sounds, I believe writing poems helped me cure myself of those insufferable snobberies that once stood like dirty glass between me and a world I wanted desperately to confront and be accepted by. If so, some poems must be the best I could find in myself. That's a good feeling to have. As long as they are my best, I don't care how good they are. That makes me one of the luckiest survivors.

Richard Hugo

JAMES WRIGHT

I think I met him in a cafe. He was seated and I was standing. Someone was seated across from him. We said how much we admired each other's work and went on too long until he made some wisecrack about how silly we were being. That broke the ice.

I'm surprised to find that *The Green Wall* was published as late as 1957, surprised because I was jealous of Jim's success and fame and by 1957 I should have known better. Once I got to know him, my jealousy seemed ridiculous. Ultimately I would realize that all jealousy is ridiculous. But for a brief time I resented James Wright — four years younger than me and already an established poet. What was worse, he deserved his reputation. I realized that when I read *The Green Wall*. I knew nothing then of the pressures of "success," especially on someone like Jim. The luckiest thing that ever happened to me was the obscurity I wrote in for many years.

Theodore Roethke, my wife and I were invited for dinner at the Wrights'. Libby served ham, boiled potatoes, vegetables, bread and salad. Roethke prided himself on being a gourmet, and I worried about what he would say to such a plain meal. (He had once remarked about "the swill served by Seattle hostesses" and that utterance had found its way back to a very fine cook who only a few days before had had him to dinner. She never forgave him and years later when she was into voodoo she took credit for Roethke's death.) I was relieved when Roethke simply said, "Very good, Libby." Later we got into a discussion on writing poems. I remember Jim saying, "It's rhythm finally that makes it work, isn't it?" Roethke nodded.

Gooseprairie, Washington, on the bank of the Bumping River. Jim, Libby, my first wife and I rented a large cabin there. Jim had no interest in fishing, but Libby went with me to the river and we caught several small trout. Libby remarked on how strongly they pulled on the line. That night we cooked the fish. Soon after dinner, three elk appeared in the meadow outside the cabin. We stood on the porch and marveled at their dignity, their long necks erect as they ran off slowly and proudly with their sure gait.

That night we drank all our beer, which was plenty. Jim and I talked about humor writers. Eventually we discussed Benchley. We agreed Thurber and Perelman were more polished artists, but Benchley seemed funnier, one who revealed the absurdity of everyday existence. He was also insidious. We started quoting him from memory, and couldn't stop. Though we soon ran out of quotes, we went on, repeating passages over and over. Our laughter seemed like it would never stop. We were howling. Tears ran down our faces. We never tired of Benchley stories, no matter how often we told them.

The next morning, we went to a local store run by Ed and Zetta Bedford. Like others who live in remote places, they had abandoned gentility years ago. They were neither friendly nor polite. And they charged plenty for beer, knowing we were miles from the next store. On another trip with other friends, I once stopped Ed Bedford, who was driving in the mountains, and asked directions to the Upper Bumping River. He immediately started to yell at me angrily: What in hell was I doing up there. I had no business fishing the Upper Bumping when the Lower Bumping had plenty of fish. The roads were bad and we'd all better get the hell out of there. He had just towed some people out of the mud and damn it he was tired of us city people coming there and causing him trouble.

Bedford only increased my resolve to go on. The fishing that day in the Upper Bumping was splendid.

Jim and I took instant dislike of the Bedfords. For years afterwards we called each other Ed, and our wives Zetta. We grabbed at ploys like the Bedfords, and we hung on with an obsessive grip.

Jim and I liked the humor inherent in hostility. We both loved Alfonso Bedoya (in *Treasure of the Sierra Madre*), his voice rising in progressive anger saying, "Badges? What badges? I don't have to show you no stinking badges." We used to say that to each other on occasion, often substituting "poems" for "badges" or "beers" or "kindness." Jim also was fond of Bogart's line, "They're not putting anything over on Fred C. Dobbs." He loved the absurdity of the name Fred C. Dobbs, the way it implied a lack of distinction.

Somewhere along the way of our early days together in Seattle, we either invented or stole the line, "Get out of the car, and get out of the car fast." We used to say it to each other often, trying to affect the accent of a New York gangster. For some unknown shared personal reason, we found that funny. We seldom tired of anything no matter how often we repeated it.

Jim gave a reading one night at Hartman's Bookstore in the University district. He read a couple of poems by Jean Clower and one of mine. He also read bits from earlier writers he loved, H.L. Mencken, Ring Lardner and I think Robert Benchley. That was typical of him. He was always generous to other writers, known or unknown. I think he was a unique writer in that he loved to read as much as he loved to write, and he had the most genuine appreciation of writing I've ever seen in anyone. He was anything but snobbish, and one of his loves included Max Shulman's *The Feather Merchants*, a popular humorous book about World War II and a soldier who stayed in the States for the duration. It didn't bother Jim that the "literary merits" of what he read and loved were not up to the standards presumed by his profession. Reading was too important to bother with "good taste."

My wife and I took Jim, Libby and their son Franz to our favorite spot, Lake Kapowsin. It was natural for us to want to share places we loved with others. But in our innocence, we failed to recognize that not everyone's sensibility was the same. Some people we took there looked on that lake with disdain or disinterest. The Wrights didn't let us down. They loved it too.

We picnicked at a table above the lake. When Jim sat on one end of a bench, it started to tilt and he caught himself awkwardly on one hand and giggled. I still couldn't interest him in fishing but he did go out in the row boat with me, and together we admired the dark water, so rich it fed new young trees that grew out of dead logs. The mossed stumps, the cattails and the redwinged blackbirds that perched in those cattails and swayed with them, the monster heron who climbed from some obscure place in the acres of rushes and reeds and authoritatively swept over the water. That bird had a right to feel superior, and we knew it.

On the way home, as we neared the U.S. Naval facility at Pier 91 in Seattle, Franz, perhaps five at the time, suddenly shouted,

"Look. Look. It's our country's flag." Jim and I said that to each other whenever we saw an American flag. Like other obsessively repeated private jokes, it never failed to amuse us.

I suppose because we were both from working class backgrounds and because we felt the consequences of those backgrounds in ourselves, we favored stylish, graceful, near-elegant Sugar Ray Robinson over that rough Utah miner, Gene Fullmer. Jim and I watched the fight at my place. Fullmer was tough. He had never been knocked down. He looked like you couldn't knock him down with a top maul.

I can't recall the round. Robinson was keeping his right hand busy with a series of short chops and short hooks to Fullmer's face. Fullmer was blocking the blows well. Suddenly Robinson, who must have shifted his weight to his left foot, caught Fullmer on the chin with what looked like a short left upper-cut. The blow didn't seem all that powerful (Robinson's knockout punches always seemed too smooth to be anything but light taps) but Fullmer stopped for a moment, then tumbled over. Jim and I were screaming as the count neared ten. We exploded with joy when the ten came. We danced. We sang. We laughed. Mostly we laughed and traded our own descriptions of what had just happened.

A mutual friend, who supported Fullmer, was a dreadful needler and Jim couldn't wait to phone him. The barrage went on for some time. I remember Jim saying, "Don't give me that shit. Next you'll be telling me it was a tank job."

We also saw the second Robinson-Bobo Olson fight, I think. Perhaps we just talked about it afterward. Robinson put Olson away with a similar move, shifting his weight to his left foot and throwing a quick left that seemed like nothing more than a crisp, light blow. Jim said more than once that Olson fell asleep on his feet. It was a good description. Olson didn't fall so much as he crumbled, didn't crumble so much as he slowly melted down into the canvas. That was the second time Robinson knocked Olson out, and both fights came after Olson had been knocked out by Archie Moore, when he had added some pounds and tried to fight light heavyweight. Jim was sure Olson had never recovered from the Moore knockout. "Moore changed Olson's jaw to glass," Jim told me. Jim once told me that he'd rather write the poems of — I can't remember what poet he was in love with at the time — than do anything else except win the heavyweight championship of the world.

If you saw the old graveyard in Mukilteo, Washington, and didn't feel the urge to write a poem, you probably had no soul. The graveyard was only one vacant lot, next to a big white house with red trim. Most of the people buried there were children or Chinese who had died in the early part of the century. A few tall pines grew at the back edge, and beyond that the land fell off to railroad tracks below and the sea beyond the railroad tracks. I wondered once what Valery would have made of that graveyard and that sea.

I took Ken Hanson there, but I think someone else took Jim. I don't remember being there with him. Anyway, the three of us ended up with Mukilteo poems. We decided to try to publish them together. How we decided on that I don't know, for Jim had left Seattle by then. I think it was in the late fifties and Jim had taken his first teaching position at the University of Minnesota.

Ken and I asked Jim if he would handle the submission. We agreed to a common title, settling on Ken's "Grave at Mukilteo." Ken felt, as I did, that since Jim's reputation was soaring and we were unknown, that his submitting the poems increased our chances of getting the three in print together. In one letter, I suggested in my shameful ambitious way that Jim try *The New Yorker* first. Jim had been in *The New Yorker* and so had Ken. I hadn't but I was sure I wanted to be.

Jim turned the idea down. He sent me a letter and said that he was sure my lines about a boy getting his first in the tall grass back of Laroway and Wong (invented names on gravestones) would insure rejection by *The New Yorker*. "*The New Yorker,*" he wrote, "just automatically assumes that their readers neither fuck nor die." Later he got them taken by the now long defunct *New Orleans Poetry Journal*.

Twenty years later, J.D. Reed, James Welch and I would try the same thing again. This time the subject was a bar in Dixon, Montana, and the title agreed on would be mine, "The Only Bar in

174

Dixon." And where else would they appear but in *The New Yorker*.

One of Jim's favorite stories, one he told me several times, was about a radio program he'd heard one night late while riding in a car in Pennsylvania. It seems that a radio station in Clint, Texas, had a powerful transmitter located across the border in Mexico. Since the transmitter was outside the U.S., the FCC had no control over what the station broadcast. The commercials were the pits, according to Jim. That particular night the powerful station was coming in clear in Pennsylvania and an oily voiced announcer was giving a pitch for a porous plastic figurine of Jesus. The figurine was hollow and had a cork in the top of Christ's head. The announcer's big line was, "Pour beet juice in Christ and he bleeds for you." Jim would repeat that line several times, imitating the announcer's voice and drawing out the word, "bleeds." Then he'd start to giggle at the tastelessness of it and say, "Bottom of the barrel. Bottom of the damned barrel."

It was while we were living in a rented brick house in early 1960 that Jim returned from Minneapolis to defend his PH.D. thesis, a brilliant one on Dickens. He stayed with us for a month. He was drinking more than I'd ever seen him drink and he talked ceaselessly. He found a record he liked in our collection, something by Delius, and he played it over and over every moment he was in the house. At times he was great fun, but of course he was also trying, telling the same stories over and over, playing the same record for eight or ten hours at a stretch.

He came home one day from his thesis defense, and soon after, when he was drunk, kept saying, "I made it. I really made it." He got hung up that night on a review he'd published, a most favorable review, of a poet who, he'd learned after the review came out, suffered from cerebral palsy. He was afraid people would think he knew about the poet's condition before he wrote the review and so had written the review out of kindness or perhaps sentimentality. I argued that he had, after all, commented only on the poems and had used quotes from those poems to support his approval of the book. I couldn't see how the poet's health had anything to do with it. Somewhere during that long evening, I must have gotten through because, as he was about to go to bed, having just washed down a fried egg sandwich with a big glass of "dago red" in a most sloppy hedonistic way, egg and wine coursing down his chin, he suddenly screamed, "You're right. You're right. What the hell has cerebral palsy to do with poetry. Dear (poet's name), fuck you." My wife and I went to bed giggling.

He stayed on, playing the Delius constantly. He seldom stopped either talking or reading aloud from some book. To survive, it was necessary to ignore him and the music at times, to blot it all out — the same music, the same talk, the same reading, again and again. A few times we made excuses, left the house with Jim in it, and made our way to a tavern where we could talk with each other and where the juke box had more than one tune to play.

He was there when we were evicted, two sad young people who couldn't fit in a world of well-kept lawns and revered gardens and nice clean houses. We found a house, not far away, but old, wooden, rundown, in a neighborhood that didn't take itself seriously. Students, laborers and old poor retired people lived there, people who didn't care how we lived. When Jim saw it, he said, "It's more like us." I felt good he'd included himself.

A few friends came to help us move. Jim drank wine and read aloud from some book while the rest of us carried out boxes and boxes of books and records, and our few other possessions. Our friends shot Jim dirty looks as they struggled by with loads or came back for more. He was oblivious to the situation, that he was the only one not doing any work. Jim and I shared that too, a distaste, even a fear of physical work. I remember when they had moved, Libby had done all the packing. She had to do the driving as Jim never learned to drive a car. At least he hadn't yet in the early sixties. I believe Jim, like me, felt acute anxiety when faced with physical work. I'm still that way. When I mow the lawn, I do it so fast I wear myself out and end up panting and sweating. I could never paint a house. I can't pace myself, couldn't find the patience. It isn't laziness. It's an inability to work calmly and easily, a desire to have the job done and out of the way.

Jim stayed on a few days in our new find. We were far more relaxed. Not only was the junky old house "more like us," but our landlord and landlady, whom I had known slightly before, had gone to California. The landlord had to run from a serious traffic violation committed while drunk, one of many on his record, rather than stand trial before a new traffic judge out to make a name for himself by handing out harsh sentences. Our landlord faced six months in jail if he didn't leave the state. All we had to do was mail the rent every month. Besides, the rent was considerably less than that for the brick home and we had more money for the essentials, beer and what Jim called "That great American philosopher, James Beam."

The day he left, we took him to the train, relieved he was going. He had found the Delius almost the moment we'd moved into the new rental and his behavior hadn't changed in the new surroundings. Yes, we were glad he was finally going. Or were we? An unexpected thing happened in the railroad station. We stood there yelling old jokes, jokes really only between us, things like "Look. It's our country's flag." or "Get out of Seattle, Bedford, and get out fast." And we were still yelling them when the train pulled out. Then he was gone and we suddenly turned to each other, my wife and I, and shrugged with a sadness we both felt. We didn't have to say it: some winning energy, tiresome yet important, had just left our life. We felt empty now that he was gone.

I saw him a few months later, on purpose. It was in the fall of 1960. My first book had been accepted by Minnesota Press, thanks to Jim. When he found out I'd submitted it there, Jim walked into the Minnesota Press offices and told them he strongly supported my work. I suspect that's why they took it.

I had decided to use my vacation (I was working at Boeing Company) to see Jim and Libby. I took the train to Minneapolis and a cab to their house. He and Libby were buying the house and he told me that 'owning' a home was a great relief — the idea that no one could throw you out. It was a real source of stability, he told me, and we, my wife and I, should try it. Stability was important to him, I knew, for by then he'd been hospitalized with a nervous breakdown. Libby too had been having problems and, as I recall, had been taking electric shock treatments though she wasn't taking them when I was there. Their house was old, plain and homey. Jim took me to the English department and introduced me to some of his colleagues. I sensed some strain in

177

some of them, uneasy feelings in Jim's presence.

One night we went to a faculty party, and it was there I began to feel Jim's alienation from the others. One young man was particularly disdainful of Jim, and of me as well. He made no effort to hide his sneers when Jim or I spoke. He was in every sense a bourgeois. In him I saw the one quality I've seen in many minor academics and cannot find sympathy for. He had acquired knowledge not out of love of the works he'd read, but to appear superior to others. That he felt superior to Jim and to me was only too evident. I remember his name and learned only recently he has died. I have to add that I've been lucky enough in the last few years to know some of the great academics, such as J. Hillis Miller and Louis Martz, and I've never seen in them any trace of that presumed superiority. Maybe that's why they are superior. Whatever, I saw in that young man the difficulty Jim must have had as a member of a university faculty.

Jim stayed up drinking back at his house and once I woke up to go to the bathroom. It must have been four in the morning and though I was groggy, I remember hearing Jim on the phone. He was talking to a colleague and was quite hostile. In my fog I worried about him and his future.

I went to a class of Jim's and heard him lecture. He was good, I thought, and the students seemed to like him. I left Minneapolis shortly after that and would not see Jim again for seven years.

A year or two later, out west, Jim Dickey told us that Jim Wright had been fired at Minnesota. It was an odd dismissal, sudden and complete. No extra year to look for another job, normal in such cases.

I'm hazy on this next bit. I remember I was in Bloomington, Indiana, and had received a letter from Robert Bly, with a copy of the letter from Allan Tate to Jim, specifying the reasons for Jim's dismissal. Bly urged me to write on Jim's behalf and felt it had been Tate's duty to back Jim and protect Jim, the way Heilman had protected Roethke at Washington. I tried to write a letter but felt futile. It bothered me that I didn't believe the reasons he gave were the real reasons Jim had been let go. I'd been in the work-a-day world long enough to know that people are seldom dismissed for incompetence. They are usually dismissed because other people don't like them, though incompetence is given as the official reason. Besides, I'd heard Jim lecture and didn't think he was incompetent, despite Tate's letter and the "evidence."

The next time I saw Jim was in 1967 in New York, where he had taken a job at Hunter College. He had remarried and I met Annie for the first time. Jim and I were both quite drunk and I recall very little of that brief meeting except that he told me they had been right at Minnesota to fire him. He didn't elaborate. He simply said he'd deserved it.

1972 was a great year at the University of Montana. Allen Ginsberg, Gary Snyder and Mark Strand read there that year, and then Jim came, not to read, just to visit. He seemed much as he had been in Seattle in 1960. He drank constantly and he played one record, a Stan Getz recording, all day and all night until he went to bed. He was on his way to give the Roethke reading in Seattle but generously offered to read for nothing at Montana. I think we got him some money at the last minute.

When he awoke in the morning, he would drink a water tumbler full of straight bourbon. Then he would return to bed for two more hours. His energy was at the usual high level and he talked ceaselessly. I had been living alone for eight years. I'd had to stop drinking the year before Jim's arrival, and at times had to block him out to keep my sanity, it seemed. One Sunday, to escape his constant chatter I turned on the TV and watched a movie. He kept talking but I put the volume high enough to crowd him out and directed all my attention to the film. At one point in the evening he suddenly cried, "Oh, my God, Dick. I can't stop talking. No wonder I have no friends."

During that visit I told him of a minor crackup I'd had at Iowa the year before and how ashamed I'd felt afterward. "I've had six," he said. I was astounded. I'd never known Jim had had six breakdowns. And all had resulted in hospitalization. I'd seen so little of him over the years I had no idea of the crippling depths of his anguish.

He would walk around the house naked for hours. "In the army," he said, "they called me Adam in the Barracks."

Jim said a lot of things that visit. I remember some of them well. He was genuinely happy in his new marriage and he hoped

179

I'd marry again too. "It's hard to find someone who knows what being a poet means," he said. "Annie knows. She's rare."

Once he started talking about the older generation of poets, Tate, Ransom, mostly. "We really did something, Dick, our generation. We really made a break from all those guys and that stuff they peddled." He also told me, while we were mentioning our divorces, that he felt, looking back on it, that he and Libby had to get married to escape Martin's Ferry. Neither of them could have done it alone.

The morning of the day he was to read, I found an article in the newspaper about a man who had gone into St. Peter's in Rome and started beating on Michaelangelo's *Pieta* with a hammer. He'd managed to damage it before they could stop him. I mentioned it to Jim who was shaving. Later, when I was shaving, I knew he was reading the same article because he yelled, "Oh, Jesus Christ, does he have to be named Lazlo Toth?"

Jim gave a good reading that afternoon. Students and faculty alike loved it. He was in good form though somewhat drunk. In his remarks between poems he indicated once that he did not believe in God. That was a typical attitude in many poets of my generation, especially those who had come from working class backgrounds and who had suffered the boredom and repression of churches that today seem long out of date.

After the reading, a young woman approached Jim and started arguing with him. She was, she declared, a Christian. Her accent was Scandinavian, perhaps Swedish. Her religious fanaticism reminded me of some dotty old women in my hometown during the depression, especially a Mrs. Morley who couldn't talk about anything except Christ, Our Savior. Jim surprised me by inviting the young woman to come with us.

She didn't let up in the car. How could we survive without accepting Christ? Only Jesus would lead to true happiness. Then I did something very unusual for me. I suddenly pulled the car over and ordered her out. (I didn't think to say, "Get out of the car, and get out of the car fast.") Jim reproached me a bit. "You shouldn't have done that, Dick."

I replied, "I had to listen to that shit when I was a kid. I sure as hell don't have to listen to it now."

"It's important to them," he said quietly.

Jim had read in the afternoon because that night a well-known scholar and social critic was scheduled to speak. By the time I got Jim fed at some local restaurant we were late to the lecture. We didn't get to hear most of the talk. When we arrived, the speaker was advising people to change their lives. If you have a job in the Post Office, quit and become a fireman for a while. I sensed Jim's hostility and realized I should not have brought him. He was drunk and the speaker was upsetting him.

When time came for questions from the floor Jim was on his feet instantly, shouting, "Have you ever been to ————" he gave some address in New York that sounded as if it could be Harlem.

The speaker cooly answered that the address sounded specious to him.

"It may be specious to you, but if you go there and start advising people on their lives you'll get answered with a knife," Jim screamed. I knew what was bugging him. The speaker had presumed that workingclass people enjoyed the same cavalier mobility as upper-middle-class people. That they could just change jobs with no emotional complications. Jim had seen his father enslaved to a lousy factory job during the depression and knew what terrible fears bind people to jobs. I knew too. For years I assumed that if I lost a job I might very well never find another.

But I felt a little embarrassed that the speaker suddenly found himself in an inhospitable situation in Montana. My colleagues told me afterward that Jim's outburst was understandable and that his reaction was justified. Jim told me later that he resented the condescension with which the speaker had treated the Montana audience. "These are sophisticated people here," Jim said, "and he had no right to take a superior attitude." I wasn't sure Jim was right. The speaker had struck me as smooth and a bit cold, but I'm not truly sensitive to condescension and so had missed that, if in fact it had been there at all.

Jim turned out to be a big hit and several people said to me at the party later, "I like your friend." I spoke to the lecturer briefly and tried to be as gracious as I could without seeming to patronize him for I was still embarrassed and, while I couldn't agree with the substance of his talk, I did want the man to feel good about Montana hospitality. Jim, at some point, sidled up to him and said, "Have you ever had a job?"

Until he left, Jim went on with the same pattern, playing the Stan Getz record over and over. Getting out of bed in the morning, drinking a water glass full of straight bourbon, then going back to bed for a couple of more hours. He attended my workshop, which I held at my house, and in answer to a question from a student, loudly announced that Roethke had been a "prick." Roethke did have an unfortunate way of putting students down or dismissing them, and I wondered if the speaker had, with what Jim termed condescension, reminded him of some painful memories involving Ted.

Alone with him for hours at a time in my house, I couldn't help noticing a peculiar change in him that had happened over the years. When he talked about his past he seemed to be trying to replay old pain, but there was something phony about it, as if the pain were no longer there to be relieved, though the anguish in his remark about having no friends was real. I wondered if a doctor hadn't made some breakthrough. I felt the very real hope that he was in much better shape than he realized. Now if he could reduce his drinking. It was killing him.

A bad thing happened during Jim's final night there. He tried direct dialing a Seattle number and in his drunkenness kept getting it wrong. I asked him to call the operator to get "credit" for the wrong numbers he'd dialed. He couldn't seem to do that right, either. I said, "Here, I'll do it." I must have let some irritation show in my voice because he suddenly flew into a rage. He glared at me and stood with clenched fists and threatened me. "No one talks to me like that," he yelled. Only an hour before he had bragged about slugging a colleague at a party in Minneapolis, and I had no doubt he wanted to slug me then. In a disdainful voice he offered me a hundred dollars to help pay my telephone bill.

I was frightened, but somehow managed to placate him. I assured him everything was all right. It was the only time the strain of being sober and alone in the house long days with a drunk had shown in my voice. I felt terrible about it and, after I got him to bed, I sat there shaking.

The next day I took him to the plane. He was drunk again by the time we left the house. At the airport I watched him board the plane, his legs slightly spread to insure his balance as he climbed the aerostairs. I believed I would never see him alive again.

Not so many months later Jim published a long glowing essay on my work in the *American Poetry Review*. I was touched and grateful. He was too honest to say anything he didn't mean. But I couldn't help wondering if he was trying to make up for that bad scene his last night in Missoula. I hoped he didn't feel he had to.

I next saw him in December 1975 (I think). I gave a reading at the YMHA Poetry Center, with Thom Gunn. I didn't know Jim was in the audience. I wanted to give a good reading because several people I admired were there — Richard Howard who introduced us, Stanley and Laura Kauffmann, Stanley and Jane Moss, and Jeff Marks who had come from Philadelphia. I knew where those good people were sitting, and though I was reading for them maybe more than for those I didn't know, I avoided looking at them while I read — I suppose I glanced once or twice at Richard Howard who sat in the first row and so could be easily seen despite the lights that made much of the audience obscure from the stage.

After the reading, people collected in the lobby and Gunn and I went out to greet our fans. To my surprise Jim and Annie were there. Jim told me he didn't drink now. I kept hugging them. I hugged them over and over. We said almost nothing.

The next time I saw Jim was the last time. January 1980, at The White House. Mrs. Carter had invited American poets to a national celebration honoring American poets. I'm not sure how the poets invited had been selected.

After hearing Philip Levine, Maxine Kumin and Sterling Brown read, I went upstairs with the others to meet the President, the First Lady and Mrs. Mondale. I was dazzled by it all, not just the White House, or meeting the President — though I had never met an American President before — but by the numbers of poets I admire. It was manic. I would start saying hello to one poet and another would be on my back: Hey, Dick. Reporters asked me questions — I was amazed they knew who I was. A glamorous blonde society lady talked to me at length about something or other. But mostly, poets. Seeing all those remarkable people reminded me more strongly than ever that poets are people I like. With a few exceptions, poets seem to me among the best people

I've met. I was dizzy with it all, happy and talking too fast in my excitement, not making much sense I suppose. Just sort of babbling. Not really in control.

Then someone tapped my shoulder. It was Jim, Annie was behind him. He looked fine but his voice sounded terribly strange, like it was coming from another throat, almost as if he were acting as a dummy to a ventriloquist somewhere nearby.

"Dick," he said, "I don't want you to hear any rumors and wonder what is going on. I have throat cancer." The news would have been unbelievable anywhere. There, it was bewildering as well. "They'll operate in about three weeks and they expect to get it all. It will be all right."

In that swirl of poets and reporters and politicans, I can't recall how long we talked or how we got separated. A couple months later I came into my house in Missoula and Matt, my stepson, told me Jim's death had just been announced on National Public Radio.

I should let this go at that. But I don't want to. I have to say that Jim Wright did a lot of things for me and I know that I'll go out inconsolable because I did far less for him. Now there's no way I can make up for it. I wrote three poems for him, one after he was gone. None were worthy of him and that's why I haven't included any of them here. So, I want to say, I wish I had done something for him. But then I remember a thing Jim's Grandmother used to say, and he was fond of quoting, "You wish in one hand and you shit in the other and see which one fills up the fastest."

No one carried his life more vividly inside him, or simultaneously in plain and in eloquent ways used the pain of his life to better advantage. What maims others often beyond repair maimed him too, but in some miraculous way it also nourished his great talent. It was miraculous too that his obsessive repetitive mind never limited his artistry.

In 1963, my first wife and I found ourselves in the Greyhound Bus Station in Wheeling, West Virginia. When I think of Jim I sometimes also think of that depressing place, the pathetic looking people, poor and discouraged. I knew that Martin's Ferry was across the river, but I couldn't see it. I asked someone where it was, and the man pointed upstream across the river as if my gaze might penetrate the bank that stood between me and the place where Jim had started, and just once I would see it.

But the bank held solid and firm, and now I let that bus station say a lot about where Jim came from and why it was necessary for him to leave, to get away. And why he did get away. And why he didn't.

Richard Hugo

The ringing woke him out of a dream. He grabbed the phone in the darkness and said his customary "Yello."

George Calley sounded even more intense than usual. "Claude's at Carver's trailer," the Boise FBI man said. "He's getting ready to take off again. Meet us at the Thunderbird Motel in Winnemucca."

"When?"

"As soon as you can get there."

Still in his pajamas, the sheriff dialed his overnight dispatcher and ordered her to round up his team. It was a few minutes before 5:00 A.M., Sunday, April 18, four days after the Winnemucca meeting with the FBI. He was wide awake. In his mind's eye he saw Claude Dallas coming out of the trailer in his pigeon-toed walk, hands in the air. Fifteen and a half months was a long time.

The county's official patrol cruiser was a white Chevy sedan that he'd bought cheap from a car-rental agency in an effort to stay within his ruined budget. The car was a rolling collection of wreckage with only one attractive feature: a high-speed gearbox. Stuffed inside when it headed south at dawn were four veterans of the case: Nettleton, State Trooper Rich Wills, Deputy Sheriff Gary Olsen and Allen Bidwell, chief of police of Homedale. The trunk overflowed with armament including the sheriff's personal submachine gun.

Nettleton stomped the accelerator with his cowboy boot. Maybe the car could take the strain and maybe it couldn't, but he and his friends weren't going to miss the final act even if it meant crawling the rest of the way. Whipsawing the Chevy along a twisting dropoff a thousand feet above Squaw Creek Canyon, he heard a small voice from the back. "Tim, nothing personal, okay? But I'd really appreciate it if you'd slow down to sixty-five on these curves marked thirty-five."

He slowed a little, then resumed speed. "Sheriff," Gary Olsen said in the middle of a flat stretch, "I just thought I should tell ya. We're doing a hundred and twenty."

"The gauge says eighty," Nettleton said. Eighty was the highest number.

"I timed it with the markers."

They barely slowed down for the little town of Jordan Valley, Oregon, where a sign said, TOUGH TIMES DON'T LAST FOREVER. TOUGH PEOPLE DO. Nettleton's riders hoped it was true. They ended up driving just under two hundred miles in two and a half hours. "How'd you get here so fast?" Frank Nenzel asked when they knocked at his door at 9:30 A.M.

Allen Bidwell answered, "We flew."

Two other FBI men had driven up from Reno with Nenzel. Bureau aircraft and additional agents were due in from San Francisco. The Butte Division SWAT team was expected momentarily and the Las Vegas team was on the road. All were graduates of the FBI's special school at Quantico, Virginia, but the separate teams had never worked together as a unit. Briefings would have to be held before they could make their move.

A small delegation led by Nevada State Trooper Jim Bagwell was detailed to watch Craig Carver's trailer from a distant bluff. They found a remote parking place north of Paradise Hill and walked nearly three miles along the foothills to avoid being seen from Poverty Flats. With them they carried a 25X spotting scope, binoculars and portable two-way radios. Their instructions were to maintain radio silence except in emergencies.

The temperature was above freezing, but there was a cold wind from the north. When they arrived on station, Craig Carver's old Ford pickup was gone and everything was quiet below.

At Nenzel's request, Nettleton and Rich Wills borrowed a Cessna and took Polaroid shots from high up. No one was in sight around noon as they sortied high above the tin-roofed trailer surrounded by junked cars and trucks. When they returned to the motel, SWAT members were assembling in ceramic bulletproof vests, military boots and olive-drab camouflage coveralls. Following bureau niceties, their M-16's were locked on semiautomatic. Nettleton realized that he would be the only lawman at the scene with an automatic weapon. Then he remembered Stan Rorex, the Humboldt sheriff's investigator whose Reising submachine gun had been conspicuous in the earlier investigations. He started to ask why Rorex and Sheriff Frank Weston weren't present but decided it was none of his business.

Stan Rorex was working a burglary case on his day off when the dispatcher reached him by radio. "What's your twenty?" he was asked.

"Shelton antelope range."

"We need you back in Winnemucca."

"It'll be a few more hours anyway. I gotta take a report."

Five minutes later his radio crackled again and he recognized the voice of Sheriff Frank Weston. "Stan? You got an hour and a half to get back."

"I'm a hundred and forty miles out."

"Get back here!"

"Sheriff, I'm driving my new four-wheel-drive Jimmy. I don't want to burn it up."

"I don't care if you *blow* it up. Get back!"

Rorex wondered what was up. If it was a homicide, Weston would have said so. Then he remembered that his wife and children had planned to spend the day patching the roof. Maybe someone had fallen.

"Frank," he said, "can you tell me what it is?"

"I can't now. *Just get in here!*"

He'd never heard such urgency in Weston's voice. He thought, It has to be something personal. Something I've done, maybe. He wants to tell me in my face. God, I hope it isn't the family . . .

*   *   *

He reached the office at 2:30 P.M. and found the sheriff pacing the floor of his office. As usual, every blow-dried gray hair was firmly in place, but he was wearing boots instead of his customary highly shined street shoes. "Come on," he said, grabbing his hat. "We got an FBI briefing at three."

En route Rorex learned that Weston had dropped into the building on this quiet Sunday and spotted an FBI man on his way to the city police department. "They were going to leave us out," the sheriff complained. Rorex knew that certain cops had been spreading the rumor that Weston was incompetent and Rorex trigger-happy. They'd probably brainwashed the FBI. He couldn't think of another explanation.

On the bluff, the spotting team watched impatiently and maintained radio silence. In this fourth hour of their vigil, the wind had become a factor. Alkali caked their mouths and noses, and there was no place to shelter. "I'd rather be getting shot at," Bagwell complained.

Something moved below, and he grabbed the scope. Craig Carver's pickup truck, white with a black top, was moving along the dirt road so slowly that it wasn't even raising dust. Five miles an hour, the state trooper figured, and wondered why.

The pickup stopped outside the trailer and a man climbed out. After a while he began tinkering with the truck, driving it a few feet, going under the hood again, then retesting. He loaded something on the homemade flatbed. It looked as though he was preparing to leave.

Frank Weston and Stan Rorex listened and watched as a SWAT member outlined the plan of attack. A Cessna 206 would fly cover. A Huey would deposit the Butte SWAT team in the desert behind Carver's place, and the Las Vegas teams would take up positions on both sides. On signal, the units would pinch in and make the arrest. To the eager Rorex, it sounded like a fine plan, except that it was all FBI.

He had to admit that the agents seemed professional. He watched as a spindly young SWATman changed from a business suit into fatigues: Clark Kent in the phone booth. Someone else was issuing .223 ammunition by the box. Over in a corner a leader was warning the helicopter pilots to land at least five hundred yards from the trailer; Dallas had been seen practicing marksmanship on his back. The same agent walked up to Rorex. "How well do you know the area?"

"Real well."

"We'd like you to set up here." The FBI man pointed on a map to a spot between the trailer and the Little Humboldt River, hundreds of yards from the action. "You'll serve as a roadblock, and you'll also keep observers away from the fire zone."

Rorex said to himself, *A roadblock?* Why, if Claude can get hold of some wheels, that's exactly where he'll head. He'll try to reach the willows along the river and then he'll be gone. "I need a man," he said. "Gimme a marksman or something."

"We don't have one to spare. Our Vegas team isn't here and everyone else is assigned."

Rorex got the feeling that he was being discounted, but he pressed his demand until Idaho Trooper Rich Wills was assigned to work with him.

Before leaving the motel, Rorex whispered to his boss, "Frank, do you see what could happen?"

"Yeah," Weston replied. "Claude'll try to get to the river."

"Straight over me."

"Well, I know you'll take care of it if he does."

Driving away from the motel, Rorex asked Rich Wills, "Whatcha got for a weapon?"

"I don't," the Idaho trooper said. "I'm assigned to take pictures."

Rorex handed over his new .44 magnum revolver. They stopped at a general store and bought film and extra shells, then doubled back to the sheriff's office for an M-1 Garand rifle. His Reising submachine gun was already in the truck along with another pistol. They were ready.

The two sheriffs, Nettleton and Weston, gravitated together in the Thunderbird briefing room. Target time was 4:00 P.M., but the SWAT team from Las Vegas still hadn't arrived and the operation was on hold. An FBI agent assigned them to perimeter patrol, a sort of free-safety position in football parlance. He asked Nettleton, "How bad do you want Dallas alive?"

The sheriff had to think before answering. "I don't want him to get away from the flat," he said slowly. "It's his choice whether he's alive or in a box. But I *would* like to have Bill Pogue's body, and who can tell us but Claude?"

By 5:00 P.M. Stan Rorex and Rich Wills had been at their assigned post on 101 Ranch Road for over an hour. Wills watched the trailer through binoculars. Craig Carver had been joined by another man, shorter and stubbier. If FBI information was correct, it was the fugitive. An observaton plane was a dot high above and every few minutes the voice of the pilot or Harry Capaul came over the radio. Eight miles to the south, a helicopter carrying the Butte SWAT team held a circular pattern over Dutch Flat Road. "What the hell are they waiting for?" Rorex said.

"They must be on the way," Wills said.

"FBI," Rorex said. "You know what that stands for? 'Fuckin' Buncha Idiots'." He looked west. The sun glowed red atop the Bloody Runs. "They got an hour," he observed. "After that we can forget it."

It was almost dark by the time the convoy of lawmen sped past George Nielsen's bar and turned northeast on the two-lane Highway 8A toward Paradise Flats. On a signal the cars pulled off the road a mile from the trailer to let the long-delayed Las Vegas personnel catch up, necessitating another short briefing. The assault force was now at strength.

The experienced SWAT units from Vegas moved up first, flanking Carver's trailer on the potholed dirt road. Nettleton and Weston stayed a half mile behind at a trailer owned by an elderly couple. Weston was still complaining about the FBI's high-handedness. "Relax, Frank," Nettleton said. "We got box seats at the greatest sight anybody can ever see."

At ten minutes before six, a big black Huey topped a nearby ridge and came out of the sun at a hundred and fifty knots. It cleared the trailer and butterflied down in the desert so briefly that the last member of the Butte team had to jump about six feet. Then it lifted up and reversed direction. Less than a quarter mile from the trailer the pilot spun tight high-speed circles and hit the siren. His amplified voice announced, "This is the FBI. Claude Dallas, come out with your hands up!"

Dallas burst through the trailer's window in a shower of glass. At the far end of the lot, Craig Carver flopped on his face, his arms and legs spread.

The ground parties moved up from opposite directions, some of the SWAT members trotting behind the open doors of their cars for cover. An agent shouted, "This is the FBI. Put your hands over your heads and don't move. Do . . . not . . . move!''

Carver slipped between junked trucks and disappeared. Dallas grabbed a rifle, jumped into the pickup truck and drove down the driveway toward the potholed access road. As FBI cars cut him off from both directions, he spun the truck and aimed for the back fence, his tires throwing sawdust and debris and light blue smoke.

He narrowly missed the trailer, careened past onto an alkali flat dotted with hummocks of sand and rabbitbrush and greasewood two or three feet tall. From the rear the truck looked like a hydroplane in lumpy seas, bouncing in the air, flopping hard, then bouncing again, leaving a wake. As the lawmen raced up the access road to head him off, Dallas steered toward the farms along the river. It was almost dark.

The two sheriffs saw the truck break out and moved in to back up the operation. As they aproached the trailer they noticed Carver on foot. "Isn't anybody gonna do anything with him?" the Humboldt sheriff asked.

"I think we better pick him up," Nettleton said. By now Dallas's truck was slaloming under the power lines to hold off the pursuing helicopter, while FBI vehicles continued to give chase. Nettleton thought, It's like watching sheep being worked by a dog, except that this time there's a whole flock of dogs and only one sheep. The image was reassuring.

He held his submachine gun on Carver while Weston applied the cuffs. Then they deposited the fence-maker in the back of a wrecked car while they secured the area around the trailer. As they were finishing up, gunfire resounded across the flats. A boy of eight or ten appeared on a bike. "What's going on?" he asked.

"Kid," Nettleton said, "you better get back."

The boy rode to a bush and stared at the cars whirling around the desert like waterbugs. Nettleton shouted, "*Kid! Get the hell outa here!*" The boy didn't budge.

The radio was cluttered with traffic. Pilot Norman Smith, "Hawkeye," to his crewmates on three hundred missions in Vietnam, reported that Dallas had fired on his Cessna; he'd seen the telltale "blue winks." The Huey tried to herd the fleeing truck toward FBI positions. Smith saw more muzzle flashes. He asked the helicopter if it had been hit. "No," the pilot radioed back, but a few seconds later he reported that he'd taken two hits in the fuselage.

SWAT leader Guilland broke in. "Green light," he said calmly. "Green light." It was the clearance to open fire.

Dallas had bounced and jounced nearly a mile in the general direction of the river when Stan Rorex and Rich Wills broke from their fixed post and helped to head him off. The fleeing Ford turned sharply, went through another fence, and stopped. A line of barbed wire trailed across its tailgate. The light was going and the fox was at bay. The radio crackled: "Take him out."

Rorex heard a shot and saw something shiny poking from the truck window. He'd been shot at before, but he'd never returned fire. He grabbed his Reising and hosed off the magazine in one long burst. He tried to keep his pattern low, but the range was too long for accuracy. He threw the submachine gun in the car and grabbed his M-1 Garand, knelt and began to fire. SWAT teams were shooting from the opposite side, and the Cessna added to the confusion by raising great clouds of dust.

After eleven rounds from the World War II rifle, Rorex noticed that Dallas's silhouette was gone. My God, he thought, I've killed him. The radio called for a cease-fire.

High on the bluff, Nevada State Trooper Jim Bagwell and his fellow observers watched as Dallas dived from the truck, crawled about a hundred yards, then flattened out in brush. The SWAT members were too distant to see where he'd gone. The helicopter doubled back toward Carver's trailer, picked up the farthest team and dropped it two hundred yards from the truck. As the agents closed the perimeter, Bagwell swept the range with his spotting scope and realized that they might overshoot their target.

"Isn't that a sight!" Frank Weston said. The SWAT teams were leapfrogging toward the truck, using dips and brush for cover. One man bobbed up at a time as the unit advanced in rhythm.

Nettleton said to himself, Those boys are heading straight into Dallas's guns. It's dark and there's dust all over the goddamn place and they won't see him till they're in his face. And then they'll be dead. I wonder whose widow we'll have to call tonight. He was filled with awe and fear and wonder.

The new silence was broken only by the twitterings of night birds settling back down. SWAT leader Guilland moved ahead on hands and knees. When he was about sixty yards past the truck, a meek voice said, "Don't shoot. I'm over here."

Off to one side, a man lay on his back, his elbows on the ground and his arms and hands in the air. Guilland raised the snout of his M-16 and called out, "Keep your hands where they are. *Don't move!*"

The man said, "I'm not gonna do anything."

The others came running when they saw their leader stand up and point toward the spot where Dallas lay next to his rifle. There was blood on his heel and his forehead, but he insisted that he wasn't hit. The SWAT leader kept him covered while another agent picked up the loaded .30-.30. It was eight minutes after six. The operation had taken twenty-two minutes.

Guilland called in the black Huey and ordered Dallas to stand. The "mountain man" was wearing Levi pants, sneakers and a multicolored shirt. His trapper's hat was missing. He appeared to have a small wound in the right ankle, just below the calf muscle.

Agents pushed in. One read the wounded man his rights and another said, "Move, you son of a bitch!" Frank Nenzel patted him down and found a speedloader in his pocket. They handcuffed him and put him aboard the helicopter for the ride to Winnemucca and the hospital.

An inspection of the truck showed why he'd stopped. A strand of barbed wire had ripped off a battery cable. There were nine bullet holes in the doors. Two revolvers lay on the front seat: a .22 and a .357, both loaded. Stan Rorex snapped pictures, including one of SWAT members standing behind the truck with their rifles. In their coveralls and grins, they looked like a party of slightly drunken hunters.

On the way to Winnemucca, the last car to pass the Paradise Hill Bar gave a long blast on its siren. It was a little message for George.

                    *   *   *

Dallas's wound was treated at the Humboldt General Hospital.
Dr. Michael Stafford said it was "a mass of shot around the ankle.
The largest fragment was about a quarter inch. It was almost like
birdshot . . . quite superficial really." Apparently a bullet had
shattered a metal part and turned it into a light spray of shrapnel.

The doctor said he was impressed by Dallas's attitude. "He was
very relaxed. I can understand now why people who knew him
talked about how much they liked him back when it happened. He
was very cordial."

On this quiet Sunday evening, head nurse Liz Nielsen was off
duty. Other nurses took care of the celebrity, and when Stan Rorex
arrived to help with security, he heard Dallas telling one of them,
"Be sure to say hello to your dad." Another attendant was
consoling the wounded man. "It's really too bad," she said.
Rorex turned away so she wouldn't see the look on his face.

Later that night, lawmen met briefly with reporters. FBI Agent
George Calley was asked what had brought Dallas back to
Humboldt County. "I believe with the exposure in the media,
everywhere you looked," he said, "maybe that drove him back."

Tim Nettleton said, "It's just like a dog that you kick in the
side. He runs in a big circle and then comes back home." Had
they expected to take the fugitive alive? "I figured he'd be
tougher than that," the sheriff said. "But he didn't walk on water
or anything. He's just a man. Our boys outmanned, outgunned
and outmaneuvered him. It was surrender or die."

Humboldt County Undersheriff Steve Bishop said, "We knew
what his potentials were. Some of it was potential and the rest of it
you might call a myth. You can get anything out of a myth. You
can make a myth as big as you want."

Jack Olsen

THE WINGED WORM

In the late spring of 1942 I slouched before the sporting goods counter of the general store in New Meadows, Idaho. I was an acolyte in a posture of dreamy, informal worship. Stories had converted me — the stories my father and uncles traded around the kitchen stove.

Home from the woods, they talked with their galluses down, reminiscing about the old homestead in Long Valley forty miles away, where as boys they caught native trout on bent pins. The water, my father would say, sweeping the flat of his hand in a wide circle, was black with them. They fought over the hook. Or, my uncle added with a wink, jumped into your hip pocket.

So I had saved money from my various enterprises — a dollar a week for the lawn in summer, in winter a dime for splitting two days' kindling — until I could stand thus, flush with power, before the oak counter with a glass top. From the jumble of tackle on display I finally picked the most ill-matched old-fashioned reel with traveling guide and star drag (a miniature of the kind designed for swordfish); fifty-pound test sturgeon line; gut leader, a book of number eight snelled hooks, and three immense, garish salmon flies.

In my memory now nothing else remains but a huge painting, behind the counter, of Custer's Last Stand, with bursts of fire and smoke from gun muzzles and twisted bodies of horses and men. The storekeeper is gone too, but for his Cheshire Cat expression of mingled mirth, pity, and perhaps a secret satisfaction at having cleared his inventory of so many misfits at once.

When the snow was almost gone from the mountains behind the mill, the war receded. All winter we had hunted Jerries and Nips with wooden guns, but now it was June and time to fish. Second grade safely under our belts, I and my best friend, Don Adair, dug two cans of fat worms and hiked to Good Creek on our own. The stream was roaring back in the canyon, milky and nearly out of its banks. The old man had warned me about this situation: it was spawning season; there wouldn't be many but they might be big.

We worked all afternoon, scrambling through willows, catching clothes and our new gear on branches, wading back and forth across the creek in shallows, our pants chill on goosebump legs.

Worm after worm grew pale and spongy in the water, disintegrated or was torn from the sharp steel, bumping along the bottom in the current. We plunged on from one hole to the next, shouting encouragement to each other. Already we were into the peculiar, timeless space that fishermen know. Heat and cold, sun and flies, scratches and sprains — they occur at the perimeter of one's mind. In the still center there is only a pure, excruciating alertness.

I stood on the old two-by-twelve plank that jutted over a deep pool. Farm kids had placed it there for a diving board, weighting the end with a heap of sod. The worm was now threaded on one of the yellow-and-red salmon flies — I hoped with this feathered serpent to gain the best of two worlds — and sank quickly. I ignored the small, deceptive tugs caused by the bait tumbling over rocks or submerged roots. At first, in wild anticipation, I had horsed backwards and snapped the leader on such snags. But in the course of the afternoon I had grown sensitive to nuances of shock. Now, all at once, the line tightened, then relaxed, then twitched again. The pull was sharp, purposeful. I reeled in and examined the hook. Bare. I began to shake, but managed to impale one of the four worms I had left.

Careful as a young priest, I repeated my cast, exactly. The writhing pink worm vanished again. Again the quick, hard pull. Something strong and alive signaled through the line. I jerked, and again the hook flashed up, bare and glinting wicked in the sun. I don't know how I breathed, or moved my hands, to thread on the next-to-last worm. I knew I had never before felt such waves of lust and anxiety. This time, however, nothing happened. Unbearable as it was, I had to accept the possibility that I had failed. The fish was suspicious, or perhaps gone.

I tried again, and again. Nothing. Then I cast once more, in despair — a despair that brought relief from the trembling, and a moment of insight. If he struck again, I would do nothing. I would wait, crafty. I would feed him, gain his confidence. One worm remained to me, the chance for a final act of treachery.

He struck. My hands were welded to the pole, my eyes squeezed shut. Somehow I quelled the wild bounding of my heart and did not lash back, though every nerve was howling with the desire to do so. After two hard tugs the line went slack; then came a series of twitches, and I saw that the line was moving through the water, upstream, not rapidly but steadily. Tentative, I leaned back a little. The tip of the rod dipped and the line straightened, taut as a wire. The butt of the rod, braced on my belt buckle, kicked me. I uttered some kind of sound and tried to run backwards. I fell off the board where it met the bank, one leg plunging into the icy water, the other splayed out on the grass.

Back and forth across the pool the line zipped, thrumming with an energy that short-circuited my own nerves. I could not make my hand turn the pitiful crank of the reel. I staggered to my feet and continued to run backwards, raising my arms over my head. Through the dark water now I could see it, a flashing like a broad knife in the sun. I gave a tremendous heave, falling over flat on my back. I heard a slapping in the water, looked and saw the fish, thrashing, bowing its body almost in a circle, seeming to walk on its tail over the pool until it whopped against the bank. With the intense clarity of a dream, I saw the hook separate from its jaw, the line go slack.

On its own momentum the trout went end-over-end and flopped onto the bank. There it lay for a moment, the gill covers flaring to reveal, within, combs the color of liver. I fought through loops of line as the thick, torpedo body flexed and sprang into the air, bounded and twisted laterally through the grass at the very brink. I ran on my knees, my arms wide for the embrace, and fell upon the trout. My nose was buried in mud, and my knees as well; but in between I had trapped that cold, muscular form. The force of it, squirming in the pit of my stomach, was tremendous, as if I had reversed Jonah and swallowed the whale.

I remained so, the breath sawing in and out of me, elbows clamped against my ribs and fingers hooked in the grass, until the last desperate convulsion. Then I inched aside until I could grasp the fish and half push, half squirt it further away from the bank. Finally, six feet back from the water and wedged between two large stones, the catch was secure enough so that I could actually see it, register it, know what I had done.

The thing was immense. Though perhaps only a third of my length, it was not all sparrow bones and spaces. The body was solid, as big as my leg, and the flesh felt hard as a rubber ball. Its jaws gaped fiercely, and the raked teeth, when I ran a finger along them, felt sharp as my father's coping saw. It was also beautiful. On top, the color of a green olive, with flecks of black ink; underneath, pearly white with just a hint of rose; and along the side, small perfect dots of brilliant blue, amber, yellow, and scarlet.

I did not know it at the time, and did not learn it for many years, but this moment — when the trout's life has flared out, leaving the corpse still glowing, changing color from instant to instant — this is a moment of the highest possible understanding, not merely of the art of angling, but of all human endeavor. It is in this moment that one has the chance to know how the needle of sadness and loss will always invade ecstasy, just at its peak. It is the moment when pursuit turns into triumph; the odd hollow at the crest of exaltation, the dark fear in the back of every hero's mind.

I screamed not for salvation from this awful truth but to summon Don Adair to witness Leviathan.

Don-n-n-ee-ee! Don-n-n-ee-EEEE! Lookit!

He burst through the bushes, dead leaves in his hair, sunburned and damp and sullen. One glimpse of his face and I felt myself tipping down a long slide away from the pure and poignant thrill of capture. I jabbered and gesticulated; he wowed and shook his head; we speculated on the dimensions of the fish, all the way up to two feet. But something was wrong, and both of us were quickly subdued. Later in the afternoon he caught his own, smaller but not by much, very respectable. Otherwise, our friendship might not have survived.

The lesson was driven home when we tramped happily back down the highway. A highway, in those days, was a two-lane blacktop usually empty but for the shimmering black pools of mirage. When we passed the Richfield station on the edge of town Mrs. Ross came out onto the concrete, hands on hips, mouth distending. "Floyd!" she hollered. "Floyd come see what these kids got! Lordy amighty!" She asked our ages, though she knew them well enough, told us we were fine little men, such fish and only so high. Shy and proud we hoisted the dangling bodies, stiffened now in a partial curl. Floyd emerged from the dark cave of the station, wrench in hand, khaki overalls spotted with grease. He regarded us, his wife yammering away on one side, eviscerated cars and trucks behind him.

"Pretty nice," he grunted. "Good Creek?"

"Back of Carlock's."

"Worms?"

"Yeah." We waited, yearning to go on and relate everything, just as it had happened, yet held back by some awkwardness of new, sudden growth. We were about to learn more still about the brotherhood of sportsmen, about how the chase can bring us closer, yet make us aware of the chasms of age and life and choice that divide us all.

"Shame you let 'em dry out like that," Floyd said, and turned to stride back into his cave.

Will Baker

FATHER WHITE MOUSE

The Americans who still hunt wild game for daily food live in two very different regions. One group, the northerners, inhabits ice-bound coasts and survives mostly on fish, blubber and reindeer. The other group roams tropical and semitropical forestland, where they take a great variety of game, including birds, reptiles, insects, worms, snails, and rodents.

Both these groups are of Asiatic origin, and are presumed to be related. Their common ancestors, we are told, took advantage of low water during a glacial period and hiked across the neck of land connecting Siberia and Alaska. In the next ten thousand years or so these adventurers crossed two continents, learning their way through quite a range of environments: arctic wasteland, tundra, rain forest, alpine slope, grasslands, desert, tropical jungle, bog, and delta. In the course of this journey they killed animals of all sizes, from the mastodon to the mouse, using spears, clubs, darts, snares, hooks, deadfalls, nets, springs, and finally the bow and arrow. Although they ate these creatures regularly and used their hides and bones for shelter and tools, they treated their prey with respect, sometimes with reverence. They told stories featuring animals or their spirits and usually they held such tales to be true, or even sacred.

The hunting story is therefore a very old, respectable way of communicating important knowledge, and I approach it with trepidation. But since, as everyone knows, both these groups of hunters are shrinking away rapidly and since, therefore, the opportunity to tell true stories about them is also vanishing, I must risk this imperfect and amateur account. It is the true story of how my son the monkey was killed by an Ashaninka hunter and mourned by choruses of Old MacDonald's Farm.

In the beginning — as the Ashaninka say — I knew nothing about the forest. Or only a very little. I knew that in some regions the rivers are huge and the people go about in canoes with outboard motors, while in others there are high mountains shrouded in fog and here everyone walks, except the white newcomers. These newcomers come in single-engined planes on days when the clouds drift apart.

The Ashaninka survive in these mist-haunted forests and also along certain rivers that unravel from the white cape of the Peruvian Andes. They are Arawak speakers, linked to the Caribbean and Central America by dugout canoe, and to the whole Amazon basin by their reliance on manioc for strong drink, cotton for their sacklike cushma gown, and palm fronds for the roof over their heads. They do not know how long they have been in these hills, or where they came from, and they do not appear much bothered by their ignorance.

In small thatch huts on the slopes above river courses, they live a very simple life, a kind of life that is probably not very different from that of the forerunners who first drifted into the country on that long trek from the northern snowfields. The women grow the cotton for the cushma and dye, spin and weave it themselves. They also dig, peel, steam, and masticate the yucca root (manioc) which they then put into a wooden trough of water. Overnight bacteria in the saliva ferment this mixture into *masato*, a strong beer everyone drinks every day.

The men make bows of palm heartwood, and arrows from cane, tree resin, fire-hardened spikes, and feathers. They also clear land with axe and machete, burn the slash, and plant yucca, corn, coffee, tobacco, cocoa, banana, and papaya. While these things are growing, they go hunting for deer, pig, tapir.

Usually they begin these tasks at dawn and work at them until the sun reaches the place we call one o'clock. Then they go home to the masato trough and refresh themselves and talk and sing and laugh until dark. In the childish and backward view of the Ashaninka, that is apparently what makes life worthwhile. Only a few of the young, mostly the men, have acquired higher ambitions. They disappear for months and come back wearing sunglasses, polyester pants, wristwatches, and an uneasy expression.

One day the clouds parted and a plane jounced down on the little grass runway. There was only one passenger. This was Big White Mouse, the foolish romantic. He had always been big, shy, and myopic, but he actually got his name only a decade ago, during the brief war at Wounded Knee, South Dakota. There he discovered that he did not have the courage to fire a rifle at other men and could not therefore pretend to the hand of a beautiful Sioux woman with a wooden leg and one of the bravest hearts he had ever known. But that is another story, and these blows to his pride did not in any case cure his foolish romanticism, which was rooted in a distant connection, on his father's side, to Quannah's Comanches.

White Mouse maintained a curiosity about the Asiatic far-travelers and mighty hunters who figured in his ancestry. Four years ago he had lived for a few months among the Ashaninka, who, in exchange for beads, shotgun shells and knives, tolerated his filming and note-taking. Now he was back, smiling and waving and bearing a new sack of trade stuff, wanting to know specifically about the hunter's life. Not just to *know*, he declared, but to experience, to *become* a hunter himself. One of his friends from the previous visit, after a shrewd look at the new machete and box of cartridges, agreed to serve as his instructor. This was Carlos, the Small Brown Jaguar.

They waited a few days for a rain to blow through. During this time White Mouse visited several hearths, drank much masato, and worked to remember how to laugh. The procedure was as follows: he came and sat in a palm-thatch hut, where people first greeted, then ignored him. After several minutes of this careful avoidance, a wife would bring a gourd bowl of masato to each man. A few monosyllables were then exchanged. A respectful belching. Another bowl. A little story, perhaps, about the last hunt. Another bowl. After twenty minutes the serious laughter began, a laughter peculiar to the Ashaninka, a high, sustained whoop of hilarity that rang clear across the river. Men collapsed backward on grass mats, rolled from side to side, spilled their drink. Sometimes White Mouse had an inkling of the source of this merriment; often he did not, though he entertained the suspicion that he was himself — his great hands and feet and spectacles — often the cause of amusement.

After several bowls of masato, he even felt like playing to this ridicule, as he had seen the Ashaninka themselves do when they tripped or bumped into things in the course of the afternoon's revelry. He sang them some of his own native songs: *Comin' 'Round the Mountain, Worried Man Blues,* and *Old MacDonald Had a Farm.* This latter number especially delighted people. The children made him sing it again and again. They loved the ducks and turkeys and tried to learn the words, but always confounded the chorus: here quack, there oink, everywhere a gobble-cluck. White Mouse in his turn grew uproarious at their mishaps, and everyone had a wonderful time.

Then one day the weather improved and Carlos jerked his head toward the mountains and took down his single-shot sixteen gauge. White Mouse, it was agreed, would practice with the bow and arrow. They set off into the trees, bushes, ferns, and creepers, following a trail that was only a foot-wide slot through the green wall. Besides his weapons, White Mouse carried in a shoulder bag a camera, film, cleaning solution for his new contact lenses, spare spectacles, pen, and notebook.

For perhaps two hours, the sun burning ever brighter through the thinning clouds, they walked. Occasonally Carlos halted to listen or utter a bird call, but most of the time he merely moved along, in a fashion that appeared more and more marvelous to White Mouse. The Small Brown Jaguar did not seem to be hurrying at all. He shambled along, pigeon-toed, with the shotgun over his shoulder or at his side, head erect and not apparently watching the trail at all. Without effort he crossed ridge after ridge.

Yet the Mouse, a full head taller than the cat, could not keep up, though he hastened and hurried and hassled without rest. The bow and arrows caught on vines and branches. His running shoes slipped on the wet rocks and roots. The heat was suffocating and sapped his strength. Blinking away sweat, he watched his instructor narrowly, trying to divine his secret. For one thing, bare feet appeared to grip the terrain better. He noted also that Carlos's toes, never confined, spread very wide. There was something undulating, snake-like, about the shamble, an even glide uphill or down. Try as he would to imitate this glide, White Mouse ended always in a gasping, sweating, stumbling, unlovely trot, and he always came last.

When they reached one of the clear, cool rills that trickled down deep, rocky notches in the mountain's flanks, White Mouse plunged his hands and arms and face in the water and moaned. Then for a few moments his impressions were sharp and clear: the mighty trunks draped with vines, some as thick as hawsers; the dense net of blades and thorns and twisted limbs; the fecund, spongy humus that was itself a miniature jungle where mushroom, moss, fungus, slug, and ant thrived.

But White Mouse saw these things only fleetingly, or Carlos was ever impatient to glide onward, so his apprentice had to scramble after, dripping and muttering. In early afternoon Carlos paused to relieve him of his camera bag, for the terrain grew steeper. Sometimes they climbed above the clouds and caught a glimpse of further, higher mountains, dark blue with distance. Many times the Brown Jaguar darted or drifted from the trail for a few minutes, whistling or cooing his calls, but returned always empty-handed, noncommittal. Occasionally he stopped to point at a scuff mark in the mulch on the forest floor, and uttered names, some of which the White Mouse knew — pig, deer, tiger — although all the marks except the tiger's looked the same to him.

When the sun was midway in its fall to the mountain tops, White Mouse grew afraid. He did not know how many kilometers they had walked in the last seven hours, but guessed in excess of twenty-five. His legs trembled and knotted, bringing sharp gasps. There was a fire in his lungs. He was almost twenty years older than his teacher, and he had spent several of those years sitting and staring at the pages of books. He stopped more and more often, covering less and less ground between stops. His own bloodstream was a continuous thunder in his ears. His thoughts became fragmentary and disconnected, like a dream. He suspected that there were snakes near, coiled in the leaves.

Carlos turned aside from the trail and pried a roughrinded fruit, like a huge brown hand grenade, from a low palm whose fronds seemed to spray straight from the earth. He popped out the segments with a knife point and cut the top of each segment to reveal five small chambers, containing a mouthful of cool, sweet liquid. After several of these greedy draughts White Mouse thought himself refreshed. He was also given a stalk from another small plant and instructed to chew it for sustenance. Carlos held his arm up to indicate the angle of the light. *Tarde*, he said, and shook his head. *Tarde.*

They went on, and within a few hundred yards they struck another steep upslope. White Mouse staggered, fell to the ground, and could not seem to get up. His breathing was an insane rasp, in and out, interrupted by occasional bleats. As his vision darkened, he perceived his companion squatting beside him. The Jaguar waited, suppressing a yawn. Finally White Mouse raised his head, whimpering, and the other considered him attentively. Then the Jaguar spoke, a rare occurrence. *"No muere,"* he said. "Not die."

White Mouse considered this advice, grasping finally the real situation, and found it good. He did not want to die ignominiously in the dirt like a foolish, middle-aged romantic. His instructor likewise did not relish packing out a corpse, or even leaving it to rot. Galvanized, the Mouse managed to get to his feet and formulate a question. How far was the nearest house and fire where they could sleep? Carlos puzzled, then arrived at one hand with fingers spread wide. Five kilometers. An uncle, a *koki*, lived there.

Once erect, White Mouse developed rapidly a system of locomotion, a spare, efficient system which allowed no hazard of fantasy or speculation. Five thousand meters, perhaps six thousand strides. These could be counted. One could take them one at a time. He began, fastening his mind to the count, and only the count, maintaining a pure faith that he would not fall.

After 924 they reached a small creek and White Mouse succeeded in kneeling, rinsing his mouth, and rising. Setting out again, he discovered that he could keep count subliminally as far as 30, freeing his imagination. Perhaps, he allowed himself to hope, Carlos had made a generous estimate. On the other hand, he already knew that a kilometer was an elastic thing to these people; it could stretch as well as contract.

He thought of the march of Progress; each stride a year. He passed the Norman Conquest, the Gutenberg Bible, the Declaration of Independence. Just before he reached the driving of the golden spike to complete the Transatlantic Railroad, he saw something in the gloom ahead. He saw the broad leaves of a banana tree. White Mouse exerted himself not to shake, or cry, and as they approached the bare, packed earth around the thatched hut where dark figures moved about a fire, he even laughed. A loud, long laugh.

After a very brief and perfunctory period of ignoring the newcomers, Koki laughed too, very happy. He and his wife and seven-year-old boy and newborn girl lived many miles from the river and did not have frequent visitors. The hut had no walls, as is customary in this place, and they could see everything the family owned. Except for two or three aluminum pots, a flour sack, and a hand mirror, everything was of wood or bone or feathers or cotton or gourd. Everyone but the baby girl had bright orange *achiote* smeared on both cheeks, and the woman wore a bunch of parrot feathers on the shoulder of her cushma. She apologized because there was only a little masato, and nothing to eat but a few snails and baked yucca. Koki, meanwhile, went carefully through their bags and examined everything, as was the custom here. He wondered at the camera, and if the contact lens solution was drinkable.

They began to swill masato instead. Koki put on his woven headdress with the three-foot bright red feather and took out his wooden flute. He tootled for a while, then grabbed White Mouse by the waist and made him dance. Carlos told the story of the day with many gestures and bird calls, and made Koki and his wife laugh by relating how White Mouse had walked, fallen, and moaned. White Mouse re-enacted the scene for their amusement, indicating how Carlos had yawned, and they whooped for a long time. Then White Mouse sang Old MacDonald several times. Koki was so excited he held the Mouse's hand and patted him on the head.

Now and then they took one of the snails from the coals and picked out the steaming meat with a bone splinter, or dipped a chunk of hot yucca in a gourd of salt. White Mouse washed these tidbits down with many bowls of masato, between verses of his song. He recombined the few words he knew into crude sentences: *Good to eat! Snails! I am big! Masato! Good masato! We sing!* He was almost crazy with happiness to be in a place where he could lie down by a fire and merely hold out his bowl to have it filled. And this drink tasted rich and complex and powerful, served to him by Koki's young, pretty wife. He fell back on the bamboo mat with a wild giggle. White Mouse decided he liked drinking her cool, sweet spit.

Far into the night they celebrated, reeling drunkenly around the fire, laughing themselves into a stupor, playing the flute, and singing. Carlos pointed to a black hole in the cotton scarf of stars in the sky. It was, he said, bitten out by a tiger. White Mouse tried to take out his contacts in the dark and dropped the left one in the dust. On all fours, he howled at the hole in the sky.

Koki played monkey, imitating this Mouse, with his strange sighs, belches, and a laugh like a snake hissing or a dog barking. With one hand he fondled the Big Mouse face in the dark to know its expression, whether it was asleep yet or still smiling. He whispered in the Mouse ear and put his head on the hairy chest to listen for messages of the heart. He was, he said, the Mouse's uncle too. Still, he could not keep his nephew awake. Mouse went to sleep with the hands still roaming over him, a skull banging into his skull in its enthusiasm, an old song crooning over him.

The next part of the story is about patience. We are not ready yet to reveal how Big White Mouse became father of monkeys, just as two hunters are in no hurry to greet one another, nor is anyone in too much of a rush to drink a few bowls of masato. As the Ashaninka say, death comes soon enough; there is no reason to hurry.

The next morning they did not return to the village, as White Mouse had expected. They went on into the forest, higher into the mountains, to the house of Carlos's brother. From there they roamed for some days, traveling with the brother's sons-in-law, young men hungry to hunt. White Mouse discovered that, although he still had difficulty keeping up, he could walk all day without falling down and moaning at sunset. He looked around more, saw more, learned new words. His companions always spotted game first, but they directed him to certain slow-moving birds and squirrels, let him shoot his arrows. Twice he grazed a wing, and before the startled quail could leave its perch Carlos blew it into a cloud of feathers and a soft, tumbling heap.

They politely gave him these birds as if they were his. He plucked the carcasses bare, tied them to his belt with thin vines they pointed out to him, and in camp ceremoniously gave the meat back to his teachers. That, too, was custom. A boy learning to hunt must give away his first half-dozen kills, so he will learn perseverence. White Mouse also plucked and carried the big wild turkeys his friends bagged, and once he gutted and packed a deer. He was delighted to perform these small services, easy for one of his bulk, in exchange for his instruction and the meat and masato given him each evening. Also — it had become a ritual — he would sing Old MacDonald every night, and now a few of the children had mastered some verses and sang with him.

One day Koki and his family came into camp bringing Carlos's wife and two sons, so with the other brother and two married daughters and all their children there were twenty or more people around several fires. To feed so many it was necessary to hunt seriously every day. The women went out with baskets to gather snails, and sometimes they traveled some way with the hunters, a few children in tow as well.

White Mouse had to laugh at himself to see how Carlos's wife, five feet tall and six months pregnant with a big basket tumplined from her brow, navigated easily the very trails where he had thought he would expire. Some of the boys eight and ten, dirty cushmas flapping like bat wings, also flew up and down the mountainside where he had only days before staggered and cried out. He could understand at last how these people had made their way from Siberia to Greenland, from Saskatchewan to the Mojave, from Cape Cod to the Everglades, from Oaxaca to the Cordilleras to the Amazon to Tierra del Fuego, from ice cap to ice cap. They simply glided, in no hurry, stopping in delight over a stray snail or a fresh tiger track.

The journey took ten thousand years. It required patience. White Mouse observed examples of this virtue, chief among which was the long afternoon spent killing a *tsamiri*, one of the four kinds of turkey, a big one that took refuge high in a giant pentandra tree after Carlos broke its wing. The bird was perhaps a hundred feet up, and the shells lacked the authority to reach it (the Peruvian government limits the powder and shot load of cartridges available to the public). Andres, a son-in-law who accompanied them, had five arrows and White Mouse had three. At full draw, an arrow had force enough to drive through the tsamiri. But the bird hunkered on a branch amid fairly thick cover, so a marksman had to try to thread the shaft through leaves and random vines, aiming also into bright sun.

For an hour they shot one barrage after another, listening as each shaft whipped through the foliage in its arc back to earth. Inevitably, they lost the arrows one by one: some stuck in the branches aloft, others vanished in the dense undergrowth. White

Mouse tried to aim carefully, and once a shot sped true, but he had achieved care at the expense of reducing his draw a bit, so the arrow merely tapped the bird on the chest, its power exhausted, and fell back. His companions whooped merrily at this turn of events, and whooped again when Andres, with his smooth, sudden draw and soft release, twice nicked feathers from the tail.

Finally Andres had but two arrows and White Mouse had none. For another thirty minutes they watched while the pair of shafts hissed into the tree and dropped back clean, waited while Andres ferreted them out and resumed his firing position. White Mouse wondered at the efficiency of this strategy, speculated on the return in protein for such an expenditure of time and energy. But finally an arrow flew perfectly, touching not a twig or leaf before it spiked the turkey through the breast. The great wings spread and flapped in surprise; the body tilted, cartwheeled off the branch, flopped perhaps eight or ten feet and then hung upside down, the wings still beating feebly, fouled somehow in a branch.

White Mouse's cry of relief and triumph died on his lips. Carlos and Andres whooped in joy. Another defeat! Hw delightful! They began to shake the thickest vines, hoping to dislodge their quarry. White Mouse helped them, swinging like Tarzan on a three-inch cable, howling his frustration. For half an hour they kept up this sport, until their arms were sore from the yanking and whipping back and forth. Andres tried his last arrow and it stuck high in the trees. Surely now they would quit, White Mouse thought. The sun was almost at the ridgetop and they were miles from home.

But when he looked again Andres had cut a long strip of tough bark from a sapling. With the bark he hobbled himself, linking his ankles perhaps a foot apart. Then he hopped to another tree, a very slim and very tall tree perhaps fifty feet away from the big pentandra. He began to climb, gripping and hoisting with his arms, his weight acting to brace his bound feet against the trunk. He went up perhaps twenty yards without stopping, rested briefly, then made another ten, bringing him to a point opposite the dangling bird. There he rested again, calling down to Carlos, the two of them laughing.

He proceeded to break out sections of branch and strip off their leaves, making clubs some three feet long, which he hurled at the bird in the neighboring tree. To take aim, however, he had to balance on narrow branches, hanging by one hand and throwing with the other in an attempt to whirl the club through a narrow avenue in the foliage. Below, the other two watched and waited, occasionally pulling on a vine to set the dead bird swaying. Six clubs. Ten clubs. Eighteen clubs. Twenty-one clubs.

When the last sunlight was caught in the treetops where he worked, Andres struck the tsamiri and it tumbled over one branch, then another, and plummeted to earth. The hunter came after, sliding down the trunk in a spray of bark dust to the ground littered now with feathers and broken branches. He was grinning like a demon. White Mouse hurried to secure the heavy bird in a length of vine and sling it from his shoulder. The firm of Plucker and Packer, he thought to himself, tired and happy. They glided down the trail and he guessed the long effort was worth it, since with the masato there would now be quite a story.

Their best day, the monkey day, began with the killing of two more turkeys. These birds, weighing between six and twelve pounds, were black with white and gray trim, difficult to see in the crisscrossing shadows of the jungle. They could race along the ground or fly into the tops of great trees. When Carlos or Andres found one they stalked it with a swift tenacity that amazed White Mouse as much as their shambling glide on the trail. Whistling at the bird to maintain contact, they crouched and wormed through the labyrinthine undergrowth, appearing briefly in one opening and then — How? Covering such distance in so little time? — reappearing in another.

The first two monkeys were handled much differently. As soon as they heard the squeak and chatter, Carlos and Andres set up a racket of their own. They clamped leaves between their lips and made perfectly the sucking kiss sound, and they broke off branches and switched them against tree trunks. Carlos waved high one of the bright red shotgun shells.

White Mouse watched intently and soon he saw the antic pair skittering through the branches overhead. They were very small, smaller than the turkeys, with long, questionmark tails. The tiny faces seemed ancient, framed by beard and brow the color of frost. They peered and gesticulated with nervous hands, shrieked, hopped and swung nearer. Soon they were no more than twenty feet away, directly above. Carlos sucked at his leaf. Andres, eyes glittering, slid an arrow across the bow and hooked it on the string.

One of the monkeys paused, sat upright on a branch. Andres bent the bow, held, released. The arrow darted up like a swallow and with a sound like a sudden, sharp sigh, impaled the monkey. She was instantly excited, gyrating around the shaft, fondling it anxiously, squealing. The red spike protruding from her back clattered clumsily in the branches.

Her mate grew frantic. He raced higher in the tree, returned, plucked urgently at her shoulder, shrieked in her ear. But she grew more and more preoccupied with the stake driven through her, dragging it this way and that along the branch. Andres waited until her fretful mate hesitated beside her, then drew again, released, and the second arrow slanted up, slowed into his flesh, stopping halfway through. Now he too spun in irritation and surprise, forgetting her as she had forgotten him, and the hunters below laughed uproariously at this demonstration of inconstant fidelity.

The death-dance went on and on, the monkeys chattering less but active still in picking and wrenching at the wicked skewers that robbed them of mobility and grace. The hunters' amusement ebbed at last, so Andres clambered into the tree and threw the small, squirming bodies to the ground. Carlos recovered them, gripped them by the neck and pulled out the bloody shafts. Holding each firmly against a log, he pressed with a hard thumb under the matchstick ribs, until the little walnut skulls turned aside, teeth bared, and the bodies began to spasm.

When both lay limp in the grass, White Mouse was handed a large leaf and a length of vine to wrap them in. But he seemed reluctant, and his companions remarked it. These *tsitsi* look like children, he said. Carlos ran a finger along the Mouse's forearm, saying, You are hairy like they are. Perhaps this is my son, my daughter, White Mouse said and attempted a careless smile. The others laughed loud at this possibility. Yes, they said, your son. Carry him home. We will roast him and eat him.

They headed back by another trail, and before long they heard a rustling in the treetops some distance into the forest. Andres produced a little bamboo whistle and blew on it, producing a chortling call. Something answered, so they crouched under a tree and called again. After a time the chortling was quite near, and

White Mouse saw finally the dark, rangy forms pouring through the high branches. *Oshtero,* the spider monkey, with long, crooked black arms and hooking tail. They were much larger than the tsitsi, and much more circumspect, moving like liquid shadows.

Carlos and Andres were alert, thrilled. They slipped away after the band of monkeys, darting so quickly through the brush that White Mouse soon lost sight of them. In a while he heard a shot, far away, so he sat down to wait, having nothing to do but brush ants away from the little leaf package of meat. When his companions returned they were dragging a big female by her long arms. More of your relatives, they said to White Mouse. A too-curious woman. They seemed quietly elated. There would be plenty to eat for everybody on this day. As there were no more cartridges and the shadows were long again, they set off homeward.

In laughing deference to the Mouse's sensibilities, they did not make him pack his big relative. Andres lashed her knees to her elbows, and with a loop of the tough bark slung her on his shoulders, so that she faced back down the trail. White Mouse, coming behind, often caught her nodding stupidly at him, her lower lip drooling blood. One forearm was lashed in such a way that her leathery palm seemed raised in hearty farewell.

They reached camp after sundown and threw the carcasses on a woven grass mat by the hearth. Then they dropped themselves on the split bamboo platform with sighs of luxurious fatigue. The women hurried to bring bowls of masato, freshly made, and to build up the fires. Three young men from another camp a few kilometers away had stopped by for the night, and these newcomers inquired eagerly about the hunt, the three monkeys, and the immense, silent white man. Carlos began the tale, which recalled exactly the wanderings of the morning. He repeated the calls of the birds and monkeys, gestured to indicate their direction. There were digressions on various subjects, some frivolous, and much banter back and forth.

Squatting or lounging on the platform, their earth-colored cushmas drawn about them, slashes of orange paint on their cheeks, this group of men looked like a flock of voluble roosting birds to the Mouse. He could not follow most of the jokes, but joined into the whooping occasionally. Soon enough, he knew, it would be time for his song. Meanwhile he watched as the women heated a huge aluminum pot of water. When it was steaming, Carlos's wife seized the big spider by one arm and leg and dunked her head-down in the pot. A little girl had brought a candle and in its flickering light he saw the knife peeling away the black fur, revealing a little ivory doll's head and pathetically shrunken shoulders.

The recounting of the hunt had now involved White Mouse, who was being examined by the newcomers. They insisted he stand back-to-back with them, to demonstrate his great height, and hold up his wide paws against their small slender hands. With his limited stock of words and much miming he told them how he was good and they were good and the masato was good, how he had panted and Carlos had yawned, how they had shot arrow after arrow at the wounded tsamiri. These tales were well received, and when without thinking he let a resounding fart there was general, enthusiastic acclaim.

Andres reminded him to tell of his son and daughter. This anecdote made White Mouse the center of affectionate attention. He was urged to reveal the dense pelt under his shirt front. The men gathered to tug at the hair here and also on his forearms. Indeed, they said, he must be related to tsitsi and oshtero, and soon he could have his son and daughter for dinner. They pointed and White Mouse saw that the two small monkeys, blackened and shirveled, reclined on a frame of green branches above one smoking fire. By another, Carlos's woman had exposed with her blade a pale, skimbleshanks adolescent girl with the head of a Moorish dwarf. Jerked by knife strokes, the head seemed to nod to him.

Everyone drank more *masato*, snacking also on the snails. It took a certain trick with the bone splinter to hook out the spiral of soft, streaming meat. There was much laughing now, much silliness, more farting. Young men went off to secure bigger logs and build the fires higher, for on those ridges in the winter season nights are very cool. Koki and another young man tootled on their flutes, and soon the children gathered around the Mouse to beg for their favorite song.

The Mouse had drunk a very great deal, like the other men, so he lay flat on his back on the platform and sang loudly to the roof. Over and over he built up to the quack-quacks and oink-oinks, but except for Carlos's elder son no one could get them anywhere near straight, and as he had at last begun to understand, this was the right approach, for among these people nothing was so humorous as failure.

He was roused finally and presented with a tiny forearm, hand still attached, smoked to a crisp. There was an expectant pause, and all the brown, open faces with solid white teeth bared in a grin were turned to him. He pretended to demur and they whooped. He accepted the arm and they whooped even louder. He tasted and frowned, rolled his eyes, began at last to chew mournfully, and the laughter came rolling over him like a waterfall. There goes your son, they called to him. Your daughter is next.

White Mouse laughed too, and as long as he did not watch the boys cracking the little skull and using its curved sections to spoon out two or three bites of brain, he even enjoyed the meat moderately, though it was dark and had an odd scent. After his meal he drank and sang and laughed until he fell asleep, was awakened and caroused some more, then fell asleep again on mats thrown down before the fire. The newcomers were given the honor of sleeping curled against him, their feet almost in the coals, and throughout the night they murmured laughter or fragments of his song into his ear.

White Mouse slept well, not tormented with foolish, romantic dreams. He knew he was only a plucker and packer, and would never be a true hunter, but his failure was also fun. These people would bring him meat, perhaps merely because he was large and hairy and would sing. They were also polite and would not let him die in the dirt from his awkwardness. They ignored his arrival; they would ignore his departure; in between everyone would drink a lot and have a good time.

A few weeks later, waiting in the village for the little plane to come, he heard the children on their way to school. They were singing.

Odd MicDunow ed a furm
Ee-yi ee-yi yooo

The voices were pure and thoughtless. He saw the small figures filing through the trees, cushmas fluttering, cotton shoulderbags stuffed with books. Unlike their parents, they could read and write.

Addonis furm ed a dock,
Ee-yi ee-yi yooo!

He thought of the plane that would come, of the other planes that flew over, bearing the Japanese and their survey instruments or the soldiers, of the road that was being built into the village.

Widda quick-quock air
Ana quick-quock dare . . .

He was all at once sad and afraid. Many, many people were coming this way; people who no longer hunted or believed in hunting or understood other people who did. Then in another instant he thought of how he must learn to laugh, no matter what, even sad and afraid. This at least he could learn from them. This at least he could take away.

Ana quick-a-quick quock
Air-dare quock-aquock . . . oink . . .

The voices dissolved into giggles, growing fainter, and then he heard the distant, mosquito-like drone of the approaching airplane.

Will Baker

THE THREE KINGS: HEMINGWAY, FAULKNER, AND FITZGERALD

Some boys, alas, do not come to serious reading, nor God knows to serious writing, precisely like hounds to round steak. Though, then again, special boys sometimes do.

I remember a few years ago reading in *Exile's Return*, Malcolm Cowley's wonderful book on the Twenties, the teenage correspondence between Cowley and Kenneth Burke. It is pretentious, chin-pulling stuff sent from Burke's parents' apartment in Weehawken to Cowley's house in Pittsburgh, dwelling chiefly on whatever were the palmy literary aspirations just then dawning on those two little booksniffs. It was 1915. Cowley was just leaving for Harvard, having already, he boasted, banged through Kipling, Congreve, and Conrad, plus a dozen other of the greats. Burke — poet and teacher to be — was contemplating his first grand tour of France, rhapsodizing about how much he loved the moon and all those things that didn't fit him out for literature, while advertising himself as "somewhat of an authority on unpresentable French novels" and the lesser Chopin — altogether things that they must both blush at now. But still, I thought: What smart boys they were! And what remarkable letters! They had already read more, I realized, digested it better, gotten it down for quicker recall, and were putting it to fancier uses at seventeen than all I'd read, understood, remembered, or could hope to make use of to that very moment. Or maybe ever. And my hat was, and continues to be, off to them.

Until I entered college at Michigan State, where I'd come from Mississippi in 1962 to learn to be a hotel manager, my own reading had been chiefly of the casual drugstore and cereal box type. Whatever came easy. And what *I* was doing when I wasn't reading Congreve or Kipling or Faulkner, Hemingway, or Fitzgerald at an early and seasoning age was whirling crazy around Mississippi in a horrible flat-black '57 Ford Fairlane my grandparents had bought me; fecklessly swiping hubcaps and occasionally cars, going bird hunting on posted land with my buddy-pals, snarfling school girls, sneaking into drive-ins, drinking, fighting, and generally entertaining myself fatherlessly in the standard American ways —

ways Cowley and Burke never write about that I've seen, and so probably knew little about firsthand.

Though, in truth, my "preparation" strikes me as the more usual American one, starting off from that broad middle ground between knowing nothing and knowing a little *about* something. Conceivably it is the very plane Faulkner and Fitzgerald and Hemingway themselves started out from at my age, or a couple of years younger — not particularly proud of their ignorance, but not sufficiently daunted by it to keep them (and me) from barging off toward appealing and unfamiliar terrains. They were novelists, after all, not experts in literature. And what they wrote about was people living ordinary lives for which history had not quite readied them. And it is, I think, a large part of why we like them so much when we read them. They were like us. And what they wrote about reminded us of ourselves and sanctioned our lives.

Reading was, in truth, my very problem in Mississippi. While I always read faster and with more "comprehension" than my school grade was supposed to (I used to pride myself, in the tenth grade, that I could read as well as any Ole Miss freshman), I was still slow, slow. Slow as Christmas. And I am still slow, though more practiced now. I have thought that had I been evaluated by today's standards, I'd have been deemed a special student and held back. Whereas in Mississippi, 1960, I was decidedly college prep.

I have also realized, since then, that I may well and only have changed from hotel management to the study of literature in college not so much because I loved literature — what did I know? — but because it was a discipline for the slow (i.e., careful). And I'll admit as well that at Michigan State knowing about Faulkner, Hemingway, and Fitzgerald, which I began to do that first year, was a novelty to set one comfortably and creditably apart from one's fraternity brothers from Menomonie and Ishpeming, who by that time were already sunk greedy-deep into packaging engineering, retailing theory, and hotel management — all those necessary arts and sciences for which Michigan State has become justly famous.

I remember very distinctly the first time I read anything by F. Scott Fitzgerald. I read the story "Absolution," in my first

English literature class at MSU. It was 1962. And I remember it distinctly because it was the first story assigned for class, and because I didn't understand anything that happened in it.

"Absolution" was written by Fitzgerald in 1924, when he was twenty-seven, hardly older than I was when I read it. In it, a fantasizing little Minnesota schoolboy lies in Holy Confession, then gets mistakenly forced to take Communion with an impure soul. Later, and in a state of baleful terror, the boy — Rudolph Miller — confesses what he's done to the same priest, who absolves him peevishly, only then promptly and in Rudolph's presence suffers his own spiritual crack-up, giving up his senses to a giddy rhapsody about glimmering merry-go-rounds and shining, dazzling strangers — all, we suppose, because he'd done nothing more venturesome than be a priest all his life. Little Rudolph sits by horrified. But in his wretchedness he has figured out already that private acts of pride and comfort matter more than public ones of abstraction and pretense. And while the priest writhes on the floor, howling like a lunatic, Rudoph slips away, having acknowledged something mysterious and consequential that will last him all his life.

End of story.

It is one of Fitzgerald's very best; youthful innocence brought into the alembic of a tawdry, usurping experience. A genuine rite of passage. Real drama.

I did not understand it because even though my mother had been a convent girl in Ft. Smith, still occasionally sat in on masses, and, I believe, wished all her life and secretly that she could be a Catholic instead of a married-over Presbyterian, I did not know what absolution meant.

That is, I did not know what the word meant, and indeed what all the trouble was about. A considerable impediment.

Nor was I about to look it up. I was not big on looking things up then. It could've been that I had heard of F. Scott Fitzgerald before. Though I don't know why I would have. He was not from Mississippi. But you could argue that Americans up to a certain age, and at that particular time, were simply born knowing who F. Scott Fitzgerald was. Ernest Hemingway and William Faulkner, too. It's possible they were just in the American air. And once we breathed that air, we knew something.

It is also true that if I knew *about* F. Scott Fitzgerald — likewise Hemingway and Faulkner — before I knew them hands-on, through direct purchase of their published work, say for instance, as I had read hungrily through some Mississippi dowager's private stacks, opened to the bookless boy who craved to read and to learn (the way it happens in French biographies, though not in mine), it is because by that time, 1961-62, all three were already fully apotheosized; brought up to a plane of importance important Americans always seem to end up on: as celebrities, estranged from the rare accomplishments that first earned them notice.

What I didn't know, though, was what absolution meant, nor anything much of what that story was about. If I had, it might've changed my life, might've signaled me how to get along better with my own devious prides and festerings. But I was just too neck-up then in my own rites of passage to acknowledge anybody else's. And while I may even have known what that expression meant, I couldn't fathom the one Fitzgerald was writing about.

So my first experience with him gave me this: Puzzlement. Backed up by a vague, free-floating self-loathing, I was, after all, not very studious then, and I balanced that habit with a vast ignorance I was not aware of. I was pledging Sigma Chi at the same time.

I know I knew who William Faulkner was by at least 1961. He *was* from Mississippi, though I had not read a word he'd written about it. When I got to Michigan State, though, we immediately became part of the important territory I was staking out for myself. He, and Ross Barnett, and a kind of complex, swinish liberalness I affected to keep black guys from stomping on me on general principle.

I *had* laid eyes on William Faulkner. At the Alumni House at Ole Miss in the fall in 1961. Or at least I remember thinking I had. And in any case I certainly told people at Michigan State I had — tightening my grip on things rightly mine. But I know I had never read anything of his, or even of Eudora Welty's — who lived only a few blocks from me and whom I used to see buying her lunch at the steam table at the Jitney Jungle grocery, where our families shopped, but never bothered to inquire about, though her niece, Elizabeth, was in my class.

I had, by the time I left high school, strangely enough, read Geoffrey Chaucer. He was unavoidable in senior English. I could (and still can) recite from memory the first fourteen lines of the Prologue to *The Canterbury Tales*, in Middle English, without giving one thought to what any of it signifies.

I had also "written" a term paper on Thomas Wolfe by then, though I hadn't read a word he'd written either. I had been given Andrew Turnbull's biography of Wolfe and had boosted most of my text straight from there, verbatim and unconsidered. I got a B.

I do remember, somewhere in this period, noticing that a friend of mine, Frank Newell, had a copy of *The Wild Palms*. It was on his bookshelf at home, in the old green-tinted and lurid Random House dust jacket with the pastel wild palms on it. I thought that Frank Newell's family were literary people because of that. And I thought *The Wild Palms* was probably a novel about Florida. In a year I would read my first Faulkner, in the same English class in college: "A Rose for Emily." And I liked it immensely. But I was surprised to know Faulkner wrote some scary stories. Somehow I had expected something different from a man who'd won the Nobel Prize.

As for Hemingway, I remember that best of all. I knew who he was by at least 1960, when I was sixteen, because my mother liked him. That is, she liked *him*.

I, of course, had not read a word, and I can't be absolutely certain my mother had, though she was a reader. Books like *The Egg and I* and *Lydia Bailey* went around our house in Mississippi, and we both had put in a lot of time in the Jackson Public Library, where it was either cool or warm at the right times of the year and where I would browse in comfort through the *National Geographics*.

What she liked about Hemingway was, I think, the way he looked. His picture had been in *Life* or *Look* in the Fifties, looking about like the Karsh photo that's still sometimes seen in magazines. A rough yet sensitive guy. A straight-talking man of letters in a fisherman's sweater. The right look.

She also liked something he'd said in public about dying, about how dying wasn't so bad but living with death till it undignified you was poison, and how he would take his own life when that happened to him, which I guess he did. That my mother liked, too. She kept the quotation on a three-by-five card, written in her own hand, stuck inside the phone book, where I would occasionally see it and feel craven embarrassment. She admired resolution and certainty about first principles. And so, I suppose, did I, though not with enough interest to hunt up a novel of Hemingway's and see what else there was to it. This was about the time my father died of a heart attack, at home, in my arms and in her presence. And we — she and I — became susceptible to certain kinds of rigor as stanches against grief and varieties of bad luck. For a while during this period she kept company with a big, burly-bluff guy named Matt, who was married and drove a powerful car and carried a .45 caliber pistol strapped to the steering column (I liked him very much) and who growled when he talked and who might've seemed like Hemingway to someone who knew absolutely nothing about him, but who had a notion.

In any case, though, my mother, who was born in northwest Arkansas, in a dirt-floor cabin near the Oklahoma line and the Osage Strip, and who has now died, was, importantly, the first person I knew of who was truly Hemingwayesque. And that included Ernest Hemingway himself.

These, then, were the first writers' names to be chalked, if obscurely, onto my remarkably clean slate, a fact vouched true to me by my ability to remember when I knew of them and by my dead reckoning that before that time I knew of no writers at all — except Geoffrey Chaucer and a part of Andrew Turnbull that I stole. I arrived at 1962, the year I would first read William Faulkner, Scott Fitzgerald, and Ernest Hemingway, remarkably ignorant for a boy of eighteen; as unlettered, in fact, as a porch monkey, and without much more sense than that idle creature of what literature was good for, or to what uses it might be put in my life. Not at all a writer. And not one bit the seasoned, reasonable, apprentice bookman customary to someone who before long would want to be a novelist.

For these three kings, then, a kingdom was vacant.

And so I read them, badly. At least at first.

It was in the dog days of the New Criticism that I read *The Sun Also Rises, Absalom! Absalom!,* and *The Great Gatsby.* We were

222

being instructed to detect literature's most intrinsic worth by holding its texts aloof from life and history, and explicating and analyzing its parts to pieces. Close reading, this was known as. And my professors — one, a bemused, ex-second-string football player from Oregon; and the other, a gentle, strange-suited, bespectacled man with the picturesque, Hemingway name of Sam Baskett — put us through our formalist/objectivist paces like dreary drill sergeants. Point of view. Dramatic structure. Image. Theme. Hemingway and Faulkner were still alive at that time, and Fitzgerald managed somehow to retain his contemporariness. And there was, among us students, a fine, low-grade brio that here we were reading new work. Probably my teachers admired these men's writing. Generationally they were much more under the thumb of their influence than I could ever be, and possibly they had wanted to be writers themselves once. (One told me that people who wanted to be writers should take jobs as fire watchers and live alone in towers.) But they still chose to teach literature to satisfy a weary system, and in any case it was in these dry classroom anatomies that I first learned exactly what meaning meant.

Symbols, I remember, were very much on my teachers' minds then, and so on mine. I was not yet *reading like a writer*. Indeed, I was just learning to read like a reader — still slowly — so that I never really got onto the symbol business as straight as I might've. But we Jessie Weston'ed the daylights out of poor Hemingway and Fitzgerald; unearthed wastelands, identified penises, fish, and fisher kings all over everywhere. From my sad underlinings and margin notes of that time, I can see that Dr. T.J. Eckleburg, the brooding, signboard optometrist, was very important to my reading of *The Great Gatsby*. He meant God, fate, decadence, evil and impotence, and was overlord of the wasteland — all qualities and identities I could not make fit together, since they seemed like different things, and since my sense of meaning dictated that assignments only be made one to one.

Jake Barnes's mystery war wound likewise supplied me no end of industry. For a time everyone in that book was wounded, or at least alienated very badly. Many things are marked "Ironic." Many things are marked "Imp." And everywhere I could I underlined *rod, bull, bandillera, worm,* and noted "Symb."

Of course, I paid no special attention to the lovely, lyrical celebration of comradeship among Jake and Bill and the Englishman, Harris, there on the Irati — a passage I now think of as the most sweetly moving and meaningful in the novel. Nor to the passage in *Gatsby* where Nick tries to say how Gatsby must've felt at the sad end of things, when he had "paid a high price for living too long with a single dream." I suppose I was just too young for all that, too busy making things harder, getting my ducks set in a straight row.

This, as I've said, was around the time I read "Absolution," and was completely puzzled by it. I was not, however, puzzled by Faulkner, whose gravity and general profusion so daunted the Michiganders I sat beside in class, since he resisted our New Critical shakedown like a demon. There was really just too much of everything in *Absalom! Absalom!* Life, in words, geysering and eddying over each other, so that just being sure what was what and who was who became challenge enough to make you beg off choosing among what things might formally *mean* — a valuable enough lesson, certainly for anyone who wants to learn about anything, ever.

Faulkner dazzled me, of course, as his writing inevitably will. But being from where he was from, I was already acquainted with the way the white man's peculiar experience in that particular locale over time begot the need to tell, to rehearse, explain, twist, revise, and alibi life clear out of its own weirdness and paradox and eventually into a kind of fulgent, cumulative, and acceptable sense. Begot, in fact, so much larruping and fabricating that language somehow became paramount for its own sake (a fresh idea to me) and in turn begot its own irony, its own humors, and genealogy and provenance.

That, I came to understand, was meaning, too.

For me, reading Faulkner was like coming upon a great iridescent glacier that I had dreamed about. I may have been daunted by the largeness and gravity and variety of what he told. But he never puzzled me so as to make me feel ignorant, as I had been before I read him, or when I read "Absolution." To the contrary. When I read *Absalom! Absalom!* those years ago, everything came *in* to me. I got something. Somehow the literal sense of all I did and didn't understand, laid in the caress of those words — all of it, absolutely commensurate with life — suddenly seemed a pleasure, not a task. And I loved it.

Before, I don't believe I'd known what made literature necessary; neither what quality of life required that it be represented, nor what quality in literature made such abstractings a good idea. In other words, the singular value of written words, and their benefit to lived life, had not been impressed on me. That is, until I read *Absalom! Absalom!*, which, among other things, sets out to testify by act to the efficacy of telling, and to recommend language for its powers of consolation against whatever's ailing you.

I point this out now because if anything I read influenced me to take a try at being a writer — even on a midget scale — it was this pleasure I got from reading Faulkner. I wrote my first story about this time, a moody, inconclusive, not especially Faulkner-like domestic minidrama called "Saturday," which I liked. And putting those events together makes me understand now how much the wish to trade in language as a writer traces to a pleasure gotten from its use as a reader.

Not that it has to be that way. For some writers I'm sure ideas come first. For others, pictures. For others, probably symbols and Vico. But for me it was telling, in words. I don't think I ever read the same way after that but began to read, in my own way, like a writer. Not to satisfy a system, but to take whatever pleasure there was from language, no matter what I understood or could parse. And that, I am satisfied now, is the way one should always read. At least to start.

In the spring of 1964, my wife and I — barely not children and certainly not yet married — drove in an old Chrysler north from East Lansing up into the lake counties where most of Hemingway's Michigan stories are set — Charlevoix, Emmet, Jordan and Petoskey, picnicked on beaches where the rich Chicagoans used to come summers, boated on Walloon Lake, staying in a little matchstick motel across the straits in St. Ignace just to say we'd been there and seen the bridge that wasn't there when Hemingway wrote about the country.

Though I was there to get a closer, more personal lowdown on those stories; stories I had been reading that spring, had loved on instinct, felt intensely, but that had also sparked my first honest act of literary criticism: namely, that I felt they never *ever* quite said enough. They forbore too much, skimped on language, made too much of silences. As if things were said only for the gods, and the gods didn't tolerate that much. And I was there, I suppose, curious and nervous about silences, to tune in on things with some experience of my own. It seems romantic now. And it probably *was* silly. But it was my way of taking things seriously and to heart. My way of reading.

What I didn't understand, of course, and certainly didn't learn marching around those woods fifty years too late, was that these were a young man's stories. And their severe economies — I think of "Indian Camp," because it was my special favorite — were the economies and silences of a still limited experience, an intelligence that wasn't finished yet, though certainly also a talent masterful at mining feelings with words, or at least at the nervy business of stripping words in such a pattern as to strand the feelings nicely inside the limits of the story.

It was a young man's aesthetic, and ideal for impressing another young man.

But I wanted badly to know why that Indian had killed himself! And I did not understand why Nick's father wouldn't just come out, while they were heading home in the boat, and say it. Tell us. Telling was what writing did, I thought. And I wasn't savvy enough myself *not* to be told. Faulkner would've told it. He'd have had Judge Benbow or Rosa Coldfield spill it out. Fitzgerald would've had somebody try to explain later on, in another city in the Middle West.

Hemingway, though, was after something he thought was purer. Later, I read in *Death in the Afternoon* that he aimed for the "sequence of motion and fact which made the emotion." Whereas, if you said a thing — explained it — you could lose it, which is what Jake Barnes says. And indeed what you lost was the feeling of the thing, the feeling of awe, terror, loss. Think of "Hills Like White Elephants," a story I admire and that students love because it seems so modern. No one says *abortion* in it. Yet the feeling of abortion — loss, puzzlement, abstraction — informs every slender, stylized gesture and line, and the story has a wonderful effect.

But the embryo writer in me, even then, wanted more. More language spent. More told so that I could know more of what went on there and feel it in the plush of the words. A man had died. And I wanted the risk the other way, risking the "blur" Hemingway so distrusted — an effect caused by a writer who has not seen something "clearly," yet who still needs to get at a truth by telling it. The world, for me, even back in 1964, seemed too various, too full, and literature too resourceful to draw such rigid lines about life just to preserve a feeling.

To me, Hemingway kept secrets rather than discovered them. He held the overcomplex world too much at arm's length either because he wouldn't on principle or couldn't say more. And for that reason I distrusted him. He valued accuracy and precision over truth, and for that reason, despite his effects, he seemed a specialist in what he himself called "minor passions." Even today, when I am always surprised at how much broader a writer he is than I remember, he still seems like a high school team captain with codes, a man who peaked too early and never went on to greater, harder feats.

Not, of course, that I didn't take with me something valuable from Hemingway, namely a deference for genuine mystery. I may now know what absolution means and why the Indian kills himself — too many doctors, too much pain and indignity. I may know beyond much doubt what was Jake Barnes's wound. But I also learned that for anyone, at any time, some things that matter can't be told, either because they're too important or too hard to bring to words, and these things can be the subject of stories. I think I learned that first and best reading Hemingway, learned the manners and protocols and codes a story observes when it comes round something it thinks is a consequential mystery. I may still prefer that mystery, once broached, be an inducement, not a restraint, to language, a signal to imagination to begin saying whatever can be said. But to have learned of that mystery at an early age is no small thing. And my debt for it is absolute.

From this highly reactive time, my memories of Fitzgerald are, at best, indistinct. I made my way through *The Great Gatsby*, exclusively settling matters of point of view and Dr. Eckleburg's significations. Then I simply left off, my memory retaining only the faraway beacon light on Daisy Buchanan's boat dock (it was

"Imp."), and Gatsby floating dead in his swimming pool, a memory I soon confused with the beginning of the movie *Sunset Boulevard,* in which the corpse played by William Holden, not Nick Carraway, tells the story.

What I *was* attentive to, though, in my bird dog's way, were the subliterate runs and drumbeats of words, their physical and auditory manifestations, the extremes of utterance and cadence, what Sartre called the *outside* of language. It is undoubtedly one reason I liked Faulkner best, since he offers so much to the poorly educated but overly sensitized.

And my belief was that these etherish matters were matters of literary style. And like all novices, I became preoccupied with that.

What followed, then, was a partitioning up of literature into Faulkneresque and Hemingwayesque, leaving a kind of stylistic no-man's-land for all the other people. To me, Fitzgerald, by having the softest drumbeats, the fewest linguistic extremes and quirks, the rarest ethers, didn't really seem to have much of a style, or if he did he had a poor, thin one.

It seems feasible that one could think that putting Fitzgerald midway between the great putter-inner and the great taker-outer casts a kind of convenient cosmos map of the male soul and its choices. Though what I was doing twenty years ago, when I was almost twenty, was just confusing style with idiosyncrasy and making myself its champion.

Not that it was entirely my fault.

My ex-quarterback of a professor (we'd heard he'd played behind Terry Baker, and so had had plenty of time for reading) had assigned us all to write a paragraph in either "the style of Hemingway" or "the style of Faulkner" — a miserable, treacherous task to assign any student, but particularly to one who had begun to write. (Though I now understand it was designed chiefly to kill class time.)

But we all wrote. And when we read our paragraphs aloud, mine produced the profoundest response from my instructor. He stopped me three sentences in and complained to all that my Hemingway sounded like everybody else's Faulkner, and that I clearly was not much good for this kind of thing.

I was badly stung. I liked style, whatever it was. And I believed I could be its master. Only I saw I needed to study it harder — Hemingway and Faulkner in particular, and what was so odd about them that I couldn't imitate them separately.

Nobody, though, was asking me to write a paragraph in the style of Fitzgerald at this time. *Fitzgeraldian* was not a word. And so for this reason he fell even more completely below my notice.

It is notable to me that somewhere in this period someone placed in my hands, for reasons I do not remember, a copy of Arthur Mizener's gossipy, pseudo-scholarly biography of Fitzgerald, *The Far Side of Paradise,* the edition with the Van Vechten photo on the front, a smiling, wide-faced Fitzgerald practically unrecognizable from the Princetonian-Arrow shirt profile on the Scribner's books.

Reading Mizener was a big mistake for me. His biographer's interest was the archly anti-New Critical one of mutually corroborating art and life. And since Fitzgerald, at least for a time, had lived a very, very *rich* life, there set on for me a long period in which I could not distinguish accurately all he'd done from all he'd written: the profligacy, the madness, the high style and helling around, ruinous wives, prep schools, the Plaza, Princeton, New York, Paris, Minnesota, Hollywood. I read the other novels, the stories and notebooks. And though I didn't exactly forget them, they just fell to his life. *He* seemed smart and too clever and poignant and overweening. But the books almost always faded back into Fitzgerald myth, into imputation, half-fact, lie, remembrance, and confession — annals where even now for me they have their truest resonance.

Today, I still believe it's as much his failure as mine that I remember as much about him as I do, but can sort out so little of his work. And that his life — vulnerable, exemplary, short writer's life — save for a brilliant novel and a few excellent short pieces, makes a better story. It is tempting to think that, like Dick Diver and Amory Blaine and Anthony Patch, he represents some promising but spoilable part of our American Self-conception. And since that is not exactly tragic, it is maybe more appealing and exemplary to us as biography than illusion.

Recently I read *The Great Gatsby* again, for possibly the fourth time (I know people who brag they read it every year). Fitzgerald wrote it before he was thirty, and as I get older it only gets better. I believe it is one of the maturest, more sophisticated and seamless books I have read, and I don't fault myself for not getting it back in 1964, since it has, I think, more to teach an older man than a young one.

And I have found its style: its elegant economies and proportionings, the sleek trajectory of its complex little story, the strategy of withholding Gatsby until his place is set, Fitzgerald's certain eye for the visual detail and, once observed, for that detail's suitability as host for his wonderful, clear judgment about Americans and American life — a judgment, Wilson said, "saturated with twentieth-century America."

The essence of Fitzgerald's style finally was that he itched to say something smart on the page, and made his novels accommodate that. It is why as a young man he was always better in shorter, manageable forms, and why a savvy young man might've learned plenty from him without ever having to mimic. And it is why I had such a hard time at first, my own ear then being chiefly to the ground.

Faulkner, of course, was the best of all three, and the very best of any American writing fiction in this century. It is not even discredit to Hemingway and Fitzgerald to say so. Liking Faulkner or not liking him is akin to liking or not liking the climate in some great territorial expanse. It seems like tautology. Whereas Hemingway and Fitzgerald, I sense, come to our affections more like the weather does, passingly.

No writer, including Henry James, minted more robust characters freshly and indelibly into our American literary memory. All those Snopeses, Temple Drake, Thomas Sutpen, Benjy Compson, Dilsey. A bear. No writer has exceeded his own natural regionalism (that dark American literary peril), or survived the codification of his style, or confessed apparently less of his personal life as grandly as Faulkner has. No one braves as much in a sentence. No one is as consistently or boisterously funny as Faulkner while remaining serious and dramatic. And, of course, no American writer this century has been so influential — impressive is the best word — both in the restraining effects of his work on other writers, and in the most generous ways as well: his work always urges all of us if not to be more hopeful, at least to be

230

more various, to include more, see more, say more that is hopeful and surprising and humorous and that is true.

I loved Faulkner when I read him first. He stumped the symbolizers, the mythologizers, the taxonomists, the *pov* guys dead in the brackets in East Lansing. He would not reduce so as to mean more. And that I liked.

Though it seemed to me, then, as it did ten years later when I was writing a novel set in Mississippi — my home too — that that was because he'd appropriated everything there was. It was even possible to want to write like Faulkner without knowing you did; to want to put down some sense of a life there without realizing it existed first in his sentences. Until the end of the Fifties — 1963 — I am convinced, a large part of *everybody's* idea of the South came from William Faulkner, whether they'd read him or not. He was in the American air, as I said before. And that went for the air southerners breathed too, since we could see how right he'd gotten it, and since, of course, he was ours.

How can I measure what it was worth to read Hemingway, Fitzgerald, and Faulkner back then in the Sixties? Influence on a writer is a hard business to assess, and I'm not sure I would tell the truth if I could, since real influence means being affected by the weather in another writer's sentences, sometimes so much that you can't even imagine writing except in that weather. And no one who's any good ever wants to write like anyone else.

One truth is that my generation of writers — born mostly in the Forties — has not lived "the same life, the generic one" that Lowell speaks about in his elegy for his friend John Berryman. We have not all prized or even read the same books. We have not all had or aspired to teaching jobs. We do not all know one another. Lowell, of course, was probably wrong about his generation, since, from what I can tell of his thinking, it included only about fifteen people. But of my own, I am sure we are too many, too spread out and differently inclined ever to have been influenced similarly by another generation's writers.

Another truth is that I don't remember a lot of those books anymore. And I never read them all to start with. A fellow I met recently, who had spent time in a North Vietnamese prison, asked me if I thought Francis Macomber's wife shot him on purpose.

And I had no idea. In my mind I had confused that story with *The Snow of Kilimanjaro*, and when I went back to figure out the answer, I was surprised. (Of course, Hemingway being Hemingway, I'm still not 100 percent sure what happened.)

Likewise, when I began to think on this essay, I chose a Faulkner novel just to graze over for atmosphere, one I thought I hadn't read — *Sanctuary* — but knew to be easy because of what Faulkner had written about it. Only now that I've finished it, I really can't be certain if I'd read it years ago or not. Odd. But there you are.

Still, as a little group, they seem to have traversed the Sixties and Seventies intact, despite the fact of a unique and intense war's being on then, and of immediate life's altering so rapidly and irrevocably. To me, they seem far away, their writing become *literature* finally. But that is only because I don't read them so much, and when I do it is usually to teach readers who were being born just when Hemingway and Faulkner were dying.

Though *their* pleasure seems certain.

I have always assigned classes to read "Babylon Revisited," Fitzgerald's bitter, touching story about Charlie Wales, the man who comes to Paris to reclaim his daughter, lost to him by the calamities of the Twenties, and the Crash, and by his own bad luck and improvidence. It is one of my favorite stories. And there is always a sentiment among students that it keeps its currency because of the Thirties' similarities — at least in my students' minds — to those years since the Sixties were over.

Faulkner still seems to excite the awe and affection he excited in me, though no one — correctly — wants to write like him. Only Hemingway, I detect, can occasionally exert a genuine and direct influence on young writers' "style." His old, dour, at-war-with-words correctness seems to ride the waves of austerity, ascending in tough, Republican times, and declining when life seems abler to support grand illusions.

As writers whose work taught me serviceable lessons about writing at a formative age, all three get high marks for mentorship — a role Hemingway cared much to fill, and that Faulkner, if we take to heart the sarcasm of his Nobel address, probably thought was ridiculous.

By 1968, when I had started graduate school in California, people were still talking about Faulkner, Hemingway, and

Fitzgerald, though primarily just as Dutch uncles to our own newborn artistic credos. We were all tiny savages then, trying on big boys' clothes. Though it was still good to be able to quote a particular novel — *As I Lay Dying* was popular — or to own something specific one of them had reportedly said and be able to unsheathe it fast. *The Crack-Up* was highly prized as a *vade mecum*, along with the *Paris Review* interviews and *A Movable Feast*.

Anyone who actually *wrote* like Faulkner or Hemingway was, of course, thought to be washed up from the start. But with their books, others' faults could be neatly exposed, crow and humble pie served to order. We were being read to by Richard Brautigan, taught by E. L. Doctorow, and imitating Donald Barthelme. But we were still interested in how those older men got along in the world where there were no grants or teaching jobs, and how they acted out their parts. One fellow in my class actually asked us all to call him Papa. And when I remember that, I need no better proof that they were in our lives, still behind us all, like Mount Rushmore in the Santa Ana hills.

Speaking selectively, I know I learned from the economies of *The Great Gatsby* how to get on with things narrative; how to get people in and out of scenes and doors and sections of the country by seizing some showy detail and then going along to whatever was next.

From Hemingway I learned just how little narrative "Instrusion" (we talked that way) was actually necessary to keep the action going, and I also learned to value the names of things, and to try to know how things worked as a way of dominating life and perfecting its illusion. There was, as well, the old workshop rapier that said Hemingway's famous dialogue, when actually spoken aloud, sounded like nothing more than an angry robot on Valium, and not like real talk. Yet locked within is the greater lesson that the page is officially different from the life, and that in creating life's illusion, the page need not exactly mimic — need not nearly mimic, really — and, moreover, that this very discrepancy is what sets art free.

From Faulkner I'm sure I learned that in "serious" fiction it is possible to be funny at the expense of nothing — a lesson also discernible in Shakespeare; that it is sometimes profitable to take risks with syntax and diction, and bring together words that ordinarily do not seem to belong together — the world being not completely foregone — and in this small way reinvent the language and cause pleasure. And finally, from Faulkner, that in representing life one needs to remember that many, many things do not stand to reason.

They were all three dead, of course, before I had written a word. Already kings. But still, I and my generation might have learned from them just what time in life our words could start to mean something to someone else — nervy business, when you think of it. They all wrote brilliant books in their twenties. We might also have learned that great literature can sometimes be written by amateurs who are either smart enough or sufficiently miscast to need to take their personal selves very seriously. In this way we might've learned some part of what talent is.

And last, we might've learned from them that the only real *place* for a writer in this country is at the top of the heap. That the only really satisfactory sanction available, the one our parents could appreciate as happily as the occupations they wanted for us — the law and banking — is success, and the personal price for success is sometimes very high, and is almost always worth it.

What I remember of them, though, is something else again, different from what they taught me. Though by saying what I actually remember, or some of it, I may say best why for me and possibly for people like me, they are three kings.

I remember, for instance, what Nick Carraway said about all our personalities, and Gatsby's in particular: that they are only "an unbroken series of successful gestures."

I remember that Hemingway gave up his first good wife, and never forgave himself for it, and that Fitzgerald kept his until she helped ruin him. (On the eve of my marriage I remember asking my soon-to-be-wife to please read *The Beautiful and the Damned*, and to promise not to ruin me in that particular way.)

I remember Hemingway saying, "It is certainly valuable to a trained writer to crash in an airplane that burns."

I remember Darl Bundren in *As I Lay Dying*, describing his sister Dewey Dell's breasts as "mammalian ludicrosities which are the horizons and valleys of the earth."

I remember Horace Benbow saying to a man already doomed, "You're not being tried by common sense . . . You're being tried by a jury."

I remember where I learned what a bota bag was and how it was used — important gear for a fraternity man.

I remember where I learned what it meant to have *repose* — *Tender Is the Night* — and that I didn't have it.

I remember that dead Indian very distinctly.

I remember what Fitzgerald said — sounding more like Hemingway than our version of Fitzgerald, but really speaking for all three writers — that "Life was something you dominated, if you were any good."

And last, I remember what Fitzgerald wrote in his notebook about Dick Diver: "He looked like me."

This is the important stuff of my memory: objects, snapshots, odd despairs, jokes, instructions, codes. Plain life charted through its middle grounds. Literature put to its best uses, the very thing I didn't know when I started.

These men were literalists, though they could be ironic. They were writers of reference. They were intuitors and observers on small things for larger purposes. They were not zealots, nor politicians. Not researchers nor experts nor experimenters. They seemed to come to us one to one. And though Faulkner could seem difficult, really he was not if you relented as I did.

Their work, in other words, seemed like *real* work, and we gave up disbelief without difficulty and said willingly, "This is our writing." They wrote to bring the news. And they were wondrous at that task. They wrote a serious, American literature that a boy who had read nothing could read to profit, and then read for the rest of his life.

"You've got to sell your heart," Fitzgerald said, and write "so that people can read it blind like braille." And in a sense, with their work they sold their hearts for us, and that inspires awe and fear and even pity. Reverence suitable for kings.

Richard Ford

LOST

Now and then people disappear in the far north and are never heard from again. For various reasons: they are lost, drowned or frozen to death. It was common enough in early days when so many were traveling the country on foot and by water and often alone. Yet in recent memory whole planeloads of people have dropped out of sight, the fuselage with its frozen bodies found years later in a snowdrift on a remote mountainside.

I remember one spring morning when a group of men came down the road at Richardson. We watched them as they searched the roadside thickets and probed the snowdrifts with poles. They were looking for an old woman who had left her house near Big Delta a few evenings before, and had not come back. Family and neighbors thought she may have walked in her half-sleep into the nearby river, to be swept away under the ice. But they couldn't be sure. They went on down the road, a scattered troop of brown and grey soon lost to view in the cold sunlight.

And there was the fellow who disappeared from his Quartz Lake trapline a few winters back. Said to be a little strange in his head and mistrustful of people, he had been long absent in the bush when a search was begun by his brother and the police. Though the country was flown over and searched for weeks, he too was never found alive. But two or three years later someone hunting in the backcountry came upon a pair of legbones and some scraps of blue wool cloth with metal buttons. Most of the bones had been carried off by animals, and it was impossible by then to say who he was or what had happened to him.

There are people lost in more ways than one. Like the man named Abrams, active for a while in the Birch Lake area many years ago. Despondent over something or other, he walked away from camp one late winter day and did not come back. No one followed him then, but he was found eventually in an old cabin up on one of the Salcha River tributaries, dead. He had cut both his wrists, and bled to death lying in a makeshift bunk.

I was told once of the end of a man whose name will have to be Hanson, since I cannot remember his real name. He drove mail by dogsled in an early day, out of Fairbanks and up the Tanana beyond Big Delta. It was sixty below zero one January day when he stopped at Delta on his way upriver. He was urged not to continue, but to stay at the roadhouse for a day or so and wait for a promised break in the weather. An experienced man, he decided to go on. He was well-dressed for it, and carried a good robe on his sled. But his dogs whined in the foggy, windless cold, and would rather have stayed.

A few days later his dogs came back, dragging the sled behind them, but without Hanson. The cold had broken by then, and men went out, following the sled trail back upriver. Some thirty miles on they found Hanson crouched beside a stack of driftwood, his arms folded on his chest, and his head down. He did not move or speak when they walked up on him. One of the men touched him, and found that they had been calling to a stone. At his feet were the charred makings of a fire that had never caught.

Though I have never been lost in the woods, I have known that momentary confusion when a strange trail divided or thinned out before me, and I have stopped there on a hillside in the wind-matted buckbrush and willows, wondering which of the many possible roads I ought to take. I have come home late through the woods at night and missed my trail underfoot, to stand undecided, listening for something in the darkness: the wind moving aloft in the trees, the sound of a dry leaf skittering over the snowcrust, or the sudden crashing of an animal disturbed.

Fred Campbell told me once of being shut in by fog on Buckeye Dome one fall day, a fog so thick he could not see the ground at his feet. He lost all sense of place and time, and wandered that day in an endless and insubstantial whiteness. It seemed to him at times that he was not walking on earth, but was stranded in a still cloud, far from anything he could touch or know. Toward evening the sun burned a hole in the mist, and he found his way down into familiar woods again.

That lostness and sinking of things, so close to the ordinariness of our lives. I was mending my salmon net one summer afternoon, leaning over the side of my boat in a broad eddy near the mouth of Tenderfoot. I had drawn the net partway over the gunwale to work on it, when a strong surge in the current pulled the meshes from my hand. As I reached down to grasp the net again I somehow lost hold of my knife, and watched half-sickened as it slipped from my hand and sank out of sight in the restless, seething water.

Poling upriver in the fall, maneuvering the nose of my boat through the slack, freezing water; or wading over stones and gravel in the shallowing current, while the boat tugged behind me at the end of a doubled rope; or again, as I floated down on the turbulent summer water, swinging my oars in response to the driftpiles looming swiftly ahead: how easily I might be spilled and swept under, my boat to be found one day lodged in driftwood, an oar washed up on the sand, and myself a sack weighted with silt, turning in an eddy.

A drowsy, half-wakeful menace waits for us in the quietness of this world. I have felt it near me while kneeling in the snow, minding a trap on a ridge many miles from home. There, in the cold that gripped my face, in the low, blue light failing around me, and the short day ending, in those familiar and friendly shadows, I was suddenly aware of something that did not care if I lived. Or, as it may be, running the river ice in midwinter: under the sled runners a sudden cracking and buckling that scared the dogs and sent my heart racing. How swiftly the solid bottom of one's life can go.

Disappearances, apparitions; few clues, or none at all. Mostly it isn't murder, a punishable crime — the people just vanish. They go away, in sorrow, in pain, in mute astonishment, as if something decided forever. But sometimes you can't be sure, and a thing will happen that remains so unresolved, so strange, that someone will think of it years later; and he will sit there in the dusk and silence, staring out the window at another world.

John Haines

WOLVES

There were wolves in the country, but they too were more like shadows — a track now and then in the thin fall snow, a distant voice, a shape in the moonlight. There were not many of them in those years, the caribou having long since left that part of the country. Once they had been common, and I was told that Canyon Creek two miles west of the homestead had in early days been called Wolf Canyon because of the number of wolves that were sighted there. My old neighbor, Billy Melvin, swore to me that one night a large pack of wolves had gone down Banner Creek in deep snow, so many of them that the trail they left behind was firm enough to drive a team and sled over.

In mid-October of one year I killed a big moose on Cabin Creek, and left the four quarters cached upon a few poles and concealed under a heap of spruce brush. It was hard-freezing weather, and I had no fear of the meat spoiling. A few days later my wife and I and one of our dogs returned from home with a block and tackle to hang up the quarters. An inch of snow had fallen in the meantime, and everything that moved on foot left its mark to be seen.

Within three miles of the cache I found a large, fresh wolf track in our trail. It was joined by another, and then another. Three wolves were going before us, heading toward Cabin Creek. We walked on more quickly as we saw that their tracks remained steady in our trail. I began to worry that they would find our cache — in my imagination I saw our winter's meat exposed by the wolves, fouled and half-eaten. Leaving the dog with my wife, I hurried on ahead as fast as I could with my pack and rifle, going nearly at a run over the frozen moss.

When I reached our small cabin on the hill overlooking the creek, I stopped and carefully surveyed the brushy flat where I had killed the moose. No sign of the wolves. I went on down into the creek bottom to the meat cache. Sure enough, the wolves had found it, and their tracks were all around in the fresh snow. One of them had climbed on the brushpile and pulled away a few of the boughs. But whether they had been spooked by our coming behind them or had found the cache unnatural and therefore dangerous, they did not touch the meat. All three of them had left the cache and gone up the creek toward Shamrock divide. That afternoon and the next morning we dragged the heavy quarters to the hill behind the cabin, and hung them high from a rack between two spruce trees. Neither wolf nor lynx nor anything else bothered the meat that winter.

And once on a cool and overcast September afternoon when we had gone to the river to check the salmon net, we heard what might have been a short cry, and saw a brownish wolf loping upriver on the dry sandbars.

There was no ravenous wolf pack in full tongue chasing the dog-sled homeward, nor a ring of bright and famished eyes waiting beyond the bivouac fire to be kept at bay by a blazing brand flung now and then into the darkness; nor from the darkness yelps and whimpers and the smell of singed fur — or so a story went that I read once many years ago.

But listen. One winter night I was awakened by something — a board in the housewall cracking in the frost. I got out of bed, went to the door and looked out the window to the cleared slope beyond the yard. Deep snow and bright moonlight lay on the hillside. I saw four dark shapes there, moving slowly uphill toward the timber. My field glasses were hanging from a nail close to the door; I quickly reached for them and put them up to my eyes. In that bright light I saw the wolves clearly — three of them grey and white, and one nearly black in the lead.

They did not stay long in the open; the timber was close, and they were soon absorbed in its shadows. But one of them paused for a moment and looked down toward the cabin, arrested by the rattling of a chain as one of our dogs came out of his shelter to look. Though it stood half in the shadow of the birches, I could see clearly the intent wolf face, its eyes and small ears, and the grey coat of fur standing thickly in the mottled moonlight. And then it too was gone. I opened the door and stood briefly in the cold on the open porch. But there was not a sound in that moonlit stillness.

The next morning when it was light I walked up the hill and found their tracks in the snow. They had come up from the river, crossed the road not far from our cabin, and gone up through the woods toward Banner Creek. The snow was loose and dry, and the wolves had plowed through it, each one leaving a shallow trough behind him. It was only in the hard snow by the roadside that I found a pair of firm, clear prints, and knew without question that they had indeed been wolves and not the phantoms of sleep.

Once before on a bright spring afternoon one of our dogs woofed and pointed its muzzle toward the river. Down there on the glittering, windswept expanse of snow we saw five wolves traveling downriver. I thought at first they might be a family of coyotes, but when I looked with the glasses I saw that they were too large and heavy-bodied. At the sound made by our dog, three of them halted and looked up toward the house. It was a long rifle shot even with a scope, four hundred yards or better, and steeply downhill into that sunny glare; I was only briefly tempted to try it. The wolves went on, trotting swiftly over the hard snowcrust, and were soon out of sight around the bluffs. Our four dogs barked and howled, but no answer came from the river.

Something like an answer came one night toward spring a few years later. We were awakened by a sound coming faintly through the walls of the cabin, like a distant singing. We got out of bed, and since it was a mild, clear night we went outdoors and stood in the snow to listen.

Far across the Tanana, a mile or more to the south of us, a group of wolves was singing. I call it singing, not howling, for that is what it was like. We could distinguish three, perhaps four voices until they all broke off in a confused chorus. Their voices sank into distant echoes on the frozen river, and began again. A light and uncertain wind was blowing out there, and the sound grew and faded as the air brought it toward us or carried it away southward. It might have come across a thousand years of ice and wind-packed snow, traveling as the light of stars from a source no longer there.

The singing was brief, a few short minutes. Chilled by the night air, we turned to go back indoors. Night, a breezy darkness, claimed the icebound river, and the only sound was the distant throb of a diesel rig on the road toward Fairbanks.

John Haines

THE ART OF PULLING HEARTS

The trapping year has its own calendar, and everything fitted a niche in the months and days. The far north summer passed quickly, a round of gardening and berry-picking, of fishing and wood-cutting — a chopping and hauling and stacking that never stopped for long under the great span of daylight. In late August darkness returned, with the glitter of frost in the mornings. Fall came on with its ice and color, with the late rush to dig potatoes and gather in the garden and greenhouse crop. The river channels shrank, the water slowly cleared of silt, and pan ice clung in the eddies. Fishing ended with the nets dried and put away, the boat hauled out on a sandbar and secured for the winter. With luck, the hunt was over and a moose was hanging in the shade. The last swans passed overhead with distant cries, and the woods were quiet.

Snow came and melted, and came again, a patchy whiteness over the fallen debris of summer. Sometime in October the first good snowfall came and remained on the ground; anything that moved upon it left its sign to be read. November came, and the snowfall deepened with the cold, falling at night far below zero. I would go for a long hike over the hills one day to look at the fur sign, or I might see while hunting late that the marten were in good number that year. At home I sorted traps and looked over snares, deciding what to do. I felt the season steady on its downward track as I paused there, weighing my choices: three months travel in the dark, or a winter at home with my books and thoughts. The two things squared off — needs and wants. My decision to trap sometimes came almost as an afterthought. I had a moose down somewhere back in the hills, and in no time a marten or two would find it and attempt to feed on the meat while it was hanging in the woods. I set a couple of traps then and there. The signs looked good, and besides I had to come and haul the meat home, didn't I? The sled was taken from storage, the harness checked and mended. The dogs were restless.

My traps were a scattering of sizes and sorts, from the small number 1 jumps I used for marten, to the larger double-spring

Victor and Newhouse made for fox, for coyote and beaver. Some of these had teeth — ugly, grim-looking things that were dangerous and hard to set. I had bought a few of them out of a bin in Fairbanks once, years before I knew what I needed and wanted; others were given to me, or I found them in one place or another. They piled up, in boxes at home or hung from nails on the wall of a camp. To save myself some of the work of packing them, I often left my marten traps hanging in trees along the trail, to be used the following season. They got a little rusty there in the weather, but it didn't seem to matter. And once because I found the advice in a book, I boiled all my traps in a strong brew made from spruce twigs and bark. This was supposed to rid the traps of their metal odor and to protect them from rust. Maybe it did, but to the marten and lynx I trapped it seemed of no importance one way or the other.

Whatever was needed, the country always provided somehow — out of its soil and snow, and from those found tools, the dulling coils and edges men leave behind. I made lynx snares from strands of old windlass cable rescued from a dump on one of the mining creeks. Time in the late fall afternoons when the long grey light filled the porch windows, and I sat there unraveling cable, working with cutters and pliers, while my thoughts strayed outward to the river below the house and returned to the task at hand. Five or six strands were about right, twisted together and knotted at the ends in a figure eight. Sometimes I found it best to heat the wire over a flame to make it easier to work with or to change its color; the brightness burned to a dull metallic blue or grey, and was not so easily seen in the woods. When I had ten or a dozen snares made I wound them into small coils, tied them together, and hung the bundles from nails on the workshop beams. I had other snares that were factory-made, with fancy metal locks, but I found them to be too long for most uses and wasteful of wire. I cut them down, making two out of one. Great numbers of snares were needed, for many would fail and be lost in the woods.

However I came to it, from hints in books, or from the remarks of old neighbors, I understood quite early that I should not trap the country too hard. There was once a common attitude, and I suppose it may still be found, that one could move into a country, trap it of everything on four legs, and then move on. But that would not do for me. Though my awareness of these things was still half-formed, I seemed to have had it in me as an instinct to care for the country that I might live in it again. Most animals in an unsettled land are not trap-shy. It is possible to catch every marten and mink in the country, and the same will be true for lynx. A country trapped too hard, as my own Redmond creeks and hills had once been, may take a long time to recover, and a man living there will face lean years of his own making. As I watched the woods and listened to the talk of old trappers, I saw that it was best to leave a little seed in the country, and to trap according to the scarcity and abundance of the fur sign. It was all too uncertain at best; too many things intervene to make any cropping of the wild a secure and reliable thing, as if life had no purpose beyond our own uses for it. That year of great abundance may return, and the woods flourish; but the rabbits will leave us again some day, and nothing we can think of to do will bring them back until they are ready. The trapping year turned on the winter solstice, a twilight world of lasting shadows and soft grey light. A cold sun clearing the mountains far to the south, the daylight hardly begun when it ended. I became a creature of the dusk, to be out early and home late, to begin in the dark and end in the dark. A trudging and packing, watching, and marking of the days. December went by, January and February. Perceptibly the days grew longer and the light stayed, though the cold often remained, deepening at nightfall. Marten season closed, beaver season opened and ran until April. A quickening came to the woods, felt in the long light and the sudden day of warmth. My mind began its return from snow and darkness to sunlight once more, to seeds and pots of earth.

And then with the onset of thaw in late spring, it was over. The traps were pulled, hung up or stored away, the snares gathered in from the woods. I made my last trip with the sled and dogs over a softening trail, and put away harness and sled for the summer. The furs were counted and admired, the money already spent in mind. Some new things learned, some disappointments.

Decisions for next year: a new trail needed to a farther creek, and a cache to be built there. One of the dogs has been acting up. So, as the sun gains power, and water drips from the cabin eaves, another year.

As I write this now, many things come to mind, half-buried under the stored up debris of the years: scraps from books, words of advice, murmurs, glimpses into forgotten days and habits. I want to make a great list of them, as if in a moment they would pass from my mind forever.

The catalogue is endless. I begin with water sets and trail sets, with blind sets and cubby sets, with drowning stones and balance poles. The vocabulary clinks with chains and rasps with nooses. The exercise of an ancient cunning, schooled in the forest so far back that its origin is forgotten, the ruses handed down by voice and page, or rediscovered by the hand and eye in practice. So innocent a device as a "stepping stick," a length of dry willow, casually dropped across the trail, to lie there much as nature might have felled it; the trap set just beyond it and to one side, so that the forefoot of the animal comes squarely down as it walks or lopes along.

I hear these words from a dead man's journal: "I will first describe the most successful set I know of . . ." A dead log spans a gully; it is so old that the bark has slipped and fallen, and the branches rotted away. But halfway across there is one dry stub standing crookedly in the air. And from it a round noose is suspended, propped above the log to bar the way. Something will cross there, who knows what; but come snowfall and a moonless night, we may find the creature hanging.

"A rabbit's head hung in a hollow tree . . ." My list tells of baits and how to use them, of spoiled fish and rotted guts. How once on someone's advice I dragged a ripe chunk of moose paunch behind me for a couple of miles, setting traps as I went. It worked, too. Every marten that crossed my trail turned and followed it. I saw that foxes and coyotes liked to dig through the snow on the river bars for a dead salmon stranded in the fall. So I buried a piece of fish in the snow where I saw old tracks, and set my trap above it; I covered it all with snow and hoped for a little wind.

"This scent is made as follows: take equal parts of rabbit, skunk and muskrat, with two mice added, chop fine, place in a covered jar and allow to stand in the sun . . ." And so the baits are refined into lures and scents, reek of soured meats, of urine saved and droppings preserved. Rich and disturbing, the whole obscene and fascinating craft and science of it, set down, stored away in mind, to be searched out one day when its use is needed.

So many intricate methods of death, brooded upon and perfected. Once in an old book I found a chapter called "The Art of Pulling Hearts." It told how to kill small animals by reaching with a deft hand under the ribcage where the heart jumped and pounded — and with a sure pull downward the heartstrings snapped.

I became reasonably skilled at what I did, almost as if I'd been born to it, and this sometimes gave me trouble. I could not avoid thinking of the animals I caught, and of my own motives and craft. I lay awake at night, watching my trail in the snow overhead, and saw myself caught in a trap or snare, slowly freezing to death. I felt the cold grip of the metal, the frost in my bones. A pair of great yellow eyes seemed to stare at me from the darkness, and looked into my soul. Very likely I bestowed on the creatures more capacity for pain and suffering than they possess, but there was no way to be sure of this. Their lives and deaths haunted me like a wound in my own flesh.

Especially painful things would sometimes happen. Once on the river I caught a neighbor's dog in a coyote snare. He was long dead when I found him, the wire drawn up so tightly around his neck that his head was nearly severed from his body. The snow and torn bushes gave evidence of a terrible struggle. I removed the snare from his neck with difficulty, and dragged the frozen body onto the midchannel ice to let the river have him. I told myself that it was not my fault; the neighbor, who lived several miles away, was careless and let his dogs run loose in the country. They often ran in a pack, and were a menace to young moose. Nevertheless, my regret over it was so keen that I set no more snares on the river close to home.

246

It was partly because of this persistent identification that I did not often attempt to trap beaver, though they were fairly common on the river sloughs. I disliked the idea of it to begin with, they were such hardworking animals, the engineers of the woods and waters, and too often pitted against carelesss men with their traps and guns, their roads and culverts. But at the same time, beaver were one of the few furs consistently worth money on the market, and three or four good pelts in those days would buy a lot of beans and bacon.

I caught my first beaver late one spring in a small pond on lower Tenderfoot. I put in a lot of time for that beaver, walking the six miles both ways from Richardson in a cold wind. I had little experience in it, and knew mostly what I had read and had been told by other trappers. And what it amounted to was work.

Snow covered the pond ice, and the beaver house was a large, irregular mound in the still-wintry landscape. I had a two-inch chisel mounted on a heavy six-foot pole. With this and a small shovel to clear the ice chips as I worked, I cut a hole two or three feet down in the ice. The brown pond water, released from its ice prison, surged up, foaming and bubbling, filling the hole to its brim. Sometimes the water kept on coming, staining the snow and flooding the ice around me. When that happened, I retreated to the shoreline where I cut some brush and poles to stand on while I continued to work with my chisel, making the hole large enough to take my trap.

I used the standard number 4 beaver trap and baited it with a fresh piece of aspen. Other baits might be used — cottonwood was best, but willow would do, and aspen was handy close to the pond. From spruce poles cut near the pond I built a rough sort of tripod, nailed and wired together. The trap was set at the bottom of this, the bait stick nailed above it and blazed with the axe so that the white wood showed through the green bark to attract a beaver in the murky water. The entire contraption was let down into the water until the lower half of it, with trap and bait, was below the ice and resting on the bottom of the pond. The water in the open hole soon froze in the subzero air, and the set was fixed like concrete until I came next time to chop it loose.

All this had to be done with care, and at the right distance from the shoreline and the beaver house, or the work would go for nothing. After cutting a hole and testing the depth with a stick, I occasionally found that the water was too shallow. There was nothing for it then but to move farther out on the ice and try again. A twig standing up from the pond bottom, or a troublesome growth of weeds, might set off the trap before a beaver found it. Beaver were scarce on the ponds, and to me in my inexperience they seemed to be exceptionally wise. Twice I pulled up a trap to find it sprung and the bait stick gone.

But I came one bright morning to find my beaver at last. It came out of the water at the end of the trap chain, drowned and dripping. I looked at it there on the sunlit ice with mingled triumph and regret. It was big and dark, and must have weighed nearly forty pounds. It made a wet and heavy load in the basket going home to Richardson over the hill.

It was hard work and low wages. Some of the old people used to say that there were few things more demanding. To stand out there in that amazing frost and handle the burning iron, often with thin gloves, or nothing at all on your hands, if the work must be done with care. Cold hands and cold feet, numbed and aching fingers. Nothing to eat all day but a frozen doughnut, or a piece of dried meat and a handful of snow. As Fred Campbell would sometimes say of himself as he danced up and down beside his trail on a cold morning, trying to stay warm, "whining like a pup" for the frost — "It was *that* cold!"

And it was not the cold alone, though that could be brutal enough. Traveling on the river ice and in the creek bottoms, there was always danger of stepping into overflow water and getting wet to the skin. Many a far North trapper could tell of breaking through thin ice and plunging into knee-deep water, of the race to shore to build a fire, to warm and dry himself. If you got anything frozen out there, far from home and shelter, it was just too bad.

I have an image of myself bent over on the ice in Tenderfoot, my nose feeling as if it was about to split open in the minus-forty degree frost; cursing, muttering to myself, as I tried with thick mitts or dead fingers to get that damned trap set just right. And come back days or weeks later to find no animal caught, but wind and snow over the set, the bait gone, the trap sprung, and nothing there at all for the time and work.

There were quiet days at home, in camp, skinning marten. The small carcass thawed overnight in a cool part of the cabin. In the morning I began with a knife, working down from the tail and back legs, pulling the skin from the cold, still-partly frozen body. A small-bladed knife was best around the toes and head. When the nose and lips came free, I stretched the wet skin inside out on a narrow board made for that purpose, and tacked it there, a thin splint holding the tail down flat.

I dried the skins carefully away from the heat, turning them on the boards, making the best of the work. And then with a few of my best furs I caught a ride to Fairbanks one morning — a long, cold ride in the back of someone's pickup, maybe. I made the rounds of the furbuyers in town, finally taking a price, never enough, but something, enough to buy the few things we needed. With a sack of groceries I caught a ride home through the dark on the long, empty highway.

If success in the woods can be put into numbers, or measured at all with its many hidden rewards, my own was never great, but varied according to the fur supply and the time I was willing to give to trapping. In one good winter I have record of, I caught twenty marten, a couple of lynx and one or two foxes. I was paid less than three hundred dollars for these when I sold them. That was a lot of money to us then, two-thirds of the year's income. And as I say that, I realize again how little we needed to live on in those years, and how important that little could be.

Not long ago, while stopped in a small settlement in Yukon Territory, I saw a local notice of fur prices for the coming fall. As I glanced over the list, I was astounded. $350 for a prime lynx! $250 for a red fox. Coyote to $150. And so on down to the always reliable marten, mink and beaver. I thought back to my own days with envy. We were lucky to get $30 for a lynx, and the average was $15. You could hardly give away a fox skin, and except for the occasional bounty money, coyote were better left in the woods. As

249

I turned away from the price list, I felt as if I'd spent a good part of my life in a bleak and impoverished age.

But as necessary as it seemed to be, and as welcome as the money was, I never really liked selling my furs. They were more to me than money — the satisfaction of a good job done, and the clean fur shining in the light. I felt the pride had gone into my pocket when they were sold.

I think of myself during those years as a passionate amateur, an intense and respectful intruder on an ancient domain. My trails and cabins were real, the dogs and much else, and I lived much of the time as if no other life or work could ever matter. But trapping was not for me the single, lifelong occupation it has been for others. I would yield to them the greater claim — masters and serious men in their own right, as many of them have been. But what I did had its own seriousness, and I learned from it what I wanted. Another lifetime, perhaps, I might have remained and let the wilderness take me.

When some of the adventure of it had worn off, and we had another source of income, I did not trap again. But it was always there, a thing I could do if I had to, though my dogs were gone, sleds and harness sold, and fur prices lower than ever.

If I consider it now, with many details forgotten, prices and much else put aside, what I return to is the deep wonder of it. How it was to go out in the great cold of a January morning, reading the snow, searching in the strongly slanted shadows for what I wanted to see. And there were books to be read there, life-histories followed sometimes to their end: a bit of fur matted in the stained ice, the imprint of an owl's wing in the snow.

A strange, mixed enjoyment. The smell of something victorious, to have worked that hard in the cold, and gotten something for my labor, to have outwitted that creature, set the trap or snare, and caught it. To discover by morning light something that lived and moved by night, and of which I had known nothing before but a footpad left in the snow.

There might come that morning after a storm when I went with snowshoes to break out a trail in the deep drifts and wind; all the tree limbs bent over with snow, and no trail to be seen, the traps buried out of sight. It was far, far back in time, that twilight country where men sometimes lose their way, become as trees confused in the shapes of snow. But I was at home there, my mind bent away from humanity, to learn to think a little like that thing I was hunting. I entered for a time the old life of the forest, became part fur myself.

Sometime there may come to us in a depleted world, the old hunter's dream of plenty. The rich country, full of game, fish and fur, bountiful as it once was. The bear, the moose, and the caribou. The woods are thick with rabbits; the marten crossing and recrossing, their paired tracks always going somewhere in the snow under the dark spruces. And carefully, one foot before the other, the round, walking track of the lynx: they never seem to hurry. Beaver in the ponds, a goshawk beating the late winter thickets like a harrying ghost; and now and then the vague menace of a wolf passing through.

This, or its sometime shadow; the country dead, and nothing to see in the snow. Famine, and the great dream passing.

John Haines

THE "HERO" OF THE EAGLE'S NEST

The "Hero of Berchtesgaden" sits on the cement floor of his welding shop in Dos Palos, California, repairing a broken John Deere axle.

The corrugated metal building is typical of the small repair shops which can be found in any agricultural community. It happens to be one of the cooler spots in town, and on a hot day it is not unusual to find it filled with sweating farmers looking for a good place to sit and discuss the world situation while Alvin Baker gets their machinery running again.

Like most welding shops, it is by no means neat and, because of the clutter, hardly anything looks out of place — not even the Army trunk with a peeling serial number: 0113552. Resting farmers simply use it as another place to sit.

There are exceptions: the crystal wine glasses lining a shelf above the workbench, their beauty in striking contrast to the blackened, greasy tools and parts scattered about. The crystal is exquisitely engraved with a German eagle in whose talons rests a circled swastika. Under the outspread wings are the letters A.H.

There aren't as many as there used to be. Over the years, an occasional careless swipe of a hand or hard slam of the door has reduced one after another to glittering bits of trash. When it happens, Baker just shrugs and goes on with his work.

Some people know him as a biker, welder, builder of houseboats, trade instructor at the high school, clarinet player, tenor with the barbershop quartet, and inventor and producer of such devices as the Baker Bead Breaker, for motorcycle tires; the Baker Quick Hitch, for tractors; or a device for removing springs from the valves of small engines.

But some of the local people also know Alvin Baker as the Hero of Berchtesgaden, the man who set out to capture Adolf Hitler singlehanded.

He's a gregarious man who is seldom seen without a smile, but it takes some prodding to get him to speak about his exploits during World War II, and how those glasses with Adolf Hitler's initials came to rest on his workshop shelf. When he does tell the story, it usually comes in bits and pieces of self-deprecating humor, punctuated by the sputter of melting metal and flashes of light from his arc welder.

At the beginning of the war, Baker joined the National Guard in South Dakota. Because of his aptitude he was soon sent to Officers' Candidate School at Fort Belvour, Virginia, where he was commissioned an officer with the Combat Engineers.

"I always like to tear things apart and put them back together," he says, sparks from the electrode bursting against his welder's helmet. "I really didn't care about the war. I only went to be a hero and to get away from home. There wasn't much excitement in Wolsey."

There wasn't much on the beaches at Marseilles, either. Baker expected to be met by withering German fire; the landing party marched in with no opposition whatsoever. All the restaurants were open and doing a thriving business. "Instead of welcoming us with open arms, one Frenchman chewed me out for getting sand on his sandwich."

He laughs again while acrid smoke rises from a crackling white-hot bead moving steadily down the broken axle.

"I thought I would never get my chance to make the papers," he jokes. "I wanted a personal parade when I got home." In February of 1945 Capt. Alvin Baker got his big break, orders to move into Bavaria and take the town of Berchtesgaden.

One of Hitler's favorite retreats, known as the Eagle's Nest, lay high above the town. In this clifftop stronghold above his villa, Hitler and his generals would make war plans and the Fuhrer enjoyed taking evening walks with his mistress, Eva Braun, along the stone path overlooking the valley.

"They thought Hitler might have gone there to die," Baker muses. "He loved the place."

Patton was rushing toward Eagle's Nest. After the town of Berchtesgaden was occupied, orders were given to stay away until he arrived, but Baker couldn't. He decided to scale the cliffs.

"I knew I could take him by surprise," Baker intones solemnly, the crinkles at the corners of his eyes hidden by the smoked glass on his helmet. "He hadn't expected to come up against the likes of a South Dakota dirt farmer."

He didn't want to take a large force. "I grabbed Cpl. Kondragowitz and moved out; I wanted to get him myself." They found the large elevator, which moved Hitler and his supplies to Eagle's Nest, stopped halfway up the shaft. So the captain and the corporal proceeded to climb the rock wall. It was treacherous, but because they could walk up a high bank of snow at the foot of the mountain, the climb was not as long as they had anticipated.

Eagle's Nest was deserted. When they couldn't find Hitler, Baker and Kondragowitz gathered what they could.

"All Hitler's personal things were marked." Baker stops welding and opens the Army trunk. Inside are a piece of tablecloth, a painting of Hitler, a folded rug, a German Luger, brass candleholders, eating utensils, a pillowcase monogrammed with the initials A.H., an arm band, and an elevator panel. "I wanted people to know that I was the one who got the drop on old Adolf." He continues the story and the welding.

From the conference table Baker cut off a piece of tablecloth with which to wrap the glasses. Everything was rolled into a carpet taken from Eva Braun's room.

Still, Baker was convinced Hitler was hiding in the area. "I just wouldn't admit defeat." He decided the German leader was in the elevator. Why else would it be midway up the shaft?

"I pulled an ax off the wall and told the corporal to watch the loot." Baker climbed down the shaft and onto the roof of the elevator. Armed with only his carbine and a bayonet, he chopped through the roof. It was empty.

Only then, Baker says wryly, did he realize it was "a damned stupid trick. If Hitler had been there he would have been surrounded by SS guards."

As proof of at least making the attempt to capture Hitler, he unscrewed the elevator control panel, tied it around his neck and brought it back up the shaft. By this time, he says, several Frenchmen had also made the climb and were gathering up armloads of Hitler's possessions and throwing them down the mountainside to cries of "Vive la France."

The corporal had found the wine cellar and they sat around the conference table and had a drink. He needed the rest. "I had been ready to capture Adolf Hitler. What a disappointment not to find him."

But his priorities soon changed. "What I had struck was a blow for the free enterprise system." He and the corporal took their carpet bundle of goods and tossed it over the side; there was no other way to get it down the mountain.

"We had to keep it from the French," Baker says. "It's a wonder anything survived."

They reached Berchtesgaden just in time to stop a fight between a sergeant and a private. The private had found Hitler's Mercedes hidden in town and the sergeant had confiscated it.

It was the most beautiful vehicle Baker had ever seen. Applying Army diplomacy to the controversy, he turned to the sergeant and "thanked him for holding the car for me."

"It had an inch of armor plating in the floor," Baker recalls. "The engine was all chrome and the doors and windows were bulletproof." But the pride of "ownership" was nearly as short-lived for the captain as it had been for his subordinates. Eventually, he says, the car was "liberated by a colonel."

Undaunted, Baker says he still felt that "I was the man who singlehandedly went after Hitler."

However, not long afterward he read an article in *Stars and Stripes:* "Vandals Destroy Hitler's Elaborate Elevator."

It was a crushing blow for the Hero of Berchtesgaden. "I thought I better stay low. They might have gotten me for looting or wanted me to pay for the damned elevator. You can never be sure about the Army."

But he still has Hitler's glasses, and sometimes puts them to good use. Baker sets the welder aside and removes his helmet. He wipes Hitler's glassware with a rag and passes it around. He pulls a bottle of wine from a Quaker State oil case.

"We like to celebrate special occasions with them; like good crops, International combines, and," he points to the newly repaired axle, "very fine welding beads."

Rich Baker

AFTER THE HURRICANE

I walk the beach at Galveston with some consistency. My path is consistent — up and down a stretch of Pirate's Beach north to the State Park and south to the horse stables. My timing is irregular: that is, before the hurricane, a month later, seven months after that, the next year. A sense of how dwellings stood before the hurricane enables me to size up the material loss, the destruction. This sense is a general one. It's not so much a familiarity with architectural styles in beachfront property; not so much a knowledge of what kind of buildings existed but rather a sense of where buildings once stood. Their absence is unmistakeable. In afterthought, trying to reconstruct a house, only the obvious details come to mind: a Spanish tile roof, the silhouette at sunrise, lounge chairs on a cedar deck. Unlike decay in cities, haunted houses and derelict ruins that have earned woeful, even frightening reputations through years of neglect or abuse, a hurricane instantly changes an occupied, modern beach house with all amenities into a ruin.

Loss is inconsistent. When destruction is so sudden, it undercuts decay. A derelict house signifies loss; that is, it has lost those aspects which characterize a home: occupants, caretakers, furnishings, decorations, heat, smells, noise. Dereliction implies decay but the process of deterioration is difficult to witness. Perhaps a gutter falls one winter, a shutter unhinges the next. Dilapidation is a cumulative process of inattention and neglect.

There are similarities between loss and decay. You can define decay in terms of loss. Take for instance food that has lost freshness. Unless the aging process adds a distinction or a refinement of taste as in a cured ham or an aged cheese, the loss of freshness signifies decay. Loss, on the other hand, cannot be defined in terms of decay.

I can identify three stages of loss along this small strip of Texas coastline. The greatest, to use a superlative to signify an absence or non-existence, is total, absolute loss. Once a house stood on this section of beach; a vacant lot is all that remains. Absence is unmistakeable to those who once knew the house. Like the return to a childhood neighborhood after many years, the neighborhood as it now exists is experienced through the memory of what things

256

were like before, a long time ago. Change is measured by a comparison with the past; there would be no concept of change unless there was a sense of the original state.

Possibly there are remnants; a toaster half buried in the sand, its cord not even frayed; a circular iron staircase leading to the open air, or a sidewalk that ends between two palms. A ridiculous scene: a couch at high tide. Domestic articles make haunting beach debris. Since beaches are pristine by definition, any item washed ashore is considered debris. Even a beautiful mother-of-pearl shell evidences the death of the creature that once inhabited it. A couch at high tide is incongruous. Impossibly cumbersome, a couch could not have washed ashore. There are likewise no telltale signs of a prolonged ocean float, no barnacles, no seaweed bits. It's conceivable that a mattress might wash ashore. Mattresses are somewhat mobile. Who hasn't seen abandoned mattresses under freeways, in the woods? But a beached davenport, a drift-sofa? Impossible. A seagull pecks stuffing from the arm-rest like a vulture pecks a corpse.

One building site retains the support poles a house once stood upon: equidistant rows of wooden poles emerge from white sand like some ancient monument, an earth sculpture in a wasteland. I admire the lean visage. In this case the foundation retains its integrity; it is true to itself: it is intact. But can a foundation be judged alone? Isn't a foundation obligated to that which is built upon it? Is it less of a foundation if it is no longer supporting, upholding anything?

In a list that begins with absence and builds from there, the opposite from assuming a whole and subtracting the lost parts, the second greatest loss after the vanished dwelling is the collapsed dwelling. Ruin is complete in both instances; likewise the essence of shelter and occupancy is missing in both. Yet the remains of the collapsed dwelling evidence structuring of some sort; only the order, the sense of cohesion, integration, is absent. Like a pile of Lincoln Logs that were once set upright and given an order, the elements of a collapsed house invite restructuring yet the pieces are not round and smooth but splintered, shattered and irrevocably entangled.

Hurricane beach rubble has a distinct character. Demolition sites in cites are barren, that is, the rubble is predominately wooden slats, plaster, shards, pipes and broken glass. The salvage workers have removed doors, frames, knobs and fixtures, and auctioneers have carted away the furnishings. But the collapsed beach house includes domestibles: rugs, utensils, draperies. The resulting heap is consequently larger, fuller, ripe with context.

Refrigerators, for example, do not collapse. In a flattened house debris pile, a refrigerator would still occupy a large, rectangular space. Even refrigerators from vanished houses, I think, must have landed somewhere intact — a garage perhaps, the bottom of a bayou, a shopping mall parking lot. Could a wind that wiped out a home disintegrate a refrigerator? Suddenly I place a great faith in the indestructability of refrigerators. What amount of tumbling, if indeed a refrigerator was blown from its location, what amount of tumbling over sand, over pavement would it take to dislodge a door, break up the metal body? Surely there must be refrigerators out there that appeared after a hurricane, appeared more or less intact — maybe a door was missing, a side dented or a corner crushed. I resolve to write my name and address on the inside of my refrigerator when I get home, not on the door — hinges are not indestructible. Below my name I'll offer a reward to the locator of this refrigerator, like the note in the bottle set to sea or the message attached to a helium filled balloon. In the advent of a hurricane I'll be able to chart the progress of a dislodged refrigerator, the errant appliance.

Earthquakes also cause structures to collapse but with a noted difference. Earthquakes are accompanied by dust — dust dislodged from ancient buildings, dust rising from the impact of buildings falling to the dirt, dust freed from plaster walls. Beach rubble is not dusty. Maybe the wind dispersed any dust at the time of the loss of cohesion, the collapse. Maybe plaster is an anomaly in beach houses. Sand, unlike dirt, has distinct morphologies and weight. Sand does not readily take flight. Even if sand was stirred up by a heavy wind, the resulting sandstorm would not be powdery or dusty. Sand is clean.

I circle the mound of a collapsed dwelling. The mound configuration is not symmetrical but the center is the tallest section. One year after the hurricane, I'm startled to find no evidence of decay. It is characteristic to find mold and moisture in backyard leaf piles. The deterioration is slow but nevertheless noticeable. At the beach there is no mold. Does the salt in the air and sand inhibit this process? There is no rust, either. The chrome dinette chair leg sticking out of the mound, pointed skywards, still gleams.

It occurs to me that a vocabulary of ruin is sketchy, as is a vocabulary of chaos. We tend to define things by the order we place on them, or by their relationship to an order that surrounds them. Take a chair, for instance. A chair has four legs, a seat, and a back, and it is used for sitting. But how to describe a part of a chair precisely? A portion of a chair ripped apart by a hurricane? It can be very cumbersome to dissect the parts and name individually which parts remain e.g. the front leg on the right-hand side as you face the chair is attached to one-third of the seat, broken at odd angles with the ladder-back in disarray since the third rung is missing, the fourth splintered . . . etc.

Consider the fitted bedsheet. Only a portion of the floral print of carnations and lilies, an elasticized corner, is visible between two nondescript masses of debris. The bedsheet appears fresh, crisp even though it is wrinkled and bunched. Like the cottons I hang out to bleach naturally in the sun, perhaps this sheet's spanking white background benefits from the prolonged exposure. How else to explain the lack of deterioration?

Another fragment invites speculation: a lone light bulb, no, two unscathed light bulbs couched in pockets of sand. The pockets were created by the global shape; over the year wind drove sand particles up and around the fragile spheres. The encroaching sand now cushions the bulbs. Unharmed, ironic in their persistence, their fragility, the bulbs offer their testimonies. Sand particles did not scratch the surface of the glass. I'm tempted to take a bulb home to try it out, to prove to myself some further irony: See this bulb? While the entire house including the socket in which the bulb was screwed has collapsed and disintegrated, broken up around it, this delicate object of light, warmth and domesticity is untouched.

Some houses are missing decks, chimneys or walls. It is the partial structure, a remaining edifice that distinguishes the third stage of loss. One house has the roof and front wall gone. Did the roof blow off in one piece like the errant refrigerator? Or, did it fall apart plank by plank, Spanish tile by Spanish tile? I peer into the interior. The drapes billow by a window; the carpeting is beige; the sofa matches. It is embarrassingly intimate. I find myself versant in the life style of an owner I never knew. I know the color and floor plan of the kitchen, the pattern of false brick paneling around the fireplace.

In the chaos of shock following disintegration, in the footsteps of disaster, someone has to pick up the pieces, try to make sense of the randomness. There is talk of fate and destiny. To count miracles, the unharmed light bulbs, re-establishes a continuity, lessens the qualifier total, as in total disaster. It is a relief to witness disorder outside of oneself, in an isolated heap of ruin on an otherwise undisturbed beach. Yet, by focusing on the ironies of mishap, the odd bits of rubble, the dislocations and chaos, I reconfirm my own mortality. This is sobering. I know I will die, my body decay, my belongings scatter. Death may come at any time and quicker than a hurricane which upheaves and howls for hours on end. Even if I comprehend this mortality, it doesn't mean I know how to prepare for it. In fact, I can only watch in silence and dismay.

Marilyn Stablein

INTRUSIONS IN ICE

Language confirms a knowledge of ice. We marvel at snow cultures — their abundant snow vocabularies. We assume a vocabulary of ice and snow does not exist in the English language. This is only partly true. English lexicons provide many words depicting the textures, movements and accumulations of ice and snow. But the majority of words are borrowed from other languages. At what point is a word, in the terminology of ice, adopted into the official, everyday usage. Or, does that matter?

Serac and *moulin*, for example, are borrowed from the French language. The words have other meanings besides those referring to conditions located within a glacier. Perhaps the ice definitions are only the third or fourth in a list of usages. Specifically, *serac* and *moulin* refer to conditions located within a crevasse of a glacier. *Serac* is a pinnacle; whereas, *moulin* is the crevasse itself, or the actual vertical shaft or cavity. I can't help but think of "Le Moulin Rouge," a painting of a Parisian nightclub where women kick up their skirts, toes in the air over their heads. Gaiety, pomp. To add *rouge* to *moulin*, adds warmth, a blush, a color to an otherwise colorless crevasse.

Moulin also depicts the way the crevasse was formed, that is, by the slow seepage of water; surface water falling through a crack. This dripping water cuts through the ice like a rotating blade. That is why the image of a mill, a machine that perpetuates a repetitive action, stimulated early glaciologists to apply the French word for mill, i.e. *moulin*, to the eroding crevasse.

To mill also means to move in a circle, an eddying mass. The word windmill conjures up both the graceful revolution of sails in the wind, as in wind curtains, and at the same time the grinding of the millstone inside the mill, pulverizing the grains, eroding a solid mass by constant friction.

The movement of glaciers was not discovered until 1861. Early geologists were correct in classifying glaciers as metamorphic rock, but as with other rock surfaces, glaciers were assumed to be stationary. As it happened, a climbing party led by a Dr. Hamel was swept away by an avalanche on the Glacier de Bossons, on Mt. Blanc in Switzerland.

The party was lost at an altitude of 14,784 feet in the year 1820. Ordinarily the white on white, the melting and retreating process associated with glaciers is difficult to witness. But forty-one years after the tragedy, the remains of Dr. Hamel's team clearly turned up at the snout of the glacier, that is, at 4,400 feet.

Calculations were then made: if the total descent was 10,384 feet in forty-one years, then the descent per annum was 10,384 divided by forty-one, that is, two hundred and fifty-three feet per year or, an incredible eight and a half inches a day.

A geologic film crew traveled to the Cascade mountain range to film an avalanche in slow motion, and chart patterns, routes and behavior of shifting snow. As the photographer set up his camera and tripod downhill and away from the path of the intended avalanche, two others walked to a nearby ridge, discharged guns and yahooed in unison. When their ruckus failed to trigger a loosening of snow, they ignited twenty-eight sticks of dynamite.

This worked; the snow was dislodged. The ensuing snowballing wall not only roared towards the camera but quickly overpowered the photographer, intently peering through his frost-resistent lens.

The film that was retrieved when his body was dug out from under thirty feet of snow is valuable today in beginning geology classes since it depicts accretion in snow walls: an enormous icy mass billows like a mushroom-shaped cloud yet moves full speed ahead until the entire screen is so white, it blacks out.

In the early 1800's, a Mr. Frederick Tudor successfully exported ice from New England. In 1832 he shipped a total of 4,352 tons of ice from Fresh Pond, Cambridge to Havanna, Cuba and points south. Ice blocks were cut from the surface of rented ponds, insulated with non-conducting materials such as sawdust and hay, and stored in ice-houses. From the ice-houses the blocks were transported to vessels for the journey to foreign markets.

In spite of the costs of sawing, splitting, lifting and towing large blocks of ice together with the costs of storage and transportation, the ice trade was quite profitable. In Calcutta and China, ice sold for two cents a pound. Even though the American ice was shipped a great distance, it sold for half the price of indigenous varieties. Mr. Tudor monopolized the ice trade for four years.

In India, indigenous methods for harvesting ice were both time consuming and labor intensive. When the December temperatures dropped enough to induce water to freeze, the operations of the ice-pits began. The ice-pits consisted of thousands of earthen pots, set in rows and insulated in the shallow beds with sugar-cane leaves, rice straw or grass. When the shallow beds were kept perfectly dry to produce evaporation, the water froze in the clay pots overnight.

To operate the ice production, on a crisp evening, with a frosty edge in the air, the ice-makers beat on hand drums to signal the coolies in the bazaar to come to the ice-pits. Hundreds of coolies: men, women and children, were employed filling every pot, which measured ten inches across, with water. At 3 a.m. the chief ice-maker would check the pots and if an inch or two of ice had frozen on the surface, he sounded the drums, this time calling the coolies back to harvest the ice. The coolies then knocked the ice out of the pots with long-handled tools, and scooped the chunks into baskets. When the baskets were full, the coolies would carry them on their heads to a central ice-house, and toss the contents into a great pit.

Inside the pit, men supplied with shoes, blankets and heavy wooden mallets would beat down the ice into a hard, flat mass. Afterwards the ice was covered with mats and straw. Ice was collected in this fashion, inches at a time, from December until early March. When the ice-houses opened for business in the beginning of May, after a good harvest, the supply would last the local British community until the middle of August.

Although the Himalayas, source of countless glaciers, were far closer than New England, no merchants undertook the job of harvesting glacial deposits and transporting the bulk back down to the plains. The indigenous ice harvested from the ice-fields and beaten into a mass, dissolved more rapidly than the frozen pond ice from America. The superior ice, it was said, was the American ice.

When Mr. Tudor first exported his harvest, the phenomena of consumer ice was unprecedented in southern countries. Now only rare ice with purported efficacious qualities is exported from one region to another. Pre-pollution era ice from glacial caches in Greenland, for example, are sold in department stores in

Manhattan. The 100,000 year old Greenland ice demonstrates a superior "staying power." When the ice does melt, crackling noises accompany the release of air compressed for thousands of years. The price for thirty-five ounces is listed as $7.00. The Japanese also import ice from Greenland. The ice, aged and pure, is claimed to be a cure-all for hangovers. Consequently imported Greenland ice is available in cocktail lounges and bars at inflated prices.

When defining the ephemeral visual phenomena known as mirage, it is curious to note that mirages are classified as "superior" or "inferior." That is, in a world defined in terms of ice, even the mirages of ice are superior to those produced by other conditions. Perhaps the superiority of these *fata morganas* is explained by larger and more realistic images.

Robert E. Peary, en route to the North Pole, confidently named a series of ice peaks rising in the distance, "Crocker Land." Subsequent efforts to find and locate the mountain range, however, have proved fruitless. The peaks, rising deftly between the horizon and the sky, were grand figments of an hallucination on ice, or one of the more concrete examples of a superior mirage.

To animate a substance, or to describe an inanimate substance in animated terminology, is fairly common. *Snow eater*, for example, is a gusting wind that has a warm temperature. The blowing appears to melt, or eat snow. *Nieve penitente* is another example. In this case the characteristic form of a kneeling penitent is equated with a certain top-heavy accumulation of snow. Usually melting is caused by the sun overhead, bearing down on snow. Wind can also erode from above. When the ground is warmer than the air, however, irregular melting from underneath produces mushroom-like shapes. The small base and top-heavy umbrella give the illusion of kneeling human figures, snow pilgrims, naive penitentes, frozen in prayer.

Movement as in *ice falls* or *avalanches* determines a behavior of sorts, a pattern of motion. All living things move, if not externally, then always internally. Being implies motion; motion implies being. A *galloping glacier* is a glacier that retreats or advances with great speed, like a mustang, covering a kilometer a day or more.

What about the reverse? It is also common to give inanimate qualities — geologic or climatic in terms of ice — to describe a person. For example, her veins became iced; her smile broke the ice, cold shoulders and the tip of the iceberg. Ice in terms of behavior is descriptive of undesirable situations or reactions. Even snow as an adjective or verb as in "a snow job," or to be "snowed under," implies deceipt, sham, or an overabundance to the point of fatality.

In the hierarchy of ice terminology, *brash* has little status. *Brash* is a nautical term for small fragments of ice that have been crushed and collected by wind or water currents to amass near the shore. Perhaps it is because the ice is crushed and of indeterminant size and shape, a haphazard of semi-frozen water — as at the bottom of a soft-drink cup after the drink is consumed — the ice loses its distinct sharp-edge. This softening must account for the term *brash,* a term that can also mean, when applied to behavior, impertinence, rashness or impudence.

Sludge, like *brash*, because of the mixture of water and ice, has inferior associations. Mud, mire, ooze and slush, like sludge, are equally the "bottom of the barrel." This is predictable if you consider the combination of the letters *s* plus *l* plus either an *o* or a *u*. Not one word that begins with these combinations of letters has a reputable connotation. Consider: slob, slobber, slog, slop, slope, slosh, sloth, slough, sloven, slow, slow-witted, slug, sluggish, slum, slumber, slump, slur and slut. The evidence is overwhelming.

When ice is isolated into fragments as in *brash* or *sludge*, the vulnerability accounts for the lower status. Ice that asserts its dominion over water, that is, ice in solid blocks and chunks, is far superior.

There are no vehicles in Tibet. There are wheels but no vehicles. The wheels revolve from the movement of fire, water, and air. Wheels are three-dimensional cannisters stuffed with prayers and relics like a Buddha's tooth. For every revolution of a prayer-wheel, each prayer inside — there are said to be thousands — is believed to be recited. To harness the elements of fire, water and air or wind to produce good karma by reciting prayers is more useful than any vehicular transportation. The wheels, for the Tibetans, are better used in praying than in moving carts or wagons along bumpy mountain paths.

There are *yogas*, physical maneuvers and practices in Tibet, special powers that if developed, may enable one to move very rapidly over the surface of the earth in a type of speed walking, or flying. Perhaps this explains the absence of vehicles. If every Tibetan practiced speed walking, vehicles would just get in the way. Besides vehicles take up road space and are costly to operate. Vehicles cannot negotiate the high mountain passes. Consider the price of a gallon of gasoline carried by pack mule to the Tibetan plateau.

But none of the *yogas*, i.e. dream *yoga* breath *yoga*, body *yoga*, etc. are practiced or learned for the sake of business or pleasure. Does that mean the Tibetans are not playful? All work is holy work, the scriptures say, but is there no holy play?

Likewise there are no winter sports in Tibet. No ice-skating, bobsledding, no skiing, cross-country sleighing and so on. Is it because Tibetans face such hardships in the day-to-day life in a snowbound country that they take no pleasure in winter sports?

Certain beasts inhabit snowy regions: snow leopards and polar bears are two varieties. Snow leopards stalk smaller animals which nest and burrow in ice. The bears fish arctic seas. These predators skillfully eke out an existence in frozen wastelands and frigid waters. They thrive, where over the years, others failed. Witness the stilled and stuffed replicas of wooly mammoths which haunt the icy chambers of science museums.

In Tibet, an abominable snowman, or *yeti*, is rumored to survive in icy regions at very high altitudes. Prints, more footlike than paw, by this two-legged creature, link the beast to man, another two-legged creature. Since the prints are located in snow, the term "snowman" seems logical. But over the years the adjective "abominable" has been consistently linked with this unknown snow creature. Considering the miracle of survival in an icy clime, the term "abominable" seems unreasonable. Isn't survival itself a cause for marvel?

Some rumors persist to account for such a loathsome description. The depth of print, for example, is an indication of an immense, weighty being. Perhaps obesity is a reason for the derisive term. Of course hairyness, an undesirable characteristic associated with beasts, assures the creature the necessary warmth needed to survive in sub-zero weather. But what distinguishes a healthy coat of fur from an overgrown, shaggy, matted skin? Is length or unevenness of hair an abomination?

Or consider the prints: longish, a recognizable heel and toes. Are the footprints overly broad, flat, huge, pigeon-toed or otherwise a sign of deformity or ugliness?

Shrieks have been reported. Feces photographed. But is an eerie cry abominable? Is one feces specimen more odious than another? Turds are turds. Since heat conducts, ripens odors, frozen turds probably do not even stink.

The beast must prey on other creatures since no plants grow in icy altitudes to support a herbivore. Is fear the abomination? Fear of some weighty, shaggy, clumsy, fleeting — since none have been captured, killed or retrieved — carnivore.

I remember a visit to the zoo. "Do Not Feed the Animals," warned signs outside the primate area.

Mother looked at the sign, sighed and looked at me. "To feed is to supply sustenance of some kind," she said. "Surely ice doesn't count as sustenance. What's water anyway . . . what harm is a little water?"

Of course, I agreed.

We took the ice cubes from our waxed-paper soft-drink cups and took turns throwing in a cube. Our noses pressed the wire, chain-link fence.

A monkey spotted the white chunks, swooped down from his branch, picked up a piece of ice and popped it into his mouth.

What did the monkey think of the ice as it melted into not much more than saliva? Do monkeys have saliva? Is it white? Did he feel the cold? Did he shiver? Do monkeys shiver?

As quickly as he popped the cubes into his mouth, they melted into nothingness. He grew perplexed. He tested the cubes, shoving them around, sniffing, batting the ice back and forth between his hands.

When all the ice had melted, he looked up as if to ask us, "What, no more?"

Marilyn Stablein

THE BARN AND THE BEES

My parents and I were driving along Boone's Ferry Road early one Sunday morning with a ripe load of horse manure in the back of the family station wagon when we saw a hand-lettered sign nailed to a telephone pole: "2 x 4 is 25 cents, 2 x 6 is 50 cents." There was so much fog on the glass we had to open the side window to see an arrow in red crayon pointing up a road to the west. Even the steam from the hot stuff behind us couldn't blunt the chill that went through me. Up that road was a barn I had admired since I was a child, and I knew it had fallen. In the same moment I felt the thrill of honest greed.

Twenty minutes later I stood alone in the jumbled ruin of red boards, straw, and the sweet stink of old dairy. No one was around, except the swallows careening overhead where the eaves had been and their nests hung once. Like me, they clung to the vacancy of the familiar. Blackberry vines had held the barn upright for years, and now that it was down the vines trailed over the tangle, dangling in a veil from the south and east walls that still stood crooked somehow. I scrambled up a slanted timber wedged into the pile to survey the place. The deep litter I stood on had a fragile architecture to it, not quite fallen clear down in a crisscross balance of long sagging rafters propped in chaos, with bent tin roofing over half-collapsed rooms where the side bays had been, the rusted stanchions wrenched into twisted contraptions, and everywhere tangles of baling wire and splintered fir siding. The heap made a ticking sound as it settled in the heat. There seemed to be too much light on it all, the fragrant old mystery bleached away and done. Then I heard a low hum from the dark southeast corner.

Lifting a jagged sheet of tin aside, I clambered into the long tunnel of slanted posts and rafters down the nave, stepping from one nail-studded board to the next, putting my body through a snake's contortions without a snake's grace, every pop and squeak of wood on wood a warning, every ping of corrugated tin in the deadfall. I passed a boat filled with hay, its bow beached on a bale that sprouted green, its keel turned to earth. I passed a wagon with no wheels, split in half where a beam had dropped through its bed to the floor. Mice scattered before me, and a bumblebee struggled out from a ball of wool, its nest that had fallen gently to a new niche in the rusted skull-hollow of a drinking pan. I had to inhabit what was left of this palace before it came all the way down, and the bees were beckoning me from their half-shattered hive now thirty feet ahead.

Others were in church. I was in a trance. In the honey-sweet gloom of the back corner I stepped up onto a patch of floor. This dusty vestibule had the privacy of prayer, the solitude of visible history. The combs hung down from a four-by-four rough-cut brace on the wall, and the bees massed quietly there, working. The small back door opened onto acres of blackberry, and a thorned vine held it ajar with a double turn around the knob. Inside, a scatter of oats glittered on the threshold. A wheelbarrow stood mounded with jars. A curry comb worn down to nothing hung from a nail on the wall where each knot-hole was mended with the rusted lid from a tin can. If I stirred, my boot would crush broken glass, so I held still and watched the bees climb each others' backs to toil, to turn over pollen and flower-sap in their mouths in a flurry of wings and touch. The blunt, heavier shapes of a few drones waited among them to be fed — so inept they could not lick their own food from underfoot. The queen must have been on the inner combs, laying like mad at this season for the main summer honeyflow. From one mating flight, one meeting with a drone, she bore children all her life. If I stood in the dark, they would not bother me. It was light and work each gave her custom to, spinning out through the open door on the quickly tightening spiral of her errand.

I crawled out and away, the fragrance of the hive, the quiet of that dark corner filling me. Across a field, in what must originally have been the farmhouse, a neighbor of the barn in a heap gave me its owner's phone number, along with a sad look. "They finally got it," she said through the screen door, as she brushed a wisp of hair aside. "I was hoping they'd forget to." She was going to say more, but a child shouted and she closed the door instead. Back home, I called and asked for Peter. It's best not to talk about money at first.

"Howdy," I said. "I was wondering about your plans for the scrap from that barn off Boone's Ferry Road."

"Yeah? Well I don't want anyone in there, the shape it's in. On account of my liability."

"I can understand that, but I noticed some boards piled out in front, and there *was* a sign about it."

"Sign? I didn't put up any sign. Must have been the guy I hired to tear it down. We're stalled on account of some bees in there."

"I can take care of those bees for you."

"Listen, you take care of those bees, and you can take anything you like. I've got to get everything out of there. Some guy complained to the County about it being a fire hazard, and they gave me a week. But do you really think there's anything worth saving? What do you want it for?"

"I want to build a barn."

In the short light at five a.m. I was there in my bee-gloves and veil, mechanic's coveralls and tall rubber boots, threading my way down the tunnel of boards and tin by memory and luck. I carried a hive-box and a spray bottle of water and a soft brush. Bees never sleep, but they generally don't fly when they're chilled. I found them as they would be at that hour, packed together on the combs with a low, sociable hum. Once the sun hit that wall behind them, they would fly.

I stepped on the wrong board, the architectural balance above me groaned and shifted, a dozen bees lifted off with an altered pitch to their buzz, and the whole hive quickened. In their sudden, ordered turmoil, I was seeing a mood-change inside a friend's brain, something naked and fair. I waited without a word. Bits of straw flickered away as the guard-bees settled back onto the wall and climbed into the mass that quieted with their return. The warm scent of wax and honey came my way. Through the doorway, mist settled over the gray sweep of the blackberry meadow. It was in full blossom, and the bees must have been working it hard. I could see the white wax over capped honey cells whenever the mass of bees parted like a retreating wave from the comb's upper rim. There would be sweet enough to keep them alive once I dampened their wings, carved away the comb entire, and swept the chilled bees into the hive-box I carried. Through my veil I saw them in the cleft they had chosen, their little city compact with purpose in a neglected place.

By dawn I had them boxed, sealed in and humming in the shade beside my car. A few had escaped my work, had followed me, then doubled back with the buzz of anger sinking to a different note. No one is quite sure what stray bees do when the home hive is destroyed and the swarm disappears without them. They might follow other bees to a foreign hive and try to take on its scent and be admitted. Or they might hang around the old vacancy, working the local blossoms and resting under a leaf until their wings are too frayed to hold in the air. Bees die when they sting, or when work finally shatters their wings.

Several days after the wall that had harbored the hive came down, I would still see a few bees hovering precisely where the combs had been. At midafternoon I would turn over a board with the print of wax across its grain — some panel or brace that had boxed in the hive — and find a solitary bee fingering the pattern like a disbelieving relative reading by braille the name new-carved on a tombstone. I shared their nostalgia for a shape in the air. And so did others, in their own ways. As I worked on the lumberpile, neighbors came by in little groups or alone to leave with me some story about the barn, and to seek some scrap of it to carry away.

First came three boys to watch me work, to pick their way around the heap so glorious with its ramps and tunnels, its pedestals of triumph and hollows of secrecy. When the pile shifted under them, they leaped off and skittered away, then came back with their father from across the road. They wanted a treehouse made, and he wanted to see the barn. He was in his yard-work clothes, not in a hurry.

"You know the woman that used to live in that old farmhouse and own this barn was a strange one," he said to me, while the boys scattered again toward the ruin. "She'd show up at our place every fall to trade walnuts for whatever we had to trade. We always took the unshelled ones, her hands were so dirty. Or maybe they were dark from the hulling. She had gunny sacks tied around her feet with baling wire."

"When was this?" I asked.

"Before they were born." He gestured toward the three boys now waltzing along a beam thrust like a bowsprit from the pile. "Looks like I'd best get them home."

271

The four of them went away carrying the small roof from the ventilator cupola. It had somehow stayed intact, riding the whole structure down as it fell, and ending perched on top of the heap. As they drifted across the road, they looked like four posts under the Parthenon.

Next came a gentleman in pressed yellow slacks and a shirt with a little alligator over his heart. His hands were clean and thin. He watched me labor for a while in silence.

"Hard work for a Sunday," he said. I stood up and let the sweat cool on my face.

"Well, I wanted to save some of these boards," I said. "The barn's gone, but there's some lumber left."

"Eyesore. I'm glad to see it finally come down." I looked at the mouth that had said this. I had nothing to say. Away across the pasture a solitary maple stood dark in its neglected shade.

"But say," he said, "I need a board to repair the rail on my deck — two-by-four, about twelve feet long . . ." He skirted carefully around the perimeter of the pile, picking at the ends of likely boards clinched firmly into the weave of collapse, now and then looking my way appealingly. I knew who had called the County about the fire hazard, about the old barn settling too slowly deeper into moss and blackberry, the stack rattling in winter storms and the tin roof pinging through each summer's heat. I pulled an eighteen-foot clear-grained length of fir from the stack I had plucked of nails, and he went off with it at an awkward march, holding the board far out to the side of his body with his fingertips. Soon I paused in my work to hear the whine and ring of his powersaw toiling through the wood. I counted seven cuts, then silence.

The woman who had bought the farmhouse, who had given me the owner's name, came down to offer a glass of lemonade. The cold sweat from the glass ran down my wrist.

"I never let my kids go inside." She squinted into the patches of darkness where walls still leaned together. "They get into enough trouble as it is. But I always felt we owned the barn, along with the house — even though we didn't. You should have seen the place when we moved in; a car in the back yard filled with apples; a drawer in the kitchen packed with red rubber bands, and another with brown ones; mice in the walls and a possum in the attic. The house had been empty a long time too."

I set the glass down, and bent to my work, wrestling heroically with a long two-by-six mired deep in the hay.

"Are you going to keep these Mason jars?" She nodded toward a dozen blued quarts lolling in the grass.

"You'll use them before I do." I shook the sweat out of my eyes to watch her cradle eleven of them somehow in her arms, with one clenched tight under her chin. She started out with a crooked smile to walk hunched and slow up the lane toward a yard littered with bright toys.

"I'll come back for the glass," she called over her shoulder. Then she turned slowly, like a ship halfway out of harbor. "Or bring it up to the house for a refill."

The afternoon was a long season of history, a plunge into the archeological midden of my own midwestern ancestors, a seduction of my hands by wood the flanks of the milkers polished. What was a stall of straw but a nest for stories, even under the naked, open light of the sky? Burlap lace around a jar blue with time held something without a name but kin to pleasure. I had to stop, I had to walk away from it, to visit the outlines of the pasture and the farm, to carry the glass to the farmhouse so I could know the rooms of its people, to walk again and rest from the persistent unity of the ruin, to lie down in purple vetch and listen to bee-women sip and dangle on the small blossoms. When the sun woke me and I stood up, there was a shape of my own dwelling in the grass.

By now I had a stack of white, six-by-six posts that had held the stanchions in a row, a heap of two-by-fours in random lengths dried hard as iron, twenty-four sheets of tin rusted on the bottom side from generations of cattle-steam and piss in hay, a whole raft of two-by-sixes in twenty-foot lengths, each dried and set precisely to the same roof-sag. When I built my barn, I would turn them over so the roof began with a slight swell. Over time, they would sag back flat and right.

I was just admiring my favorite stick — the four-by-eight haybeam from the gambrel's point, complete with a patch of lichen where it had thrust out into the weather, and a rusted iron ring bolted through that had pulleyed up ton after ton of feed — when a red sports car came creeping along the nail-studded road.

I glanced at the clouds reflected in the windshield when it stopped, then lowered the beam to the ground.

The driver waited inside, watching me, or finishing a song on the radio, just long enough to show he was in no hurry, then climbed out slow, slid his hands into his pockets, and looked at the sky.

"Name's Peter. Finding anything good?" He stood by his car.

I pointed a crowbar at the hay-beam. "Just what you see: lumber with rot on both ends but some good wood in the middle."

"What about the bees?"

Right there." I aimed the crowbar at the hive-box humming quietly in the blackberry shade. "I caught all but a few."

"A few?"

"Five."

He nodded slowly, like a bear with ponderous thoughts. "I think I might want those doors," he said, nodding toward the two big wagon doors slapped face-down where they had fallen. He started gingerly around the heap's perimeter in his rubber running shoes. "My wife likes antique stuff — you found anything like that? It doesn't have to be pretty, so long as it's old. My own idea of old is black-and-white TV, but she sees it different."

"There's a wheelbarrow with the bottom rotted out and one handle gone — something like that?"

"She'd love it. Could you wheel it out and leave it by the doors? The County's given me a week to scrape this down to bare dirt. Anything left after Friday will cost me a fine. And the man I hired to take it all down should be along soon. He may have stuff he wants too." He looked at the sky. A quick rain had begun, and he backed away toward the car. "Try to have everything you want out pretty quick. And don't get hurt."

He paused to say more, looked at the ground, then turned and folded himself carefully into the car. The crowbar was warm in my hand, and slick with sweat. The rain felt good. The lights of the car came on, flickered to high-beam, then died as the windshield wipers started to wag. He backed out the long track across the field, his tires spinning a few times on the wet grass.

A cloud moved and sunlight rippled glistening across the field after him. The lumber around me began to steam. My footing was slick but the air was clean. As I worked with steel-hafted hammer in my right hand and crowbar in my left, swinging each long board through the loving rhythm of lift, pound and tease, roll and balance, flip, shove and drop-slap to the stack of clean lumber, I heard the unique machine of the fallen barn flex in the heat, the rippled ping when tin changes its mind, the shriek of a sixteen-penny nail jerked from the sheath rust wedded it to for seventy years, the see-saw rub and grabble of a rafter waggled from the heap, and in a pause the plop of sweat sliding off my elbow to a stone. Before me loomed the raw, steaming tangle of chaos with a history of order, a flavor of tradition, the stiff, wise fiber of old growth; behind me, stacks of lumber rose with a new barn intrinsic in each board, in the rivet of right work I had yet to do to knit it all together again. My hands were twin apprentices to the wreck, to the knowing fragments of joinery still buried there.

As I curled my spine over the tangle to grasp a clear length of one-by-twelve fir, two causes made my task hard: the persistence of the builder, circa 1910, and the haste of the wrecker, 1980. The builder had known how to make things hold, clinching nails that bound the battens down, and pinning the whole fabric of the walls with extra braces scarfed to the frame wherever it might be vulnerable to the wind's pivot or gravity's drag. The wrecker, on the other hand, was in a hurry.

Maybe he heard the bees when he first drove up, and decided not to go inside at all. Maybe the doors were so woven with thumb-thick ropes of blackberry he didn't take the time to pry them apart and find the mahogany skiff locked together with bronze screws, or the wagon bed, the kerosene lamp, its wick last trimmed before he was born, now crushed flat under a three-hundred-pound stick of fir. He never saw the stack of two-by-six spare joists, ten foot long and clear. Those the farmer had set aside for years of so much hay even this cathedral wasn't ample enough. With them he would lay an extra hay-floor over the stanchion alley. Instead, the wrecker threw a grappling hook high over the roof an l pulled it all down. That must have brought out the bees to kiss l im in the eyes. I found the hook abandoned — it had stabbed into ι punky rafter with twenty feet of rope dangling where the wrecker had cut it away and fled. I coiled the rope and hung the hook from a volunteer cherry at the field's edge.

Somewhere way down Boone's Ferry Road I heard the low hum of a big bike coming. I heard it slow for the turn, and accelerate with a roar the last two-hundred yards up the side-road toward me. Then it came popping and growling over the field. A nail came out for the crowbar and flipped past my face. I was listening too hard and not watching what I did. I turned.

My face was small and double in the dark glasses on the upturned face of the Gypsy Joker idling his big Harley ten feet away. On the shoulder of his black jacket were stitched the red names of his friends or victims: *Rick, Joe, Rollo.* When the engine rumbled and faded and coughed dead, the black leather of his gloves creaked as he flexed his right hand free.

"Finding some good stuff, buddy?" My double body was still in his glasses. His beard pointed to the field behind me. "I had a nice stack of boards all pulled out over there, but some bastard went and hauled them away."

"Oh, that was me," I said.

"Was, huh?"

"Peter said I get the bees out, I could take any lumber I wanted."

"You talked to Peter about it? I guess that's okay. But what about those bees? Christ, I blow up my truck trying to pull this wreck down, then these bees come busting out with my number in their tails. I don't mess with them little guys. No way." He looked around, raised his hand to his shades, but left them on. "They gone?"

"They're gone," I said.

"Well, hey, soon as I get my truck fixed I'm gonna start hauling this pile to the super dump, so take everything you can." His head turned toward my Chevy low in the grass, then slowly back to me. "I'm on fixed rate. The less I have to haul, the better. Jesus, take it all for firewood. You ain't never going to get another chance like this." He kicked his smoking bike to life with a roar, and had to shout. "I tell you what: I wreck buildings for my living, and I never see pickings easy as these." With a tight nod he turned the bike and bounced across the field, a shrug and hunch restoring his solitude as he waggled away through the grass.

Wind riffled over the mounds and valleys of the blackberry patch, lifting off a harvest of white petals that skimmed across the

276

swell. The two swallows twittered as they spiraled overhead, and a cricket, undisturbed by catastrophe, began to chant from somewhere near the fallen barn doors.

Along toward dusk, as I began sliding the longest boards onto the roof of my car named The Duchess, I saw a little boy come furtively down from the farmhouse, through the lilac hedge, through the wild hawthorn grove and out to the edge of the barn's debris. From the slow bob and swivel of his head, I could read how his gaze followed the outlines of the building that had stood there — first around the footing-wall perimeter, then down the stanchion bay, out into the central floor where the wagon had been, up some invisible ladder to the loft, then south to the back wall. He looked at me. I was part of the treachery. He was polite and said nothing. I began to wrestle a twenty-foot six-by-six, authentic with manure, onto the car.

"It wasn't dangerous," he said quietly, and I knew it was. I got the beam to the balancing joint and stopped to rest.

"Did you go in there a lot?"

"Just sometimes."

"What was it like?"

"It was always dark, and you had to know where you were going. There was broken glass, too, a whole floor of it. But I put a board across it so I could walk."

"What about the ladder?" I said, once I had the beam all the way up at rest on the car roof.

"I knew the good steps to step on. You just go slow, and hold onto other things at the same time. And there were bees in there. They never hurt you. I came up that close." He held his hand in front of his eyes. His face was a blur against the pale swathe of the hawthorn. "They kept working. They never bothered you. Once I even tasted some of their honey that dropped down on the straw." He looked back at me. "What are you going to build here, mister?"

"I'm not going to build anything here," I said, reaching for another board so he wouldn't go away. "Someone just wanted the barn taken down."

"What happened to the bees?"

"They're right there. Can you hear them?" I pointed to the hive-box that glowed a dull white and hummed. We both stood still.

By dark I unloaded the mossy timbers and curve-cured boards at my home, carried them one at a time around the house through the memorized tunnel of plum arch, apple tree, grape arbor. I stacked them in different ways, season by season, putting them to bed under tin, listening to the rattle of rain and fitting them in mind on my pillow to an old shape that would happen simply by happening slow. Whenever I hefted a timber so heavy I feared for my collarbone, or teased a splinter from my palm, I remembered how these boards stood face-to-face in a forest harvesting nineteenth-century light, how they slid through the saws side by side, how the green-chain grader's crayon marked them with a C for clear or an S for standard.

Clinched together in the first barn-shape, wood had a memory, and the boards in my yard now curved again for sun and water with a tree's wish, with the honest warp of their character, with history visible in every stress-ripple, every seam of bark or pitch, every conk-wither or knot. The tight grain of slow growth held steady long. But the oldest memory was of earth. Where any board had touched down to the damp floor below architecture, rot took root, branching upward into heartwood.

I sawed the rot-softened wood away, planed each curve straight, measured the length of firm timber, and began to build the barn again. My industry was slow. The building inspector told me to hurry.

"One hundred and eighty days without visible progress cancels your original permit," he said. "Better get going." But he forgave me. I kept working, resting, remembering the design in the air where the swallows flew. I started remodeling before it was done. The building inspector forgave me even that. Then he retired. His replacement warned me, and then forgave me.

At five a.m. in 1984, I am in the loft. Dust-colored rafters join in marriage above me. The hay-beam behind my head aims toward sunrise. Soon the blackberry pasture out this window will blossom. Soon the bees, daughters of the daughters of the bees I took care of, will winnow out from their white box beyond the pear tree into sunlight.

Kim R. Stafford

A FEW MILES SHORT OF WISDOM

A few nights in your life, you know this like the taste of lightning in your teeth: Tomorrow I will be changed. Somehow in the next passage of light, I will shed reptilian skin and feel the wind's friction again. Sparks will fly. It's a hope for the right kind of fear, the kind that does not turn away.

A few miles short of Wisdom, Montana, I flipped open my sleeping bag at the top of Lost Trail Pass. Starlight prickled my shoulders with cold's tattoo. At midnight there, August meant less than altitude. A long day's winding drive from La Grande had left me numb with the car's buzz, and abrupt dark silence was impossible to believe. But the tall stems of the trees made no sound. My ears were clouded with engine throb and tire whine. The whisper of stars I thought I heard was only a tune my head-bone played. Where I slid into the thin summer bag, I felt a bump of rock dent the small of my back. Sleep blurred my eyes, but I begged the rock to keep me wakeful. Tomorrow, I would drive down a valley that had burned my imagination, a place early trappers called The Big Hole. Tomorrow, Wisdom. The trees' utterance was a pitchy fragrance.

Why did I wish to stay awake? Sometimes stories from thoughtful travelers you trust, or some old book you believe, or the mind's own credulous pilgrim named Imagination will make a place dazzle in anticipation. Tomorrow, The Big Hole. And there was the battlefield that books and travelers and my mind made shine like an icon. Tomorrow, wisdom — if my hunch could be true. Where Joseph and the Nez Perce band were attacked at dawn one year after Custer died, I meant to stand apart from my own life and listen. I meant to stand apart from my century, if I could. The people who raised me would recede, and I would stand apprentice to the place itself. If wisdom could be portable from history, I might read it there in some configuration of the ground. Then sleep.

Midmorning of the next day, I sat faint in the car parked at headquarters for the Big Hole National Battlefield. By the rear-view mirror, pine-scattered hills were a blur of heat. Revelation was not going as planned. Dawn had come and gone. On my sleeping bag flung over the back seat, the dew had long dried, and sweat now trickled off my nose. Traveling alone, I had taken the exploratory vow: I will not eat until I learn from this place. I was untaught, and faint.

The personnel at headquarters, the tan-suited rangers inside their buff museum built to suggest a Nez Perce tipi, had tried hard to prepare an experience for me. Beyond the glass-cased photographs and furs, the guns and arrows, they had ushered me into a little auditorium for my command performance of the slide show. I had sat alone among the gray folding chairs while an artist's sketches of the battle flashed before me scene by scene, and a strident male voice on the tape loop told what the sound effects were to mean — the pulse of firing guns, a woman's scream, hoofbeats from invisible horses — while the watercolor faces of the stern and the doomed went flickering through their show. Then suddenly the music came up and it was over. A little motor whirred, and curtains were automatically drawn aside from the windows facing west. There was the battlefield below, on a flat place by the river. Sun had bleached the replica lodge-poles gray. One cloud dragged its shadow toward Canada. On the sill of the view window, two flies had died side by side.

Now, in the car, leaning back against the hot head-rest, I understood the chronology, and the battlefield's topography. From my vantage point at headquarters, I had seen the signs strung out along the river where named warriors had fallen, and the pine-thicket knoll where the U.S. Army had been surrounded and pinned down when the tide of battle turned against them. I saw where they had their all-day chance to think on Custer's fate, before the Nez Perce slipped away by night, ending their thirty-six hour siege, abandoning their joyless victory for flight. I could follow the events and feel, in my faint of hunger, a shred of what the original cast of this drama lived. But where I sat in the car, all this was nothing. The windshield wore the small debris of shattered yellow bugs.

What did I expect? The past wears an armor that thickens, and I was a fool to think hunger and a wish could pierce it. I had learned the dates and the map, had seen in photographs a long-braided

280

woman and the anguish of old men. I had browsed on books in the National Battlefield gift shop, and I was fed full with history, with news that stays facts:

During the morning of August 9, 1887, . . . 163 soldiers of the U.S. 7th Infantry and 33 civilian volunteers endured a 36-hour siege as the final scene in the Battle of the Big Hole. The battle began with a dawn attack by the military force upon a camp of 800 Nez Perce men, women and children encamped in 89 tipis on the grassy bank across the river . . . Follow the trail and explore the military defensive positions. Recreate the struggle of the besieged men and the hostile feelings of the surrounding Nez Perce warriors.

I folded the brochure, and closed my eyes. My government was trying hard to help me. They had made a building and a show. They had scratched out a trail and numbered it, had given me a brochure with matching numbers. I would follow the path. I was grateful. Still my heard was a vacant room. I had one more try.

Inside, at the headquarters reception desk, a ranger with his flat-brim hat on the desk beside him was tallying information from the guest register.

"I bet you get people from all over." I faced him over the glass display case filled with books and souvenirs.

"Excuse me one moment," he said. "1984 to date, out-of-state 87 percent total." His tanned fingers worked the blue ballpoint as if it were a shovel, scooping figures off one page and tossing them neatly onto another. Then he looked up at me. "Yes, from all over the world. Have you had a chance to sign the register?"

"Right here." I pointed to the word "Oregon." The space for my remark was blank, but the column above that blank was filled with "Beautiful display," "Very moving," "Worth the drive," "Howdy from Texas," "My third visit and better than ever." The ranger glanced at me, then turned away to usher a couple wearing identical sunglasses into the small auditorium for the slide show. I could hear the music begin as he closed the door behind them.

"I'm curious," I said. "How many Nez Perce people visit the battlefield?"

The ranger turned to the register, then to his tally. "We had a woman from Iowa last year who said she was one-fifth Nez Perce." He looked into the air between us for a moment, then back at me. There was a pause, and I could hear the muffled pulse of gunfire from the auditorium. My eyes asked the obvious question, and he answered it.

"We know others visit the battlefield itself," he said. "They just don't come here to the Visitor Center to sign the book." He looked into the air again. We both knew this was the part of the show about the Nez Perce warrior named Rainbow — how he was shot as he ran through the mist, how his comrade Five Wounds would have to die the same day by the vow they had shared. We heard the tapered scream of Rainbow's wife, a century distant through the auditorium wall. My eyes asked him again. This time he paused. I had to say it.

"When do they visit the battlefield?" I looked out the window behind him, as he studied my face.

"They come at night," he said, "and no one sees them." He paused again. "They have their ceremonies in the place, and we respect that." Something brushed my sleeve. He turned. A woman held out four postcards and a dollar bill.

"This has been marvelous, just marvelous. I must tell my daughter. Her children would love this. They're in Chicago, you know. Don't get west very often." The postcards in her hand hovered over a huge open purse, like hawk wings over a nest. Suddenly they plunged inside and her hand escaped just as the purse snapped shut. "But maybe with these pictures I can get them to come. We could drive down from Butte, make a day of it. Wouldn't that be nice?"

"It beats Chicago. I've been to O'Hare," the ranger said.

"O'Hare!" The woman glanced at the ceiling with a smile, crossed herself, spun around, and moved gradually away.

The ranger picked up his pen, but I waited. I could tell from the music the slide show was almost over.

"The ceremonies," I said. He held his pen up like an artist's brush. Now the question was in his eyes: how can I trust what I tell you to be safe? Perhaps I have said too much already.

"We don't know much about the ceremonies, just that they happen." We both looked into the air, not at each other. We looked into a box of wind from another time, a box suspended between us, a wind blind to his uniform and my traveling clothes, a box of storm air where the real voices resided and twenty centuries made a number with no meaning. I asked the inevitable question.

"How do you know about the ceremonies? Is there evidence left at the site?"

He looked hard at me, then away. In the auditorium, the little motor whirred to pull curtains aside from the west window. "In certain places," he said, looking toward the auditorium door, "they leave ribbons hanging from the trees." The door opened, and the woman came out before her man. The skin around their eyes was pale. In one smooth motion, they both put on their sunglasses.

On the trail to the battle overlook, the sharp-toed print of a doe's hoof was centered on the print of a woman's spike-heeled shoe. The woman came yesterday, the doe at dawn. I stepped aside, leaving that sign in the dust.

But where were the ribbons? Now hunger-vacancy sharpened my sight instead of dulling it. Wind stirred every pine limb with light, green urgency flickering in the heat, lags of color calling every tree a monument. Ribbons? Ceremony? The wind was hilarious and sunlight a blade across my forehead. All along the trail, numbered stakes held cavalry hats of blue-painted wood to mark known positions where soldiers suffered or died. On the high ground above the trail, stakes painted to resemble the tail feathers of eagle marked the known positions of Nez Perce snipers who held the soldiers pinned down all through the afternoon. Feather Feather. Hat Hat Hat. Feather. Tree. Wind. Straw-pale brochure in my hand. Brochure folded into my pocket. Vacancy. Tree. Wind. Ribbon.

Far uphill, at mirage distance, a ribbon shimmered orange from a twig of pine. Off-trail, pine duff sank softly beneath my feet. Trees kept respectfully apart. Earth sucked dry by roots from other pines made them scatter. A gopher had pushed open a hole, and cobweb spangled the smallest dew across it. Then the climb thinned my attention to one small spot of color the wind moved.

Orange plastic ribbon crackled between my fingers — the kind surveyors use to mark boundaries. Not it. Not the wisdom of the place. Not the secret her sunglasses obliterated, not the message that woman from Iowa went home without. Not the secret the ranger guarded, then whispered.

A girl's voice spoke from the grove: "The Nez Perce had only 10 snipers on the high ground, but the soldiers weren't sure how many were there." She stopped and looked about, then led her parents and sister on along the trail, reading to them from the brochure in her hand. Somehow, she did not stumble, and they padded away through their little flock of dust and disappeared toward the river. A bird's trill broke from the willow thicket where they had passed, a watery trill. Patience settled into my mind, like a fossil leaf pressed between centuries. I threaded the trees like a memory. A crow drifted over. A single pine bough stirred, as if the wind were a compact traveler roving before me.

When I found the ribbons they were red and blue. Five strands flickered half a fathom long from a single branch of the pine growing where Five Wounds died. The ribbons knotted at eye-level swung new in the breeze, and between my feet a single strand of older ribbon had fallen, bleached white by snow and sun. The age of this custom made me dizzy. The five ribbons on the limb were new as the soft needle-growth sprung from the pine candles. The faded ribbon on the ground lay among sun-bleached needles. The sun-white ribbon on the ground took me back to the hopeful recollections of bead, fur, and photograph cased in glass at the museum, while the five new ribbons conveyed me to the ceremonies of night. I stood so long the sun moved, and a cool shadow rose out of the ground.

Beside my left foot a red ant carried some white crumb by an intricate path: all the long length of a pine needle, careening impossibly over a shattered cone, then up a thin tongue of grass to tumble and rise and struggle on. Following the ant, I saw flecks of blue in its path, and then I was lying down to see tiny blue glass beads strung out along the path of the thread that had held them until it rotted to nothing. So. Before the ribbons marked this place, an older ribbon. Before an older ribbon marked this place, the beads. And before the beads? The ant was skirting around a gray sphere half-sunk into the ground: a round musket ball of lead.

A century collapsed into this moment of ground, where generations of private celebration grew outward from one story. This square yard of pine duff bound a guest register that could never be tallied, only renewed, only inhabited by the night-faithful memory that walked in the form of the people. Twenty steps east from the tree with the ribbons a ton of granite hewn to a block and polished was carved with the story as the U.S. Army had lived it through. That was one way to remember 1877: carve the truth in stone and draft a platoon of guardians, write books and print brochures and script slide shows and build a hall to house them all, then carve a trail with numbers like a tattoo on the hill. I was grateful for all that. All that can make a visitor ready to know. But that public way is not knowing in itself, only a preparation for knowing. Knowing is a change of heart, physical, slower than the eye's travel across a page of text, or across a stone dressed with words.

The books, the message on stone, the trail's configuration would all have to be revised by an act of will; the ribbons were either renewed or lost by the very nature of their fragility. Sun and rain destroyed them. Flowers withered, and the ribbons.

Suddenly in the heat a kind of fear chilled me — fear about my fellowship with the sometimes acquisitive tribe of patriots named America. Even in small things, we wish to map our conquest of the planet and the past. My own childhood collections flickered through my mind: stamps, stones, leaves pressed in a Bible, insects stilled by cotton soaked with alcohol and pinned to styrofoam in a box. And arrowheads. Smoky obsidian and blood-red flint. Modern habit is to lay such things away safe behind glass, and I had learned that habit well. I knew how to lift each bead with tweezers, plot and take each bullet up, sift them all out from the dust and alter them from a part of the world to an illustration of it. Could I leave the bones of the story still, and carry only its breath away in my mouth? Or would I thread five beads on a pine needle souvenir, saying softly to myself no one would know them gone?

I heard the girl's voice reading along closer through the grove, as she led her family toward the story of Five Wounds. His promise to Rainbow, sworn brother, to die the same day in battle. If one died, the other would die before day ended. And Rainbow had died. The ribbons were a part of Five Wounds' promise. He was a hundred years dead and they were new.

From wooden hats staked to the ground I could see where soldiers lay flat to earth in knots of two and three across the slope. The thin grass of pine shade moved, and wind made the trees glisten as sunlight shifted in them, but the hats held still as skulls, each where a soldier lived out his one day's bright terror or luck. But then Five Wounds came sprinting out from the willows into the slot of a shallow ravine, dashing his death-alley straight into the guns of these little hats in crossfire. He knew they had him before the one long breath of his run turned to blood in his mouth, but he lurched to the brow of the ravine to fall at my feet beneath these ribbons, beneath the bullets scattered later by night to heal his name, and now beneath the low voice of this girl practicing the ceremony of literate culture with a paper in her hands:

"Five Wounds charged up the gulch and was killed without a doubt . . ."

"What are the ribbons for?" her little sister said, interrupting. Leaning on each other, the parents stepped back, gentled by fatigue. The girl stopped reading and looked up.

"What ribbons?" Her eyes squinted for distance, then focused on the paper again. "It doesn't say."

Driving on, I was tipsy with gratitude. Fenceposts passing fast out the open window were pine with the bark left on, and they chirred like insects — whisp, whisp, whisp, whisp — down the long straight road heat blurred. The mountains stood up in a blue ring distant around the valley. Sage entered me, then a hint of cut hay, then the wind-twisted fragrance of smoke and manure from a little clutter of ranch buildings at the long, tapered end of its drive. After a few miles, Wisdom itself was a truck filled with horses saddled and stamping fitfully, a wall of deer antlers below a TV satellite dish, country music aching from loudspeakers nailed to the trading post facade, and a poster at the bar advertising a rodeo memorial for two teenagers killed in a car wreck: "Only working cowboys within a hundred-mile radius of Wisdom will be eligible for the purse."

The wisdom was behind, and I was sailing out the highway banked on the long curves the river led east, past fields where ponies put their ears forward to the passing snap of my fingers in the wind, and on into the open country that somehow forgot to get changed from plain gray sage and rocky bluffs, from ravines dark with willow shade and stone litter glittering down a hillside where hard rain scattered it, and the trees getting scarce for the long dry of days like this.

I was changed. The ribbons had pulled the sky right down to the ground, and tethered my soul to a story. If I was not changed, not wise, I had a way to become so. I possessed a vision-book of one moment, a story small as the pitchy pith of juniper seed to nibble for the rest of my life.

Then I saw the bear, and stopped the car. It was a young bear, about my size and black as lightning's footprint, rambling northeast along the south-facing slope of the river gully, in the direction the Nez Perce survivors of the battle had taken toward Canada. When I climbed out and the car door made a sound, the bear didn't shy suddenly off to the side like I've seen bear do, or coyotes feeling the bullet-blast of human sight graze their shoulders. Wind riffled the bear's fur, and it turned slowly to look over its shoulder from about a hundred yards off. Even at that distance, I could see the close squint of eyes, the nostril-flare of pertinent curiosity. She lifted her nose to know me by the thin daylight, she turned away, head swung down, and ambled away over the open slope of sage, climbing toward the bluffs at the crest of my sight.

The afternoon still: a wisp of wind-whistle in sage, and the little rattle of stone where the bear's paws swung along. I felt history receding with the click and scatter of her steps, as if I saw the last run of a river trail away down the geologic trough of its bed. What made seeing not enough? What made me want to meet that shaggy woman, not merely see her sip the wind over her shoulder and turn away?

In the car I stared at the choke, the odometer, the radio. The paltry pleasures of speed and distance were mine. How had exhilaration evaporated so fast? The dwindling hummock of the bear was approaching the ridge as I turned the key and swung out, cruised a half mile out of sight around the bend, killed the engine and coasted to a stop, left the white car's pod, the road's gray vine, and climbed toward the ridge. A need for quiet now — now that the bear's scent would follow the wind toward me as her path met mine. She would not know I was there. Now she would come close enough with her poor eyes to see my shape rise up.

At the brow of the ridge, along her natural way, I crouched breathless among sage scrub abuzz with insect tremor and sound. The ground fell away to my left toward the river's long curve. To my right stretched miles of open sage. The only hidden ground lay before me, toward the afternoon sun. There, I had seen the bear aim straight this way. There was no alternative for her but to come up over the hump of ground to meet me. If she turned, I would surely see her on the open ground to either side. From here, I would see first the black hackles of her back like a ruffled wave over the sage horizon, then the bobbing rims of her ears, then her small, close-set eyes, her lips pulled back to pant — and then I would stand up slowly.

My fear brightened the hillside as with sweat. Every tongue of sage leaf glittered, and the sand before me was exact with sunlight. I faced west, where the breeze at my face trembled cool with rumor and scent: the smoky scent of bruised stone, the thin sweet fragrance of crushed grass. Soon, it would be bear. Soon my heart would stop its percussive haste. I would stand, and speak. Some compliment. Some respectful word.

Wind rattled the dry sticks of the sage. My bones held an old juniper's arthritic stance. The sun moved, and an ant came toward me, crossed a fathom of epic sand, and disappeared into the shade I cast. Blank wind chilled my face. Somehow, the bear slipped past my vision by some private tunnel of its own power.

The risk I took to meet the bear was a responsibility greater than being husband, father, or son. But it was not enough. I was no true citizen of wisdom, but spent all I had on being afraid. So busy with fear, I had not enough hospitality for danger and change. There was only dwindling light on the place itself.

I stood up dizzy with regret, stumbled back to the car, slid in the key, drove east, drove two hundred miles east by a path of dash-lined curves, of skid marks and guard rails dented with rust, of gas-stop exits numbered monotonous, of passing and being passed by the wind-tailed trucks made brazen by their size, drove miles of signs promising greater distances to Bozeman than Butte, to Billings than Bozeman, and miles of travel without change. And Change was my sworn brother — that we would die the same day, as Five Wounds swore to Rainbow, and fulfilled.

The day ended in Billings, where the librarians were meeting. They had come by air and car from Missoula, Boise, Seattle, Portland, and smaller cities. They talked about change, and tradition. After the banquet, I stood at the podium, the microphone one breath's distance from my lips, and spoke: The Role of the Humanist in a Technological Age. I was not able to tell what I was learning, only what I had learned — too long before to be true. There was kind applause, and draining of the last wine. At the end, at midnight in the twenty-third floor conference suite, among the swirl of my smart companions, good people of my tribe holding their drinks in clear cups that tingled with the buzz and din of talk — at the end I saw the crowd divide when lightning began to play over the city below us. Some drew back against the wall. "Should we really be up here? Is the basement safer now? The stairwell . . . ?"

But some set down their champagne cups to press outward against tall windows, as lightning came faster toward us over the grid of streets, the jagged light that started fires that night all over Montana. I stepped toward the bright hot ribbons hanging down, and the din of our talk was hushed. One light on every thing: antenna, automobile, hilarious newspaper debris, the dark distant hills. In a flash our party's reflection in the window eclipsed — the ribbons hanging down, and a girl's voice telling the story, the burnt ozone scent of change come through sage to meet me.

Still, I am afraid. A man of my own tribe trusted me with the story of the ribbons, and I trust you with the beads. He may have been wrong, and I may be wrong. I would let the place alone, but it will not let me alone.

They say in Japan stands a building filled with national cultural treasures so valuable no steel door, no lock is strong enough to protect them from thieves. Instead of such a door, the state has hired an old man to watch the building in case of fire. He slowly walks about the building, then rests in the shade. Tied by thread to the simple door-latch, a note from the Emperor explains the supreme value of the treasury inside. There is no other lock.

I would make such a note for a square yard of ground in Montana, a few miles west of Wisdom.

Kim R. Stafford

LOOKING FOR A LOST DOG

The most valuable thoughts which I entertain are anything but what I thought. Nature abhors a vacuum, and if I can only walk with sufficient carelessness I am sure to be filled.

Henry David Thoreau

I started off this morning looking for my lost dog. He's a red heeler, blotched brown and white, and I tell people he looks like a big saddle shoe. Born at Christmas on a thirty-below-zero night, he's tough, though his right front leg is crooked where it froze to the ground.

It's the old needle-in-the-haystack routine: small dog, huge landscape, and rugged terrain. While moving cows once, he fell in a hole and disappeared. We heard him whining but couldn't see him. When we put our ears to the ground, we could hear the hole that had swallowed him.

It's no wonder human beings are so narcissistic. The way our ears are constructed, we can only hear what's right next to us or else the internal monologue inside. I've taken to cupping my hands behind my ears — mule-like — and pricking them all the way forward or back to hear what's happened or what's ahead.

"Life is polyphonic," a Hungarian friend in her eighties said. She was a child prodigy from Budapest who had soloed on the violin in Paris and Berlin by the time she was twelve. "Childishly, I once thought hearing had mostly to do with music," she said. "Now that I'm too old to play the fiddle, I know it has to do with the great suspiration of life everywhere."

But back to the dog. I'm walking and looking and listening for him, though there is no trail, no clue, no direction to the search. Whimsically, I head north toward the falls. They're set in a deep gorge where Pre-Cambrian rock piles up to ten thousand feet on either side. A raven creaks overhead, flies into the cleft, glides toward a panel of white water splashing over a ledge, and comes out cawing.

To find what is lost is an art in some cultures. The Navajos employ "hand tremblers," usually women, who go into a trance and "see" where the lost article or person is located. When I

291

asked one such diviner what it was like when she was in trance, she said, "Lots of noise, but noise that's hard to hear."

Near the falls the ground flattens into a high-altitude valley before the mountains rise vertically. The falls roar, but they're overgrown with spruce, pine, willow, and wild rose, and the closer I get, the harder it is to see the water. Perhaps that is how it will be in my search for the dog.

We're worried about Frenchy because last summer he was bitten three times by rattlesnakes. After the first bite he walked toward me, reeled dramatically, and collapsed. I could see the two holes in his nose where the fangs went in, and I felt sure he was dying. I drove him twenty miles to the vet; by the time we arrived, Frenchy resembled a monster. His nose and neck had swollen as though a football had been sewn under the skin.

I walk and walk. Past the falls, through a pass, toward a larger, rowdier creek. The sky goes black. A blue ocean seems to stretch between, and the black sky hangs over like a frown. A string of cottonwoods whose new, tender leaves are the color of limes pulls me downstream. I come into the meadow with the abandoned apple orchard. The trees have leaves but have lost most of their blossoms. I feel as if I had caught strangers undressed.

The sun comes back, and the wind. It brings no dog, but ducks slide overhead. An Eskimo from Barrow, Alaska, told me the reason spring has such fierce winds is so birds coming north will have something to fly on.

To find what's lost; to lose what's found. Several times I've thought I might be "losing my mind." Of course, minds aren't literally misplaced — on the contrary, we live too much under them. As with viewing the falls, we can lose sight of what is too close. It is between the distant and close-up views that the struggle between impulse and reason, logic and passion takes place.

The feet move; the mind wanders. In his journals Thoreau wrote: "The saunterer, in the good sense, is no more vagrant than the meandering river, which is all the while sedulously seeking the shortest course to the sea."

Today I'm filled with longings — for what I'm not, for what is impossible, for people I love who can't be in my life. Passions of all sorts struggle soundlessly, or else, like the falls, they are all noise but can't be seen. My hybrid anguish spends itself as recklessly and purposefully as water.

Now I'm following a game trail up a sidehill. It's a mosaic of tracks — elk, deer, rabbit, and bird. If city dwellers could leave imprints in cement, it would look this way: tracks would overlap, go backward and forward like the peregrine saunterings of the mind.

I see a dog's track, or is it a coyote's? I get down on my hands and knees to sniff out a scent. What am I doing? I entertain expectations of myself as preposterous as when I landed in Tokyo — I felt so at home there that I thought I would break into fluent Japanese. Now I sniff the ground and smell only dirt. If I spent ten years sniffing, would I learn scents?

The tracks veer off the trail and disappear. Descending into a dry wash whose elegant, tortured junipers and tumbled boulders resemble a Japanese garden, I trip on a sagebrush root. I look. Deep in the center of the plant there is a bird's nest, but instead of eggs, a locust stares up at me.

Some days I think this one place isn't enough. That's when nothing is enough, when I want to live multiple lives and be allowed to love without limits. Those days, like today, I walk with a purpose but no destination. Only then do I see, at least momentarily, that everything is here. To my left a towering cottonwood is lunatic with birdsong. Under it I'm a listening post while its great gray trunk — like a baton or the source of something — heaves its green symphony into the air.

I walk and walk: from the falls, over Grouse Hill, to the dry wash. Today it is enough to make a shadow.

Gretel Ehrlich

TO LIVE IN TWO WORLDS: CROW FAIR AND A SUN DANCE

June. Last night, alone on the ranch, I tried to pull a calf in a rainstorm. While attempting to hold a flashlight in one hand and a six-foot-long winchlike contraption called a "calf puller" in the other, I slipped in the mud and fell against the cow's heaving flank. I yelled apologies to her over thunder so concussive that friends at a neighboring ranch claimed "it shook the handles loose from the coffee cups." On my feet again, I saw rain undulate down hay meadows and three theaters of lightning making simultaneous displays: over Red Basin's tipped-up mesas a thick root of lightning drilled straight down; closer, wide shoals of it flashed like polished car hoods all being lifted at once; and in the pasture where I fumbled with a chain, trying to fasten it around the calf's emerging front feet, lightning snapped sideways like flowered vines shot from a cannon over my shoulders. In that cadaverous refulgence, the calf was born dead. The next morning, clear and cool after a rainless month of hundred-degree heat, I tightened my lariat around his hocks and, from the rubbery, purplish afterbirth they had impaled, dragged him behind the pickup out of the pasture.

Implicated as we westerners are in this sperm, blood, and guts business of ranching, and propelled forward by steady gusts of blizzards, cold fronts, droughts, heat, and wind, there's a ceremonial feel to life on a ranch. It's raw and impulsive but the narrative thread of birth, death, chores, and seasons keeps tugging at us until we find ourselves braided inextricably into the strand. So much in American life has had a corrupting influence on our requirements for social order. We live in a culture that has lost its memory. Very little in the specific shapes and traditions of our grandparents' pasts instructs us how to live today, or tells us who we are or what demands will be made on us as members of society. The shrill estrangement some of us felt in our twenties has been replaced a decade or so later by a hangdog, collective blues. With our burgeoning careers and families, we want to join up, but it's difficult to know how or where. The changing conditions of life are no longer assimilated back into a common watering trough. Now, with our senses enlivened — because that's the only context we have to go by — we hook change onto change ad nauseam.

On a ranch, small ceremonies and private, informal rituals arise. We ride the spring pasture, pick chokecherries in August, skin out a deer in the fall, and in the enactment experience a wordless exhilaration between bouts of plain hard work. Ritual — which could entail a wedding or brushing one's teeth — goes in the direction of life. Through it we reconcile our barbed solitude with the rushing, irreducible conditions of life.

For the fifth consecutive year I helped my neighbors Stan and Mary move their cattle through four 6,000-acre pastures. The first morning we rode out at three. A new moon grew slimmer and slimmer as light ballooned around us. I came on two burly Hereford bulls sniffing the cool breeze through the needles of a white pine, shaded even from moonlight as if the severe sexual heat of their bodies could stand no excess light. All week we moved cows, calves, and bulls across washes of ocher earth blooming with purple larkspur, down sidehills of gray shale that crumbled under our processional weight like filo pastry. Just before we reached the last gate, six hundred calves ran back; they thought their mothers, who had loped ahead, were behind them. Four of us galloped full tilt through sagebrush to get around and head off this miniature stampede, but when we did catch up, the calves spilled through us in watery cascades, back to the last pasture, where we had to start the gather all over again. This midseason roundup lasted six days. We ate together, slept, trailed cattle, and took turns bathing in the big galvanized tub at cow camp. At the end of the week, after pairing off each cow with the proper calf, then cutting them out of the herd — a job that requires impeccable teamwork and timing between rider and rider and rider and horse — we knew an intimacy had bloomed between us. It was an old closeness that disappears during other seasons, and each year, surprised afresh by the slightly erotic tint, we welcomed it back.

July. Last night from one in the morning until four, I sat in the bed of my pickup with a friend and watched meteor showers hot dance over our heads in sprays of little suns that looked like white orchids. With so many stars falling around us I wondered if daylight would come. We forget that our sun is only a star destined to someday burn out. The time scale of its transience so far exceeds our human one that our unconditional dependence on its life-giving properties feels oddly like an indiscretion about which we'd rather forget.

The recent news that astronomers have discovered a new solar system in-the-making around another sun-star has startled us out of a collective narcissism based on the assumption that we dominate the cosmic scene. Now we must make room for the possibility of new life — not without resentment and anticipation — the way young couples make room in their lives for a baby. By chance, this discovery came the same day a Kiowa friend invited me to attend a Sun Dance.

I have Indian neighbors all around me — Crow and Cheyenne to the north, Shoshone and Arapaho to the south — and though we often ranch, drink, and rodeo side by side, and dress in the same cowboy uniforms — Wrangler jeans, tall boots, wide-brimmed, high-crowned hats — there is nothing in our psyches, styles, or temperaments that is alike.

Because Christians shaped our New World culture we've had to swallow an artificial division between what's sacred and what's profane. Many westerners, like Native Americans, have made a life for themselves out in the raw wind, riding the ceremony of seasons with a fine-tuned eye and ear for where the elk herd is hidden or when in fall to bring the cattle down. They'll knock a sage hen in the head with a rock for dinner and keep their bearings in a ferocious storm as ably as any Sioux warrior, but they won't become visionaries, diviners, or healers in the process.

On a Thursday I set off at two in the morning and drove to the reservation. It was dark when I arrived and quiet. On a broad plain bordered in the west by mountains, the families of the hundred men who were pledging the dance had set up camps: each had a white canvas tipi, a wall tent, and a rectangular brush arbor in a circle around the Lodge, where for the next four days the ceremony would take place. At 5 A.M. I could still see stars, the Big Dipper suspended in the northwest as if magnified, and to the east, a wide bank of what looked like blood. I sat on the ground in the dark. Awake and stirring now, some of the "dancers" filed out of the Lodge, their star quilts pulled tightly over their heads. When they lined up solemnly behind two portable johns, I thought

I was seeing part of the dance. Then I had to laugh at myself but at the same time understood how the sacredness of this ceremony was located not just in the Lodge but everywhere.

Sun Dance is the holiest religious ceremony of the Plains tribes, having spread from the Cheyenne to the Sioux, Blackfoot, Gros Ventre, Assiniboine, Arapaho, Bannock, and Shoshone sometime after the year 1750. It's not "sun worship" but an inculcation of regenerative power that restores health, vitality, and harmony to the land and all tribes.

For the hundred dancers who have volunteered to dance this year (the vow obligates them to dance four times during their lives) Sun Dance is a serious and painful undertaking; called "thirsty standing," they eat no food and drink no water for four days. This year, with the hundred-degree heat we've been having, their suffering will be extreme. The ceremonies begin before dawn and often last until two or three in the morning. They must stay in the Lodge for the duration. Speaking to or making eye contact with anyone not dancing is forbidden, and it's considered a great disgrace to drop out of the dance before it is over.

Sun Dance was suppressed by the government in the 1880s, and its full revival has only been recent. Some tribes practiced the ceremony secretly, others stopped. George Horse Capture, a Gros Ventre who lives near me and has completed one Sun Dance, has had to read the same sources I have — Dorsey, Kroeber, and Peter Powell — to reeducate himself in his tradition.

"Did you sleep here last night?" an old man, one of the elders of the tribe, asked. Shrunken and hawk-nosed, he wore a blue farmer's cap and walked with a crudely carved pine cane. "No, I drove from Shell," I answered, sounding self-conscious because I seemed to be the only white person around. "Oh . . . you have a very good spirit to get up so early and come all this way. That's good . . . I'm glad you are here," he said. His round eyes narrowed and he walked away. On the other side of the shed where the big drum was kept he approached three teenage girls. "You sober?" he asked. "Yes," they replied in unison. "Good," he said. "Don't make war on anyone. If you're not drunk, there's peace." He hobbled past me again out into the parched field between the circle of tents and the Lodge. Coleman lanterns were being lighted and the tipis behind him glowed. He put both hands on top of the cane and, in a hoarse voice that carried far across the encampment, sang an Arapaho morning song: "Get up, Everyone get up . . . ," it began, followed by encouragements to face the day.

The sky had lightened; it was a shield of pink. The new moon, white when I had arrived, now looked blue. Another voice — sharp, gravelly, and less patient, boomed from the north, his song overlapping that of the first Crier's. I looked: he was a younger man but bent at the shoulders like a tree. He paced the hard ground as he sang, and the tweed jacket he wore, which gave him a Dickensian look, hung from him and swayed in the breeze. Now I could hear two other Criers to the south and west. The four songs overlapped, died out, and started again. The men, silhouetted, looked ghostlike against the horizon, almost disembodied, as though their age and authority were entirely in the vocal cords.

First light. In the Lodge the dancers were dressing. Over gym shorts (the modern substitute for breechclouts), they pulled on long, white, sheath skirts, to which they fastened, with wide beaded belts, their dance aprons: two long panels, front and back, decorated with beads, ribbons, and various personal insignias. Every man wore beaded moccasins, leaving legs and torsos bare. Their faces, chest, arms, and the palms of their hands were painted yellow. Black lines skittered across chests, around ankles and wrists, and encircled each face. Four bundles of sage, which represents healing and breath, were tucked straight up in the apron fronts; thin braided wreaths of it were slipped onto the dancer's wrists and ankles, and a crown of sage ending in two loose sprays looked like antennae.

Light begets activity — the Lodge began filling up. It's a log arbor, forty yards across, covered with a thatchwork of brush. Its sixteen sides radiate from a great center pole of cottonwood — the whole trunk of a hundred-year-old tree whose forked top looked like antlers. A white cloth was tied with rope around the bark, and overhead, on four of the pine stringers, tribal members had hung bandanas, silk cowboy scarves, and shawls that all together form a loose, trembling hieroglyph spelling out personal requests for health and repair.

Alongside the dancers, who stood in a circle facing east, a group of older men filed in. These were the "grandfathers" (ceremonially related, not by blood) who would help the younger dancers through their four-day ordeal.

The little shed against which I had leaned in the pre-morning light opened and became an announcer's stand. From it the drum was rolled out and set up at the entrance to the Lodge.

Light begets activity begets light. The sky looked dry, white, and inflammable. Eleven drummers who, like "the grand-fathers," were probably ranchers sat on metal folding chairs encircling the drum. A stream of announcements in both Arapaho and English flooded the air. Friends and relatives of the dancers lined up in front of the Lodge. I found myself in a group of Indian women. The drumming, singing, and dancing began all at once. It's not really a dance with steps but a dance of containment, a dance in place. Facing east and blowing whistles made of eagle wing bones in shrill unison, the men bounced up and down on their heels in time to the drumbeat. Series after series of songs, composed especially for Sun Dance, were chanted in high, intense voices. The ropey, repeating pulse was so strong it seemed to pull the sun up.

There were two important men at the back of the Lodge I hadn't noticed. That their faces were painted red, not yellow, signified the status of Instructor, Pledger, or Priest. The taller of the two held a hoop (the sun) with eagle feathers (the bird of day) fastened around it. The "grandfather" standing in back of him raised the hoop-holding hand and, from behind, pushed the arm up and down in a wide, swinging arc until it took flight on its own.

I felt warmth on my shoulder. As the sun topped the horizon, the dancers stretched their arms straight out, lifting them with the progress of the sun's rising. Songs pushed from the backs of the drummers' throats. The skin on the dancers' chests bounced as though from some interior tremor. When the light hit their faces, they looked as if they were made of sun.

The sunrise ceremony ended at eight. They had danced for nearly two hours and already the heat of the day was coming on. Pickups rambled through camps, children played quietly everywhere. Walking to a friend's camp, I began to understand how the wide ampleness of the Indian body stands for a spirit of accomodation. In the ceremony I had just witnessed, no one — dancer, observer, child, priest, or drummer — had called attention to himself. There was no applause, no frivolousness. Families ambled back to their camps as though returning from a baseball game. When I entered my friend's brush arbor (already a relief from the sun) and slid behind the picnic table bench she handed me a cup of coffee I'd been hoping for. "They're dancing for all of us," she said. Then we drained our cups in silence.

Though I came and went from the Sun Dance grounds (it was too hot to stand around in the direct sun) the ceremonies continued all day and most of each night. At nine the "runners" drove to the swamp to cut reeds from which they fashioned beds for the dancers. The moisture in the long, bladelike leaves helped cool the men off. At ten, special food eaten by the dancers' families was blessed in the Lodge, and this was surely to become one of the dancers' daily agonies: the smell of meat, stew, and fry bread filling the space, then being taken away. The sunrise drummers were spelled by new ones, and as the songs began again those dancers who could stood in their places and danced. Each man was required to dance a certain number of hours a day. When he was too weak or sick or reeling from hallucination, he was allowed to rest on his rush mat.

"What happens if it rains during Sun Dance?" I asked my Kiowa friend. "It doesn't," she answered curtly. By eleven, it was ninety-nine degrees. We drove west away from the grounds to the land she owned and went skinny-dipping in the river. Her brown body bobbed up and down next to my white one. Behind us a wall of colored rock rose out of the water, part of a leathery bluff that curved for miles. "That's where the color for the Sun Dance paints comes from," my friend's husband said, pointing to a cave. He'd just floated into view from around an upstream bend. With his big belly glinting, he had the complacent look of a man who lords over a houseful of women: a wife, two daughters, a young tutor for his girls. The night before, they'd thrown an anniversary party at this spot. There were tables full of Mexican food, a five-piece Mexican band whose members looked like reformed Hell's Angels, a charro with four skinny horses and a trick-riding act, two guests who arrived from the oil fields by helicopter, and a mutual friend who's Jewish and a Harvard professor who popped bikini-clad out of a giant plywood cake.

The men in the Rabbit Lodge danced as late as the party-goers. The next morning when I arrived at four-thirty the old man with the cane walked directly to me. "Where's your coat? Aren't you cold?" he asked gruffly, though I knew he was welcoming me. The dancers spit bile and shuffled back and forth between the johns and the Lodge. A friend had asked one of them how he prepared for Sun Dance. He replied, "I don't. There's no way to prepare for pain." As the dancers began to look more frail, the singing became raucous. The astounding volume, quick rises in pitch, and forays into falsetto had an enlivening effect on all of us. Now it was the drummers who made the dancers make the sun rise.

Noon. In the hottest midday sun the dancers were brought out in front of the Lodge to be washed and freshly painted. The grandfathers dipped soft little brooms of sage in water and swabbed the men down; they weren't allowed to drink. Their families gathered around and watched while the dancers held their gaze to the ground. I couldn't bring myself to stand close. It seemed a violation of privacy. It wasn't nudity that rendered the scene so intimate (they still had their gym shorts on), but the thirst. Behind me, someone joked about dancing for rain instead of sun.

I was wrong about the bathing scene. Now the desolation of it struck me as beautiful. All afternoon the men danced in the heat — two, eight, or twenty of them at a time. In air so dry and with their juices squeezed out, the bouncing looked weightless, their bodies thin and brittle as shells. It wasn't the pain of the sacrifice they were making that counted but the emptiness to which they were surrendering themselves. It was an old ritual: separation, initiation, return. They'd left their jobs and families to dance. They were facing physical pain and psychological transformation. Surely, the sun seared away preoccupation and pettiness. They would return changed. Here, I was in the presence of a collective hero. I searched their faces and found no martyrs, no dramatists, no antiheroes either. They seemed to pool their pain and offer it back to us, dancing not for our sins but to ignite our hearts.

Evening. There were many more spectators tonight. Young Indian women cradling babies moved to the front of the Lodge. They rocked them in time with the drums and all evening not one child cried. Currents of heat rose from the ground; in fact, everything seemed to be rising: bone whistles, arms, stars, penises, the yeast in the fry bread, the smell of sage. My breasts felt full. The running joke in camp was about "Sun Dance Babies." Surely the expansive mood in the air settled over the tipis at night, but there was more to it than that. Among some tribes a "Sacred Woman" is involved in the ceremony. The sun is a "man power" symbol. When she offers herself to the priest, their union represents the rebirth of the land, water, and people. If by chance a child is conceived, he or she is treated with special reverence for a lifetime.

Dawn. This morning I fainted. The skinny young man dancing in front of me appeared to be cringing in pain. Another dancer's face had been painted green. I'm not saying they made me faint — maybe I fainted for them. With little ado, the women behind me picked me up. Revived and feeling foolish, I stood through to the end. "They say white people don't have the constitution to go without water for so many days," a white friend commented later. It sounded like a racist remark to me. She'd once been offered a chance to fast with a medicine man and refused. "I think it has more to do with one's concepts of hope and fear," I mumbled as she walked through the field to her car.

Afternoon. At five, only two dancers were standing. Because of the heat, the smell of urine had mixed with the sage.

Later in the evening I stood next to two teenage boys from Oklahoma. Not realizing I was old enough to be their mother, they flirted with me, then undercut the dares with cruelty. "My grandmother hates white tourists," the one who had been eyeing my chest said to me. "You're missing the point of this ceremony," I said to him. "And racism isn't a good thing anywhere." They walked away, but later, when I bumped into them, they smiled apologetically.

When I had coffee in a friend's brush arbor during a break in the dancing, the dancer's wife looked worried. "He looks like death warmed over," she said. A young man with black braids that reached his belt buckle was dangling a baby on each knee; I've never seen men so gentle and at ease with children. A fresh breeze fanned us. The round-the-clock rhythm of drumbeats and dancing made day and night seem the same. Sleeping became interchangeable with waiting, until, finally, there was no difference between the two.

Sunday. Two American flags were raised over the Lodge today — both had been owned by war veterans. The dance apron of a man near me had U.S. Navy insignias sewn into the corners. Here was a war hero, but he'd earned his medal far from home. Now the ritual of separation, initiation, and return performed in Vietnam, outside the context of community, changes into separation, benumbment, and exile.

Throughout the afternoon's dancing there was a Give-Away, an Indian tradition to honor friends, relatives, and admirers with a formal exchange of gifts. In front of the announcer's stand there was a table chock-full of food and another stacked high with Pendleton blankets, shawls, and beadwork. The loudspeaker overwhelmed the drumming until all the gifts were dispersed. Pickups streamed through the camps and a layer of dust muted the hard brightness of the day. After his first Sun Dance one old man told me he had given nearly everything he owned away: horse, wagons, clothes, winter blankets. "But it all comes back," he said, as if the day and night rhythm of this ceremony stood for a bigger tidal cadence as well.

Evening. They've taken the brush away from the far side of the Lodge. Now the dancers face west. All hundred men, freshly painted with a wild dappling of dots, stripes, and crooked lines, bounced up and down vigorously and in short strokes waved eagle fans in front of their bodies as if to clear away any tiredness there.

When I asked why the Sun Dance ended at night, my friend said, "So the sun will remember to make a complete circle, and so we'll always have night and day." The sun drained from the dancers' faces and sank into a rack of thunderclouds over the mountains. Every movement coming from the Lodge converged into a single trajectory, a big "V" like a flock of birds migrating toward me. This is how ritual speaks with no words. The dancing and whistling surged; each time a crescendo felt near, it ebbed. In the southwest, the first evening star appeared, and the drumming and singing, which had begun to feel like a hard dome over my head, stopped.

Amid cries of relief and some clapping I heard hoarse expulsions of air coming from dancers, like whales breaching after being under water too long. They rushed forward to the front of the Lodge, throwing off the sage bracelets and crowns, knelt down in turn by wooden bowls of chokecherry juice, and drank their first liquid in four days.

The family standing next to me approached the Lodge cautiously. "There he is," I heard the mother say. They walked toward the dancer, a big, lumbering man in his thirties whose waist, where rolls of fat had been, now looked concave. The man's wife and father slid their arms around his back, while his mother stood in front and took a good look at him. He gave her the first drink of sweet water from his bowl. "I tried to be there as much as possible today. Did you see me?" his wife asked. He nodded and smiled. Some of the young children had rushed into the Lodge and were swinging the flattened reeds that had been the dancers' beds around and around in the air. One of the drummers, an energetic man with an eccentric, husky voice, walked up to a group of us and started shaking our hands. He didn't know us but it didn't matter. "I'm awfully glad you're here," he kept saying, then walked away laughing ecstatically. The dancer I had been watching was having trouble staying on his feet. He stumbled badly. A friend said he worked for Amoco and tomorrow he'd be back in the oil fields. Still supporting him with their arms, his family helped him toward their brush arbor, now lit with oil lamps, where he would vomit, then feast.

It's late August. Wind swings down the hay meadows from high cornices of rimrock above the ranch like guffaws of laughter. Since Sun Dance several images recur: the shaded, shell-like bodies of the dancers getting smaller and smaller; the heated, expanding spectators surrounding them. At the point of friction, a generosity occurs. The transition to autumn is a ritual like that: heat and cold alternate in a staccato rhythm. The magnetizing force of summer reverses itself so that every airplane flying over me seems to be going away. Heat lightning washes over and under clouds until their coolness drops down to us and then flotillas of storms bound through as though riding the sprung legs of a deer. I feel both emptied and brimming over.

A week later. I'm camped on a hill next to an anthropologist and his wife. He's Indian, she's white, and they drove here on what he calls his "iron pony" — a motorcycle — to attend Crow Fair. "You see I had to marry one of these skinny white women so we could both fit here," he explained as they squeezed onto the seat. He was as round and cheerful as the chrome gas tank his belly rested on. Surrounding us were the rolling grasslands that make up the middle Yellowstone Valley, site of the summer councils held by the warring Crow, Sioux, Blackfoot, and Cheyenne. the Wolf Mountains to the south step up into pitched rises, crowned with jack pines. The dark creases in the hills are dry washes, now blackened with such an abundance of ripe chokecherries they look clotted with blood. On a knob nearby, recently signed with fire, is Custer's battlefield. "If there was any yellow hair left on that sonofabitch, it's gone now," a Crow friend who had fought the fire said. The Crows, of course, were the ones scouting for Custer, but it seems to have been a temporary alliance, having more to do with their animosity toward other tribes than a love for any white man.

Crow Fair is a five-day country fair — Indian style. It's different from ours because their roots are nomadic, not agricultural. Instead of the horse pulls, steer judging, and cake stands, they have all-night sessions of Indian dancing, a traditional dress parade, and a lengthy rodeo augmented by horse racing and betting. Looking down from the hill where I pitched our borrowed tent, the encampment of well over five hundred tipis could have been a summer council at the turn of the nineteenth century except for the pickups, loudspeakers, and the ubiquitous aluminum folding chairs. Inside the sprawl of tipis, tents, and arbors was a circle of concession stands, at the center of which stood the big open-air dance arbor.

My young friend Ursula, who was visiting from Cambridge, asked if these Indians lived here all the time. Indians don't, of course, still live in tipis, but the encampment looked so well-worn and amiable she wasn't wrong in thinking so. Part of the "wholeness" of traditional Indian life that the tipi and circular dance arbor signify is the togetherness at these powwows. Indians don't go home at night; they camp out where the action is, en masse, whole extended families and clans spanning several generations. It's a tradition with them the way sending our kids to summer camp is with us.

305

Two days before the fair started, the pickups began to roll in with tipi poles slung over the tailgates. Brush was cut, canvas unrolled, and in twelve hours a village had been made. Tipis and tents, reserved mainly for sleeping, were often as plush as an Arab's. Inside were wall-to-wall rugs, hanging lanterns, and ceremonial drums. Outdoor kitchens were arranged under canvas flies or inside a shady brush arbor with packing crates turned on end for shelves, and long picnic tables were loaded with food. With barely any elbow room between camps, even feuding tribes took on a congenial air, their children banding together and roving freely.

At the morning parade you could see the splendors of traditional moccasins, but what interested me more were the contradictions: the Sioux boy in warrior dress riding the hood of a Corvette; vans with smokey windows covered with star quilts and baskets; the roar of new wave music coming from the cars. John Whiteman, the last surviving Custer scout, rode on the back of a big ton truck with his tiny wife, who had hoisted up a brown-and-white-striped umbrella to shade herself from the sun. They were both, someone said, well past 110 years old.

Ursula and I were the first ones at the rodeo because everyone else seemed to know it would start late. The young, cigar-smoking man who sold us our tickets turned out to be an Eskimo from Barrow, Alaska. He'd come south to live with what he called "these mean Plains Indians."

The Crow crossed into this valley in the late 1700s and fought off the Shoshone to claim territory that spread between the Big Horns, the Badlands, and the Wind River Mountains. Trappers, like Osborne Russell, who hunted right along with them, described the Crow as tall, insolent, and haughty, but submissive when cornered. Russell met one chief who had hair eleven feet long, and said their beadwork was "excessively gaudy." The Crows were so pinched geographically by raiding Sioux and Blackfeet they adopted a militaristic style, still evident in the way they zipped around camp in police cars with "Executive Security Force" emblazoned on the doors. Endowed with a natural horse-handling ability, they became famous horse thieves.

The rodeo got under way after an off-key rendition of "God Bless America" (instead of the national anthem). A local band, aptly named "The Warriors," warmed up on the stand in front of us. While the rough stock was run into the bucking chutes they played "He's Just a Coca-Cola Cowboy." As testimony to their enthusiasm for horses, the rodeo, usually a two- or three-hour affair, lasted seven hours.

Before the all-night session of dancing began we made the circuit of concession stands. Between the corn dogs and Indian tacos — fry bread topped with beans and hot sauce — was an aisle of video games. Between the menudo and the caramel apples were two gambling tents — one for bingo, the other for poker. You could eat corn barbecued in the husk Navajo style and a hunk of Taos bread, or gulp down a buffalo burger and a Coke, the one cooked by a Navajo from Shiprock, the other by an Ogalalla Sioux. Ursula had her ears pierced and bought a pair of opalescent earrings; I bought a T-shirt with the words "Crow Fair" across the front, and around and around we went until the dancing began.

Dark. Instead of the tamping, rigid, narcotic bounce of Sun Dance that seemed to set into motion a chronic tremor, one that radiated out of the Lodge to knock against our legbones and temples, the dances at Crow Fair were show-offish and glittering. These Society, War, Animal, and Contest Dances served no direct purpose these days, the way some religious dances do. "What you're seeing out there is a lot of dyed turkey feathers and plastic elk teeth, and kids doing the Indian disco," a friend commented. He's an Italian from Saint Louis who married a Kiowa woman when he was sixteen and together they moved to Wyoming to live with the Shoshone. Incongruity delights him as much as tradition. "We assimilate a little this way, and a little that way. Life is only mutation."

The dance arbor was lit by mercury vapor lamps hung from one forty-foot power pole at the center — no bonfires or Coleman lanterns here. The ceremonies started with a long prayer in English during which a Crow child in front of me shot off a toy gun, aiming first at the preacher, then at himself, then at me. Six separate drum groups set up around the periphery with names like Night Hawks, Whistling Elk, Plenty Coups, Magpie, and Salt Lake Crows. Although participants had come from a great number of tribes — Assiniboine, Apache and Shoshone, Sioux, Kiowa, and Arapaho — what we saw was only Plains-Indian dancing.

307

Performed in a clockwise motion, as if following the sun, the dancers moved in long lines like spokes on a wheel. Anyone could dance, and it seemed at times as if everyone did. Families crowded in around the dance space with their folding chairs and Pendleton blankets — babies and grandmothers, boys and fathers, mothers and daughters, all dressed fit to kill. The long succession of dances began: Girls' Fancy Shawl, Boys' Traditional, Fast and Slow War Dance, a Hoop Dance, a Hot Dance, and a Grass Dance. Intertribal dances — open to anyone — alternated with contest dances that were judged. Participants wore Coors numbers pinned to their backs the way bronc riders do. The costumes were elaborate. There were feathers dyed magenta and lime green, then fluffed at the tips; great feather bustles attached to every backside; and long straps of sleighbells running from ankles to hips. The Hot Dancers wore porcupine-hair roaches on their heads, the War Dancers carried straight and crooked lances, the Society Dancers wore wolf heads with little pointed ears, and the women in fringed buckskin dresses carried elegant eagle fans. One young man, who seemed to be a loner, had painted black stripes across his face and chest so thickly the paint ran together into a blackface. Later, we discovered he was white. A good many white people danced every night. One couple had flown in from Germany; they were Hot Dance aficionados, and when I tried to talk to them I found out they spoke only German and Crow. A blond boy of ten said he had driven north from Arizona with his adopted Apache parents. After eating a cheesy, dripping box of nachos, he went out to win his contest.

I squeezed through the delicious congestion of bodies, feathers brushing my cheeks, and circled under the eaves of the arbor. One boy, who couldn't have been older than three, in war bonnet and bells, shuffled out into the dance circle. The Mylar balloon tied to his hand was shaped like a fish. Four boys dancing near the power pole crouched low, jerking their heads and shoulders in the Prairie Chicken Dance. The Fast Dancers spun by, like wheels of fireworks, orbiting at twice the speed of the others.

Outside the arbor was a residual flux: crowds of Indian teenagers ambled past the bright concession stands, behind which a ribbon of headlights streamed, and behind them glowed rows of tents and tipis.

The arbor closed at 3 A.M., and we walked up our hill and went to bed. A couple of drunks stumbled by. "Hey. What's this? A tombstone?" one of them said as he kicked the tent. When no one answered, he disappeared in the brush. Later, the 49ers, a roving group of singers, began their encampment serenade. They sang until dawn every night of the fair so that even sleep, accompanied by their drumbeats, felt like a kind of dancing.

Crow Fair days are hot; Crow Fair nights are cold. A rumbling truck woke me. It was the septic tank man (he was white) pumping the outhouses. Some Livingston, Montana, friends who had arrived late were scattered around on the ground in sleeping bags. I brushed my teeth with water I'd brought for the radiator. The dance arbor, abandoned and dreary at midday, was getting a facelift from a cleanup crew. All the action was elsewhere: when I walked toward the bluffs behind the camp, I discovered two hundred children splashing in the Little Big Horn River.

That afternoon I visited Gary Johnson's camp. He's a bright, sly Crow drummer. Over some beadwork repairs he was swatting flies. "You killed our buffalo, I'll kill your flies," he said with a sardonic grin as I pulled up a chair. A small boy had taken Gary's drumstick and had beaten the metal top of a beer cooler until it was covered with dents. "Let him play, let him play," Gary admonished the boy's mother. "That's how we learn to make music." To be a drummer is to be a singer too, the voice used as percussively as the drum is musically. "I'd like to steal this boy. He and I would sing every night."

Every turn of the nomadic Crow life was once marked by movement and music. There were dances to celebrate birth, puberty, marriage, or death. There were healing dances and hunters' dances and contrary dances, in which all movement was done in reverse. There were dances to count coup, welcome strangers, honor guests, to cement alliances and feuds. Songs weren't composed but received whole from animals, plants, or storms. Antelope gave mothers lullabies, thunder and wind gave medicine songs, bears taught hunting songs.

Carlos Castaneda gave us talking bushes, but few of us realized how common these transmissions had become in aboriginal America. When I asked Gary about his pink-and-red-striped tipi — the only one of its kind in camp — he explained: "That's a

309

medicine tipi. Somehow I inherited it. The creek water rose up and told the guy living in it to dress and live like a woman. That was to be his medicine. So he became a *berdache* (a transvestite)." He gave me a serious look. "I'll do anything in that tipi, but I'll be damned if I'm going to sleep in it."

D. H. Lawrence described the Apache ceremonies he saw as "the feet of birds treading a dance" and claimed the music awakened in him "new root-griefs, old root-richnesses." In the next three nights I saw the quick, addled movements of blue grouse, feet that worked the ground like hooves, or else massaged it erotically with moccasins. One of the nights, when almost everyone had gone, I thought I heard women singing. It turned out to be teenage boys whose strange, hoarse voices convulsed and ululated in a falsetto. Gary was there and he drummed and danced and his son and wife danced, all the repetitions redoubled by multiple generations. How affectionately the shimmering beadwork traced the shapes of their dreams and threaded them back to the bodies that dreamed them.

It had been raining on and off all evening. The spectators and all but a few dancers had left. Shoals of garbage — pop cans, hot-dog wrappers, corn husks, and pieces of fry bread — drifted up against the wooden benches. I knew I had been riding an ebb tide here at Crow Fair. I'd seen bead workers' beadwork, dancers' dance steps, Indianness for the sake of being Indian — a shell of a culture whose spontaneous force had been revived against great odds and was transmitting weak signals. But transmitting nonetheless. The last inter-tribal dance was announced. Already, three of the drum groups had packed up and were leaving the arbor when five or six Crow men, dressed like cowboys, walked onto the grass. In boots, not moccasins, and still smoking cigarettes, they formed a long line and shuffled around and around. The shrill, trembling song that accompanied them could empower anyone listening to turn away from distraction and slide their hands across the buttocks of the world — above and beyond the ceremonial decor that was, after all, the point of all this. At the last minute, a young boy jumped up and burst into a boiling, hot-stepping Fast Dance, his feathered headdress shaking down his back like lightning. I wondered how much of this culture-straddling he could take and what in it would finally be instructive to him. Almost under his bounding feet a row of young children were sleeping on blankets laid out for them. Their feather bustles were bent and askew and a couple of moccasins were missing. A very tall Crow man with long braids but skin so light he might actually have been white began picking up the children. One by one, and so gently none of them woke, he carried them away.

Gretel Ehrlich

LENSES

You get used to looking through lenses; it is an acquired skill. When you first look through binoculars, for instance, you can't see a thing. You look at the inside of the barrel; you blink and watch your eyelashes; you play with the focus knob till one eye is purblind.

The microscope is even worse. You are supposed to keep both eyes open as you look through its single eyepiece. I spent my childhood in Pittsburgh trying to master this trick: seeing through one eye, with both eyes open. The microscope also teaches you to move your hands wrong, to shove the glass slide to the right if you are following a creature who is swimming off to the left — as if you were operating a tiller, or backing a trailer, or performing any other of those paradoxical maneuvers which require either instincts or a grasp of elementary physics, neither of which I possess.

A child's microscope set comes with a little five-watt lamp. You place this dim light in front of the microscope's mirror; the mirror bounces the light up through the slide, through the magnifying lenses, and into your eye. The only reason you do not see everything in silhouette is that microscopic things are so small they are translucent. The animals and plants in a drop of pond water pass light like pale stained glass; they seem so soaked in water and light that their opacity has leached away.

The translucent strands of algae you see under a microscope — Spirogyra, Oscillatoria, Cladophora — move of their own accord, no one knows how or why. You watch these swaying yellow, green, and brown strands of algae half mesmerized; you sink into the microscope's field forgetful, oblivious, as if it were all a dream of your deepest brain. Occasionally a zippy rotifer comes barreling through, black and white, and in a tremendous hurry.

My rotifers and daphniae and amoebae were in an especially tremendous hurry because they were drying up. I burnt out or broke my little five-watt bulb right away. To replace it, I rigged an old table lamp laid on its side; the table lamp carried a seventy-five-watt bulb. I was about twelve, immortal and invulnerable, and did not know what I was doing; neither did

312

anyone else. My parents let me set up my laboratory in the basement, where they wouldn't have to smell the urine I collected in test tubes and kept in the vain hope it would grow something horrible. So in full, solitary ignorance I spent evenings in the basement staring into a seventy-five-watt bulb magnified three hundred times and focused into my eye. It is a wonder I can see at all. My eyeball itself would start drying up; I blinked and blinked.

But the pond water creatures fared worse. I dropped them on a slide, floated a cover slip over them, and laid the slide on the microscope's stage, which the seventy-five-watt bulb had heated like a grill. At once the drop of pond water started to evaporate. Its edges shrank. The creatures swam among algae in a diminishing pool. I liked this part. The heat worked for me as a centrifuge, to concentrate the biomass. I had about five minutes to watch the members of a very dense population, excited by the heat, go about their business until — as I fancied sadly — they all caught on to their situation and started making out wills.

I was, then, not only watching the much-vaunted wonders in a drop of pond water; I was also, with mingled sadism and sympathy, setting up a limitless series of apocalypses. I set up and staged hundreds of ends-of-the-world and watched, enthralled, as they played themselves out. Over and over again, the last trump sounded, the final scroll unrolled, and the known world drained, dried, and vanished. When all the creatures lay motionless, boiled and fried in the positions they had when the last of their water dried completely, I washed the slide in the sink and started over with a fresh drop. How I loved that deep, wet world where the colored algae waved in the water and the rotifers swam!

But oddly, this is a story about swans. It is not even a story; it is a description of swans. This description of swans includes the sky over a pond, a pair of binoculars, and a mortal adult who had long since moved out of the Pittsburgh basement.

In the Roanoke valley of Virginia, rimmed by the Blue Ridge Mountains to the east and the Allegheny Mountains to the west, is a little semi-agricultural area called Daleville. In Daleville, set among fallow fields and wooded ridges, is Daleville Pond. It is a big pond, maybe ten acres; it holds a lot of sky. I used to haunt the place because I loved it; I still do. In winter it had that airy scruffiness of deciduous lands; you greet the daylight and the open space, and spend the evening picking burrs out of your pants.

One Valentine's Day, in the afternoon, I was crouched among dried reeds at the edge of Daleville Pond. Across the pond from where I crouched was a low forested mountain ridge. In every other direction I saw only sky, sky crossed by the reeds which blew before my face whichever way I turned.

I was looking through binoculars at a pair of whistling swans. Whistling swans! It is impossible to say how excited I was to see whistling swans in Daleville, Virginia. The two were a pair, mated for life, migrating north and west from the Atlantic coast to the high arctic. They had paused to feed at Daleville Pond. I had flushed them, and now they were flying and circling the pond. I crouched in the reeds so they would not be afraid to come back to the water.

Through binoculars I followed the swans, swinging where they flew. All their feathers were white; their eyes were black. Their wingspan was six feet; they were bigger than I was. They flew in unison, one behind the other; they made pass after pass at the pond. I watched them change from white swans in front of the mountain to black swans in front of the sky. In clockwise ellipses they flew, necks long and relaxed, alternately beating their wide wings and gliding.

As I rotated on my heels to keep the black frame of the lenses around them, I lost all sense of space. If I lowered the binoculars I was always amazed to learn in which direction I faced — dazed, the way you emerge awed from a movie and try to reconstruct, bit by bit, a real world, in order to discover where in it you might have parked the car.

I lived in that circle of light, in great speed and utter silence. When the swans passed before the sun they were distant — two black threads, two live stitches. But they kept coming, smoothly, and the sky deepened to blue behind them and they took on light. They gathered dimension as they neared, and I could see their ardent, straining eyes. Then I could hear the brittle blur of their wings, the blur which faded as they circled on, and the sky brightened to yellow behind them and the swans flattened and darkened and diminished as they flew. Once I lost them behind

314

the mountain ridge; when they emerged they were flying suddenly very high, and it was like music changing key.

I was lost. The reeds in front of me, swaying and out of focus in the binoculars' circular field, were translucent. The reeds were strands of color passing light like cells in water. They were those yellow and green and brown strands of pond algae I had watched so long in a light-soaked field. My eyes burned; I was watching algae wave in a shrinking drop; they crossed each other and parted wetly. And suddenly into the field swam two whistling swans, two tiny whistling swans. They swam as fast as rotifers: two whistling swans, infinitesimal, beating their tiny wet wings, perfectly formed.

Annie Dillard

TEACHING A STONE TO TALK

1.

The island where I live is peopled with cranks like myself. In a cedar-shake shack on a cliff — but we all live like this — is a man in his thirties who lives alone with a stone he is trying to teach to talk.

Wisecracks on this topic abound, as you might expect, but they are made as it were perfunctorily, and mostly by the young. For in fact, almost everyone here respects what Larry is doing, as do I, which is why I am protecting his (or her) privacy, and confusing for you the details. It could be, for instance, a pinch of sand he is teaching to talk, or a prolonged northerly, or any one of a number of waves. But it is, in fact, I assure you, a stone. It is — for I have seen it — a palm-sized oval beach cobble whose dark gray is cut by a band of white which runs around and, presumably, through it; such stones we call "wishing stones," for reasons obscure but not, I think, unimaginable.

He keeps it on a shelf. Usually the stone lies protected by a square of untanned leather, like a canary asleep under its cloth. Larry removes the cover for the stone's lessons, or more accurately, I should say, for the ritual or rituals which they perform together several times a day.

No one knows what goes on at these sessions, least of all myself, for I know Larry but slightly, and that owing only to a mix-up in our mail. I assume that like any other meaningful effort, the ritual involves sacrifice, the suppression of self-consciousness, and a certain precise tilt of the will, so that the will becomes transparent and hollow, a channel for the work. I wish him well. It is a noble work, and beats, from any angle, selling shoes.

Reports differ on precisely what he expects or wants the stone to say. I do not think he expects the stone to speak as we do, and describe for us its long life and many, or few, sensations. I think instead that he is trying to teach it to say a single word, such as "cup," or "uncle." For this purpose he has not, as some have seriously suggested, carved the stone a little mouth, or furnished it in any way with a pocket of air which it might then expel. Rather

316

— and I think he is wise in this — he plans to initiate his son, who is now an infant living with Larry's estranged wife, into the work, so that it may continue and bear fruit after his death.

2.

Nature's silence is its one remark, and every flake of world is a chip off that old mute and immutable block. The Chinese say that we live in the world of the ten thousand things. Each of the ten thousand things cries out to us precisely nothing.

God used to rage at the Israelites for frequenting sacred groves. I wish I could find one. Martin Buber says: "The crisis of all primitive mankind comes with the discovery of that which is fundamentally not-holy, the a-sacramental, which withstands the methods, and which has no 'hour,' a province which steadily enlarges itself." Now we are no longer primitive; now the whole world seems not-holy. We have drained the light from the boughs in the sacred grove and snuffed it in the high places and along the banks of sacred streams. We as a people have moved from pantheism to pan-atheism. Silence is not our heritage but our destiny; we live where we want to live.

The soul may ask God for anything, and never fail. You may ask God for his presence, or for wisdom, and receive each at his hands. Or you may ask God, in the words of the shopkeeper's little gag sign, that he not go away mad, but just go away. Once, in Israel, an extended family of nomads did just that. They heard God's speech and found it too loud. The wilderness generation was at Sinai; it witnessed there the thick darkness where God was: "and all the people saw the thunderings, and the lightnings, and the noise of the trumpet, and the mountain smoking." It scared them witless. Then they asked Moses to beg God, please, never speak to them directly again. "Let not God speak with us, lest we die." Moses took the message. And God, pitying their self-consciousness, agreed. He agreed not to speak to the people anymore. And he added to Moses, "Go say to them, Get into your tents again."

It is difficult to undo our own damage, and to recall to our presence that which we have asked to leave. It is hard to desecrate a grove and change your mind. The very holy mountains are keeping mum. We doused the burning bush and cannot rekindle it; we are lighting matches in vain under every green tree. Did the wind use to cry, and the hills shout forth praise? Now speech has perished from among the lifeless things of earth, and living things say very little to very few. Birds may crank out sweet gibberish and monkeys howl; horses neigh and pigs say, as you recall, oink oink. But so do cobbles rumble when a wave recedes, and thunders break the air in lightning storms. I call these noises silence. It could be that wherever there is motion there is noise, as when a whale breaches and smacks the water — and wherever there is stillness there is the still small voice, God's speaking from the whirlwind, nature's old song and dance, the show we drove from town. At any rate, now it is all we can do, and among our best efforts, to try to teach a given human language, English, to chimpanzees.

In the forties an American psychologist and his wife tried to teach a chimp actually to speak. At the end of three years the creature could pronounce, in a hoarse whisper, the words "mama," "papa," and "cup." After another three years of training she could whisper, with difficulty, still only "mama," "papa," and "cup." The more recent successes at teaching chimpanzees American Sign Language are well known. Just the other day a chimp told us, if we can believe that we truly share a vocabulary, that she had been sad in the morning. I'm sorry we asked.

What have we been doing all these centuries but trying to call God back to the mountain, or, failing that, raise a peep out of anything that isn't us? What is the difference between a cathedral and a physics lab? Are not they both saying: Hello? We spy on whales and on interstellar radio objects; we starve ourselves and pray till we're blue.

4.

I have been reading comparative cosmology. At this time most cosmologists favor the picture of the evolving universe described by Lemaitre and Gamow. But I prefer a suggestion made years ago by Valery — Paul Valery. He set forth the notion that the universe might be "head-shaped."

The mountains are great stone bells; they clang together like nuns. Who shushed the stars? There are a thousand million galaxies easily seen in the Palomar reflector; collisions between and among them do, of course, occur. But these collisions are very long and silent slides. Billions of stars sift among each other untouched, too distant even to be moved, heedless as always, hushed. The sea pronounces something, over and over, in a hoarse whisper; I cannot quite make it out. But God knows I have tried.

At a certain point you say to the woods, to the sea, to the mountains, the world, Now I am ready. Now I will stop and be wholly attentive. You empty yourself and wait, listening. After a time you hear it: there is nothing there. There is nothing but those things only, those created objects, discrete, growing or holding, or swaying, being rained on or raining, held, flooding or ebbing, standing, or spread. You feel the world's word as a tension, a hum, a single chorused note everywhere the same. This is it: this hum is the silence. Nature does utter a peep — just this one. The birds and insects, the meadows and swamps and rivers and stones and mountains and clouds: they all do it; they all don't do it. There is a vibrancy to the silence, a suppression, as if someone were gagging the world. But you wait, you give your life's length to listening, and nothing happens. The ice rolls up, the ice rolls back, and still that single note obtains. The tension, or lack of it, is intolerable. The silence is not actually suppression; instead, it is all there is.

5.

We are here to witness. There is nothing else to do with those mute materials we do not need. Until Larry teaches his stone to talk, until God changes his mind, or until the pagan gods slip back to their hilltop groves, all we can do with the whole inhuman array is watch it. We can stage our own act on the planet — build our cities on its plains, dam its rivers, plant its topsoils — but our meaningful activity scarcely covers the terrain. We do not use the songbirds, for instance. We do not eat many of them; we cannot befriend them; we cannot persuade them to eat more mosquitoes or plant fewer weed seeds. We can only witness them — whoever they are. If we were not here, they would be songbirds falling in the forest. If we were not here, material events like the passage of seasons would lack even the meager meanings we are able to muster for them. The show would play to an empty house, as do all those falling stars which fall in the daytime. That is why I take walks: to keep an eye on things. And that is why I went to the Galapagos islands.

All this becomes especially clear on the Galapagos islands. The Galapagos islands are just plain here — and little else. They blew up out of the ocean, some plants blew in on them, some animals drifted aboard and evolved weird forms — and there they all are, whoever they are, in full swing. You can go there and watch it happen, and try to figure it out. The Galapagos are a kind of metaphysics laboratory, almost wholly uncluttered by human culture or history. Whatever happens on those bare volcanic rocks happens in full view, whether anyone is watching or not.

What happens there is this, and precious little it is: clouds come and go, and the round of similar seasons; a pig eats a tortoise or doesn't eat a tortoise; Pacific waves fall up and slide back; a lichen expands; night follows day; an albatross dies and dries on a cliff; a cool current upwells from the ocean floor; fishes multiply, flies swarm, stars rise and fall, and diving birds dive. The news, in other words, breaks on the beaches. And taking it all in are the trees. The *palo santo* trees crowd the hillsides like any outdoor audience; they face the lagoons, the lava lowlands, and the shores.

I have some experience of these *palo santo* trees. They interest me as emblems of the muteness of the human stance in relation to all that is not human. I see us all as *palo santo* trees, holy sticks, together watching all that we watch, and growing in silence.

In the Galapagos, it took me a long time to notice the *palo santo* trees. Like everyone else, I specialized in sea lions. My shipmates and I liked the sea lions, and envied their lives. Their joy seemed conscious. They were engaged in full-time play. They were all either fat or dead; there was no halfway. By day they played in the shallows, alone or together, greeting each other and us with great noises of joy, or they took a turn offshore and body-surfed in the breakers, exultant. By night on the sand they lay in each other's flippers and slept. Everyone joked, often, that when he "came back," he would just as soon do it all over again as a sea lion. I concurred. The sea lion game looked unbeatable.

But a year and a half later, I returned to those unpeopled islands. In the interval my attachment to them had shifted, and my memories of them had altered, the way memories do, like particolored pebbles rolled back and forth over a grating, so that after a time those hard bright ones, the ones you thought you would never lose, have vanished, passed through the grating, and only a few big, unexpected ones remain, no longer unnoticed but now selected out for some meaning, large and unknown.

Such were the *palo santo* trees. Before, I had never given them a thought. They were just miles of half-dead trees on the red lava sea cliffs of some deserted islands. They were only a name in a notebook: "*Palo santo* — those strange white trees." Look at the sea lions! Look at the flightless cormorants, the penguins, the iguanas, the sunset! But after eighteen months the wonderful cormorants, penguins, iguanas, sunsets, and even the sea lions, had dropped from my holey heart. I returned to the Galapagos to see the *palo santo* trees.

They are thin, pale, wispy trees. You walk among them on the lowland deserts, where they grow beside the prickly pear. You see them from the water on the steeps that face the sea, hundreds together, small and thin and spread, and so much more pale than their red soils that any black-and-white photograph of them looks like a negative. Their stands look like blasted orchards. At every season they all look newly dead, pale and bare as birches drowned in a beaver pond — for at every season they look leafless, paralyzed, and mute. But in fact, if you look closely, you can see during the rainy months a few meager deciduous leaves here and there on their brittle twigs. And hundreds of lichens always grow on their bark in mute, overlapping explosions which barely enlarge in the course of the decade, lichens pink and orange, lavender, yellow, and green. The *palo santo* trees bear the lichens effortlessly, unconsciously, the way they bear everything. Their multitudes, transparent as line drawings, crowd the cliffsides like whirling dancers, like empty groves, and look out over cliff-wrecked breakers toward more unpeopled islands, with their freakish lizards and birds, toward the grieving lagoons and the bays where the sea lions wander, and beyond to the clamoring seas.

Now I no longer concurred with my shipmates' joke; I no longer wanted to "come back" as a sea lion. For I thought, and I still think, that if I came back to life in the sunlight where everything changes, I would like to come back as a *palo santo* tree, one of thousands on a cliffside on those godforsaken islands, where a million events occur among the witless, where a splash of rain may drop on a yellow iguana the size of a dachshund, and ten minutes later the iguana may blink. I would like to come back as a *palo santo* tree on the weather side of an island, so that I could be, myself, a perfect witness, and look, mute, and wave my arms.

6.

The silence is all there is. It is the alpha and the omega. It is God's brooding over the face of the waters; it is the blended note of the ten thousand things, the whine of wings. You take a step in the right direction to pray to this silence, and even to address the prayer to "World." Distinctions blur. Quit your tents. Pray without ceasing.

Annie Dillard

TOTAL ECLIPSE

1.

It had been like dying, that sliding down the mountain pass. It had been like the death of someone, irrational, that sliding down the mountain pass and into the region of dread. It was like slipping into fever, or falling down that hole in sleep from which you wake yourself whimpering. We had crossed the mountains that day, and now we were in a strange place — a hotel in central Washington, in a town near Yakima. The eclipse we had traveled here to see would occur early the next morning.

I lay in bed. My husband, Gary, was reading beside me. I lay in bed and looked at the painting on the hotel room wall. It was a print of a detailed and lifelike painting of a smiling clown's head, made out of vegetables. It was a painting of the sort which you do not intend to look at, and which, alas, you never forget. Some tasteless fate presses it upon you; it becomes part of the complex interior junk you carry with you wherever you go. Two years have passed since the total eclipse of which I write. During those years I have forgotten, I assume, a great many things I wanted to remember — but I have not forgotten that clown painting or its lunatic setting in the old hotel.

The clown was bald. Actually, he wore a clown's tight rubber wig, painted white; this stretched over the top of his skull, which was a cabbage. His hair was bunches of baby carrots. Inset in his white clown makeup, and in his cabbage skull, were his small and laughing human eyes. The clown's glance was like the glance of Rembrandt in some of the self-portraits: lively, knowing, deep, and loving. The crinkled shadows around his eyes were string beans. His eyebrows were parsley. Each of his ears was a broad bean. His thin, joyful lips were red chili peppers; between his lips were wet rows of human teeth and a suggestion of a real tongue. The clown print was framed in gilt and glassed.

To put ourselves in the path of the total eclipse, that day we had driven five hours inland from the Washington coast, where we lived. When we tried to cross the Cascades range, an avalanche had blocked the pass.

A slope's worth of snow blocked the road; traffic backed up. Had the avalanche buried any cars that morning? We could not learn. This highway was the only winter road over the mountains. We waited as highway crews bulldozed a passage through the avalanche. With two-by-fours and walls of plyboard, they erected a one-way, roofed tunnel through the avalanche. We drove through the avalanche tunnel, crossed the pass, and descended several thousand feet into central Washington and the broad Yakima valley, about which we knew only that it was orchard country. As we lost altitude, the snows disappeared; our ears popped; the trees changed, and in the trees were strange birds. I watched the landscape innocently, like a fool, like a diver in the rapture of the deep who plays on the bottom while his air runs out.

The hotel lobby was a dark, derelict room, narrow as a corridor, and seemingly without air. We waited on a couch while the manager vanished upstairs to do something unknown to our room. Beside us on an overstuffed chair, absolutely motionless, was a platinum-blond woman in her forties wearing a black silk dress and a strand of pearls. Her long legs were crossed; she supported her head on her fist. At the dim far end of the room, their backs toward us, sat six bald old men in their shirtsleeves, around a loud television. Two of them seemed asleep. They were drunks. "Number six!" cried the man on television, "Number six!"

On the broad lobby desk, lighted and bubbling, was a ten-gallon aquarium containing one large fish; the fish tilted up and down in its water. Against the long opposite wall sang a live canary in its cage. Beneath the cage, among spilled millet seeds on the carpet, were a decorated child's sand bucket and matching sand shovel.

Now the alarm was set for six. I lay awake remembering an article I had read downstairs in the lobby, in an engineering magazine. The article was about gold mining.

In South Africa, in India, and in South Dakota, the gold mines extend so deeply into the earth's crust that they are hot. The rock walls burn the miners' hands. The companies have to air-condition the mines; if the air conditioners break, the miners die. The elevators in the mine shafts run very slowly, down, and up, so the miners' ears will not pop in their skulls. When the miners return to the surface, their faces are deathly pale.

Early the next morning we checked out. It was February 26, 1979, a Monday morning. We would drive out of town, find a hilltop, watch the eclipse, and then drive back over the mountains and home to the coast. How familiar things are here; how adept we are; how smoothly and professionally we check out! I had forgotten the clown's smiling head and the hotel lobby as if they had never existed. Gary put the car in gear and off we went, as off we have gone to a hundred other adventures.

It was before dawn when we found a highway out of town and drove into the unfamiliar countryside. By the growing light we could see a band of cirrostratus clouds in the sky. Later the rising sun would clear these clouds before the eclipse began. We drove at random until we came to a range of unfenced hills. We pulled off the highway, bundled up, and climbed one of these hills.

2.

The hill was five hundred feet high. Long winter-killed grass covered it, as high as our knees. We climbed and rested, sweating in the cold; we passed clumps of bundled people on the hillside who were setting up telescopes and fiddling with cameras. The top of the hill stuck up in the middle of the sky. We tightened our scarves and looked around.

East of us rose another hill like ours. Between the hills, far below, was the highway which threaded south into the valley. This was the Yakima valley; I had never seen it before. It is justly famous for its beauty, like every planted valley. It extended south into the horizon, a distant dream of a valley, a Shangri-la. All its hundreds of low, golden slopes bore orchards. Among the orchards were towns, and roads, and plowed and fallow fields. Through the valley wandered a thin, shining river; from the river extended fine, frozen irrigation ditches. Distance blurred and blued the sight, so that the whole valley looked like a thickness or sediment at the bottom of the sky. Directly behind us was more sky, and empty lowlands blued by distance, and Mount Adams. Mount Adams was an enormous, snow-covered volcanic cone rising flat, like so much scenery.

Now the sun was up. We could not see it; but the sky behind the band of clouds was yellow, and, far down the valley, some hillside orchards had lighted up. More people were parking near the highway and climbing the hills. It was the West. All of us rugged individualists were wearing knit caps and blue nylon parkas. People were climbing the nearby hills and setting up shop in clumps among the dead grasses. It looked as though we had all gathered on hilltops to pray for the world on its last day. It looked as though we had all crawled out of spaceships and were preparing to assault the valley below. It looked as though we were scattered on hilltops at dawn to sacrifice virgins, make rain, set stone stelae in a ring. There was no place out of the wind. The straw grasses banged our legs.

Up in the sky where we stood the air was lusterless yellow. To the west the sky was blue. Now the sun cleared the clouds. We cast rough shadows on the blowing grass; freezing, we waved our arms. Near the sun, the sky was bright and colorless. There was nothing to see.

It began with no ado. It was odd that such a well-advertised public event should have no starting gun, no overture, no introductory speaker. I should have known right then that I was out of my depth. Without pause or preamble, silent as orbits, a piece of the sun went away. We looked at it through welders' goggles. A piece of the sun was missing; in its place we saw empty sky.

I had seen a partial eclipse in 1970. A partial eclipse is very interesting. It bears almost no relation to a total eclipse. Seeing a partial eclipse bears the same relation to seeing a total eclipse as kissing a man does to marrying him, or as flying in an airplane does to falling out of an airplane. Although the one experience precedes the other, it in no way prepares you for it. During a partial eclipse the sky does not darken — not even when 94 percent of the sun is hidden. Nor does the sun, seen colorless through protective devices, seem terribly strange. We have all seen a sliver of light in the sky; we have all seen the crescent moon by day. However, during a partial eclipse the air does indeed get cold, precisely as if someone were standing between you and the fire. And blackbirds do fly back to their roosts. I had seen a partial eclipse before, and here was another.

What you see in an eclipse is entirely different from what you know. It is especially different for those of us whose grasp of astronomy is so frail that, given a flashlight, a grapefruit, two oranges, and fifteen years, we still could not figure out which way to set the clocks for Daylight Saving Time. Usually it is a bit of a trick to keep your knowledge from blinding you. But during an eclipse it is easy. What you see is much more convincing than any wild-eyed theory you may know.

You may read that the moon has something to do with eclipses. I have never seen the moon yet. You do not see the moon. So near the sun, it is as completely invisible as the stars are by day. What you see before your eyes is the sun going through phases. It gets narrower and narrower, as the waning moon does, and, like the ordinary moon, it travels alone in the simple sky. The sky is of course background. It does not appear to eat the sun; it is far behind the sun. The sun simply shaves away; gradually, you see less sun and more sky.

The sky's blue was deepening, but there was no darkness. The sun was a wide crescent, like a segment of tangerine. The wind freshened and blew steadily over the hill. The eastern hill across the highway grew dusky and sharp. The towns and orchards in the valley to the south were dissolving into the blue light. Only the thin river held a trickle of sun.

Now the sky to the west deepened to indigo, a color never seen. A dark sky usually loses color. This was a saturated, deep indigo, up in the air. Stuck up into that unworldly sky was the cone of Mount Adams, and the alpenglow was upon it. The alpenglow is that red light of sunset which holds out on snowy mountaintops long after the valleys and tablelands are dimmed. "Look at Mount Adams," I said, and that was the last sane moment I remember.

I turned back to the sun. It was going. The sun was going, and the world was wrong. The grasses were wrong; they were platinum. Their every detail of stem, head, and blade shone lightless and artificially distinct as an art photographer's platinum print. This color has never been seen on earth. The hues were metallic; their finish was matte. The hillside was a nineteenth-century tinted photograph from which the tints had faded. All the people you see in the photograph, distinct and detailed as their faces look, are now dead. The sky was navy blue. My hands were silver. All the distant hills' grasses were finespun metal which the wind laid down. I was watching a faded color print of a movie filmed in the Middle Ages; I was standing in it, by some mistake. I was standing in a movie of hillside grasses filmed in the Middle Ages, I missed my own century, the people I knew, and the real light of day.

I looked at Gary. He was in the film. Everything was lost. He was a platinum print, a dead artist's version of life. I saw on his skull the darkness of night mixed with the colors of day. My mind was going out; my eyes were receding the way galaxies recede to the rim of space. Gary was light-years away, gesturing inside a circle of darkness, down the wrong end of a telescope. He smiled as if he saw me; the stringy crinkles around his eyes moved. The sight of him, familiar and wrong, was something I was remembering from centuries hence, from the other side of death: yes, *that* is the way he used to look, when we were living. When it was our generation's turn to be alive. I could not hear him; the wind was too loud. Behind him the sun was going. We had all started down a chute of time. At first it was pleasant; now there was no stopping it. Gary was chuting away across space, moving and talking and catching my eye, chuting down the long corridor of separation. The skin on his face moved like thin bronze plating that would peel.

The grass at our feet was wild barley. It was the wild einkorn wheat which grew on the hilly flanks of the Zagros Mountains, above the Euphrates valley, above the valley of the river we call *River*. We harvested the grass with stone sickles, I remember. We found the grasses on the hillsides; we built our shelter beside them and cut them down. That is how he used to look then, that one, moving and living and catching my eye, with the sky so dark behind him, and the wind blowing. God save our life.

From all the hills came screams. A piece of sky beside the crescent sun was detaching. It was a loosened circle of evening sky, suddenly lighted from the back. It was an abrupt black body out of nowhere; it was a flat disk; it was almost over the sun. That is when there were screams. At once this disk of sky slid over the sun like a lid. The sky snapped over the sun like a lens cover. The hatch in the brain slammed. Abruptly it was dark night, on the land and in the sky. In the night sky was a tiny ring of light. The hole where the sun belongs is very small. A thin ring of light marked its place. There was no sound. The eyes dried, the arteries drained, the lungs hushed. There was no world. We were the world's dead people rotating and orbiting around and around, embedded in the planet's crust, while the earth rolled down. Our minds were light-years distant, forgetful of almost everything. Only an extraordinary act of will could recall to us our former, living selves and our contexts in matter and time. We had, it seems, loved the planet and loved our lives, but could no longer remember the way of them. We got the light wrong. In the sky was something that should not be there. In the black sky was a ring of light. It was a thin ring, an old, thin silver wedding band, an old, worn ring. It was an old wedding band in the sky, or a morsel of bone. There were stars. It was all over.

3.

It is now that the temptation is strongest to leave these regions. We have seen enough; let's go. Why burn our hands any more than we have to? But two years have passed; the price of gold has risen. I return to the same buried alluvial beds and pick through the strata again.

I saw, early in the morning, the sun diminish against a backdrop of sky. I saw a circular piece of that sky appear, suddenly detached, blackened, and backlighted; from nowhere it came and overlapped the sun. It did not look like the moon. It was enormous and black. If I had not read that it was the moon, I could have seen the sight a hundred times and never thought of the moon once. (If, however, I had not read that it was the moon — if, like most of the world's people throughout time, I had simply glanced up and seen this thing — then I doubtless would not have speculated much, but would have, like Emperor Louis of Bavaria in 840, simply died of fright on the spot.) It did not look like dragon, although it looked more like a dragon than the moon. It looked like a lens cover, or the lid of a pot. It materialized out of thin air — black, and flat, and sliding, outline in flame.

Seeing this black body was like seeing a mushroom cloud. The heart screeched. The meaning of the sight overwhelmed its fascination. It obliterated meaning itself. If you were to glance out one day and see a row of mushroom clouds rising on the horizon, you would know at once that what you were seeing, remarkable as it was, was intrinsically not worth remarking. No use running to tell anyone. Significant as it was, it did not matter a whit. For what is significance? It is significance for people. No people, no significance. This is all I have to tell you.

In the deeps are the violence and terror of which psychology has warned us. But if you ride these monsters deeper down, if you drop with them farther over the world's rim, you find what our sciences cannot locate or name, the substrate, the ocean or matrix of either which buoys the rest, which gives goodness its power for good, and evil its power for evil, the unified field: our complex and inexplicable caring for each other, and for our life together here. This is given. It is not learned.

The world which lay under darkness and stillness following the closing of the lid was not the world we know. The event was over. Its devastation lay round about us. The clamoring mind and heart stilled, almost indifferent, certainly disembodied, frail, and exhausted. The hills were hushed, obliterated. Up in the sky, like a crater from some distant cataclysm, was a hollow ring.

You have seen photographs of the sun taken during a total eclipse. The corona fills the print. All of these photographs were taken through telescopes. The lenses of telescopes and cameras can no more cover the breadth and scale of the visual array than language can cover the breadth and simultaneity of internal experience. Lenses enlarge the sight, omit its context, and make of it a pretty and sensible picture, like something on a Christmas card. I assure you, if you send any shepherds a Christmas card on which is printed a three-by-three photograph of the angel of the

Lord, the glory of the Lord, and a multitude of the heavenly host, they will not be sore afraid. More fearsome things can come in envelopes. More moving photographs than those of the sun's corona can appear in magazines. But I pray you will never see anything more awful in the sky.

You see the wide world swaddled in darkness; you see a vast breadth of hilly land, and an enormous, distant, blackened valley; you see towns' lights, a river's path, and blurred portions of your hat and scarf; you see your husband's face looking like an early black-and-white film; and you see a sprawl of black sky and blue sky together, with unfamiliar stars in it, some barely visible bands of cloud, and over there, a small white ring. The ring is as small as one goose in a flock of migrating geese — if you happen to notice a flock of migrating geese. It is one 360th part of the visible sky. The sun we see is less than half the diameter of a dime held at arm's length.

The Crab Nebula, in the constellation Taurus, looks, through binoculars, like a smoke ring. It is a star in the process of exploding. Light from its explosion first reached the earth in 1054; it was a supernova then, and so bright it shone in the daytime. Now it is not so bright, but it is still exploding. It expands at the rate of seventy million miles a day. It is interesting to look through binoculars at something expanding seventy million miles a day. It does not budge. Its apparent size does not increase. Photographs of the Crab Nebula taken fifteen years ago seem identical to photographs of it taken yesterday. Some lichens are similar. Botanists have measured some ordinary lichens twice, at fifty-year intervals, without detecting any growth at all. And yet their cells divide; they live.

The small ring of light was like these things — like a ridiculous lichen up in the sky, like a perfectly still explosion 4,200 light-years away: it was interesting, and lovely, and in witless motion, and it had nothing to do with anything.

It had nothing to do with anything. The sun was too small, and too cold, and too far away, to keep the world alive. The white ring was not enough. It was feeble and worthless. It was as useless as a memory; it was as off kilter and hollow and wretched as a memory.

When you try your hardest to recall someone's face, or the look of a place, you see in your mind's eye some vague and terrible sight such as this. It is dark; it is insubstantial; it is all wrong.

The white ring and the saturated darkness made the earth and the sky look as they must look in the memories of the careless dead. What I saw, what I seemed to be standing in, was all the wrecked light that the memories of the dead could shed upon the living world. We had all died in our boots on the hilltops of Yakima, and were alone in eternity. Empty space stoppered our living days wrong. With great effort we had remembered some sort of circular light in the sky — but only the outline. Oh, and then the orchard trees withered, the ground froze, the glaciers slid down the valleys and overlapped the towns. If there had ever been people on earth, nobody knew it. The dead had forgotten those they had loved. The dead were parted one from the other and could no longer remember the faces and lands they had loved in the light. They seemed to stand on darkened hilltops, looking down.

4.

We teach our children one thing only, as we were taught: to wake up. We teach our children to look alive there, to join by words and activities the life of human culture on the planet's crust. As adults we are almost all adept at waking up. We have so mastered the transition we have forgotten we ever learned it. Yet it is a transition we make a hundred times a day, as, like so many will-less dolphins, we plunge and surface, lapse and emerge. We live half our waking lives and all of our sleeping lives in some private, useless, and insensible waters we never mention or recall. Useless, I say. Valueless, I might add — until someone hauls their wealth up to the surface and into the wide-awake city, in a form that people can use.

I do not know how we got to the restaurant. Like Roethke, "I take my waking slow." Gradually I seemed more or less alive, and already forgetful. It was now almost nine in the morning. It was the day of a solar eclipse in central Washington, and a fine adventure for everyone. The sky was clear; there was a fresh breeze out of the north.

The restaurant was a roadside place with tables and booths. The other eclipse-watchers were there. From our booth we could see their cars' California license plates, their University of Washington parking stickers. Inside the restaurant we were all eating eggs or waffles; people were fairly shouting and exchanging enthusiasms, like fans after a World Series game. Did you see . . . . . ? Did you see . . . ? Then somebody said something which knocked me for a loop.

A college student, a boy in a blue parka who carried a Hasselblad, said to us, "Did you see that little white ring? It looked like a Life Saver. It looked like a Life Saver up in the sky."

And so it did. The boy spoke well. He was a walking alarm clock. I myself had at that time no access to such a word. He could write a sentence, and I could not. I grabbed that Life Saver and rode it to the surface. And I had to laugh. I had been dumbstruck on the Euphrates River, I had been dead and gone and grieving, all over the sight of something which, if you could claw your way up to that level, you would grant looked very much like a Life Saver. It was good to be back among people so clever; it was good to have all the world's words at the mind's disposal, so the mind could begin its task. All those things for which we have no words are lost. The mind — the culture — has two little tools, grammar and lexicon: a decorated sand bucket and a matching shovel. With these we bluster about the continents and do all the world's work. With these we try to save our very lives.

There are a few more things to tell from this level, the level of the restaurant. One is the old joke about breakfast. "It can never be satisfied, the mind, never." Wallace Stevens wrote that, and in the long run he was right. The mind wants to live forever, or to learn a very good reason why not. The mind wants to know all the world, and all eternity, and God. The mind's sidekick, however, will settle for two eggs over easy.

The dear, stupid body is as easily satisfied as a spaniel. And, incredibly, the simple spaniel can lure the brawling mind to its dish. It is everlastingly funny that the proud, metaphysically ambitious, clamoring mind will hush if you give it an egg.

Further: while the mind reels in deep space, while the mind grieves or fears or exults, the workaday senses, in ignorance or idiocy, like so many computer terminals printing out market prices while the world blows up, still transcribe their little data and transmit them to the warehouse in the skull. Later, under the tranquilizing influence of fried eggs, the mind can sort through this data. The restaurant was a halfway house, a decompression chamber. There I remembered a few things more.

The deepest, and most terrifying, was this: I have said that I heard screams. (I have since read that screaming, with hysteria, is a common reaction even to expected total eclipses.) People on all the hillsides, including, I think, myself, screamed when the black body of the moon detached from the sky and rolled over the sun. But something else was happening at that same instant, and it was this, I believe, which made us scream.

The second before the sun went out we saw a wall of dark shadow come speeding at us. We no sooner saw it than it was upon us, like thunder. It roared up the valley. It slammed our hill and knocked us out. It was the monstrous swift shadow cone of the moon. I have since read that this wave of shadow moves 1,800 miles an hour. Language can give no sense of this sort of speed — 1,800 miles an hour. It was 195 miles wide. No end was in sight — you saw only the edge. It rolled at you across the land at 1,800 miles an hour, hauling darkness like plague behind it. Seeing it, and knowing it was coming straight for you, was like feeling a slug of anesthetic shoot up your arm. If you think very fast, you may have time to think, "Soon it will hit my brain." You can feel the deadness race up your arm; you can feel the appalling, inhuman speed of your own blood. We saw the wall of shadow coming, and screamed before it hit.

This was the universe about which we have read so much and never before felt: the universe as a clockwork of loose spheres flung at stupefying, unauthorized speeds. How could anything moving so fast not crash, not veer from its orbit amok like a car out of control on a turn?

Less than two minutes later, when the sun emerged, the trailing edge of the shadow cone sped away. It coursed down our hill and raced eastward over the plain, faster than the eye could believe; it swept over the plain and dropped over the planet's rim in a twinkling. It had clobbered us, and now it roared away. We blinked in the light. It was as though an enormous, loping god in the sky had reached down and slapped the earth's face.

Something else, something more ordinary, came back to me along about the third cup of coffee. During the moments of totality, it was so dark that drivers on the highway below turned on their cars' headlights. We could see the highway's route as a strand of lights. It was bumper-to-bumper down there. It was eight-fifteen in the morning, Monday morning, and people were driving into Yakima to work. That it was as dark as night, and eerie as hell, an hour after dawn, apparently meant that in order to *see* to drive to work, people had to use their headlights. Four or five cars pulled off the road. The rest, in a line at least five miles long, drove to town. The highway ran between hills; the people could not have seen any of the eclipsed sun at all. Yakima will have another total eclipse in 2086. Perhaps, in 2086, businesses will give their employees an hour off.

From the restaurant we drove back to the coast. The highway crossing the Cascades range was open. We drove over the mountain like old pros. We joined our places on the planet's thin crust; it held. For the time being, we were home free.

Early that morning at six, when we had checked out, the six bald men were sitting on folding chairs in the dim hotel lobby. The television was on. Most of them were awake. You might drown in your own spittle, God knows, at any time; you might wake up dead in a small hotel, a cabbage head watching TV while snows pile up in the passes, watching TV while the chili peppers smile and the moon passes over the sun and nothing changes and nothing is learned because you have lost your bucket and shovel and no longer care. What if you regain the surface and open your sack and find, instead of treasure, a beast which jumps at you? Or you may not come back at all. The winches may jam, the scaffolding buckle, the air conditioning collapse. You may glance up one day and see by your headlamp the canary keeled-over in its cage. You may reach into a cranny for pearls and touch a moray eel. You yank on your rope; it is too late.

Apparently people share a sense of these hazards, for when the total eclipse ended, an odd thing happened.

When the sun appeared as a blinding bead on the ring's side, the eclipse was over. The black lens cover appeared again, backlighted, and slid away. At once the yellow light made the sky blue again; the black lid dissolved and vanished. The real world began there. I remember now: we all hurried away. We were born and bored at a stroke. We rushed down the hill. We found our car; we saw the other people streaming down the hillsides; we joined the highway traffic and drove away.

We never looked back. It was a general vamoose, and an odd one, for when we left the hill, the sun was still partially eclipsed — a sight rare enough, and one which, in itself, we would probably have driven five hours to see. But enough is enough. One turns at last even from glory itself with a sigh of relief. From the depths of mystery, and even from the heights of splendor, we bounce back and hurry for the latitudes of home.

Annie Dillard

THE GIFTS

Cold, clear, and calm in the pale blue morning. Snow on the high peaks brightening to amber. The bay a sheet of gray glass beneath a faint haze of steam. A November sun rises with the same fierce, chill stare of an owl's eye.

I stand at the window watching the slow dawn, and my mind fixes on the island. Nita comes softly down the stairs as I pack gear and complain of having slept too late for these short days. A few minutes later, Ethan trudges out onto the cold kitchen floor, barefoot and half asleep. We do not speak directly about hunting, to avoid acting proud or giving offense to the animals. I say only that I will go to the island and look around; Ethan says only that he would rather stay at home with Nita. I wish he would come along so I could teach him things, but know it will be quieter in the woods with just the dog.

They both wave from the window as I ease the skiff away from shore, crunching through cakes of freshwater ice the tide has carried in from Salmon River. It is a quick run through Windy Channel and out onto the freedom of the Sound, where the slopes of Mt. Sarichef bite cleanly into the frozen sky. The air stings against my face, but the rest of me is warm inside thick layers of clothes. Shungnak whines, paces, and looks over the gunwale toward the still-distant island.

Broad swells looming off the Pacific alternately lift the boat and drop it between smooth-walled canyons of water. Midway across the Sound a dark line of wind descends swiftly from the north, and within minutes we are surrounded by whitecaps. There are two choices: either beat straight up into them or cut an easier angle across the waves and take the spray. I vacillate for a while, then choose the icy spray over the intense pounding. Although I know it is wrong to curse the wind, I do it anyway.

A kittiwake sweeps over the water in great, vaulting arcs, its wings flexed against the touch and billow of the air. As it tilts its head passing over the boat, I think how clumsy and foolish we must look. The island's shore lifts slowly in dark walls of rock and timber that loom above the apron of snow-covered beach. As I approach the shelter of Low Point, the chop fades and the swell is smaller. I turn up along the lee, running between the kelp beds

337

and the surf, straining my eyes for deer that may be feeding at the tide's edge.

Near the end of the point is a narrow gut that opens to a small, shallow anchorage. I ease the boat between the rocks, with lines of surf breaking close on either side. The waves rise and darken, their sharp edges sparkle in the sun, then long manes of spray whirl back as they turn inside out and pitch onto the shallow reef. The anchor slips down through ten feet of crystal water to settle among the kelp fronds and urchin-covered rocks. On a strong ebb the boat would go dry here, but today's tide change is only six feet. Before launching the punt I meticulously glass the broad, rocky shore and the sprawls of brown grass along the timber's edge. A tight bunch of rock sandpipers flashes up from the shingle and an otter loops along the windrows of drift logs, but there is no sign of deer. I can't help feeling a little anxious, because the season is drawing short and our year's supply of meat is not yet in. Throughout the fall, deer have been unusually wary, haunting the dense underbrush and slipping away at the least disturbance. I've come near a few, but these were young ones that I stalked only for the luxury of seeing them from close range.

Watching deer is the same pleasure now that it was when I was younger, when I loved animals only with my eyes and judged hunting to be outside the bounds of morality. Later, I tried expressing this love through studies of zoology, but this only seemed to put another kind of barrier between humanity and nature — the detachment of science and abstraction. Then, through anthropology, I encountered the entirely different views of nature found in other cultures. The hunting peoples were most fascinating because they had achieved deepest intimacy with their wild surroundings and had made natural history the focus of their lives. At the age of twenty-two, I went to live with Eskimos on the arctic coast of Alaska. It was my first year away from home, I had scarcely held a rifle in my hands, and the Eskimos — who call themselves the Real People — taught me their hunter's way.

The experience of living with Eskimos made very clear the direct, physical connectedness between all humans and the environments they draw existence from. Some years later, living with Koyukon Indians in Alaska's interior, I encountered a rich new dimension of that connectedness, and it profoundly changed my view of the world. Traditional Koyukon people follow a code of moral and ethical behavior that keeps a hunter in right relationship to the animals. They teach that all of nature is spiritual and aware, that it must be treated with respect, and that humans should approach the living world with restraint and humility. Now I struggle to learn if these same principles can apply in my own life and culture. Can we borrow from an ancient wisdom to structure a new relationship between ourselves and the environment? Or is Western society irreversibly committed to the illusion that humanity is separate from and dominant over the natural world?

A young bald eagle watches nervously from the peak of a tall hemlock as we bob ashore in the punt. Finally the bird lurches out, scoops its wings full of dense, cold air, and soars away beyond the line of trees. While I trudge up the log tide flats with the punt, Shungnak prances excitedly back and forth hunting for smells. The upper reaches are layered and slabbed with ice; slick cobbles shine like steel in the sun; frozen grass crackles underfoot. I lean the punt on a snow-covered log, pick up my rifle and small pack, and slip through the leafless alders into the forest.

My eyes take a moment adjusting to the sudden darkness, the deep green of boughs, and the somber, shadowy trunks. I feel safe and hidden here. The entire forest floor is covered with deep moss that should sponge gently beneath my feet. But today the softness is gone: frozen moss crunches with each step and brittle twigs snap, ringing out in the crisp air like strangers' voices. It takes a while to get used to this harshness in a forest that is usually so velvety and wet and silent. I listen to the clicking of gusts in the high branches and think that winter has come upon us like a fist.

At the base of a large nearby tree is a familiar patch of white — a scatter of deer bones — ribs, legs, vertebrae, two pelvis bones, and two skulls with half-bleached antlers. I put them here last winter, saying they were for the other animals, to make clear that they were not being thoughtlessly wasted. The scavengers soon picked them clean, the deer mice have gnawed them, and eventually they will be absorbed into the forest again. Koyukon elders say it shows respect, putting animal bones back in a clean, wild place instead of throwing them away with trash or scattering them in a garbage dump. The same obligations of etiquette that bind us to our human community also bind us to the natural community we live within.

Shungnak follows closely as we work our way back through a maze of windfalls, across clear disks of frozen ponds, and around patches of snow beneath openings in the forest canopy. I step and wait, trying to make no sound, knowing we could see deer at any moment. Deep snow has driven them down off the slopes and they are sure to be distracted with the business of the mating season.

We pick our way up the face of a high, steep scarp, then clamber atop a fallen log for a better view ahead. I peer into the semi-open understory of twiggy bushes, probing each space with my eyes. A downy woodpecker's call sparks from a nearby tree. Several minutes pass. Then a huckleberry branch moves, barely twitches, without the slightest noise . . . not far ahead.

Amid the scramble of brush where my eyes saw nothing a few minutes ago, a dim shape materializes, as if its own motion had created it. A doe steps into an open space, deep brown in her winter coat, soft and striking and lovely, dwarfed among the great trees, lifting her nose, looking right toward me. For perhaps a minute we are motionless in each other's gaze; then her head jerks to the left, her ears twitch back and forth, her tail flicks up, and she turns away in the stylized gait deer always use when alarmed.

Quick as a breath, quiet as a whisper, the doe glides off into the forest. Sometimes when I see a deer this way I know it is real at the moment, but afterward it seems like a daydream.

As we work our way back into the woods, I keep hoping for another look at her and thinking that a buck might have been following nearby. Any deer is legal game and I could almost certainly have taken her, but I would rather wait for a larger buck and let the doe bring on next year's young. Shungnak savors the ghost of her scent that hangs in the still air, but she has vanished.

Farther on, the snow deepens to a continuous cover beneath smaller trees, and we cross several sets of deer tracks, including some big prints with long toe drags. The snow helps to muffle our steps, but it is hard to see very far because the bushes are heavily loaded with powder. The thicket becomes a latticed maze of white on black, every branch hung and spangled in a thick fur of jeweled snow. We move through it like eagles cleaving between tumbled columns of cloud. New siftings occasionally drift down when the treetops are touched by the breeze.

Slots between the trunks up ahead shiver with blue where a muskeg opens. I angle toward it, feeling no need to hurry, picking every footstep carefully, stopping often to stare into the dizzying crannies, listening for any splinter of sound, keeping my senses tight and concentrated. A raven calls from high above the forest, and as I catch a glimpse of it an old question runs through my mind: Is this only the bird we see, or does it have the power and awareness Koyukon elders speak of? It lifts and plays on the wind far aloft, then folds up and rolls halfway over, a strong sign of luck in hunting. Never mind the issue of knowing; we should assume that power is here and let ourselves be moved by it.

I turn to look at Shungnak, taking advantage of her sharper hearing and magical sense of smell. She lifts her nose to the fresh but nebulous scent of several deer that have moved through here this morning. I watch her little radar ears, waiting for her to focus in one direction and hold it, hoping to see her body tense as it does when something moves nearby. But so far she only hears the twitching of red squirrels on dry bark. Shungnak and I have very different opinions of the squirrels. They excite her more than any other animal because she believes she will catch one someday. But for the hunter they are deceptive spurts of movement and sound, and their sputtering alarm calls alert the deer.

We approach a low, abrupt rise, covered with obscuring brush and curtained with snow. A lift of wind hisses in the high trees, then drops away and leaves us in near-complete silence. I pause to choose a path through a scramble of blueberry bushes and little windfalls ahead, then glance back at Shungnak. She has her eyes and ears fixed off toward our left, almost directly across the current of breeze. She stands very stiff, quivering slightly, leaning forward as if she has already started to run but cannot release her muscles. I shake my finger at her as a warning to stay.

I listen as closely as possible, but hear nothing. I work my eyes into every dark crevice and slot among the snowy branches, but see nothing. I stand perfectly still and wait, then look again at Shungnak. Her head turns so slowly that I can barely detect the movement, until finally she is looking straight ahead. Perhaps it is just another squirrel . . . I consider taking a few steps for a better view.

Then I see it.

A long, dark body appears among the bushes, moving deliberately upwind, so close I can scarcely believe I didn't see it earlier. Without looking away, I carefully slide the breech closed and lift the rifle to my shoulder, almost certain that a deer this size will be a buck. Shungnak, now forgotten behind me, must be contorted with the suppressed urge to give chase.

The deer walks easily, silently, along the little rise, never looking our way. Then he makes a sharp turn straight toward us. Thick tines of his antlers curve over the place where I have the rifle aimed. Koyukon elders teach that animals will come to those who have shown them respect, and will allow themselves to be taken in what is only a temporary death. At a moment like this, it is easy to sense that despite my abiding doubt there is a shared world beyond the one we know directly, a world the Koyukon people empower with spirits, a world that demands recognition and exacts a price from those who ignore it.

This is a very large buck. It comes so quickly that I have no chance to shoot, and then it is so close that I haven't the heart to do it. Fifty feet away, the deer lowers his head almost to the ground and lifts a slender branch that blocks his path. Snow shakes down onto his neck and clings to the fur of his shoulders as he slips underneath. Then he half-lifts his head and keeps coming. I ease the rifle down to watch, wondering how much closer he will get. Just now he makes a long, soft rutting call, like the bleating of a sheep except lower and more hollow. His hooves tick against dry twigs hidden by the snow.

In the middle of a step he raises his head all the way up, and he sees me standing there — a stain against the pure white of the forest. A sudden spasm runs through his entire body, his front legs jerk apart, and he freezes all akimbo, head high, nostrils flared, coiled and hard. I can only look at him and wait, my mind snarled with irreconcilable emotions. Here is a perfect buck deer. In the Koyukon way, he has come to me; but in my own he has come too close. I am as congealed and transfixed as he is, as devoid of conscious thought. It is as if my mind has ceased to function and I only have eyes.

But the buck has no choice. He suddenly unwinds in a burst of ignited energy, springs straight up from the snow, turns in mid-flight, stabs the frozen earth again, and makes four great bounds off to the left. His thick body seems to float, relieved of its own weight, as if a deer has the power to unbind itself from gravity.

The same deeper impulse that governs the flight of a deer governs the predator's impulse to pursue it. I watch the first leaps without moving a muscle. Then, not pausing for an instant of deliberation, I raise the rifle back to my shoulder, follow the movement of the deer's fleeing form, and wait until it stops to stare back. Almost at that instant, still moving without conscious thought, freed of the ambiguities that held me before, now no less animal than the animal I watch, my hands warm and steady and certain, acting from a more elemental sense than the ones that brought me to this meeting, I carefully align the sights and let go the sudden power.

The gift of the deer falls like a feather in the snow. And the rifle's sound has rolled off through the timber before I hear it.

I walk to the deer, now shaking a bit with swelling emotion. Shungnak is beside it already, whining and smelling, racing from one side to the other, stuffing her nose down in snow full of scent. She looks off into the brush, searching back and forth, as if the deer that ran is somewhere else, still running. She tries to lick at the blood that trickles down, but I stop her out of respect for the animal. Then, I suppose to consummate her own frustrated predatory energy, she takes a hard nip at its shoulder, shuns quickly away, and looks back as if she expects it to leap to its feet again.

As always, I whisper thanks to the animal for giving itself to me. The words are my own, not something I have learned from the Koyukon. Their elders might say that the words we use in prayer to spirits of the natural world do not matter. Nor, perhaps, does it matter what form these spirits take in our own thoughts. What truly matters is only that prayer be made, to affirm our humility in the presence of nurturing power. Most of humanity throughout history has said prayers to the powers of surrounding nature, which they have recognized as their source of life. Surely it is not too late to recover this ancestral wisdom.

It takes a few minutes before I settle down inside and can begin the other work. Then I hang the deer with rope strung over a low branch and back twice through pulley-loops. I cut away the dark, pungent scent glands on its legs, and next make a careful incision along its belly, just large enough to reach the warm insides. The stomach and intestines come easily and cleanly; I cut through the diaphragm, and there is a hollow sound as the lungs pull free. Placing them on the soft snow, I whisper that these parts are left here for the other animals. Shungnak wants to take some for herself but I tell her to keep away. It is said that the life and awareness leaves an animal's remains slowly, and there are rules about what should be eaten by a dog. She will have her share of the scraps later on, when more of the life is gone.

After the blood has drained out, I sew the opening shut with a piece of line to keep the insides clean, and then toggle the deer's forelegs through a slit in the hind leg joint, so it can be carried like a pack. I am barely strong enough to get it up onto my back, but there is plenty of time to work slowly toward the beach, stopping often to rest and cool down. During one of these stops I hear two ravens in an agitated exchange of croaks and gurgles, and I wonder if those black eyes have already spotted the remnants. No pure philanthropist, the raven gives a hunter luck only as a way of creating luck for himself.

Finally, I push through the low boughs of the beachside trees and ease my burden down. Afternoon sun throbs off the water, but a chill north wind takes all warmth from it. Little gusts splay in dark patterns across the anchorage; the boat paces on its mooring line; the Sound is racing with whitecaps. I take a good rest, watching a fox sparrow flit among the drift logs and a bunch of crows hassling over some bit of food at the water's edge.

Though I feel utterly satisfied, grateful, and contented, there is much to do and the day will slope away quickly. We are allowed more than one deer, so I will stay on the island for another look around tomorrow. It takes two trips to get everything out to the skiff, then we head up the shore toward the little cabin and secure anchorage at Bear Creek. By the time the boat is unloaded and tied off, the wind has faded and a late afternoon chill sinks down in the pitched, hard shadow of Sarichef.

Half-dry wood hisses and sputters, giving way reluctantly to flames in the rusted stove. It is nearly dusk when I bring the deer inside and set to work on it. Better to do this now than to wait, in case tomorrow is another day of luck. The animal hangs from a low beam, dim-lit by the kerosene lamp. I feel strange in its presence, as if it still watches, still glows with something of its life, still demands that nothing be done or spoken carelessly. A hunter should never let himself be deluded by pride or a false sense of dominance. It is not through our own power that we take life in nature; it is through the power of nature that life is given to us.

The soft hide peels away slowly from shining muscles, and the inner perfection of the deer's body is revealed. Koyukon and Eskimo hunters teach a refined art of taking an animal into its component parts, easing blades through crisp cartilage where bone joins bone, following the body's own design until it disarticulates. There is no ugliness in it, only hands moving in concert with the beauty of an animal's making. Perhaps we have been too removed from this to understand, and we have lost touch with the process of one life being passed on to another. As my hands work inside the deer, it is as if something has already begun to flow into me.

When the work is finished, I take two large slices from the hind quarter and put them in a pan atop the now-crackling stove. In a separate pot, I boil scraps of meat and fat for Shungnak, who has waited with as much patience as possible for a husky raised in a hunter's team up north. When the meat is finished cooking I sit on a sawed log and eat straight from the pan.

A meal could not be simpler, more satisfying, or more directly a part of the living process. I wish Ethan was here to share it, and I would explain to him again that when we eat the deer its flesh is then our flesh. The deer changes form and becomes us, and we in turn become creatures made of deer. Each time we eat the deer we should remember it and feel gratitude for what it has given us. And each time, we should carry a thought like a prayer inside: "Thanks to the animal and to all that made it — the island and the forest, the air, and the rain . . ." We should remember that in the course of things, we are all generations of deer and of the earth-life that feeds us.

Warm inside my sleeping bag, I let the fire ebb away to coals. The lamp is out. The cabin roof creaks in the growing cold. I drift toward sleep, feeling pleased that there is no moon, so the deer will wait until dawn to feed. On the floor beside me, Shungnak jerks and whimpers in her dog's dreams.

Next morning we are in the woods with the early light. We follow yesterday's tracks, and just beyond the place of the buck, a pair of does drifts at the edge of sight and disappears. For an hour we angle north, then come slowly back somewhat deeper in the woods, moving crosswise to a growing easterly breeze. In two separate places, deer snort and pound away, invisible beyond a shroud of brush. Otherwise there is nothing.

Sometime after noon we come to a narrow muskeg with scattered lodgepole pines and a ragged edge of bushy, low-growing cedar. I squint against the sharp glare of snow. It has that peculiar look of old powder, a bit settled and touched by wind, very lovely but without the airy magic of a fresh fall. I gaze up the muskeg's easy slope, and above the encroaching wall of timber, seamed against the deep blue sky, is the brilliant peak of Sarichef with a great plume of snow streaming off in what must be a shuddering gale. It has a contradictory look of absoluteness and unreality about it, like a Himalayan summit suspended in mid-air over the saddle of a low ridge.

I move very slowly up the muskeg's east side, away from the breeze and in the sun's full warmth. Deer tracks crisscross the opening, but none of the animals stopped here to feed. Next to the bordering trees, the tracks follow a single, hard-packed trail, showing the deer's preference for cover. Shungnak keeps her nose to the thickly scented snow. We come across a pine sapling that a buck has torn with his antlers, scattering twigs and flakes of bark all around. But his tracks are hardened, frosted, and lack sharpness, so they are at least a day old.

We slip through a narrow point of trees, then follow the open edge again, pausing long moments between each footstep. A mixed tinkle of crossbills and siskins moves through the high timber, and a squirrel rattles from deep in the woods, too far off to be scolding us. Shungnak begins to pick up a strong ribbon of scent, but she hears nothing. I stop for several minutes to study the muskeg's long, raveled fringe, the tangle of shade and thicket, the glaze of mantled boughs.

Then my eye barely catches a fleck of movement up ahead, near the ground and almost hidden behind the trunk of a leaning pine, perhaps a squirrel's tail or a bird. I lift my hand slowly to shade the sun, stand ahead still, and wait to see if something is there. Finally it moves again.

At the very edge of the trees, almost out of sight in a little swale, small and furry and bright-tinged, turning one direction and then another, is the funnel of a single ear. Having seen this, I soon make out the other ear and the slope of a doe's forehead. Her neck is behind the leaning pine, but on the other side I can barely see the soft, dark curve of her back above the snow. She is comfortably bedded, gazing placidly into the distance, chewing her cud.

Shungnak has stopped twenty yards behind me in the point of trees and has no idea about the deer. I shake my finger at her until she lays her ears back and sits. Then I watch the doe again. She is fifty yards ahead of me, ten yards beyond the leaning tree, and still looking off at an angle. Her left eye is clearly visible and she refuses to turn her head away, so it might be impossible to get any closer. Perhaps I should just wait here, in case a buck is attending her nearby. But however improbable it might be under these circumstances, a thought is lodged in my mind: I can get near her.

My first step sinks down softly, but the second makes a loud budging sound. She snaps my way, stops chewing, and stares for several minutes. It seems hopeless, especially out here in an open field of crisp snow with only the narrow treetrunk for a screen. But she slowly turns away and starts to chew again. I move just enough so the tree blocks her eye and the rest of her head, but I can still see her ears. Every time she chews they shake just a bit, so I can watch them and step when her hearing is obscured by the sound of her own jaws.

Either this works or the deer has decided to ignore me, because after a short while I am near enough so the noise of my feet has to reach her easily. She should have jumped up and run long ago, but instead she lays there in serene repose. I deliberate on every step, try for the softest snow, wait long minutes before the next move, stalking like a cat toward ambush. I watch beyond her, into the surrounding shadows and across to the muskeg's farther edge, for the shape of a buck deer; but there is nothing. I feel ponderous, clumsy-footed, out-of-place, inimical. I should turn and run away, take fear on the deer's behalf, flee the mirrored image in my mind. But I clutch the cold rifle at my side and creep closer.

The wind refuses to blow and my footsteps seem like thunder in the still sunshine. But the doe only turns once to look my way, without even pointing her ears toward me, then stares off and begins to chew again.

I am ten feet from the leaning tree. My heart pounds so hard, I think those enchanted ears should hear the rush of blood in my temples. Yet a strange certainty has come into me, a quite unmystical confidence. Perhaps she has decided I am another deer, a buck attracted by her musk or a doe feeding gradually toward her. My slow pace and lapses of stillness would not seem human. For myself, I have lost awareness of elapsed time; I have no feeling of patience or impatience. It is as if the deer has moved slowly toward me on a cloud of snow, and I am adrift in the pure motion of experience.

I take the last step to the trunk of the leaning pine. It is bare of branches, scarcely wider than my hand, but perfectly placed to break my odd profile. There is no hope of getting any closer, so I slowly poke my head out to watch. She has an ideal spot: screened from the wind, warmed by the sun, and with a clear view of the muskeg. I can see muscles working beneath the close fur of her jaw, the rise and fall of her side each time she breathes, the shining edge of her ebony eye.

I hold absolutely still, but her body begins to stiffen, she lifts her head higher, and her ears twitch anxiously. Then instead of looking at me she turns her face to the woods, shifting her ears toward a sound I cannot hear. A few seconds later, the unmistakable voice of a buck drifts up, strangely disembodied, as if it comes from an animal somewhere underneath the snow. I huddle as close to the tree as I can, press against the hard, dry bark, and peek out around its edge.

There is a gentle rise behind the doe, scattered with sapling pines and clusters of juniper bushes. A rhythmic crunching of snow comes invisibly from the slope, then a bough shakes . . . and a buck walks easily into the open sunshine.

Focusing his attention completely on the doe, he comes straight toward her and never sees my intrusive shape just beyond. He slips through a patch of small trees, stops a few feet from where she lies, a long moment. She reaches her muzzle out to one side, trying to find his scent. When he starts to move up behind her she stands quickly, bends her body into a strange sideways arc, and stares back at him. A moment later she walks off a bit, lifts her tail, and puts droppings in her tracks. The buck moves to the warm ground of her bed and lowers his nose to the place where her female scent is strongest.

Inching like a reptile on a cold rock, I have stepped out from the tree and let my whole menacing profile become visible. The deer are thirty feet away and stand well apart, so they can both see me easily. I am a hunter hovering near his prey and a watcher craving inhuman love, torn between the deepest impulses, hot and shallow-breathed and seething with unreconciled intent, hidden from opened eyes that look into the nimbus of sun and see nothing but the shadow they have chosen for themselves. In this shadow now, the hunter has vanished and only the watcher remains.

Drawn by the honey of the doe's scent, the buck steps quickly toward her. And now the most extraordinary thing happens. The doe turns away from him and walks straight for me. There is no hesitation, only a wild deer coming along the trail of hardened snow where the other deer have passed, the trail in which I stand at this moment. She raises her head, looks at me, and steps without hesitation.

My existence is reduced to a pair of eyes; a rush of unbearable heat flushes through my cheeks; and a sense of absolute certainty fuses in my mind.

The snow blazes so brightly that my head aches. The deer is a dark form growing larger. I look up at the buck, half embarrassed, as if to apologize that she has chosen me over him. He stares at her for a moment, turns to follow, then stops and watches anxiously. I am struck by how gently her narrow hooves touch the trail, how little sound they make as she steps, how thick the fur is on her flank and shoulder, how unfathomable her eyes look. I am consumed with a sense of her perfect elegance in the brilliant light. And then I am lost again in the whirling intensity of experience.

The doe is now ten feet from me. She never pauses or looks away. Her feet punch down mechanically into the snow, coming closer and closer, until they are less than a yard from my own.

Then she stops, stretches her neck calmly toward me, and lifts her nose.

There is not the slightest question in my mind, as if this was certain to happen and I have known all along exactly what to do. I slowly raise my hand and reach out . . .

And my fingers touch the soft, dry, gently needling fur on top of the deer's head, and press down to the living warmth of flesh underneath.

She makes no move and shows no fear, but I can feel the flaming strength and tension that flow in her wild body as in no other animal I have ever touched. Time expands and I am suspended in the clear reality of that moment.

Then, by the flawed conditioning of a lifetime among fearless domesticated things, I instinctively drop my hand and let the deer smell it. Her dark nose, wet and shining, touches gently against my skin at the exact instant I realize the absoluteness of my error. And a jolt runs through her entire body as she realizes hers. Her muscles seize and harden; she seems to wrench her eyes away from me but her body remains, rigid and paralyzed. Having been deceived by her other senses, she keeps her nose tight against my hand for one more moment.

Then all the energy inside her triggers in a series of exquisite bounds. She flings out over the hummocks of snow-covered moss, suspended in effortless flight like fog blown over the muskeg in a gale. Her body leaps with such power that the muscles should twang aloud like a bowstring; the earth should shudder and drum; but I hear no sound. In the center of the muskeg she stops to look back, as if to confirm what must seem impossible. The buck follows in more earthbound undulations; they dance away together, and I am left in the meeting-place alone.

There is a blur of rushing feet behind me. No longer able to restrain herself, Shungnak dashes past, buries her nose in the soft tracks, and then looks back to ask if we can run after them. I had completely forgotten her, sitting near enough to watch the whole encounter, somehow resisting what must have been a prodigious urge to explode in chase. When I reach out to hug her, she smells the hand that touched the deer. And it seems as if it happened long ago.

For the past year I have kept a secret dream, that I would someday come close enough to touch a deer on this island. But since the idea came it seemed harder than ever to get near them. Now, totally unexpected and in a strange way, it has happened. Was the deer caught by some reckless twinge of curiosity? Had she never encountered a human on this wild island? Did she yield to some odd amorous confusion? I really do not care. I would rather accept this as pure experience and not give in to the notion that everything must be explained.

Nor do I care to think that I was chosen to see some manifestation of power, because I have little tolerance for such dreams of self-importance. I have never asked that nature open any doors to reveal the truth of spirit or mystery; I aspire to no shaman's path; I expect no visions, no miracles except the ones that fill every instant of ordinary life.

But there are vital lessons in the experience of moments such as these, as if we live them in the light of wisdom taken from the earth and shaped by generations of elders. Two deer came and gave the choices to me. One deer I took and we will now share a single body. The other deer I touched and we will now share that moment. These events could be seen as opposites, but they are in fact identical. Both are founded in the same principles, the same relationship, the same reciprocity.

Move slowly, stay quiet, watch carefully . . . and be ever humble. Never show the slightest arrogance or disrespect. Koyukon elders would explain, in words quite different from my own, that I moved into two moments of grace, or what they would call luck. This is the source of success for a hunter or a watcher, not skill, not cleverness, not guile. Something is only given in nature, never taken.

I have heard the elders say that everything in nature has its own spirit and possesses a power beyond ours. There is no way to prove them right or wrong, though the beauty and interrelatedness of things should be evidence enough. We need not ask for shining visions as proof, or for a message from a golden deer glowing in the sky of our dreams. Above all else, we should assume that power moves in the world around us and act accordingly. If it is a myth, then spirit is within the myth and we should live by it. And if there is a commandment to follow, it is to approach all of earth-life, of which we are a part, with humility and respect.

Well soaked and shivering from a rough trip across the Sound, we pull into the dark waters of the bay. Sunset burns on Twin Peaks and the spindled ridge of Antler Mountain. The little house is warm with lights that shimmer on the calm near shore. I see Nita looking from the window and Ethan dashes out to wait by the tide, pitching rocks at the mooring buoy. He strains to see inside the boat, knowing that a hunter who tells his news aloud may offend the animals by sounding boastful. But when he sees the deer his excited voice seems to roll up and down the mountainside.

He runs for the house with Shungnak, carrying a load of gear, and I know he will burst inside with the news. Ethan, joyous and alive, boy made of deer.

Richard K. Nelson

DOWN IN MY HEART

I'll just sit here by your bed, George, and talk to you quietly tonight, maybe for a long time, because I don't know when I'll get a chance again. I don't know whether you can hear me or not, but I'll talk along anyway, in hope.

It's getting dark outside; you can hardly see the trees along the drive now, and the lamps near the gate are on. There were a few flakes of snow when I came out from town, but I can't tell now whether it is snowing. The whole hospital is quiet, and the man in charge of this floor said I could stay as long as I wanted to. It's unusual, he said, but they don't know what to make of your case. If you would only eat — but I won't say anything about that. The man said they were giving you just enough to keep you going — but I won't say any more about it.

I want to talk through to you, George, a collection of stories I made of what happened to us in the war years. I don't know whether you can hear it, or whether anyone ever will; but I want to say these things, because we are a lost people — you and I and some others — and we saw an event that few others could experience, a big event that made us silent and engulfed us quietly.

I'll tell it slow, George, and maybe you can hear me. You are one of the main characters, and I want you to look back with me at the story. It's dark outside now. It is the spring of 1942. The wind is blowing.

"When the mob comes," George would say, "I think we should try surprising them with a friendly reaction — take coffee and cookies out and meet them."

"As for me," Larry would say, "I'll take a stout piece of stove wood, and stand behind the door, and deal out many a lumpy head — that's what they'd need."

"Well, I don't know about you all," Dick would say, "but I intend to run right out of that back door and hide in the brush — 'cause I don't want my death on any man's conscience."

When are men dangerous? We sat in the sun near the depot one Sunday afternoon at McNeil, Arkansas, and talked cordially with

353

some of the men who were loafing around in the Sabbath calm. Bob was painting a watercolor picture; George was scribbling a poem in his tablet; I was reading off and on in *Leaves of Grass* and enjoying the scene.

When are men dangerous? It was March 22, 1942. The fruit trees at the camp farm were in bloom. We had looked at them as we went by, starting on our hike, and we stopped while I took a picture of George and Bob with our two little calves. We spoke of the war and of camp and of Sunday as we hiked through the pine woods and past the sagging houses. We knew our way around; we had done soil conservation work during our months in camp, in the fields beside our path. Not all had been friendly, it is true. Our project superintendent had warned us against saying ''Mr.'' and ''Mrs.'' to Negroes, and we had continued to use the terms; and one stormy night when no doctors would come out, some of the men in camp had given first aid to a Negro woman, whose husband had led them through the dark woods to the cabin where the woman lay screaming. Thus we had become friends with some of our neighbors. With some of them we had made friends, but it was harder with others, and we went to town inconspicuously, with care, no more than two at a time; and we were in most ways the quiet of the land, and unobserved, we thought.

When we had hiked into McNeil we had found a few men loafing around in the shade. The stores were closed; Main Street extended a block each way from the depot and then relaxed into a sand road that wandered among scattered houses. We too relaxed for our Sunday afternoon. Bob set up his drawing board; George got out his tablet and pen; and I sat leaning against a telephone pole and began to read — among dangerous men.

It takes such an intricate succession of misfortunes and blunders to get mobbed by your own countrymen — and such a close balancing of good fortune to survive — that I consider myself a rarity, in this respect, in being able to tell the story, from the subject's point of view; but just how we began to be mobbed and just where the blunders and misfortunes began, it is hard to say. We might have lived through a quiet Sabbath if it had not been for Bob's being an artist; or, especially, if it had not been for George's poem; and on the other hand we might have become digits in

Arkansas's lynching record if Walt Whitman had used more rhyme in his poetry.

About eight of the townsmen gathered to look over Bob's shoulder as he painted. His subject was a dilapidated store across the street. The men were cordial and curious. I asked them questions about their town. The only time we were abrupt was when they asked where we were from. "Magnolia," Bob said, and quickly changed the subject to their town baseball team. One of the onlookers edged up behind George and looked over his shoulder, while George went on with his composing and revising — unheeding.

I went back to my book, and I'll never be able to remember whether I was reading, when it happened, "Come, I will make the continent indissoluble . . ."

I looked up. The onlooker, a handsome young man, well-dressed, and with tight skin over the bridge of his nose, had snatched George's poem and was reading it.

"What's the idea of writing things like this?" he challenged. "If you don't like the town, you haven't any right to come around here." I was familiar with the edge on his voice. He knew we were CO's.

George stood up, straight, with his arms hanging at his sides, his face composed, and remonstrated that he hadn't meant the poem to be read — he was just trying to write, trying to express his own feelings.

"Here," George said, "I don't want the poem; I'll take it and throw it away." The young man held the poem away from George's outstretched hand and took his discovery a few steps away to show it to another townsman. The two muttered. The first man returned. He scrutinized Bob's drawing, while George and I stood without moving and Bob went on painting — a little faster. What could we do when men were dangerous?

The young man spoke, not directly to us but to the other townsmen, some of whom had drawn nearer, about our being CO's. There was more muttering, in which we began to hear the quickening words — "yellow" and "damn." At first these words the men said, about us, to each other; then the faces were turned more our way when the words were said. A short, strong man broke into action, went to where Bob was still sitting, and grabbed the drawing board.

"Why, sir!" Bob said, and looked up as if in surprise.

"We'll take care of this," the short man said. He started to rip the drawing paper from the board, but another man stopped him.

"Save that for evidence." The short man raised the board over his head to break it over a piece of iron rail set like a picket near the depot; then he stopped, considered, caressed the board, and settled down to hold it under his arm and to guard the evidence.

"We ought to break that board over their heads," someone suggested. Several others repeated the idea; others revised the wording, expanded the concept, and passed the saying along. Some spoke of "stringing them up."

George got constructive. "I guess I'll go home," he said; "I don't think they like me here." He started to leave the circle — by now there were about fifteen men around.

"Hey, you; you're not going any place," one said.

"Don't let him leave," said another.

George came back and sat down.

A man at the edge of the group — a beautiful man to us — said, "Let's call the sheriff." This call was in turn echoed around. To our great relief someone actually crossed the street to call. The tension, however, was far from ended.

The young man who had started the inquisition turned to me. "What were you doing?"

"I was reading a book." I held it up — *Leaves of Grass.* "A poetry book."

"What's that in your pocket?" he asked, pointing to my shirt pocket. I explained that it was a letter which I had written.

"But you said you hadn't written a letter," he accused. The group of men shifted their feet. I explained that I had been reading a book immediately before, but that earlier I had written a letter. The questioner demanded it, arm outstretched. The others were watching these exchanges, sometimes retiring to the edge of the group to talk and then elbowing back. By now about twenty-five were present.

The questioner considered and then accepted my suggestion that he wait for authority before taking the letter. He turned away, and he and others tried to argue with George about his convictions on war. George wouldn't say much — just that he considered war the wrong way of attaining ends many agreed to be good.

Then the young man veered, in the midst of the discussion of war, to an accusation that George's writing was not poetry. There was an implication that if it wasn't poetry it might be something else — like information for the enemy. George said that he thought what he had written — it was being circulated constantly through the crowd, exciting rumbles of anger wherever it passed — was poetry, and that poetry didn't need to rhyme. This opinion brought snorts from the crowd. The young man said that poetry always rhymed. *Leaves of Grass* throbbed under my arm, but I said nothing.

Drawing down one side of his mouth and looking sideways at George, the young man said, "Where did you go to school?" He grabbed the book from under my arm and opened it at random. He read a passage aloud to the lowering group, to prove that poetry rhymed. He started off confidently, read more and more slowly, and finally closed the book with a snap.

"Well, that may be poetry," he said, "but what you wrote ain't." The crowd was a little taken aback. It shifted its feet.

By this time I had a chance to look over a shoulder and read George's poem, which I hadn't yet seen. It certainly was unfortunate — a Sandburgian description of McNeil beginning, "McNeil! Hmph! Some town, McNeil . . ." An alert bystander clucked at a line in the poem: "And loaded freighters grumble through at night."

"There!" he said. "That's *information*. That's them troop trains!" We lost all we had gained from Whitman.

By this time, though, some of the group were arguing about why Bob painted. None of them could understand his insistence that he painted for fun. "But what are you painting *that* for?" they asked, pointing to the old store building. "It must be for a foreign power," one said.

"I don't think a foreign power could use a picture of this store in McNeil," Bob said. The chief prosecutor bristled.

"That's just where you're wrong, Bub — it's little towns like McNeil that's the backbone of the country, and Hitler knows it."

Bob was stunned by the contextual force of the remark; he was silent.

During all of this heckling and crowding we were merely quiet and respectful. We didn't know what else to do. We learned then rapidly what we later learned about other provokers — including policemen — that almost always the tormentor is at a loss unless he can provoke a belligerent reaction as an excuse for further pressure or violence.

Every few minutes a car would come to a stop near us to spout out curious people. The news was getting around; later we discovered that towns five or ten miles away had begun to hear about the spies almost as soon as the group began to form around us. The people of Arkansas stood off and talked, nodding their heads and reading — with more interest than most poets can hope to arouse — George's blunderbuss of a poem.

Finally, to our great relief, the police car from Magnolia rolled up. A policeman was driving; a man in plain clothes, who turned out to be a Federal revenue man, was beside him. The policeman gave us the first friendly word in a long time.

"That your work?" he asked Bob, nodding toward the picture still held by the evidence man. "That's pretty good."

The two representatives of the law took over, got our names, and gravely considered the indictments of the crowd. My letter was brought to light by the surrounding chorus of guards. The revenue man read it carefully, the onlookers craning over his shoulder. He retired to a new group. They read it. The officers took my camera, which had been confiscated by our guards, for evidence. They took *Leaves of Grass*. The policeman came back to the car, where we were standing. He was the first man we had seen in a long time who didn't either stare at the ground when looked at or glare back.

The revenue man circulated around through the crowd for at least half an hour, talking to local leaders. The mob at its greatest numbered not more than sixty, or possibly seventy-five. All assurances given, the revenuer came back to the car; and our two rescuers — our captors in the eyes of the mob — whisked us back to camp, where we created a sensation as we rode down past the barracks in the police car.

The mob scene was over; our possessions were returned to us — except for the picture, the poem, and my letter, which were placed on exhibit at the Magnolia police station to satisfy inquirers that all precautions were being taken. At camp we doubled the night watch, for fear of trouble; but nothing happened.

And the next morning, before work, we three stood before the assembled campers — about one hundred men, clothed in various shades of denim and of bits from the ragbag, and seated on long wooden benches — and gave our version of what had happened, in order to quiet rumors and to help everyone learn from our experience. The argument about poetry got a big laugh, as did Bob's "Why, sir!" Before leaving that barracks hall we had to talk over the mobbing thoroughly; for it signified a problem we had to solve: When are men dangerous? How could we survive in our little society within a society? What could we do?

For that occasion, our camp director, a slow-talking preacher of the way of life taught by Jesus Christ, gave us the final word:

"I know you men think the scene was funny, in spite of its danger; and I suppose there's no harm in having fun out of it; but don't think that our neighbors here in Arkansas are hicks just because they see you as spies and dangerous men. Just remember that our government is spending millions of dollars and hiring the smartest men in the country to devote themselves full time just to make everyone act that way."

We remembered, and set out to drain more swamps and put sod in more gullies in Arkansas.

William Stafford

GROWING UP GAME

When I went off to college my father gave me, as part of my tuition, 50 pounds of moose meat. In 1969, eating moose meat at the University of California was a contradiction in terms. Hippies didn't hunt. I lived in a rambling Victorian house which boasted sweeping circular staircases, built-in lofts, and a landlady who dreamed of opening her own health food restaurant. I told my housemates that my moose meat in its nondescript white butcher paper was from a side of beef my father had bought. The carnivores in the house helped me finish off such suppers as sweet and sour moose meatballs, mooseburgers (garnished with the obligatory avocado and sprouts), and mooseghetti. The same dinner guests who remarked upon the lean sweetness of the meat would have recoiled if I'd told them the not-so-simple truth: that I grew up on game, and the moose they were eating had been brought down, with one shot through his magnificent heart, by my father — a man who had hunted all his life and all of mine.

One of my earliest memories is of crawling across the vast ..rinent of crinkled linoleum in our Forest Service cabin kitchen, dow 1 splintered back steps, through wildflowers growing wheat-high. I was eye-level with grasshoppers who scolded me on my first solo trip outside. I made it to the shed, a cool and comfortingly square shelter that held phantasmagoric metal parts; they smelled good, like dirt and grease. I had played a long time in this shed before some maternal shriek made me lift up on my haunches to listen to those urgent, possessive sounds that were my name. Rearing up, my head bumped into something hanging in the dark; gleaming white, it felt sleek and cold against my cheek. Its smell was dense and musty and not unlike the slabs of my grandmother's great arms after her cool, evening sponge baths. In that shed I looked up and saw the flensed body of a doe; it swung gently, slapping my face. I felt then as I do even now when eating game: horror and awe and hunger.

Growing up those first years on a forest station high in the Sierra was somewhat like belonging to a white tribe. The men hiked off every day into their forest and the women stayed behind in the circle of official cabins, breeding. So far away from a store, we ate venison and squirrel, rattlesnake and duck. My brother's first rattle, in fact, was from a King Rattler my father killed as we watched, by snatching it up with a stick and winding it, whiplike, around a redwood sapling. Rattlesnake tastes just like chicken, but has many fragile bones to slither one's way through; we also ate salmon, rabbit, and geese galore. The game was accompanied by such daily garden dainties as fried okra, mustard greens, corn fritters, wilted lettuce (our favorite because of that rare, blackened bacon), new potatoes and peas, stewed tomatoes, barbecued butter beans.

I was four before I ever had a beef hamburger and I remember being disappointed by its fatty, nothing taste and the way it fell apart at the seams whenever my teeth sank into it. Smoked pork shoulder came much later in the South; and I was twenty-one, living in New York City, before I ever tasted leg of lamb. I approached that glazed rack of meat with a certain guilty self-consciousness, as if I unfairly stalked those sweet-tempered white creatures myself. But how would I explain my squeamishness to those urban sophisticates? How explain that I was shy with mutton when I had been bred on wild things?

Part of it, I suspect, had to do with the belief I'd also been bred on — we become the spirit and body of animals we eat. As a child eating venison I liked to think of myself as lean and lovely just like the deer. I would never be caught dead just grazing while some man who asn't even a skillful hunter crept up and konked me over the he d. If someone wanted to hunt me, he must be wily and outwitting. He must earn me.

My father had also taught us as children that animals were our brothers and sisters under their skin. They died so that we might live. And of this sacrifice we must be mindful. "God make us grateful for what we are about to receive," took on a new meaning when one knew the animal's struggle pitted against our own appetite. We also used *all* the animal so that an elk became elk steaks, stew, salami, and sausage. His head and horns went on the wall to watch us more earnestly than any babysitter, and every Christmas Eve we had a ceremony of making our own moccasins for the new year out of whatever Father had tanned. "Nothing wasted," my father would always say, or, as we munched on sausage cookies made from moosemeat or venison, "Think about who you're eating." We thought of ourselves as intricately linked to the food chain. We knew, for example, that a forest fire meant, at the end of the line, we'd suffer too. We'd have buck stew instead of venison steak and the meat would be stringy, withered-tasting because in the animal kingdom, as it seemed with humans, only the meanest and leanest and orneriest survived.

Once when I was in my early teens, I went along on a hunting trip as the "main cook and bottle-washer," though I don't remember any bottles; none of these hunters drank alcohol. There was something else coursing through their veins as they rose long before dawn and disappeared, returning to my little camp most often dragging a doe or pheasant or rabbit. We ate innumerable cornmeal-fried catfish, had rabbit stew seasoned only with blood and black pepper.

This hunting trip was the first time I remember eating game as a conscious act. My father and Buddy Earl shot a big doe and she lay with me in the back of the tarp-draped station wagon all the way home. It was not the smell I minded, it was the glazed great, dark eyes and the way that head flopped around crazily on what I knew was once a graceful neck. I found myself petting this doe, murmuring all those graces we'd been taught long ago as children. *Thank you for the sacrifice, thank you for letting us be like you so that we can grow up strong as game.* But there was an uneasiness in me that night as I bounced along in the back of the car with the deer.

What was uneasy is still uneasy — perhaps it always will be. It's not easy when one really starts thinking about all this: the eating game, the food chain, the sacrifice of one for the other. It's never easy when one begins to think about one's most basic actions, like eating. Like becoming what one eats: lean and lovely and mortal.

Why should it be that the purchase of meat at a butcher shop is somehow more righteous than eating something wild? Perhaps it has to do with our collective unconscious that sees the animal bred for slaughter as doomed. But that wild doe or moose might make it without the hunter. Perhaps on this primitive level of archetype and unconscious knowing we even believe that what's wild lives forever.

My father once told this story around a hunting campfire. His own father, who raised cattle during the Depression on a dirt farm in the Ozarks, once fell on such hard times that he had to butcher the pet lamb for supper. My father, bred on game or their own hogs all his life, took one look at the family pet on that meat platter and pushed his plate away from him. His siblings followed suit. To hear my grandfather tell it, it was the funniest thing he'd ever seen. "They just couldn't eat Bo-Peep," Grandfather said. And to hear my father tell it years later around that campfire, it was funny, but I saw for the first time his sadness. And I realized that eating had become a conscious act for him that day at the dinner table when Bo-Peep offered herself up.

Now when someone offers me game I will eat it with all the qualms and memories and reverence with which I grew up eating it. And I think it will always be this feeling of horror and awe and hunger. And something else — full knowledge of what I do, what I become.

Brenda Peterson

WE ARE OUTCASTS

A gray gloom settled down over our family. Sumiko was ill. Always during the winter she had asthmatic attacks, but this particular winter was the worst. The little black kitten, Asthma, which Mrs. Matsui had given her because, she said, black cats could cure asthma, mewed all day long and rubbed its back against the bed. Almost every day Dr. Moon climbed the long flight of stairs and walked through the hotel without a glance at our rough-looking hotel guests who stared rudely at him. His large, clean, pink-scrubbed hands were strong and tender as he turned Sumiko over and thumped on her thin shoulder blades. Sumiko, wheezing heavily, submitted to the doctor's examination. Her eyes were black and alert as she tried not to look frightened. Dr. Moon told Father he was concerned about Sumiko's cough and the drop of blood she had spit out. He would send a specialist to see her.

Soon a short, burly man with sandy hair, growing wreathlike on his bald head bustled into the hotel. He was Dr. Stimson, director of the King County Tuberculosis Department. Father stuttered as he thanked him for taking time to come and see Sumiko, but Dr. Stimson waved Father's stumbling words aside, "No trouble, no trouble. It's my job. Well, how's the young lady feeling this morning?"

His bright blue eyes peered intently at Sumiko through thick glasses as he examined her. Dr. Stimson said Sumiko must have an X ray taken of her chest. He gave us a pamphlet describing the North Pines Sanitarium and how it took care of sick children. There were bright appealing photographs of children in sun suits and floppy white hats playing in a beautiful garden. A shuddering chill seized me. Did Sumiko have to go away? She was just six. She would be so unhappy away from all of us.

One morning Mother carefully dressed Sumiko and took her to the city clinic for an X ray. Then we waited for the fatal news with a sense of heavy foreboding. Mother moved about as if she were walking in a dream. As I sat by Sumiko's bedside, sewing dresses for our dolls, Sumiko asked me suddenly, "Do I have to go away?"

"Maybe . . ." I tried to find the right words. "It's not definite yet, Sumiko, but if you do have to, you will go to a wonderful place. It'll be just like going on a real vacation, Sumiko." I tried to be enthusiastic. "There're lots of beautiful trees and flowers and you'll go on walks and picnics with other boys and girls, all dressed in white shorts and sun hats. And you'll eat lots of ice cream, and when you come back you'll be so tanned and husky, we won't recognize you at all."

"Really?" Sumiko's enormous eyes sparkled. "How do you know?"

"I read all about it. You'll just play all day, sleep a lot and eat plenty of good food. Golly, I wouldn't mind going!"

As I talked, I thought I heard a door close but no one was in the parlor. Much later, I learned that it had been Father. He had overheard our conversation about the wonderful sanitarium and had started to laugh, but a sob came out instead. He quickly left and locked himself in the kitchen where he could cry undisturbed.

That evening Dr. Stimson came. We stood, gray-lipped, quietly waiting to hear the verdict. Dr. Stimson's eyes twinkled as he told us that Sumiko did not have tuberculosis. We cried with relief as we hugged Sumiko, swathed in a heavy flannel nightgown and smelling of camphor oil. Like a thin little sparrow burrowed deep in its nest, Sumiko cocked her Dutch-bobbed head at us and spoke carefully so as not to wheeze or cough. "I'm glad I don't have to go on that vacation!"

Dr. Stimson said Sumiko must have plenty of milk, rest and sunshine. So Father and Mother decided to rent a cottage by the sea for the summer. Father said, "Yes, we must do it this summer. We'll start looking right away for a suitable place near Alki Beach."

I leaped into the air and did ten cartwheels in a row. Sumiko, sitting hunched over in Mother's bed, rasped out a gurgling chuckle, but Henry said, "Aw, who cares about Alki. That's sissy stuff."

Henry would be going to the farm in Auburn, as he did every summer, to pick berries. It was customary for Japanese parents to send their sons to rural areas to work on farms where they could harden their muscles and their self-reliance under the vigilant eyes of a Japanese farmer. Henry was proud that he was going off to work to earn his own living, something that girls could never do.

But Sumiko and I dreamed about a little white cottage by the beach, planning in detail how we would spend our days. We would wake with the sun no matter how sleepy we might be, put on our bathing suits and dash out for an early morning dip. We would race back to our cottage, rout Mother and Father out of bed and have a wonderful big breakfast together. We would see Father off to work, help Mother with the house chores and prepare a lunch basket to spend the rest of the day on the beach. Every evening Father would join us at the beach and he would build a roaring bonfire for us. We would watch the evening sun melt the sky into a fiery mass of purple and magenta and wait until the last streak of wine had faded into the blackness behind Vashon Island. Then we would walk slowly back to the cottage, deeply tired and content. A brisk shower to rinse off the sand, the seaweed and salt water, then to bed. And all night we would listen to the muffled rhythmic beat of the ocean waves on the black sands.

Early one day, Mother and I set out to Alki to find a cottage near the beach where we always picnicked. We found a gray house with a FOR RENT sign on its window, just a block from the beach. One side of the house was quilted with wild rambler roses and the sprawling green lawn was trim behind a white-painted picket fence. When I pressed the doorbell, musical chimes rang softly through the house. A middle-aged woman wearing a stiffly starched apron opened the door. "Yes, what can I do for you?" she asked, looking us over.

Mother smiled and said in her halting English, "You have nice house. We like to rent this summer." Mother paused, but the woman said nothing. Mother went on, "How much do you want for month?"

The woman wiped her hands deliberately on her white apron before she spoke, "Well, I'm asking fifty dollars, but I'm afraid you're a little too late. I just promised this place to another party."

"Oh," Mother said, disappointed. "That's too bad. I'm sorry. We like it so much."

I swallowed hard and pointed to the sign on the window. "You still have the sign up. We thought the house was still open."

"I just rented it this morning. I forgot to remove it. Sorry, I can't do anything for you," she said sharply.

Mother smiled at her, "Thank you just the same. Good-by." As we walked away, Mother said comfortingly to me, "Maybe we'll find something even nicer, Ka-chan. We have a lot of looking to do yet."

But we scoured the neighborhood with no success. Every time it was the same story. Either the rent was too much or the house was already taken. We had even inquired at a beautiful new brick apartment facing the beach boulevard, where several VACANCY signs had been propped against empty windows, but the caretaker told us unsmilingly that these apartments were all taken.

That night I went to bed with burning feet. From my darkened bedroom, I heard Mother talking to Father in the living room. "Yes, there were some nice places, but I don't think they wanted to rent to Japanese."

I sat bolt upright. That had not occurred to me. Surely Mother was mistaken. Why would it make any difference? I knew that Father and Mother were not Americans, as we were, because they were not born here, and that there was a law which said they could not become naturalized American citizens because they were Orientals. But being Oriental had never been an urgent problem to us, living in Skidrow.

A few days later, we went to Alki again. This time I carried in my purse a list of houses and apartments for rent which I had cut out from the newspaper. My hands trembled with a nervousness which had nothing to do with the pure excitement of house-hunting. I wished that I had not overheard Mother's remark to Father.

We walked briskly up to a quaint, white Cape Cod house. The door had a shiny brass knocker in the shape of a leaping dolphin. A carefully marcelled, blue-eyed woman, wearing a pince-nez on her sharp nose, hurried out. The woman blinked nervously and tapped her finger on the wall as she listened to Mother's words. She said dryly, "I'm sorry, but we don't want Japs around here," and closed the door. My face stiffened. It was like a sharp, stinging slap. Blunt as it was, I had wanted to hear the truth to wipe out the doubt in my mind. Mother took my hand and led me quickly away, looking straight ahead of her. After a while, she said quietly, "Ka-chan, there are people like that in this world. We have to bear it, just like all the other unpleasant facts of life. This is the first time for you, and I know how deeply it hurts; but when you are older, it won't hurt quite as much. You'll be stronger."

Trying to stop the flow of tears, I swallowed hard and blurted out, "But Mama, is it so terrible to be a Japanese?"

"Hush, child, you mustn't talk like that." Mother spoke slowly and earnestly. "I want you, Henry, and Sumi-chan to learn to respect yourselves. Not because you're white, black or yellow, but because you're a human being. Never forget that. No matter what anyone may call you, to God you are still his child. Mah, it's getting quite warm. I think we had better stop here and get some refreshment before we go on."

I wiped my eyes and blew my nose hastily before I followed Mother into a small drugstore. There I ordered a towering special deluxe banana split, and promptly felt better.

The rest of the day we plodded doggedly through the list without any luck. They all turned us down politely. On our way home, Mother sat silent, while I brooded in the corner of the seat. All day I had been torn apart between feeling defiant and then apologetic about my Japanese blood. But when I recalled the woman's stinging words, I felt raw angry fire flash through my veins, and I simmered.

We found Sumiko sitting up in bed, waiting for us with an expectant smile. Mother swung her up into the air and said gaily, "We didn't find a thing we liked today. The houses were either too big or too small or too far from the beach, but we'll find our summer home yet! It takes time." I set my teeth and wondered if I would ever learn to be as cheerful as Mother.

Later in the evening, Mr. Kato dropped in. Father told him that we were looking for a cottage out at Alki and that so far we had had no luck. Mr. Kato scratched his head, "Yahhh, it's too bad your wife went to all that trouble. That district has been restricted for years. They've never rented or sold houses to Orientals and I doubt if they ever will."

My face burned with shame. Mother and I had walked from house to house, practically asking to be rebuffed. Our foolish summer dream was over.

Somehow word got around among our friends that we were still looking for a place for the summer. One evening, a Mrs. Saito called on the phone. She lived at the Camden Apartments. She said, "My landlady, Mrs. Olsen, says there is a small apartment in our building for rent. She is a wonderful person and has been kind to us all in the apartments, and we're practically all Japanese. You'd like it here."

Mother said to me afterwards, "See, Ka-chan, I told you, there are all kinds of people. Here is a woman who doesn't object to Orientals."

The Camden Apartments was a modest, clean building in a quiet residential district uptown, quite far from Alki.

Mrs. Marta Olsen, a small, slender, blue-eyed woman took charge of the business end of the apartment while her husband and her three brothers were the maintenance men of the large building. Marta said to Mother in her soft Scandinavian accent, "I'm sorry we don't have a place large enough for the whole family."

The modest apartment on the fourth floor was just large enough to accommodate Mother and Sumiko in the one bedroom while I occupied the sofa in the living room. Father and Henry, we decided, would stay at the hotel, but join us every evening for dinner. Marta assured us that by winter we would be all together in a larger apartment which would be vacated.

Of course, we were grateful for even this temporary arrangement, especially when we found the Olsens to be such warm, friendly folks. Marta and her husband were a middle-aged childless couple; but they apparently looked upon all the children living in the apartments as their own, for they were constantly surrounded by chattering, bright-eyed youngsters. Marta was always busy baking her wonderful butter cookies for them. It was not too long before Sumiko and I were enjoying them ourselves, and Marta and Mother were exchanging their favorite native recipes.

That summer Sumiko and I pretended we were living in the turret of a castle tower. We made daily swimming trips to Lake Washington, surrounded by cool green trees and beautiful homes. But deep in our hearts we were still attached to Alki Beach. We kept comparing the mud-bottom lake and its mosquitoes to the sparkling salt water of Puget Sound, its clean, hot sands and its fiery sunsets.

Mother was more than content with the apartment. Its windows opened up unlimited vistas of beautiful scenery. Straight across we could see a bridge rise up to meet Beacon Hill where on its crest the soft yellow building of the Marine Hospital stood magnificently alone, its soaring clean lines etched sharply against the sky. On clear days we could see the icy beauty of Mount Rainier loom up in its splendor, and in the evenings we watched the brilliant diamond lights of the Rainier Valley Highway strung across the soft blue velvet of the summer night. All this inspired Mother to stand at the bay window at odd hours of the night in a poetic trance. Once she caught a hauntingly beautiful moonlight scene and a *tanka* materialized in her mind, which she interpreted for us:

> *In the spring-filled night*
> *A delicate mauve*
> *Silken cloud*
> *Veils the moon's brilliance*
> *In its soft chiffon mist.*

The words used in *tanka* were quite different from spoken Japanese. *Tanka* was written in five, seven, five, seven, seven accents in five lines, totaling exactly thirty-one syllables, never more, never less. In reciting the poem, it was sung melodiously in a voice laden with sentiment and trembling emotion to give it proper meaning and effect. The expression *nali keli* was often employed in these poems. Whenever we wanted to tease Mother, we added this expression to every sentence we uttered. We nudged each other whenever we caught Mother standing in front of a bubbling rice pot, lost in thought. "Mama, *gohan kogeri nali keli!* the rice scorcheth.

Mother smiled at our crude humor, but we had to admit that there was something in *tanka,* the way Mother used it. With it, she gathered together all the beauty she saw and heard and felt through that window and pulled it into our little apartment for us to enjoy. Sometimes the night was blotted out with heavy fog and we could see nothing. Then Sumiko and I would sit curled on the davenport, reading and listening to the radio while Mother sat in her armchair, mending or sewing, as she listened to the sounds of a fog-bound city. At the end of the quiet evening she would recite to us the *tanka* which she had created.

Kiri no yo no
Hodoro ni fukete
Samu zamu toh
Okibe no fune ka
Fue nali kawasu

The fog-bound night
Ever deepening in somber silence
Tinged with chilling sadness
Could those be ships far off at sea
Echoing and re-echoing their deep foghorns?

On such evenings I felt suddenly old, wondering that I could like such a melancholy poem. It reminded me of the way I had come to feel about my summer experience, half sad and half at peace with the world.

Gradually I learned in many other ways the terrible curse that went with having Japanese blood. As the nations went, so went their people. Japan and the United States were no longer seeing eye to eye, and we felt the repercussions in our daily lives.

International matters took a turn for the worse when Japan's army suddenly thrust into Shanghai. City officials, prominent men and women were interviewed and they all shouted for punishment and a boycott on Japanese goods. People stopped patronizing Japanese shops. The Chinese who were employed by Japanese resigned their jobs, one after another.

I dreaded going through Chinatown. The Chinese shopkeepers, gossiping and sunning themselves in front of their stores, invariably stopped their chatter to give me pointed, icicled glares.

The editorial sections of the newspapers and magazines were plastered with cartoons of hideous-looking Japanese. The Japanese was always caricatured with enormous, moon-shaped spectacles and beady, myopic eyes. A small mustache was perched arrogantly over massive, square buck teeth, and his bow-legged posture suggested a simian character.

When stories about the Japanese Army on the other side of the Pacific appeared in the newspapers, people stared suspiciously at us on the streets. I felt their resentment in a hundred ways — the way a saleswoman in a large department store never saw me waiting at the counter. After ten minutes, I had to walk quietly away as if nothing had happened. A passenger sitting across the aisle in a streetcar would stare at me coldly.

One beautiful Sunday afternoon a carload of us drove out into the country to swim at the Antler's Lodge. But the manager with a wooden face blocked our entrance, "Sorry, we don't want any Japs around here."

We said, "We're not Japs. We're American citizens." But we piled into the car and sped away trying to ignore the bruise on our pride.

Even some of the older Japanese were confused about the Nisei. Whenever a Japanese freighter crept into the harbor to pick up its cargo of scrap metal or petroleum, a group of angry citizens turned out as pickets in protest. Quite often Nisei college students walked up and down the dock with them, wearing sandwich signs, "Halt the oil and stop the Japs!" It shocked the sensibilities of the community elders. They muttered, "Who do these Nisei think they are? Don't they realize they, too, have Japanese blood coursing through their veins?"

About this time the Matsui's son, Dick, became the talk of the folks of the Tochiki-ken prefecture. Dick had studied electrical engineering through the International Correspondence Course and had just accepted an important job with the Goto firm in Japan. The townfolk buzzed with excitement everytime someone decided to pull up stakes and go to Japan.

I remember one heated argument about Dick's decision at Mr. Wakamatsu's cafe, where Father had taken me for lunch. Mr. Sakaguchi, hotel manager and one-time president of the Seattle Japanese Chamber of Commerce, and Mr. Sawada, a clothing salesman, joined us.

"I say Dick's a smart lad to be going to Japan!" Mr. Sakaguchi pounded the table so hard all the coffee cups rattled in their saucers. "Where else could Dicku get a real man's job? Certainly not here!" As he stuck out his lower lip, his round bald head made him look like an octopus.

Mr. Sawada shook his head thoughtfully. "I don't know about that, Sakaguchi-kun. It's Dicku's own decision, but if I were his parents, I would advise him to think twice about it. After all, Dicku's an American citizen; his future is here."

I liked Mr. Sawada. He was a man of gentle humor and understanding. His wife had died many years ago, leaving him with three children to rear. All his life, he worked hard as a salesman. He walked many miles every day on his route and he always walked with firm deliberate footsteps as if he were determined not to show his weariness. Mr. Sawada was one of the happiest and proudest men I knew, for one of his fondest dreams was coming true. His brilliant eldest son, George, was studying medicine.

"A future here! Bah! Words, words!" Mr. Sakaguchi exploded. "How many sons of ours with a beautiful bachelor's degree are accepted into American life? Name me one young man who is now working in an American firm on equal terms with his white colleagues. Our Nisei engineers push lawn mowers. Men with degrees in chemistry and physics do research in the fruit stands of the public market. And they all rot away inside."

Mr. Sawada insisted quietly. "That's why I think our young men should go to the Midwest or East. Jobs, all kinds of them, are open to Nisei, I hear. Take Nagai's son, for example. He took a good civil service job as an engineer in Wisconsin."

"Nagai's boy is one in a million. Most of us don't know a soul out there. You can't just go out there without contacts. I'm telling you Dicku's the smart one. With his training and ability to use both the English and Japanese language, he'll probably be a big shot one of these days in the Orient." Mr. Sakaguchi continued to prod Mr. Sawada, "Now be frank, Sawada-kun, if you had a good job waiting for you right now in Japan, wouldn't you pick up and leave?"

Mr. Sawada replied firmly, "And leave my children? No, I wouldn't. I've lived here too long. My wife is buried here. All my friends are here. I haven't kept in touch with my relatives in Japan so I'd be a stranger, if I were to return now. Life certainly has its peculiar twists, doesn't it?"

"Indeed!" Father agreed. "After the young ones were born, our roots sank deeper here. This is our children's home, and it has become ours."

When Dick had been offered the attractive job, Mrs. Matsui came to tell us about it. She felt as proud as if the Emperor himself had bestowed a personal favor upon her family. When Mother wondered how Dick would like Japan, a country which he had never seen, Mrs. Matsui said, "Dicku feels that it's the place for him. He would work himself right up to the top without having to fight prejudice."

She said Dick had been developing an intense dislike of America over the years, and she traced it to a certain incident which Dick had never been able to forget. At work one summer at the Pike Place Public Market, a white man selling vegetables at a nearby stall had shouted at him peevishly, "Ah, why don't all of ya Japs go back to where ya belong, and stop cluttering up the joint."

Young and trigger-tempered, Dick had flung back, "Don't call me 'Jap.' I'm an American!"

The man had flung his head back in derisive laughter, and Dick would have torn off his apron and flung himself at him if his friends hadn't held him back.

Mrs. Matsui continued, "Dicku never forgot those words. He said that that was what every white man in this country really thought about us. He refused to go to the university because he said it was just a waste of time and money for a Nisei."

Then Dick had plunged into the correspondence course with fury, determined to be on his own so he would not have to work for a white man. When the agent from Japan approached him, Dick had snatched at the bait.

People of the same mind with Mr. Sakaguchi flatly stated, "What's so terrible about it? It's better for a man to go where he's welcome. You can't waste a man's talent and brains without wrecking his spirit."

On the other hand, young men like Jack Okada, Henry's college friend, were scornful of Dick's decision. "Dick's a fool. He thinks he's going to be kingpin out there with an American education. Those big companies can make use of fellows like him all right, but Dick's going to find himself on a social island. The Japanese hate us Nisei. They despise our crude American manners."

On the day when Dick was to sail for Japan, everyone of the Tochigi-ken prefecture turned out at Smith Cove to give him a send-off. Mother and I represented our family. Confetti and streamers laced the air as hundreds of Japanese milled around on the dock in tight circles, bowing and making their formal farewells. When the ship shuddered, sounding its deep bass horn, we fought our way through the crowd to Dick. Mrs. Matsui was smiling bravely like a samurai mother sending her son off to war. I managed to slide an arm through the crushing wall of bodies and pumped Dick's perspiring hand. He acknowledged my best wishes with an unsmiling face. In the bright sun, his face was drawn and white, making him look young and uncertain, and I wondered if Dick was having a change of heart at the last minute. Another warning horn vibrated through the air. Dick, his arms loaded with gifts and shopping bags full of fruits and packages, fought his way up as the gangplank swung off the dock. It rattled up to the lip of the ship and a sailor walked the deck, vigorously striking a brass cymbal, drowning out all conversation. It was a moment of incomparable confusion and loneliness, the clash of the cymbal mixed with the hurried last-minute farewells and the flowing tears. Another blast of the horn, then from the deck of the ship, the measured strain of "Auld Lang Syne" floated out over our heads. More confetti showered down, colored serpentines snaking swiftly through the air. Everyone was shouting, "*Sayonara* . . . good-by, good-by!"

Mrs. Matsui suddenly burst into tears. Mr. Matsui, standing erect beside his wife, solemnly waved his straw hat at the small figure of his son on the ship, slipping away in the distance. I wanted to flee from Smith Cove. It was no longer the shining shore where the Issei had eagerly landed many years ago, but the jumping-off place for some of their young, looking to Japan as the land of opportunity. We had all felt as Dick had, one time or another. We had often felt despair and wondered if we must beat our heads against the wall of prejudice all our lives.

In the privacy of our hearts, we had raged, we had cried against the injustices, but in the end, we had swallowed our pride and learned to endure.

Even with all the mental anguish and struggle, an elemental instinct bound us to this soil. Here we were born; here we wanted to live. We had tasted of its freedom and learned of its brave hopes for a democracy. It was too late, much too late for us to turn back.

Monica Sone

COMING INTO THE COUNTRY

With a clannish sense of place characteristic of the bush, people in the region of the upper Yukon refer to their part of Alaska as "the country." A stranger appearing among them is said to have "come into the country."

Donna Kneeland came into the country in April, 1975. Energetically, she undertook to learn, and before long she had an enviable reputation for certain of her skills, notably her way with fur. Knowledgeable people can look at a pelt and say that Donna tanned it. In part to save money, she hopes to give up commercial chemicals and use instead the brains of animals — to "Indian tan," as she puts it — and she has found a teacher or two among the Indian women of the region, a few of whom remember how it was done. The fur is mainly for sale, and it is the principal source of support for her and her companion, whose name is Dick Cook. (He is not related to Earl Cook, of the Capital Site Selection Committee.) A marten might bring fifty dollars. Lynx, about three hundred. Wolf, two hundred and fifty. They live in a cabin half a dozen miles up a tributary stream, at least forty and perhaps sixty miles from the point on the border meridian where the Yukon River leaves Yukon Territory and flows on into Alaska. The numbers are deliberately vague, because Cook and Kneeland do not want people to know exactly where the cabin is. Their nearest neighbors, a couple who also live by hunting and trapping, are something like twenty miles from them. To pick up supplies, they travel a good bit farther than that. They make a journey of a couple of days, by canoe or dog team, to Eagle, a bush community not far from the Canadian boundary whose population has expanded in recent years and now exceeds a hundred. For three-quarters of a century, Eagle has been an incorporated Alaskan city, and it is the largest sign of human material progress in twenty thousand square miles of rugged, riverine land. From big bluffs above the Yukon — five hundred, a thousand, fifteen hundred feet high — the country reaches back in mountains, which, locally, are styled as hills. The Tanana Hills. The tops of the hills are much the same height as New Hampshire's Mt. Washington, Maine's Mt. Katahdin, and North Carolina's Mt. Mitchell. Pebble-clear streams trellis the mountains, descending toward the opaque, glacier-fed Yukon, and each tributary drainage is suitable terrain for a trapper or two, and for miners where there is gold.

For Donna Kneeland, as many as five months have gone by without a visit to Eagle, and much of the time she is alone in the cabin, while her man is out on the trail. She cooks and cans things. She grinds wheat berries and bakes bread. She breaks damp skins with an old gun barrel and works them with a metal scraper. A roommate she once had at the University of Alaska went off to "the other states" and left her a hundred-and-fifty-dollar Canadian Pioneer parka. She has never worn it, because — although her cabin is in the coldest part of Alaska — winter temperatures have yet to go low enough to make her feel a need to put it on. "We've had some cool weather," she admits. "I don't know how cold, exactly. Our thermometer only goes to fifty-eight." When she goes out at such temperatures to saw or to split the wood she survives on — with the air at sixty and more below zero — she wears a down sweater. It is all she needs as long as her limbs are active. Her copy of "The Joy of Cooking" previously belonged to a trapper's wife who froze to death. Donna's father, a state policeman, was sent in to collect the corpse.

Donna is something rare among Alaskans — a white who is Alaska-born. She was born in Juneau, and as her father was biennially transferred from post to post, she grew up all over Alaska — Barrow, Tok, Fairbanks. In girlhood summers, she worked in a mining camp at Livengood, cooking for the crew. At the university, which is in Fairbanks, she majored in anthropology. In 1974, she fell in love with a student from the University of Alberta, and she went off to Edmonton to be with him. Edmonton is Canada's fourth-largest city and is the size of Nashville. "In Edmonton, every place I went I could see nothing but civilization. I never felt I could ever get out. I wanted to see something with no civilization in it. I wanted to see even two or three miles of just nothing. I missed this very much. In a big city, I can't find my way out of a paper bag. I was scared to death of the traffic. I was in many ways unhappy. One day I thought, I know what I want to do — I want to go live in the woods. I left the same day for Alaska."

In Alaska, where "the woods" are wildernesses beyond the general understanding of the word, one does not prudently just wander off — as Donna's whole life had taught her. She may have lived in various pinpoints of Alaskan civilization, but she had never lived out on her own. She went to Fairbanks first. She took a job — white dress and all — as a dental assistant. She asked around about trappers who came to town. She went to a meeting of the Interior Alaska Trappers Association and studied the membership with assessive eyes. When the time came for a choice, she would probably have no difficulty, for she was a beautiful young woman, twenty-eight at the time, with a criterion figure, dark-blond hair, and slate-blue, striking eyes.

Richard Okey Cook came into the country in 1964, and put up a log lean-to not far from the site where he would build his present cabin. Trained in aspects of geophysics, he did some free-lance prospecting that first summer near the head of the Seventymile River, which goes into the Yukon a few bends below Eagle. His larger purpose, though, was to stay in the country and to change himself thoroughly "from a professional into a bum" — to learn to trap, to handle dogs and sleds, to net fish in quantities sufficient to feed the dogs. "And that isn't easy," he is quick to say, claiming that to lower his income and raise his independence he has worked twice as hard as most people. Born and brought up in Ohio, he was a real-estate appraiser there before he left for Alaska. He had also been to the Colorado School of Mines and had run potentiometer surveys for Kennecott Copper in Arizona. Like many Alaskans, he came north to repudiate one kind of life and to try another. "I wanted to get away from paying taxes to support something I didn't believe in, to get away from big business, to get away from a place where you can't be sure of anything you hear or anything you read. Doctors rip you off down there. There's not an honest lawyer in the Lower Forty-eight. The only honest people left are in jail." Toward those who had held power over him in various situations his reactions had sometimes been emphatic. He took a poke at his high-school principal, in Lyndhurst, Ohio, and was expelled from school. In the Marine Corps, he became a corporal twice and a private first class three times. His demotions resulted from fistfights — on several occasions with sergeants, once with a lieutenant. Now he has tens of thousands of acres around him and no authorities ordinarily proximitous enough to threaten him — except nature, which he regards as God. While he was assembling his wilderness dexterity, he spent much of the year in Eagle, and he became, for a while, its mayor. A single face, a single vote, counts for a lot in Alaska, and especially in the bush.

The traplines Cook has established for himself are along several streams, across the divides between their headwaters and on both banks of the Yukon — upward of a hundred miles in all, in several loops. He runs them mainly in November and December. He does not use a snow machine, as many trappers in Alaska do. He says, "The two worst things that ever happened to this country are the airplane and the snow machine." His traplines traverse steep terrain, rocky gullies — places where he could not use a machine anyway. To get through, he requires sleds and dogs. Generally, he has to camp out at least one night to complete a circuit. If the temperature is colder than thirty below, he stays in his cabin and waits for the snap to pass. As soon as the air warms up, he hits the trail. He has built lean-tos in a few places, but often enough he sleeps where he gets tired — under an orange canvas tarp. It is ten feet by ten, and weighs two and a half pounds, and is all the shelter he needs at, say, twenty below zero. Picking out a tree, he ties one corner of the tarp to the trunk, as high as he can reach. He stakes down the far corner, then stakes down the two sides. Sometimes, he will loft the center by tying a cord to a branch above. He builds a lasting fire between the tree and himself, gets into his sleeping bag, and drifts away. Most nights are calm. Snow is light in the upper Yukon. The tarp's configuration is not so much for protection as to reflect the heat of the fire. He could make a closed tent with the tarp, if necessary. His ground cloth, or bed pad, laid out on the snow beneath him, is the hide of a caribou.

He carries dried chum salmon for his dogs, and his own food is dried moose or bear meat and pinole — ground parched corn, to which he adds brown sugar. In the Algonquin language, pinole was "rockahominy." "It kept Daniel Boone and Davy Crockett going. It keeps me going, too." He carries no flour. "Flour will go rancid on you unless you buy white flour, but you can't live and work on that. I had a friend who died of a heart attack from eating that crap. It's not news that the American people are killing themselves with white flour, white sugar, and soda pop. If you get out and trap thirty miles a day behind dogs, you can damned well tell what lets you work and what doesn't.'' From a supplier in Seattle he orders hundred-pound sacks of corn, pinto beans, unground wheat. He buys cases of vinegar, tomato paste, and tea. Forty pounds of butter in one-pound cans. A hundred pounds of dried milk, sixty-five of dried fruit. Twenty-five pounds of cashews. Twenty-five pounds of oats. A forty-pound can of peanut butter. He carries it all down the Yukon from Eagle by sled or canoe. He uses a couple of moose a year, and a few bear, which are easier to handle in summer. ''A moose has too much meat. The waste up here you wouldn't believe. Hunters that come through here leave a third of the moose. Indians don't waste, but with rifles they are overexcitable. They shoot into herds of caribou and wound some. I utilize everything, though. Stomach. Intestines. Head. I feed the carcasses of wolverine, marten, and fox to the dogs. Lynx is another matter. It's exceptionally good, something like chicken or pork.''

With no trouble at all, Dick Cook remembers where every trap is on his lines. He uses several hundred traps. His annual food cost is somewhere under a thousand dollars. He uses less than a hundred gallons of fuel — for his chain saws, his small outboards, his gasoline lamps. The furs bring him a little more than his basic needs — about fifteen hundred dollars a year. He plants a big garden. He says, ''One of the points I live by is not to make any more money than is absolutely necessary.'' His prospecting activity has in recent years fallen toward nil. He says he now looks for rocks not for the money but ''just for the joy of it — a lot of things fall apart if you are not after money, and prospecting is one of them.''

In winter on the trail, he wears a hooded cotton sweatshirt, no hat. He does use an earband. He has a low opinion of wool. ''First off, it's too expensive. Second off, you don't have the moisture problem up here you have in the States.'' He wears Sears' thermal long johns under cotton coveralls, and his feet are kept warm by Indian-made mukluks with Bean's felt insoles and a pair of wool socks. He rarely puts on his parka. ''You have to worry up here more about overdressing than about underdressing. The problem is getting overheated.'' Gradually, his clothes have become rags, with so many shreds, holes, and rips that they seem to cling to him only through loyalty. Everything is patched, and loose bits lap as he walks. His red chamois-cloth shirt has holes in the front, the back, and the sides. His green overalls are torn open at both knees. Half a leg is gone from his corduroy pants. His khaki down jacket is quilted with patches and has a long rip under one arm. His hooded sweatshirt hangs from him in tatters, spreads over him like the thrums of a mop. "I'll tell you one thing about this country," he says. "This country is hard on clothes."

Cook is somewhat below the threshold of slender. He is fatless. His figure is a little stooped, unprepossessing, but his legs and arms are strong beyond the mere requirements of the athlete. He looks like a scarecrow made of cables. All his features are feral — his chin, his nose, his dark eyes. His hair, which is nearly black, has gone far from his forehead. His scalp is bare all the way back to, more or less, his north pole. The growth beyond — dense, streaked with gray — cantilevers to the sides in unbarbered profusion, so that his own hair appears to be a parka ruff. His voice is soft, gentle — his words polite. When he is being pedagogical, the voice goes up several registers, and becomes hortative and sharp. He is not infrequently pedagogical.

A decade and more can bring deep seniority in Alaska. People arrive steadily. And people go. They go from Anchorage and Fairbanks — let alone the more exacting wild. Some, of course, are interested only in a year or two's work, then to return with saved high wages to the Lower Forty-eight. Others, though, mean to adapt to Alaska, hoping to find a sense of frontier, a fresh and different kind of life. They come continually to Eagle, and to Circle, the next settlement below Eagle down the Yukon. The two communities are about a hundred and sixty river miles apart, and in all the land between them live perhaps thirty people. The state of New Jersey, where I happen to live, could fit between Eagle and Circle. New Jersey has seven and a half million people. Small wonder that the Alaskan wild has at least a conceptual appeal to certain people from a place like New Jersey. Beyond Circle are the vast savannas of the Yukon Flats — another world. Upstream from Circle are the bluffs, the mountains, the steep-falling streams — the country. Eagle and Circle are connected only by river, but each of them is reachable, about half the year, over narrow gravel roads (built for gold mines) that twist through the forest and are chipped out of cliffsides in high mountain passes. If you get into your car in Hackensack, Circle is about as far north as you can go on North America's network of roads. Eagle, with its montane setting, seems to attract more people who intend to stay. In they come — young people in ones and twos — from all over the Lower Forty-eight. With general trapping catalogues under their arms, they walk around wondering what to do next. The climate and the raw Alaska wild will quickly sort them out. Some will not flinch. Others will go back. Others will stay on but will never get past the clustered cabins and gravel streets of Eagle. These young people, for the most part, are half Cook's age. He is in his middle forties. He is their exemplar — the one who has done it and stuck. So the newcomers turn to him, when he is in town, as sage and mentor. He tells them that it's a big but hungry country out there, good enough for trapping, maybe, but not for too much trapping, and they are to stay the hell off his traplines. He does not otherwise discourage people. He wants to help them. If, in effect, they are wearing a skin and carrying a stone-headed club, he suggests that technology, while it can be kept at a distance, is inescapable. "The question," he will say, "is how far do you want to go? I buy wheat. I use axes, knives. I have windows. There's a few things we've been trained to need and can't give up. You can't forget the culture you were raised in. You have to satisfy needs created in you. Almost everyone needs music, for instance. Cabins may be out of food, but they've all got books in them. Indian trappers used deadfalls once — propped-up logs. I wouldn't want to live without my rifle and steel traps. I don't want to have to live on a bow and arrow and a deadfall. Somewhere, you have to make some sort of compromise. There is a line that has to be drawn. Most people feel around for it. Those that try to be too Spartan generally back off. Those who want to be too luxurious end up in Eagle — or in Fairbanks, or New York. So far as I know, people who have tried to get away from technology completely have always failed. Meanwhile, what this place has to offer is wildness that is nowhere else."

A favorite aphorism of Cook's is that a farmer can learn to live in a city in six months but a city person in a lifetime cannot learn to live on a farm. He says of newcomers, "A lot of them say they're going to 'live off the land.' They go hungry. They have ideas about everything — on arrival. And they've got no problems. But they're diving off too high a bridge. Soon they run into problems, so they come visiting. They have too much gear and their sleeping bags are too heavy to carry around. They are wondering where to get meat, where and how to catch fish, how to protect their gear from bears. you can't tell them directly. If you tell them to do something, they do the opposite. But there are ways to let them know.''

Cook seems to deserve his reputation. In all the terrain that is more or less focussed on the post office at Eagle, he is the most experienced, the best person to be sought out by anyone determined to live much beyond the outermost tip of the set society. He knows the woods, the animals, sleds, traps, furs, dogs, frozen rivers, and swift water. He is the sachem figure. And he had long since achieved this status when a day arrived in which a tooth began to give him great pain. He lay down in his cabin and waited for the nuisance to pass. But the pain increased and was apparently not going to go away. It became so intense he could barely stand it. He was a couple of hundred miles from the most accesible dentist. So he took a pair of channel-lock pliers and wrapped them with tape, put the pliers into his mouth, and clamped them over the hostile tooth. He levered it, worked it awhile, and passed out. When he came to, he picked up the pliers and went back to work on the tooth. It wouldn't give. He passed out again. Each time he attacked the tooth with the pliers, he passed out. Finally, his hand would not move. He could not make his arm lift the pliers toward his mouth. So he set them down, left the cabin, and — by dogsled and mail plane — headed for the dentist, in Fairbanks.

John Borg came into the country in 1966. He was a mailman, on vacation, and he pitched his tent by American Creek a mile out of Eagle. The Army had brought him to Alaska in the nineteen-fifties — just before Alaska became a state — and (in his phrase) ''plain opportunity'' was what had caused him to stay. He carried letters around Anchorage for a number of years while opportunity in other forms withheld itself. And then he found Eagle. From birth he had been at home among low populations in open settings. He had grown up in Spirit Township, in the hills of northern Wisconsin, and had gone to Rib Lake High School, thirteen miles away. Now here was a town smaller by far than any he had known — some log cabins and a few frame buildings aggregated on a high bank above a monumental river. It seemed to him beautiful in several respects. "The quality of the people who lived here at the time is what made it particularly attractive." In 1968, he and his wife, Betty, took over the Eagle Roadhouse, providing bunks and board for exploration geologists, forest-fire fighters, and anyone else who might happen into Eagle. Before long, they had the propane franchise; and Borg became, as well, the regional Selective Service registrar, and president of the Eagle Historical Society, and the local reporter for the National Weather Service, and the sole officer (at this river port of entry) representing the United States Customs Service, and — on the payroll of the United States Geological Survey — the official observer of the Yukon. Borg had left Anchorage because half of the people of Alaska lived there and that was "just too many." Now, hundreds of miles distant in the bush, he was on his way to becoming a one-man city. Inevitably, with his postal background, he also became the postmaster — of Eagle, Alaska 99738 — and, as such, he is the central figure in the town. He is a slim, fairly tall man, who looks ten years younger in a hat. He was born in 1937. He has a narrow-brimmed cap made from camouflage cloth that, once on his head, is unlikely to come off, indoors or out, and gives him a boyish, jaunty air as he cancels stamps, weighs packages, and exercises his quick, ironic wit. There is a lightness about him, of manner, appearance, and style, that saves him from the weight of his almost numberless responsibilities. One place where the hat comes off is in the small log cabin called Eagle City Hall. Inside are a big iron stove, benches for interested observers, and a long table, where Borg sits with the Eagle Common Council. His bared forehead is a high one — an inch or two higher than it once was. His eyes seem lower beneath it. His regard is uncommonly stern. Shadows come into his mustache, which turns into an iron brush. The youth in the post office has been returned to sender. Behind the heavier demeanor at the head of the Council table is John Borg the Mayor.

The post office is in a small cabin about a hundred yards from the riverbank at an intersection of unpaved streets — the heart of town. Borg owns the building and rents it to the United States.

He arrives there by eight in the morning, after checking the height of the river (when the river is liquid). Because this is where the Yukon enters Alaska, its condition at Eagle is of considerable interest to the two dozen villages in the thirteen hundred river miles between the Canadian boundary and the Bering Sea. Borg also reads instruments that react to the weather, and he turns on the Weather Service's single-sideband radio to attempt to send facts to Anchorage. Eagle is not in perfect touch with the rest of the world. Signals get lost. Fairbanks, urban center of the northern bush, would be the more appropriate place to call, because, among others, the bush pilots of Fairbanks want the information. But the radio gets through to Fairbanks only about one time in five. Success in reaching Anchorage is about eighty per cent. So Borg calls Anchorage, toward four hundred miles away, and the word — of the river, of the weather, of an emergency — is relayed back north to Fairbanks.

"KCI 96 Anchorage. KEC 27 Eagle. Clouds now, six to eight thousand feet. Visibility, fifteen miles. Winds, calm. River, thirty-eight and falling. Water temperature, thirty-six degrees." The air in the night went down to twenty-eight. Yesterday's high was fifty. Right now, the air is at forty-five on an uncertain morning under volatile skies — May 13, 1976. It is mail day, the country's substitute for organized entertainment, but there is no guarantee that the plane will come through. It comes two, three, occasionally four times a week. The weather is inconstant, mutable. Squalls of snow may be shoved aside by thunderheads that are soon on the rims of open skies. Borg's records show that on a July day in the nineteen-sixties the thermometer reached ninety-six. During a night in January, 1975, the column went down to seventy-two degrees below zero. Borg says the air was even colder by the river. While this is the coldest part of Alaska, it is also the hottest and among the driest. Less than four feet of snow will fall in all of a winter, and about a foot of total precipitation (a figure comparable to New Mexico's) across the year. There is a dusting of new snow, Borg comments, on the mountains down the river.

The foyer stirs. The post office has a miniature lobby, a loitering center, with a small grid of combination boxes, public notices, and a wicketless window framing Borg himself. Camouflage hat. Faded plaid shirt. "What can I do for you?"

Lilly Allen (in her twenties) has a cartful of textbooks to ship back to the University of Nebraska. High school in Eagle is by correspondence, and is controlled from filing cabinets in Lincoln. The teachers are in Nebraska. Lilly is the resident supervisor.

Jim Dungan comes in, slowly, hands Borg a letter, and makes no move to go. He leans forward on his crutches and draws on his pipe. Dungan has more time even than his fellow-townsmen do this year, as a result of an accident. He says, often, "I'll be off these crutches soon. I won't be wearing them all my life, that's for sure." There are lead weights on the crutches today. Borg asks about them, and Dungan says they are divers' weights, and that when his leg gets better he will slip them into pockets in his wet-suit when he dives for gold. One on each crutch, the weights total fifty pounds. They are not there to create a vanity of muscles but to build his stamina, to keep him in condition.

"It's easy to get out of condition," Borg remarks. "All you have to do is nothing."

Bertha Ulvi and Ethel Beck, Indian sisters, come in to mail raingear to Ethel's husband, who is working in the Arctic for the Alyeska pipeline consortium.

A plane goes overhead. Borg, busy at the scales, says it's not the mail plane — just Jim Layman in his Taylorcraft. A few minutes later, he hears another plane, and says, "No. That's not it. That's Warbelow, coming up from Tok." Borg doesn't have to go out for a look. From the sound alone, he can usually say where an aircraft is coming from, what kind it is, and who is flying it.

Eagle is a dry community. Its leading bootlegger comes in and posts a letter, followed by his closest competitor. They, in turn, are followed by Elva Scott, Sage Cass, Horace Biederman, Sarge Waller (an alumnus of the Marine Corps), and Jack Boone. With dark furry hair and a dark furry beard, Boone appears to be part bear and part wolf. "You've got a bunch of weird individuals in this town," he observes. And he adds, "Me included."

On one wall of the post-office lobby is a thick sheaf of notices about fugitives all over the United States who are "WANTED BY FBI." They include descriptions, fingerprints, and pictures of people who appear to have arrived long since in Eagle.

Roy Miettunen comes in with a letter — a rare public appearance. He likes to talk, but he stays in his cabin; you have to go to him. In the warmer weeks of the year (a short season), he works his claim on Alder Creek, far out in the mountains, sluicing gold. He once prematurely used up his food, and he walked out in eleven days, eating squirrels. It takes more than squirrels to keep Roy Miettunen in form. He lost more than sixty pounds, and came out of the woods weighing two thirteen. He speaks slowly, firmly, attractively. With his great frame and his big head, his unfrivolous jaw, he looks more sergeant than Sarge. He was, long ago, of the Seattle police. In his cabin he has eighteen rifles, thirty-four pistols, and two swords.

A visitor from the state Department of Highways, concerned about the condition of a stretch of local road, comes in and speaks with Borg about the use of his Cat. The term Cat derives, of course, from the Caterpillar Tractor Company, of Peoria, Illinois, and, in the synecdochical way that snow machines in Canada are generally called Ski-Doos and snow machines in the Alaskan upper Yukon are called sno-gos, all bulldozers of any make or size are called Cats. John Borg's Cat is a forty-two-horse John Deere, with a seven-foot blade. Borg mentions forty dollars an hour as the asking price for his Cat — at work with him on it. The State of Alaska hems but does not completely haw. Borg nods at thirty-eight.

Anton Merly appears, and Jack Greene, followed by Ralph Helmer, who now runs the roadhouse. He has a letter for his grandmother near Spokane. She is in her eighties, and the letter is in acknowledgement of her birthday. He tells Borg that he lived for three years on her farm after his parents were divorced. "That was a very beneficial thing in my life, although I didn't realize it at the time." Helmer, about a dozen others, and the central buildings of the city of Eagle are supplied with electricity at thirty-five cents a kilowatt-hour by a private power company consisting of Carlie Ostrander and John Borg. They have two diesel generators, which can put out twelve kilowatts over an effective radius of a thousand yards. Borg sells power to the post office. But his home cabin, in the woods far back from the river, is out of range. He has a small generator there to run the washing machine and power tools, but the cabin does not use electric light.

Kay Christensen comes in. She has no letter. She wants to speak to Borg about plowing up her garden with his Rototiller. Borg accepts the job. In the eighteen-nineties, Jack McQuesten, a storekeeper celebrated in the country, used to plow his garden with a moose.

The sky was clear at 7 A.M. Then cumulus built up, and some rain fell, and now, at eleven, comes the dinning sound of hail. Dan Kees, a relative newcomer, talks about the hail in West Virginia, where he is from, and Borg listens. Borg is a member of the Bible Chapel, politically the strongest unit in Eagle, and Kees is his pastor. Kees wears a cowboy-style hat, so wide-brimmed it could be looked upon as a stunted sombrero. He is technically a missionary here. That is, the church headquarters at Glennallen, Alaska, pays him. His parishioners are referred to locally as "the bloc," "the group," "the Christians," "the fundamentalists." They also include the families of Ralph Helmer, Ron Ivy, the Ostrander brothers, and Roger Whitaker, the regional constable. In the spectrum of Eagle society, the fundamentalists are all the way over in the ultraviolet, beyond the threshold of visible light. Dick Cook and the young people of the river (the wheat grinders, meat hunters, trappers — liberal, certainly, and in some ways lawless) are at the opposite end, deep into the infrared. A few whites are married to Indians. The Indians number less than fifty, and almost all live three miles upriver, outside the plat of the town. Philosophically, they are as close to the river people as they are to anyone else. Across the middle span of the society are — among others — drifters, merchants, visionaries, fugitives, miners, suburbanites, and practitioners of early retirement. There is something of the rebel in everyone here, and a varying ratio between what attracts them to this country and what repels them in places behind. "Never put restrictions on an individual" is probably page 1, line 1 of the code of the bush. But people here encounter restrictions from governments state and federal, from laws to which they do not all subscribe, and — perhaps to an extent just as great — from one another. Compressed, minute, Eagle is something like a bathysphere, lowered deep into a world so remote it is analogous to the basins of the sea. The people within look out at the country. John Borg remembers regretfully when there was more room to move around inside.

He takes from a wall a photograph of someone in Eagle holding a gold pan full of hailstones the size of eggs, and shows the picture to Kees, possibly to imply that hail like that could destroy a place like West Virginia. The stones falling now are scarcely half an inch thick. Their clatter is considerable, but is not enough to kill the sound of a Cessna 207, up there in the storm with the incoming mail. Borg loads up a van and drives out to the airstrip, which is halfway between the town and the Indian Village. The strip, for the moment, is white as winter. The hail continues, but the skies are broken, and around the gray clouds are wide bays of blue. Borg has collected mail here at sixty below zero, coming out from town on a snow machine for half a ton of Christmas cards arriving one month late. The 207 flares, lands, and taxis up, its wings like snare drums under the pounding stones. The pilot gets out, catches some hail, and examines it. The stones, in shape, resemble Hershey's Kisses. He looks back into the storm and sees seven geese fighting their way through the same airspace he was in moments before. "How would you like to get *that* in the eyeballs?" he says, with feeling for the geese. The pilot, new in Alaska, is from New Jersey. There is a passenger or two. A small roll of chain-link fence comes off the plane. An Indian family is expecting it, and is on hand to pick it up. Borg stuffs the van with mailbags and cardboard cartons. The wing of the 207 is now coated with slush. "That will raise hell with the airfoil," says the pilot, and Borg produces a broom. He sweeps three hundred pounds of slush off the airplane, and the pilot returns to the air.

People throng the post office like seagulls around a piling, like trout at the mouth of a brook. Many, of both races, wear sweatshirts and windbreakers on which are stencilled the words "Eagle, Alaska." Make what they will of the country, they seem to yearn for contact with the outside world. On days when the mail plane does not come, the human atmosphere is notably calmer than it is now. With a sheet of plywood against his postal window, Borg blocks himself away while he and his wife, whose head tops out at his shoulder blades, do the sorting. As letters go into the boxes, the doors open and slap shut. The babble declines. Many stand and read without dispersing to their cabins. Viola Goggans is baffled by something to do with wheel bearings. Borg gives her a short lesson in their function and potential flaws. Almost gingerly, he hands Lilly Allen a package that — as he knows from her many inquiries — contains a beautifully crafted dulcimer. He is obviously relieved that it has come at last. Sara Biederman, an Indian who lives in the town, is having trouble with the legal phraseology of a letter from Fairbanks. She comes to the window and hands the letter to Borg. "It says there's fourteen hundred and ninety-eight dollars due on your truck and if the money is not paid they will come and get the truck," he tells her. Michael David collects mail and packages, for himself and others in the Indian Village. He is young, slim, without expression. A headband holds his long black hair. Michael David is the Indian Village Chief. "He's got an awful uphill grade in front of him," remarks his counterpart, the Mayor.

John McPhee

REQUIEM FOR THE OUTFITTER TO THE SISTERHOOD

Whenever I go to a Roman Catholic funeral in Missoula, Montana, I make a point of counting the rabbis. My most recent tally turned up thirty-nine plus one. I hesitate to say forty because one was a maverick, and, from years' experience of inner Church circles, I recognized him as the current target for the Clerical Supplier or "Outfitter to the Sisterhood," as he was known to me during thirty-odd years in the convent.

The *rabbis* or *rabats* are the black clerical fronts that support the Roman collar. Sleeveless, backless, and in these respects, not unlike the shrouds of Evelyn Waugh's Loved Ones, they extend to the clerical waist and reassure the faithful that the priest is not just another one of us. The fortieth rabat was blue — Electrifying Blue — and exemplified for me the whole complex of docility and contradiction in the Church today, with its near-fatal consequences for the merchant who so carefully built his mail-order market on the separatist appeals of tradition and exclusiveness.

Like every closed group, the Church has its own vocabulary, and the enterprising business man, cultivating a specialized market, will try to speak as the Romans do. He may not be very good at it, and there's the sport. His task is further complicated by the evolution in Religious Orders since Vatican II and the growing sense of individualism among priests and nuns — a spirit expressed in their dress.

Twenty years ago the Outfitter's sales pitch appeared under a motto misquoted from "the great Apostle Paul": "Be Constant in Season and Out of Season." Then, lest the merchant should rush in where angels feared to tread, he meekly apologized for "introducing a biblical reference in this secular letter." But, as he explained, it "expresses exactly our attitude to you at all times. It is our credo. It is the rock upon which our business is built."

Lately this rock looks more and more like sand, predictable in its shifts as those three-minute wonders that save us from the hard-boiled breakfast; and I confess to a certain nostalgia as I re-read the lyrical appeals of yesteryear:

"Hitch your wagon to a star" is the excellent advice of Emerson in one of his clever essays, where he urges us ever to strive for perfection . . . This we are always trying to do for you.

Passing over Emerson's cleverness for the moment, let us latch onto that star-drawn wagon in quest of the perfect Knee Warmers for nuns. Apparently prayer cannot warm them, for this particular item continued to occupy a prominent position in the catalogues for another decade, taking its place beside all-wool bed caps, foot warmers, armlets, wristlets and Full Fashioned Tights (waist to toe) which came, like everything else, in black and white. It would have required a far more imaginative stretch to relate them to anything as sophisticated as a body stocking and the most revealing thing about them was that they were termed ideal for nuns and children.

Today, as some of my friends still in the Order rummage through the bursar's junk mail, it's hard for them to find much from the Faithful Outfitter to the Sisterhood. What has happened to "the Nun's Store within Your Door" (Copyright, 1953) in all the upheaval of *aggiornamento?* Time was when the Outfitter's name, like that of the holy foundress, was a household word in most convents where he did a booming grooming business in black serge and unbleached muslin. His catalogue was often found beside the New Testament on the community room shelves where the specialized magazines he advertised in reinforced the message.

Two decades ago, before the decline in priestly and religious vocations, nearly 165,000 nuns and more than 52,000 priests in the United States alone provided a stable market for miles of black serge, mountains of standard luggage, and oceans of indelible laundry marking ink. Besides, there were the products everybody uses: toiletries, indispensable notions like thread, and (in calced orders) shoe laces. These last were available in lengths all the way from 27 to 72 inches, a fact that may have had some bearing on the home accident toll in convents.

The dedicated Outfitter-Watcher now has his eye on Dallas where a company called Creative Image pushes contemporary habits not identifiable by Order and custom-made habits for communities of 200 or more. The catalogue of "the West Coast

Convent Supplier," in Glendale, California, ranges alphabetically over armlets, chapel veils, clippers and chemises through overshoes and storm rubbers all the way to Sisters' Umbrellas with the dangerous name of Black Magic. The Thread of Life Knee Warmers are still there, but shoe laces stop at 36 inches, and it's apparent that, as the trend towards Career Apparel catches on in banks and department stores, nuns' unwillingness to return to uniform will keep them out of step. Once powerful appeals to tradition and exclusiveness no longer work, and the interim emphasis on carefree polyester and the Sisters' "active life in this modern world" is already outmoded, as the sisters do their best to shake the baby doll image presented by the Outfitter professing to sell clothes "designed to keep up with your pace."

The simple truth is that most nuns would be glad to have a crack at anonymity, and mass-produced "contemporary habits," which look like schoolgirl uniforms with a Marlene Dietrich veil, won't do. For anyone who really understands the emotional investment in vesture that many of us had made, the change seems incredible.

Several years ago, at a national convention, a sister rose to her feet in response to somebody's casual reference to "a nun."

"We're not *nuns*," she insisted, invoking the technical distinction between solemn and simple vows, "and we don't like to be called *nuns*." Replay for several minutes of floor time. I sat there on the poets' panel, amused at the speaker in her modified habit, thinking about my "Blue Nun" poem and my complete willingness to be called a nun until the day arrived when I could be called an ex-nun. After being a member of a religious community for a while one quite forgot the strangeness of its language to secular ears. Shortly after I "entered" the convent I was introduced to my "angel," a specially-appointed guide who would pilot me through the cloistered air with all its ethereal thinness until I learned to adapt my very breathing to the general law. I was shown the "black room" where black serge garments were cleaned and pressed and the "white room" where the starched coifs, bandeaux and collars enjoyed separate-but-equal facilities.

All through the "not-nun's" homily the whole phenomenon of separatism abetted by specialized vocabulary continued to absorb me, and even now I've barely begun to deal with its implications. I had read Erving Goffman's *Asylums* and had been both enlightened and cast down by his study of the characteristics common to total institutions — prisons, mental hospitals, the military and the monastery. He even illustrated his points with long citations from the Rule of St. Benedict, one of three or four models for all subsequent religious rules.

I understood the important role of uniform dress because I had already experienced the hostility that greeted any departure, however trivial, from the religious habit. The first problem came when I shortened my black underskirt to seven inches from the floor after twice tearing it to ribbons in a bicycle chain. I reasoned that the dress regulations were not made with bicycles in mind — everyone rode them on our sprawling Fort Wright College campus — and that the law did not bind in impossible cases. My second dress code violation consisted in wearing a blue wool hand-knit scarf, the gift of a student who had had the foresight to ask my superior's permission before presenting it to me. It seems unbelievable now that so much energy was consumed in matters of so little consequence, or that it required so much courage to risk the disapproval of one's peers as well as superiors, but those outside the church may understand by recalling what happened when students first began wearing beards and long hair or draping themselves in the American flag. Besides, I had a long history of conformism: one of my recurring dreams starting from high school days involved forgetting to wear my uniform to school and spending all day in a vain attempt to get home to remedy the oversight. Freud would call it the dream of nakedness, but this interpretation fails to take account of the dressing down I had witnessed when a superior discovered that three freshmen in cool pastels had sent their uniforms to the cleaners on the same day.

One or two of my friends in the sisterhood were much braver than I. I remember one who had jested with her colleagues about the undue significance attached to the habit. Apparently word of her heresy reached official ears, and one day when she was walking towards the dining room a few paces behind the provincial superior, that ramrod figure turned to demand abruptly, "And what makes you think you'd be any more relevant in a hot pink suit?" Another responded to a tight-lipped superior's injunction against a cape shorter than the regulation by removing the cape altogether and returning unabashed to an art exhibit. My hot pink friend, several months later, took the black serge from her habit, converted it into a pants suit — the first on our campus — and wore it to a banquet, where, with modestly downcast eyes, she proclaimed herself the only nun present still wearing the habit. She is the same person who ran the most successful booth at a campus fund-raising fest, where she sold all the sensible black walking shoes beloved of the counter-culture, along with the black wadded winter capes and matching hoods or "caplins," to which any sister unlucky enough to catch cold used to be condemned for the winter. The garments were snapped up at five dollars apiece by students in granny dresses who came back to buy seconds for Christmas presents and to ask for the ultimate authentic detail, a cape or a hood with the original user's name still sewed in place according to convent regulations.

By the time all this was going on the Outfitter had already entered a schizophrenic phase. A 1966 check of nine catalogues indicated that the Old Faithful Outfitters were still gushing, although one reminded the curious that it is "easier to find a new customer than to keep a satisfied one."

A different, but related, challenge confronted the customer. Change can be upsetting to those for whom the religious congregation and its time-honored regalia loom larger than the Church, and here the Outfitter could be remarkably sensitive. Jamieson, for example, eased its customers over the hurdles with professional finesse:

"An item in ever-increasing demand is a short sleeve blouse for Sisters, and Jamieson has just the blouse for you. We have purposely made it short sleeve since we have found that many Communities . . . want to add their own sleeves in their own particular styling . . ." And when you buy mantles and aqua capes (No, it isn't a *color*, it's a *rain* cape) you can specify the appropriate collar: Dominica or Ursula and know that nothing will be out of order.

In easy narrative fashion, Jamieson's allayed any worries about changing the garb. "This community approached Jamieson," we are told, "after prominent national designers failed in the task."

One thinks of how they might have failed. In the colorful manner in which Marianne Moore failed to name the Edsel, say? "We developed a model that was adopted," the copywriter continued, "and since that time we have made many thousands of veils and collars of easy care, wash-n-wear materials, to the great satisfaction of the sisters who wear them."

But the reader must not be allowed to think it was easy: "This community knew what they wanted in the way of design, but they couldn't find a suitable material and the design was so difficult they couldn't find anyone to manufacture it for them, that is, until they came to us; we found that one of our flame-proof, crack-resistant, guimpe materials was ideal for the job and calling upon our long experience, found a manufacturing method that worked and is working to this day, as we continue to produce this item." Thus technology triumphs and the Fire Department as well as the sisters can relax until the next crisis or simply read on to discover that the fascinating Sisters of Mercy House Habit is "made from the same fabric that is used for the uniforms of the United States Government Health Service." If you can't be fire-proof, be hygienic, but don't demand too much of this world's goods. After all these examples and more like them we were forced to agree with Jamieson that "in this changing world of the Nun, when so many communities are changing the design of their habits and headpieces, it is very important . . . to be aware of Jamieson's ability to serve . . . in these very important areas . . ."

For some time afterwards the New and the Old locked in combat, and nowhere did one find more graphic evidence of the conflict than in the catalogues of the more enterprising Outfitter, who wanted to have it both ways. Soothingly, he assured us that his "watchwords — Quality, Service and Guaranteed Satisfaction . . . never will change." yet he now headed his inside-front-cover sales letters with "SOMETHING NEW" and proceeded in chatty fashion to tell us that he had bought out a local competitor and could, therefore, offer a wider selection of apparel fabrics. His approach might be quietly cautious as in this description of *New! Bathing Suits*: "Widely acclaimed because they are designed for today's modern Sister, with tradition still in mind." But in the same catalogue, nuns addicted to scrupulous measurement would find the "Anti-Back Ache Hem Marker: Every Convent Needs

One." Utility and conformity, in fact, were far more powerful appeals than style, and Sisters' pockets (Order by Waist Size) appeared as regularly as holsters in a catalogue of children's toys. Incongruities multiplied with Yawitz' Equestrian Type Pants (loose knee, open gore) in the lingerie section and Jamieson's perennial 72-inch shoe laces tangled in the 1967 catalogue with hair spray, car coats, trim-fit undergarments and a brochure showing sixteen styles of bathing suits.

All the emphasis used to be on tradition and exclusiveness. In fact, one enterprising firm represented its century-long service record by a gallery of family portraits inside the front cover. Each was tagged with name, dates of birth and death and a sanctimonious R. I. P. for those who had passed beyond. Having surveyed this devoted family group, one of whom, the caption informed us, was "beloved by all who knew him," the reader was all the more ready to consider the lower half of the page. There he found "the laity's gift problems made easy." One had simply to send a check or money order with the name and address of the nun he wished to remember, and a gift certificate would be sent to her, insuring her choice of merchandise exactly suited to her needs.

And even in 1962, catalogue customers could still get hung up on the family portraits. New York's "Century-Old Catholic Firm" boasted 125 years of continuous service. Ecumenism notwithstanding, the company ignored the Sacred Art Commissions and kept a front-cover niche for a very bad statue of the Blessed Virgin. It grieved me to learn that "Our brother Redmond McCosker," "A Patient Man of Great Faith," had gone to his eternal reward in 1959, bringing the total of RIP's to five and leaving a lone McCosker in the subordinate role of secretary-treasurer, while some dark horse with an Italian name was president. But in a world of unbridled change, it was reassuring to know that McCosker's bras were "correctly designed for the Sisterhood," and that swimwear was discreetly billed as "Bathing Necessities." Furthermore, the black poplin suit had short sleeves and a high neck, with a one-piece undergarment of wool jersey to render the whole idea innocuous. Impartially sized in small, medium and large, each of the two pieces came to only $4.95.

Complete coverage, which used to be something the insurance companies touted, gradually became the Number 1 selling-point for nuns' swimwear, but the bathing suits were there to stay. In Neil Doherty's 1966 catalogue, an assurance in 24-point type attached to an asterisk after the index entry for bathing suits, reminded customers that, "We are currently designing our 1966 line of beachwear for the Sisterhood. Please write for color brochure after the first of the year." And Jamieson's lined up eight selling points starting with economy and durability, ranging through careful tailoring and fit and ending with snag-proof zippers. Both conservative and lively colors appeared. Some suits with skirts or half skirts and others with "boy style" legs. No bikinis. But no apologies either. "Such fun to wear — a bright, cheery floral design in the new angel skin (?) latex fabric. You'll enjoy . . ." And all of these excellent selling points were topped off with a warning note: "Medical authorities advise that for hygienic purposes; (*sic*) each Sister should have and use her own swimsuit. Swimsuits should not be exchanged."

Names were a different matter. They must be exchanged. Chosen with one eye on the cloister gate-receipts, they reflected the gradual transition from withdrawal to involvement. True, the evolution had not yet produced consistency, but this was merely one more indication that change is nearly always intermittent and gradual. In the fifties the labels were clear: Cloister Cloth, Disciplined Cloth, Cathedral Veiling. Once in a while, to be sure, the speaker would slip out of character, especially when singing the glories of a nationally advertised product. He might refer to a deodorant sold "in the Sensational Plastic Spray Bottle" or speak of slippers "for after school comfort." But one would seldom find misnomers to match those of the seller catering to secular trade. House slippers, purchased perforce from the local retailer and not from the Complete Outfitter to the Sisterhood, might bear the distractingly profane name of Honeybugs. On the other hand, to show how keen the competition could become among dealers in religious goods, one company advertised Coverall Church Aprons and St. Christopher Key Cases; another listed a St. George Armband; and still another, no doubt an *avant-garde* liturgist, specialized in "*Rorate Coeli*" raincapes (from the opening prayer of the Mass for the Sunday before Christmas: *"Drop down dew, ye heavens*, from above; and let the clouds rain the just. Let the earth be opened and bud forth a savior . . ."*)* for nuns.

The nomenclature of the sixties was at once more secular and more daring: "NU-EVE, the Most Fitting Name in Panties" was saved only by the fact that Mary is commonly referred to as the Second Eve. But no such sanction could be urged for Lollipop Panties, also spelled Lolypop. The Institution Supply Co. offered Padre Coth — "Forever Black" — woven for the ecclesiastical trade — and "Eminence" underwear for men with cardinalatial ambitions. John F. McEvoy, whose 1965 catalogue headlined a 75-year service record over the Michelangelo *Pieta*, was a curious compound of convention and innovation. Million-Miler luggage traveled between covers sealed with the emblem of The Religious Dry Goods Association, "Your Sign of Safe Buying." Instinctively, one sensed that Religious Goods were drier than their profane counterparts; but the stress on Wash 'N' Wear synthetics was confusing.

Lanoue's Shoes ("The Finest Nun's Shoes Come from Lanoue") were equally promiscuous: Victoria, Superior, Chapel, Candidate, Novice and Academy mingled shamelessly with Kush N'Arch, Forward Thrust, Stroller, Medic, Koolie and Scout, and with such familiars as Patty, Peggy, Marion and Cindy. Shoes were not the only items obtainable from this supplier. Hosiery, luggage, scissors and manicure sets, along with everything for foot care, crowded his catalogue. And the busy nurse or teacher who still wanted a perfect fit was invited to "Send all the markings in the most comfortable shoes you are now wearing . . . When these sizes are not readable, draw an outline of your foot, while seated, with no pressure on the foot. Hold pencil straight in vertical position."

If a multiplicity of duties does not wholly account for such shopping procedures, perhaps some of the outmoded rules of cloister may. In some orders one or more sisters might be designated to shop for the entire community. These "extern sisters," as they were sometimes called, might have a difficult task arranging for all the highly personalized problems of anatomy and taste in communities of a dozen or more members, even though regulations sharply limited the range of diversity. At least one order I know of routinely required that rolls of linoleum be brought out to them on the sidewalk because the Rule forbade them to enter the stores. Others were not allowed to dine in company with laymen, so any type of public event that required the sisters' presence beyond mealtime would necessarily involve a restaurateur willing to provide sequestered dining facilities.

In all of the early catalogues I have studied, merchandise was displayed without benefit of models, but I foresaw the day when some *avant-garde* producer would superimpose his custom-made Benedictine mantle on a picture of St. Gertrude or his Carmelite veil on a portrait of St. Therese of Lisieux, the Little Flower. Meanwhile, he had already hit upon the device of sketching fifty-one distinct types of nuns' headgear on the title page of his catalogue, thus conveying the impression that every sister with a head, however hidden, shopped there.

Time has altered that, too. More and more of the Outfitters came to believe that even if clothes didn't make the man, the model makes the mantle. By 1964, sketched demurely, she had begun to replace the disembodied garments and the headless dress forms, until in 1967, convincingly photographed, she took her place, head high on the Jamieson cover, no longer looking dowdy and shapeless like the 1962 McCosker postulants in their ankle-length skirts and sensible shoes, but trim, clear-eyed and intelligent, wearing a practical tailored coat, her hair showing beneath the simple headdress. In the Jamieson's and the Tirrell's of that period, the artists had given us models of everything, including the action-fit bra. But Yawitz, Doherty, McCosker, Fitzpatrick, McEvoy and Institution Supply continued to treat pajamas and underwear as if they were wholly spiritual. Lowered eyes seemed to have less to do with prayerful recollection than with showing off the length of one's eyelashes — possibly Jamieson's subliminal approach to eyelash curlers in the 1970 catalogue.

As a matter of fact, pajamas had only been admitted to the catalogues a short time before. They were not quite as new as the Credit Card Service, but their omnipresence marked the passing of an era. They reminded us that successful advertising was predicated on demand. Where no market exists, one must be developed. And here, the man with something to sell must be pardoned if he gently insists on multiplying our needs or persuading us to follow the crowd — even *our* crowd. Instead of assuring us that we must be content with whatever is assigned to our use, as the Rule emphasizes, he meant to establish the superiority of his product. It was not surprising that, in doing so, he sometimes created a ludicrous picture of convent life. Consider, for example, the effect produced by this 1952 catalogue entry:

That's why Sisters in thousands of convents have demanded McCosker's No. 70 Underwear for over 20 years.

Pondering that passage, I once ruefully reflected that in some convents it would take twenty years. But the Sister Purchaser's overwork could hardly be blamed on poor McCosker. After all, his policy was immediate delivery and rapid turnover. In fact, one might almost have said that, for him, the voice of the customer, like that of the old-fashioned cloister bell, was Heaven's own command.

What had happened, I wondered, to "America's Outstanding Underwear Value" in ten years. Had it died with the last of the brothers or survived with the shoe strings? I looked at the 1962 catalogue (Why was our latest McCosker's four years out of date? Was it indicative? And of what? Sisters demanding underwear?) On page 22 I found the FAMOUS NUMBER 70. The type size had grown to 60-point. The illustration had expanded to fit the width of the page and two insets had been added to demonstrate the sag-proof shoulder and comfortable non-binding cuff. The copy had changed too. "Every Garment Cut Full Size," I read. "Not an inch has been skimped . . . every size is *full*. That's why Sisters in thousands of convents have demanded *McCosker's No. 70 Underwear for over 30 years.*"

I closed the book, convinced that the world, inside the cloister as well as out, was moving ahead and that the day was not too far away when the nun, like her secular sister, would simply go downtown, shop for her clothes like anybody else and use the Outfitter's catalogue to press wild flowers.

That prediction has been largely verified. One searches in vain for the giants of the nuns' mail-order market only to find a few wholesale suppliers of easy-care synthetics, a few expensive tailors of clerical clothing, and more religious goods houses that go in for marginal items such as electric-blue rabbis. In an odd way, we have come full circle, for the rabbi-rouser still aims at the conformist. His customer, too nervous to dress like a layman, especially on state occasions, yet uneasy about his old-fashioned image, is a pushover for commercial compromise.

The priest in the blue rabbi may have been signaling that, although he was one with his brothers in marking a good man's passage to eternity, he was not just another diocesan priest, but a member of Ignatius Loyola's shock troops. Perhaps he overshot the mark in ways that only the experienced Outfitter could truly appreciate.

Madeline De Frees

TO WORK AND KEEP KIND

Of the multitude of spoken and unspoken injunctions handed on from parents, teachers, and friends, there are a simple few the heart selects and pursues with an instinctive recognition. My title comes from Stanley Kunitz's plea to the ghost of his father at the end of the poem "Father and Son":

O teach me how to work and keep me kind.

It is just these necessities I've seen Stanley Kunitz exemplifying to young writers over the past twelve years.

The character of Kunitz's own work and his dedication to the work of writers whose talents he has encouraged over the years, continues to inspire and amaze me. The impression is of an energy not unlike that of the salmon he writes so movingly about in "King of the River":

> *dare to be changed*
> *as you are changing now*
> *into the shape you dread*
> *beyond the merely human.*

His energy is indeed full of changes, of transformations informed by that final knowledge of our human fatedness which commands us, as he says in the poem, to "increase and die." His faith in my own endeavors to write poetry and to teach has been a guiding force at the very heart of my writing and living.

The first time I heard Kunitz's name was when Theodore Roethke read aloud to us a Kunitz poem entitled "The Science of the Night" in the spring of 1963. After Roethke's sudden death that summer Stanley Kunitz came to the University of Washington to read his poems in a special program to commemorate Theodore Roethke. It was the fall of 1963. I had just been swept away as only the young can be by the vision of a life dedicated to the writing of poetry. All summer I'd been washing dishes at night in a restaurant. Days I worked in the newsroom of my hometown paper as a reporter and girl Friday, hoping to be able to afford to

403

return to college. On the occasion of Mr. Kunitz's reading, I was dispirited. Sick at heart. Roethke was gone.

When Kunitz was ushered into the packed lecture hall and seated in the chair directly in front of mine, it was as if an emissary from Roethke had suddenly arrived. I was so shaken by the sense of this that I remember thinking I should ask Mr. Kunitz to sign his book of poems for me — a daring act indeed since I had denied myself such a request of Roethke out of an assumption that this was probably beneath his dignity. But I was too far gone in need to honor such a scruple now. Nonetheless, my hand refused to make the short reach over the back of the chair to proffer the book. I'm laughable to myself in that moment, but caught too by the earnestness of such attachments to those who shepherd anyone's first tottering gestures in the attempt to write. Not until thirteen years had passed would my hand extend the same book of poems into those of Mr. Kunitz.

But the voice that gave his poems that day, full of unsentimental consequence and self-mended yearning, seems to have imprinted itself onto my psyche. I know now, as I didn't then, that the deep recognitions I felt had to do most probaby with our common search for our fathers. Kunitz's own father had died as a suicide in a public park the spring before he was born. My father was alive, but distanced from me by drinking and spiritual torments which divided him from everyone. While Kunitz attempted to resurrect his father in order to gain the time they'd never had, I seemed pitted against the clock of my father's life in an effort to construct a language of the heart that would, I hoped, reach him and consequently my own life, before it was too late.

By comparison, I had a bounty of time with my father; and because I seized on my task early, I think my poems finally did give solace to my father. Yet since his death, I've felt closer to the mysterious ramifications of the loss Kunitz must have lived from the start. There is the cold withdrawal at the end of "Father and Son" as the father's ghost turns toward his son "the white ignorant hollow of his face." And, in a similarly eerie moment, the ghost of Abraham Lincoln coexists with a contemporary likeness which bears his "rawboned, warty look, / a gangling fellow in jeans" and then gives way to "that other one / who's tall and lonely." Kunitz has been haunted a lifetime by the sense of one who has been banished forever from the kingdom of the living. Perhaps this is what gives his poems such a strong reserve of mystery — this feeling of presences which have the power to outlast their corporeal forms.

Recently I used the word *mystery* in speaking to a group of writing students in Urbana, Illinois, and they looked at me as if I'd just suggested they all dig wells and drink only well water from that day forward. Mystery in poems seemed an anachronism. "I need my grottoes," I said. There was a blank look on their faces. At this point I reached for Kunitz's book of essays, *A Kind of Order, A Kind of Folly*, turned to the chapter entitled "Seedcorn and Windfall," and read to them:

Poets today tend to be clearer — sometimes all too clear. A poem is charged with a secret life. Some of its information ought to circulate continuously within its perimeter as verbal energy. That, indeed is the function of form: to contain the energy of a poem, to prevent it from leaking out.

It is this sense of a secret inner life which nourishes the poems, signals its taboos and rituals as they limit or instruct access, that I value in Kunitz's poetry and person. Yet this containment never intends to obfuscate meaning arbitrarily. His mysteries arrive without exertion as a natural extension of his spirit-finding voice.

In 1973 I was attending classes at the Iowa Writers' Workshop when I purchased Kunitz's translations of Anna Akhmatova. I had so far not found a female poet in English who wholly captured my imagination. Akhmatova, through Kunitz, came powerfully alive for me. I sat at the kitchen table in the small upstairs apartment and began the poem "Stepping Outside." It was directed to Akhmatova, telling her how she had allowed me to face some of the hardships of my life through her own example of strength. In a rush of gratitude I typed the poem and sent it off to Stanley Kunitz, whom I had never met.

Having since received many such gifts myself from those who've read my poems or essays, I now understand what a rare thing it was when I took from my mailbox a reply from Kunitz. So often the best intentions to thank or to inquire further toward such volunteer correspondents have been delayed or have escaped me altogether in the rush of travel or teaching. All the more to wonder at the magnanimous reply he made, asking me to send more poems for publication in the *American Poetry Review*. It was to be my poetic debut — the first time a group of my poems would appear in a poetry magazine with a large national circulation. I felt "discovered," and the loneliness of my strivings seemed, at last, to have won an advocate.

Three years later I was able to arrange a meeting when Kunitz accepted an invitation to read his poems at Kirkland College in upstate New York. I had just joined the teaching staff there. My personal life was a shambles. I was recently divorced from my poet husband and was unsure what I should do next. Kunitz arrived sans luggage, sans poems. I remember our first task together was to search in the library for periodicals which carried his most recent poems. We talked all the while of Roethke, and I remember a feeling of childlike jubilation on my part — not that of meeting, but of reunion. This visit, crucial as it was, renewed my resolve toward my own writing and confirmed me in the steps I had just taken to leave my unhappy marriage. The fresh reserve of energy that allowed me to leave America for Ireland shortly afterward also had something to do with the encouragement Kunitz had given me. There I was to write most of the poems which formed the heart of my second book, *Under Stars*.

Since then an intimacy so akin to that of father and daughter has developed that I fear mentioning it as such. Maybe I'm afraid it is some spell which allows this inheritance. Also, I know I'm not the only beneficiary. I have good sisters in his affection — Louise Gluck, Carolyn Forche, Cleopatra Mathis, Mary Oliver, Olga Broumas — my friends and some of the leading poets of my generation. And there are others — Michael Ryan, Daniel Halpern, Robert Hass, Gregory Orr — writers who have likewise benefited from his wisdom and support.

I remember his journey to the Northwest in 1978 for a writers' conference in Port Townsend, and how he drove with me an hour away to go fishing with my father and me for salmon. He caught a beautiful fifteen-pound salmon that day, and we photographed it near my mother's rhododendrons before taking it back to Port Townsend for our supper. My mother led Stanley around her flower garden and they developed an instant rapport — she reciting the names of plants and he often recognizing something aloud before she could tell him, thereby presenting, as unobtrusively as possible, his own credentials as an accomplished gardener.

At some point they got into a lively, but friendly argument about which was the oldest known tree in the world. My mother insisted it was the Bristlecone Pine. Stanley argued that it was the *Metasequoia glyptostroboides*, commonly known as the Dawn Redwood. *"Pinus aristata,"* my mother declared, and stood firm. Over the next several years I passed clippings from various newspapers and gardening journals proving one or the other case back and forth between them. Clearly neither was going to lose this debate. My mother had proudly displayed her own Bristlecone Pine to Stanley before he left, and this caused Stanley to say to me at the end of one of our visits in the East, "I'd like to give your mother a Dawn Redwood. Sometime I will."

The time must have seemed appropriate to him after my father's death in 1982. The idea of the tree had accumulated sufficient significance. I followed instructions and went to the nursery to make the purchase for Stanley. The next day, to my mother's delight and surprise, a truck arrived with the Dawn Redwood. It was planted a little distance from its adversary, the Bristlecone Pine. This seems to have settled the contest between them, and in its place are my mother's ministrations toward the tree itself, referred to now simply as "Stanley's tree."

I tell this story to commemorate the longevity of the man himself as we celebrate his poetry, criticism, and his many personal gifts to the entire literary community in his eightieth year, and to bring us back to kindness, without which the work we do would be bereft of its deepest rewards. Stanley Kunitz's gifts to the literary community and to me personally amount to a debt that can only be answered with thanks and with love, which isn't an answer — but more like two trees, each reputed to be the oldest living tree in the world, growing silently upward, side by side.

Tess Gallagher

MY FATHER'S LOVE LETTE 'S

It's two days before Christmas and I have checked myself into the Dewitt Ranch Motel. "We don't ask questions here," says the manager, handing me the key to number 66. I let him think what he thinks.

The room is what I need, what I've been imagining for the past two days — a place with much passing and no record. I feel guilty about spending the money, but I've trusted my instincts about what it will take to get this writing done. For the past week I've been absorbed with student manuscripts and term papers. At the finish, I discover I have all but vanished. Coming to the motel is a way to trick myself out of anonymity, to urge my identity to rise like cream to the top again.

I had known from the first moments of being asked to write about my influences as a writer that I would want to get back to the child in me. For to talk of influences for a writer is essentially to trace the development of a psychic and spiritual history, to go back to where it keeps starting as you think about it, as an invention of who you are becoming. The history which has left its deepest imprint on me has been an oral and actual history and so involves my willingness at a very personal level. It involves people no one will ever know again. People like the motel room I write this in, full of passing and no record. The "no record" part is where I come in. I must try to interrupt their silence. Articulate it and so resurrect them so that homage can be paid.

To speak of influences, then, is not to say "Here, try this," only "This happened and this is what I think of it at this moment of writing."

I want to begin with rain. A closeness, a need for rain. It is the climate of my psyche and I would not fully have known this if I had not spent a year in Arizona, where it rained only three glorious times during my entire stay there. I begin with rain also because it is a way of introducing my birthplace on the Olympic peninsula in Washington State, the town of Port Angeles. The rain forest is a few miles west. The rain is more violent and insistent there. Port Angeles lies along the strait of Juan de Fuca and behind the town are the Olympic Mountains. The Japanese current brings in warm

408

air, striking the mountains, which are snow-covered into June.

It is a faithful rain. You feel it has some allegiance to the trees and the people, to the little harbor with its long arm of land which makes a band of calm for the fishing boats and for the rafts of logs soon to be herded to the mills. Inside or outside the wood-framed houses, the rain pervades the temperament of the people. It brings an ongoing thoughtfulness to their faces, a meditativeness that causes them to fall silent for long periods, to stand at their windows looking out at nothing in particular. The people don't mind getting wet. Galoshes, umbrellas — there isn't a market for them here. The people walk in the rain as within some spirit they wish not to offend with resistance. Most of them have not been to Arizona. They know the rain is a reason for not living where they live, but they live there anyway. They work hard in the logging camps, in the pulp mills and lumberyards. Everything has a wetness over it, glistening quietly as though it were still in the womb, waiting to be born.

Sudden Journey

Maybe I'm seven in the open field —
the straw-grass so high
only the top of my head makes a curve
of brown in the yellow. Rain then.
First a little. A few drops on my
wrist, the right wrist. More rain.
My shoulders, my chin. Until I'm looking up
to let my eyes take the bliss.
I open my face. Let the teeth show. I
pull my shirt down past the collar-bones.
I'm still a boy under my breast spots.
I can drink anywhere. The rain. My
skin shattering. Up suddenly, needing
to gulp, turning with my tongue, my arms out
running, running in the hard, cold plenitude
of all those who reach earth by falling.

Growing up there, I thought the moss-light that lived with us lived everywhere. It was a sleepy predawn light that muted the landscape and made the trees come close. I always went outside with my eyes wide, no need to shield them from sun bursts or the steady assault of skies I was to know later in El Paso or Tucson. The colors of green and gray are what bind me to the will to write poems.

Along with rain and a subdued quality of light, I have needed the nearness of water. I said once in an interview that if Napoleon had stolen his battle plans from the dreams of his sleeping men, then maybe I had stolen my poems from the gray presence of water.

The house I grew up in overlooks the eighteen-mile stretch of water between Canada and America at its far northwest reach. The freighters, tankers, tugs, and small fishing boats pass daily; and even at night a water star, the light on a mast, might mark a vessel's passage through the strait. My father was a longshoreman for many of these years and he knew the names of the ships and what they were carrying and where they came from: the *Kenyo Maru* (Japanese), the *Eastern Grace* (Liberian), the *Shoshie Maru* (Japanese) — pulp for paper, logs for plywood, lumber for California. He explained that *maru* was a word that meant that the ship would make its return home. I have been like these ships, always pointed on a course of return to this town and its waters.

On Saturdays my father would drive my mother and my three brothers and me into town to shop and then to wait for him while he drank in what we called the "beer joints." We would sit for hours in the car, watching the townspeople pass. I noticed what they carried, how they walked, their gestures as they looked into the store windows. In other cars were women and families waiting as we were, for men in taverns. In the life of a child, these periods of stillness in parked cars were small eternities. The only release or amusement was to see things, and to wonder about them. Since the making of images is for me perhaps 90 percent seeing and 10 percent word power, this car seeing and the stillness it enforced contributed to a patience and a curiosity that heightened my ability to see. The things to be seen from a parked car were not spectacular, but they were what we had — and they promoted a fascination with the ordinary. My mother was an expert at this:

410

"See that little girl with the pigtails. I bet she's never had her hair cut. Look there, er father's taking her in there where the men get their hair cut." And sure enough, the little girl would emerge twenty minutes later, eyes red from crying, one hand in her father's and the other clutching a small paper sack. "The pigtails are in there."

Every hour or so my mother would send me on a round of the taverns to try for a sighting of my father. I would peck on the windows and the barmaid would shake her head *no* or motion down the dim aisle of faces to where my father would be sitting on his stool, forgetting, forgetting us all for a while.

My father's drinking, and the quarrels he had with my mother because of it, terrorized my childhood. There is no other way to put it. And if coping with terror and anxiety are necessary to the psychic stamina of a poet, I had them in steady doses — just as inevitably as I had the rain. I learned that the world was not just, that any balance was temporary, that unreasonableness could descend at any minute, thrashing aside everything and everyone in its path.

Emotional and physical vulnerability was a constant. Yet the heart began to take shelter, to build understandings out of words. It seems that a poet is one who must be strong enough to live in the unprotected openness, yet not so strong that the heart enters what the Russian poet Akhmatova calls "the icy calm of unloving." Passion and forgiveness, emotional fortitude — these were the lessons of the heart I had no choice but to learn in my childhood. I wonder now what kept me from the calm of not loving. Perhaps it was the unspoken knowledge that love, my parents' love, through all was constant, though its blows could rake the quick of my being.

I was sixteen when I had my last lesson from the belt and my father's arm. I stood still in the yard, in full view of the neighbors. I looked steadily ahead, without tears or cries, as a tree must look hile the saw bites in, then deepens to the core. I felt my spirit reach its full defiance. I stood somehow in the power of my womanhood that day and knew I had passed beyond humiliation. I felt my father's arm begin to know I had outleaped the pain. It came down harder. If pain could not find me, what then would enforce control and fear?

I say I entered my womanhood because I connect womanhood with a strong, enduring aspect of my being. I am aware, looking back, that women even more than children often serve a long apprenticeship to physically and psychically inflicted threat and pain. Perhaps because of this they learn more readily what the slave, the hostage, the prisoner, also know — the ultimate freedom of the spirit. They learn how unreasonable treatment and physical pain may be turned aside by an act of will. This freedom of spirit is what has enabled poets down through the ages to record the courage and hopes of entire peoples even in times of oppression. That women have not had a larger share in the history of such poetry has always seemed a mystery to me, considering the wealth of spiritual power that suffering often brings when it does not kill or maim the spirit. I can only assume that words have been slow in coming to women because their days have, until recently, been given over so wholly to acts, to doing and caring for.

During these periods of abuse I did not stop loving. It was our hurt not to have another way to settle these things. For my father and I had no language between us in those numb years of my changing. All through my attempts in the poems, I have needed to forge a language that would give these dead and living lives a way to speak. There was often the feeling that the language might come too late, might even do damage, might not be equal to the love. All these fears. Finally no choice.

The images of these two primal figures, mother and father, condense now into a vision of my father's work-thickened hands, and my mother's back, turned in hopeless anger at the stove where she fixed eggs for my father in silence. My father gets up from the table, shows me the open palms of his hands. "Threasie," he says, "get an education. Don't get hands like these."

Out of this moment and others like it I think I began to make a formula which translates roughly: words = more than physical power = freedom from enslavement to job-life = power to direct and make meaning in your own life.

There were few examples of my parents' having used words to transcend the daily. The only example was perhaps my father's love letters. They were kept in a cedar chest at the foot of my bed. One day I came across them, under a heap of hand-embroidered pillowcases. There were other treasures there, like the deer horn used to call the hounds when my father had hunted as a young man. The letters were written on lined tablet paper with a yellow cast to it. Written with a pencil in a consistently erratic hand, signed "Les" for Leslie and punctuated with a brigade of XXXXXs. I would stare at these Xs, as though they contained some impenetrable clue as to why this man and woman had come together. The letters were mainly informational — he had worked here, was going there, had seen so-and-so, would be coming back to Missouri at such and such a time. But also there was humor, harmless jokes some workman had told him, and little teasings that only my mother could have interpreted.

My mother's side of the correspondence was missing, probably because my father had thrown her letters away or lost them during the Depression years when he crossed the country, riding the rails, working in the cotton fields, the oil fields, and the coal mines. My mother's lost letters are as important to remember as those I found from my father. They were the now invisible lifeline that answered and provoked my father's heart-scrawl across the miles and days of their long courtship. I might easily have called this essay "My Mother's Love Letters," for they would have represented the most articulate half of the correspondence, had they been saved. That they are now irrevocably lost, except to the imagination, moves them into the realm of speculation. The very act that my mother had saved my father's love letters became a sign to me as a child that love *had* existed between my parents, no matter what acts and denials had come after.

As with my parents, invisible love has been an undercurrent in my poems, in the tone of them, perhaps. They have, when I can manage it, what Marianne Moore called iodine and what I call turpentine. A rawness of impulse, a sharpness, a tension, that complicates the emotion, that withholds even as it gives. This is a proclivity of being the signature of a nature that had learned perhaps wrongheadedly that love too openly seen becomes somehow inauthentic, unrealized.

My father's love letters were then the only surviving record of my parents' courtship and, indeed, the only record that they ever loved each other, for they never showed affection for one another in front of us. On a fishing trip years after I'd left home, my father was to remark that they had written to each other for over ten years before they married in 1941.

413

My father's sleep was like the rain. It permeated the household. When he was home he seemed always to be sleeping. We saw him come home and we saw him leave. We saw him during the evening meal. The talk then was of the ILWU longshoremen's union and of the men he worked with. He worked hard. It could be said that he never missed a day's work. It was a fact I used in his defense when I thought my mother was too hard on him after a drinking bout.

Stanley Kunitz has seen the archetypal search for the father as a frequent driving force for some poets, his own father having committed suicide before his birth. It occurs to me that in my own case, the father was among the living dead, and this made my situation all the more urgent. It was as if I had set myself the task of waking him before it was too late. I seemed to need to tell him who he was and that what was happening to him mattered and was witnessed by at least one other. This is why he has been so much at the center of my best efforts in the poems.

The first poem I wrote that reached him was called "Black Money," this image taken from the way shoveling sulfur at the pulp mills had turned his money black. He had come to visit me in the Seattle apartment where I lived as a student and I remember telling him I'd written this poem for his birthday. I had typed it and sealed it into an envelope like a secret message. He seemed embarrassed, as if about to be left out of something. Then he tore the envelope open and unfolded the poem. He handed it back to me. "You read it to me," he said. I read the poem to him and as I read I could feel the need in his listening. I had finally reached him. "Now that's something," he said when I'd finished. "I'm going to show that to the boys down on the dock."

Black Money

His lungs heaving all day in a sulphur mist,
then dusk, the lunch pail torn from him
before he reaches the house, his children
a cloud of swallows about him.
At the stove in the tumbled rooms, the wife,
her back the wall he fights most, and she
with no weapon but silence
and to keep him from the bed.

414

In their sleep the mill hums and turns
at the edge of water. Blue smoke
swells the night and they drift
from the graves they have made for each other,
float out from the open-mouthed sleep
of their children, past banks and businesses,
the used car lots, liquor store, the swings in the park.

The mill burns on, now a burst of cinders,
now whistles screaming down the bay, saws jagged
in half light. Then like a whip
the sun across the bed, windows high with mountains
and the sleepers fallen to pillows
as gulls fall, tilting
against their shadows on the log booms.
Again the trucks shudder the wood framed houses
passing to the mill. My father
snorts, splashes in the bathroom,
throws open our doors to cowboy music
on the radio, hearts are cheating,
somebody is alone, there's blood in Tulsa.
Out the back yard the night-shift men rattle
the gravel in the alley going home.
My father fits goggles to his head.

From his pocket he takes anything metal,
the pearl-handled jack knife, a ring of keys,
and for us, black money shoveled
from the sulphur pyramids heaped in the distance
like yellow gold. Coffee bottle tucked in his armpit
he swaggers past the chicken coop,
a pack of cards at his breast.
In a fan of light beyond him
the Kino Maru pulls out for Seattle,
some black star climbing
the deep globe of his eye.

As the oldest child, I seemed to serve my parents' lives in an
ambassadorial capacity. But I was an ambassador without a

country, for the household was perpetually on the verge of dissolving. I cannot say how many times I watched my father go down the walk to the picket fence, leaving us forever, pausing long enough at the gate to look back at us huddled on the porch. "Who's coming with me?" he would ask. No one moved. Again and again we abandoned each other.

Maybe this was the making of my refugee mentality. And perhaps when you are an emotional refugee you learn to be industrious toward the prospect of love and shelter. You know both are fragile and that stability must lie with you or it is nowhere. You make a home of yourself. Words for me and later poems were the tools of that home-making.

Even when you think you are only a child and have nothing, there are things you have, and as Sartre has already told us, one of these things is words. When I saw I had words and that these could affect what happened to me and those I loved, I felt less powerless, as though these might win through, might at least mediate in a life ruled as much by chance as by intention.

These ambassadorial skills I was learning as a child were an odd kind of training for the writing of poems, perhaps, but they were just that. For in the writing of the poem you must represent both sides of the question. If not in act, then in understanding. You must bring them into dialogue with one another fairly, without the bias of causes or indignation or needing too much to be right. It requires a widening of perspective, away from oversimplification — the strict good or bad, wrong or rightness of a situation. The sensibility I've been attempting to write out of wants to represent the spectrum of awareness. In this way the life is accounted for in its fullness, when I am able.

I have spoken of words as a stay against unreasonableness, and they are often this — though more to one's solitude than to the actual life. My father came to his own words late, but in time. I was to discover that at seventy he could entertain my poet friends and would be spoken of afterward as someone exceptional in their experience. He told stories, was witty, liked to laugh. But in those early days, my father was not a man you could talk with. He would drive me to my piano lessons, the family's one luxury, without speaking. He smoked cigarettes, one after the other. He was thinking and driving. If he had had anything to drink during these times it was best to give him a wide berth. I was often afraid of him, of the violence in him, though like the rain, tenderness was there, unspoken and with a fiber that strangely informed even the unreasonable. If to be a poet is to balance contraries, to see how seemingly opposite qualities partake of, in fact penetrate, each other, I learned this from my combative parents.

3 A.M. Kitchen: My Father Talking

For years it was land working me, oil fields,
cotton fields, then I got some land. I
worked it. Them days you could just about
make a living. I was logging.

Then I sent to Missouri. Momma
come out. We got married.
We got some kids. Five kids.
That kept us going.

We bought some land near the water.
It was cheap then. The water
was right there. You just looked out
the window. It never left the window.

I bought a boat. Fourteen footer.
There was fish out there then.
You remember, we used to catch
six, eight fish, clean them right
out in the yard. I could of fished to China.

I quit the woods. One day just
walked out, took off my corks, said that's
it. I went to the docks.
I was driving winch. You had to watch
to see nothing fell out of the sling. If
you killed somebody you'd
never forget it. All
those years I was just working
I was on edge, every day. Just working.

You kids. I could tell you
a lot. But I won't.

It's winter. I play a lot of cards
down at the tavern. Your mother.
I have to think of excuses
to get out of the house. You re
wasting your time, she says. You're wasting
your money.

You don't have no idea, Threasie.
I run out of things
to work for. Hell, why shouldn't I
play cards? Threasie,
some days now I just don't know.

This long childhood period of living without surety contributed
in another way to my urge to write poetry. If I had to give one word
which serves my poetry more than any other, it might be
"uncertainty." Uncertainty which leads to exploration, to the
articulation of fears, to the loss of the kind of confidence that
provides answers too quickly, too superficially. It is the poet's
uncertainty which leaves her continually in an openness to the
possibilities of being and saying. The true materials of poetry are
essentially invisible — a capacity or the constant emptying of the
house of the word, turning it out homeless and humbled to search
its way toward meaning again. Maybe "poem" for me is the act of
a prolonged beginning, one without resolution except perhaps
musically, rhythmically — the word "again" engraved on the fiery
hammer.

After my youngest brother's death when I was twenty, I began
to recognize the ability of poetry to extend the lives of those not
present except as memory. My brother's death was the official
beginning of my mortality. It filled my life, all our lives, with the
sense of an unspoken bond, a pain which traveled with us in
memory. It was as though memory were a kind of flickering
shadow left behind by those who died. This caused me to connect
memory firmly to the lie of the spirit and finally to write poems
which formalized the sharing of that memory.

I have been writing about my progress toward a life in words and poems, but my first love was actually paint. As a child I took great pleasure in the smell of linseed, the oil of it on my fingers, the tubes of oil paint with their bands of approximate color near the caps, the long-handled brushes. I had heard somewhere that artists taught themselves by copying other painters. But the only paintings we had in the house were those in some Bible books a salesman had sold my mother. I began to copy these with oil colors onto some rough paper I'd found in a boxcar near the paper mill below our house. I remember especially my painting of Jacob sleeping at the foot of a heavenly stairway, with several angels descending. They each had a pair of huge wings, and I wondered at the time why they didn't just fly down, instead of using the stairs. The faces of these angels occupied a great deal of my efforts. And I think it is some help to being a poet to paint the faces of angels when you are ten.

I finished the Jacob painting and sent it to my grandfather in Missouri. He was a farmer and owned a thousand-acre farm of scrub oak, farmland, and riverbed in the Ozarks. My mother had been raised there. Often when she had a faraway look about her, I imagined she was visiting there in her thoughts.

My Mother Remembers That She Was Beautiful

The falling snow has made her thoughtful
and young in the privacy
of our table with its netted candle
and thick white plates. The serious faces
of the lights breathe on the pine boards
behind her. She is visiting
the daughter never close
or far enough away to come to.

She keeps her coat on, called into
her girlhood by such forgetting.
I am gone or yet
to happen. She sees herself
among the townspeople, the country glances
slow with fields and sky

as she passes or waits
with a brother in the hot animal smell
of the auction stand: sunlight,
straw hats, a dog's tail
brushing her bare leg.

"There are things you know.
I didn't have to beg," she said, "for anything."

The beautiful one speaks to me
from the changed, proud face and I see
how little I've let her know
of what she becomes. Years
were never the trouble, or the white hair
I braided near the sea
on a summer day. Who
she must have been
is lost to me through some fault
in my own reflection and we will have to go on
as we think we are, walking for no one's sake
from the empty restaurant into the one color
of the snow — before us, the close houses,
the brave and wondering lights of the houses.

Children sometimes adopt a second father or mother when they
are cut off from the natural parent. Porter Morris, my uncle, was
the father I could speak with. He lived with my grandparents on
the farm in Windyville, Missouri, where I spent many of my
childhood summers. He never married, but stayed with the farm
even after my grandparents died. He'd been a mule trainer during
the Second World War, the only time he had ever left home. He
loved horses and raised and gentled one for me, which he named
Angel Foot because she was black except for one white foot.

I continued to visit my grandfather and my uncle during the five
years of my first marriage. My husband was a jet pilot in the
Marine Corps. We were stationed in the South, so I would go to
cook for my uncle during the haying and I would also help stack the
hay in the barn. My uncle and I took salt to the cattle. We sowed a
field with barley and went to market in Springfield with a truckload

of pigs. There were visits with neighbors, Cleydeth and Joe Stefter or Jule Elliot, when we sat for hours telling stories and gossiping. Many images from my uncle's stories and from these visits to the farm got into the long poem "Songs of the Runaway Bride" in my first book.

My uncle lived alone at the farm after my grandfather's death, but soon he met a woman who lived with her elderly parents. He began to remodel an old house on the farm. There was talk of marriage. One day my mother called to say there had been a fire at the farm. The house had burned to the ground and my uncle could not be found. She returned to the farm, what remained of her childhood home. After the ashes had cooled, she searched with the sheriff and found my uncle's skeleton where it had burned into the mattress springs of the bed.

My mother would not accept the coroner's verdict that the fire had been caused by an electrical short-circuit, or a fire in the chimney. It was summer and no fire would have been laid. She combed the ashes looking for the shotgun my uncle always kept near his bed and the other gun, a rifle, he hunted with. They were not to be found. My mother believed her brother had been murdered and she set about proving it. She offered a reward and soon after, a young boy walking along the roadside picked my uncle's billfold out of the ditch, his name stamped in gold on the flap.

Three men were eventually brought to trial. I journeyed to Bolivar, Missouri, to meet my parents for the trial. We watched as the accused killer was released and the other two men, who had confessed to being his accomplices, were sentenced to five years in the penitentiary for manslaughter. Parole would be possible for them in two to three years. The motive had been money, although one of the men had held a grudge against my uncle for having been ordered to move out of a house he'd been renting from my uncle some three years before. They had taken forty dollars from my uncle, then shot him when he could not give them more. My parents and I came away from the trial stunned with disbelief and anger.

Two Stories

*to the author of a story taken from the death of
my uncle, Porter Morris, killed June 7, 1972*

You kept the names, the files
of who they were, mine
gone carnival, ugly Tessie.
It got wilder but nothing
personal. The plot had me
an easy lay for a buck.
My uncle came to life
as my lover. At 16
the murderer stabbed cows
and mutilated chickens. Grown,
you gave him a crowbar that happened
to be handy twice. Then you made him
do it alone. For me
it took three drunks, a gun, the house
on fire. There was a black space
between the trees where I told you.

The shape of my uncle
spread its arms on the wire springs
in the yard and the neighbors
came to look at his shadow
caught there under the nose
of his dog. They left that angel
to you. Your killer never
mentioned money. Like us he wanted
to outlive his hand in the sure blood
of another. The veins of my uncle streaked
where the house had been. They watched
until morning. Your man found a faucet
in an old man's side. His pants
were stiff with it for days. He left
the crowbar on Tessie's porch like a bone.

My weapon was never found.
The murderers drove a white
stationwagon and puked
as they went. They hoped
for 100 dollar bills stuffed
in a lard can. But a farmer
keeps his money in cattle
and land. They threw his billfold
into the ditch like an empty
bird. One ran away. Two stayed
with women. I kept the news
blind. You took it from my mouth,
shaped it for the market, still
a dream worse than I remembered.

Now there is the story of me
reading your story and the one
of you saying it
doesn't deserve such care.
I say it matters
that the dog stays by the chimney
for months, and a rain
soft as the sleep of cats
enters the land, emptied
of its cows, its wire gates pulled down
by hands that never dug
the single well, this whitened field.

    I tried to write it out, to investigate the nature of vengeance, to disarm myself of the anger I carried. I wrote two poems about this event: "Two Stories" and "The Absence." Images from my uncle's death also appeared in "Stepping Outside," the title poem of my first, limited-edition collection. I began to see poems as a way of settling scores with the self. I felt I had reached the only possible justice for my uncle in the writing out of my anger and the honoring of the lie that had been taken so brutally. The *In Cold Blood* aspect of my uncle's murder has caused violence to haunt my vision of what it is to live in America. Sometimes, with my eyes wide open, I still see the wall behind my grandfather's empty bed, and on it, the fiery angels and Jacob burning.

I felt if my uncle, the proverbial honest man, could be murdered in the middle of the night, then anything was possible. The intermittent hardships of my childhood were nothing compared to this. I saw how easily I could go into a state of fear and anger which would mar the energy of my life and consequently my poems for good. I think I began, in a steady way, to move toward accepting my own death, so that whenever it would come before me as a thought, I would release myself toward it. In the poems I've written that please me most, I seem able to see the experience with dead-living eyes, with a dead-living heart.

My own sense of time in poems approximates what I experience in my life — that important time junctures of past and present events via memory and actual presences are always inviting new meanings, revisions of old meanings, and speculation about things still in the future. These time shifts are a special province of poems because they can happen there more quickly, economically, and convincingly than in any other art form, including film. Film is still struggling to develop a language of interiority using the corporeal image, while even words like *drum* or *grief* in poems can borrow inflection from the overlap of words in context, can form whole new entities, as in a line from Louise Bogan's poem "Summer Wish": "the drum pitched deep as grief."

Since my intention here has been to emphasize experiential influences rather than literary ones, I must speak of the Vietnam War, for it was the war that finally caused me to take up my life as a poet. For the first time since I had left home for college, I was thrown back on my own resources. My husband and I had met when I was eighteen and married when I was twenty-one. I was twenty-six when he left to fly missions in Vietnam. I'd had very little life on my own. It became a time to test my strengths. I began working as a ward clerk in a hospital, on the medical floor. I did this for about five months, while the news of the war arrived daily in my mailbox. I was approaching what a friend of that time called an "eclipse." He urged me to leave the country. It was the best decision I could have made, as I look back now.

My time in Ireland and Europe during the Vietnam War put me firmly in possession of my own life. But in doing this, it made my life in that former time seem fraudulent. The returning veterans, my husband among them, had the hardship of realizing that many Americans felt the war to be wrong. This pervasive judgment was a burden to us both and one that eventually contributed to the dissolution of our marriage.

I began to experience a kind of psychic suffocation which expressed itself in poems that I copied fully composed from my dreams. For a while, this disassociation of dream material from my life caused the messages to go unheeded. But gradually my movement out of the marriage began to enact the images of dissolution in the poems. It was a parting that gave me unresolvable grief, yet at the same time allowed my life its first true joys as I began a full commitment to my writing. I think partings have often informed my poems with a backward longing, and it was especially so with this one.

I returned to Seattle in 1969 and began to study poetry with David Wagoner and Mark Strand at the University of Washington. My family did not understand what I was doing. Why should I divorce and then go back to college to learn to write poetry? It was beyond them. What was going to become of me now? Who would take care of me?

Trees have always been an important support to the solitude I connect with the writing of poetry. I suspect my affection and need of them began in those days in my childhood when I was logging with my parents. There was a coolness in the forest, a feeling of light filtering down from the arrow-shaped tops of the evergreens. The smell of pitch comes back. The chain-saw snarl and a spray of wood chips. Sawdust in the cuffs of my jeans. My brothers and I are again the woodcutter's children. We play under the trees, but even our play is a likeness to work. We construct shelters of rotten logs, thatch them with fireweed, and then invite our parents into the shelters to eat their lunches. We eat Spam sandwiches and smoked fish, with a Mountain Bar for dessert. After a time, my parents give me a little hatchet and a marking stick so I can work with them, notching the logs to be cut up into pulpwood to be made into paper. My brothers and I strip cones from the fallen trees,

425

milking the hard pellets with our bare hands into gunnysacks, which are sold to the Forestry Department for ten dollars a bag. There is a living to be made and all of us are expected to do our share.

When I think of it now, it is not far from the building of those makeshift shelters to the making of poems. You take what you find, what comes naturally to the hand and mind. Ther was the sense with these shelters that they wouldn't last, but that they were exactly what could be done at the time. There were great gaps between the logs because we couldn't notch them into each other, but this allowed us to see the greater forest between them. It was a house that remembered its forest. And for me, the best poems, no matter how much order they make, have an undercurrent of forest, of the larger unknown.

To spend one's earliest days in a forest with a minimum of supervision gave a lot of time for exploring. I also had some practice in being lost. Both exploring and being lost are, it seems now, the best kind of training for a poet. When I think of those times I was lost, they come back with a strange exhilaration, as though I had died, yet had the possibility of coming back to life. The act of writing a poem is like that. It is that sense of aloneness which is trying to locate the world again, but not too soon, not until the voice has made its cry, "Here, here, over here," and the answering voices have called back, "Where are you?"

My mother and father started logging together in 1941, the year my mother traveled from Missouri by bus to marry my father. As far as she knows, she was the only woman who worked in the woods, doing the same work the men did. She was mainly the choker-setter and haul-back. She hauled the heavy steel cable, used to yard the logs into the landing, out over the underbrush to be hooked around the fallen trees. My mother's job was a dangerous one because the trees, like any dying thing, would often thrash up unexpectedly or release underbrush which could take out an eye or lodge in one's side. She also lifted and stacked the pulpwood onto the truck and helped in the trimming of the branches. She did this work for seven years.

There is a photograph of my mother sitting atop two gigantic logs in her puffed-sleeve blouse and black work pants. It has always inspired me with a pride in my sex. I think I grew up with the idea that whatever the rest of the world said about women, the woman my mother was stood equal to any man and maybe one better. Her labor was not an effort to prove anything to anyone. It was what had to be done for the living. I did not think of her as unusual until I was about fourteen. I realized then that she was a wonderful mechanic. She could fix machines, could take them apart and reassemble them. None of the mothers of my friends had such faith in their own abilities. She was curious and she taught herself. She liked to tinker, to shift a situation or an object around. She had an eye for possibilities and a faculty for intuitive decision-making that afterward looked like knowledge. I feel I've transferred to the writing of poems many of my mother's explorative methods, even a similar audacity toward my materials.

"What happened to those letters?" I ask my mother over the telephone. I don't tell her I'm at the Dewitt Ranch Motel writing this essay. I don't tell her I'm trying to understand why I keep remembering my father's love letters as having an importance to my own writing.

"Well, a lot of them were sent to the draft board," she says. "Your dad and I were married November of forty-one. Pearl Harbor hit December seventh, so they were going to draft your father. A lot of men was just jumping up to get married to avoid the draft. We had to prove we'd been courting. The only way was to send the letters, so they could see for themselves."

"But what happened to the letters?"

"There was only about three of them left. You kids got into them, so I burnt them."

"You burnt them? Why? Why'd you do that?"

"They wasn't nothing in them."

"But you kept them," I say. "You saved them."

"I don't know why I did," she says. "They didn't amount to anything."

I hang up. I sit on one of the two beds and stare out at an identical arm of the motel which parallels the unit I'm in. I think of my father's love letters being perused by the members of the draft board. They become convinced that the courtship is authentic. They decide not to draft him into the war. As a result of his having written love letters, he does not go to his death, and my birth takes place. It is an intricate chain of events, about which I had no idea at the start of this essay.

I think of my father's love letters burning, of how they might never have come into their true importance had I not returned to them here in my own writing. I sit in the motel room, a place of much passage and no record, and feel I have made an important assault on the Great Nothing, though the letters are gone, though they did not truly exist until this writing, even for my parents, who wrote and received them.

My father's love letters are the sign of a long courtship and I pay homage to that, the idea of writing as proof of the courtship — the same blind, persistent hopefulness that carries me again and again into poems.

Tess Gallagher

HOLDING TO THE LAND

Wind-driven snow weathervaned cattle in my calving lot as large-animal veterinarian Les Pannetier walked to the polled Hereford bull clamped in my squeeze chute. In the wind, which chilled me through my coveralls, Pannetier pulled off his coat and rolled his shirt sleeves to the elbow; he dipped his hands in soapy water and ran his fingers along the bull's swollen jaw. Concentrating on the softball-sized knots beneath the hide, he lanced and washed each one clean. "Lump jaw," he said. "Well along at that." And he seemed a bit apologetic as he ran through my options: lengthy and expensive treatment, selling the bull as a canner at the local auction ring, or slaughtering him for home meat. At best, he said, treatment might stop the infection (actinomycosis) from progressing further, but the real damage had already been done. The jawbone had been honeycombed by the bacteria; the bull would be permanently disfigured, and was likely sterile, too, a result of fever accompanying the infection.

Pannetier pried open the animal's mouth and pulled the heavy tongue to one side. "Take a look here," he said. So I looked. Not real nice right before lunch. Pockets of infection were embedded in the decaying gums, and it was obvious at first glance that it wouldn't be long before my bull began to lose his teeth. As I stared into that gullet, I saw how I'd be losing more than just an expensive animal. He was to have been the key to upgrading the grass-fed range stock my father and I raise here in central Montana. He'd been a gamble and a sacrifice, and, gentled by good treatment, he'd become a 1,500-pound buddy. A registered Hilger bull, he couldn't be replaced: the Hilger family ranch, where his line had been developed, went under last year, the old folks bowing to the pressures of rural development and age.

"Handsome animal," Pannetier said. "But you can't do much with him like this. They'd just take him away from you at the auction in Butte."

"Then let's treat him," I said. "Give him the works, if it's that or the rifle."

Five weeks later, with the infection now stopped, the bull began to lose his teeth. Rather than watch him starve, I butchered him.

The dream dressed out to 400 pounds of hamburger. Bull meat: hard chewing and tough to swallow.

Most Americans have notions about farming, that tilling of soil and spring branding of calves, vague notions, nostalgic or romantic, perhaps, of hardy folks handling land and livestock in careful and considered ways; of energetic, weathered men; of people who live in the quiet dignity of fields and pastures, guided, perhaps, by personal ethics more elevated than those of, say, real estate salesmen. And we know from newspapers, magazines, and the evening news that these same people are right now facing any number of serious economic problems. Farmers are in debt: they owed just under $50 billion at the start of the 1970s, and now owe about $200 billion. Perhaps 40,000 farmers (there are roughly 650,000 full-time farmers in the country, and many more part-time ones) have debts equal to 70 percent or more of their assets. And those assets are shrinking: the value of farmland dropped 12 percent in the United States last year, and more than 20 percent on the Northern Plains. It was the steepest drop since 1933, in the middle of the Depression. The agricultural sector is slower to get into a recession, but also slower to come out of one — there has been little recovery on the farm. The worldwide recession of 1981 slashed demand for American products, and the strength of the dollar continues to make the cost of buying American too great for many countries.

Here in the semi-arid West, where farmers more often call themselves ranchers, we also face the special tests of a severe climate: the wind in most of Wyoming, the hard winters along the length of the Continental Divide, especially harsh in places like Winter Park and the Big Hole Valley. And there is the everlasting threat of drought on the eastern plains. Yet hundreds of small outfits somehow manage to stay in business, struggling along in debt or at least not making much money — in 1983, the average Montana farmer netted $13,083. These are the family places, where two or more generations have owned and worked the same land, where small may be 400 or 4,000 acres, where jobs in town often support the ranch in lean years.

In Montana, most ranchers, along with raising cattle, do a certain amount of farming, growing grain and hay to feed the livestock in the winter. But just imagine farming this: a steep,

430

windburned landscape littered with boulders the size of banks, where even during wet years the hills and fields burn brown in July, where the only source of water, other than deep wells, is an aspen-lined creek, so shallow in summer you're hard pressed to water a saddle horse. Call this Jefferson Creek. Imagine it in the heart of Montana, where my father and I ranch, and where we farm a hundred acres of dry-land hay ground — land cleared one stump at a time by my grandfather and his father with two-man crosscut saws, dynamite, and teams of Belgian horses.

This has been cattle country for a hundred years, though in certain places terraced buffalo trails still contour the muscled hills. It's country that can wear you out and make you proud, make you exult in what is and what isn't there. Until recently, the only signs of man in vast stretches of this country were the grassed-over berms of backfurrows turned by long forgotten walking plows, and lonesome lilac bushes that bloom each spring, reminders of homesteads gone bust. In the 1980s, however, the name of the game has become change — rapid change which is accelerating beyond our wildest whiskey dreams. As if rocky soil, Dust Bowl summers, and killing frost weren't enough, we now see just beyond our wire boundary fences power lines, new roads, and modular homes on grasslands that had remained unchanged in most senses in recent geological time. And what is happening here is not an isolated, quirky accident; it exemplifies, rather, trends almost everywhere in the West today wtihin a twenty- or thirty-mile radius of small cities — from the outskirts of Cheyenne and Jackson, Wyoming, to Montana's Paradise and Bitterroot valleys, to places like Idaho Falls and Coeur d'Alene.

It is happening just beyond the tree line on the far side of our creek — what Idaho farmer Burt Trueblood calls "the people problem." It goes like this: in the mid-1970s, young professionals with salaried jobs in town decided they would rather be young professionals with homes in the country. Toward this end, they borrowed heavily to build expensive houses on short acres of land in one or another recently subdivided stand of pine. Contractors roaded the country to death and built, built, built, until today those secluded stands of pine look just like town. Thousands of acres of big-game habitat and pasture have been destroyed by people who, for the most part, consider themselves conservation-minded.

Their conservation, however, seems most often focused on the extremes of pristine wilderness and ecological disasters, while ignoring the farmland in between.

Lately, local developers have come up with a new wrinkle: "Limerock Country Living." This living takes place on twenty-acre parcels of open white-rock ridge land with covenant restrictions so lax a school bus might qualify as a permanent dwelling. These parcels are for people who like a view, so first thing, after signing their thirty-year mortgage, they get a D-8 Caterpillar and cut a road up through the buffalo trails to the highest, driest point on their property. From there they can gaze down at the daily demolitions in the new open-pit mine off north . . . . and make plans to chop their twenty acres into five-acre plots in order to avoid the sinister mathematics of high-interest, long-term loans.

The native bunchgrass, which sustained the buffalo and forty generations of cattle, is fenced into squares too small to support a goat year-round. Erosion begins with each new excavation. Knapweed, leafy spurge, and Dalmation toadflax get started in every patch of disturbed soil, and their seeds are spread by wheeled vehicles which drive everywhere in that open country that wheeled vehicles *can* drive. But as each twenty-acre parcel gets fenced or subdivided into smaller pieces, less and less space is left for new folks to roam. Their ATVs, Jeeps, and saddle horses soon stand idle as the horrors of Banvel, Tordon, Roundup, and 2,4-D are brought to bear on the weeds.

A landscape once capable of supporting a wide variety of wildlife, upland birds, and domestic stock begins — as soon as it is arbitrarily partitioned, without consideration for the lay of the land — to die. Country once full of life declines into a pastel-sided desert, glittering with the accumulated junk of humanity and patrolled by bands of feral dogs. A way of life requiring dry grass and space is squeezed out in favor of one requiring only on-ramps to town. Unlike the ranchers who preceded them, these countrified city workers produce little or nothing for themselves from the land they so arrogantly occupy. Instead, they turn their new homes in the country into castles of consumption. And what they consume, they bring from town — reversing the symbiotic farm/town relationship dating back probably to the invention of the plow.

Change, of course, is nothing new in America. Progress, and rural suspicion of it, have been constant themes in our history and literature. Early in the nineteenth century, when much of the continent still remained unexplored, James Fenimore Cooper had Natty Bumppo, the venerable trapper of the *Leatherstocking Tales*, declare in disgust:

What the world of America is coming to, and where the machinations and inventions of its people are to have an end, the Lord, He only knows. I have seen, in my day, the chief who, in his time, had beheld the first Christian that placed his wicked foot in the region of York! How much has the beauty of the wilderness been deformed in two short lives!

The trapper, looking back toward better times, saw that from the very beginning of our history there had been no harmony — nor could there ever be — between untrammeled progress and the natural landscape.

Development, in the form of economic colonialism, first arrived in the West in the 1820s, as fur traders poled their way upriver from St. Louis to take what wealth they could from the natives and the land. The French boatman Jourdannais, in A. B. Guthrie's panoramic novel *The Big Sky,* was just such a man, out for a fast buck in raw materials that he intended to process and ship back to the growing towns and cities as cheaply as possible. This sort was followed by mine owners, timber cutters, and then utility consortiums — all seeing the land as a source of quick wealth, and not as the source of life itself. As the glory days of the fur trade dim in Guthrie's novel, a man named Peabody arrives from the East, itching to bring in more people, to settle the country. Unlike Jourdannais, Peabody looks not to what can be quickly taken, but to the future:

When country which might support so many actually supports so few, then, by thunder, the inhabitants have not made good use of the natural possibilities . . . That failure surely is justification for invasion, peaceful if possible, forcible if necessary, by people who can and will capitalize on opportunity.

433

That sounds fine if you're an invader, not an invadee, and lots of folks out West have taken Peabody's advice over the years, including a coal company bearing his name that is currently razing eastern Montana — a company which insists that Montana's grassland is a price worth paying for neon light and video game arcades in distant towns. If you haven't had the opportunity to watch a GEM (Giant Earth Mover) in action, scooping sixty cubic yards of coal and sod at a bite, believe in this: it is a wondrous reaping of "natural possibilities." All that power, efficiency, and technology, all that alien iron brought to bear on one grassy spot, makes you tremble. And it makes you wonder, too, how much coal would have to be dug to generate the immense amount of energy required to build a machine of that size in the first place. How many months of digging? How many years?

Since World War II, trends in farming have "progressed" along much the same lines. In the 1940s, my grandfather traded the draft horses he and his father had depended on for thirty-five years for Ford tractors that turned out a mind-boggling twelve-drawbar horsepower. Progress. He could plow all day and not have to fuss with harnesses and hot horses when he came home in the dark. In the 1960s, we moved on to twenty-horsepower tractors, and then, in the 1980s, to forty-five-hp models. Peanuts. Up north, the wheat farmers are using four-wheel-drive brutes equipped with air conditioning and TV and with engines rated from 600 horsepower on up. This is good, we've been led to think; or, more accurately, to accept *without* thinking. And if big is good, then the bigger the better.

As the idea of bigger machines gained acceptance in the 1950s and 1960s, so did the notion of bigger farms. We came to believe that one man farming 400 acres with one tractor was more efficient, and thus better, than four men farming 100 acres apiece with smaller machines. Those who could and felt so compelled expanded, buying or leasing smaller, poorer farms and "modernizing" them into ever larger units. In the process, folks who were content with what they had came to be seen in the same light as the smaller machines with which they farmed: outmoded, inefficient, expendable. Insurance companies, entertainment conglomerates, petrochemical corporations, high-tech industries, even paper cup and candy companies bought ranches in the West and invested heavily (wrote off heavily too) in their modernization, this at a time when rapidly rising land values made buying agricultural land increasingly more difficult for farmers and ranchers. Large farming became known as agribusiness, the business end often operated by executive non-farmers in distant cities. The family farmer, who lived where he worked, came to be seen as a picturesque anachronism, his antiquated way of life often seeming to stand in the way of progress.

During the 1950s and 1960s the myth that scientific advances and increased efficiency would enable America's farmers to feed the world really took hold. We were assured that advanced farming techniques would increase yields, that technological "breakthroughs" could perpetually improve harvests. In the 1970s, especially, as the threat of worldwide famine became clear, big farmers were encouraged to get bigger, to produce at maximum capacity by plowing down even their windbreaks and ditch banks (and replacing them with automated sprinkler systems, which operate not by gravity but on expensive electricity). Our government urged us down the path of maximum size, maximum specialization, maximum mechanization, and maximum production — to be achieved, however, with a mimimum of farmers. Only now are voices beginning to be raised that all this maximizing is exhausting our topsoil, and that by century's end we may be witnessing shortages, not surpluses.

The great dream of American agriculture has been to make the desert bloom. And it has been done. Yet in the semi-arid West, where rapid population growth and water-hungry industries have greatly increased the demand for clean water, aquifers have begun to show signs of depletion. In *To Quench Our Thirst,* a study of the nation's growing water shortage, David A. Francko and Robert G. Wetzel write:

Throughout the West, these varied and enormous demands for water have resulted in chronic water shortfall conditions unparalleled since the Dust Bowl days of the 1930s. In many areas of the region the situation has become so acute that choices between food production and energy development may have to be made.

Expansionism and production-oriented reliance on super-mechanization, as well as an increasing dependence on expensive oil and electricity, have hurt farmers, except perhaps the very small operators who have clung to what they know will work over the long run. Good farming practices, including the spreading of manure and the rotation of crops, have been ignored by progressive-thinking agribusinessmen who have favored — thus increasing their dependence upon — expensive chemical fertilizers and sprinkler irrigation. Yet higher production often creates surplus, which in turn leads to lower prices. As with the GEM coal shovels, one wonders when, exactly, that point of diminishing returns is reached, when farmers must increase their debts and ruin their soil to produce more of that which is progressively worth less.

There are so many snags like this in our thinking these days, so many Catch-22s. As a people, we have accepted the routine condemnation of small farms for their smallness, yet we casually condone the subdivision of these places into even smaller "ranchettes." We fear the millions of unemployed, hungry, and homeless in our cities, yet do little to prevent the ranks of displaced farmers from adding to their numbers. Indeed, we seem to take a kind of patriotic pride in the knowledge that fewer of us can produce more, just as fewer of us with advanced weapons can kill more. We store great quantities of surplus food in warehouses and hide cheese in caves, yet the Physician Task Force on Hunger in America recently reported that hunger is at epidemic proportions. The five o'clock news shows us not only the starving multitudes in Africa but farm families in Iowa who subsist on potatoes rejected by local wholesalers *because they can't afford to buy food.* How could things have gotten so out of hand in our land of plenty that farmers have to worry about buying food, when it's farmers who *raise* the food?

We drown in statistics yet have little hope of finding the truth. But last fall, back at the ranch, my father and I took two truckloads of 600-pound feeder calves to market, calves which in 1972 went for more than ninety cents a live pound. Last September we got sixty to sixty-five cents and felt plenty lucky. During those twelve years, gasoline prices increased 300 percent and the price of machinery went up 250 percent or more. And of course everything else we bought, from boots to toothpaste, went up too.

If you work ten-hour days to lose money, sooner or later you'll sour on the notion that your rewards must be internal. The frustration at just trying to break even has taken on a new edge this past year. Montana now has a suicide hotline for people in agriculture: (406) 653-2492. It's not toll free. Last November, the Montana Department of Agriculture released a study showing that 45 percent of the state's farmers and ranchers believe they will go out of business in the next five years if current conditions persist. It's no wonder farmers are found hanging from the rafters in their barns.

Most small farmers don't want subsidized solutions or temporary bailouts; they want a price for their product that at least keeps pace with inflation, interest rates, and production costs. Farmers receive less than thirty cents of every dollar consumers spend for food — the remaining seventy cents being added for transportation, processing, packaging, marketing, and advertising. Together, these activities take only a fraction of the *time* required to produce the food in the first place.

One night last winter, while looking for a lame calf, I met my downstream neighbor, on foot too, trying to find a cow he figured would calve that night. At a distance he looked like the scarecrow in *The Wizard of Oz*, his canvas jacket, jeans, and rubber boots a patchwork of home-sewn thrift. Despite the cold we stopped to chat over the top strand of our boundary fence, and when the talk turned to ranching he said, "Well, we're sure not in it for the money."

His remark has come to haunt me at odd times, like when I'm on my knees in the mud, up to both elbows inside a cow, trying to turn her calf. Although I might not tell him this to his face, it sometimes seems we're in it because of dreams: the faithful, ongoing dreams that come with being the third or fourth or fifth generation to work the same heartbreaking piece of ground. For many of us there is a continuous myth-making process, a steady reinventing and renewal of ourselves which is generated and defined by one aspect of our rural lives more than by anything else: our sense of place.

But the myths are wearing thin. The lonesome horseman, once the central image of Western myth, now lives in an Airstream out behind the swather shed, and he leaves, when his skills are no longer needed, not for the wilderness but for a job that often seems demeaning in town. "Successful" ranchers have evolved into country club trustees with winter homes in Arizona and pilot's licenses to help them keep track of the land they own.

At night, satellite television brings a stream of Western imagery so incompatible with our experience we wonder if we're ranching on the same planet. Yet the domestic power plays of *Dallas* are just plain more interesting than Grandpa's stories about the coming of the two-bottomed plow. But when Grandpa dies . . . when he's gone, so are most of his tales about how things were when the land was young — stories about men and horses, about feuds and friendships, about bloodletting and forgiveness, about brute strength and dumb courage; stories which became, somehow, part of our own lives — stories which, in pre-TV times, magically sustained us by fostering local legends, personal myths, and our ideas about how we, as Westerners, ought to act. And, without much thinking about it, we let these mythic notions lead us toward a commitment to stay on, to invest our loyalty and dreams in the places from which we grew, even as these places changed before our eyes like a conjurer's trick.

Last spring I attended the Montana Myths Project conference in Helena, our state capital. Perhaps three hundred people met at the Colonial Inn to explore the effects Western myths have had on our sense of ourselves. One of the speakers, a Crow Indian named Jeanne Peace-Windy Boy, described eloquently the savage process of dispossession that her people still face, emphasizing that today's contracts and agreements often seem to be no more binding than those signed in the 1870s. As she spoke, I remembered a story fragment I'd heard twenty-five or thirty years before. In the winter of 1909-10, my grandfather and his father witnessed on their weekly trips to town a large encampment of Indians on the outskirts of Helena. The Indians were kept under military guard for the duration of that winter, on the ground where the Colonial Inn now stands. These people were en route to reservations, having been forced from land they'd owned for centuries by the governmental processes homesteaders believed would safeguard *their* rights of private ownership. As I listened to Jeanne Peace-Windy Boy, I realized how many farmers and ranchers I know who feel certain — whether they will openly admit it or not — that they are facing the same dispossession that cost those Indians their land only a hundred years ago. "Invasion," as Peabody said, "peaceful if possible, forcible if necessary . . ."

Since we do without many of the things most Americans take for granted — weekends off, new cars, up-to-date appliances — we have come to think of ourselves, by comparison, as poor. My father worked six days a week for thirty years before he bought his first new vehicle, which, fifteen years later, he uses every day and still refers to as his "new" truck. My old pickup, which I use almost every day, is thirty-five years old. Stories about the repossession of $100,000 tractors have become commonplace on the evening news, yet there has been little mention of the thousands of farm and ranch families who have for years sacrificed a standard of living most Americans would see as ordinary, even minimal. These families — who may have no indoor plumbing, central heating, or telephone, who work by lantern light in the barn because there is no electricity except at the house — run operations where earnings get plowed back into the place, where outbuildings may be in better repair than bedrooms. While often free of debts, these families are usually considered poor, their living conditions dismissed as backward, even embarrassing for youngsters who bring friends home to visit Mom and Pop on the farm.

Most embarrassing of all, perhaps, is that we still work with our hands. Hand labor in our culture has become associated with the most pejorative terms in our language: *wetback, redneck, nigger.* Farmers are perceived as inarticulate, unsophisticated, dull, and incapable of doing much else besides farming. Our society's emphasis on upward mobility, hypercleanliness, and ease serves to draw ever greater distinctions between farmers and middle- and upper-class Americans. The belief that handwork is undignified, dirty, even disgusting is reinforced by our schools, our television, and our advertising. To *like* working outdoors in all kinds of weather, often using tools invented centuries ago, seems downright simple-minded.

439

We find we have skills that are no longer valued by the vast majority of Americans. In spite of a mushrooming rural population, our sense of isolation grows. We see ourselves as a few, surrounded by many, with more on the way. We feel less secure, more vulnerable to violence from outside.

And here on Jefferson Creek, we've come to worry not only that greedy outsiders will try to take control of our land, but that one of the adjoining ranches will sell, opening the floodgates for development right on the creek. We vacillate: one day we swear we'll tough it out, maybe circle up our balers and defend the old homestead with Grandma's pearl-handled Colt; a few days later, we speak seriously of selling to anybody with that kind of cash. Increasingly, we don't know how to act; we are surrounded by an alien culture which we see as oppressive and beyond our power to understand. And there will be no moving farther west. This is it.

When, finally, you're faced with the choice of continuing an operation which seems less viable every day or retiring young and financially secure, you realize that maybe it's a way of life you've been after all along, and not the good life. But when you admit that you're clinging to a doomed way of life, no matter what your reasons, a distance begins to grow between you and your past, between you and your land, between you and yourself. What ranching often comes down to today is a last chance of acting out what your best dreams have demanded you ought to be.

Ralph Beer

TRANSCENDENTALISM AND THE AMERICAN ROAD

It is several years since I last climbed up in a tractor-trailer to pop spurs into its high behind. The allusion to horses cinches. There is an intense relationship between men and their trucks, and latterly, women and their trucks. Faces, modes and metiers change. It is still the same old road.

Some trucks have eighteen gears. At night I still sometimes lie in bed listening to the throb and cracking as somebody feels for the slot, double-clutches, and gooses it riding on in. I'm a romantic, sometimes, but I am not a romantic about the road.

There is such a thing as creative truck driving. I want to talk about that as I run San Francisco/Boston while also talking about American transcendentalism. Thoreau was its practitioner and Emerson its prophet. They lived in an age of expanding technology, but it was not a seventy mile an hour technology. That put a limit on what they could see when they look at Nature, and Nature was one of their big subjects.

Great efforts can sometimes be seen as allegories. People make all kinds of journeys, whether they drive trucks or study mathematics. I speak of the feel of the thing while discussing Emersonian notions of Nature, The Mind Of The Past, and Experience as they fit with the thrust of high powered machinery over the road. If you have some other road, a corn field or a business office, a salesroom or a bank, who can say that they have always been the driver instead of the driven?

The start is made a little after midnight; and if the start is from San Francisco it might as well have been from Des Moines or Tallahassee or Portland, either Maine or Oregon. The road map carries the route and is similar to the palm of the hand. Lifelines on the palm are usually the deepest and best marked. So it is with the map, the major north-south and east-west routes section and square and explain the rough parallelogram that is the USA. It is a mathematical disorder that makes a lot of sense.

Clear night, maybe cloudy night, rainy night or snow. It is terrible to put tire chains on a truck, so that in the north you are always thinking about snow. Blue lights over the ready-line at the truck stop. Rig checked, lubed, whistling on a high diesel whine, surging on idle. Sharp stink of number two diesel.

The cab smells. That is one of the things that makes a truck personal. The cab smells of the hours and days and weeks of sitting in that small area of intimate cubic feet; staring into the sun, sweating, farting, smoking, drinking coffee, writing the log. The cab is office, bedroom, kitchen. A lot of house-keeping goes on in any truck.

In addition, the cab smells of itself. Leather, graphite, household oil on the appliances. The smell of rubber, the bite of ammonia used on the windshield and mirrors. After a few months of living in a truck the smell is as familiar as the morning smile of that lovin' lover you've always dreamed of and probably won't have; but imagination is real.

And I'd turn over and she'd be asleep and then she'd wake up and I would be young again.

But smell is also real and it is not imagination. After living with it so long one knows immediately when there is disturbance. Time to find a truck stop with a laundry. Time to wash the sheets and blankets.

And a truck sounds. It is the subtle, unthought of noises that, missing, would first make you uncomfortable and would finally make you pull over. Slight sighs and cushionings of the five hundred dollar custom seat, the rattle of pencils in the chartbox, the bare hum of vibration in the doghouse cover; these and perhaps two dozen tiny others live as a current beneath the roar of the engine, growl of gears, hiss of compressed air from the brakes and the rush of drumbeats from the stacks. And a truck is tactile. All good truckers are nuts about cleanliness. When it did not feel clean I can remember having a hard time driving.

And visual. The way, after midnight, that the marker lights cast suggestions of gold leaf and shadow to edge the west coast mirrors, the red cast of the directionals, and the green glow that is made into a suggestion on the dash by turning down the rheostat. In the west coasts the van rises, the center and rear markers following down the road like yellow stars drawn to the sun system of the headlights.

It is your truck and in a way it is you. The imaginary lover is real enough but you've never kissed that smile; and sometimes it

happens that given the chance you would not let it happen —
unless maybe you were drinking — because love can cause pain,
but as long as the hands are ten-two on that wheel and everything
is done right that truck will break no hearts. Climb up after the
last cup of coffee, settle into the feel of the rig, and pull it yelling
into the road.

We all have our tools and they become part of us.

Speed. In the years after I quit trucking the word took grim
overtones as the drug culture expanded and meth buzzed and
zonked and ripped through systems already high on the out front
crash of rock music. Speed. On the road it means something else.
Speed is constancy, taking advantage of every lull in the landscape
that gives temporary advantage. Finally, it is also the ability to
stay awake. The driver of a large truck thinks in terms of wind,
engine rpms, grades.

Whales play off the California shores, and since Melville they
have been a symbol of the forces of nature, a contrast to the
freeways out of San Francisco that are always busy, blinks of red
tail lights and flashers exclaiming in pips against the blue
flourescence that illuminates the Bay Bridge. In the mirrors the
city rises, people choked, intolerably beautiful, intolerably mean.
Insurance companies parade battalions of manicured secretaries
and wide-tie, narrow-eyed guys who diddle claims and joke of
mistresses. Chinese slugging it out against the high cost of living
in the city; Chinese making it, climbing over the backs of other
Chinese. In North Beach, Italians. Red wine, cappucino, Caruso
records on the juke.

Golden Gate Park, echoes and pekin ducks, Japanese tea
garden, acres of grass and flowers, the Brundage collection . . .
aquarium, animals, the once known hippie hill, and screwing in
the bushes. Echoes and God and Ginsberg.

San Francisco. Stop at the toll gate, make sure of the receipt
against taxes, and haul one ass and sixty thousand pounds of truck
and load out of there.

Man should not be a writer, Emerson says. He should be Man
writing. We should not be truckers either, but ourselves driving a
truck.

It is even better than that, Ralph Emerson. You rode trains,
ships and coaches. Did you ever walk the working bridge of that

ship, or stand high in the cab of a long-nosed eight wheeler that screamed like faith down the narrow line of silver tracks, tracks that disappear like the point of an arrow into darkness. There's a transcendental high, the point being that it could not be attained without the use of the machine. It transforms Nature. It transforms life.

Kick through the gears, feel the hump of the load, gather rpms and hoard them; rev, grab, line the tach just under the red jumping over point. At seventy miles an hour a lot of things are happening. Listen.

There is a great hand of wind pushing the mirrors. There is thunder in the stacks. Bounce, thrust, kick of the van which is laying two thousand square feet of aluminum sail against any quartering wind. Thump and hum of 10/22 tires, the song of nylon and weight; power wailing like the hammers of hell as overdrive comes singing in and you smash thirty tons down a narrowing road that is silver in vivid moonlight.

Lots of times; just one singing bunch of times when it was late and the cops were oiling the red, scratchy fire of the night shift from their eyes with coffee, I would turn off the lights and drive like a dark banshee under that moon. Shadows then of fence posts, trees, the dark squatting farmhouses; all the antithesis of wind because they stand and break the flow. Open road, open engine, wind lifting the trailer so that the rig weighed less and howled like a pagan hymn. Lots of times. I *was* the wind.

Emerson would understand this. Kidding each other, a friend and I write letters back and forth. The Emersonian view of Nature (my friend says) is something like an x-ray, and something like $E = MC^2$, but that is too mechanical . . . to which I add that I'll buy the formula if we can include the expression that $Pi = 3$. Emerson knew, and tries to tell us about Nature, about us. Nature does not give a damn. Its expression is there, and it is we who must give a damn and be willing sometimes to drive without headlights. Everything costs and not much can be bought with money.

The transcendentalists paid in different ways.

"Where is the literature which gives expression to Nature?" Thoreau knows as he asks. ". . . would be a poet who could impress the winds and streams into his service, to speak for him; who nailed words to their primitive senses . . ."

Aye. Thoreau was doing it and paying the price. I read Wild Apples and taste and dream. Something sensual there, intimated, and I indignantly wonder why men cannot admit that they are deprived of the original pain and fury of giving physical birth. Since Freud there has been much nonsense. What appears on the page must be no more narrow than a barrel, and only half as long . . . and here comes that long, high truck with a squall like passion thrusting down the tunnel of night, grooving between the fenceposts.

High. High. Nature translated by machine, oblivious for a time of the hunching butts of men and the spreading legs of women. The liquids are all in the crotch of the engine, the churning crankshaft, the spitting injectors.

Of course there is sex. It helps sell Bibles. Of course, Henry. Shit yes. Of course, Sigmund. But sex is as natural, or can be, as Nature. Should we fear either or both in combination?

Nature transformed, transcendent. I once saw fifty miles away and blazing over the flat run of land what at first I took to be artillery practice. No storm could be so, I thought, and I was raised beside huge rivers which are natural channels of storm. Approaching, like a Stephan Crane metaphor of War as machine; the storm sweeping and throwing flame that illuminated red through the black, high-arching clouds. The storm closing with dragons in its teeth, ozone and enamel on its breath, and I, a charging Don Quixote screaming horsepower and song, defiance and the virtue of then dedicated loins. The crash, the shock, and you meet the thunder, thundering in, become the thunder.

In Oregon there was once a sunset sky of piling clouds that were like tumbled and dying roses on a casket.

No doubt our own preoccupation with sex causes us to look askance at the transcendentalists, that suspects illumination through repression. Thank then, those origins that allow all of us to be laughable. We accuse them of being preoccupied? Puritan mentality. The kind of mind that cannot conceive Christ never sweating, never walking across dusty country, never stepping behind a tree to take a leak?

Strange thoughts as the road unreels. Who was that woman named Mary, not his mother, the other one?

Thinking collapses the road time. There was a twist and howling coming over the mountains, the rig slowed to a walk while the engine strolled high and vibrant. After Donner Pass sunlight hit a domain, a valley between mountains that extended flat for thirty miles and is visible its length. Streams in the valley, the high waters of higher and melting snow. Green-fading, rusty orange corn that is stumpy, and the yellow linoleum of wheat, polished and glossy in the sun. King Arthur ruled such a place. A kingdom. Kick it in the ass, rev on over the top. Reno ahead. Transcendental low.

The journey that some of us make . . . it is easy to tell who stays home; they are those who will not admit that at one time or another in their lives they were not capable of any ill, or any beauty, no matter how great.

Aggie's Truck Stop. Where the fleet seat to meet and treat; to greet the heat of hustled meat, to eat the ass of cold defeat, ere bleating nickle-less onward.

And the Hopefull roll her onto the ready line after buying fuel for Nevada. First buck's worth of nickles is free. Chow better than average, and the jackpot lights clang songs of tinkle-bell glory; the beer cold and the machines hot, except for that phallic handle you are jerking. Going to be a come down, going to be a bust.

One of the ways my truck was different was this: On the flat snout of the cab was painted, "Somewhere i have never traveled." I blessedly nigh had to break the fingers of a sign painter to get him to make the i small, and it would not be until years later that I would realize that it takes some learning, takes some sense, to deserve the knowledge that humility does not mean humiliation. The painter had been right; but then, who of us has not been a sophomore at something, sometime.

It is easy to lose the money, and it makes you want to hump some stranger even when you know what's happening. Beer churning in the gut, a hundred bucks down the tube of the dollar slot, regret and loneliness knotting in the throat. Neon and clanging. The thick, beer tasting thought that maybe it would be good to catch a ride to town, invest a couple hundred at twenty-one, make a bundle. The beer wins. You lose.

Catch a ride back to the truck stop, the neon still winking in a ticking, precise, chronometer action; spelling the seconds of the day, the night, the day, your days. The truck is sitting there. Silent.

"You be okay?" The guy driving is hot to get rid of you. Hot to get inside and blow dough.

The answer. "Sure." Knowing it's a lie, hoping somewhere down inside it's the truth. Wire the company for an advance, get some sleep. Ethan Brand must have made this trip once in his search for the unforgivable sin. Did Hawthorne know it?

Where is the solace of Nature now? The sky is beginning to burn in the east. Clouds are as pink and blue as the caucus over a first born kid, and it makes no difference. This is not nature and the machine. This is the road. There is no consolation, only sleep. Later, waking, the beer is still heavy and there are smells in the cab but the nose is no good. Tonight, or late this afternoon, will see you back out there like some dumb Kerouac on the prod.

The log book is a sustained metaphor of lies. Catch up the log, juggle the time, fake repairs. More coffee, free in the trucker's lounge that is kept exclusive from tourists, and a trembling leg when you clutch too hard. Rig out of balance because the head is out of balance, but the fading light is clear and unrestrained. In the use of language we are taught not to mix metaphors, and yet Nature mixes hers every day. This probably means that the expert in language is a dogmatist and not a theologian.

In Arkansas I once drove through every kind of weather in a twenty mile stretch.

Rainbow and fog, hail and snow and the high whistle of an arctic wind gave over to sunshine warm as toes in thick socks. It ended prophetic, I hoped, the water-glazed macadam glistening like a benediction with white and frosty hail melting in the ditches.

Kick it on through Winnemucca, Wells and Elko. Jake Holman of *The Sand Pebbles* came from Wellco, Nevada, and Richard McKenna who wrote the book was too soon dead.

Sharp winds sometimes burst at night through the mountains, and the lights of on-coming traffic drunkenly scatter along the road with staggers of incipient death. The wind knocks the van, sobers a man as he rolls the window, and in fifty or a hundred miles the lungs are as clean as they'll ever be. Normal breathing, but the cold wind rimes the fine cutting edges of the teeth. Stars and shadows, animals bounding like spirits down the white line of

447

road, to either swerve off into darkness, or die in the splat of a mechanized purgatory run by the hand of a trucker who is not then man driving a truck. A rabbit, possum or cat causes a liquid thump running under the tandem. Sometimes they get caught under the box where they are not seen for a couple of days. In summer you follow the smell and pry them out in pieces with a stick. Animals and mechanized man; must there be combat? To me the whale has always seemed like a personification of Nature — Whale, Nature — Nature, Whale . . . they sound the same . . . and who is Ishmael?

One drives like a redundancy, the long road unwinding, and the break with Nevada is at dawn; descending then to the salt flats where other drivers with racing engines are looking for answers. Thinking of eternity at four hundred miles an hour across the eternal land.

Utah. Roadrunners without hangovers. Hawks and salt, sage and lime. The busy hive of Salt Lake City wears the sign of the Bee with the same grim judgment which bestowed on Hester Prynne her A; but Salt Lake City shows not the first sign of progress toward sainthood.

It is not only necessary not to lie, it is necessary to tell the truth without apology.

Emerson thought a lot about what he termed The Mind Of The Past. He was not exactly speaking of history. Now The Mind Of The Past begins to unroll, for here the weather is dry, and where the salt does not gather too thick a nail will last for years. The nail in the board means nothing, unless one thinks of the hand that held the hammer that drove the nail that went through the board that fit onto the house . . . The Temple rises about cheap, hump-em-as-you-ketch-em motels, and cheaper hamburger joints where the grill is not hotter than the pavement — which is hot. Hot. The truck whirls beside the shrinking lake to hook left, then right, above the city where it enters onto that long, long road.

They came, the Mormons; ass back and horse back, or on foot and staggering. Fifteen miles a day, twenty miles a day, four miles a day. They panted in that sun and they dared to keep on dreaming and they built a temple to their God which is hardly more peculiar than most gods; but the real temple they built was to the tenacity of the human spirit that was afraid but willing to lay bones

448

along the sun-cracked trails of Utah. The truck sings high when it gets clear of the hills. It eats up their best day's journey in fifteen minutes.

I've seen it everywhere, the spirits crowd in, not insisting, sometimes even disinterested. They come in the dark nights and along the smoking highways of the Cumberlands where the roadside is overgrown and mist rises from the road like the fingers of ghosts. The land is peopled then, alive with dead, just choose your part of the country and look. Cherokee starving under the sainted auspices of Andrew Jackson, bodies dangling from limbs, black, red, white. The great American democracy where everyone dead is equal. At least that is true in the mist ridden intrusion of headlights.

The sacred Cod and John Henry; and those same Indians apologized to the animal's spirit after they killed it because that was reverent and right.

Nature and the past do not live on perception alone. They have meaning because of the sweat.

Utah is a hot breeze. Coming across the engine has been as regular as a metronome, the tach wired in place. Roll it on into Colorado. The painter, Fred Remington, may have made everyone's face look the same, but he sure knew how to draw a horse. Stop for fuel, try to win a thirty-thirty rifle off a two bit punchboard knowing that the owner of the joint was the guy who got the first punch. Tired. Adjust the log. Sleep, but not much, because there is still a lot of road. Aluminum and fibre glass cabs heat quickly in the sun, and three other rigs are stealing the only shade. There are forest birds calling out there, reminding, but nobody is preaching. The first mountain bluebird I ever saw was at a crossroads in Montana. It looked like heaven's little finger.

"Doubtless we have no unanswerable questions," says Emerson. Doubtless. We sometimes have to grow enough to realize what the questions are, though. The trancendentalists were big on capacity, and we seldom have a chance to continually test our transcendental capacity. You get that chance when you drive a truck. Sometimes in peculiar ways. I can remember the face of the only man I ever almost killed and how he saw it coming and said the right things; he was sorry, after all, that he had hogged the road.

449

It is more than Nature except as we are natural. The road is artificial, the truck is a construction with no characteristic of a whale, and so the combinations that go into something like sleeplessness come from individual capacity. On the northern route it is possible to run coast to coast in three days. The central route takes longer. A hundred thousand miles a year for a trucker is nothing. The record is nearly half again that much. You learn not to sleep.

Fatigue is when the spirits come. They arrive, sliding silently in behind eyes that are lighting double images in the brain while you're thinking of all the wrong things you ever did in your life. Pictures and voices rise in the mental vision, and until one adapts to the sleeplessness there is only one technique to keep from running off the road. Drive until it is at the danger point, then slap the face until welts are raised while repeating, "this is silly, this is silly." In a little while the timelessness sets in. The dreamlike quality takes over and the pictures and voices are clear and formed.

At one time I could drive for thirty hours with no more than forty minutes sleep while doing everything right. It is as illegal as the government.

The picture that bit me most was an actual photograph I had once seen. It was not a woman; neither mother, lover, wife. It was of a child. Me. A picture of me at five years of age.

Curly hair, fatuous camera grin . . . and innocence. The promise in that child. What happened? We all have a piece of John Calvin's puritan and iron-ass conscience in us. Even Emerson. Especially Thoreau. No one was, is, safe.

For instance, I imagined the other day that I was in that supermarket of which Alan Ginsberg wrote, and I was walking along with Jonathan Edwards, the puritan preacher, when we met the beards of Ginsberg and Walt Whitman. We peered at each other, questioning around containerized tides and bottle ripples; and Edwards' God sent us a storm. Whitman's sent soft rain. Mine got down on its knees and prayed for us . . . praying to who? And Ginsberg's laughed and passed around a joint, explaining that in order to protect one's idealism it is necessary to be a cynic; but not a really, really cynic, for one must sooner or later genuinely laugh at oneself — between bouts of fury.

The pictures and voices slide in and out, grandmothers and aunts, lovers and the face of my first shy love, a girl no more than a child who died at thirteen.

The rig sings an undercurrent of power across Colorado and into Kansas. Denver folds in the mirrors, a dangerous town loaded with booze and dough and bad drivers . . . something special in that line about Denver. The undercurrent transmits the past like words over a phone. It is going to take hours to get across, yet the words assure, distract, teach. It is the creative imagination that so many have and so few use unless they are willing to drive before the wind. That truck does not blush if blank verse is spoken into the whistle around the west coast mirrors.

Christopher Marlowe gets mixed up with Clarence Darrow; and farms slide past on the Kansas flat where homesteaders were once narrow minded but generous . . . and Margaret Fuller whispers, "I am lost in this world, I sometimes meet angels, but of a different star from mine." But she spoke to The Mind Of The Past and to Beethoven, so it may be that Kansas does not hear. There is always something to read in a truck. A disposable library bought and read during layovers, to be lost each housecleaning. "Books," Emerson says, "are for idle moments."

Ephraim McDowell links arms with Lister and Priestly. The three men smile. History becomes a living museum where everyone is assed in side by side. The shot from a German luger is flat across the scenery, but the dying scream is 13th century Eskimo.

The Mind Of The Past comes riding on the transmitting current of the timeless feel, and, by golly damn, there you find that you have pulled that box all the way to Kansas City. Now it is time to seriously sleep, but best to take one light breath of whiskey first and read a chapter. It takes a while to come down. The timelessness does not want to contradict itself and end.

"Son, are you all right?" . . . a fading voice.

"No sir."

"If you'd just listen . . ."

"Your ways don't work, sir. For me." And then the gospel according to Thoreau declares that the old have nothing useful to tell the young. Count the age, remember a laughing sixty year old guy who once helped you load, figure that you understand . . . hope so, anyway.

Kansas City is just one of the good places to get laid. After twelve hours sleep there is an accumulation of urine and loneliness that causes a bump in the pants. Rub the sleep from road stained eyes, straighten the perspective by shaking the head, and step out into Nature.

The scream of a diesel revving in the shops at the truck stop bangs like a drummer in an echo chamber. In the restaurant tired waitresses walk on rubber heels that phlunk like a worn out pinball. Some truckers carry a motorcycle in their van so they can tour the town they are in. Some have been in a truck stop in every town in the USA, and have seen nothing of those towns — like pilots flying to an unending succession of airports.

It will be evening soon. Possible to speak carefully, be with someone, stay sober and still catch the best part of the morning road.

The search for love. Every man and every woman who ever lived probably believed that there was an address called home, but many do not know the address and so it is necessary to constantly knock on doors, smile at faces, question, question — are you the one?

Meet her in a joint over beer, a single beer because both of you have a business to run. Twenty dollars. Thirty dollars, depends on the woman and whether she has her own room — to which you flee; she perhaps running from the memory of some man and you with memory of a woman. It is frightening to say "I love you." This is supposed to save everybody some trouble.

Pretty girl, hair curled on her shoulders, and she doesn't look tough at all. You watch her take off the shirt, the small ribs, the dark, erected nipples, tiny mama-wrinkles on the belly show she's been caught at least once. "Are you the one? It's all right what you do, if you truly are the one." And you wonder why you think of a prostitute as a girl and not a woman . . . and the answer echoes from Abram Terz's Chorus, "Any little tart can make you feel like a schoolboy — it's not fear, but reverence . . ."

The attempt is to make love but it ends up a screw. Possible sometimes to close the eyes and catch an occasional sliding

452

glimpse of dream; but this is not natural, and this is not love. This is the road.

"Without action thought can never ripen into truth." Emerson chided the scholars of his day for the kind of thinking that rises from lack of motion. He was right, of course. One often does not know how to do a thing right or think rightly about it, until it has been done transcendentally wrong. Nor is it possible to identify all the good things that exist in bad situations: a peculiar and individual variety of goodness. If only there were not the schedule and you could learn to know this woman, if only you had not paid for it in the first place. Sometimes she even says she hopes you will come back, and maybe it isn't a lie.

Experience. Crack that big bastard over the river at midnight and wail it into Missouri, then north through Illinois. A sleigh-ride now. Freeways open ahead like concrete flowers. The tandem hums and sings, the pace of the rig eager like homeward running horses. I know a philosopher who has chosen instead to be a blacksmith. Hooves in his hands, sweat, knowing of horses. I imagine wind in wild manes under a running, summer storm.

Birth, life, death. The circle is not sufficient and we sometimes forget creation. Yet, why are even the most reduced in imagination and resources often found to be collectors of buttons or matchbooks?

Experience explains itself in many ways. In Kentucky there is a two-level run called Dive Bomber hill, over a mile of drop with a rock face at the end. The road hooks left and up the next mountain. I've seen drivers hold back a thousand revs, hit that sweeping ninety degree turn at sixty, hang their wheel left, then right and goose out that last thin line of power. The trailer actually picks up and walks across the road. It saves time on the next grade.

Intuition is developed by experience. Everyone who loves a job knows more about that job than can ever, ever be explained. Coming over the back side of a hill you almost always know if there is trouble ahead a long time before you can possibly see it. Cattle in the road, a wreck, the cops. Experience creates.

The journey that some of us make, but that is the only similarity, for each has a road that requires individual decisions.

Fuel, coffee, more fuel. There will be one more stop for sleep before entering Pennsylvania. Ohio has good truck stops

453

and chickenshit cops. They will stop a rig for a burned out marker light. The cab smells of beer and sweat, the feet stink and are moist in Wellington boots.

Emerson did not even know how much he knew, and that is because his thought and experience were different. Sometimes he does not examine things that could stand examination. He never recognized the difference between power and force; does not show that it is force that comes chopping from the barrel of a machine gun; that power is what supplied the gun, the ammunition, the gunner and the direction to point. It is also power, and that a great power, that silences the gun. In classrooms, offices, field jobs, wherever I've met another Pilgrim, he or she was glad for that distinction. It helps when you have to make decisions.

The truck skims and hums and sums the road like it was a collection of ideas.

Nature. "The mass of men lead lives of quiet desperation." Thoreau writes that, and from the high cab of an over-the-road truck it is possible to add, "With frequent realizations of transcendental awareness." It is not the best solution, but it is where a lot of us start.

The Mind Of The Past. It throbs, rolls and beats. In Pennsylvania at the glaring lights of the port of entry there is no trouble in remembering that in New York, proper Dutch ladies once played kickball with the severed heads of Indians as proper Dutch gentlemen, who supplied the heads, cheered.

Experience. It has been a long, long run. Pennsylvania is the come down. The game is to avoid road checks and play the extended speed-up, slow-down stunts that Pennsylvania police seem to require. The truck sounds tired, the engine cresting out a little below where it ought to be; because the engine is you and you are it, and for this run the two are inextricably mixed. The engine is nothing but force. The way to power that obviates ignorance and gunners may be to abandon that engine, be undeceived by its howling illusion; to become, perhaps, a man writing. Others on this road have made similar decisions: after all, birds must run on a beach somewhere, and somewhere there must be an address. Time soon to climb down. Time soon to knock on doors, smiling, asking.

454

The road collapses fast. Across the nether end of New York, a run over mountains into Massachusetts, and soon the unloaded rig will hit the shops for a clean up. There will be a little time; time to walk along the harbor with its commerce, its fleets, its fish-smelling, rope-smelling perfume.

There is wind in the mirrors, the tires bawl and yell, and runs of sunlight lie across fields partly obscured by bumpy clouds. On this ocean whales also play offshore, and as one catches overdrive he mentally kneels . . . "Our Father who art in somewhere . . . the Whales will always win, dear Father, the Whales already have won — pity poor we who believe we are victorious; and when the Whales win again it may be that we will once more discover nature and ourselves."

Outside Boston, the long haul made, the rig surging and mumbling like a complaining old person rocking in the sun. Close it down, walk away on tired legs that are suddenly getting back a little of their spring, feet that want to move like young wisdom. There'll be another beer in town, another book. Will there also be the nerve to once more try to say, I love you.

Sure there will, as long as you can stay willing to run before the wind. Transcendentalism was never pure. It was always a process that led to the discovery of truth . . . and so it teaches finally that we must tell no lies, love each other as soon as we can come to love ourselves, and then be unafraid to take our chances.

Jack Cady

FLIP

Let me call her Ruth here.

She came to the ranch on one of the first pale chilly days of an autumn, hired to cook for us for a few months, and stayed on in our lives for almost three years. Her time with us is a strange season all mist and dusk and half-seen silhouettes, half-heard cries. There is nothing else like it in the sortings of my memory. Nor is there anything now to be learned about why it happened to be her who became my father's second wife and my second mother, for no trace of Ruth — reminiscence, written line, photograph, keepsake — has survived. It is as if my father tried to scour every sign of her from our lives.

But not even scouring can get at the deepest crevices of memory, and in them I glimpse Ruth again. I see best the eyes, large and softly brown with what seemed to be some hurt beginning to happen behind them — the deep trapped look of a doe the instant before she breaks for cover. The face was too oval, plain as a small white platter, but those madonna eyes graced it. Dark-haired — I think brunette. Slim but full breasted. And taller than my mother had been, nearly as tall as Dad. A voice with the grit of experience in it, and a knowing laugh twice as old as herself.

Not quite entirely pretty then, this taut, guarded Ruth, but close enough to earn second looks. And the mystery in her could not be missed, the feeling that being around her somehow was like watching the roulette wheel in the Maverick make its slow, fanlike ambush on chance.

Even how Ruth came to be there, straight in our path after Dad turned our lives toward the valley, seems to have no logic to it. Never before or since did I see anyone quite like her on a ranch. Ranch cooks generally were stout spinsters or leathery widows, worn dour and curt by a life which gave them only the chore of putting meals on the table for a dozen hungry men three times a day. So alike were cooks usually that the hired men seldom bothered to learn their names, simply called each one *Missus*.

But Ruth didn't fit Missus, she was Ruth to everybody. Those eyes were the kind which caught your glance on the streets of Great Falls or Helena, where young women went to escape to a store job and the start toward marriage and a life they hoped would be bigger than the hometown had offered — city eyes, restless eyes. Yet here Ruth was in the valley, passing the syrup pitcher along the cookhouse table, and for all anyone could tell, she seemed ready to stay until she came upon whatever she was looking for.

Her first reach had been badly out of aim — a marriage, quickly broken, to a young soldier. *He was home on a furlough one time,* a voice from his family tells it, *and met her and married her in such short time; really they weren't even acquainted.* Dad must have known about that jagged, too-quick marriage; the valley kept no such secrets. But living womanless had left us wide open for Ruth. To me, an eight-year-old, she was someone who might provide some mothering again. Not *much* mothering, because she kept a tight, careful mood, like a cat ghosting through new tall grass. But the purr of a clever voice, fresh cookies and fruit added to my lunchbox, even a rare open grin from her when I found an excuse to loiter in the kitchen — all were pettings I hadn't had. And for Dad, Ruth must have come as a sudden chance to block the past, a woman to put between him and the death on the summer mountain.

It happened faster than any of us could follow. This man who had spent six careful years courting my mother now abruptly married his young ranch cook.

Ruth, Dad. They were a pairing only the loins could have tugged together, and as with many decisions taken between the thighs, all too soon there were bitterest afterthoughts.

I remember that the drumfire of regret and retaliation began to echo between them before we moved from the ranch in early 1948, only months after the wedding. The ranch itself had plenty of ways to nick away at everyone's nerves. Any sprinkle of rain or snow puttied its mile of road into a slick gumbo, the pickup wallowing and whipping as Dad cussed his way back and forth. Yet the place also was too dry for good hay or grain, and too scabbed with rock up on the slopes where the cattle and sheep had to graze. Dad had begun to call it *this-goddamn-rockpile,* the surest sign that he was talking himself into dropping the lease. For her part, Ruth likely was ready to leave after the first night of howling coyotes, or of a cougar edging out of the Castles to scream down a gulch. Working as a cook on the big ranches out in the open expanse of the valley was one thing, but slogging away here under the tumbled foothills was entirely another. Ruth's mouth could fire words those soft eyes seemed to know nothing about, and the ranch primed her often. I can hear her across the years:

Charlie, I don't have to stay here, I didn't marry this hellforsaken ranch . . . I got other places I can go, don't you doubt it . . . Lots of places, Charlie.

And Dad, the jut notching out his jaw as it always did when he came ready for argument: *Damn it, woman, d'ye think we can walk away from a herd of cattle and a band of sheep? We got to stay until we get the livestock disposed of. You knew what you were getting into . . .* And always at the last, as he would hurl from the house out to another of the ranch's endless chores: *Will-ye-forget-it? Just-forget-it?*

But nothing was forgotten, by either of them. Instead, they stored matters up against one another. *The time that you . . . I told you then . . .* There came to be a full litany of combat, and either one would refer as far back as could be remembered.

If they had fought steadily the marriage might have snapped apart before long and neither would have been severely hurt. But they bickered in quick seasons. Weeks, maybe a month, might pass in calm. Saturday nights, we went to dances in the little town of Ringling. Dad and Ruth whirled there by the hour. Often my Uncle Angus called the square dances, and I would watch Dad in a circle of flying dancers while a burring voice so close to his cried: *Swing your opposite across the hall, now swing your corners, now your partners, and promenade all!* Sometime after midnight, I would stretch on a bench along the dancehall wall with a coat over me and go to sleep. I would wake up leaning against Ruth's shoulder as the pickup growled down the low hill to the ranch buildings. The murmurs I heard then between Dad and Ruth would go on for a day or two. But eventually, a blast of argument, then no talking, sulking. Sometimes Ruth would leave for a day or two. Sometimes Dad *told* her to leave, and she wouldn't. At last, one or the other would make a truce — never by apology, just some softened oblique sentence which meant that the argument could be dropped now. Until Ruth felt restless again; until Dad's unease twisted in him once more.

I watched this slow bleed of a marriage, not yet old enough to be afraid of exactly what might happen but with the feeling creeping in me that the arguments in our house meant more than I could see. Joking with me as she sometimes did, Ruth would grin and her face come down close to mine: *If your hair gets any redder, you're gonna set the town on fire, you know that?* Dad talked in his usual soft burr when I rode in the pickup with him: *Son, let's go fix that fence where Rankin's cows got in. There's not enough grass on this place for our own without that honyocker's cows in here, too. Hold on, I'm gonna give her snoose to get up this sidehill . . .* But when they were together, I so often heard a hard edge in what they said to each other, a careful evenness as they talked over plans to leave the ranch as soon as they could.

For what was happening, I can grasp now, was the misjudgment greater by far than their decision to be married: their mutual refusal to call it off. Each had a fear blockading that logical retreat. Dad would not admit his mistake because he wanted not to look a fool to the valley. On that he was entirely wrong; the only mystification anyone seemed to have was why he kept on with a hopeless mismatch. *I couldn't see that, going on with that marriage, with that little child you in the midst of it,* a woman of the valley once cried to me. *Ruth thought everything should come in a cloud for her. But she had hate in her, she was full of hatefulness . . . What was Charlie thinking of to let that go on?* For her part, Ruth would not face up to another split, would not let another broken marriage point to her as an impossible wife. Since neither could see how to call a halt to the mismarriage, it somehow was going to have to halt itself. But before it did, the pair of them would make two mighty exertions to stay together.

Perhaps because this arrival of Ruth in our lives is a riffle of time which everyone around me later tried to put from mind, memory hovers stubbornly here. Memory, or the curious nature, perhaps, that keeps asking exactly what the commotion was about. For on the edge of this fray between Dad and Ruth I begin to see myself, and here at the age of eight and nine and ten I was curiosity itself. If I inscribe myself freehand, as Dad did with the unfading stories he told me of his own young years, the words might be these: *I was a boy I would scarcely know on the street today. Chunky, red-haired, freckled — the plump face straight off a jar of* strawberry jam. *Always wearing a small cowboy hat, because I seared in the sun. Under that hat, and inside a name like no one else's. Ivan: EYE-vun, amid the Frankie-Ronny-Bobby-Jimmy-Larry-Howie trill of my schoolmates. Dad was amazed with himself when he at last discovered that he had spliced Russian onto the Scottish family name; he and my mother simply had known someone named Ivan and liked the sudden soft curl of the word — and besides wanted to* how up *Dad's least favorite brother, who had recently daubed* junio; *onto a son.*

The name, together with the hair and freckles, gave me attention I wasn't always sure I wanted. At Dad's side in the saloons I sometimes met men who would look down at me and sing out: 'Now the heroes were plenty and well known to fame/Who fought in the ranks of the Czar/But the bravest of all was a man by the name/Of Ivan . . . Skavinsky . . . Skavar!' I consoled myself that it was better than being dubbed Red or Pinky, which I also heard sometimes in the saloons. And once in a great while, in his thoughtful mood as if remembering a matter far away, Dad would call me 'Skavinsky.' It made a special moment, and I prized it that way.

People who remember me at this age say I was something of a small sentinel: 'You always were such a little sobersides.' 'You was always so damned bashful it was hard to get a word out of you.' All right, but how jolly was I supposed to be, with a mother dead and the next one in a sniping match with my father? I believe that much of what was taken to be my soberness was simply a feeling of being on guard, of carefully watching life flame around me. Of trying not to be surprised at whatever else might happen.

I can tell you a time, as my father storied so many of his into me: Dad and Ruth and I are walking toward the movie house, on some night of truce in the family. We are at the end of the block from the building when I notice Kirkwood coming down the street. Kirkwood is a school classmate, but a forehead taller than I am, and with that head round as a cannonball and atop square shoulders you could lay bricks on. Kirkwood can never be counted on to behave the same from one minute to the next, and now he bears down on us, yelps 'Hullo, Ivy!' and takes a swipe at my hat.

The worst prospect I can think of is coming true: the great given rule of boyhood is not to make you look silly in front of your *grownups, and Kirkwood is toe-dancing all over it. Now he has put on a hyena grin and falls in step with me. He glances toward Dad and Ruth, then skips at me and knocks the hat from my head.*

'Kirkwood-I'll-murder-you!' I rasp as lethally as I can and clap the hat down over my ears. It sends his delirium up another notch, and he skips in for another whack at the hat. Dad and Ruth no longer can pretend not to notice and begin to glance back at the sniggering and muttering behind them.

Kirkwood giggles; this time when I hear him scuffling close, I swing around with my right arm stiff in what I now understand was a right jab. Kirkwood runs his round jaw into it and bounces flat onto the sidewalk. He wobbles up, looks at me dazedly, then trots off in a steady howl. I hustle toward the movie house where Dad and Ruth are waiting and watching. Both are grinning as if they have mouths full of marshmallows.

But I was less sure of my feelings. It was as if I had been through a dream that I knew was going to happen. Not in every detail — who could foresee even Kirkwood gone that batty? — but in its conclusion: that from the instant Kirkwood rambled into sight, he was aimed onto my fist. It somehow seemed to me there ought to be an apprehension about such certainty, some questioning of why it had to be inexorably so. But it was a questioning I could not handle, and what I felt most was the curious intensity of having seen it all unfold, myself somehow amid the scene as it swept past me. Somehow a pair of me, the one doing and the one seeing it done.

It was exactly that twinned mix — apprehension and interestedness — that I felt all during Ruth's startling time in our lives.

Now the awaited move, when we at last would put the ranch and its zone of combat behind us. Put them behind us, in fact, in a way as wondrous to me as it was unexpected, for Dad and Ruth faced toward White Sulphur Springs and undertook the last livelihood anyone could have predicted of either of them: they went into the cafe business.

The Grill, across the street from the Stockman, had come up for rent. It was the third and smallest eating place in a town which had not quite enough trade for two. There was the barest smidgin of reason to think of Ruth coping with such an enterprise; with her

461

years of cooking for crews, she at least could handle a kitchen. But for Dad, the notion had all the logic of a bosun's mate stumping ashore to open up a candy shop. Yet somehow Dad and Ruth, this pair who had never been around a town business of any sort and who already were finding out that they flinted sparks off each other all too easily — somehow they talked one another into trying to run the Grill together, and somehow they turned out to have a knack for it.

The knack, of course, was nine-tenths hard work. *Those two took on that place like a house afire.* But when Dad sorted through his savvy, there was use there, too. From all the ranches behind him, he knew enough about purchasing provisions, and better yet, he knew the valley and its people. He put up new hours for the Grill. It would stay open until after the last saloon had closed.

There at the last of the night and the first hours of morning, the Grill found its customers: truckers on their runs through the pitchy dark, ranchers heading home from late business in Helena or Great Falls, some of the Rainbow crowd trying to sober up on black coffee and T-bone. Steaks and hashbrowns covered Ruth's stove, and Dad dealt platters of food until his arms ached. Saturday nights I was allowed to stay up as late as I wanted — on Dad's principle of fathering, that I might as well have a look at life sooner than later — and I looked forward to the pace of that last night of the week like a long, long parade coming past.

Just at dusk, ranch hands would begin to troop in for supper, minutes-old haircuts shining between their shirt collars and hat brims, because *Well, I gotta go in and get my ears lowered* was the standard excuse to come to town for a night of carousing. As the dark eased down and the war-whoops from the crowds in the Maverick and the Grand Central came oftener, the cafe would begin to receive the staggerers who had decided to forget the haircut after all and get right on with the drinking. They were a pie crowd, usually jabbing blearily at the fluffiest and most meringue-heaped possibilities in the countertop case. Sometime in mid-evening, Lloyd Robinson would arrive, suspiciously fingering down a coin for a cup of coffee and demanding to know if my freckles weren't from a cow's tail having swiped across me. Soon after him, as if the town's two prime bellies couldn't be long apart, it would be Nellie crashing in, chortling with delight and

spinning a joke off the first item he spotted: *That jam jar, now —
did you hear about the Swede at the breakfast table?* 'Yiminey,'
he says, 'I yoost learn to call it yam and now they tell me it's yelly.'

Then if there was a dance in the hall behind the Rainbow, the
night would crest with two tides of customers: one which filled the
cafe as soon as the dance ended, and a second made up of those
who had gone off to drink some more until the first wave cleared
out. And at last, sometime after two in the morning, would come
the phone call from Peter McCabe thirty yards across at the
Stockman: *Save us three, Charlie.* Dad would put aside a trio of
T-bone steaks, and before long, Pete and his night's pair of bar
help would be straddling in to the counter and trading the night's
news with Dad. A few hours before Sunday dawn, the Grill would
close and we would step out the door into the emptied town.

A quieter flow of eaters presented themselves too, I was to
notice — the town's oldtimers, the pensioners, the sheepherders
and cowpokes hanging on from yesteryear. As I have told, the
Stockman, where Pete McCabe was known to be the kind of a
fellow who would set up a drink even when the pension check
hadn't yet come to pay for it, drew most of these oldtimers,
sometime in the night, sometime through the week. Now, over
across the street, Dad was good for an emergency meal as well.
How many times I heard one or another of them, joking so as not to
seem begging, ask Dad for a meal *on account* — on account, that
was, of being broke. Weeks and months and even years
afterward, one or another of them might stop him on the street and
say, *Charlie, here's that Grill money I've been owing you.*

Ruth, I think, never objected to those meals Dad would jot on the
tab. They might fight over a spilled holder of toothpicks, but not
that long apologetic rank of "accountants." Out on the valley
ranches, she had seen in the crews clopping to her supper table the
men who were growing too old for the work they had done all their
lives, and soon too old for anything but those lame rounds of the
saloons along Main Street.

Age was making that same wintry push on the one person Ruth
seemed steadily to hold affection for, too. She had been raised by
her grandmother — her family so poor and at war with itself it had
shunted her off there — and regularly she went across the Big

Belts to the next valley to see the old woman. Several times, on an afternoon off from the cafe, she took me on those visits.

Creased and heavy, stiff in the knees and going blind, the grandmother was the most ancient woman I had ever seen, and her house the shadowiest and most silent. The grandmother spent her days entirely in the dim kitchen, finding her way by habit through a thickening haze of cataract webs. When we stepped in past the black kitchen stove and the drab cabinets lining the walls, the grandmother would peer toward us and then begin to talk in a resigned murmur, eyes and legs giving way above and below a body not yet quite willing to die, and Ruth, listening, would be a different person, softer, younger, seeming to feel the grandmother's aches as her own.

But whatever Ruth took from those visits seemed to stop at our own doorsill. Time and again, she and Dad faced off, and then they would go full of silence for a day or more. Or worse, one would be silent and the other would claw on and on.

If nothing else set them at each other, there always was the argument about our small herd of cattle, which Dad had kept after all when we left the ranch and which he was pasturing now in the foothills of the Big Belts. He drove out each morning to pitch hay to the cattle, then came back to work in the cafe from mid-afternoon until closing. On weekends, I went with him to the cattle, and only then would hear out of him the few tiny snatches of music he knew, his absentminded sign of contentment. A forkful of alfalfa to the cows, then *But the squaws ALONG the YuKON . . . are-good-enough-for-me:* a tuneless minute of whistling and looking out across the valley to the pinnacles of the Castles, then *When it's SPRINGtime in the ROCKies . . .*

Whether or not Ruth knew he was out there singing and whistling amid the cows, she did suspect that Dad had not given up intentions of ranching. Dad suspected, just as rightly, that neither of them could keep up the day-and-night pace of the cafe work for long, and that our income soon was going to have to come from livestock again.

In the meantime, we had become town people, and I had the time to myself to roam White Sulphur. Once, in one of the off-balance tributes I would get used to in the valley, someone beside Dad in a saloon caught me studying up at him and blurted:

464

That kid is smarter than he knows what to do with. Which was right enough, and yet I did know enough to keep my eyes moving through the town, reading whatever of it showed itself. The rememberings from that have lasted as a kind of casing which goes into place over the earlier odyssey with Dad through the saloons, a second and wider circle across undefined territory, and this time on my own.

The plainest fact I found, so plain that it seemed to me then it never could change, was that White Sulphur totally lived on livestock. All the places I liked best had the sounds and smells and feels which came one way or another from the herds and flocks out on the leathered slopes of grassland. In the creamery where Dad bought milk and butter for the cafe, the air hung so heavy with the dampness of processing that it was like walking against pillows, and everyone talked loudly out of the sides of their mouths to be heard over the rumble of churns. Nearby, the grain elevator took a noise like that and tripled it, the roaring clank of conveyors carrying off wheat and barley and oats somewhere into the high box of tower. At the railroad shipping pens, the noises came directly from the livestock. In their best of times sheep go through life in a near-panic, and their frenzied bleating as they were wrangled up the chutes into boxcars grew to a storm of sound. And the cattle, when they were pastured near the pens a day or so before shipping could be heard all across town — a constant choir of moaning, like wind haunting into ten thousand chimneys at once.

White Sulphur was as unlovely but interesting as the sounds of its livelihood. A teacher who had arrived just then to his first classroom job would remember to me: *The town didn't look too perky. It had been through the Depression and a world war, and obviously nobody had built anything or painted anything or cleaned anything for twenty years.*

Sited where the northern edge of the valley began to rumple into low hills — by an early-day entrepreneur who dreamed of getting rich from the puddles of mineral water bubbling there, and didn't — White Sulphur somehow had stretched itself awkwardly along the design of a very wide T. Main Street, the top of the T, ran east and west, with most of the town's houses banked up the low hills on either side of the business area at its eastern end. To the west

465

lay the sulphur slough, the railroad and shipping pens, and the creamery and grain elevator. The highway, in its zipper-straight run up the valley, snapped in there like the leg of the T onto Main Street. Much of the countryside traffic, then, was aimed to this west end of town, while all the saloons and grocery stores and cafes — and the post office and the druggist and the doctor and the two lawyers, since it took two to fight out a court case — did business at the east end.

This gave White Sulphur an odd, strung-out pattern of life, as if the parts of the community had been pinned along a clothesline. But it also meant there was an openness to the town, plenty of space to see on to the next thing which might interest you. Even the school helped with this sense of open curiosity, because it had been built down near the leg of the T where two of the town's main attractions for a boy also had ended up — the county jail, and the sulphur slough.

Since the nine saloons downtown fueled a steady traffic of drunks, the jail was kept busy, and most schooldays we had a fine clear view of the ritual there. It was only a few dozen yards from the diamond where we played work-up softball to where the brick jail building perched atop a small embankment. Just in from the edge of this embankment, a wire clothesline had been looped between two fat posts. Right there, the prisoners often had a morning recess at the same time as ours. They were sent out to pin their bedding on the clothesline and beat some cleanliness into it — and, I suppose, to huff some of the alcohol out of themselves. Sheepherders who had come in from the mountains for their annual binge, the regular winos from the Grand Central who were tossed in jail every few months to dry out, once in a while a skinny scuffed-up cowboy from one of the Rankin ranches — there they would be, on the embankment before us like performers on a stage.

Most of the men I could recognize from my nights downtown with Dad. But one morning a single inmate came out, a slender man I didn't know but whose face I seemed to have seen before. The softball game stopped as we all puzzled at that strange familiar face. The instant before any of us figured it out, one of my classmates rushed to get his words into the air first: *Hey, that's my dad!* His face the replica of the man's, he looked pleadingly from one to another of us. Desperation knowing only bravado to call on, one more time he cried it — *That's my dad!* — before we faced around, shame fixed in the air, toward the next batter.

At the bottom of the slope from the school grounds, as if it had seeped down from the overflow off the prisoners' bedding, lay the sulphur slough which gave White Sulphur its name. On cold days, the slough steamed and steamed, thin fog puffs wisping up from the reeds, as if this was where the entire valley breathed. Any weather, the water stewed out an odor like rotten eggs. At the slough edge nearest the school stood a tiny gazebo, a rickety scrap from the town's days when it had tried to be a resort. Either as decoration or a roof against bird droppings, the gazebo sheltered a small hot spring. A corroding cup hung on one pillar of the gazebo, and if you dared to touch it, then you could dare the taste of the sulphur spring water.

One of my classmates — of course, Kirkwood — downed the water as if it were free lemonade. His grandfather, a nasty-faced character who indeed gave every sign that he might live forever, had convinced him that the stuff was a positive elixir for a person's insides. After Kirkwood had slurped down a cupful, I would reluctantly sip away. What bothered me even worse than the taste was the rancid look of the spring. The sulphur water had layered its minerals into a kind of putty on stones and clay and even the underwater strands of grass, and the spring always was coated with this sickly whitish curd, as if something poisonous had just died there. And yet, nowhere else had anything like this steaming place, and so the slough and its baleful water drew us.

White Sulphur had other lures I thought must be the only ones of their kind in the universe — the giant carcasses of buildings to be poked into. Late in the last century, when the town had figured it might grow, a few grandiose buildings had been put up, and they had not yet fallen down entirely. Near the sulphur slough stood the remains of the Springs Hotel, a long box of gingerbread-work and verandas which had been built for resort-goers who came to take the waters. I seem to remember that whatever was left of this building was so treacherous none of us would go out on its floor more than a few feet from the wall; you could fall through the sagging floorboards to some black awfulness below. Another awfulness clung to the Springs Hotel's past. The story was that someone had been killed diving into its swimming pool, that White Sulphur dwindled away from being a resort after that. The public death of that diver was epitaphed in the hotel's blind gape of windows and the broken spine of ridgepole. A boy stepped uneasily here, and stepped away not quite knowing what it was that brought him back and back.

Across town loomed a huger wreck, cheerier and much more inviting. This one was called the Old Auditorium — a sharp comedown from its original name, the Temple of Fun. It had been built in the 1890's by an earnest group of local businessmen — a magazine writer who happened through town described the type as *exerting every nerve to prosper* — who totally misjudged the town's need for a structure of that size. Probably there never had been enough people in the entire county to fill the place, even if they all had been herded in at gunpoint for culture's sake.

Built of brick, with a shingled dome rising from the middle of the roof like a howdah on the back of a great red elephant, and a forest of chimneys teetering unevenly around the edge, the temple had never been finished by its exhausted backers, although it was complete enough to use for school recitals and graduation ceremonies by the time the 1925 earthquake shook it onto the condemned list. A dozing dinosaur of a building, it had been collapsing little by little ever since the earthquake. Now the remains stood over us, roofless, ghostlike, magical as a wizard's abandoned castle.

I think it must have been not only the size and gape of the place, but the glacial spill of red brick that attracted me. Oddly, since in the early days White Sulphur had its own brickyard and a number of substantial buildings besides the Temple of Fun had been put up, the town had come through the years into a clapboard, take-it-or-leave-it appearance which made brick-built respectability seem very rare. And here was the largest stack of the reddest brick I could imagine. I could prowl in — windows and doors had vanished long since — and amid the clattering emptiness walk the old stage, study out from the dilapidated walls where rooms had been. Echoes flew back to me as if the auditorium had stored all the sounds from its prime years. It stood as a kind of cavern of history for a few of us, a place where you could go off into an expanse of both space and time.

One other large brick building graced White Sulphur, and if the old auditorium was a cave to be sought out, this next was a man-made mass you could not avoid. You came to it — the Sherman Hotel — as you walked up Main Street; three massive stories of brick and cornicework snouting out into the thoroughfare as firmly as a thumb crimping into a hose.

At the very start of White Sulphur's history there had been a dispute about where Main Street ought to run. The doctor who held the land at the west end of town banked too heavily on the notion that some judicious slough drainage and timber roadbedding would draw the route along his holdings. A rival laid out a plat to the east of him, complete with a 25-foot jog away from the direction of the slough and directly out into the path mapped out for Main Street. In some wink of confusion or bribery, the rival survey was accepted by the authorities, the town grew up along the misjointed plat lines, and for the next sixty years, the big brick hotel built at the boundary of the muddle squatted halfway into Main Street.

In the hotel lobby, a wide high window had been installed near the outer edge of this prowlike jut to take advantage of the outlook. Sitting there in a leather chair you could watch the cars come, straight as fence wire, until suddenly they had to angle off. Old men hobbled into the hotel to lobby-sit the afternoon hours away and watch the cars do their surprised swerve around them. It made a pastime, and the town didn't have many.

For some reason I can't summon back, once in those years Dad and I checked into the Sherman Hotel for a night. The room was worse than we had expected, and worse even than the hotel's run-down reputation. A bare lightbulb dangled over a battered bed; I think there was not even a dresser, nightstand, or chair. The bedsprings howled with rust. Sometime in the skreeking night, Dad said: *Call this rattletrap a hotel, do they? I've slept better in wet sagebrush.*

And yet, dismal as it was, the cumbersome hotel did some duty for the town. The teacher arriving to his job stepped from the bus there and went in to ask the clerk if there were lockers for his baggage for a day or two. *Just throw it there in the corner,* he was

told. *But I'd like to lock it away, everything I own is in there . . .*
The clerk looked at him squarely for the first time: *Just throw it in the corner there, I said.* When the teacher came back in a day or so, all was in the corner, untouched.

One last landmark from those years, the gray stone house called the Castle. It speared up from the top of the hill behind the Stockman, a granite presence which seemed to have loomed there before the rest of the town was ever dreamed of. Actually, a man named Sherman had built it in the early 1890's, with bonanza money from a silver lode in the Castle Mountains. He had the granite blocks cut and sledded in by ox team from the mountains, and from a little distance, the three-story mansion with its round tower and sharp roof peaks looked like one of the sets of fantasy pinnacles which poke up all through that range. So in name and material and appearance, all three, old Sherman built for himself an eerie likeness of the Castles which had yielded up his fortune.

If the outside was a remindful whim, the inside of the Castle showed Sherman's new money doing some prancing. It was said he had spared nothing in expense — woodwork crafted of hardwoods from distant countries, crystal dangles on every chandelier, a huge water tank in the attic which sluiced water down to fill the bathtubs in an instant, a furnace which burned hard hot anthracite coal shipped all the way from Pennsylvania. All this was known only by rumor as I would circle past, because Sherman had been in his grave for twenty years and the Castle now stood with boards across its windows and swallows' mud nests clotted onto the fancy stonework.

Those were the relic faces of White Sulphur, the fading profiles of what the town had set out to be. Other features presented themselves to me, too, off the faces of the thousand people who lived in White Sulphur then, and a second thousand dotted out on the ranches from one far end of the county to another. Of all those twenty hundred living faces, the one clearest ever since has been our madman's.

What had torn apart Henrik's brain — defect of birth, some stab of illness or accident — I have never known. But he hung everlastingly there at the edge of town life, gaping and leering. His parents, old and made older by the calamity which had ripped their son's mind, would bring Hendrik to town with them when they came for groceries. Slouched in their pickup or against the corner of the grocery, Hendrik grimaced out at us like a tethered dog whose mood a person could never be entirely sure of.

He was able to recognize friends of the family, such as Dad, and make child's talk to them — innocent words growled out of a strongman's body. And somewhere in the odds and ends of his mind he had come up with the certain way to draw people to him. He would gargle out loudly what could have been either plea or threat: *YOU god uh CIGuhREDD?*

No one would deny this pitiful spectre a cigarette, and Hendrik would puff away with a twisted squint of satisfaction, his eyes already glowering along the street for his next donor. Dad, who was uneasy around any affliction but was fond of Hendrik's family, always lit the cigarette carefully and said a few words, while I peeked up at the rough man. If he happened to look down at me, it was like being watched by the hot eye of a hawk. All through this time, I can pick out again and again that scene of poor clever lunatic Hendrik, and a town uneasy under his glare.

In that time I puzzled up into three other faces which were strange to me — the black faces of Rose Gordon, Taylor Gordon, and Bob Gordon. The Gordons, I know now, were one of the earliest and most diligent families of White Sulphur. The parents of Rose and Taylor and Bob had come in during the town's short heyday of mining wealth, and Mother Gordon had become the town's laundress: *Momma's back-yard looked like a four-mast schooner comin' in.* But to me, the three Gordons could have been newly set down from the farthest end of the world, where people were the color of night. They were very black — Rose in particular had a sheen dark as ink. Their faces were unlined, not crinkled at the corners of the eyes as Dad's and the other ranch men's were. And their voices chimed amid the burrs and twangs of everyone else downtown.

Taylor Gordon was a singer. Every so often he would perform at the high school auditorium, singing the spirituals he had heard from his mother as she worked at her wash tubs. His tenor voice could ripple like muscle, hold like a hawser across the notes: *Swing low, sweet chaaaariot . . .* The strong, sweet sound had carried him to New York, where he sang in concert halls and on the radio and had been declared by a national magazine as "the latest

471

rival to Paul Robeson.'' He also had gone through money as if he were tossing confetti into the streets of Harlem, and when the Depression hit, he promptly ended up back in the valley herding sheep.

But he brought with him New York stories such as no one in the valley had ever heard or dreamed of. Of his writer friend Carl Van Vechten: *He was a big Dutchman, he had very buck teeth, rabbit teeth like, and weighed about two hundred pounds, let's say, and was six feet tall. But he wasn't what they called a potbellied six . . . . . He liked sometimes to wear a phantom red shirt, reddest red I ever saw. He wore rings, y'know, exotic rings, something that would stand out, or a bracelet, somethin' like that. Bein' a millionaire he could do those things. I remember one night we went to a party. Carl and I was dressed as in Harlem, dressed in kind of satire. Some man gave both of us sam hill. He said, 'You got somethin' to offer the world. You don't have to do anything out of the ordinary, just be yourselves.' Carl laughed and said, 'Well, can't we have a little FUN?'* Of a black man who Taylor said had a magic with words and deeds: *When everybody was broke, a lot of people would go to Father Divine and get the best meal in the world for thirty-five cents, see. And you'd be surprised — white, black, blue, green and the other, they'd eat in Father Divine's because you could get a meal you couldn't pay two dollars for downtown for thirty-five cents, including ice cream dessert. And he had 'em lined up, you'd thought a baseball game was goin' on.* Of how people in Harlem could tell where a man was from just by the scar on his face: *By the brand that was on him, y'see. They could tell where he'd been in a fight. If you were shootin' craps, you more or less would be bendin' down when you got cut and that way you'd get it across the forehead here. Whereas if you were playin' poker, you were more apt to be settin' up, then you'd be apt to get this one here across the cheek. Then if you were playin' what they called 'skin,' why you'd apt to get this other. So y'see, if a fella was cut here, he was from Greechyland, if he was cut this other way he was from Selma, Alabama, and so on and so on.*

Now, either Taylor or Bob owned the building the post office was in, and the pair of them lived on the second floor. Taylor came and went in a bold erect style, always with some new plan for singing in New York again or making a fortune from some gadget he had invented. He also took pride in being the one writing man the valley had ever had. Taylor was a talented storyteller — it was as if his voice put a rich gloss on anything it touched — and while he had been in New York singing at society parties, white writers such as Van Vechten urged him to make a manuscript of his stories of early-day White Sulphur. They steered him to a publisher and illustrator, and shepherded his guesswork grammar into print as a memoir with the title *Born to Be*.

The book with his name on it naturally impressed Taylor into thinking he could do another. This time there was no help, and no publisher. The failure worked on his mind for years; eventually he saw conspirators. The man who published his first book had become John Steinbeck's publisher as well, and for the rest of his life, Taylor told anyone who would listen that Steinbeck and the publisher had pirated his second book idea and made it into *The Grapes of Wrath*.

While Taylor built that phantom swindle in his mind, Bob Gordon crashed back and forth between street and room, a desperate drinker even by White Sulphur standards. I would see him sometimes when I went to the post office for the mail, off somewhere in his plodding stagger. I remember that he wore suspenders, one of the few men in town who did, and the straps made a slumping X across his big back as they slid down his shoulders. Brothers indeed, Taylor and Bob, in desperation as well as in skin, the one daydreaming of New York and second fame, the other fumbling for his next bottle of whiskey.

Rose Gordon lived apart from her brothers, both in place and behavior. She was the one in the family who had chosen to be courtly toward the white faces all around, and a time or two a week she came along Main Street, a plump dark fluff of a woman, with her constant greeting, *How do you do? And how are you today?* Rose had extreme faith in words and manners. The death of any old-timer would bring out her pen, and a long letter to the *Meagher County News* extolling the departed. She was especially fond of two groups in the valley's history, the Scots who had homesteaded in the Basin and elsewhere around the valley, and the Indians who had worn away before the tide of settlement.

Her passion for the Indians, fellow sufferers for the dusk of their skin, was understandable enough. *They were the first ladies of this land,* she would declare of the Indian women she had seen when she was a girl, and the saying of it announced that Rose Gordon knew ladyship from personal experience. But the transplanted Scots, my father's family and the others who had never seen black faces before and in all likelihood didn't care for them when they did? It was their talk. The lowlands burr, the throaty words which came out their mouths like low song, captivated Rose.

She was as entranced with the spoken word as Taylor was with the written, and the oration she had given when she was valedictorian of her high school class of five students in 1904 — that oration given from a rostrum in the old auditorium, a large American flag fastened square and true along the back stage wall — had been the summit of her life. When I had become a grown man, she astonished me once by reciting word-for-word the climax of that oration sixty years before: *I gave my address on the progress of the Negro race. I ended, I said: 'The colored soldiers have earned the highest courage, and they won unstinted praises by their bravery, loyalty and fidelity. They have indeed been baptized into full citizenship by their bloodshed in defense of their country, and they have earned the protection of that honorable emblem, the Stars and Stripes!*

While Rose held those words in her memory as if they were her only heirloom, other street voices plaided White Sulphur life for me as well. The twang which gritted out of Lloyd Robinson and the other Missourians: *You could of talked all day long and not said that . . . Seen anything of that long-geared geezer who was gonna break that gelding for me? . . . That Swede don't know enough to pound sand in a rat hole . . .* In June, mosquitoes would come in a haze off the Smith River, and the mosquito stories would start: *Bastards're so big this year they can stand flatfooted and drink of a rainbarrel . . . saw one of 'em carry off a baby chick the other day . . . yah, I saw two of 'em pick up a lamb, one at each end . . .* Any time of year, the muttering against Rankin and his vast holdings in the valley: *That goddamn Rankin's so crooked he couldn't sleep in a roundhouse . . . so tight he squeaks . . . so mean the coyotes wouldn't eat him . . .* One rancher or another proud of a new woven-wire fence: *Horse-high, bull-strong, and hog-tight . . . .* Another, defending himself against the notion that his saddle horse was the color and quality of mud: *No, by God, she's more of a kind of tansy-gray, the color of a cat's paw . . .* Nellie in the Grill, shaking over early morning coffee: *I got lit up like a church last night . . . Went home and threw my hat in the door first. It didn't come back out, so I figured I was safe . . .*

And always, always, the two voices which went at each other just above my head. *Ruth, where the hell you been? If you think you can just walk off and leave me with the cafe that way, you got another think coming . . . Mister, I didn't marry you to spend all my time in any damn cafe. Where I go is my business . . .* The look in my direction, then: *Better leave us alone, Ivan . . .* But the voices would go on, through the walls, until one more silence set in between my father and my second mother.

The silences stretched tauter until a day sometime in the autumn of 1948, when the Grill and our town life came to an end. Dad and Ruth could agree on one thing: the tremendous hours of cafe work were grinding them down. They gave up the lease, and now bought a thousand head of sheep and arranged to winter them at a ranch on Battle Creek in the Sixteen country, not far from the Basin where Dad had grown up.

There seemed to be no middle ground in the marriage. Not having managed to make it work while under the stare of the entire town, now the two of them decided to try a winter truce out in what was the emptiest corner of the county, just as it had been when Peter and Annie Doig came there to homestead a half-century before and as it is whenever I return now to drive its narrow red-shale road. Gulch-and-sage land, spare, silent. Out there in the rimming hills beyond the valley, twenty-five miles from town, Dad and Ruth would have time alone to see whether their marriage ought to last. *Could* last.

And I began what would be a theme of my life, staying in town in the living arrangement we called *boarding out*. It meant that someone or other, friend or relative or simply whoever looked reliable, would be paid by Dad to provide me room-and-board during the weekdays of school. It reminds me now of a long visit, the in-between feeling of having the freedom to wander in and out but never quite garnering any space of your own. But I had some knack then for living at the edges of other people's existences, and in this first span of boarding out — with friends of Ruth, the

Jordan family — I found a household which teemed in its comings-and-goings almost as the cafe had.

Indeed, *We call it the short-order house around here,* Helen Jordan said as deer season opened and a surge of her out-of-town relatives, armed like a guerrilla platoon, swept through. Ralph Jordan himself came and went at uneven hours of the day and night, black with coal dust and so weary he could hardly talk: he was fireman on the belching old locomotive called Sagebrush Annie which snailed down the branch-line from White Sulphur to the main railroad at Ringling. Ralph with a shovelful of coal perpetually in hand, Helen forever up to her wrists in bread dough or dishwater — the Jordans were an instructive couple about the labor that life could demand.

And under their busy roof, I was living for the first time with other children, their two sons and a daughter. The older boy, Curtis, thin and giggly, was my age, and we slept in the same bed and snickered in the dark at each other's jokes. Boarding out at the Jordans went smoothly enough, then, except at the end of each week when Dad was to arrive and take me to the Battle Creek ranch with him. Friday night after Friday night, he did not arrive.

Whatever Dad or Ruth or I had expected of this testing winter, the unlooked-for happened: the worst weather of thirty years blasted into the Sixteen country, and Dad and Ruth found themselves in contest not so much with each other now, but with the screaming white wilderness outside.

As bad winters are apt to do, this one of 1948-49 whipped in early and hard. Snow fell, drifted, crusted into gray crystal windrows, then fell and drifted and crusted gray again. Dad and his hired man pushed the sheep in from the pastures to a big shed at the ranch buildings. Nothing could root grass out of that solid snow. The county road began to block for weeks at a time. Winter was sealing the Sixteen country into long frozen months of aloneness, and I was cordoned from the life of Dad and Ruth there.

At last, on the sixth Friday night, long after I had given up hope again, Dad appeared. Even then he couldn't take me to the ranch with him; he had spent ten hours fighting his way through the snow, and there was the risk that the countryside would close off entirely again before he could bring me back to town Sunday night. *Tell ye what we'll do, Skavinsky. Talk to that teacher of yours and*

476

see if you can work ahead in your schoolwork. If she'll let you, I'll come in somehow next Friday and you can come spend a couple of weeks out at the ranch.

All week, whenever the recess bell rang I stayed at my desk and flipped ahead in one text or another, piling up lesson sheets to hand to the bemused teacher. Before school was out on Friday, Dad came to the door of the classroom for me, cocking his grin about clacking in with snowy overshoes and a girth of sheepskin coat.

The highway down the valley was bare, a black dike above the snow, as he drove the pickup to the turnoff toward Battle Creek. Then the white drifts stretched in front of us like a wide storm-frothed lake whose waves had suddenly stopped motion to hang in billows and peaks where the wind had lashed them against the sky.

The very tops of fenceposts, old gray cedar heads with rounded snow caps, showed where the road was buried. Between the post tops, a set of ruts had been rammed and hacked by Dad and the few other ranchers who lived in Sixteen country.

Dad drove into the sea of snow with big turns of the steering wheel, keeping the front wheels grooved in the ruts while the rear end of the pickup jittered back and forth spinning snow out behind us. Sometimes the pickup growled to a halt. We would climb out and shovel away heavy chunks like pieces of an igloo. Then Dad would back the pickup a few feet for a running start and bash into the ruts again. Once we went over a snowdrift on twin rows of planks another of the ranchers had laid for support, a bridge in midsea. Once we drove entirely over the top of a drift without planks at all.

Where the road led up to the low ridge near the old Jap Stewart ranch, we angled between cliffs of snow higher than the pickup. Near Battle Creek, with our headlights fingering past the dark into the white blankness, Dad swerved off the road entirely and sent the pickup butting through the smaller drifts in a hayfield. It had started to snow heavily, the wind out of the Basin snaking the flurries down to sift into the ruts. I watched the last miles roll up on the tiny numbers under the speedometer as Dad wrestled the wheel and began his soft Scots cussing: *Snow on a man, will ye? Damn-it-to-hell-anyway, git back in those ruts. Damn-such-*

weather. Hold on, son, there's a ditch here somewhere . . . The twenty-fifth mile, the last, we bucked down a long slope to the ranch with the heavy wet flakes flying at us like clouds of moths. Dad roared past the lighted windows of the ranch house and spun the pickup inside the shelter of the lambing shed. *Done!* he said out into the storm. *Done, damn ye!*

To my surprise, Battle Creek was not living up to its name, and Dad and Ruth were getting along less edgily there than they ever had. It may have been that there simply was so much cold-weather work to be done, feeding the sheep, carrying in firewood, melting snow for water because the pump had frozen, that they had little stamina left over for argument. Or perhaps they had decided that the winter had to be gotten through, there simply was no route away from one another until spring. Whatever accounted for it, I slipped into its bask and warmed for the days to come.

Each morning, Ruth stood at the window sipping from a white mug of coffee, watching as Dad and the hired man harnessed the team to the hay sled. Then, if Dad had said they needed her that day, she would pull on heavy clothing and go out and take the reins while the men forked hay off to the sheep. Dad helped her in the house, the two of them working better together at the meals and dishes than they had when they were feeding half the town in the Grill. The pair of them even joked about the icy journey to the outhouse which started each day. Whoever went first, the other would demand to know whether the seat had been left good and warm. *It damn well ought to be,* the other would say, *half of my behind is still out on it.* Or: *Sure did, I left it smoking for you.*

The ranch house had been built with its living quarters on the second floor, well above the long snowdrifts which duned against the walls. A railed porch hung out over the snow the full length of the house, and from it the other ranch buildings were in view like a small anchored fleet seen from a ship's deck. The lambing shed, low and cloud-gray and enormously long, seemed to ride full-laden in the white wash of winter. Most of the time, the sheep were corralled on the far side of the shed, their bored bleats coming as far as the house if the wind was down. Not far from the lambing shed stood the barn, dark and bunched into itself, prowing up out of the stillness higher than anything else in sight. A few small sheds lay with their roofs disappearing in drifts, swamped by this cold ocean of a winter. Battle Creek flowed just beyond those sheds, but the only mark of it was a gray skin of ice.

In this snow world, Dad and his hired man skimmed back and forth on the hay sled, a low wide hayrack on a set of runners pulled by a team of plunging workhorses. I rode with the men, hanging tight to the frame of the hayrack prowing above where the horses' hooves chuffed into the snow. When the men talked, their puffs of breath clouded fatly out in front of their faces. Our noses trickled steadily. Dad put a mitten against my face often to see that my cheeks weren't being frostbitten.

The winter fought us again and again. Our dog crashed through the ice of Battle Creek, and the wind carried the sound of his barking away from the house. We found the shatter where he had tried to claw himself out before the creek froze him and then drowned him. A blizzard yammered against the back wall of the house for two days without stop. Outside the snow flew so thick it seemed there was no space left between the flakes in the air, just an endless crisscross of flecks the whiteness of goose down. When Dad and the hired man went to feed the sheep, they would disappear into the storm, swallowed, thirty feet from the window where Ruth and I watched.

An afternoon when the weather let up briefly, I climbed the slope behind the house, to where a long gully troughed toward Battle Creek. Snow had packed the gulch so full that I could sled down over its humps and dips for hundreds of feet at a time. Trying out routes, I flew off a four-foot shale bank and in the crash sliced my right knee on the end of a sled runner as if I had fallen against an axe blade.

That moment of recall is dipped in a hot red ooze. The bloody slash scared out my breath in a long *uhhhhh*. A clench ran through the inside of me, then the instant heat of tears burned below my eyes. The climb from the gulch was steep. Now the burning fell to my leg. Blood sopped out as I hobbled to the house with both hands clamped over my wound, and Ruth shook as she snipped away the heavy-stained pants leg. The cut, she quickly told me, did not live up to its first horrific gush; it was long but shallow and clean, and dressings easily took care of it. In a few days, I could swing my leg onto the hay sled and again ride with the men above the horses' white-frosted heels.

The two weeks passed in surges of that winter weather, like tides flowing in long and hard. On the last morning, no snow was falling, but Dad said so much had piled by then that we could get to town only by team and sled. Ruth said she wanted to go with us. Dad looked at her once and nodded.

Dad and the hired man lifted the rack off the hay boat and fixed a seat of planks onto the front pair of sled runners. Inside that seat, blankets piled thickly onto the heavy coats we wore, we sat buried in warmth, almost down in the snow as the horses tugged us along on the running bob. Harness buckles sang a *ching-tink, ching-tink* with every step of the horses. Dad slapped the reins against the team's rumps and headed us toward the hayfields along Battle Creek. The road would be no help to us, drift humped onto drift there by now. We would aim through meadows and bottomlands where the snow lay flatter.

The grayness stretching all around us baffled my eyes. Where I knew hills had to be, no hills showed. The sagebrush too had vanished, from a countryside forested with its clumps. One gray sheet over and under and around, the snow and overcast had fused land and sky together. Even our sleigh was gray and half-hidden, weathered ash moving like a pale shadow through ashen weather.

Dad headed the team by the tops of fenceposts, and where the snow had buried even them, by trying to pick out the thin besieged hedge of willows along the creek. I peeked out beside Ruth, the two fogs of our breath blowing back between us as the horses found footing to trot. More often, they lunged at the snow, breaking through halfway up their thick legs. Dad talked to the horses every little while: *Hup there, Luck, get your heft into it . . . Pull a bit, damn ye, Bess . . . Up this rise, now, get yourself crackin' there . . .* Their ears would jab straight up when they felt the flat soft slap of the reins and heard Dad's voice, and they would pull faster and we would go through the snow as if the sled was a running creature carrying us on its back.

The twin cuts of our sled tracks, the only clear lines the snow had not yet had time to seize and hide, traced away farther and farther behind us. Except for the strides of the horses and Dad's words to them, the country was silent, held so under the weight of the snow. In my memory that day has become a set of instants somewhere between life and death, a kind of eclipse in which hours did not pass and sound did not echo, all color washed to a flannel sameness and distance swelling away beyond any counting of it. We went into that fog-world at one end of Battle Creek and long after came out at the other, but what happened in between was as measureless as a float through space. If it was any portion of existence at all, it did not belong to the three of us, to that winter which had frozen all time but its own.

After that ghostly trip, I went back to my boarding family and Dad and Ruth went on with the struggle against the winter. It was another month or so before Dad arrived to take me to the ranch again. This time, we drove across the drifted world inside a plowed canyon, the slabs and mounds of frozen snow wrenched high as walls on either side of the thin route. *We've had a D-8 'dozer in here, the government sent it out when it looked like we were all gonna lose the livestock out here. I had to get a truckload of cottonseed cake sent in for the sheep, the hay's goin' so damn fast. They put the bumper of that truck right behind the 'dozer and even so it took 'em sixty-six hours to make it to the ranch and back, can ye feature that? That load of cottoncake is gonna cost us $2500 in transportation, but we had to have 'er.* I looked at him as if he'd said the moon was about to fall on us; $2500 sounded to me like all the money in the state of Montana. But Dad grinned and talked on: *You should of been out here to see all the snowplowin'. After they 'dozed out our haystacks, the crew was supposed to go up and 'doze out Jim Bill Keith's place. I was the guy that was showin' them the way, ridin' the front end of that Cat. Hell, I got us lost on the flats up here — same damn country I grew up in, ye know — and we 'dozed in a big circle before we knew what was goin' on. Plowed up a quarter of a mile of Jim Bill's fence and didn't even know it. Blizzardin', boy it's been ablowin' out here, son. They came out in one of those snow crawlers to change Cat crews — changed 'em with an airplane when they first started, but the weather got so bad they couldn't fly — so here they come now in one of these crawlers, and the guy drivin' is drunker'n eight hundred dollars. I thought he was gonna bring that damned crawler through the window of the house . . .* I laughed with him, but must have looked worried. He grinned again. *We're doin' okay in spite of it all. Haven't lost any sheep yet, and that high-priced cottoncake gives us plenty of feed. If this winter don't*

481

last into the summer, we're even gonna make some pretty good money on the deal.

Then in the next weeks came an afternoon when Dad saddled a horse and plunged off through the below-zero weather to the neighboring Keith ranch. *He came up here wanting to borrow some cigarettes, and some whiskey.* Probably the truce with Ruth was wearing through by then. Dad idled in the kitchen, talking and drinking coffee with Mrs. Keith while waiting for Jim Bill and his hired man to come back from feeding their cattle. *I remember, yes, your dad had ridden up on a little sorrel horse and he was sitting in the kitchen with Flossie, and he kept looking out at this kind of a red knob out here on the hill. He looked and he looked, and pretty soon he jumped up and yelled: 'It's broke, it's broke!' and he ran outside. And that winter was broke. The hired man and I came riding home with our earflaps rolled up and our coats off, and our mittens stuck in the forkhole of the saddle. Just like that.*

The chinook which had begun melting the snowdrifts even as Dad watched did signal the end of that ferocious winter, and somehow too it seemed to bring the end of the long storm within our household. Before, neither Dad nor Ruth had been able to snap off the marriage. Now they seemed in a contest to do it first, like a pair tugging at a stubborn wishbone.

Near the start of summer, Ruth announced she was leaving, this time for all time. Dad declared it the best idea he'd ever heard out of her. Alone with Ruth sometime in the swash and swirl of all this, I asked why she had to go. She gave me her tough grin, shook her head and said: *Your dad and me are never gonna get along together. We're done. We gave it our try.*

Why it was that the two of them had to endure that winter together before Ruth at last could go from Dad, I have never fathomed. Perhaps it was a final show of endurance against one another, some way to say *I can last at this as long as you can.* But that long since had been proved by both, and it is one of the strangenesses of this time that they had to go on and on with the proof of it. A last strangeness came over these years even after Ruth had vanished from us, and the divorce been handed down, one last unrelenting echo of it all. Dad no longer would even refer to Ruth by name. Instead, he took up something provided by one of the onlookers to our household's civil war. Naturally, the valley had not been able to resist choosing up sides in such a squabble, and a woman coming to Dad's defense reached for anything contemptible enough to call Ruth. At last she spluttered: *Why, that . . . that little flip!* For whatever reason, that Victorian blurt rang perfectly with Dad, put him in the right in all the arguments he was replaying in his mind. From the moment the surprising word got back to him, he would talk of Ruth only as *Flip, that damned Flip.*

Ruth went, and Flip stayed, one single poisoned word which was all that was left of two persons' misguess about one another. I have not seen Ruth for twenty years, nor spoken with her for twenty-five. But for a time after those few warring years with my father, her life straightened, perhaps like a piece of metal seethed in ire for the anvil. She married again, there was a son. And then calamity anew, that marriage in wreckage, and another after that, the town voice saying more than ever of her *She thinks everything should come in a cloud for her but she has hatefulness in herself,* until at last she had gone entirely, *disappeared somewhere out onto the Coast, nobody's cared to keep track of her.*

The son: I am curious about him. Was he taken by Ruth to see the grandmother blinking back age and blindness? Did Ruth stand with him, white mug of coffee in her hand, to watch snow sift on a winter's wind? But the curiosity at last stops there. When Dad and Ruth finally pulled apart, the one sentiment I could recognize within me — have recognized ever since — was relief that she had gone, and that the two of them could do no more harm to each other.

Once more Dad had to right our life, and this time he did it simply by letting the seasons work him up and down the valley. He went to one ranch as foreman of the haying crew, on to another to feed cattle during the winter, to a third for spring and the lambing season.

When school started and I could not be with him, he rented a cabin in White Sulphur and drove out to his ranch work in the morning and back at night. During the winter and in spring's busyness of lambing, I usually boarded with Nellie and his wife in their fine log house. Nellie's wife was a world of improvement from Ruth — a quiet approving woman, head up and handsome.

In the pasture behind their house she raised palomino horses, flowing animals of a rich golden tan and with light blond manes of silk. The horses seemed to represent her independence, her declaration away from Nellie's life of drinking, and she seemed to think Dad was right in letting me be as free and roaming as I was. It occurs to me now that she would have given me her quiet approving smile if I had come home from a wandering to report that I'd just been down at the Grand Central watching a hayhand knife a sheepherder.

And after her season of calm, Dad began one for us together. When the summer of 1950 came, he bought a herd of cattle, and we moved them and ourselves to a cattle camp along Sixteenmile Creek.

There our life held a simpler pace than I could ever remember. The two of us lived in a small trailer house, the only persons from horizon to horizon and several miles beyond. Dad decided to teach me to shoot a single-shot .22 rifle, using as targets the tan gophers which every horseback man hated for the treacherous little burrows they dug. We shot by the hour, rode into the hills every few days to look at the cattle, caught trout in the creek, watched the Milwaukee Railroad trains clip past four times every day.

Then I had my eleventh birthday — five years since my mother had died — and it seemed to trigger a decision in Dad. Something had been working at him, a mist of despond and unsteady health which would take him off into himself for hours at a time. One evening in the first weeks after my birthday, after he had been silent most of the day, he told me a woman would be coming into our lives again.

His words rolled a new planet under our feet, so astonishing and unlikely was this prospect. Ruth had come and gone without much lasting effect, except for the scalded mood Dad showed whenever he had a reason to mention her. But the person he had in mind now cast a shadowline across everything ahead of us, stood forth as the one apparition I could not imagine into our way of life. My mother's mother.

In the night, in mid-dream, people who are entire strangers to one another sometimes will congregate atop my pillow. They file into my sleeping skull in perplexing medleys. A face from grade school may be twinned with one met a week ago on a rain-forest trail in the Olympic Mountains. A pair of friends I joked with yesterday now drift in arguing with an editor I worked for more than a thousand miles from here. How thin the brainwalls must be, so easily can acquaintanceships be struck up among these random residents of the dark.

Memory, the near-neighborhood of dream, is almost as casual in its hospitality. When I fix my sandwich lunch, in a quiet noon, I may find myself sitting down thirty years ago in the company of the erect old cowboy from Texas, Walter Badgett. Forever the same is the meal with Walter: fried mush with dark corn syrup, and bread which Walter first has toasted and then dried in the oven. When we bite, it shatters and crashes in our mouths, and the more we eat, the fuller our plates grow with the shrapnel of crumbs. After the last roaring bite, Walter sits back tall as two of the ten-year-old me and asks down: Well, reckon we can make it through till night now? *I step to the stove for tea, and come instead onto the battered blue-enamel coffee pot in a sheepherder's wagon, my father's voice saying* Ye could float your grandma's flat-iron on the Swede's coffee. *I walk back toward my typewriter, past a window framing the backyard fir trees. They are replaced by the wind-leaning jackpines of one Montana ridgeline or another. I glance higher for some hint of the weather, and the square of air broadens and broadens to become the blue expanse over Montana rangeland, so vast and vaulting that it rears, from the foundation-line of the plains horizon, to form the walls and roof of all of life's experience that my younger self could imagine, a single great house of sky.*

Now the mood moves on, the restless habit of dream and memory, and I come to myself in a landscape of coastal western-ness so different in time and place from that earlier one. Different, yet how readily acquainted.

Ivan Doig

My father never had dates while we lived alone together in Seattle, or he had none that I knew about. I didn't wonder why. He was saving himself for my mother. But once he surprised me. It was the day before Christmas, and he hired a cleaning lady to scrub our rooms. Before she arrived from the referral service he sent me away to a double feature downtown. I arrived home before I was expected. The cleaning lady's instruments of work were leaning against the back porch railing, and the house was just as I had left it. The cleaning lady, maybe sixty, was as skinny as a broom, and drunk. She pinched me on the cheek. I wasn't friendly. She joshed my father. There was a smudge of lipstick on his cheek, and his necktie was loose. He looked to me like a clown, but he couldn't know why, couldn't see the lipstick on him. He could see the cleaning lady's smudged lips, though, and right away he opened great distance between her and himself.

"You can leave now," he said.

"I haven't cleaned up yet, honey," she said. She was saucy, unmindful of my father's short temper.

"That's all right," he said. "Some other time." He was surprisingly courtly.

The cleaning lady stood up stiffly, as if on her dignity. "It's not as easy as that, honey, *some other time* . . ." She was mocking my father, on Christmas Eve.

"Here, take this," he said. He gave her a twenty. She blew him a kiss, and left laughing.

I asked my father if he had kissed her.

"Of course not. Jesus, how could you think that?"

"There's lipstick on your cheek."

"Oh, that," he said, touching his cheek, blushing. "Well, yes, there was an office party, pretty girl there, red hair, nice popsie, about twenty-five, just a friendly kiss, very pretty . . ."

As though "pretty" made a difference. It made a difference.

My father's work at Boeing was as liason between design engineering, and production, just what he had done at Lockheed for the XP-38 and at North American for the XP-51. Now the project was the XB-52, and this was the Atomic Age, aviation had changed, was all business. My father had not changed, was not all business, and if his easy way with regulations won him admirers who worked under his charge on the mockup and prototype of the bomber, it also drew the attention of people without much sense of humor.

It drew the attention of the FBI. My father was careless with papers and blueprints, and didn't always lock his desk at night. This was a nuisance, but nothing to cause the heavy trouble about to come down on him after his security check. My father required a "Q" clearance — virtually an atomic clearance — for his work, and the FBI had just accumulated a meticulous record of his life.

It was late August, 1951. I remember because it happened the day after the unlimited hydroplane race near the Floating Bridge. Our Chris-Craft Riviera had just been "repo'd" (my father's word for "repossessed," a word he had such frequent occasion to use he abbreviated its three syllables to two), and we were watching the big inboard hydroplanes thunder around the markers from my own little racing runabout, *Y-Knot*. The boats were powered by airplane engines, Allisons and Rolls-Royces, sometimes two engines, and they could surpass two hundred miles per hour. One of the boats back in the pack was a gray, ungainly thing with two supercharged in-line engines, and on a straightaway it began to move up. The engines were winding high, the superchargers screaming, and my father touched my arm.

"Look away," he said. "That guy's about to blow."

I looked sharp, saw the boat hobbyhorsing a little. "What?" I asked my father. "What did you say?"

"He's pushed those Allisons too far. They won't take that much. There. He's gone."

And I looked where the boat had been, and there wasn't any bo anymore.

Let's go," my father said. "That's all she wrote."

The next day the FBI came to visit. It was Sunday. They identified themselves and my father told me to leave the room. Two of them talked to him. I tried to hear what they said. They were polite, serious. My father didn't raise his voice. When he said something, which wasn't often, they didn't interrupt him. When they left they shook hands with him, and with me. One of them reminded him not to leave town, they'd be in touch. My father said of course, he'd be at home.

A few hours later he packed the MG and we drove to Port Angeles and took the ferry to Canada: Victoria, on Vancouver Island My father checked us into the Empress, and I heard him use the name Saunders Ansell. The Empress was huge, and my father knew his way around it. He said that was where he'd been, "with a friend," when I flew to Seattle from Florida. We had tea with cakes and cookies and crustless sandwiches cut into thirds and quarters. My father looked at me across the tea table in the fancy lobby and said I needed a decent jacket. We went to the best haberdasher in Victoria, where he bought me a Black Watch tartan jacket. It came with brass buttons with a crest stamped on them, and my father insisted that these be removed, and replaced with solid, heavy, plain brass buttons. I was proud of my picture in the mirror. I reminded me of someone who had been raised to eat cucumber sandwiches in the lobby of the Empress.

My father was distracted. The next day we drove out the island to a place called Wilcooma Lodge, perched on the side of a fjord. We ate smoked salmon and looked at the water. My father drank whiskey with Lon Chaney, Jr., a guest, and when he came to bed he woke me up. He sat on the edge of my bed, rocking back and forth, holding his head in his hands. He was drunk, but he wasn't angry this time. He was sad.

"I've done awful things," he said.

"What things?" I asked him, afraid he might tell me.

"I don't know." His hands were in front of his face, held there like a mask. "Jesus, a man like me, power to waste life, engines of destruction . . . Sometimes, old man, it weighs heavy, believe me. Very, very, very heavy indeed."

Then he gave me specifics. He had drawn the line with the XB-52, had argued against its development as an atomic bomber. He couldn't allow another Hiroshima, Nagasaki, he already had "enough blood on his hands." He was in trouble because of his anti-atomic position, "deep trouble." The FBI wasn't finished with him.

We stayed a week. I was proud of my father's courage, the risk he was running. We rowed up the fjord, talking about old times. My father put his arm around me a lot, said he wanted me to be anything at all I wanted to be, as long as it served other people. He told me again how important it was that we tell the truth to each other, hang the cost. He said he thought maybe Rosemary wouldn't come to Seattle, but that was all right, maybe we'd travel south, see how she and Toby were doing.

He taught me to drive. I got three miles down the gravel driveway of Wilcooma Lodge, shifting pretty well, and then I lost it on an easy right-hander. The left fender and door were goners, but my old man managed to laugh about it, told our English hosts I had "pranged her into a ditch." He told me "never mind, you'll get the hang of it."

That day he made a long call to Seattle, and when he hung up he got a tow truck for his car. We followed in a taxi to the Seattle ferry, and boarded early, after the MG was put in the hold. We watched people come up the gangplank, slowly at first, then more frantically as the ferry prepared to shove off.

"Tell you what," my father said. "I'll bet you a buck someone misses the boat."

"If the boat's gone, how can we tell?"

"We have to see him miss it."

"I don't know . . ."

"I'll do you better. Someone has to miss the boat, and be so goddamned mad that he shakes his fist at us, jumps up and down, and throws his hat on the ground."

"I'll take it. A buck."

"If he throws his hat on the ground, and jumps up and down on it, you'll owe me two bucks, okay?"

"Deal."

We had the hawsers aboard, were slipping into the channel. "Look," my father said, pointing. I owed him two bucks, and fifteen years later I paid him.

We stood out on the windward railing all the way to Seattle. It was a clear night, dry and cold, and we saw the sun go down toward Asia and for an instant, like a flashbulb, light up the Olympic range. My father laid his arm over my shoulder. I wanted to comfort him.

"Is it going to be okay?" I asked him.

"Yes," he said.

And this was so, for the time being. Much later I learned what happened. The FBI had traced him back, stumbling over debts and a few scrapes with the police, some heavy drinking, the kinds of things the FBI finds when it looks. All the way back to his first job at Northrup. Here was a careless man, a good engineer, a patriotic American. Then, abruptly, in 1936, he disappeared. Groton hadn't heard of him, except to tell someone in Birmingham it hadn't heard of him. Yale hadn't heard of him. The Sorbonne didn't know what the hell it was being asked to verify, *what* school of *aeronautiques?* My father hadn't, as he claimed, been born in New York, at Columbia Presbyterian Hospital. Who was he? Where had he come from? Here was a man in close proximity to atomic bombers who seemed to have been dropped into this country, a few years before a world war, from nowhere. Here was a man obliged to answer some questions.

He answered them, somehow. Boeing kept him on. I can't imagine why. Probably cost-plus saved him. Cost-plus government contracts have saved many another. Boeing's profit was a fixed percentage of its costs; the higher its payroll, the more the company earned. My father was of some use to Boeing, imperfect as he was. And perhaps the FBI decided that even a man with bad character can be a patriot.

A few weeks after our flight to Canada and my father's return to Boeing, Alice, "Tootie," my stepmother, arrived.

Alice came in with the century. When I met her in a high corner room of the Olympic Hotel she was fifty-one, and looked older. My father, forty-three, looked her age. She had been twice married, widowed, and then divorced. Her first husband was a chemical magnate (his firm, Sandoz, developed LSD) and a prig. Alice cherished his memory, and was proud that he had considered himself undressed without his spats. He wore pince-nez, and was by all accounts a very serious gentleman.

Her second husband was different. He stroked a Harvard eight that won Henley, was a member of Porcellian and a class marshal. That was about it for him, though. He liked Mexico — the sun, the hours and the spirits — and he spent Alice's money fast, capital as well as interest. Like my father, he was younger than she.

I liked Alice. She had a musical voice, trained to its vibrato precision by singing coaches and finishing schools. I liked the pretty white hair she wore piled on top of her head, and her formality. She was fastidious, but didn't seem cold. She was big, I guess "Rubenesque" is the euphemism, and she put on airs, but they were the airs of a schoolmarm, and I found them comfortable, at first. Later, when she pronounced the *is* in isolate" to rhyme with the *is* in "Sis," I'd straighten her out, and still later I'd mock her. But then, just thirteen, I reckoned she must know something I didn't know.

My father introduced us with pride; he "knew we'd love each other." I'd had no warning about Alice, had never heard of her, before he took me to her room. She and my father kissed when she opened the door, but this was friendly, not at all carnal. I don't know what I thought my father and this woman were to each other, but I didn't think of their association as a betrayal of my mother.

I was wrong. Later I learned that Duke had known Alice since we lived in Old Lyme. He had met her in Boston, and they had spent much time there together, hobnobbing with her ex-husband's Harvard friends. They had rendezvoused in Paris while we lived in Sarasota, and my father had been with this nice lady at the Empress in Victoria when I left Sarasota, and at Wilcooma Lodge when I visited in Seattle.

Rosemary was outraged when Duke told her about Alice. I, of course, applied a double standard to my parents, but it was easy to rationalize: There was always between Alice and my father the sense of an arrangement rather than a passion. They liked each other, and then they didn't, but I never felt ardor ebb or flow between them. But I was a kid, and saw what I wished to see.

I didn't know, or even sense, that my appearance repelled Alice. I was wearing pale-green gabardine trousers when she met me, and these were held in place by a quarter-inch white patent leather belt. Over a shiny shirt with representations of brown-skinned islanders at play beneath palm trees I wore the tartan jacket my father had so recently bought me, and the jacket she especially despised. She was also disappointed in my table manners. We ate that first night at Canlis's, a fancy restaurant high on a hill overlooking Lake Union, and I worked through the courses pretty

491

fast. She finally said, "Please don't wolf your food," and I said, "I'm a Wolff, why not?" Duke laughed, and told me to slow down. I noticed Alice's neck go blotchy red, but I didn't know yet that this was a danger signal, *We Are Not Amused*.

The next morning she took me to the Prep Shop at Frederick & Nelson. The clothes were laughably uncool but I indulged the nice lady, let her trick me out cap-a-pie. I stood firm on the question of my hair, so the boys at St. Bernard's and Collegiate, where Alice's son had been schooled, would not have recognized me as one of their own. That second night we ate in the Cloud Room of the Camlin, and I watched my father's measured moves with his eating equipment while he talked to me and Alice listened, now and then touching the corner of her linen napkin to the corner of her mouth.

"I spoke with Rosemary this morning." My father had never called her *Rosemary* to me before, always *your mother*. "We've decided that a divorce makes sense, better for her and for me." He didn't wait for me to say anything, but there was nothing I wanted to say. "You'll stay with me, of course." I nodded, took a bite of roast sirloin. "Toby'll stay with his mother. He needs her, and it's fair." I nodded. "I guess there's not much more to say about this. You know how she feels?" I nodded. "Well. How would you feel about Alice staying here in Seattle?"

"Duke," Alice said, motioning him to quit now.

"Living with us, I mean," my father said.

"Oh, Duke! Give the child time!"

I tried to get a whole asparagus into my mouth without dripping hollandaise on my new flannels. "Okay with me," I said. "Fine," I said, smiling at the nice lady across the table.

We moved to a big house on Lake Washington, northeast of the Sand Point Naval Air Station. I got a new, faster boat, specially made for me. I had the whole top floor of the house and could play whatever music pleased me, as loud as I wanted. I didn't see much of my school friends, and Duke didn't see much of his Boeing friends. Alice wasn't comfortable around them. I began to hear how differently they talked, the gaffes they committed. My father wouldn't wear a tie every night to dinner but I had to, and at first I liked this.

The MG went up on blocks when the cold weather came, and Duke and Alice bought a brand-new Buick Roadmaster Estate Wagon, with Brewster green metal, wood trim and Dyna-Flo transmission. They were married in a civil ceremony at home the day his divorce came through, and some of his pals from MG rallies teased him about the Buick, its automatic transmission and four air holes ("Ventaports") in the hood. Alice let me sample the fish house punch while I helped her make it, and I enjoyed the lightheaded sensation. Some of Duke's friends whistled when they saw the house and the spread: smoked salmon, caviar, oysters, a Smithfield ham. I liked the impression we seemed to make, but I saw that my father did not, and that when people told him he "must've struck gold" Alice's neck went red. By now I knew what that meant.

My father got drunk and went to the garage with some friends from the MG club. They ran the engine, talked about old times, bragged about their cars. My father made me sit behind the wheel while he told again how I had "pranged" the car, and I blushed. Then he told his friends that he was keeping the MG for me till my sixteenth birthday, and I was so excited I honked the horn.

After the men and their wives left I was sent to bed. I heard an argument, much worse than anything between Duke and Rosemary, a shouting match. Alice didn't seem to fear him. He came upstairs, sat on my bed. He was breathing heavily, and I was afraid.

"Did this whole goddamned thing for you."

"What, Dad?"

"Don't *what, Dad* me! D'you think I wanted this?"

"I don't know."

"You know all right. Just don't have the guts to take responsibility."

He sounded as though he hated me. "Tell me what I've done," I asked. I was being a lawyer.

"Jesus," he said. Then he mimicked me: *"Tell me what I've done!* Nothing, kiddo, and you'll never do anything, either."

Then he left, slowly negotiating the narrow stairs, swearing. I heard one last thing before he pitched out the front door, and drove away in the Buick:

"That's all she wrote, Arthur."

493

A few weeks later I overheard a discussion between my father and stepmother about money, a temperate discussion about stocks and shares, annual yield, "the tax picture." I asked my father who paid for what these days. He didn't react to the question as though it were delicate. He told me his salary at Boeing was high, he had had a promotion. Moreover, he said, he had finally come into his father's estate, half a million dollars. I said that was wonderful, we were rich, right? It wasn't polite to speak of these things, my father explained to me. Gentlemen did not discuss money. Besides, while his was tied up in investments Alice would carry many of the petty household expenses. She was sensitive about these matters, my father explained, so I was never, never, never to speak to my stepmother about money, his or hers. I was to rest assured that there was plenty.

To believe the fable of the inheritance required great will, an appetite for credulity I can now credit only by assuming that I preferred this fabulous notion to the transparent reality that my father was a grifter, living off a woman who didn't seem inclined to give anything away free. I think I *couldn't* have believed in the half million. Maybe I didn't care. I was safe; as my father said, there was plenty now, wherever it came from.

Seattle couldn't hold them. On the last day of January, two months after they were married, Duke quit his job. Alice had wearied of the provincialism of the "jumping-off-place for Alaska," and of having water pour on her head every time she stepped outside. My father had been offered a job in Tennessee, with a jet-engine test center. He would have a raise in pay to twelve hundred a month and great responsibility. Incredibly, he had managed to push through the same resume that had so recently provoked the FBI.

It was decided that we would make a proper trip of it, ship our household things and the MG and my boat and motor (this time, for sure, they went where I went), and drive southeast in the Buick. Alice and I would come to know each other, my father thought, if we traveled three thousand miles together in an automobile. We got to know each other.

There were pleasant moments. We drove south along the coast to Los Angeles, putting into the Benson in Portland, the Palace in

San Francisco and the Bel Air in Los Angeles. I took on a patina of sophistication, and when Alice treated me to dancing at the Coconut Grove in the Ambassador, where we listened to Gordon MacRae and I drank creme de menthe frappe, I decided that here was a life to suit me. I saved menus (Chasen's, Romanoff's — where my father, for a sawbuck, seemed to be known by the owner — The Brown Derby and the Polo Lounge). I went alone to *Mister Roberts*, my first live play, and expressed opinions about it. My father took me to hear Billie Holiday at a simple club near Watts, and then Jack Teagarden, whose bass player called out to him when the set ended, "Duke, you old scoundrel." This was the musician who had shipped out to Europe with my father after he got the boot from the University of Pennsylvania, "after your dad left college." He let Duke buy him drinks. Alice — who wanted me to call her "Tootie," which I couldn't — went back to the Bel Air. The bass player said my dad could have been okay on guitar if he'd stuck with it. I kept a matchbook from that place.

The next morning my father and stepmother drove me to the coast somewhere near Venice, where Elgin Gates now had his own boat and motor dealership and his own Caddy. Gates offered to let me drive his D-class hydro, good for sixty and more, a marvel of a boat, if I came back the next day. Duke and Alice were happy to take me back, but I was more interested in the city now. I thought I'd like to be a night owl, studied the way my father dressed, bought *Confidential* to read about scandals in places like the Coconut Grove and not just to study pictures of Abbe Lane's cleavage.

I learned to eat salad with a salad fork. To order oil and vinegar rather than Thousand Island. To accept cheese, and to order meat rare rather than well done. I was almost ready for an artichoke.

They showed me Carlsbad Caverns and the Grand Canyon, but I wasn't much interested. New Orleans lay ahead, jazz and Brennan's. My father was amused, for a while, and then not so amused. My wisdom was gaining too fast on his own. Somewhere in Texas we passed a car in a ditch, with an ambulance and state troopers at hand. Two miles down the road my father said, as though to himself:

"That was a Roadmaster, just like this one."

"No," I said a mile later, "it was a Super. It only had three holes."

We traveled another ten miles. "You argue too much; it's getting to be a habit, and you're wrong most of the time."

Alice was asleep in the back seat. We were trying to make Dallas before dark.

"I'm not arguing, just telling you it was a Super. It had three holes. Roadmaster has four. Like ours."

My father pulled to the side of the road. Sighed. "We've come about twenty miles past that car," he said. "If I go back it'll cost us forty miles, an hour out of our day, our lives. It's not necessary. It's not even interesting. The car was a Roadmaster, that's all."

"I'll bet you ten bucks it was a Super. I looked right at it, three holes."

My father didn't take my bet. He turned us around and headed us west, into the sun. The sun woke up Alice. She asked questions; I answered them. My father was silent. She said she couldn't believe a grown man would let his child run him all over the map this way. I thought I didn't like her. I had begun to think this earlier, hearing my stepmother make notional pronouncements about me when she knew I was well within earshot. My father drove on. He was silent. Alice was disgusted. I was happy, couldn't wait to make them count those three damned Ventaports, and get this sorted out. I almost mentioned my father's glasses to him, but something made me think this was a bad idea. When we reached the place where the Buick Super had gone into the ditch it was gone. A Texas highway patrolman was measuring a skid mark. My father asked where they had taken the wreck. The patrolman told him: the town was off the highway, five miles down yonder dirt road.

"Just ask him what kind of car it was," Alice said.

"Yeah," I said, "ask him, he'll tell you."

My father said nothing. He drove five miles to a crossroads gas station and let me sit for a minute looking out my window at the wrecked Buick Roadmaster. I figured Alice had switched cars on me. It was just like her, and by then I knew that money could get any job done.

*   *   *

496

I drove the Porsche flat out along Nod Hill Road, just as my father drove his Ferrari, a three-liter Ghia-bodied roadster he had "bought" when he "bought" my Porsche, using the third Jaguar in his stable as a down payment for both cars and promising to make killer monthly payments, which he never made. Alice was by now resolute in her antagonism to his financial caprices, and would have no part of his toys or the debts he accumulated on behalf of his toys. She was rightly aghast when she first saw the Porsche, and this further alienated me from her.

One night, with fog drifting across Nod Hill Road, my father and I nearly hit head on. We were drunk, and just managed to nose our cars into opposite ditches. We met in the middle of the road at the sharp right-hander near the wall of a sheep pasture and hugged and laughed: wouldn't that have been something, setting the old lady free of us and our damned cars at a single swipe!

My father finally did bang his Ferrari into that stone wall and three weeks later, sixteen and a half, I rolled my Porsche over a different stone wall. The girl with me was thrown clear and got off cheap, with five stitches behind her ear. I smashed my nose, had it stitched together by a sleepy intern in South Norwalk, and tried to sleep off a concussion. My father sat by my bed slapping me awake. I laughed at him walking around in his pajamas in a public building, but he wasn't laughing anymore. I was a tinhorn "Porfirio" with a "completely false set of values."

It was decided I should work that summer before my last year at Choate. The previous summer I had been fired for indolence after three weeks cutting grass and trimming hedges as an apprentice to Raymond Massey's Wilton grounds keeper, but this was to be a serious enterprise. I was hired by Tolm Motors in Darien, where Duke had his cars and mine tuned and repaired. (He had now traded himself down from the Ferrari to a Mercedes 190SL, and me from the wreckage of the Porsche to a VW). He owed Tolm so much that he muscled me into my summer job: they were nice to me so that if he ever paid any bills he might pay them first. My job at seventy-five cents an hour was pleasant and educational. I washed and waxed the sports cars of clients who had brought them for repair. My partner in this work was a black bachelor, George, about forty-five. In light of his superior experience he was paid two bits more an hour than I was paid. We became friendly; I talked to him about Choate and he listened, and soon knew the names of my teachers and friends, answering strophe with antistrophe:

"George, I've had it up to here with Bill Morse."

"That boy too damned big for his britches. A nice one 'longside the head bring him down to size, yessir."

I resolved to teach George about the great jazz musicians who had enriched the culture of his people, but when I got permission to bring a record player to the garage where we worked alone with hoses and brushes and chamois cloth, George said he didn't cotton to jazz, he preferred the classics, Kostelanetz and Ezio Pinza. Never mind, it was my machine, and I arbitrated a settlement, two picks for me, one for him, thus: "Rockin' Chair," "Struttin' with Some Barbeque," "Some Enchanted Evening."

One day I suggested that George come to dinner at home in Wilton and then blow it out with my father and me in Westport.

"Shit," he said, "you don't know nothin'."

For reasons beyond my understanding I was trusted by Tolm to take delivery of its new Jaguars, Triumphs, and Mercedes from distributors in New York. Once or twice a week I'd come to work dressed like a Choatie, wearing a bow tie, saddle shoes, and a seersucker jacket, and take the train to New York to fetch a car. The last car I picked up was a gray gull-winged Mercedes 300SL, still covered with dock grime and shipping grease. The seats were black glove leather. It was explained that the car's speed during break-in was governed by a restraint on the accelerator that prevented me from exceeding eighty in top gear, but this could be overridden in an emergency, breaking a lead seal and placing in peril the car's warranty. Coming down the long hill at Stamford on the Merritt Parkway there was an emergency. I wanted urgently to drive Tolm Motors' new car a hundred and fifty, and I did. Tolm Motors, finding the lead seal broken, was cross and fired me, cutting its losses and resigning itself to a place at the bottom of Duke's action pile. I said goodbye to George, promised to stay in touch.

"No, you got bigger fish to fry, won't be thinkin' 'bout old George."

"Bullshit, George."

"Yeah," George said, the last word from him the last time I saw him.

The night I wrecked my Porsche I had been drinking at Rip's Lounge. The pianist and organist from Sarasota had opened a nightclub in a shopping center in White Plains. It was as dark as Dick's hatband in there; the walls were fish tanks, bubbling greenly. Rip wore a white dinner jacket when he played. It set off his brilliantined black hair to good advantage, he thought. I went there with Duke, a Choate friend, and our dates. My date was a plain-talking blonde, Buster Crabbe's daughter, and when my father said he had been her father's friend, I didn't believe him. Her father, after all, had been somebody, Tarzan! Duke had in fact been his friend in Miami, where they swam together in an aquatic circus. Nevertheless, Susie Crabbe preferred my Choate friend, Jack, and so did Jack's date prefer Jack. I studied this injustice while a wonderful jazz guitarist, Mundell Lowe, played solo. And when he was finished, Rip, who considered himself the headliner, began to play and I talked too loudly, to Jack.

"Where do you think we'll be in ten years from now?"

"I don't know," Jack said. "Who knows?"

"Who do you think's going to do better?"

"What do you mean by better?" Jack asked.

"You know. I know. We'll know then. Listen, we'll know."

My father was annoyed. "Shut up and listen to the music."

"Tell you what," I told Jack, "let's get together in ten years and ·e what's happened to us."

"You're serious."

"Bet your ass I'm serious!" My voice had risen. Rip looked hard at our table. Duke looked hard at Rip.

"Okay," Jack said, "a deal. A hundred I'm happier, better off, further ahead. Ten years from now."

Our dates giggled as we seized hands. People stared at us. Rip quit "Autumn in New York" abruptly, left the stand. As he passed our table he muttered something, probably to me. My father was drunk now, and pugnacious. Maybe Rip had said something to him, we had disrupted our friend's set, it was his club. Rip headed downstairs to the men's room, and I followed him. At the bottom of the stairs he put his arm around me like a buddy, and was about to lecture me, I think, on good manners, when we were spun around by Duke's shout from the top of the stairs.

"Take your hands off him, greaser!"

"What!" Rip shouted. "What did you say?"

"I know you in and out, pal." My father was shaking his finger.

"Come down here you fake sonofabitch," Rip said. "You're all air, always have been, just a crummy, deadbeat talker, come on down, let's get this over."

"I'm no fool," my father said. "You've got a gun."

"I don't need it for you." Rip pulled the revolver from his shoulder holster.

"Don't shoot me!" my father yelled.

Rip tried to hand it to me, but I backed away. It was the snubnose he had shot at rabbits in Florida. I begged them to stop. Rip threw his pistol on the floor.

"If I come after you," my father said, "you'll pick it up; you're a mob guy, I know all about you."

Rip picked up the gun, shook out the bullets, threw the gun in a trash basket, beckoned with his hand, said quietly: "Come down here, I don't want to fight in front of my customers."

"Fuck yourself," my father said.

Rip started upstairs fast. I followed, grabbing at his coat, and by the time I reached him he was at the front door of his club, watching my father drive away, leaving rubber. There was no point chasing him, his Ferrari was too fast.

"He's chickenshit," Rip said.

"No," I said, "he isn't." But I knew he was.

I was not good to Choate, but neither was Choate good to me. Piety, courtesy, self-importance, smugness, and a killing dose of homily characterized the Choate I knew. Choate's business was to define and enclose. Alice understood this from her son's experience, and even before I arrived for summer school she wrote Seymour St. John: "Choate will do wonders for Jeff. Learning to share and also to accept restrictions pleasantly." Then another letter: "It will help Jeff, he will become accustomed to restrictions."

Cookie-cutting has its virtues. It's worth something to be taught that neighbors have rights, that conventions are not prima facie malign, that rules are not always provocative. At Choate, though, cookie-cutting was a fixation. The boys we called "straight arrows" thrived. The rest of us — "negos," carpers, corner-cutters, and wise-apples — bucked the system, and some had fun. The happy ones knew what they were doing, but I didn't. I said *no* by reflex, wouldn't take the bit, see the point, play the game, join the team. I was ashamed of myself, and bitter that Choate didn't love me. I should have understood that boys who don't join the team cannot expect to be loved by the team.

Most of the masters at Choate and many of the boys felt I laughed too quickly and too often at things sacred to them: the score of the Deerfield game, the election of class officers, our privilege not to be permitted to smoke. Seymour St. John's farewell message to my graduating class, published in the 1955 yearbook, *The Brief,* closed with an unidentified quotation "from one of my heroes." It is vintage homily, just the kind of stuff we heard at chapel every evening after dinner, and before lunch on Sunday: "The ideals which have lighted my way, and time after time have given me new courage to face life cheerfully, have been Kindness, Beauty, and Truth."

Perhaps. There were no black students at Choate, and someone once asked the Head why. There were no black students at Choate, said the Reverend St. John, because it was unfair to elevate the aspirations of Negroes by inviting them to a school whose customs, requirements, and academic standards were beyond their reach. Yet, he said, all were equal in the eyes of the Lord. So he invited a black preacher to sermonize to us every year. This was a huge man with a musical voice, a Robeson bass; he had the most cultivated of accents, the product of education at Trinity College, Cambridge. The Head beamed to hear him speak. The last time I heard him, I deployed alarm clocks throughout the chapel, and they rang at five-minute intervals for almost an hour. *Mea culpa*, it was the weak link who did this. My father had done it too, at the Clark School. It was just dumb, easy mischief, not so much the work of an angry young man as of a temperamental brat.

The spring of my fifth-form year I visited the Head for a heart-to-heart. I was in trouble. I had run up bills. From way back, midway through my first year, this had been a problem. Here's a note from George Steele in 1952: "I have had to write your parents about your Bookshop bill. Now, ere the new year, I expect you to get yourself out of your difficulties." Then came a wire to my father, with a copy to Steele, from St. George's Inn, where we were sometimes allowed to eat dinner, and in whose basement some of us smoked, a vice punishable by immediate expulsion: THE AMOUNT OF $49.19 ACCRUED BY YOUR SON JEFFREY WOLFF HAS NOT BEEN PAID. IF IT IS NOT PAID IN FULL BY THE FIFTEENTH OF THIS MONTH WE WILL BE FORCED TO TURN THE ACCOUNT OVER TO OUR ATTORNEY FOR COLLECTION.

But the immediate cause of my trouble was a breach of school regulations, sort of. Fifth-formers were obliged to be present at a specified number of meals each week, and attendance was usually recorded by a master, seated at each round table of twelve. At Sunday supper, however, the masters were free, and we signed ourselves in. I came to the dining hall, signed in, bowed my head for the Head's appreciation of our many bounties, gulped a glass of milk and left for a proper meal at St. George's. A straight arrow, aware that I had exhausted my outside dining privileges, turned me in to Mr. Steele. The Penguin took the position that I had, in effect, lied, had breached the Honor Code, was subject to the consideration of the Honor Committee.

On the Honor Committee was a boy I knew well. He was as dumb as a shoe. Three weeks earlier he had stolen my sweater. I saw him leave my room with it and retrieved it from his drawer. I had worn it every day since, in front of him. I was wearing it now. He frisked with me, told me there was no place at Choate for liars, that I wasn't good enough for his wonderful school. Others in the room, the class of the class ahead of me, nodded. I sat silent, no defense, of course they were right, the sweater was nothing weighed against my breach of honor, I was low, a miserable thing, verily.

They were sports. I was let off with a warning. I went to see the Head, and he told me I didn't deserve to remain in his school. When I left his office I felt soiled, diminished, and beyond reach. I believed the man despised me, and was right to despise me. Now I find a generous memo in my file, a record of our talk:

Jeff Wolff came in June 3rd to say that he had just recently had a change of heart and hoped he might have an opportunity to prove himself in the year ahead. As nearly as I could judge, Jeff was completely sincere and not motivated — primarily at least — by a

fear that he would not be allowed to continue at Choate next year.
He admits that he has been less than honest, sloppy, and generally
useless in his approach to School life. I told him he would have to
be 100 percent in very way in his Sixth Form year or we just could
not keep him. I suggested that this might be more of a challenge
than Jc 'f wanted to accept, but he insisted that this was just the
way he wanted it to be.

I left the Head's office and wanted to be alone. There was only
the chapel. At Choate I was never alone, except there. I loved
chapel for this, sang the hymns with gusto, even reverence. Alone
in the chapel I banished resentments. I prayed to be better. I
tried. My *Brief* biography is illustrated with a poorly drawn
cartoon of a boy studying book titled *Being One of the Boys.* I
studied the subject diligently, to my shame. Had myself
confirmed by the Head, in the Head's faith. Joined the Altar Guild
and the Scholarship Committee. Sang with the choir, the glee
club, and the Maiyeros (pipsqueak Whiffenpoofs). I tried to make
the football team: "Fine effort," the coach said, "willing. Going
to be a hard competitor to stop. Fought hard as a guard. Good
development." But I wasn't good enough, and so I became a
cheerleader. Good God! I'd rather confess I was a pickpocket. My
friends were amused. I was perplexed.

The Maiyeros gave a concert at Miss Porter's, in Farmington. I
fell in love with a girl from Philadelphia. She liked me, for a while,
and visited me for a day and night in Wilton during her Christmas
vacation. I had hoped she would stay longer, but she lost interest
quickly. She seemed uncomfortable with my father; Duke wasn't
what she knew on the Main Line. She was quiet, reserved, not
pretty, handsome, with mannish shoulders. I liked her for good
reasons, and as usual I liked her too well. I wanted her to love me;
I boasted, labored to charm, dropped names, felt her slip away,
heard her telephone the New York, New Haven and Hartford to
ask about an earlier train. We drove to the Norwalk station in
silence. At the station she told me there was no need to wait for
her train, but I did. We waited five minutes together; she
pretended to read a book.

That night I wrote her a letter, twenty or thirty pages, maybe fifty. Falsehood on falsehood. *Bons mots* from *Bartlett's* that I hoped weren't familiar, because I displayed them as my own. References to my upcoming social season, so busy with coming-out parties in Boston and New York. The summer looked full too, Pater would be off as usual doing polo at Brandywine and Myopia. I'd be playing the eastern tennis circuit, Longwood, Newport Casino, had a fair chance to advance to a ranking if I could sharpen the backstroke, but squash at the Racquet Club was playing hob with my wrist. And so on and on and on . . . I even quoted, as a closing epigraph, a line or two from Sophocles, in Greek: *Thus do flies to gods like little boys to men*, or something. I signed off, finally, "affectionately."

This letter was probably worse than I have represented it here. I know I wrote it on Racquet Club stationery (taken from a cache my father had cadged when Frank Shields took him to lunch to sell him the temporary use of towels), and I know I sealed the envelope with wax from a Christmas candle and stuck Duke's crest, engraved on a salt shaker he had given Alice as a wedding gift, in the wax.

That night my father found the letter, opened it, read it. He didn't bring it to me. He destroyed it first, and then came to my room and woke me. He knew the toll, to the penny; he was so gentle. He didn't quote the letter at me, or refer to it. He told me I was better than I thought, that I didn't need to add to my sum. I had warmth, he said; warmth and energy were the important things. These were a long time paying off sometimes, but they paid off. Honesty was the crucial thing, he said, knowing who I was, being who I was. What he said was so; I knew it was so. I didn't even think to turn his words against him, he was trying so hard to save me from something, to turn me back. I had this from him always: compassion, care, generosity, endurance.

*   *   *

I had never seen kindred dying or dead. No one I knew well was killed in a car or a war. None drowned, or fell from a great height, or was shot hunting. My dead were strangers. When I was a cub on the night police beat for *The Washington Post* I was sent to a

504

tough neighborhood near Howard University to look at someone who had been hurt. It was raining, late at night. A cop said something about knife wounds, and gestured. The thing lay covered by a piece of oilskin, with its feet in a brimming butter. The cop obligingly pulled back the poncho, for the merest instant, like a stripper flashing the last bit just at the blackout. He grinned at me while I scribbled in my notebook: *coal in a croker sack . . . blood: pretty, a dash of red on a blackbird's wing.* (I assumed the corpse was black: the bad street, the knife, the late hour, the law's indifference, even the rain suggested that the corpse was black, and it was.) I returned to the newsroom to compose a memorial drenched in mist and metaphysics, but the night city editor was interested only in the man's name and address, age and occupation, and I knew none of these. I should at least have asked his name.

And once I saw a stain on Route 301, on the Eastern Shore of the Chesapeake Bay Bridge. It was said by gawkers to have been a man changing a tire. A truck highballing north had whacked him; the stain was still wet in the low October sun, more rust than red, and greasy. The remains of the man who had been changing his tire formed an imperfect disc, about four feet across. The first rain would clean him away.

Just those two experiences of death, or just those two close up. One of my best friends killed himself a few days after I had spent a merry week with him. I had come to America from Cambridge to visit him at the Harvard Business School, where he was a student and not performing as well as he had expected himself to perform. A few days after he announced his engagement to a girl he seemed to love, who seemed to love him back, he parked his car near the emergency room of a hospital near his family's house. He lay across the front seat, stuck the muzzle of a pump gun in his mouth, and pulled the trigger with his toe. I had come home for the engagement party but was back in England when he did it.

I don't know why he shot himself. People spoke of a dark history I knew nothing about, and a few mentioned the confusions of love, but most people believed he was disappointed by his performance at the business school. None of these reasons seemed much like reasons to me.

Now, driving home from Kay's terrace where I had just learned of my father's death, trying to think of my father, I thought instead of Kay's husband. He wore a wooden leg, got around well on it, elaborated jokes about it. He had flown wearing it in the Air Corps, and had escaped from a German POW camp wearing it. People who knew this man loved him, while he was alive. But he shot himself in a spectacularly cruel way, perhaps not calculated to do maximum hurt to his four children and three stepchildren, but having that end, and the damage he did to his wife was incalculable. Driving to my in-laws' house I thought of that suicide. Why would anyone choose so casually to empty so much life from himself?

There was a message to telephone the police in California. There would be an autopsy; they suspected suicide. In the room where my father died, the police told me on the telephone, were many empty liquor bottles and empty barbiturate pillboxes. Much later the police told me that the general squalor of the scene — my father lying on his stomach naked, his head under a chair, "legs and feet together pointing eastward" in the language of the death report — combined with the awful smell in the dank, tiny room to argue, even to case-hardened cops, hopelessness. This suicide was no mystery. It made sense to me. I thought my father had every reason to welcome death, and I had always assumed he would try to control his history to the very end. *It's nothing.* But the autopsy a few days later revealed a death from congestion of his arteries; probably, when he died, he wanted to live forever.

From my in-laws' house I telephoned my mother, and told her as much as I knew, and for the first time I heard my mother weep. I telephoned Ruth Atkins, and when I had finished with the telephone about suppertime, Priscilla asked me if I wanted to eat. I said I wasn't hungry. She said she was sleepy, and would go to bed. I followed her to the guest room, expecting her to mourn with me. She wouldn't. I grew angry to the point of violence. I didn't understand her coldness, but I do now.

I had felt ashamed of my father in her father's house, and now I was ashamed of my shame, and ashamed to be there at all, under that roof. It was as though to accept their hospitality were to collaborate in their judgment of my father. I thought I knew what they thought of him, and I knew what they thought of me. Sometimes in that house I felt Priscilla look at me through her parents' eyes, and I thought that house in Narragansett was a place where my father would not have been made to feel welcome. I tried to forget the night of his death that neither had he been welcome those past ten years in my own house, and in my eagerness to forget this I repudiated all of them, my wife and her parents, and now Priscilla says she has never seen me so cold or so angry. She withdrew, would not dishonor any of us by seeming to feel what she did not. I wanted her to love my father now. I wanted to love my father now. How could she, if I could not? She had never seen him, had heard his voice once across telephone wires. We had promised him and ourselves a visit to California, but we never went. Every time we settled on a date to show my father his first grandson, and then his second, something happened, he got put away again or pulled a fast move on me or we decided we'd rather visit Madrid, ski in Austria.

I think that for a few hours that night I hated my wife. I drove to a seedy Narragansett roadhouse, a rough bar with a tropical motif where surfers hung out. I wanted a fight. I sat at the bar drinking whiskey chased by beer, scowling and muttering at friendly strangers wearing cut-offs and clean, jokey T-shirts. The beachboys were tan, pacific, easy; surfers had no beef with me. I shut the place down and drove flat out to Kay's house. I wanted to explain to her, at once, why I had thanked God that my father was dead. I wanted her to know that my words were not an atheist's unfelt exclamation, and that they did not only display relief that my children were alive. They also meant what they seemed to mean, that I thanked someone that my father had been delivered from the world, and I had been delivered from him.

I woke my friend three hours before dawn. I had first met Kay at her California ranch nine years earlier, the day after I left my father in the San Diego jail. Two of her daughters were Priscilla's lifelong friends, and one of them I had courted. Like everyone who knew him I had idolized her husband, and he crawled out the bedroom window of our Madrid hotel room, swaying drunk on a narrow ledge ten floors above the street because I had just told him a sad story. A couple of his children helped me snag his good leg and haul him to safety, and the way they looked at him that night I guessed they had had to save him from himself many times before. A few days before he shot himself, with his wife and children as witnesses, Kay had written me to wish me well in my courtship of Priscilla, and her letter was full of energy, wit, love, and delight with the future.

It was too cold to sit on the terrace, but my friend lit the Japanese lanterns out there so we could see them from the living room. Above the fireplace a motto was cut into the mantel: *Kind friend, around this hearthstone speak no evil of any creature.*

The morning with Kay changed me. She spoke of her dead husband and I talked of my dead father; we traded scandal for scandal, and soon we were laughing. I told how my father despised prudence, savings accounts, the *idea* of savings accounts, the *fact* of savings accounts, looks before leaps. Yes, her husband too, hobbling along the pitching deck of a sailboat he had chartered to sail solo before he taught himself to sail. It had been fun to be her husband's wife, and my father's son. This was important to understand.

Kay led me through my father's history, let me begin to apprehend him as a critic of the conventions, a man who caricatured what he despised. *Is it Yale men you like? Okay, I'm a Yale man, see how easy it is? Nothing to it but will and nerve.* My friend led me to understand how lucky I was to be free, that there was a benign side to my father's dishonor, that I had never had to explain or apologize to him any more than he had had to explain or apologize to me. Much of this, of course, was casuistry. I don't believe now that my father was truly a critic of society, or that his life was any more happy than it was defiant.

Never mind. I had come into that night alienated. I was becoming handy with repudiations of every kind, and learning to nurture anger solicitously. I had felt betrayed by my father, and wanted to betray him. Kay turned my course. She had the authority of someone who had passed through the worst of fires. I listened to her. I saw again what I had seen when I was a child, in love with my father as with no one else. He had never repudiated me or seen in my face intimations of his own mortality. He had never let me think he wished to be rid of me or the burden of my judgment, even when I had hounded him about his history, had quibbled with its details like a small-print artist, like a reviewer, for God's sake! He didn't try to form me in his own image. How could he? Which image to choose? He had wanted me to be happier than he had been, to do better. He had taught me many things, some of which were important, some of which he meant, some of which were true. The things he told me were the right things to tell a son, usually, and by the time I understood their source in mendacity they had done what good they could. I had been estranged from my father by my apprehension of other people's opinions of him, and by a compulsion to be free of his chaos and destructions. I had forgotten I loved him, mostly, and mostly now I missed him. I miss him.

When I finally left Kay's house I felt these things, some for the first time. I drove home slowly, and stopped at stop signs. The door to the room I shared with Priscilla was open when I came in, but I didn't go through that door that night. I went to my children's room. I stood above Justin, looking down at him. And then my son Nicholas began to moan, quietly at first. They did not know their grandfather was dead; they knew nothing about their grandfather. There would be time for that. I resolved to tell them what I could, and hoped they would want to know as much as I could tell. Nicholas cried out in his sleep, as he had so many times before, dragging me out of nightmares about his death with his own nightmares about his death, his dreams of cats with broken legs, broken-winged screaming birds, deer caught in traps, little boys hurt and crying, beyond the range of their parents' hearing. Sometimes I dreamt of my son bleeding to death from some simple wound I had neglected to learn to mend.

Now I smoothed his forehead as my father had smoothed mine when I was feverish. Justin breathed deeply. I crawled in bed beside my sweet Nicholas and took him in my arms and began to rock him in time to Justin's regular breaths. I stunk of whiskey and there was blood on my face from a fall leaving Kay's house, but I knew I couldn't frighten my son. He ceased moaning, and I rocked him in my arms till light came down on us, and he stirred awake in my arms as I, in his, fell into a sleep free of dreams.

Geoffrey Wolff

TRANNY MAN OVER THE BORDER

In the Plaza

— hibiscus blooms fall with heavy plops, lie sprawled on the sunny cobblestones and cement benches like fat Mexican generals, scarlet-and-green parade uniforms, gawdy and limp, too hot and tired to rise back to the rank of their branches. Later, perhaps. Now, siesta . . .

"Not good!" yells the gray crewcut American from Portland with his fifty-year face running sweat and his new Dodge Polaro sitting behind a tow truck outside the Larga Distancia Oficina. "Not three thrown in less than five thousand miles!"

Yelling from Puerto Sancto, Mexico, to Tucson, Arizona, where he'd bought his last transmission after buying his second in Oroville, California, where he'd paid without much complaint because it *is* possible to strip the gears with the hard business miles he'd put on it, but a tranny again in Tucson? And now, less than a week later? The third blown?

"Not good at all! So listen up; I'm gonna jerk the thing out and ship it back first train your direction. I expect the same promptness from you garage boys, right? I expect a new transmission down here in time for us to make the festival in Guadalajara one week from tomorrow! There's no excuse for this kinda workmanship I can tell you *that!*"

What he didn't tell the garage boys in Tucson was that he was pulling a twenty-four-foot mobile home.

"I been a Dodge man ten years. We don't want a ten-year relationship to blow up from one fluke, right?"

He hung up and turned to me. Next in line, I had been his nearest audience.

"That'll get some greasemonkeys' asses smoking in Tucson, won't it, Red?" He leaned close, as if we had known each other for years. "They aren't a bad bunch. Fact is, I hope I can find me a mechanic down here with a *fraction* the know-how as those Arizona boys."

Reaffirmation of Yankee superiority left him so flushed with feeling for his countrymen that he chose to overlook the stubbled look of me.

"What's your name, Red? You remind me of my oldest boy a little, behind that brush."

"Deboree," I told him, taking his hand. "Devlin Deboree."

"What brings you to primitive Puerto Sancto, Dev? Let me guess. You're a nature photographer. I saw you out there after those fallen posies."

"Way wrong," I told him. "It isn't even my camera. My father sent his along. He came to Sancto last year with my brother and me, and nobody took picture one."

"So Dad sent you to bring back the missed memories. He musta been a lot more impressed than I been."

"Wrong again. He sent me to bring back jumping beans."

"Jumping beans?"

"Five gallons. Dad's going to give one bean away with each quart of his new ice cream, to publicize the flavor. Not Jumping Bean — Pina Colada. We run a creamery."

" 'Debris,' huh?" He gave me a wink to let me know he was kidding. "Like in 'rubbish'?"

I told him it was more like in Polish. He laughed.

"Well, you remind me of my kid, *what*ever. Why don't you join me in the Hotel Sol bar after your call? We'll see if I remind you of your old man."

He winked again and left, roguishly tipping his fishing cap to the rest of the tourists waiting to contact home.

I found him under a palapa umbrella by the pool. His look of confidence was already a little faded, and he was wondering if maybe he shouldn't've also had a good U.S. mechanic come *with* the transmission — pay the man's way now, fight it out with the Dodge people later. I observed some of these Mexican mechanics were pretty good. He agreed they *had* to be pretty good, to keep these hand-me-downs running, but what did they know about a modern automatic transmission? He pulled down his sunglasses and drew me again into the abrupt intimacy.

"You can take the best carburetor man in the whole country, say, and turn him loose in an area he isn't qualified in, and you're going to have troubles. Believe me, numerous troubles . . ."

This truth and his drink made him feel better. The grin returned and the ungreased whine of panic was almost oiled out of his voice by his second Seagram's and Seven-Up. By the bottom of his third he was ready to slip 'er into whiskeydrive and lecture me as to all the troubles a man can encounter along the rocky road of life, brought about *mainly* by unqualified incompetents in areas where they didn't belong. *Nu*merous troubles! To steer him away from a tirade I interrupted with what I thought was a perfectly peaceful question: How many did he have with him? One eye narrowed strangely and slid over my backpack and beard. With a voice geared all the way back into suspicion he informed me that his *wife* was along and what about it.

I gaped, amazed. He thinks that I mean how many *troubles* meaning his wife or whoever meaning I'm trying to cast some snide insinuation about his family! Far out, I thought, and to calm him I said I wished *my* wife and kids were along. Still suspicious, he asked how many kids, and how old. I told him. He asked where they were and I said in school —

"But if I have to wait much longer for these jumping beans I'm going to have them all fly down. Sometimes you have to skip a little school to further your education, right?"

"Right!" This brought him close again. "Don't I wish my woman'd known that when my kids were kids! 'After they get their educations' was her motto. Right, Mother, sure . . ."

I thought he was going to get melancholy again, but he squared his shoulders instead and clinked his glass against mine. "Decent of you and your brother to take a trip with your old dad, Red." He was glad I had turned out not to be some hippy rucksack smartass ᵃfter all, but a decent American boy, considerate of his father. He twisted in his chair and called grandly for the waiter to bring us another round uno mas all around, muy goddamn *pronto*.

"If you aren't a little hardboiled," he confided, shifting back to wink at me, "they overcharge."

He grinned and the wink reopened, but for one tipsy second that eye didn't match up with its mate. "*Over*charge!" he prompted, commanding the orb back into place.

By the time the drinks arrived the twitch was corrected and his look confident and roguish again. For a moment, though, a crack had been opened. I had seen all the way inside to the look behind the looks and, oh gosh, folks, that look was dreadful afraid. Of what? It's difficult to say, exactly. But it wasn't of me. Nor do I think he was really afraid of the numerous troubles on the rocky road ahead, not even of getting stranded gearless in this primitive anarchy of a nation.

What I think, folks, looking at the developed pictures and remembering back to that momentary glimpse into his private abyss, is that this guy was afraid of the Apocalypse.

His Wife

The Tranny Man's wife is younger than her husband, not much, a freshman in high school when he was a football-hero senior, at his best.

She's never been at her best, although it isn't something she thinks about. She's a thoughtful person who doesn't think about things.

She is walking barefoot along the stony edge of the ocean with her black pumps dangling from a heel strap at the end of each arm. She isn't thinking that she had too many rum-and-Cokes. She isn't thinking about her podiatrist or her feet, spreading pudgy over the sand.

She stops at the bank of the Rio Sancto and watches the water sparkle across the beach, rushing golden to the sea. Upriver a few dozen yards, women are among the big river stones washing laundry and hanging it on the bushes to dry. She watches them bending and stretching in their wet dresses, scampering over the rocks with great bundles balanced on their heads, light little prints spinning off their feet elegant as feathers, but she isn't thinking *We're so misshapen and leprous that we have to drink more than is good for us to just have the courage to walk past.* Not yet. She's only been in town since they were towed in this morning. Nor is she asking herself *When did I forsake my chance at proportion? Was it when I sneaked to the fridge just like Pop, piled on more than a seven-year-old should carry? Was it after graduation when I had those two sound-though-crooked incisors replaced by these troublesome caps? Why did I join the mechanical lepers?*

h·r ankles remind her of the distance she has walked. Far enoug'> for a backache tonight. Looking down, her feet appear to her as dead creatures, drowned things washed in on the tide. She forces her eyes back up and watches the washwomen long enough not to appear coerced, then turns and starts back, thinking, Oh, by now he'll either be finished with the call or ready to call it off if I know him.

But she isn't thinking, as she strides chin-raised and rummy along the golden border. *They saw anyway. They know that we are The Unclean, allowed nowdays to wander among normal people because they have immunized themselves against us.*

"And if he's *not* ready I think I'll take a look around that other hotel." Meaning the bar. "See who's there."

Meaning other Americans.

His Dog

The Tranny Man has to climb the hill into the hot steep thick of it, to find the man Wally Blum says will maybe work this weekend and pull the Tucson transmission. He has to take his dog. The dog's name is Chief and he's an ancient Dalmation with lumbago. There was no way to leave him in the hotel room. Something about Mexico has had the same effect on old Chief's bladder as on the Tranny Man's slow eye. Control has been shaken. In the familiar trailerhou. Chief had been as scrupulous with his habits as back home, but as soon as they'd moved into the hotel it seemed the old dog just couldn't help but be lifting his leg every three steps. Scolding only makes it worse.

"Poor old fella's nervous" — after Chief watered two pinatas his wife had purchased for the grandchildren this morning.

"We never should have brought him," she said. "We should have put him in a boarding kennel."

"I told you," the Tranny Man had answered. "The kids wouldn't keep him, I wasn't leaving him with strangers!"

So Chief has to climb along.

The Hot Steep Thick

The map that Wally Blum scribbled leads the Tranny Man and his pet up narrow cobblestone thoroughfares where trucks lurch loud between chuckholes . . . up crooked cobblestone streets too narrow for anything but bikes . . . up even crookeder and narrower cobblestone canyons too steep for any wheel.

Burros pick their way with loads of sand and cement for the clutter of construction going on antlike all over the mountainside. Workers sleep head uphill in the clutter; if they slept sideways they'd roll off.

By the time the American and his dog reach the place on the map, the Tranny Man is seeing spots and old Chief is peeing dust. The Tranny Man wipes the sweat from under the sweatband of his fishing cap and enters a shady courtyard; it's shaded by rusty hoods and trunk lids welded haphazardly together and bolted atop palm-tree poles.

El Mecanico Fantastico

In the center of a twelve-foot sod circle a sow reclines, big as a plaza fountain, giving suck to a litter large as she is. She rolls her head to look at the pair of visitors and gives a snort. Chief growls and stands his ground between the sow and his blinking master.

There is movement behind the low vine-shrouded doorway of a shack so small that it could fit into the Dodge's mobile home and still have room for the sow. A man ducks out of the doorway, fanning himself with a dry tortilla. He is half the Tranny Man's size and half again his age, maybe more. He squints a moment against the glare, then uses the tortilla to shade his eyes.

"Tardes," he says.

"Buenas tardes," the Tranny Man answers, mopping his face. "Hot. Mucho color."

"I spik Engliss a little," says El Mecanico Fantastico.

The Tranny Man recalls reading somewhere how that was where the slur "Spik" came from. "Thank heaven for *that*," he says and launches into a description of his plight. The mechanic listens from beneath the tortilla. The sow watches old Chief with voluptuous scorn. Burros trudge past the yard. Small children drift into sight from El Mecanico Fantastico's shack; they cling to their father's legs as he listens to the Tranny Man's tale of mechanical betrayal.

When the tale finally dribbles to an end, EMF asks, "What you want for me to do?''

"To come down to that big garage where they towed it and take the danged transmission out so I can send it to Tucson. See?''

"I see, si,'' says the mechanic. "Why you don't use the big garage mecanicos?''

"They won't work on it until Monday is why.''

"Are you in such a hurry you cannot wait for Monday?''

"I already called and told Tucson I was shipping the thing back to them by Monday. I like to get on these things while they're hot, you see.''

"Si, I see,'' says El Mecanico Fantastico, fanning himself with the tortilla again. "Hokay. I come down manana and take it out.''

"Can't w   c t on it now? I'd like to be sure of getting it on that train.''

"I see,'' says the Mexican. "Hokay. I get my tools and we rent a burro.''

"A burro?''

"From Ernesto Diaz. To carry my tools. The big garage locks their tools in a iron box.''

"I see,'' says the Tranny Man, beginning to wonder how to pin down a reasonable estimate for labor, tools and a burro.

Suddenly there is a big brodie of squeals and yelps in the dust. The sow's red-bristled boar friend has dropped in and caught Chief making eyes at his lady. By the time they are pulled apart Chief has one ear slashed and has lost both canines in the boar's brick hide.

But that isn't the worst of it. Giving away all that weight has been too much for dog's aged hindquarters. Something is dislocated. He has to ride back down strapped atop a second burro. The ride pops the dislocation back in so he can walk again by evening, but he is never able afterward to lift a hind leg without falling over.

Him and His Wife Again

They've been there a week now. They are flat-tiring back from the beach to the south in a rented Toyota open-top. The left rear blew out miles back. There is no spare. And a ruptured radiator hose is spewing steam from under the dash so they can barely see the road ahead.

Finally the wife asks, "You're going to just keep *driving* it?"

"I'm going to *drive* the sonofabitch *back* to the sonofabitch that *rented* me the sonofabitch and tell him to shove this piece of broken Jap junk up his overpriced greaser *ass!*"

"Well, drop the dog and me off at the Blums' first, then, if you're going to — if we get close."

She didn't say If you're going to make a scene. There was steam and furor enough.

His Friends

The Tranny Man missed the before-siesta mail out and he's promised himself to get a letter to his sister finished to take down to the post office when it opens after siesta. He's at the Blums' rented villa, alone except for Chief. The dog is stretched on a woven mat, tongue out and eyes open. Wally Blum's at the beach surfcasting. The Tranny Man doesn't know where Betty Blum and his wife have gone.

The Blums' hacienda is not down in Gringo Gulch but up on the town's residential slopes. The yard of a shack across the canyon-of-a-street is level with his window, and three little girls smile at him across the narrow chasm. They keep calling Hay-lo mee-ster, then ducking back out of sight in the foliage of a mango tree and giggling.

That tree is the whole neighborhood's social center. Kids play in its shade. Birds fly in and out of its branches. Two pigs and a lot of chickens prowl the leafy rubble at its roots. All kinds of chickens — chickens scrawny and chickens bald, chickens cautious and chickens bold. The only thing the chickens seem to have in common is freedom and worthlessness.

The Tranny Man watches the chickens with a welcome disdain. What good can they be, too sick to lay, too skinny to eat? What possible good? Inspired by the inefficiency, he launches into his letter:

Dear Sis: Gawd, wot a country! It is too poor to know it's ignorant and too ignorant to know it's poor. If I was Mexico you know what I would do? I would attack the U.S. just to qualify for foreign aid when we whup 'em (ha ha). Seriously, it sure isn't what I had hoped, I can tell you that.

A green mango bounces off the grill of his window. More giggles. He reads the last line with a sigh and lays down his ballpoint. Wish you were here, Sissy, with all my heart. He drains his Seven-and-Seven and feels a kind of delicious depression sweep over him. A poignancy.

An accordion in one of the shacks begins practicing a familiar tune, a song popular back home a couple years back. What was it? Went *la la la* laa; *we'd fight and* neh-*ver win . . .* That was it! *Those were the days, my friend; those were the days . . .*

The poignancy becomes melancholy, then runs straight on through sentiment to nostalgia. It stops just short of maudlin. With another sigh he picks his pen up and resumes the letter:

I think of you often on this trip, Old Pal. Do you remember the year Father drove us to Yellowstone Park and how great it was? How wonderful and bright everything looked? How proud we felt? We were the first kids coming out of the Depression whose Father could afford to take his family on such a trip. Well let me tell you, things are not bright anymore and not very likely to get so. Ferinstance, let me tell you about visiting Darold, in 'Berserkly.' That about says it. You simply cannot believe the condition that nice college town has allowed itself to get into since we were there in '62 for the Russian-American track meet —

He stops again. He hears a strange clucking voice: "Que? Que?" In the yard across the way he sees a very old woman. She appears to be swaying her way along a clothesline with an odd, weightless motion. Her face is vacant of teeth or expression. She seems unreal, a trick of the heat, swaying along, clucking "Que? Que? Que?" She sways along until she reaches a frayed white sheet. She gathers it from the line and starts felling her way back to her shack. "Que? Que? Que Que?"

"Blind," says the Tranny Man, and rises to check Wally's cupboards. He's bound to have *some*thing to pick up where the Seventy-seven left off, something stronger if possible: eighty-eight . . . ninety-*nine!* He bobs this way and that around the strange kitchen, awash with sweat, rendered rudderless by the jagged apparition of the blind crone. He is drifting fast now toward the reefs.

The First Crack

The Tranny Man's wife arrives half an hour later with Wally Blum's wife, Betty, in Wally's nice little Mexican-built Volkswagen jeep loaded with gifts for the gals back home. She has barely begun telling Betty Blum how grateful she is for the ride not to mention the company when she is pulled about by her elbow and scolded so loudly for going off without taking the mail — so *unfairly* — that the world is suddenly billowing silent about her, all the street sounds ceasing, the hens not clucking, the kids not chattering on the rooftop, the mariachi not pumping his accordion . . . even the river half a mile down the hill, stopping its sparkle around the rocks. The kneeling girls are raised from their wash to listen: how will the gringa senora take it, this machismo browbeating?

"Understand?" the Tranny Man demands in closing. "*Sabe?*"

The evening leans forward from its many seats. Betty Blum begins to take blame and croon apologies in the familiar catty pussyfooting of one browbeaten senora coming to the defense of another. The unseen audience starts to sigh, disappointed. But before the Tranny Man can begin his grumpy forgiving, the Tranny Man's wife hears herself speaking in a voice stiff with care at the delivery of each syllable, telling her husband to let go of her arm, to lower his shouting, and to never treat her as though she were drawing a wage from him — *never again* speak to her like she was one of his broken machines.

"If you do I swear I'll kill you, and if I can get to him I'll kill Donald, and if I can get to them before I'm stopped I'll kill Terry and the grandchildren and then myself, I swear it before *God!*"

Both her husband and Betty stare dumbstruck at this outburst. Then the two of them exchange quick small nods: shoulda seen something like this coming . . . woman this age . . . all those rum-and-Cokes. The Tranny Man's wife is no longer paying attention. She knows she has been effective. For a moment she feels as though the intensity of this effect will set her aflame, that her flesh will melt and run off her bones.

Then the pulse of the street begins to rush again. The kids on the roof whisper excited reviews. The chickens gather in the lobby of shade under the mango branches. The accordionist doesn't resume his practicing, but, the Tranny Man's wife feels, this is out of a kind of consideration, as one musician in the twilight to another, not criticism.

The Aftermath

The Tranny Man stalks back into the hacienda: Betty Blum gives his wife a ride back to the Hotel del Sol. When she returns she has a bottle of Seagram's, a pack of cold Seven-Up and a warm smile that hints she can be as sympathetic to misunderstood husbands as to browbeaten wives.

Wally shows up with two yellowtail and the Tranny Man accepts their invitation for supper. After fish and white wine he borrows a pair of trunks from good ol' Wally and a safety pin from bountiful Betty to keep them from falling off his skinny ass, and they all go for a midnight swim. Then they come back and drink some more. He tells Wally it's always the kids that keep a marriage together, but with these kids these days! Is it worth it? Then he confides to Betty — who is still wearing the bikini that looks *damned decent* for a woman her age — how one thing the kids these days *do* have on the ball is getting rid of all those old-fashioned notions about sex being evil. It's natural! Betty could not agree more.

When he figures it is late enough that his wife has been adequately disciplined, he borrows their car to drive back to the hotel with old Chief. "I bet she's there by now," he bets.

He wins; she's asleep on the couch. It will be the last time he'd win such a bet.

The Tranny Man's Dream

Things can be trusted. Things do not break. Things are not gyps. Pull chains on light switches are not manufactured to snap off inside the fixture just to force a poor sucker to shell out *dinero* for a complete new rip-up that isn't *fair*.

His Virility

"Ten pesos for a rum-'n'-Coke? They only cost five pesos two blocks from here!"

They have been drinking at the hotel all afternoon.

"This is the beachfront," his wife reminds him. "Besides, these have straws."

The waiter rewards her logic with a grand denture display. Betty and Wally order. The drinks arrive. Betty sips her margarita like a bee choosing a blossom from acres of clover.

"Feh," she drawls. "Not great but feh-uh."

"I love the way you Miami women talk, Betty." The Tranny Man is drunk. "In fact I love all women. From the young uns with papaya titties to the old uns with experience!" He spreads his arms. "I love *all* people, actually; from these —"

He stops short. He has seen something that nips his declaration in the bud. The Tranny Man's wife follows her husband's gaze to see what has stymied this tribute. Across the beach she sees the reason in the shade of a canvas-covered icecream pushcart, wearing lime green barely to the crotch, as provocative as a Popsicle. Busted, her husband leaves it unfinished. He turns his scrutiny to the cover of the Mexican edition of *Time* that Wally has bought from a newsboy. There's a picture of Clifford Irving on the cover. He reads over Wally's shoulder, lips moving.

His wife continues to stare at the young morsel at the icecream stand, not out of jealousy, as she knows Betty Blum is silently supposing, but with a sense of sweet wonder, as one stares at a pressed flower discovered in a school annual, wondering, What had it meant when it was fresh? Where did it go? Feeling herself suddenly on the verge of finding some kind of answer she rises from the shaded table, no longer in the mood for oyster cocktail,

521

and walks across the sand toward the surf.

There is a silence as the Tranny Man frowns after her. When he looks back, Betty Blum extends him brown-eyed condolences over the salty rim of her margarita, as if to advise, Don't let her mess with your mind.

"*Time,*" declares Wally Blum, "is one of those things you can trust because you know just how much to allow for political bias."

The Tranny Man regains himself with a robust "Right!" and turns back to the question of nevermind who's Clifford Irving who's Howard *Hughes?*

The three of them walk back to the hotel restaurant and order Lobster Supreme, picking at the shells till nearly ten. Finally the Tranny Man yawns it's his bedtime and excuses himself, letting all present know by the twinkle in his roguish eye that he is far too much a man to let some menopausal bitch mess with his sleep let alone his mind! Over Wally's protests he peels two hundred-peso bills from his wallet and places them beside his plate. To Betty's request that they buy a bottle to drink up on his balcony he graciously explains that ordinarily he would be more than happy to oblige, but tomorrow is the day his new transmission should be coming in from the States, and he likes to get on these things while they're hot. Another time. He squeezes Betty's hand and turns and mounts the stairs, giving them his most erect exit.

Puerto Sancto Darkness

Here it comes again: the turmoil, the chaos, the hubbub and howls — the nightdogs again — the pre-dawn yapping that starts in the hills south and sweeps across the town, just when you were sure the sonofabitches had, at last, exhausted the shadows and were going to settle down and let you get some rest.

Old Chief whimpers. The Tranny Man burrows under his pillow cursing the night, the dogs, the town, his crazy wife who had suggested in the first place coming to this thorny wilderness, goddam her! Why *here*, he demands of the darkness, instead of Yosemite or Marineland or even the Shakespeare festival in Ashland? Why *this* goddamn anarchy of thorn and shadows?

A fair question. I had been forced to deal with it there once myself. You see, one day, not long after Betsy had announced we were finally broke, we all finally knew that my father was going to die (of course I am reminded of him by the Tranny Man — not by the person himself but by certain things particular to this type of American: the erect exit, the wink, the John Wayne way he spoke to machinery and mechanics . . . many things). The doctors had been telling us for ages that he only had so much time, but Daddy had continued to stretch that alloted time for so long that Buddy and I secretly believed that our stubborn Texas father was never going to succumb to any enemy except old age. His arms and legs shriveled and his head wobbled on his "goddamn noodle of a neck," but we continued to expect some last-minute rescue to come bulging over the horizon.

Daddy thought so too. "All this research, I figure they'll whip it pretty soon. They better. Look at these muscles jump around —"

He'd draw up a pantleg and grin wryly at the flesh jerking and twitching.

"— like nervous rats on a leaky scow."

Yeah, pretty soon, we agreed. Then one September day we were out at the goat pasture sighting in our rifles and talking about where we were going to take our hunting trip this fall, when Daddy lowered his 'ought-six and looked at us.

"Boys, this damned gunbarrel is shaking like a dog shitting peach pits. Let's take some *other* kind of trip . . ."

— and we all knew it was going to be our last. My brother and I talked it over that night. I knew where I wanted to go. Buddy wasn't too sure about the idea, but he conceded I was the big brother. We presented the plan to Daddy the next day over his backyard barbecue.

"I don't object to a journey south, but why this Purty Sancto? Why way the hell-and-gone down there?"

"Dev claims there's something special about it," Buddy said.

"He wants to show off where he hid out for six months," Daddy said. "Aint that the something special?"

"Partly," I admitted. Everybody knew I'd been trying to get the three of us down there for years. "But there's something besides that about the place — something primal, prehistoric . . ."

"Just what a man in his predicament needs," my mother put in. "Something prehistoric."

"Maybe we oughta fly up to that spot on the Yukon again," Daddy mused. "Fish for sockeye."

"No, damn it!" I said. "All my life you've been hauling me to your spots. Now it's my turn."

"A drive across Mexico would shake him to pieces!" my mother cried. "Why, he wasn't even able to handle the drive to the Rose Parade up in Portland without getting wore to a frazzle."

"Oh, I can handle the drive," he told her. "That aint the question."

"Handle my foot! A hundred miles on those Mexican roads in your sorry condition —"

"I said I can stand it," he told her, flipping her a burger. He turned to eye me through the smoke. "All's I want to know is, one: why this Puerto Sancto place? and, two: what *else* you got up your sleeve?"

I didn't answer. We all knew what was up my sleeve.

"*Oh* no you don't!" My mother swung her glare at me. "If you think you're going to get him off somewheres and talk him into taking some of that stuff again —"

"Woman, I been legal age for some time now. I will thank you to leave me do my own deciding as to *where* I go and *what stuff* I take."

Years before, at the beginning of the sixties, Buddy and I had been trying to grow psilocybin mushrooms in a cottage-cheese vat at the little creamery Daddy staked Buddy to after he got out of Oregon State. Bud made up some research stationery and was getting spore cultures sent to him straight form the Department of Agriculture, along with all the latest information for producing the mycelium hydroponically. Bud and I plumbed an air hose into the vat, mixed the required nutrients, added the cultures and monitored the development through a microscope. Our ultimate fantasy was to produce a psilocybin slurry and ferment it into a wine. We believed we could market the drink under the name Milk of the Gods. All we ever made was huge yeast-contaminated messes.

But in one of those culture kits Buddy ordered they very helpfully included a tiny amount of the extract of the active ingredient itself — I guess so we could have something to compare our yield to, were we ever to get one. Daddy brought this particular package out to the farm from the post office. He was skeptical.

That little dab of nothing?'' In the bottom of a bottle smaller than a pencil was maybe a sixteenth inch of white crust. ''All that talk I heard about those experiments and *That's* all you took?''

I dumped the powder in a bottle of Party-Pac club soda. There wasn't so much as a fizz. ''This is probably about the size dose they gave us.'' I began pouring it in a set of wineglasses. ''Maybe a little bigger.''

''Well, hell's bells, then,'' Daddy said. ''I'll have a glass. I better check this business out.''

There were five of us: Buddy, me, Mickey Write, Betsy's brother Gil — all with some previous experience — and my Lone Star Daddy, who could never even finish the rare bottle of beer he opened on fishing trips. When we'd all emptied our glasses there was still a couple inches left in the Party-Pac bottle. Daddy refilled his glass.

''I want enough to give me at least some notion . . . I'm tired of *hearing* about it.''

We went into the living room to wait. The women had gone to the shopping center. It was about sundown. I remember we were watching that last Fullmer-Basilio fight on TV. When the shopping run got back from town my mother came popping in and asked, ''Who's winning?''

Daddy popped right back, ''Who's fighting?'' and grinned at her like a goon.

In another hour that grin was gone. He was pacing the floor in freaked distress, shaking his hands as he paced, like they were wet.

''Damn stuff got down in all my *nerve ends!*'' Could that have had something to do with getting that disease? We all always wondered, didn't we?

By the merciful end of a terrible hell of a night, Daddy was vowing, ''If you two try to manufacture this stuff . . . I'll crawl all the way to Washington on my bloody hands and *knees* to get it outlawed!''

Not a fair test, he later admitted, but he was damned if he was going to experiment further. "Never," he vowed. "Not till I'm on my deathbed in a blind alley with my back to the wall."

Which was pretty much the case that September.

The three of us flew to Phoenix and rented a Winnebago and headed into Mexico, usually Buddy at the wheel while Daddy and I argued about our selection of tapes — Ray Charles was alright, but that Bob Dappa and Frank Zylan smelt like just more burning braincells.

The farther south we went the hotter it got. Tempers went up with the temperature. A dozen times we were disinherited. A dozen times he ordered us to drop him at the first airport so he could fly out of this ratworld back to civilized comfort, yet he always cooled down by night when we pulled over. He even got to like the Mexican beer.

"But keep your dope to yourselves," he warned. "My muscles may be turning to mush but my head's still hard as a rock."

By Puerto Sancto Daddy had thrown out all the cassettes and Buddy had picked up some farmacia leapers. We were all feeding pretty good. I wanted to take the wheel to pilot her in on the last leg of our journey, then, the first bounce onto a paved street in hundreds of miles I run over a corner of one of those square Mexican manhole covers and it tilts up catty-corner and pokes a hole in our oilpan. We could've babied it to a hotel but Daddy says no, leave it with him; he'll see to it while we hike into town and get us a couple rooms.

"Give me one of those pep pills before you go," he growled, "so I'll have the juice to deal with these bastards."

He took a Ritalin. We eased it on to the biggest garage we could find and left him with it. Buddy and I went on foot across the river and into town where we rented a fourth-story seafront double, then walked down to the beach action and got burned forty bucks trying to buy a kilo of the best dope I ever smoked. From a hippie girl with nothing but a tan and a promise.

We waited three hours before we gave up. On the defeated walk back through the outskirts we passed a bottled gas supply house. I spoke enough Spanish and Buddy had enough creamery credentials that we talked them out of an E tank of nitrous. By the time we'd had a hit or two in the stickerbushes and got on back to the garage, the oilpan was off and welded and back on and Daddy knew the first names and ages and family history of every man in the shop, none of whom spoke any more English than he did Spanish. He had even put together the deal for the jumping beans.

"Good people," he said, collapsing into the back of the Winnebago. "Not lazy at all. Just easy. What's that in the blue tank?"

"Nitrous oxide," Bud told him.

"Well I hope it can wait till I get a night in a hotel bed. I'm one shot sonofagun."

We all slept most of the next day. By the time we were showered and shaved and enjoying room-service breakfast on our breezy terrace, the sun was dipping down into the bay like one of those glazed Mexican cookies. Daddy stretched and yawned.

"Okay . . . what you got?"

I brought out my arsenal. "Grass, hash, and DMT. All of which are smoked and none of which last too long."

"Not another fifteen rounds with Carmen Basilio, eh? Well, I aint cared about smoking ever since a White Owl made me puke on my grandpa. What was in that tank, Bud?"

"Laughing gas," Buddy said.

To a man with thirty-five years' experience in refrigeration, that little tank at least looked familiar. "Is the valve threaded left or right?"

I held it for him, but he didn't have the strength to turn it. I had to deal it — to my father first, then my brother, then myself. I dealt three times around this way and sat down. Then we flashed, this man and his two fullgrown sons, all together, the way you sometimes do. It wasn't that strong but it was as sweet as dope ever gets . . . at the end of our trip on the edge of our continent, as the sun dipped and the breeze stopped, and a dog a mile down the beach barked a high clear note . . . three wayfaring hearts in Mexico able to touch for an instant in a way denied them by gringo protocol. For a beat. Then Daddy stretched and yawned and allowed as how the skeeters would be starting now the breeze had dropped.

"So I guess I'll go inside and hit the hay. I've had enough. Too much dipsy-doo'll make you goony."

He stood up and started for bed, his reputation for giving everything a fair shake still secure. It wasn't exactly a blessing he left us with — he was letting us know it wasn't for him, whatever it was we were into, or his hardheaded generation — but he was no longer going to crawl to Washington to put a stop to it.

He went through the latticed door into the dark room. Then his head reappeared.

"You jaspers better be sure of the gear you're trying to hit, though," he said, in a voice unlike any he'd ever used when speaking to Buddy or me, or to any of the family, but that I could imagine he might have used had he ever addressed, say, Edward Teller. "Because it's gonna get steep. If you miss the shift it could be The End as we know it."

And that is what reminds me most of the Tranny Man show. Like Daddy, he knew it was gonna get steep. But he wouldn't make the shift. Or couldn't. He'd been dragging too much weight behind him for too long. He couldn't cut it loose and just go wheeling free across a foreign beach. When you cut it off something equally heavy better be hooked up in its place, some kind of steadying drag, or it'll make you goony.

"Drive you to *distraction* is what!"

This, the Tranny Man tells me at the post office. I stopped by to see if there was any jumping-bean news. There's the Tranny Man, suntanned and perplexed, a slip of paper in each hand. He hands both notes to me when he sees me, like I'm his accountant.

"So I'm glad she took off before we both had some kind of breakdown. It's this crazy jungle pushed her over the edge if you ask me. Serves her right; she was the one insisted on coming. So there it is, Red." He shrugs philosophically. "The old woman has run out but the new transmission has come in."

I see the first note is from the *estacion de camiones,* telling him that a crate has arrived from Arizona. The second is also from the bus station, scrawled on a Hotel de Sancto coaster:

"By the time you get this I will be gone. Our ways have parted. Your loving wife."

Loving has been crossed out. I tell him I'm sorry. He says don't worry, there's nothing to it.

"She's pulled this kind of stuff before. It'll work out. Come on down to the bus depot and help me with that tranny and I'll buy you breakfast. Chief?"

The old dog creeps from behind the hotel desk and follows us into the cobbled sun.

"Pulled it lots of times before . . . just never in a foreign *coun*try before, is the problem."

Last Shot of Tranny Man's Wife

He used to do reckless things — not thoughtless or careless: reckless — like to toss me an open bottle of beer when I was down in the utility room, hot with cleaning. What could it hurt? If I dropped it there was no big loss. But if I caught it? I had more than just a bottle of beer. Why did he stop being reckless and become careless? What was it caught his attention and stiffened him into a doll? What broke all that equipment? — is what the Tranny Man's wife is thinking on her way to the American Consulate in Guadalajara to try to cash a check.

Last Shot of Tranny Man

They wouldn't let me on the plane with the ticking five-gallon can of jumping beans. I had to take the bus. At the Pemex station outside Tepic I saw the Tranny Man's Polaro and his trailer. He was letting old Chief squat in the ditch behind the station. Yeah, he was heading back. To the good old U.S. of A.

"You know what I think I'm gonna do, Red? I think I'm gonna cross at Tijuana this time, maybe have a little fun."

Winking more odd-eyed than ever. How was his car? Purring right along. Heard from his wife? Not a peep. How had he liked his stay in picturesque Puerto Sancto?

"Oh, it was okay I guess, *but —*" He throws his arm across my shoulders, pulling me close to share his most secret opinion: "— if *Disney'd* designed it there'd of been monkeys."

Ken Kesey

CONTRIBUTORS

William Kittredge is the author of *Owning It All* (nonfiction) and two collections of short fiction, *The Van Gogh Field* and *We Are Not in This Together.*

Joan Swift is best known as a poet whose collections include *This Element, Parts of Speech* and *The Dark Path of Our Names.*

John Hildebrand's nonfiction book on the Yukon is forthcoming from Houghton Mifflin.

David Quammen writes a regular column for *Outside* and is the author of two novels and a book of nonfiction.

H.L. Davis is the only author from Oregon to win the Pulitzer Prize in fiction.

Rich Ives is the author of a book of poems, *Notes from the Water Journals* and editor of three anthologies of Northwest writing.

Barry Lopez received the Pulitzer Prize for nonfiction for *Arctic Dreams.* His other books include *Of Wolves and Men, Desert Notes, River Notes* and *Winter Count.*

Thomas McGuane is widely known for his novels and has recently released a new collection of short fiction.

Clyde Rice won the 1984 Western States Book Award for his first book, published at age eighty-one.

Richard Hugo is widely known for several books of poems, including *Making Certain It Goes On*, an autobiographical collection entitled *The Real West Marginal Way* and a mystery novel.

Jack Olsen is the author of numerous novels and books of investigative journalism, including *Night of the Grizzlies* and *Son.* He lives on Bainbridge Island.

Will Baker grew up in Idaho and has lived in California and Montana and is the author of several books including *Backward: An Essay on Indians, Time and Photography* and *Mountain Blood,* which won the Associated Writing Programs first Award for Creative Nonfiction.

Richard Ford is the author of several novels, including the widely praised *The Sportswriter* and a collection of stories, *Rock Springs.*

John Haines is the author of two works of autobiographical essays and several widely praised collections of poetry. He was an Alaska homesteader for sixteen years and has now returned to Alaska after teaching and writing in other parts of the Northwest.

Rich Baker is a novelist and short story writer who recently won the Hemingway Prize.

Marilyn Stablein is the author of *The Census-Taker.*

Kim Stafford is the author of several books of poems and received a Citation for Excellence for Creative Nonfiction in the 1986 Western States Book Awards.

Gretel Ehrlich is a poet and nonfiction writer living in Wyoming. She is the author of *The Solace of Open Spaces.*

Annie Dillard has received a Pulitzer Prize for *Pilgrim at Tinker Creek* and is the author of *Holy the Firm, Teaching a Stone to Talk, Living by Fiction,* and *Encounters with Chinese Writers.*

Richard K. Nelson is an anthropologist and the author of several books, including *Make Prayers to the Raven.*

William Stafford has received numerous awards for his poetry and has also authored two collections of criticism as well as his account of World War II conscientious objectors, *Down in My Heart.*

Brenda Peterson is the author of two novels, *Becoming the Enemy* and *River of Light*.

Monica Sone, who lives in Canton, Ohio, is a clinical psychologist.

John McPhee is widely known for more than two dozen works of crative nonfiction, including *Coming into the Country*.

Madeline De Frees is a widely know poet whose collections include *Magpie on the Gallows* and *When Sky Lets Go*.

Tess Gallagher is the author of three collections of poems, a collection of short fiction and *A Concert of Tenses*, a collection of criticism.

Ralph Beer has recently published a novel, *The Blind Corral*, and lives on a ranch near Helena, Montana.

Jack Cady won the Iowa Short Fiction Award for *The Burning* and is the author of *The Well, Singleton,* and *The Jonah Watch*.

Ivan Doig is the author of three novels and two works of nonfiction, including the widely praised *This House of Sky*.

Geoffrey Wolff is the author of an autobiographical work, *The Duke of Deception*, and has recently released a new novel, *Providence*.

Ken Kesey is best known for his novels, *One Flew Over the Cuckoo's Nest* and *Sometimes a Great Notion*.

Thomas McGuane is widely known for his novels, including *Ninety-two in the Shade* and *Nobody's Angel*, and has recently released a new collection of short fiction.